NORTH CAROLINA

The History of an American State

NORTH CAROLINA

The History of an American State

JOHN L. BELL, JR. & JEFFREY J. CROW

THIRD EDITION

CLAIRMONT PRESS
Atlanta, Georgia

ABOUT THE AUTHORS

DR. JOHN R. BELL, JR., is professor of history emeritus at Western Carolina University in Cullowhee. He received his Ph.D. from the University of North Carolina at Chapel Hill. Dr. Bell is the author of *Hard Times: Beginnings of the Great Depression in North Carolina 1929-1933*. He contributed to *The History of Jackson County* and has published in various historical journals.

DR. JEFFREY J. CROW is Director of the Division of Archives and History, North Carolina Department of Cultural Resources. He received his Ph.D. from Duke University and has taught in several North Carolina colleges and universities. He has written numerous books and publications, including *The Black Experience in Revolutionary North Carolina*. From 1982 to 1993, Dr. Crow was Editor in Chief of the *North Carolina Historical Review*.

CONTRIBUTOR
James Carl Fugate, former teacher, Trexler School, Onslow County Schools, Richlands, North Carolina

EDITORIAL STAFF

EDITORIAL DIRECTOR: Kathleen Conway

DESIGNER: Robin McDonald

PHOTO RESEARCH: Robin McDonald, Marie Martin

MAPS: Magellan Geographix, Santa Barbara, California
  Lee Windham, Clanton, Alabama

PREPRESS PUBLICATION: Photographics, Inc., Birmingham, Alabama

TO THE STUDENTS

MORE AND MORE, our world is becoming a global village. Yet North Carolinians cannot be model citizens of this global village if they are ignorant of their own history and culture. North Carolinians have always had a strong sense of history. They remember places, events, and people because they want to understand better who they are and how to deal with their destiny.

This book covers more than four hundred years of the state's history – from Native American life before European settlement in 1585 to the modern industrialized society of the twenty-first century. In the course of those centuries, North Carolina has shown a special kind of independence. It has not always followed the course set by other states or even by the nation. Rather, it has often chosen to chart its own course.

North Carolina is noted for its diversity, rich culture, and cherished traditions. Its people make their living from the sea in the coastal region, the textile mills in the Piedmont, and the farms in the Mountain region. The aim of this book is to present the state's diversity and tell how different people with distinct ethnic and racial backgrounds help capture the essence of what it means to be a Tar Heel.

*Above: The North Carolina Museum of History opened in 1994. **Page i:** Built before the Civil War, the Capitol Building in Raleigh now contains executive offices. **Pages ii-iii:** View of farm and mountains from the Blue Ridge Parkway. **Pages iv-v:** Guides in colonial costume converse next to the shop of T. Bagge, Merchant, at Old Salem. **Front Cover:** The Elizabeth II, a replica of a sixteenth-century English sailing ship, anchored at Manteo. **Back cover:** Connestee Falls near Brevard.*

Top: *This diorama is one of the exhibits at the Schiele Museum of Natural History.* **Above:** *This visually impaired student explores one of the exhibits at the North Carolina Museum of Art.*

TABLE OF CONTENTS

Top: *During the summer, visitors can pan for gold at the Reed Gold Mine.* **Above:** *A full-size replica of the Wright Brothers' airplane is on display at Kitty Hawk. The original is at the Smithsonian.*

NORTH CAROLINA LAND OF MANY PLACES

NORTH CAROLINA has a varied geography. It has both white sand beaches and the highest mountains in the eastern United States. The subtropical climate nourishes large forests and many crops. North Carolina's geography has greatly influenced the way its people have lived and worked.

The earliest inhabitants of North Carolina were Native Americans. Many different tribes lived in North Carolina, each with its own language and way of living. When the early European explorers came to the New World, contact with Native Americans benefited both cultures. The Indians, however, had no immunity to European diseases and died by the thousands.

Right: The wreck of the Laura Barnes *on Cape Hatteras National Seashore.* ***Above:*** *Building on Cape Hatteras festooned with the nameplates of wrecked ships.*

CHAPTER ONE

THE GEOGRAPHY OF NORTH CAROLINA

I think in all the world the like abundance is not to be found. . . .
—Arthur Barlowe on first seeing Carolina in 1584

GEOGRAPHY IS THE STUDY of the physical features of Earth. Geography is also concerned with human beings and how they affect and are affected by their **environment** (surroundings). The geography of North Carolina has influenced the history of its people: the way they have lived and worked and shaped their society. In turn, people have influenced North Carolina's geography. They have cleared forests, drained swamps, deepened harbors, dammed rivers, and leveled hills and mountains. People have also had a harmful effect on the environment.

Let's look at how geography has affected North Carolina's history. Let's also look at how our actions have changed the environment and affected the way we live.

Left: *At 5,964 feet, Grandfather Mountain is the highest point in the Blue Ridge Mountains.* *Above:* *Charlotte is the largest city in North Carolina and the second largest banking center in the entire United States. The city is located in the southern Piedmont region.*

LOCATION

North Carolina's environment is affected by its location on Earth's surface. Located in the southeastern United States, North Carolina extends from 34° to 36° 30' north latitude. **Latitude** is the distance north or south of the equator. North Carolina is about one-third of the way from the equator to the North Pole. Other states in the same latitude include Tennessee, Oklahoma, and California. The state also extends from 75° 30' to 84° west longitude. **Longitude** is a measure of the distance east or west of the prime meridian at Greenwich, England. Going west, North Carolina is about one-fourth of the way around the world from Greenwich.

The Atlantic Ocean forms North Carolina's eastern boundary and Tennessee its western border. The state is bounded on the north by Virginia and on the south by South Carolina and Georgia. North Carolina is about 500 miles east-west by 180 miles north-south. It covers a little less than 53,000 square miles, just about the size of England.

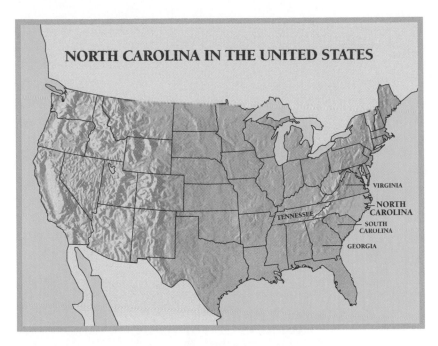

NORTH CAROLINA IN THE UNITED STATES

VIRGINIA

NORTH CAROLINA

TENNESSEE

SOUTH CAROLINA

GEORGIA

Left: This map shows North Carolina's position in the United States It is one of the South Atlantic states. **Below:** Seen from the Outer Banks, the Atlantic Ocean is vast. The ocean is a route of commerce and a source of sea-food and recreation. Its warm Gulf Stream helps moderate coastal temperatures. **Opposite page:** The Great Smoky Mountains are among the highest in eastern North America. They show the rugged beauty of the Mountain region.

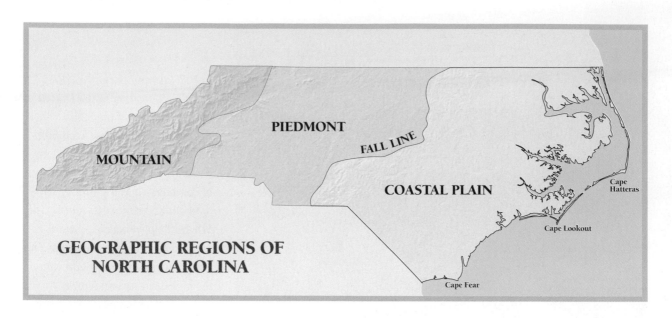

GEOGRAPHIC REGIONS OF
NORTH CAROLINA

MOUNTAIN

PIEDMONT

FALL LINE

COASTAL PLAIN

Cape Hatteras

Cape Lookout

Cape Fear

*Top: The state has three main
geographical regions. Two are
the Coastal Plain and Piedmont,
separated by the Fall Line. The
other is the Mountain region,
beginning at the Blue Ridge
Mountains.* **Above:** *Kure Beach is
at the southern end of the Atlantic
coast of North Carolina.* **Opposite
page:** *Cape Lookout National
Seashore attracts surf fishermen
from across the country.*

REGIONS OF THE STATE

North Carolina has three distinct geographical divisions. These are the
Coastal Plain, the Piedmont, and the Mountain.

THE COASTAL PLAIN

The Coastal Plain is located between the Atlantic Ocean and the Fall
Line. The **Fall Line** is an imaginary line that runs from Richmond County
to Halifax County through the places on rivers where falls are first found.
The land of the Coastal Plain rises from sea level in the east to about 500
feet in the west. The Fall Line also marks where the sandy soil of the
Coastal Plain gives way to the more rocky soil of the Piedmont.

The Coastal Plain is the site of the state's major military bases. They
include Fort Bragg, Seymour-Johnson Air Force Base, Camp Lejeune, and
Cherry Point Marine Air Station. Sunny Point on the Cape Fear is a major
ammunition shipping port. The Coastal Plain contains almost one-half
of the state's land area. It is divided into two areas: the Tidewater and the
Inner Coastal Plain.

The Tidewater

The Tidewater extends about 20 to 30 miles inland from the Atlantic
Ocean. The area takes its name from the fact that the tide rises and falls
on its rivers and sounds.

Bordering the ocean along the coast of the Tidewater is a series of barrier
islands called the Outer Banks. Parts of these islands, called **capes**, jut far
out into the ocean. The names of the three capes are Cape Fear, Cape Lookout, and Cape Hatteras. For 30 miles off the capes, ocean currents deposit

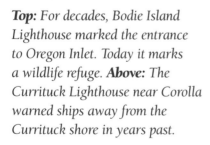

Top: For decades, Bodie Island Lighthouse marked the entrance to Oregon Inlet. Today it marks a wildlife refuge. ***Above:*** The Currituck Lighthouse near Corolla warned ships away from the Currituck shore in years past.

sands on the ocean bottom, making the waters shallow. These shallow waters are dangerous to ships. So many ships have run aground near Cape Hatteras that the area is called the "Graveyard of the Atlantic." In the 1800s, the government built lighthouses to warn ships away from the dangerous waters. These lighthouses still stand at the capes and at Bodie Island.

The Outer Banks were settled mainly by English people. Isolated through the centuries, their descendants still pronounce many words as the early English did. They made their living by fishing and lifesaving, having saved many people involved in shipwrecks along the coast.

Today, the Outer Banks form a great recreation area. Beach cottages and condominiums crowd areas like Nags Head and Ocracoke. People go there to swim, rest, relax, and fish. Congress has created two national seashores

along the Outer Banks. Called the Cape Hatteras and Cape Lookout national seashores, they stretch for 170 miles along the coast.

Across the sounds from the Outer Banks is the mainland part of the Tidewater. This area is poorly drained and contains many swamps, ponds, and streams. Between Albemarle Sound and Norfolk, Virginia, lies the Great Dismal Swamp. Although a highway runs through the swamp, it is still a wild area.

Within the Tidewater are the major coastal towns, among the oldest in the state. They include Elizabeth City, Edenton, Washington, New Bern, Beaufort, Wilmington, and Southport. The major ports of Wilmington and Morehead City are located in the Tidewater. The largest universities in the Tidewater are Elizabeth City State and UNC-Wilmington.

Salt marshes, like this one at Roanoke Island, are very valuable to the environment. They control erosion, cleanse the water, and serve as a nursery for fish.

MOVING THE CAPE HATTERAS LIGHTHOUSE

In April 1999, the candy-striped Cape Hatteras Lighthouse stood 130 feet from the ocean. Yet by August, it was 3,000 feet from the ocean. How did this happen? Did the ocean recede?

Amazingly, the 4,800-ton, 208-foot-tall lighthouse was moved. A chimney company jacked it up on steel beams, put it on steel rollers, and pushed it with hydraulic jacks along seven steel tracks. The journey ended when the lighthouse was lowered onto a 5-foot-deep concrete base far from the ocean. People who had opposed the move feared the brick lighthouse would crumble as it moved; fortunately, it did not. The move was a marvel of engineering.

Why was the move necessary? When the lighthouse was completed in 1871, it was 1,500 feet from the ocean. Over the next century, the wind and the ocean slowly eroded the shoreline and endangered the lighthouse. Erosion is a natural process; sand swept from some beaches builds up on others. Some people proposed that sand-trapping seawalls be built to protect the lighthouse. But Duke University professor Orrin Pilkey, Jr., and other scientists argued that the natural erosion process should not be hindered. They showed that over time seawalls would not stop the erosion. As a result, North Carolina became the first state to ban building beach walls except in special cases.

Top: The Cape Hatteras lighthouse in its original location. ***Above:*** A close-up showing the lighthouse raised on yellow support beams. The red panel on the front controlled the 60 hydraulic jacks used to raise and lower the lighthouse. ***Opposite page:*** The lighthouse about halfway to its new site.

The lighthouse was declared a special case, but a sandbag wall built in 1990 did not stop the erosion around it. People feared that the lighthouse would be destroyed if hit by a hurricane. They still demanded that the lighthouse be saved. Outer Bankers had an emotional attachment to it. Tourists drove hundreds of miles to see the lighthouse, the tallest in the nation. An editor wrote that it was an object of "grace, beauty, and strength." So, after years of study, the lighthouse was moved so that we and future generations could continue to enjoy it.

At one time, planters grew rice along the lower Cape Fear River. The rising and falling tides made it possible to flood and drain rice fields inside dikes. Rice is no longer grown commercially, but you can still see old rice fields at Orton Plantation near Wilmington. The state's major phosphate deposits are in the Tidewater. Phosphates are used to make fertilizers.

Many historic sites in the Tidewater area are open to visitors. Tryon Palace at New Bern is the restored colonial capitol of North Carolina. Sites of important Civil War battles are Fort Macon near Morehead City and Fort Fisher below Wilmington. At Brunswick Town on the lower Cape Fear River are the remains of a town burned by the British in 1776. Nearby is Orton Plantation. The World War II battleship *North Carolina* is docked at Wilmington.

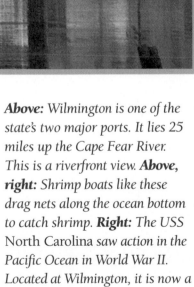

Above: Wilmington is one of the state's two major ports. It lies 25 miles up the Cape Fear River. This is a riverfront view. *Above, right:* Shrimp boats like these drag nets along the ocean bottom to catch shrimp. *Right:* The USS North Carolina *saw action in the Pacific Ocean in World War II. Located at Wilmington, it is now a museum and is open to visitors.*

Inner Coastal Plain

The Inner Coastal Plain stretches from the Tidewater to the Fall Line. The sandy soil has made this area the state's prime agricultural region. Tobacco is the main crop, but farmers also grow cotton, corn, wheat, peanuts, soybeans, vegetables, and fruit. Farmers also raise beef and dairy cattle, hogs, and poultry. Fayetteville is the largest city in the area. Other large towns and centers of agricultural trade include Goldsboro, Wilson, Rocky Mount, and Greenville.

There is also manufacturing in the Inner Coastal Plain. Lumber, clothes, tobacco products, textiles, chemicals, paper, and electric machinery are among the products produced here.

The Sandhills area of the Inner Coastal Plain is noted for its golf courses. Starting in the 1890s, wealthy northerners wintered around Pinehurst and played golf for recreation. They helped develop the area as a major golfing center.

The Inner Coastal Plain is home to many colleges and universities. The largest are East Carolina University at Greenville and Fayetteville State University. Pembroke State University is located at Pembroke. Founded to meet the educational needs of the Lumbee Indians, people of all races now attend it.

Above: *Tobacco is the state's most valuable crop. Here a farmer picks the first leaves, the largest ones at the bottom of the plant.* **Left:** *As farming declined in the Coastal Plain, factories moved in. Here a woman operates a drill press in a factory at Clinton.* **Opposite page, top:** *The sandy soil and warm weather of the Sandhills are ideal for peach orchards.* **Opposite page, bottom:** *The warm winters and scenic views attract golfers to the Sandhills.*

Above: The rich clay soils of the Piedmont produce abundant grains, tobacco, cotton, hay, and livestock. **Opposite page:** Raleigh is the state's capital. It has grown rapidly because of the nearby Research Triangle Park and the expansion of state government.

THE PIEDMONT

Lying between the Fall Line and the Blue Ridge Mountains is the Piedmont, meaning "at the foot of the mountains." The land in this area rises from about 500 to 1,500 feet. Its geography features rolling hills, hardwood forests, mineral deposits, and many water-power sites along swift-flowing streams.

The Piedmont is the center of the state's **urban** (city) population. The state's largest cities are located in the Piedmont: Charlotte, Raleigh, Greensboro, Winston-Salem, and Durham. The building of the North Carolina Railroad and the rise of the tobacco and textile industries in the 1800s helped these cities grow.

The Piedmont is also the center of manufacturing for the state. The abundant hydroelectric power in the area led to the development of its three major industries—textiles, tobacco, and furniture. Recently,

other types of manufacturing have arisen. They include food, machinery, chemicals, printing, electrical equipment, clothing, plastics, and fabricated metals.

The availability of many minerals also helped the economic growth of the Piedmont. Before 1849, North Carolina was the leading gold-producing state in the nation. The federal government minted gold coins at Charlotte. Once gold was discovered in California, however, gold mining in North Carolina declined. At one time iron ore, coal, and tungsten were mined in the Piedmont, but those deposits too declined. Talc, lithium, and feldspar are among the minerals mined in the state today. Sand, gravel, and clay are abundant in the area and are the basis for a large brick industry.

The rich clay soil of the Piedmont nourishes a variety of crops. Tobacco, corn, wheat, and soybeans are grown here. Dairy herds, beef cattle, poultry, and hogs also contribute to farm income.

The Piedmont is the state's center of higher education, boasting three major research universities. These are Duke University in Durham, the

University of North Carolina at Chapel Hill, and North Carolina State University at Raleigh. Three other important schools are the North Carolina Agricultural and Technical State University at Greensboro, the University of North Carolina at Greensboro, and the University of North Carolina at Charlotte. Wake Forest University in Winston-Salem and Davidson College in Davidson are noted for their strong liberal arts programs.

The Piedmont is also a center for the state's cultural activities. Raleigh is home to state museums of art, history, and natural science. Winston-Salem features a restored Moravian village, a museum of early decorative arts, a contemporary art gallery, a dance company, and the restored home of a tobacco manufacturer. The Mint Museum of Art is located at Charlotte. Larger cities have active symphonies and theaters. Near Asheboro is the state zoo, which promises to be one of the best in the South. Important historic sites include the Guilford Court House Battleground from the Revolutionary War, the Reed Gold Mine below Concord, and Spencer Shops near Salisbury, which house a transportation museum.

Above: The state's textile industry developed before the Civil War. Located mainly in the Piedmont, it has been one of the state's biggest employers. ***Opposite page, top:*** The furniture industry developed first in High Point and Mebane in the 1880s. Today it is one of the state's most important industries. ***Opposite page, bottom:*** Duke University is one of the leading universities in the nation. Towering over the campus, the chapel holds the tomb of the university's patron, James Buchanan Duke.

THE MOUNTAINS

Between the Piedmont and the state of Tennessee is the Mountain region. Its **elevation** (its height above sea level) ranges from about 1,500 to 6,600 feet. The mountains are part of the Appalachian chain, which runs southwest to northeast from Georgia to Quebec. At the eastern edge is a range called the Blue Ridge Mountains. At the western edge are ranges that include the Unakas and Great Smokies. In between are broad highland valleys. Connecting the eastern and western ranges are ridges like the Balsams and the Black Mountains. Some forty peaks in the Mountain region are over 6,000 feet high. At 6,684 feet, Mount Mitchell in Yancey County is the highest peak in the eastern United States.

The Mountain region was the last in the state to be settled by Europeans. The lack of roads isolated the early settlers and helped them preserve parts of their nineteenth-century culture. As a result, the mountain people have close-knit families whose ballads, manners of speech, handicrafts, and beliefs go back many years. The state's only Indian reservation is located at Cherokee. A part of the tribe refused to be removed to Oklahoma in the 1830s. Their descendants still live on the reservation and preserve their language and culture.

The Mountain region is still largely **rural** (country), with many small farms. In fact, Asheville is the only large city. As a result, agriculture is important. The leading crops are burley tobacco (which is air-cured), corn, soybeans, wheat, vegetables, and apples. A crop of increasing importance is Christmas trees. The higher elevations are ideal for growing Fraser fir, white pine, and hemlock trees. Livestock include poultry, beef cattle, and dairy herds.

*Top: The Blue Ridge Mountains mark the eastern boundary of the Mountain region. Gaps enabled early settlers to enter the mountains. **Above:** Mountain-reared Doc Watson has become one of the leading singers of folk music.*

Left: *The Appalachian Trail runs through the mountains from Georgia to Maine. The highest and most scenic parts are in North Carolina.* **Above:** *The Joyce Kilmer National Forest preserves the state's largest virgin forest. Some of the giant poplars and hemlocks are over 600 years old.*

The Pisgah and Nantahala national forests, the state's largest, are located in the mountains. These forests provide wood for logging and the lumber industry. They are also favorite sites for camping, fishing, and hunting.

Mining is an important activity in the Mountain region. Among the minerals found in this region are feldspar, olivine, kaolin, mica, asbestos, marble, talc, and gemstones. Near Franklin, tourists may still mine for precious stones, including sapphires, rubies, and garnets.

Although the Mountain region is basically rural, there is some industry. The leading industries are textiles, clothing, furniture, electrical machinery, paper, chemicals, rubber, and plastics. The largest state universities in the Mountain region are Western Carolina at Cullowhee and Appalachian State at Boone. Another important institution is the University of North Carolina at Asheville.

More recently, tourism has become very important. The 254 miles of the Blue Ridge Parkway in North Carolina attract 14 million visitors a year. The Great Smoky Mountains National Park (half in North Carolina and half in Tennessee) draws over 8 million visitors a year for camping, fishing, and hiking. The Appalachian Trail runs through North Carolina on its way from Georgia to Maine and attracts many hikers. The

mountains also have two major wilderness areas at Linville Gorge and Shining Rock. Some of the last virgin forest in the state can be found at Joyce Kilmer Memorial Forest. In the winter, skiing is popular, especially in Watauga and Avery counties.

The Carl Sandburg home at Flat Rock and the Thomas Wolfe home in Asheville introduce visitors to two great American literary figures. The Biltmore Estate in Asheville, the summer home of the Vanderbilts of New York, gives tourists a glimpse of how wealthy families lived around 1900.

Do You Remember?
1. What borders North Carolina on the north, south, east, and west?
2. What are North Carolina's three distinct geographical divisions?
3. What three capes are part of the Outer Banks?
4. What five large cities are located in the Piedmont?
5. What three major universities are located in the Piedmont?
6. Before 1849, North Carolina was the leading producer of what precious metal?
7. What is the highest peak in the eastern United States?

Above: *Asheville is the only large city in the Mountain region. Tourism, retailing, manufacturing, and medical care are important to its economy.* **Opposite page, top:** *Mountain farmers grow burley tobacco. They cut the stalks with leaves on them and air-dry them in open barns.* **Opposite page, bottom:** *Mountain farmers terrace hilly land to prevent erosion.*

Water and waterways have always been important to North Carolina. In the colonial period and later, waterways were the main highways. They were also important for turning the water wheels that powered early machinery and for turning the turbines that generated electricity. Recent periods of **drought** (long periods without rainfall) have made people aware of the need to conserve water.

THE ATLANTIC OCEAN

The largest body of water bordering the state is the Atlantic Ocean. In early days, it was like a large highway used by ships to bring settlers to North Carolina. Later, it served as a trade route. Ships still sail this ocean with goods from the many nations of the world. The state's two main ports are Wilmington and Morehead City.

The Atlantic Ocean has several features that make it important to the state. Two great **currents** (flows of water within a larger body of water, such as the ocean) meet off the coast. The Labrador Current flows south and brings cold water. The warm Gulf Stream flows north and veers out to sea near Cape Hatteras. The meeting of the two currents off Cape Hatteras has created a rich fishing ground.

The continental shelf extends along the bottom of the Atlantic from the coastline to distances of 16 to 65 miles off shore. The **continental shelf** is an underwater plain extending out from a continent. This area, which is never more than 300 feet deep, is the area where most fish are found. It is also the area where offshore oil and gas are likely to be found. Near Capes Fear, Lookout, and Hatteras, the continental shelf gets shallow. These shallows are called **shoals**. Thirty feet or less deep, these shoals may range 20 miles or more out to sea. Ships coming too close to shore sometimes run aground on the shoals.

Inlets are the places where the ocean flows between the Outer Banks toward the mainland. At high tide, the ocean flows toward the mainland. At low tide, the water flows back into the ocean. This causes strong currents in the inlets. The currents push sand along the bottom, filling in old channels and creating new ones. This makes navigation of the inlets very dangerous. The main inlets are Oregon, Hatteras, and Ocracoke.

THE SOUNDS

Between the Outer Banks and the mainland are shallow bodies of water called **sounds**. Although the water in the sounds may be 30 feet deep in places, it is usually only 3 to 5 feet deep. North Carolina has five major sounds. From north to south they are: Currituck, Albemarle, Pamlico, Core, and Bogue. Pamlico and Albemarle are the two largest. Because

Top: *Fishing is important to the coastal economy.* **Above:** *The Intracoastal Waterway enables small boats to travel from Currituck to Calabash without entering the ocean.*

WATER TRANSPORTATION AND CITIES

During the seventeenth and early eighteenth centuries, the most notable cities to arise in America were New York, Boston, Charles Town, and Philadelphia. Their growth into major cities happened in part because of their geographical locations near deep water.

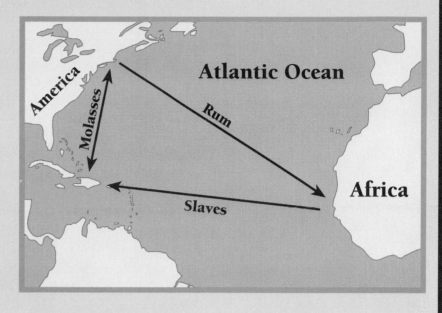

The four cities became important trading centers, exporting local commodities and importing goods from many points around the Atlantic basin. All had deep water to accommodate large ocean-going ships and smaller coastal vessels. All had harbors protected from wind and wave. All developed wharves for loading and unloading cargo. All were located on rivers, which encouraged trade with the backcountry: Charles Town at the junction of the Ashley and Cooper rivers; Philadelphia on the Delaware; New York on the Hudson; and Boston on the Charles.

Farmers and other workers produced more goods than could be used locally. They sold their goods to city merchants. The merchants sold the goods mainly to the West Indies to get money, slaves, sugar, spices, and molasses to make into rum. Profits from this trade were used to import manufactured goods from Great Britain.

Trade increased the wealth of these cities. That wealth enabled them to become important economic, cultural, and political centers.

The route used by the merchants to keep rum, molasses, and slaves flowing between America, the West Indies, and Africa was known as the Triangular Trade Route.

Albemarle and Currituck sounds have no inlets, ocean water cannot flow freely into them. Their waters are thus less salty than the others. Fresh water from rivers flows into the sounds all the time. The mingling of fresh and salty water results in *brackish* water.

An important water route called the Intracoastal Waterway runs through the sounds. Completed in the 1930s, the Intracoastal Waterway is at least 10 feet deep and runs from Maine to Texas. Large barges and pleasure boats use it constantly.

*Above: Oriental Harbor on Pamlico Sound supports recreational and fishing boats. **Oppo-site page, top:** The town of Washington developed in the nineteenth century because of its location on the Tar-Pamlico River and the Pamlico Sound. **Opposite page, bottom left:** In early days, the Neuse River, seen here at Smithfield, was an important route of commerce. **Opposite page, bottom right:** The Cape Fear River is the state's only long, navigable river flowing directly into the Atlantic Ocean.*

The sounds cover about 8 million acres; the shoal waters in the ocean cover about 6 million acres. These waters form one of the best fish breeding grounds in the eastern United States. The commercial fishing industry catches millions of dollars worth of fish a year. The most valuable finfish are menhaden, flounder, and striped bass. The most valuable shellfish are crab, scallop, and shrimp.

RIVERS

North Carolina has many rivers, most of them beginning from small streams in the Piedmont or the mountains. Only one of the rivers flows directly into the Atlantic Ocean inside the state. That is the Cape Fear River, and it is the only one that large ships can navigate.

Four sizable rivers flow into the sounds. They are the Chowan, Roanoke, Tar-Pamlico, and Neuse. Two large rivers, the Yadkin-Pee Dee and the Catawba, flow from the Piedmont into South Carolina.

The eastern continental divide lies in the mountains. East of the divide, the rivers flow into the Atlantic Ocean. West of the divide, the streams flow into one of the rivers that feed the Ohio River. These rivers are the Hiwassee, Little Tennessee, French Broad, Watauga, and New.

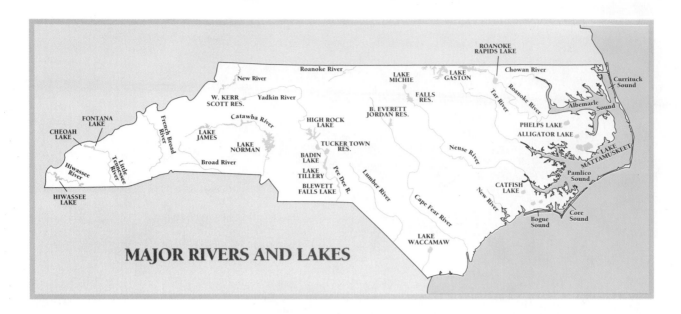

MAJOR RIVERS AND LAKES

Above: The state's rivers and lakes provide water resources for recreation, wildlife, and the generation of electrical power.
Right: The goldenrod flowers along a small inlet on Lake Mattamuskeet are in full bloom. Lake Mattamuskeet is North Carolina's largest natural lake. It is a wildlife refuge, especially for ducks and geese.

LAKES

There are about 50,000 lakes and ponds in the state. All of the natural lakes are in the Coastal Plain. The largest of these are Mattamuskeet, Phelps, and Waccamaw. In the 1920s, Lake Mattamuskeet was drained and the lake bottom farmed. It was too expensive, however, to keep the water pumped out. The lake is now a wildlife preserve.

Most of the lakes are man-made. Some of the lakes are a result of flood-protection measures. Others were created for recreation, to store water for downstream use, to generate hydroelectric power, or to cool thermo-electric power plants. The three largest man-made lakes in the state are Fontana Lake on the Little Tennessee, Lake Norman on the Catawba, and Lake Gaston on the Roanoke. The water held in these three lakes could cover Mecklenburg County with about seven feet of water.

The wake of a boat disturbs the placid surface of Lake Lure, a man-made lake near Chimney Rock in the Blue Ridge Mountains

Do You Remember?

1. What are the two great currents that meet off the North Carolina coast to create a rich fishing ground?
2. Why are the inlets so dangerous to navigation?
3. What is the only river in North Carolina that flows directly into the Atlantic Ocean?
4. Where do the rivers east of the continental divide flow? Where do rivers west of the continental divide flow?

Above: The mountains get more snowfall than other parts of the state. Many ski resorts flourish during the winter. ***Below right:*** North Carolina gets enough rainfall to grow a variety of crops and forests. Rainfall is generally heavier in the mountains and along the coast.

CLIMATE

North Carolina's climate is a *humid subtropical* one. That is, it produces distinct changes in the seasons and supports a wide variety of **flora** (plants) and **fauna** (animals).

The annual rainfall averages from 44 inches in the northern Piedmont to 70 inches in the southern mountains. Snowfall is heaviest in the moun-

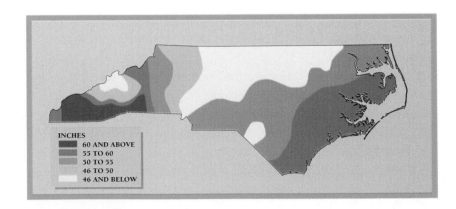

INCHES
- 60 AND ABOVE
- 55 TO 60
- 50 TO 55
- 46 TO 50
- 46 AND BELOW

tains, averaging 10 inches a year. Along the coast, snowfall averages less than 2 inches. The state goes through periodic droughts. Dry spells were bad in 1933, 1968, the late 1980s, and at the turn of the century.

Temperatures vary widely from the coast to the mountains. In July, the average temperature ranges from the 60s to the 80s. In January, the average temperature ranges from 48°F (Fahrenheit) on the coast to below 36°F in the mountains. The yearly number of frost-free days averages 270 along the coast and 130 in the northern mountains. Overall, the state can grow any crop or tree that does well in a subtropical climate. The mountain growing season, however, is too short for the cotton, peaches, plums, pecans, and figs that grow to the east. Some of the mountaintops have Canadian-type forests.

WINDSTORMS

While the climate is mild, the state does experience three kinds of windstorms. These are thunderstorms, hurricanes, and tornadoes. The most common are *thunderstorms*, caused by rapidly rising warm air and cold downdrafts. Accompanied by thunder, lightning, and blowing rain, they occur about forty to fifty days a year.

Hurricanes are storms that arise in the tropical Atlantic Ocean and cover hundreds of square miles. A storm becomes a hurricane when its winds measure 74 miles per hour. Those winds blow counterclockwise around an "eye." Warm ocean waters feed hurricanes, but, once over land, hurricanes lose speed and intensity. When they strike the coast, they may push high walls of water ahead of them. Flood damage is often as great as the wind damage. Hurricane season runs from June through November. The area around Cape Hatteras is most likely to be hit by hurricanes and the mountains the least. Over the years, hurricanes have changed the geography of the Outer Banks. Hurricane Floyd in 1999 was the most destructive storm in recent history. Heavy rains flooded the Coastal Plain, killing thirty-five people. Thousands were left homeless, and crop damage was widespread.

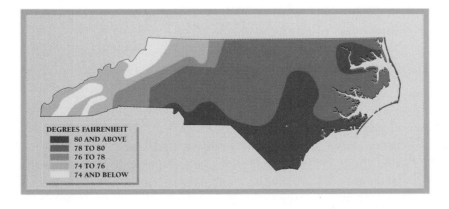

DEGREES FAHRENHEIT
- 80 AND ABOVE
- 78 TO 80
- 76 TO 78
- 74 TO 76
- 74 AND BELOW

Left: This map shows average temperatures around North Carolina during July. **Above:** *Springtime in North Carolina not only means budding flowers and trees, it also means tornado weather.*

A hurricane in 1973 destroyed these buildings near the coast. High winds and tidal floods make hurricanes destructive.

Tornadoes usually occur from March through May when very hot and cold air masses meet. Tornado winds can reach speeds of up to 500 miles an hour. The power of a tornado is awesome. When it drops from the clouds, this funnel-shaped storm damages or destroys almost everything in its path. It can demolish buildings and drive pieces of straw through telephone poles. Luckily, the destructive paths of tornadoes average less than 400 yards wide by 10 miles long. The state averages about three tornadoes a year, mainly in the Piedmont.

Do You Remember?
1. What type of climate does North Carolina have?
2. What are three kinds of windstorms experienced by North Carolina?
3. When does a tropical storm become a hurricane?
4. Which region of the state has the largest average annual rainfall?
5. What is the range of North Carolina's average July temperature?

HOW GEOGRAPHY AFFECTED DEVELOPMENT

Geography greatly influenced the history and development of the people of North Carolina. Climate and soils, waterways, and natural resources had an impact on the way the state developed.

CLIMATE AND SOILS

The fertile soil and subtropical climate with its abundant rainfall and mild temperatures have resulted in a wide variety of crops and trees in the state. Rainfall of just ten inches a year would have made it impossible to grow corn, tobacco, and cotton. The land would likely have been covered with grassy plains rather than great forests.

WATERWAYS

Ships crossing the Atlantic Ocean from Europe and Africa needed good ports to land people and cargoes. The coast of North Carolina was

This is a 1780 engraving of the harbor at Charleston, South Carolina. In early days, much trade from North Carolina went through this port and helped it grow.

dangerous and ports few. Ships could run aground on shoals and break up. The earliest towns were on Albemarle and Pamlico sounds, which could not be reached by large ocean-going ships. In colonial times, the two best ports were Beaufort and Wilmington. Both were reached by navigating shallow inlets and shifting channels.

Ship captains preferred large, safe ports. They found such ports at Charleston to the south and on Chesapeake Bay to the north. As a result, Charleston and the towns in the Chesapeake Bay area became centers of wealth, political leadership, and culture. North Carolina's ports were smaller, less prosperous, and had fewer cultural advantages. Although the state has developed docks and deepened the channels at Morehead City and Wilmington, more ships still visit Charleston and Norfolk.

Because North Carolina had few good ports, settlement spread out evenly across the state. The first colonists settled around Albemarle Sound. Later colonists made their way overland from Virginia, South Carolina, and Pennsylvania to the backcountry. Because the people were spread out, few large towns arose. North Carolina still has no single large population center and is as much rural as urban.

The lack of good ports had other results. African slaves came in largely through the ports of neighboring colonies. This made slaves more difficult to get and more expensive. Without the labor needed to farm large amounts of land, plantations in North Carolina were smaller and the planters made less money. There was much less wealth in North Carolina than in its neighboring colonies. This led one historian to refer to the colony as "Poor Carolina."

Because ports were poor and farms smaller, no large aristocracy or privileged upper class developed as in Virginia and South Carolina. No families like the Washingtons, Byrds, Jeffersons, or Laurenses provided political leadership. In North Carolina, leadership fell upon men of the "middling sort." There is a kernel of truth to the old saying that North Carolina was "a vale of humility between two mountains of conceit."

North Carolina's rivers served as highways in the early days, but these highways did not unite the people. Nor did they keep all trade within the state. The rivers of the Coastal Plain, except for the Cape Fear, emptied into the sounds.

GEOGRAPHY'S EFFECT ON HISTORY

Geography has played an important role in American history. In early days, the Atlantic Ocean was a great "highway" that brought Europeans and Africans to America. That highway was also an important trade route among the three continents.

The Appalachian Mountains were a barrier to early westward movement. But that barrier gave the young British colonies time to grow and prosper before settlers pushed over the mountains.

The great inland river systems —the Ohio, Mississippi, Missouri, Red, and Arkansas—carried farm products to New Orleans for export. The need to protect those river routes led the United States to seek control of the mouth of the Mississippi.

America's geography also helped determine the types of economies that arose. For example, New England's narrow, rocky coast fostered an economy based on manufacturing, trade, fishing, shipbuilding, and small-farm agriculture. The wide coastal plain and subtropical climate of the South led to plantations, slavery, and agriculture for export. The treeless plains beginning in Illinois were perfect for grain and livestock production. The geography of the Midwest provided not only the raw materials for industry—coal deposits in Pennsylvania, iron ore in Minnesota, limestone in the Ohio Valley—but also lakes and river systems for cheap transportation for both raw materials and finished products.

Farmers along the Virginia border found it easier to trade with Petersburg and Norfolk. The Lumber, Yadkin-Pee Dee, Catawba, and Broad rivers flowed into South Carolina, promoting trade with Columbia, Georgetown, and Charleston. The mountain rivers flowed northward and westward; trade in the mountains turned toward Virginia and Tennessee.

As you can see, the natural transportation system did not tie the sections of the state together. Each of the three sections of the state tried to advance its own interests. **Sectionalism**, an exaggerated allegiance to the interests of one's own region, developed. Politicians became more loyal to their region than to the state. By the 1890s, the railroads tied the state together, but by that time sectionalism had become deeply rooted in state politics.

NATURAL RESOURCES

Natural resources have influenced the state's history and development. The large Coastal Plain forests enabled colonists to make a living. From the longleaf pines, they made turpentine, rosin, tar, and pitch. From white oak, they made barrels. And from cypress, they made shingles. All of these items were important to foreign trade. Later, the hardwood forests of the Piedmont provided wood for the furniture industry.

Before the Civil War, gold mining brought great wealth to the state. The rich clay deposits gave rise to the brick industry and pottery making. Iron ore and coal supported early industry.

Without abundant ground water for wells and streams for reservoirs, people could not have easily settled on the land. Water resources also made the state a leader in generating hydroelectric power.

HOW PEOPLE AFFECT GEOGRAPHY

Over the years, people have gradually changed North Carolina's geography. One change has been in the number and variety of the state's plants and animals. Elk, buffalo, panthers, wolves, passenger pigeons, Carolina parakeets, and ivory-billed woodpeckers once called the state home, but no longer. In the 1950s, the use of DDT as an insect killer nearly wiped out bald eagles, bluebirds, osprey, pelicans, and peregrine falcons. The great Coastal Plain pine forests were largely cut down for lumber, tar, and turpentine. Only a few stands of the great longleaf pines remain.

Our water resources have also been damaged. Wastes from sewers, industries, and farms have polluted rivers and streams. Some fish have absorbed high levels of chemicals and are unsafe to eat. Even ground water, from which people draw drinking water in rural areas, has become polluted. Rusted metal gasoline storage tanks have released gasoline into ground water. Chemicals from industrial dumps have seeped into the ground. Some well water is unfit to drink. Silt from building projects has clogged streams and lakes and destroyed spawning areas for fish.

Motor vehicles and industry are major sources of air pollution. Gases from these sources combine with moisture to form **acid rain**. The most tragic results of acid rain may be found on mountains like Mount Mitchell, Richland Balsam, and Clingman's Dome. In a process not yet understood, acid rain and insects seem to have destroyed whole mountaintop forests of red spruce and Fraser fir. The once lush forests of beautiful evergreens are now cemeteries of dead gray trees.

Air pollution of the upper atmosphere may help to produce the "greenhouse effect" that is warming the earth. Scientists believe that increasingly warmer air may someday melt the polar icecaps and raise the levels of the oceans, submerging low-lying land like the Outer Banks.

The spraying of insecticides almost destroyed the bald eagle, but its numbers are now growing.

People are becoming more aware of the need to make the environment safer for humans, plants, and animals. Governments now prevent the filling-in of wetlands and are moving to clean the air and water by requiring better sanitary landfills. People recycle more glass, metals, and plastics to keep down the amount of garbage. It is now illegal to dump raw sewage into streams. The use of DDT has stopped. Motor vehicles must have pollution control devices to cut down on the gases they give off. Industrial waste dumps are being cleaned up.

Above left: Richland Balsam Mountain near Waynesville is covered with dead spruce trees. Scientists think that a combination of acid rain and non-native insects killed them. ***Above right:*** To save the environment, people are learning to recycle trash.

Do You Remember?

1. What three things are necessary to grow the wide variety of crops and trees in the state?
2. What was the harmful effect of DDT on the wildlife of the state?
3. What have been some of the causes of the damage to North Carolina's water resources?
4. What are the major causes of air pollution?

CHAPTER · REVIEW

Reviewing People, Places, and Terms

Define, identify, or explain the importance of the following.

1. acid rain
2. cape
3. continental shelf
4. current
5. drought
6. elevation
7. environment
8. Fall Line
9. fauna
10. flora
11. geography
12. hurricane
13. inlet
14. latitude
15. longitude
16. rural
17. sectionalism
18. shoal
19. sound
20. tornado
21. urban

Understanding the Facts

1. Where is the Fall Line in North Carolina? Why did early towns grow up along the Fall Line?
2. Why is the narrow eastern part of the Coastal Plain called "the Tidewater"?
3. Why are the coastal waters of North Carolina referred to as the "Graveyard of the Atlantic"?
4. What does *Piedmont* mean?
5. Why did so many larger businesses and factories get their start in the Piedmont region?
6. What types of crops are grown in the Mountain region?
7. What is the significance of the eastern continental divide?
8. In which region are all of North Carolina's natural lakes found?
9. How did North Carolina's coastal geography affect the settlement of the colony?
10. Why did sectionalism develop in the state?

Developing Critical Thinking

1. How does the higher elevation of the Mountain region affect the growing of crops?
2. How do you think settlement patterns of Europeans would have been affected if North Carolina's coastal waters had been deeper for ships and easier to navigate?
3. What do you think was meant by the old saying that North Carolina was "a vale of humility between two mountains of conceit"?
4. What are some ways in which the government has encouraged protection of the environment?

Applying Your Skills

1. For many years, lighthouses along North Carolina's coast have helped guide ships away from our dangerous waters. On a map, locate some of North Carolina's lighthouses. At your local library, research the Cape Hatteras Lighthouse or one of the other lighthouses along our state's coast. Draw a picture or make a model of one of the lighthouses.
2. Make a map that shows the topographical features (rivers, plains, and so on) of the county in which you live.
3. The lumber and furniture industries are important to North Carolina's economy. Collect samples of tree leaves in your area and identify these leaves using a guide book from your library. Are any of your local trees used in the lumber or furniture industries? What businesses in your county rely on wood from these kinds of trees to make their products?

4. Take hourly readings of the temperature on an outside thermometer to see how the temperature changes during the day. Determine the high and low temperatures and the average temperature for the day.

Making Connections
1. After reading the feature on page 35, why do you think the study of geography is important to the study of history?
2. Select a highway, river, or body of water in your area. Try to find out—in the library or from a local historian—what part it played in the settlement of your area. Write your findings in a brief report.
3. Identify the two largest ports in the state in terms of tonnage shipped through the port facilities.
4. How do you think large, landlocked cities such as Raleigh, Dallas, and Charlotte were able to develop without deep-water ports?

Tar Heel Trivia
- The first lighthouse along the coast of North Carolina was erected in 1795, on Bald Head Island. Bald Island is located at the mouth of the Cape Fear River.

BUILDING SKILLS: USING YOUR TEXTBOOK

Making proper use of your textbook is different from reading a novel or science fiction story. Your textbook could be thought of as having two parts: the narrative, which tells the story of the state of North Carolina, and the visual information, which makes the narrative come alive. The visual information—cartoons, illustrations, maps, charts, and captions (copy printed below or alongside illustrations)—is an important part of your study of the history of North Carolina.

The narrative is divided into sections by headings. The major headings appear in capital letters and are large, bold, centered, and underlined. Lower-level headings are set in boldface capital letters and boldface italics. These headings are like an outline of the chapter. They help you organize the information in the chapter. If you scan these headings before you begin to read, you may better understand the overall plan of the chapter.

Look over the terms, people, and places listed in the "Chapter Preview" before you begin reading. If you do not know the meanings of some of the terms, locate them in the glossary at the back of the book or in a dictionary. The terms appear in boldface type the first time they appear in the narrative. They are often defined there, or you may be able to determine the meanings by the way they are used in the sentences.

Once you begin to read the chapter, read the narrative straight through without interruption. Answer the questions labeled "Do You Remember?" These questions will help you check your understanding of what you have read. After you have read the narrative, study the photographs and their captions and any maps and charts in the chapter. Photographs help you visualize some of the people, places, and events in the chapter. The captions may point out the important information about the photograph or provide more information about the subject or events. Maps and charts help you summarize information provided in the chapter.

Try the following activities.
1. Prepare an outline of Chapter 1 using the headings in the chapter.
2. Look at the maps in the chapter. What information do the maps provide? How do they help you understand the narrative?
3. Find two captions that provide information not included in the narrative. What is that information?
4. Find and list the photographs that illustrate the geographic region in which you live. Choose your favorite photograph from the list. Why did you chose that photograph?

Be sure to follow these suggestions as you read the rest of the chapters in the textbook.

CHAPTER TWO

NATIVE AMERICANS

...these Indians are the freest People in the World....

—John Lawson

FOR THOUSANDS OF YEARS before the Europeans came, people lived in North Carolina. In 1600, they numbered about 100,000 and were organized into many tribes. A **tribe** is a group of people who share a common ancestry, language, name, and way of living. Over the centuries, the Native Americans developed their own ways of living. These peoples and their ways of living had a great effect on the development of North Carolina.

ORIGINS

The origins of the Native Americans in America are hidden in the mists of time. Many scholars believe that the Indians' **ancestors** (those people from whom one is descended) came from Asia during the last Ice Age, which lasted from about 70,000 B.C. to 10,000 B.C. The extreme cold caused the glaciers to spread and the rivers to freeze. With fewer rivers flowing into them, the oceans shrank and the sea level dropped about 300 feet. A great spruce and pine forest grew up along what is now the North Carolina coast.

Twice during this Ice Age, the Bering Sea between Siberia and Alaska disappeared. Dry land then connected Asia and North America. The ancestors of Native Americans likely crossed this land bridge into North America during both of those periods. They spread out over North and South America, arriving in North Carolina about 14,000 years ago.

We know little about the Native Americans in the *pre-contact period*, the time before the Europeans arrived. The Indians had spoken languages, but they left no written records. What we do know comes from traditions and the studies of archaeologists. **Archaeologists** are scientists who study the items left behind by ancient peoples. Archaeologists dig up and examine such items as pieces of stone, bone, pottery, and tools to discover how the people lived. These items are called **artifacts**.

CHAPTER · PREVIEW

Terms: tribe, ancestor, archaeologist, artifact, culture, atlatl, agriculture, dialect, anthropologist, clan, maize

People: Paleo Indians, Archaic Indians, Woodland Indians, Mississippian Indians, Tuscarora, Catawba, Cherokee

Places: Bering Sea, Town Creek site

Opposite page: Richard Crowe of the Qualla Reservation displays the authentic dress of the Cherokee.

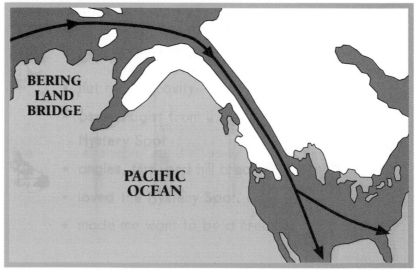

Above: *This painting depicts early Asians crossing the land bridge between Asia and Alaska during one of the Ice Ages. These Asians are thought to be the ancestors of Native Americans.* **Right:** *This map shows the location of the land bridge. Since the last Ice Age, ocean levels have risen and covered it. This land crossing is now at the bottom of the Bering Sea.*

BERING
LAND
BRIDGE

PACIFIC
OCEAN

PRE-CONTACT CULTURES

Archaeologists have grouped the pre-contact peoples into four **cultures**, or ways of life. The time frames given are estimates. One culture may have overlapped another by as much as 1,000 years.

PALEO CULTURE

The first of these cultures is called the Paleo culture. The word *paleo* means very old or long ago. The Paleo culture lasted until about 10,000 years ago. The Indians of this *paleolithic* (old stone) culture were nomadic hunters. That is, they wandered from place to place, following the herds of large animals.

The Paleo Indians chipped stone to form knives and scrapers and points for spears. With the spears, they hunted mammoth, camel, and an early kind of bison. The Paleo Indians probably hunted in small groups, creeping up on the large game animals so they could use their spears. Some of their spears had short removable shafts with points. They could then use the long part again and again.

Using only stone-tipped weapons and their ingenuity, Paleo Indians killed mammoth, as in the picture below, and other large animals.

ARCHAIC CULTURE

The word *archaic* means old. The Archaic culture covers the period from about 10,000 years ago to about 2,500 years ago. During this time, the large animals the Indians hunted for food died out. No one knows why, but a larger Indian population may have led to overhunting. To hunt smaller game, the Archaic people had to change their methods. For example, they used a short stick called an **atlatl**, which helped them throw spears with more force. Sometimes the Archaic people used a *bannerstone* on the atlatl to give it even more force. Since there were no longer herds of animals to follow, they stayed in one place longer. They then had time to fish and to gather plants, nuts, fruit, and roots for food.

The Archaic Indians shaped and polished stones and used them for bowls, tools, and pendants. They carved pipes from stone and used them for smoking. The Indians learned to boil food in soapstone bowls by dropping heated stones into the liquid. These stones were round and flat, with a hole in the middle. The cook could put a stick through the hole to move the stone from the fire to the bowl and back again.

The Archaic Indians buried the bodies of their dead with care, which means they may have believed in an afterlife.

*Top: Late Archaic peoples began to make crude pottery. **Above:** Woodland pottery was decorated in different ways. While still wet, the pottery was stamped with fabric, cord, corn cobs, or a carved paddle and sometimes carved with a tool.*

WOODLAND CULTURE

The Woodland culture developed about 1000 B.C. and lasted in North Carolina until about 1000 A.D. Like earlier groups, the Woodland people were hunters. They developed the bow and arrow for hunting, and deer was their chief game. They learned to grow crops. Using the rich land along rivers, they grew corn, squash, bottle gourds, and sunflowers. Since they no longer followed the herds, they began to build permanent villages. Their houses were round with grass roofs.

The Woodland people also gathered berries and nuts, storing the nuts in underground pits. To serve and store food, they created clay pottery, which they strengthened with small rocks and sand. Their jewelry consisted of ear spools and ornamental necklaces (called *gorgets*) made of copper and stone.

The Woodland people had great respect for the dead. They buried the dead in round pits along with items that belonged to the person such as pipes and necklaces.

MISSISSIPPIAN CULTURE

The Mississippian culture started about 700 A.D. along the Mississippi River near southern Illinois. It may have reached the southwestern mountains and the Pee Dee River area of North Carolina about the year 1300.

The Mississippian Indians were more likely to be farmers than hunters. **Agriculture** (farming) was so important to them that they had

ceremonies for planting and harvesting times. They built ceremonial centers, large cleared areas surrounded by fences to keep out enemies. Inside the fence was an earthen pyramid topped by a ceremonial building. The grounds around the base of the pyramid were used for ball games and dancing. The Town Creek site near Mount Gilead in Montgomery County is a good example of one of these centers. The Mississippians settled it about 1550, but remained for only about one hundred years. No one knows what happened to them.

Ceremonial mounds are also found in many places in western North Carolina. The largest and best preserved is in Franklin, at the old Cherokee town of Nikwasi. Other mounds were built in the Tuckaseigee, Valley, and Oconoluftee river valleys. Archaeologists do not believe that the Mississippians settled in this area, however. They think that the Cherokee adopted their ways.

The expansion of farming allowed more stable settlements and free time for the Woodland peoples. Circular houses, probably of pole, wickerwork, and bark construction, characterized Woodland settlements.

TOWN CREEK INDIAN MOUND

Over five hundred years ago, well before Columbus made his first voyage to America, a group of Native Americans moved into the area that later became part of North Carolina. These Native Americans settled in the Pee Dee River Valley in the southeastern Piedmont. The Indians, who were related to the Creek Nation, drove out Siouan tribes who lived in the area. They dominated this land for the next century, until about 1550.

The Creek did not live in one huge village, but in many villages scattered along the region's riverbanks and streams. Nearby, they built a cer-

emonial center, where they—" the people of one fire"— could gather for important events. Surrounded by a wall of logs plastered with mud and straw, this center included a burial house and priests' dwellings. Its most prominent structure was the major temple, which was located on top of an earthen mound, well above the other buildings. The site was sacred ground and was truly the focal point of Creek religious, social, and political life. In this center, the Creek held sun-worship rituals, funerals, feasts, and sporting events and celebrated victories in battle.

Today, the ceremonial center stands once again in a wide, grassy clearing surrounded by forest. Located five miles east of Mount Gilead is a reconstruction of the Creek's original fort-like ceremonial center. It is now a state historic site known as Town Creek Indian Mound. In addition to reconstructions of the major temple and other buildings, the site includes a modern museum where Creek artifacts are displayed.

*Opposite page top: A Creek priest presides over a burial in this recreation at Town Creek Indian Mound. **Below:** This is a view of the Town Creek site. These people built a palisade of logs for protection. They also dug an escape tunnel to the river bank.*

Mississippians built the Town Creek temple mound basket by basket of dirt. The mound is shaped like a pyramid with the top cut off.

The Mississippian Indians were better organized than earlier groups. They chose chiefs to lead the tribe in certain activities such as hunting and war.

Do You Remember?

1. How were the prehistoric peoples able to get across the Bering Sea to North America?
2. When did the first Native Americans arrive in North Carolina?
3. What are the four distinct pre-contact cultures archaeologists have identified?
4. What activity were the Mississippians more likely to be involved in than hunting?

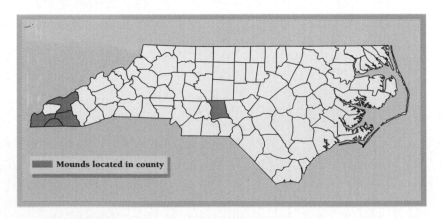

Mounds located in county

After making contact with the Indians, the Europeans began keeping records about them. The early Europeans were not the best observers, however. They thought that their own culture was superior and that the Indian culture was strange because it was different. Even so, their one-sided accounts provide more information than archaeological studies.

The earliest accounts describe the Indians by tribe and by language group. They identified twenty-eight tribes as living in North Carolina. The largest tribes were the Tuscarora, Catawba, and Cherokee. There were also many smaller tribes. Some of these died out from disease soon after their first contact with Europeans. Their names, however, remain upon the land: Cape Fear, Cheraw, Chowan, Coree, Eno, Hatteras, Neuse, Pamlico, Saxapahaw, Sugaree, Waxhaw.

The Indians spoke languages that belonged to three main families, or groups. These groups were *Algonquian*, *Iroquoian*, and *Siouan*. The tribes speaking Algonquian lived mainly along the coast. These included the Chowanoc, Moratoc, Pamlico, Roanoac, and Secotan tribes. Those speaking Iroquoian included the Tuscarora and the Cherokee. The Tuscarora lived in the Coastal Plain and the Cherokee in the Mountains. The Siouan-speaking tribes lived mainly in the Piedmont but were also in the southern Coastal Plain. The Cape

CONNECTING · HISTORY · AND · LANGUAGE

CAROLINA PLACE NAMES

Native Americans have left their mark upon North Carolina. The coastal area is full of descriptive Indian names. The name *Roanoke* is very common and is Algonquian for "northern people." The name of a river and county—Chowan—comes from the Algonquian *sorwan*, meaning "south." Other places are named for tribes: Core Sound for the Coranine or Coree tribe, Pamlico Sound for the Pamtecough and the Neuse River for the Neusick.

In the Piedmont, the Pee Dee River gets its name from the Catawba word *pi'ri*, meaning "something good." The Tuscarora word *e-eno* described the Eno River: "a great way" or "far off."

Mountain place names resound with the beautiful Cherokee language. The Nantahala Gorge gets its name from a Cherokee word meaning "land of the noonday sun." The gorge is so deep that the sun is seen only near mid-day. The word *unega*, meaning "white," is found in the names Unaka and Unicoi, mountain ranges bordering Tennessee. Cataloochee, the name of a creek and a ridge, comes from the Cherokee word *gad-a-lu-tsi*, meaning "standing in a row." It refers to the timber standing on the mountain.

These and many more beautiful Native American place names have added a lyrical richness to our language.

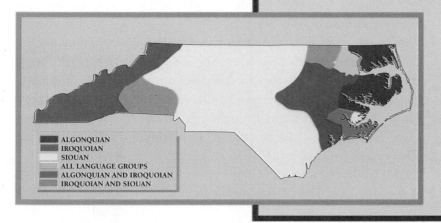

ALGONQUIAN
IROQUOIAN
SIOUAN
ALL LANGUAGE GROUPS
ALGONQUIAN AND IROQUOIAN
IROQUOIAN AND SIOUAN

John White's paintings on the Raleigh expeditions of 1584 and 1585-1586 provide much information on early Indians. This painting depicts the village of Pomelooc, located to the southwest of Lake Mattamuskeet.

Fear, Catawba, Occaneechi, Pedee, Saponi, Saura, Tutelo, and Waxhaw tribes are included in this last group.

Although tribes belonged to the same language group, they did not necessarily understand one another. The Tuscarora and Cherokee, for example, both spoke Iroquoian but could not understand each other's language. This is similar to the problem faced today by people who speak French, Spanish, and Italian. Even though all three languages come from Latin (the language of Rome), the speakers cannot understand one another unless they know the other languages.

Even within one tribe, there might be several **dialects**, or regional forms of the language. The Cherokee, for example, spoke three dialects of

Iroquoian. The Indians communicated by learning their neighboring tribe's language, by sign language, or by speaking Mobilian. Mobilian was a trading language based on Choctaw and was used throughout the Southeast.

Do You Remember?

1. Why were the European accounts of the Native Americans likely to be one-sided?
2. How many Native American tribes lived in North Carolina when the Europeans came?
3. How did the Native Americans communicate with each other since different tribes spoke different languages or dialects?

Above left: White painted the ways the Native Americans fished. Can you find a gig, a net, a weir, and spears? ***Above right:*** *Here is a chief, or "Herowan," from Roanoke. As a sign of wisdom, the men folded their arms when talking to one another.*

The manner of their attire and painting them selves when they goe to their generall huntinges, or at theire Solemne feasts.

Their ripe corne

Their greene corne

Corne newly sprong

Their sitting at meate

The place of solemne prayer

The house wherein the Tombe of their Herounds standeth

SECOTON

A Ceremony in their prayers w... strange iestures an shows dansing abowt posts carved on the tops lyke mens faces.

Left: This is White's painting of Secoton, located on the Pamlico River. The bottom house contained the bones of ancestors who had died. The ceremonial grounds next to this house were for prayer and celebration. The three fields on the right contain corn at different stages of growth. Opposite page, top left: White painted a priest who cut his hair differently and wore a rabbit skin cape. Opposite page, below left: John White painted the wife of the chief at Pomelooc carrying a child on her back. Opposite page, right: Some Indians painted their bodies when hunting and feasting, as White's painting shows. Did the red and white colors have special meaning?

Below: Swimmer, a Cherokee priest, was born about 1835. He related much of his knowledge of Cherokee lore to ethnologist James Mooney about 1887. *Right:* Today's Cherokee practice Christianity and sometimes engage in ancient religious rites.

BELIEF SYSTEMS

Although the Native Americans belonged to different tribes and spoke different languages, they had many common beliefs. All believed, for example, that many gods and spirits affected people on Earth. They believed that they must cleanse themselves inside and out to purify their spirits. They believed in an afterlife where brave warriors and faithful women were rewarded and cowards and thieves were punished.

Many beliefs are recorded in the works of **anthropologists**, scientists who study human cultures. Anthropologists interviewed Indians, mainly

Cherokee, over a hundred years ago. Many of the following beliefs, for example, were related by a Cherokee medicine man named Swimmer in the 1880s. In the 1700s, early explorers recorded similar stories.

This World

The Cherokee believed that Earth was a large island, resting on the waters. It hung from the sky by four cords, one each from the north, south, east, and west. The four directions were sacred, as was the number 4. Each direction had a special color. East was red and represented life and success. West was black, which stood for death. North was blue and indicated cold, trouble, and defeat. South was white and meant warmth, happiness, and peace. Each tribe thought that it was at the center of Earth, which it called "This World."

Above This World was the Upper World, which represented order and expectation. Cleaner and purer than This World, the Upper World lay above a sky vault of solid rock. Twice a day, the vault rose to let the sun and the moon pass below it. At night the sun returned to its starting point by passing over the sky vault so that it would not be seen. When the moon darkened from an eclipse, the Cherokee believed that a giant frog was trying to swallow the moon. They made noise to scare the frog into releasing the moon. It always worked.

Below the waters on which the earth rested was the Under World, a place of disorder and change. The Under World was the opposite of This World. For example, when it was summer in This World, it was winter in the Under World. The Under World was home to cannibals, ghosts, man-killing witches, and monsters. This World lay between the order of the Upper World and the confusion of the Under World. One could pass from This World into the Under World by entering deep water, guided by a friendly spirit.

This "buffalo man" mask was worn in ceremonies to depict the existence of ghosts, witches, and evil spirits.

Gods and Spirits

The chief gods, found in the Upper World, were the Sun and the Moon. The Sun was the main god, and she had the power of night and day, of life and breath. As a symbol of the Sun, the Cherokee kept a sacred fire burning. Keepers of the fire fed it some cornmeal or animal meat every day. The Indians believed that the Sun was kindhearted and watched over This World. In darkness, however, she was not watching and bad things could happen. The Moon was also a god, the Sun's brother. He represented rain and fertility.

The Cherokee had two other gods. One was Kanati, or the red man who lived above the sky vault in the east. Kanati's voice was thunder. The Cherokee believed Kanati was a friend and spoke of him with respect. The other god was Long Man, the river. His head rested in the hills and his feet in the lowlands. His voice could be heard in the rippling waters, and priests could interpret what he said.

Besides the chief gods, there were also lesser beings in the Under World who often helped the Indians. All of these lesser spirits had to be treated with honor so they would not become resentful and spread disease.

The Cherokee also believed in the Immortals and the Little People. The Immortals lived in the mountains, especially inside bald mountains and under Nikwasi Mound. They were invisible, except when they wanted to be seen. On one occasion, say the Cherokee, the Immortals came out from under the mound and helped to drive away an attacking tribe. The Little People were very short (about eighteen inches high) and had long hair. While they usually helped people, they were sometimes very mischievous, causing bewilderment and insanity.

The Cherokee also believed in ghosts, which were the spirits of dead persons. When a person died, if the person's ghost was not frightened away, it might stay and cause illness and death. The ghosts of murdered people, however, could not be frightened away. They remained until their murders were avenged.

The Cherokee also believed in two monsters. One was the Tlanuwa, the great hawk. The other was the Uktena, a dragon-like being. The Uktena had the body of a snake, the antlers of a deer, the wings of a bird, and sometimes the teeth and claws of a cougar. The Tlanuwa and the Uktena were mortal enemies. They usually ignored humans, but did sometimes kill them. The Cherokee believed that, just after the creation of the earth, a priest tricked the Tlanuwa into destroying the Uktena.

Animals

The Cherokee believed that there were three types of beings in This World. These were human beings, animals, and plants. Human beings and animals opposed one another. There were three kinds of animals: four-footed animals, birds, and vermin. The greatest of the four-footed animals was the deer.

Birds were important animals because they came in contact with the Upper World. Their feathers were often used in ceremonies. The most important bird was the eagle, which stood for peace and order. Its tail feathers were highly prized, and it was an honor to wear them. Falcon feathers were used to improve eyesight. Turkey buzzard feathers helped healing. The Cherokee associated the turkey and the red-bellied woodpecker with war.

Vermin included snakes, lizards, frogs, fish, and perhaps insects that were harmful to man, like fleas and hornets. Indians associated vermin with the Under World because many of them lived in water. They were afraid to kill a snake because it might want revenge. The rattlesnake, however, was different. The Cherokee believed it was once a man sent to This World to save humans from disease caused by the Sun. Eating its meat would make one fierce. Its rattles were used to scare enemies, its oil was good for sore joints, its fangs were used to draw blood during healing, and its bones were made into necklaces.

Some animals did not fit neatly into these three groups. The Cherokee believed that the owl was a witch because its eyes were spaced like a human's and it could see in the dark, unlike other birds. The bat and flying squirrel were four-footed but could also fly. The cougar was special

The Cherokee avoided most snakes, but they found ceremonial uses for the fangs and rattles of the rattlesnake.

because it could see in the dark and had claws like a bird. The frog and the turtle had four legs but lived in the water.

The bear was also a special case, for it stood on two legs like a man. The Cherokee believed that bears were once men who failed to avenge wrongs done to their people. Because this was a great crime, the men were turned into bears. Before the Indians killed any animal, they asked the animal's spirit to forgive them. But not the bear. Bear-men who would not avenge wrongs did not deserve respect.

PLANTS

Being the friends of humans, plants were used for food and to fight disease and bring healing. The most important plant and main source of food was corn.

The American Indians had over two hundred plants they used for medicine. Priests or medicine men often made a ceremony of giving out medicines. The root of bear grass was used against snakebite and rheumatism. To ease shortness of breath and to stop bleeding, the Cherokee drank a potion containing ginseng. Angelica root was good for back pain, while spicebush tea cleaned the blood. Horsemint tea brought on sweating and reduced swelling in the legs. The roots of the Venus flytrap and the pitcher plant were thought to have unusual powers because the plants fed on dead insects.

Tobacco was a special plant. When smoked in a pipe, its pure, white smoke rose up to the Upper World. As a result, the Cherokee, and most other tribes, used tobacco on ceremonial occasions when asking for blessings from the gods.

PURIFICATION

The Indians believed This World was usually orderly and predictable. While people stayed pure and behaved themselves and kept nature in balance, the spirits treated them justly. But illness and bad luck could come to people who misbehaved and polluted This World, especially by mixing things from the Upper World and the Under World. The body then had to be purified, inside and out. To cleanse the inside of the body, the person drank a black tea, usually yaupon (a type of holly). To cleanse the outside of the body, the person first spent time in a sweat house and then washed in a cold stream.

People in the tribe came from near and far to take part in the Green Corn Ceremony. The main purpose of the ceremony was to give thanks for the corn that would feed them for another year. It usually took place at the first full moon after the late corn ripened. The first day was spent feasting, cleaning all the buildings, and putting out all fires. The second day was a day of fasting. The men drank tea to cleanse themselves. During

As Native Americans developed agriculture, corn became their most important crop, a symbol of life.

the second day, the men would forgive wrongs done to them. Murder, however, was not forgiven. On the morning of the third day, everyone feasted again. That afternoon, the priest lit a new fire and carried it to the ceremonial center. From that fire the village fires were restarted. All wrongs were forgiven and the priest urged the people to remain pure so they would have good luck. Then the women joined the men in dancing. On the fourth day they feasted, danced, painted themselves with white clay, and took a ceremonial bath in a stream. Some North Carolina Native Americans still practice this ceremony.

LAW OF RETALIATION

The Cherokee had few laws. The most important was the law of retaliation. *To retaliate* means "to strike back or to get even." Believe it or not, the law of retaliation was used to prevent feuds and preserve peace within the tribe. According to this law, if one person injured another, the person harmed had the right to harm the first in a similar manner. If one person killed another, the spirit or ghost of the person who had been killed would not rest until relatives avenged the death. The dead person's kin did this by killing the killer or a close relative. The matter was then considered settled.

When one tribe killed people from another tribe, war often resulted. The Cherokee looked upon war as a way to avenge deaths and terrorize the enemy. The Cherokee did not often go to war to gain territory or property. Raiding the enemy was voluntary and a way to win honor. Warriors prepared for it by purifying themselves. Then, in small groups, they crept up on and attacked their enemies, taking trophies to show their people that the deaths were avenged. Sometimes the warriors returned with live captives.

Some tribes were mortal enemies, and they might travel hundreds of miles to make war. For some tribes, war was a way of life, a way to prove manhood and win glory. When tribes wanted to make peace, they asked a neutral tribe to arrange peace talks.

Cunne Shote, also called Stalking Turkey, was a Cherokee chief of the 1700s. In 1762 he traveled to England where he met George III. The cape and gorget shown in this painting were English gifts.

Do You Remember?

1. In the Cherokee belief system, what did the Upper World and Under World represent?
2. What were the four major gods of the Cherokee?
3. What did the Cherokee believe about the ghosts of murdered people?
4. According to the Cherokee, what were the three types of beings in This World?
5. What were three uses of plants by the Native Americans?
6. What was the purpose of the law of retaliation?

This 1797 lithograph shows a Cherokee village on the Tellico River, now part of Tennessee.

HOW NATIVE AMERICANS LIVED

Most North Carolina tribes had a mother-centered family system. Within a tribe were **clans**, groups of people who believed themselves related by blood. A clan was usually represented by a totem animal like a wolf. Women were at the center of these clans. As a result, women had a considerable voice in matters affecting the clan and the tribe.

The Family

Within the family system, a child was related by blood only to the mother, not to the father or the father's family. The parents and grand-parents, brothers and sisters, aunts and uncles, nieces and nephews, and other children of an Indian mother were her children's closest relatives. Therefore, her children could not marry any of them. Nor could they marry close relatives in their natural father's clan.

The mother's brothers were responsible for raising her children. Indian parents were loving and easy going and disciplined their children very little. John Lawson, an early English explorer, reported that a Catawba boy who almost hit him with an arrow was not even scolded.

In some tribes, mothers bound their babies to a board. This made it easier to care for the baby as the mother worked around the house or in

NATIVE AMERICAN GAMES

Scholars estimate that in 1492 there were about 2.5 million North American Indians in hundreds of tribes. Although they had different cultures and spoke over 300 languages, certain practices united them all. These practices were play, games, and sport.

Ball games were most popular among all tribes, and lacrosse was the most common game. Both men and women played it, and the number of people on a side could be 50 to 100. The game was very rough, and players sometimes broke bones. Shinny and double ball were two other popular ball games.

Foot racing was another universal and popular sport, especially in the Southwest. There, long distance runners excelled. One Cree Indian is recorded as running 125 miles in 25 hours. The Zuni could easily run 25 miles in 2 hours while kicking a ball! Speed and stamina were important because tribes communicated with one another by sending runners.

Games that children played helped prepare them for adult roles. Mudball fights were common, and children were taught not to cry when hit. Hide-and-seek taught the skills of searching and evading. Children also played archery games, wrestled, sledded, and raced on foot and on ponies.

These games and sports were common to all tribes, much as the Olympic sports are common to many nations.

The Choctaw Indians played ball games as a form of recreation. The games also helped them improve their skills for hunting and war. George Catlin caught the spirit of these games in his painting Choctaw Ball Game.

Above: This log house in the Oconoluftee Village in Cherokee is typical of eighteenth-century Cherokee dwellings. **Opposite page:** This replica of a Cherokee council house in Cherokee provides seating for representatives of the seven clans.

the fields. To the Cherokee, a flattened head was a mark of beauty. An Indian mother would bind her baby's head tightly to the board, flattening the back of the head.

Children played at games that helped them learn their adult roles. Boys learned to use the bow and arrow and girls learned to cook and tend small children. Special ceremonies marked the time when girls became women and boys became men.

Men and women married at different ages. Women just past the age of puberty were ready for marriage. Men were usually older, having had to prove themselves at hunting and war. A man and a woman who wanted to marry usually asked permission of the woman's family. After a small ceremony, the husband went to live with his wife's family and clan. Husbands and wives could divorce one another if they both agreed, and divorce was common.

Government

On the local level, Native Americans were governed by the clans. Each clan took care of its own affairs, deciding who could marry and who should be punished for wrongs.

A village was ruled by a headman. The village headman and other respected elders made up a council, which advised the tribal chief. The

Above left: The Cherokee still make baskets of split oak, cane, and honeysuckle vines. They dye the baskets with natural dyes like walnut and bloodroot. Above right: Many tribes made dugout canoes from a single log by burning and scraping out the middle.

chief rarely made an important decision without talking to the council. Decisions at council meetings were reached by agreement rather than by a majority vote. At some point in the discussions, the council simply agreed on the best thing to do. Some tribes had two chiefs, one for making war and one for making peaceful decisions.

Food

All of the Native Americans fished and hunted animals to obtain meat. Deer was their main meat, but they also ate rabbit, squirrel, bear, turkey, raccoon, and small birds. Meat was often cooked by roasting it over an open fire. This was the origin of barbecuing, a popular way of cooking meat today. Fat from bear meat made a grease that was used in many ways.

Fish was also an important part of the Native Americans' diet. They used various methods to catch fish: hook and line, traps, spearing, and nets. On inland streams, they built V-shaped rock dams with traps at the pointed end of the V. The remains of some of these dams may still be seen in mountain rivers. At night, they would build fires on piles of sand in their canoes. The firelight attracted fish like flounder and sea trout, which they then speared.

The tribes also grew a number of crops. Their chief crop was corn, which they called **maize**. Corn was prepared in many ways: ground into meal for bread, cooked in wood-ash water to make hominy, or roasted by the ear over a fire. During the winter, dried corn was stored in an air-tight crib built high above the ground.

Other crops included squash, pumpkins, beans, and sunflowers. The main fruit tree they grew was the peach. Honey and berries, fruits, and nuts gathered from the wild rounded out their diet. The Cherokee made a delicious vegetable oil for cooking and seasoning by boiling crushed hickory nuts.

Clothing

The Native Americans wore little clothing. Tanned deerskins provided breechcloths for men and apron-skirts for women. Small children often wore no clothes. During warm weather, no one wore shoes. During cold weather, the Native Americans wore moccasins, leggings, and match-coats for warmth. *Match-coats* were long, very warm capes made of furs or feathers. John Lawson, who lived among the Indians for several years, was amazed that they could sleep on the ground at night with no match-coat or other cover.

Shelter

Shelters were made from materials at hand. The Cherokee first built a framework of poles or saplings, which they then covered with bark or tree branches. Some houses were round, others rectangular. Inside were benches for sleeping and sitting. Because fleas were numerous, the benches were built higher than a flea could jump. Other furnishings included woven mats, pottery, baskets, and wooden utensils. Fires were built in the middle of the dirt floors. During the summer, the sides were opened to let in cool air. During the winter, the sides were closed to hold in the heat.

The Cherokee built log houses for winter living. A small fire kept the house very warm but filled it with smoke. This was useful when they wanted to make the body sweat out impurities. The Indians also built council houses for meetings. These council houses were larger versions of their dwellings.

Some Cherokee, like Going-back Chiltoskey, are noted for sculpting and carving. The bald eagle was thought to be special because it could fly to the Upper World.

Do You Remember?

1. What is meant by a mother-centered family system?
2. How were Native American children raised?
3. What were the three levels of Indian government? Who ruled at each level?
4. Name three foods eaten by Native Americans.

CHAPTER · REVIEW

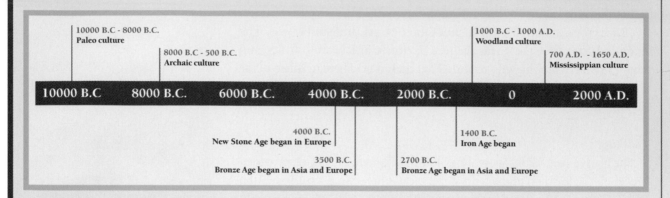

| 10000 B.C - 8000 B.C.
Paleo culture | | | | 1000 B.C - 1000 A.D.
Woodland culture | |
| 8000 B.C - 500 B.C.
Archaic culture | | | | 700 A.D. - 1650 A.D.
Mississippian culture | |

| 10000 B.C | 8000 B.C. | 6000 B.C. | 4000 B.C. | 2000 B.C. | 0 | 2000 A.D. |

4000 B.C.
New Stone Age began in Europe

1400 B.C.
Iron Age began

3500 B.C.
Bronze Age began in Asia and Europe

2700 B.C.
Bronze Age began in Asia and Europe

Reviewing People, Places, and Terms

Match each of the following words with the definitions that follow.

ancestor
anthropologist
archaeologist
clan
culture
tribe

1. A scientist who studies the origin, culture, and development of humans
2. A group of people who share a common ancestry, language, name, and way of living
3. A way of life or the way we think about and do things
4. A scientist who studies the items left behind by ancient peoples to determine how they lived
5. A person from whom one is descended
6. A group of people who believe themselves related by blood

Understanding the Facts

1. About how many Native Americans lived in North Carolina in 1600?
2. Where is the Bering Sea? Why is this sea important in understanding the arrival of the earliest people to America?
3. Why is an archaeologist's work important in understanding our culture and other cultures?
4. Which pre-contact culture do archaeologists believe was the first to grow crops?
5. What plant was used by the Cherokee in many of their ceremonies?
6. What was the Green Corn Ceremony?

Developing Critical Thinking

1. How can archaeologists tell much about a past culture by studying bits of old pottery, tools, or fragments of clothing?
2. How did changes in climate affect the migration of early peoples from one part of the world to another?
3. How do you think the Native Americans were able to survive so well before Europeans came to the New World?
4. In what ways do you think "civilized" society has demonstrated the Indians' law of retaliation?

Applying Your Skills

1. Using the description given on page 57, draw a picture of what you believe Uktena looks like.
2. Sign language was important to Native American culture and is still a method of communicating between people who cannot hear or who do not speak the same language. Develop a short

story to present to your class and devise signs with your hands that will represent the major people, places, and things described in your story.
3. Visit a local museum or historic site and ask whether it has or collects Native American artifacts. Are any on display? How large is the collection? What types of artifacts are in the collection (arrowheads, pottery, pipes, ornaments, and so on)? Report on your findings to your classmates.

Making Connections

1. Determine what Native American tribes once lived in your area. Are there any place names that came from those early tribes? Share your findings with the class.
2. In what ways did the childhood games of Native Americans prepare them for adulthood?

3. Write a brief "newspaper sports report" of a lacrosse game played by an early Native American tribe. Include in your report the names of the teams, the highlights of the game, and the score.

Tar Heel Trivia

- The Cherokee held six religious festivals each year. the main festival was the Green Corn Ceremony.
- Maize, grown by almost all the Indian peoples of the Americas, was first cultivated about 7,000 years ago in the Valley of Mexico. By the 1500s, maize had spread throughout the Americas and 200 different strains were grown.
- Archaeologists who have reconstructed and tried the atlatl have found that a man using one can pierce a 4-inch target at 40 yards.

● BUILDING SKILLS: FINDING THE MAIN IDEA ●

When you read about a topic, don't try to remember every detail. Identifying the main idea of a paragraph will help you organize information and remember more of what you read.

The main idea of a whole paragraph is often stated in the first sentence of the paragraph, although it may also appear in the second or third sentence. The other sentences in the paragraph provide supporting details. For example, the main idea of the following paragraph is stated in the first sentence. The other sentences in the paragraph provide the supporting details.

The Indians spoke languages that belonged to three main "families," or groups. These groups were Algonquian, Iroquoian, and Siouan. The tribes speaking Algonquian lived mainly along the coast. These included the Chowmanoc, Moratoc, Pamlico, Roanoac, and Secotan tribes. Those speaking Iroquoian included the Tuscarora and the Cherokee. The Tuscarora lived in the Coastal Plain and the Cherokee in the Mountains. The Siouan-speaking tribes lived mainly in the Piedmont but were also in the southern Coastal Plain. The Cape Fear, Catawba, Occaneechi, Pedee, Saponi,

Saura, Tutelo, and Waxhaw tribes are included in this last group.

What are some of the details provided by the other sentences? You are correct if you answered: the names of the three language groups, the names of the tribes included in each language group, and where each language group lived.

Do you think it is necessary to remember all the details in the paragraph? If not, which are most important? You can probably remember the names of the three language groups and where the tribes in each language group lived. But it would be difficult to remember which tribes belonged to each language group. It is not necessary to remember all details, but try to pick out the major fact from a paragraph.

Read the first paragraph under the heading "Belief Systems" on a page 54, and answer the following questions.

1. What is the main idea of the paragraph?
2. Which sentence in the paragraph states the main idea?
3. Which sentences provide supporting details?

NORTH CAROLINA IN THE NEW WORLD

RALEIGH, AMADAS, BARLOW, LANE, WHITE—all tried unsuccessfully to colonize North Carolina in the 1580s. Later, in the 1660s, King Charles II of England gave Carolina to eight of his supporters. They were successful in colonizing North Carolina.

The proprietary period was full of turmoil. Colonists had to contend with internal unrest, wars with the Native Americans, and piracy. Yet the colony of North Carolina was flourishing when the king assumed control of it in 1729.

Right: To celebrate the 400th anniversary of the first English attempts to plant a colony in the New World, the state of North Carolina launched the Elizabeth II in 1984. The replica of a sixteenth-century sailing vessel rests at anchor at Manteo. *Above:* North Carolina's most famous outdoor drama tells the story of the mysterious disappearance of the Lost Colony.

CHAPTER THREE

EUROPEAN EXPLORATION OF THE NEW WORLD

Two hours after midnight land appeared, at a distance of about two leagues from them.... Presently they saw naked people, and the admiral [Columbus] went ashore in the armed boat.... When they had landed, they saw very green trees and much water and fruit of various kinds. The admiral...took possession of the land . . . for the King and Queen [Ferdinand and Isabella]....

—Christopher Columbus

F OR CENTURIES, EUROPEANS HAD TRADED with Asia through such Mediterranean ports as Venice and Constantinople and along a land route known as the Silk Road. Many middlemen took part in the Far Eastern trade. A **middleman** is a trader who buys goods from producers and sells them to other traders or to consumers. The middlemen drove up the prices of such luxury

Left: *Marco Polo reached the Orient by land in the thirteenth century. His writings inspired Columbus.* **Above:** *This mural in the U.S. Capitol commemorates Christopher Columbus's first voyage to the New World.*

items as dyes, silk, perfumes, drugs, gold, jewels, and spices such as pepper, cinnamon, nutmeg, and cloves.

In 1477, the publication of Marco Polo's *Travels* led many Europeans to believe that China's fabulous riches could be reached by ship. The riches of the East Indies, Polo said, were "something wonderful, whether in gold or precious stones, or in all manner of spicery." First, however, Europeans would have to find a shorter trade route to the Orient.

THE SEARCH FOR NEW TRADE ROUTES

Among those looking for a trade route to the Far East was Prince Henry the Navigator of Portugal. During the early to mid-1400s, Prince Henry sent ships south along the coast of Africa in search of an eastern passage to the Indian Ocean. But it was not until 1488, long after Prince Henry's death, that Bartholomew Díaz rounded the southern tip of Africa at the Cape of Good Hope.

Another European sea captain named Christopher Columbus believed that the route to the Far East lay to the west. Like other experienced navigators of his day, Columbus believed the earth was round. Columbus thought that the distance from Portugal to Japan was less than 3,000 miles. (It was really 12,000 miles.) He also believed that no land mass would bar his way to the Orient. For years, Columbus tried to get support for his plan from the **monarchs** (kings and queens) of France, Portugal, and England. Finally, Queen Isabella and King Ferdinand of Spain agreed to finance his voyage.

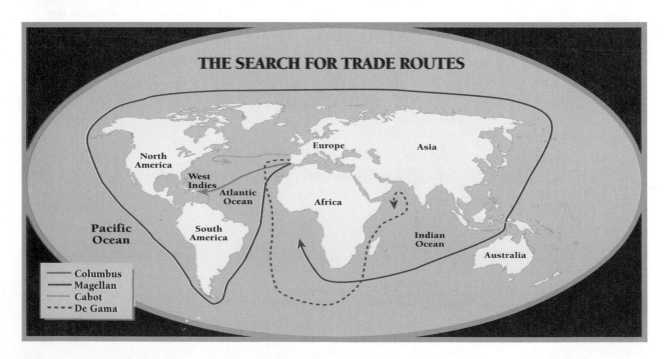

THE SEARCH FOR TRADE ROUTES

North America · Europe · Asia · West Indies · Atlantic Ocean · Africa · Pacific Ocean · South America · Indian Ocean · Australia

—— Columbus
—— Magellan
—— Cabot
- - - De Gama

On August 3, 1492, Columbus, a 41-year-old Italian, set sail from Palos, Spain, hoping to reach China and the East Indies. His ships were named the *Pinta*, the *Niña,* and the *Santa Maria*. On one of the best-known dates in American history—October 12, 1492—Columbus landed on a Caribbean island he named San Salvador (one of the Bahama Islands).

Columbus believed that the islands he had found lay off the coast of India. He even called the friendly and gentle natives he met "Indians." He believed that they could be converted easily to Christianity and hoped to make them faithful subjects of the Spanish monarchs.

In all, Columbus made four voyages to the western hemisphere (1492, 1493, 1498, 1502). In his later voyages, he explored along the coasts of Central and South America and was the first European to visit Puerto Rico, Jamaica, and the Virgin Islands. In his reports, he described the extraordinary beauty of the "New World" he found. (Europe was the "Old World.") When he died in 1506, Columbus still believed that he had discovered a westward route to the Far East's riches. Vast stores of gold and spices, he insisted, lay close at hand.

John Cabot, who like Columbus was from Genoa, Italy, also sailed west. In 1497, sailing under an English flag, he discovered Newfoundland in present-day Canada. Actually, he rediscovered it. Norsemen led by Leif Ericsson had landed in Labrador in the year 1001. They established a settlement in a region they called *Vinland*. After trying several times to colonize the area, the Norsemen fled back to Greenland. Unfriendly natives helped hasten their departure.

In 1498, Vasco da Gama sailed around Africa and reached India. An ocean trade route to the Orient had finally been found.

Amerigo Vespucci, an Italian navigator, had the honor of giving his name to the New World. In 1499, Vespucci sailed along the coast of South America. His writings caught the attention of a mapmaker who, in 1507, named the new land *America*.

In 1522, Ferdinand Magellan succeeded in reaching Asia by sailing to the west. However, his route around the tip of South America was long and hard. Europeans wanted an easier route to China and India. They were looking for the so-called **Northwest Passage**, an all-water route to Asia through the North American continent.

Top: *America was named for Amerigo Vespucci.* **Above:** *In 1498 Vasco da Gama reached India by sailing around Africa.*

Do You Remember?

1. On what date did Columbus land at San Salvador?
2. What explorer tried to establish a settlement in Labrador in 1001?
3. For whom was the New World named?

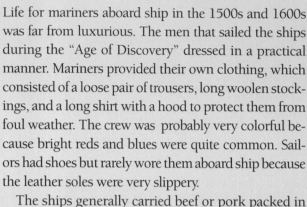
SHIPBOARD LIFE

A visit to the Elizabeth II *in Manteo gives an idea what shipboard life was like in the sixteenth century.*

Life for mariners aboard ship in the 1500s and 1600s was far from luxurious. The men that sailed the ships during the "Age of Discovery" dressed in a practical manner. Mariners provided their own clothing, which consisted of a loose pair of trousers, long woolen stockings, and a long shirt with a hood to protect them from foul weather. The crew was probably very colorful because bright reds and blues were quite common. Sailors had shoes but rarely wore them aboard ship because the leather soles were very slippery.

The ships generally carried beef or pork packed in brine (saltwater), ship's biscuit (hardtack), or sometimes salted fish. The voyage usually started out with live animals, such as chickens and pigs, but they were soon eaten. The biscuit was nothing more than a mixture of flour and water that was baked and packed away in barrels. Since food was seldom stored in the driest part of the ship, biscuit often became moldy and by the end of a voyage infested with insects. Beer, wine, and cider were the preferred drinks aboard ship because the alcohol content made them less likely to spoil. Since cook fires on board wooden ships could be disastrous, hot or warm meals were not very common.

Most mariners were very religious, and their souls were carefully looked after by the captain. At morning and evening prayers, Bible verses or passages were read and hymns sung. Aboard ship, there were strict rules against swearing and blasphemy.

Superstition also played a prominent part in life at sea. Because most sailors could not read, printed pages of any type were never destroyed for fear that the printed page might be a part of a Bible. It was also considered very unlucky to begin a voyage on a Friday because that was the day that Christ was crucified. There were good superstitions too. Sailors believed that if an infant was buried below a tree that was later used to build a ship, the spirit of the infant would protect the ship.

Discipline was strict and harsh. It was important that all members of the crew did as they were ordered because one man making a mistake could put the entire crew in peril.

FRENCH EXPLORATION

In 1524, a group of merchants in Lyons, France, convinced King Francis I that France must enter the competition for riches and empire. With the French king's backing, Giovanni da Verrazano set out to find a new route to the Orient.

Verrazano was the first European to explore the coast of North Carolina. Sailing south past Spain and then turning west into the broad Atlantic Ocean, Verrazano sighted land in March 1524, near what is now Cape Fear. He followed the coastline south for about 150 miles before turning to the north again. Verrazano was afraid he would run into the Spanish if he went too far south.

Along the coast of present-day Onslow County, Verrazano tried to send a landing party ashore. Rough seas made landing impossible, but one sailor was washed ashore. The sailor carried gifts, which he gave to the friendly American Indians who greeted him. This meeting of the Old World and the New World made both sides curious. The sailor's white skin astonished the natives. The French in turn described the Indians as larger than Europeans and more athletic.

Verrazano continued sailing north along the North Carolina coast. He could see over the Outer Banks into the Pamlico and Albemarle sounds, but he could not see the mainland in the distance. As a result, he reported that the sounds were the Pacific Ocean. For more than a **century** (one

Because of Spain's success in the New World, Francis I of France (above) supported Giovanni da Verrazano's search for a route to the Orient. Verrazano was the first European to explore the coast of North Carolina (top).

hundred years), mapmakers showed the Pacific Ocean just to the west of the North Carolina coast.

Do You Remember?

1. Who was the first European to explore the coast of North Carolina?
2. Who was likely the first white man to encounter the Native Americans in North Carolina?
3. Why did early mapmakers mistakenly show the Pacific Ocean just to the west of the North Carolina coast?

SPANISH EXPLORATION

In the fifty years after Columbus's first voyage, Spanish explorers searched the Caribbean for wealth. In 1513, Juan Ponce de León discovered Florida, and Vasco Nuñez de Balboa crossed the Isthmus of Panama to reach the Pacific Ocean. (An *isthmus* is a narrow strip of land bordered on both sides by water and connecting two larger pieces of land.)

Hernando Cortés was the first to live up to Spanish dreams of tremendous wealth. In 1519, he landed in what is now Mexico. Within two years, Cortés had conquered the native Aztec Indians, killed their ruler

In 1519 Hernando Cortés landed in Mexico and conquered the Aztec Empire.

Montezuma, and won a treasure in gold and silver. Hearing of the wealth of the Incas in Peru, Francisco Pizarro set out for the western coast of South America. In 1535, in the Andes, Pizarro defeated the Incas. In doing so, he captured the richest silver mines in the world.

In just a half century, the Spanish monarchs had an empire as large as ancient Rome's. But in building that empire, the **conquistadores** (Spanish conquerors) had destroyed three highly developed Native American cultures. The Aztec, Maya, and Inca peoples were skillful farmers and engineers, having built roads, bridges, and canals to carry water. The Mayans, who lived in Mexico and Central America, had developed a calendar more accurate than that of any European. They also had their own writing and mathematics systems. Few traces of these cultures remain—only ruins, pieces of pottery, and some language. Showing no mercy, the conquistadores leveled great Indian cities and temples and erected cathedrals and monasteries in their place.

The push to explore north of Florida came from Spanish officials in the New World. Between 1520 and 1525, Lucas Vásquez de Ayllón, a Spanish official on the island of Hispaniola, backed three voyages in search of a site for a colony. A **colony** is a group of people who settle in a distant land but who are still under the rule of their native land. Ayllón's agents explored a region between the Cape Fear and Santee rivers that the Native Americans called *Chicora*.

In 1523, the Spanish monarch named Ayllón governor of Chicora for life. But it was not until July 1526 that Ayllón tried to plant a colony there. He set out from the West Indies with a party of 500 men and women, three monks, and slaves. They landed at the mouth of a river they called Rio Jordan, which may have been the Santee River. The Ayllón colony failed when the settlers could not find suitable land.

In the sixteenth century, the Spanish also explored the region's interior. In 1539, Hernando de Soto left Havana, Cuba, with a huge group: 500 to 600 men, 200 horses, mules, dogs, and pigs. The party marched north through Florida and spent the winter of 1539-1540 at an Indian town near what is now Tallahassee.

In the spring, De Soto continued his march, moving across parts of what are now Georgia and South Carolina. Having heard about the Cherokee, De Soto turned toward western North Carolina. In May 1540, he reached the Blue Ridge Mountains. The Native Americans in the area were friendly and very helpful. While the Spaniards searched for gold (which they didn't find), the Cherokee supplied food for both them and their horses. When De Soto decided to move on, they crossed the Little Tennessee River near present-day Franklin in Macon County. There he saw the river flowing to the west (all of the other rivers they had crossed flowed east). De Soto had discovered a **tributary** of the Mississippi River. A

Top: In 1513 Vasco Núñez de Balboa crossed the Isthmus of Panama and discovered the Pacific Ocean. Above: Hernando de Soto explored much of the southeastern United States. He marched across Florida, Georgia, South Carolina, and North Carolina in 1539-1540. Eventually, he reached the Mississippi River.

EARLY NAVIGATION

Traveling by ship from Europe to the New World in the 1500s and 1600s was difficult and dangerous. Violent storms, spoiled food, starvation, and disease aboard ship took their toll; knowledge of the New World's geography, ocean currents, and weather was often sketchy. Finding the best way from Europe to a specific location in North or South America was the work of the ship's navigator. Without the skills, knowledge, and daring of their navigators, ship captains could easily stray off course and get lost—which often meant death.

In the 1500s, navigators could only estimate their ships' positions at sea. Navigators charted their courses by the stars and by using a cross-staff, which was simply a stick with a crosspiece. The navigator put the crosspiece to his eye and aimed it toward the sun to measure the angle of the sun above the horizon. Knowing this angle, he could determine the ship's latitude.

To gauge the distance the ship had traveled, the navigator multiplied the hours that had passed by the varying speed of the ship. To determine the ship's speed, the navigator stood at the front of the ship holding a rope with knots tied in it. He threw one end of the rope into the ocean and counted the number of knots that passed through his hands until the end of the rope reached the rear of the ship. Even today, the speed of a ship is measured in "knots."

In the 1500s navigators depended on a cross-staff to plot their courses. The cross-staff measured the angle of the sun above the horizon. In that way navigators could estimate their latitude.

tributary is a stream that flows into a river. In May 1541, he reached the Mississippi itself.

During the next quarter of a century, some Spaniards came into contact with the North Carolina coast. Shipwrecked sailors, Dominican priests trying to set up missions at Chesapeake Bay, and Spanish pilots all ran into the changeable weather and treacherous waters of the Outer Banks. Sometimes they were looking for a safe place in the sounds before returning to the open sea.

One reason for Spain's continuing interest in the Carolinas was the fear that France or England might try to set up a colony there. Indeed, a group of French Protestants known as Huguenots did set sail for the Cape Fear River in 1562. They landed instead at Port Royal, South Carolina. However, the French hated **Protestants** (Christian non-Catholics) so much that the Catholic monarch of France would not support the colony. Jean Ribaut, the leader of the Huguenots, asked England for help. In the end,

the French Huguenots had to abandon their colony. All would have been lost if the English had not rescued them at sea. Spain did establish the first permanent European settlement in North America. St. Augustine was founded in Florida in 1565.

Spain's search for easy riches in North America brought Captain Juan Pardo, Sergeant Hernando Boyano, and a band of about twenty-five soldiers to the Carolina region in 1566. They landed at St. Helena, South Carolina, and marched north and west. Pardo followed De Soto's route for much of the way, even visiting the same Indian villages. In the foothills of the Blue Ridge Mountains, the Spaniards built a fort where Boyano and some of the soldiers stayed during the winter. Pardo went east. When he returned to the fort in 1567, the Spaniards moved to the west through the mountains. Their route included present-day Macon, Clay, and Cherokee counties. Again, relations with the Cherokee were peaceful. Eventually, the group circled through Tennessee, Alabama, Georgia, and South Carolina.

Jean Ribaut tried to establish a colony of French Protestants at the Rio Jordan in 1562. Instead he landed at Port Royal, South Carolina. The colony failed.

Do You Remember?

1. What was the goal of the early Spanish explorers?
2. Name two of the Spanish explorers who conquered the Inca, Maya, and Aztec Indians.
3. What Spanish explorer was the first to reach the Blue Ridge Mountains in North Carolina?

At first, contacts between Native Americans and Europeans were friendly and beneficial to both sides.

The introduction of the horse had a profound effect on Native American cultures. The conquistadores brought the first horses to America. Trade among the tribes brought horses north through Mexico and into the Great Plains. There, the horse became the center of certain tribes' existence. The Apache, Comanche, Sioux, and Blackfoot used horses for hunting and warfare. In many cases, a man's wealth and standing in the tribe were measured by the number of horses he owned. The horse allowed the tribes to move around, but they had to move their camps more often to find fresh pastures.

TRADE

Trade was another result of the contact between Europeans and American Indians. The search for a Northwest Passage first brought European explorers and then traders to North America. Fishermen from a number of European countries came to the Newfoundland Banks each summer. They caught cod and other fish, which they "salted" and took back to Europe each fall. They also began trading with the Indians in the area. The Europeans quickly found that the Indians prized their tools. Since the Indians still used stone tools, they were eager to trade for steel knives, brass kettles, and other metal goods. Beads and cloth were also valued by the Indians. In exchange, the Europeans received furs.

As the demand grew in Europe for furs, especially beaver skins, some nations set up trading posts in North America. For example, the French founded Quebec on the St. Lawrence River in 1608. The Dutch built a trading post on Manhattan Island in 1624. Sweden sent a trading party to the Delaware River valley in 1638. The northern European nations, however, were more interested in trade than in colonies.

To meet the European demand for animal skins, some tribes changed their whole way of life. The Abenakis tribe of Maine, for example, spent so much time catching beaver that it had to rely on the Massachusetts tribe for food supplies. The Massachusetts tribe, in turn, spent all their time producing food in exchange for the European metal tools they received from the Abenakis.

RELIGION

The French and the Spanish made the greatest effort to convert the Native Americans to Christianity. In French Canada, Indians called the Jesuit missionaries of the Roman Catholic church the "Black Robes." When they were not able to get Native Americans to adopt European ways, the Jesuits

In 1624 the Dutch built a trading post on Manhattan Island and called it New Amsterdam. The English seized the colony in 1664 and renamed it New York.

EXPLORATIONS AND THEIR RESULTS

Over millions of years, the New World and the Old World developed different forms of plant and animal life. The New World crops such as maize (corn), beans, squash, and potatoes were more plentiful and more nutritious than such Old World crops as wheat and rye. Maize was easily grown in Europe, and within 10 years of its discovery it was being cultivated in Italy. The potato took longer to become established in Europe but ultimately had a more significant effect upon European history than maize. Other foods taken back to Europe include tomatoes, tapioca, chocolate, pineapples, avocadoes, runner beans, Jerusalem artichokes, and passion fruit. The turkey was taken back to Europe early on and was being bred in Spain in the early 1500s. The Europeans in turn introduced cattle, pigs, chickens, goats, sheep, and horses to the Americas. These exchanges improved the diets of both peoples.

Plants too made the crossing from the New World to the Old: morning glory, nasturtium, dahlia, and the tobacco plant—the Indian "weed." Smoking and chewing tobacco quickly became popular in the Old World. Tobacco became a major crop in North Carolina, and growing tobacco led to the success of the later English colonies.

The introduction of the horse to the New World made a tremendous difference in the lives of the Native Americans.

Before the coming of the Spanish conquistadores, the Aztec capital of Tenochtitlan was a thriving city of 100,000 people. Smallpox so weakened the inhabitants that they surrendered the city to Cortez.

learned the Indians' languages and traveled to the Indians to spread their message. This technique worked. Thousands of Native Americans accepted Christianity without abandoning their essential life-style. Since belief systems spread throughout all aspects of the Indian life-style, there were some changes in, for example, their values.

DISEASE

Native Americans had no **immunity** (resistance) to germs that Europeans had carried around for centuries. Explorers, traders, and settlers from England, France, and Spain brought influenza, measles, and other diseases to the Americas. These diseases killed millions of Native Americans. Smallpox, spread by direct human contact, was the most deadly. Usually, one-half to three-fourths of all Indians who had not been previously exposed to it died.

No one knows how many Native Americans were living in the New World when the Europeans arrived. Perhaps as many as 10 million Indians lived in central Mexico in 1500. A century later, fewer than 1 million remained. At first, Cortés's conquistadores failed to defeat the Aztecs. What they could not do by force, smallpox did for them. Smallpox so weakened the Aztecs that they surrendered their capital city of Tenochtitlan to Cortés. On that site, the Spaniards built what is now Mexico City.

Throughout the Americas, the story was the same. To the north, where Indians met only a few Europeans, disease left a deadly trail. In the early seventeenth century, a Frenchman noted that Canadian Indians often complained that "since the French mingle with them and carry on trade with them, they are dying fast and the population is thinning out." Four years before the Pilgrims landed at Plymouth, Massachusetts, fishermen infected local tribes with an unknown illness, probably chicken pox. A visiting Englishman said the Indians had "died on heapes, as they lay in their houses." Everywhere he traveled he saw piles of bones and skulls.

In the American South, Indians suffered the same devastation. It is estimated that 200,000 Indians lived in the South in 1685. In the half century that followed, disease, war with colonists and other tribes, enslavement, and migration reduced the South's Native Americans by as much as two-thirds. By 1730, fewer than 67,000 Indians remained. In 1685, perhaps 10,000 Indians lived east of the mountains of North Carolina. The Cherokee, who spread across much of southern Appalachia, numbered perhaps another 32,000. In 1730, less than 2,000 Native Americans lived east of the mountains, a decrease of 80 percent. The Cherokee numbered no more than 10,500, a decrease of about 65 percent.

In 1695, smallpox struck the Pamlico Indians. In 1697, it struck the Cherokee. The effects of smallpox could be traced from tribe to tribe. John Lawson, who came to North Carolina soon after 1700, wrote about the drop in the number of Native Americans in just half a century:

> The Small-Pox and Rum have made such a Destruction amongst them that, on good grounds, I do believe, there is not the sixth Savage living within two hundred Miles of our Settlements, as there were fifty Years ago. These poor Creatures have so many Enemies to destroy them, that it's a wonder one of them is left alive near us.

By 1707, smallpox had spread to the Tuscarora, the largest and most powerful tribe east of the mountains in North Carolina. The Cherokee were hard hit. Another epidemic visited the Cherokee in 1738-1739 and yet another in 1760.

In time, the Native Americans acquired enough immunity to survive the European diseases. But by that time, European expansion and the Indians' overwhelming population losses had reduced Native Americans to a minority in their own homeland.

Do You Remember?

1. What were some of the items traded between Native Americans and the Europeans?
2. Why were the Jesuits successful in converting some Native Americans to Christianity?
3. Why were European diseases so deadly for the Native Americans?

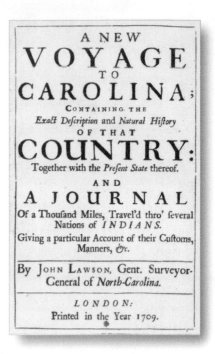

A NEW
VOYAGE
TO
CAROLINA;
CONTAINING THE
Exact Description and Natural History
OF THAT
COUNTRY:
Together with the Present State thereof.
AND
A JOURNAL
Of a Thousand Miles, Travel'd thro' several
Nations of INDIANS.
Giving a particular Account of their Customs,
Manners, &c.

By JOHN LAWSON, Gent. Surveyor-
General of North-Carolina.

LONDON:
Printed in the Year 1709.

John Lawson explored the Carolinas from 1700 to 1711. He often lived among the Indians. His journal—A New Voyage to Carolina (1709)—remains one of the most important books ever written about colonial America.

CHAPTER · REVIEW

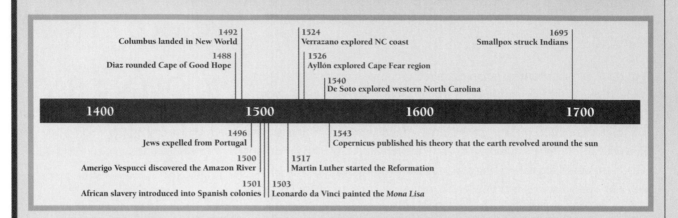

1492
Columbus landed in New World

1488
Diaz rounded Cape of Good Hope

1524
Verrazano explored NC coast

1526
Ayllón explored Cape Fear region

1540
De Soto explored western North Carolina

1695
Smallpox struck Indians

1400   **1500**   **1600**   **1700**

1496
Jews expelled from Portugal

1500
Amerigo Vespucci discovered the Amazon River

1501
African slavery introduced into Spanish colonies

1503
Leonardo da Vinci painted the *Mona Lisa*

1517
Martin Luther started the Reformation

1543
Copernicus published his theory that the earth revolved around the sun

Reviewing People, Places, and Terms

On a separate sheet of paper, write the terms from the list that could replace the underlined words in the following statements.

centuries
colonies
conquistadores
immunity
middlemen
Northwest Passage

1. <u>Merchants</u> in Italy controlled the trade routes and trade goods that passed through the Mediterranean from Asia to Europe.
2. Spanish <u>conquerors of Central and South America</u> came to the New World in search of riches, especially gold and silver.
3. Early explorers were more interested in trade than in establishing <u>permanent settlements in the New World for their sponsoring nations</u>.
4. Explorers from France and England were particularly interested in finding <u>a water route to Asia through the North American continent</u>.
5. Because they had no (a) <u>natural ability to resist disease</u>, Native Americans died by the thousands, and perhaps millions, from diseases Europeans had been exposed to for (b) <u>hundreds of years</u>.

Understanding the Facts

1. How did the publication of Marco Polo's *Travels*, which described his visits to China in the thirteenth century, affect European exploration?
2. How many voyages did Columbus actually make to the New World?
3. Explain the use of the terms *New World* and *Old World*?
4. Name the three native cultures in Mexico, Central America, and northern South America that the Spanish conquistadores conquered and then destroyed.
5. Why was Spain interested in the territory north of Florida?
6. What was the first permanent European settlement in the New World? Where was it located?
7. What effect did the introduction of the horse have on certain Native American cultures?
8. What happened to the Native American population as the result of the diseases brought to the New World by the Europeans?

Developing Critical Thinking

1. "Gold, Glory, and Gospel" are factors said to have attracted European voyages to the Americas. How do you think these factors affected European exploration and settlement of the New World?

2. How do you think Native American society would have been different if Europeans had never brought horses to the New World?

3. What might have been the effect on history if so many Native Americans had not died from diseases brought by the Europeans?

Applying Your Skills

1. Imagine that you are the leader of a Spanish expedition trying to establish a new colony along the coast of North Carolina in the 1520s. Make a list of the items you think you would need. Remember, the space on your ship is *very* limited.

2. At your local library, find a book that illustrates the great buildings constructed by the Aztec or Maya. Find another book that illustrates the great pyramids and temples of ancient Egypt. Compare the buildings of these two cultures and prepare a report for class. Include in your report maps and sketches that show when and where these buildings were constructed.

3. Use the information in this chapter and in other reference books to chart the courses of at least three explorers mentioned in this chapter.

Making Connections

1. Early navigators had to rely on crude navigation devices to help them find the New World. Try to determine the name of one navigation device used today by astronauts who are trying to find their way in the New World of space. Share your findings with your classmates.

2. Compare the technology and motivation of explorers from the 1500s and 1600s with those of today.

3. How did European-Indian contact improve the diets of both peoples?

Tar Heel Trivia

- The invention of movable type and the printing press in Germany in the 1450s revolutionized the spread of information. That invention made possible the publication of Marco Polo's *Travels* in 1477. Before then, the manuscript had circulated hand-to-hand for nearly two centuries.

- In 1604, King James I of England called tobacco "loathsome to the eye, hatefull to the nose, harmfull to the brain, [and] dangerous to the Lungs."

BUILDING SKILLS: USING TIMELINES

Keeping track of all the events you read about can be difficult. Timelines can help you remember events in the order they happened. Although a timeline can show events over a short period of time, most often it covers a period of years. Making a timeline is a useful way to organize the events that took place during a period of time. Sometimes it is impossible to include all events in a timeline; only the most important ones can be included. These important events then provide reference points for other events that occurred during the same period.

In your textbook, timelines appear in the Chapter Review section of the chapter, where they help you remember the events in the order they occurred during the chapter. They also help you place other events within the time frame of those on the timeline. You may want to expand these timelines and add other events to help you in your study of the chapter.

Look at the timeline for this chapter. It covers a period of about 200 years. On a separate sheet of paper, expand the timeline to include at least two other events you read about in the chapter that were not included on the timeline.

Try This!

Make a timeline of your life or one of your older relatives (mother, father, grandmother, grandfather, aunt, uncle). Start the timeline with the year you (or they) were born; then write in the present year. Show at least eight events in the order they occurred.

CHAPTER FOUR

ENGLISH EXPLORATION OF NORTH CAROLINA

...we have discovered...the goodliest soile under the cope of heaven.
—Ralph Lane

F RENCH, SPANISH, AND ENGLISH explorers all visited North Carolina in the sixteenth century. Spain, in particular, made many trips to the area. It was England, however, that came closest to planting the first permanent colony.

ENGLISH EXPLORATION

England and Spain were rivals in religion, politics, and trade. During the 1530s, King Henry VIII of England broke with the Catholic Church and named himself head of the Church of England. When she came to the throne in 1558, Queen Elizabeth I (Henry VIII's daughter) made sure that England remained a Protestant nation. The Spanish monarch, Philip II, was a devout Catholic who was determined to bring Christianity to the New World. Philip could not accept the presence there of England, a Protestant nation and a military rival.

At sea, the conflict between Spain and England had already turned into undeclared war. Great English sea captains such as John Hawkins, Francis Drake, and Richard Grenville captured Spanish treasure ships filled with gold, silver, and other valuable **commodities** (goods). These English **privateers** were really pirates sailing with the approval of the queen. They also attacked and burned Spanish settlements in the New World.

THE GILBERT PATENT

By the 1570s, England had grown jealous of Spain's wealthy empire in the New World. A group of merchants, adventurers, and other men led by Sir Humphrey Gilbert and Walter Raleigh believed that only by establishing English colonies in the New World could England challenge Spain.

Opposite page: Queen Elizabeth I granted patents first to Sir Humphrey Gilbert and then to Walter Raleigh to discover "remote" lands for colonization. Above: Elizabeth's chief rival was King Philip II of Spain. Deeply religious, Philip hoped to spread Catholicism to the New World and prevent England, a Protestant nation, from planting colonies there.

Terms: commodity, privateer, commerce, patent, expedition, Spanish Armada

People: Queen Elizabeth I, Sir Humphrey Gilbert, Sir Walter Raleigh, Philip Amadas, Arthur Barlowe, John White, Wingina, Granganimeo, Wanchese, Manteo, Sir Richard Grenville, Thomas Harriot, Ralph Lane, Virginia Dare

Places: Roanoke Island, Croatoan Island

English colonies would open up **commerce** (trade) and serve as bases for military operations against Spain.

On June 11, 1578, Queen Elizabeth I granted Gilbert a **patent**, an official document giving its holder certain rights. This patent allowed Gilbert to discover "remote heathen and barbarous" lands not held by any Christian ruler or people. The queen told Gilbert he could govern any colonies he set up, but he must follow English laws. In return, Gilbert was to pay Elizabeth one-fifth of all the gold and silver that was found. The patent gave Gilbert the right to colonize a huge area—from Spanish Florida to the Arctic.

During the next several years, Gilbert gathered information about America and made plans for several trips. A group of merchants from Bristol agreed to help pay for the voyages. Finally, in June 1583, Gilbert set sail for Newfoundland with six ships. On August 4, he reached the North American coast, claiming it in the name of the queen. The Canadian wilderness, however, proved too harsh for a colony. Gilbert decided to return to England. On the return trip, Gilbert's ship sank in a storm near the Azores. All hands, including Gilbert, were lost.

RALEIGH'S EXPEDITION

When Gilbert died, Walter Raleigh was already a favorite in Queen Elizabeth's court. Raleigh also happened to be Gilbert's half-brother. He moved quickly to take over Gilbert's patent, which was due to run out. On March 25, 1584, Queen Elizabeth granted Raleigh his own patent.

Raleigh began making plans for an **expedition** (journey). To captain his ships, he chose Philip Amadas and Arthur Barlowe. Simon Fernandez, who was Portuguese, was hired as pilot. John White, an artist, also joined the group. The small expedition sailed from Plymouth, England, on April 27, 1584.

THE AMADAS-BARLOWE VOYAGE

On July 13, 1584, Amadas and Barlowe reached the Outer Banks of North Carolina. They claimed the area in the name of Queen Elizabeth. Three days later, Native Americans appeared. In his record of the voyage, Barlowe described the Indians as "very handsome, and goodly people, and in their behavior as mannerly, and civill, as any of Europe." The ruler of these Roanoac Indians was named Wingina. But it was his brother Granganimeo who greeted the English.

The English gave the Indians gifts, and the natives traded deer and buffalo hides for hatchets, axes, and knives. Barlowe noted the Indians' appearance and dress, especially their copper, leather, and pearl ornaments. The women wore their hair long on both sides, while the men

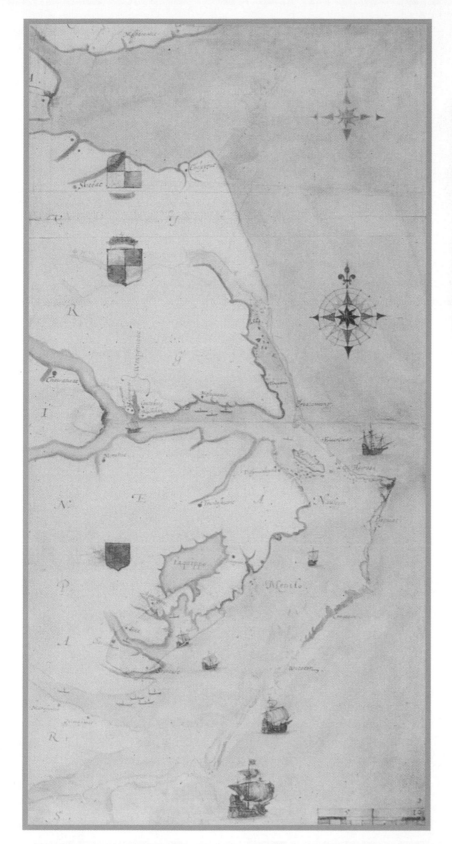

Left: *John White, a talented artist, made four and possibly five trips to the New World. His map of "Raleigh's Virginia," probably drawn in 1585-1586, appears remarkably accurate even today.* **Above:** *Walter Raleigh received a knighthood from Queen Elizabeth in 1585 because of his efforts to establish an English colony on Roanoke Island.*

SIR WALTER RALEIGH

On a chilly morning in October 1618, Sir Walter Raleigh statesman, soldier, explorer, poet stood on a scaffold in the Old Palace Yard of Westminster in London. After a silent prayer, he knelt before the chopping block. The masked executioner hesitated. "What doest thou fear?" Raleigh is reported to have asked. "Strike, man, strike!" The ax fell twice. So ended the life of a man who seemed to stand for England's ambitions and daring during the Age of Discovery.

The Roanoke voyages that Raleigh planned and supported in the 1580s were not successful in planting a permanent colony in America. Raleigh's efforts, however, clearly staked English claims to this region of the New World. His efforts also provided valuable information for those English colonists who later established Jamestown, Virginia, in 1607.

Sir Walter Raleigh, for whom North Carolina's state capital is named, never traveled to North Carolina or to the Roanoke area himself. On two occasions, however, he did explore the northern part of South America in search of El Dorado, the legendary city of gold. He never found riches in the New World, and the privileges and power that he once enjoyed in the English court ended. He lost Queen Elizabeth's favor and was hated by her successor, King James I. In 1604, the king accused Raleigh of treason, imprisoned him in the Tower of London, and fourteen years later had the English knight beheaded.

Sir Walter Raleigh never reached Roanoke Island, but he did explore parts of South America (right) in search of gold and riches. His political fortunes declined, however, and he was imprisoned in the Tower of London (above) in 1604. King James I had Raleigh beheaded in 1618 (opposite page).

had long hair on only one side. Barlowe described the Native Americans as "yellowish" in color. Most had black hair, although he did see children with reddish-brown hair.

Above all, the land's bounty impressed Barlowe. He believed that it was perfect for a colony. The soil was so rich that the natives could plant and harvest three crops of corn a year. All kinds of fruits, nuts, and vegetables grew nearby. The forests and waters were filled with animals and fish.

After spending six weeks on or around Roanoke Island, Amadas and Barlowe returned to England. They took with them some of the local crops as well as maps and watercolor drawings by John White. The explorers also took back with them Wanchese and Manteo, two of the local Indians.

Queen Elizabeth was pleased with the expedition. On January 6, 1585, she named the new land *Virginia* after herself, the Virgin Queen. She also knighted Raleigh. He already had plans for a second trip, and the queen was now prepared to help. Elizabeth contributed gunpowder, one of her ships (the *Tiger*), and an experienced military man, Ralph Lane.

Do You Remember?

1. Why was the Spanish king, Philip II, bothered by the presence of England in the New World?
2. What rights did Gilbert receive under the patent granted him by Queen Elizabeth I?
3. Who took over the Gilbert patent on Gilbert's death?
4. Why did Amadas and Barlowe believe that the Outer Banks would be a perfect place for a colony?
5. What name was given to the land explored by Amadas and Barlowe?

THE LANE COLONY

On April 9, 1585, an expedition of seven ships left England led by Sir Richard Grenville. Fernandez and Amadas served again, as did artist John White. Thomas Harriot, a brilliant scientist, also went along. Also aboard were Wanchese and Manteo, who were returning home.

They reached the northern end of Roanoke Island in July 1585, where they began building a fort. Grenville prepared to return to England. Before he left, however, something happened that was a taste of things to come. A silver cup disappeared. Grenville sent some men to the Indian village of Aquascogoc (probably on Pamlico Sound) to demand the return of the cup. When the Indians failed to produce it, Grenville's men burned the village and destroyed the corn crop.

Once on land, Ralph Lane took command of the colony of 107 men. Lane organized the colony along military lines. He divided his colony into three separate parties. One he sent to the Chesapeake Bay to search

Top: Sir Richard Grenville, who led an expedition from England to Roanoke Island in 1585, was a privateer for Queen Elizabeth. He fought the Spanish Armada in 1588 and died in a naval engagement with Spain. Above: Thomas Harriot was a brilliant scientist who published his observations of the New World in 1588.

for a deepwater harbor and places from which he could attack the Spanish. A second party remained near Roanoke Island and explored the Outer Banks as far south as Cape Hatteras. A third group he led westward in a search for silver. It was this third party that caused new problems between the colonists and the Native Americans.

The 1585 colony commanded by Ralph Lane built a fort on Roanoke Island. The site, now called Fort Raleigh, was excavated and reconstructed between 1947 and 1950.

TROUBLED RELATIONS WITH NATIVE AMERICANS

Lane believed that Wingina, the ruler of the Roanoac Indians, had a plan to destroy the colonists. According to Lane, Wingina hoped to unite the Weapemeoc, Chowanoc, Moratoc, and Mangoak tribes with his own Roanoacs to attack the English settlement. As Lane moved west to explore the Albemarle Sound and the Chowan and Roanoke rivers, he found the Moratoc and Weapemeoc villages deserted. He took the empty villages as a sign of Wingina's treachery. Desperately in need of food, Lane's party barely made it back to Roanoke Island. Once there, the poorly supplied colony continued to demand food from Wingina.

At first, Wingina seemed cooperative, but Lane was suspicious. Before Wingina could organize an attack, if indeed that was his plan, Lane struck.

On June 1, 1586, Lane and a band of twenty-seven men entered Wingina's village of Dasamunquepeuk (present-day Mann's Harbor). Wingina and his people believed Lane had come for more food and to talk about the increasing tension between them. (There had been a small fight the night before.) Instead, at a certain signal (the words "Christ our Victory"), Lane and his men attacked. Wingina was hurt, but he escaped. Edward Nugent, one of Lane's men, chased Wingina into the woods. Nugent soon returned carrying Wingina's head.

THE RETURN TO ENGLAND

The colony continued to run short of food, and relations with the Native Americans worsened. In June 1586, Sir Francis Drake arrived at Roanoke Island. For months, Drake had been raiding Spanish colonies in the West Indies. His arrival, a terrible storm, and the short supplies convinced Lane that it was time to return to England. The colonists left in such a hurry that Lane left behind three of his men who were away on an expedition.

Soon after Lane's leaving, Sir Richard Grenville returned with supplies for the settlement. After searching for Lane and his men, Grenville learned

This engraving of Raleigh's Virginia was made by Theodor de Bry in 1590. Based on White's map, it shows the Indian villages that the English colonists visited.

EARLY HISTORIC RECORDS

John White's watercolor drawings, such as those on pages 50 to 53, provide an important visual record of Raleigh's expeditions. The drawings showed Native Americans; how they farmed, fished, and cooked; and Indian ornaments, clothing, and body decorations. White also drew pictures of the birds, fish, and insects. Many of his animal drawings, however, were probably lost.

This John White painting of a box turtle shows an early example of our state reptile.

Thomas Harriot most likely learned the Algonquian language from Wanchese and Manteo during their year in England. Once in North America, Harriot became even more fluent. He talked directly with the Indians and found out a great deal about their culture and about the land's natural resources.

White and Harriot also made very accurate maps of the region. The two men spent much of the winter of 1585-1586 among the Native Americans. They surveyed the sounds, drew maps and detailed sketches of Indian villages, and learned all they could about America. When Harriot returned to England, he published his notes in *A Briefe and True Report of the New Found Land of Virginia* (1588). He wanted to convince others to settle in America, so he painted a glowing picture. In spite of the exaggeration, Harriot and White left a valuable record of North Carolina at the dawn of European colonization.

from the Native Americans that they had left with Drake. In order to hold the region for England, Grenville left fifteen of his men, along with two years' worth of supplies. Then he sailed back to England.

Do You Remember?
1. What were some of the reasons for the trouble between the colonists and the Indians?
2. What caused Lane to abandon his colony at Roanoke Island?

THE LOST COLONY

The next English attempt to colonize Roanoke Island would end in mystery. The colony started, however, with high hopes.

First, Raleigh planned the colony differently. He wanted to plant a larger colony on Chesapeake Bay, which would give the colonists a deepwater port. Second, this colony would not be a military one as Lane's had been. The new settlement would have a civil government and would include men, women, and children. Third, the settlers would have a stake in the colony, for they would receive grants of land.

THE WHITE COLONY

To be governor of the colony of 117 (including 17 women and 9 boys), Raleigh chose John White. The colonists left England on May 8, 1587, and arrived at Roanoke Island on July 22. White intended to drop off Manteo and another Indian named Towaye (who had returned with either Lane or Grenville to England) and to pick up the fifteen men Grenville had left behind. White learned, however, that most of the men had been killed in an Indian attack that might have been in retaliation for Lane's actions. Wanchese may have taken part in the attack. He had come to view the English as invaders who must be driven out.

Just as alarming, Simon Fernandez, with whom White had clashed several times during the trip, refused to take the colonists to Chesapeake Bay. With no other choice, White began rebuilding the settlement on Roanoke Island. Luckily, the houses from Lane's colony were still standing and could be repaired. On July 28, however, tragedy struck. While fishing alone for crabs some two miles from the settlement, George Howe was killed by Indians. Hoping to avoid trouble, Governor White sent Manteo and a party of twenty-one men to visit Manteo's tribe, the Croatoans. At first, the Croatoans were suspicious but then welcomed the colonists. The Indians and the English agreed to live together as friends. On Raleigh's orders, Manteo was baptized on August 13, 1587, the first person in the New World to be baptized a Protestant Christian. He was named lord of Roanoke and Dasamunquepeuk.

On August 18, Eleanor Dare, the daughter of Governor White and the wife of Ananias Dare, gave birth to "the first Christian borne in Virginia." Because of that honor, she was named Virginia.

At the end of August, Fernandez was ready to sail for England. By that time, the colony needed more supplies. The White colony, like Lane's, had arrived too late to plant crops. The colonists asked White to return to England for the food, tools, and other things they needed. Reluctantly, White agreed. He sailed on August 27, leaving behind his daughter, her husband, and his new granddaughter. White did not return for three years.

In 1588, Sir Francis Drake was too busy defending England and helping defeat the Armada to worry about the Roanoke colony.

THE DISAPPEARANCE OF THE COLONY

At the time White left Roanoke Island, Spain and England had reached the point of war. Fearing a Spanish invasion, Queen Elizabeth ordered that no ships leave England. Although Sir Richard Grenville was ready to return to the Roanoke colony in late 1587, he was not allowed to set sail.

In the spring of 1588, Governor White was allowed to take two small ships with supplies for the colony. They never arrived. White's ship was captured by French pirates, and the other ship returned to England. The approach of the **Spanish Armada** (fleet) in late July 1588 ended any hopes of helping the colonists that year. Raleigh, Drake, and Grenville were too busy defending England and defeating the Armada to worry about the Roanoke colony. It was not until 1590 that White was able to return to Roanoke with two ships. Toward sundown on August 17, 1590, White and his men neared the northern end of Roanoke Island. When they got close to the shore, White sounded a trumpet and made other noises to get the colonists' attention. There was no answer.

The next morning (which would have been Virginia Dare's third birthday), the company searched for signs of the settlers. Before he left in 1587, White had arranged a "secret code" that the colonists could use to tell

This painting imagines the baptism of Virginia Dare, the first English child born in the New World. She was the granddaughter of John White, governor of the 1587 colony.

THE SPANISH ARMADA

King Philip II of Spain sent 130 ships, the 'Invicible Armada,' to invade England. The attempt ended in disaster for Spain.

Tired of English attacks on his settlements and shipping, Spanish King Philip II plotted the invasion of England. With one crushing blow, he would bring England under his rule and restore Catholicism to that Protestant nation.

To carry out his plans, Philip built a huge fleet. Numbering about 130 ships, 19,000 soldiers, and 8,000 sailors, the fleet set sail from Spain in May 1588. The Spanish called their fleet the "Invincible Armada."

The English were prepared. They were superior seamen. Their ships were smaller, lighter, and faster, and the ships' guns had a longer range. When the Armada entered the English Channel, beacon fires announced the enemy's arrival.

Philip's attempt to invade England ended in disaster. The English sent fire ships among the Armada, severely crippling it. Badly beaten, the Spanish fleet headed north hoping to circle around Scotland, sail along the coast of Ireland, and return to Spain. But fierce storms scattered the Armada. Nineteen Spanish ships wrecked on the coasts of Scotland and Ireland, where their crews were slaughtered. Only sixty-three ships returned to Spain.

The defeat of the Armada weakened Spain's position as a naval power. The defeat also ensured England's continued pursuit of colonies and riches in the New World.

him where they were if they had had to leave. If they were in danger, they were also to carve a cross. White found the letters CRO carved on a tree, but no cross.

The fort was overgrown with grass and weeds and the houses were no longer standing. Iron bars, shot, and guns lay on the ground. Books, papers, pictures, and other items once buried in chests had been dug up and exposed to rain and weather. White discovered that his own property was ruined. Clearly, the colonists had not been there for some time. At the fort's entrance, however, White found another carved message. Five feet above the ground on a tree stripped of its bark were the letters *CROATOAN*. Again, there was no cross signaling trouble.

White took this to mean that the colonists had moved to Croatoan Island (present-day Cape Hatteras) to live among Manteo's tribe. Unfortunately, a fierce storm prevented White from reaching the island. Fearing for the safety of his two ships, White returned to England. He was never able to resume his search for the "Lost Colony."

Many historians and writers have offered theories to explain what happened to the Lost Colony. Some believe that the colonists did move south to Croatoan Island, as White thought. Others suggest they went north to the Chesapeake. Some believe they split into two groups, one of which went to the Chesapeake area, the other to Croatoan Island. Still others say they moved into the interior and settled along the Chowan or Roanoke rivers. The Lumbee Indians of Robeson County claim to be descendants of the Lost Colony. Several historians think the Indians killed the colonists. Some believe that the Spanish sailed up from Florida and destroyed the colonists. Others believe that the colonists died of starvation or disease. The colonists had no ship large enough to carry all of them back to England, so it is unlikely they tried such a dangerous voyage. Yet no one *really* knows what happened to them. *The Lost Colony*, an outdoor drama presented each year in Manteo, is about the mysterious disappearance of the English colony.

Sir Walter Raleigh also had a tragic end. James I, Elizabeth's successor, accused Raleigh of conspiring with Spain and opposing James's right to the throne. Raleigh was jailed and spent most of the last fifteen years of his life in the Tower of London. Because of his arrest, he lost all claims to Virginia. In 1618, he was beheaded.

No one knows what happened to the Lost Colony. Lumbee Indians, such as the girl pictured here, believe they are descendants of the Lost Colony.

Do You Remember?
1. Why was the second attempt at colonizing Roanoke Island started with such high hopes?
2. Why did it take White so long to return to the Roanoke colony?
3. How were the colonists supposed to let White know their location if they had to leave?

CHAPTER REVIEW

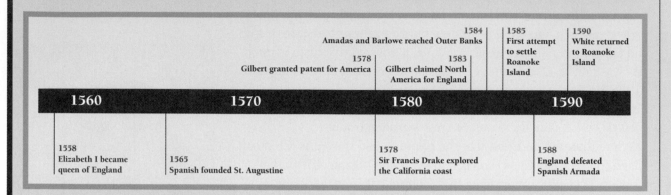

1560	1570	1580	1590

1584
Amadas and Barlowe reached Outer Banks

1578
Gilbert granted patent for America

1583
Gilbert claimed North America for England

1585
First attempt to settle Roanoke Island

1590
White returned to Roanoke Island

1558
Elizabeth I became queen of England

1565
Spanish founded St. Augustine

1578
Sir Francis Drake explored the California coast

1588
England defeated Spanish Armada

Reviewing People, Places, and Terms

On a separate sheet of paper, write the word or words that best complete each of the following sentences.

> Philip Amadas
> Arthur Barlowe
> expedition
> King Philip II
> patent
> privateers
> Queen Elizabeth I
> Walter Raleigh
> Spanish Armada
> John White

1. Relations between England and Spain in the mid-1500s were poor. Repeated attacks by English (a)_____ on Spanish ships and settlements convinced monarch (b)____ to send the (c)____ to invade and conquer England.

*2. (a)_____ gained the support of (b)_____ of England, who granted him a (c)_____ to establish a colony in the New World.

3. The first Roanoke (a)_____ was led by (b)_____ and (c)_____. They visited the area of the Outer Banks and brought back local plants, maps and watercolors by (d)_____, and two local Indians.

Understanding the Facts

1. Why did England want to establish colonies in the New World?
2. Give two reasons why Walter Raleigh was able to take over Gilbert's patent to establish an English colony in the New World.
3. What was the purpose of Amadas and Barlowe's voyage to America in 1584?
4. Why did the Lane colony fail?
5. Why did Raleigh hope to plant a colony north of Roanoke Island—in the Chesapeake Bay area?
6. List some of the differences between the first attempt to settle Roanoke Island and the second attempt.
7. Why did Governor White return to England in August 1587?
8. How did Sir Walter Raleigh die?

Developing Critical Thinking

1. If early accounts by Thomas Harriot were true that "food was plentiful," why do you think the colony continued to run short of food?
2. How do you think our view of history would be different if John White's artwork had not, at least in part, survived?
3. Would you have wanted to be a member of the Lane colony? Why or why not?

1. Select one of the John White drawings of Indian life illustrated in Chapter 2. Describe what the drawing tells about the Indians who were living in the Roanoke area when the English arrived.
2. Select one of the events mentioned in this chapter. Write a headline and a short account of the event as it might have appeared in a newspaper of the time.

Making Connections

1. John White's drawings and Thomas Harriot's notes have been invaluable sources of information for historians. What effect do you think their writings and illustrations had on English society at the time?
2. What effect did the defeat of the Spanish Armada have on the colonization of the New World?
3. In defeating the Spanish Armada, the English used smaller, lighter, and faster ships. Research information at the library, or interview someone with naval experience, to determine what types of ships our navy uses today to defend us.

Tar Heel Trivia

- Virginia Dare was not the only child born to the Lost Colonists. A child was also born to Dyonis and Margery Harvie.

BUILDING SKILLS: USING PRIMARY AND SECONDARY SOURCES

Historians often work with primary sources. *Primary sources* are documents—such as letters, diaries, and log books—written about an event by someone who was alive at that time. A *secondary source* is an account by someone who is retelling, summarizing, or interpreting the information in a primary source.

Sometimes working with a primary source is difficult because the language style is different from that used by the historian. You should also keep in mind that the author of a primary or secondary source may have been influenced by emotions or may have exaggerated his or her writing for some reason.

Below is a portion of Arthur Barlowe's report to Walter Raleigh concerning his 1584 voyage to the Roanoke Island area. Read this excerpt, as well as his comments that appear in your textbook. Then answer the questions that follow.

This island has many goodly woodes full of Deere, Conies, Hares, and Fowle, even in the midst of Summer in incredible abundance. The woods are . . . not barren and fruitless, but the highest and reddest Cedars in the world. . . . Pynes, Cypres, Sassappras, . . . and many other of excellent smell and qualtie.

The soile is the most plentiful, sweete, fruitful and wholesome of all the worlde: there are above fourteen severall sweet smelling timber trees, and the most part of their underwoods are Bayes, and such like; they have those Okes that we have, but farre greater and better. . . .

Beyond this island they call Roanoak, are maine islands very plentifull of fruits and other natural increases together with many townes and villages, along the side of the continent. . . .

Hugh T. Lefler, *North Carolina History As Told by Contemporaries* (Chapel Hill: University of North Carolina Press, 1965), pp. 5-6.

1. Is the excerpt a primary or a secondary source?
2. Was Barlowe favorably impressed with Roanoke Island? Give examples to support your opinion.
3. What did Barlowe bring back to England? Why might this be important to future expeditions?
4. Queen Elizabeth I and Walter Raleigh were pleased with Barlowe's report. Based on what you have read, what might have been included to make the report more complete?
5. What questions would you have asked Barlowe upon his return?

CHAPTER FIVE

THE COLONIZATION OF NORTH CAROLINA

I an[d] my wife, two children, and my old father have, the Lord be praised, arrived safe and sound in Carolina, and live twenty English miles from New Bern. I hope to plant corn enough this year. The land is good, but the beginning is hard, the journey dangerous.
— Unnamed German Settler

AFTER THE FAILURE OF RALEIGH'S EXPEDITIONS between 1585 and 1590, it was almost twenty years before the English tried again to plant a permanent colony in the New World. When they did, they repeated the mistakes made with the Roanoke colonies. Colonies founded to search for gold and silver did not last.

Finally, the English began to establish agriculturally based colonies that welcomed both men and women. These survived and grew. North Carolina lay at the southern edge of the first permanent English settlement in the New World.

THE VIRGINIA COMPANY

In 1606, a group of merchants and wealthy individuals in England formed the Virginia Company. King James I gave the Virginia Company a patent to establish colonies in the New World. The Virginia Company was a **joint-stock company**. During the 1500s, England had developed joint-stock companies as a way of pooling the resources of a large number of people.

Opposite page: Jamestown, Virginia, founded in 1607, became the first permanent English settlement in the New World. The arrival of Africans in 1619 helped ease a labor shortage but also planted the seeds of slavery.

CHAPTER · PREVIEW

Terms: joint-stock company, capital, indentured servant, slave, navigable, persecution, Lords Proprietors, Assembly, militia, governor, council, unicameral, bicameral, taxes, land grant, Culpeper's Rebellion, dissenter, Quakers, borough town, smuggling, royal colony

People: Sir Robert Heath, Nathaniel Batts, William Drummond, Thomas Miller, John Lawson, Baron Christoph von Graffenried, Thomas Cary, Tom Blunt, Edward Teach, Stede Bonnet

Places: Jamestown, Carolana, Albemarle Sound, Bath, New Bern, Brunswick, Wilmington

Above: One of the early leaders of Jamestown was Captain John Smith. Smith's iron-fisted leadership the first year saved the colony. *Below:* The marriage of John Rolfe and Pocahontas. Rolfe planted the first tobacco crop in 1611.

Raleigh had used one to finance his Roanoke voyages. A joint-stock company was much like a corporation of today. Investors bought shares in the company and expected to receive a part of the profits when the company discovered precious metals or opened new trade routes.

Joint-stock companies worked well for trading voyages. As a way of funding colonies, however, they failed. Most investors were looking for quick profits, which were unlikely. The early settlements founded by joint-stock companies often needed large amounts of **capital** (money and property such as supplies, tools, ships). Investors did not want to keep pouring money into colonies that produced little in return.

The Virginia Company suffered from these problems and more. The company first tried to plant a colony in Maine. But after one hard winter there, the colony failed. In 1607, the company sent 144 men and boys to the James River area of Virginia, only 104 of whom survived the trip. In May 1607, they founded Jamestown, naming it for the king.

Disease, a shortage of food, and disagreements nearly destroyed the Jamestown colony. By January 1608, only 38 of the original colonists were still alive. The colonists had not come prepared to work. They expected to make easy fortunes. Instead of planting crops, they searched for gold. Only when Captain John Smith took control in 1608 did the colony manage to avoid total collapse.

Jamestown's success was important to North Carolina for several reasons. First, John Smith heard rumors about the Lost Colony. Indians told

MERCANTILISM

England began establishing colonies in America during a period of world history known for exploration and colonization. All of the European countries wanted to establish colonies so they could be more powerful.

During the 1500s-1700s, England—and the other nations of Europe—followed policies that came to be known as *mercantilism*. An important goal was to make England largely self-sufficient. To do that, the monarchy needed to create a "favorable balance of trade" by exporting more goods than were imported. A favorable balance of trade would bring gold and silver into England and make it militarily and economically strong. Laws were enacted to regulate trade. They made it difficult for foreign merchants to import goods into England; English merchants were told to export goods only in English ships.

Colonies were to help England gain that favorable balance of trade. They were sources of such raw materials and foods as sugar, timber, rice, tobacco, and cotton, thus ending any need to import these goods from other countries. Colonies were also markets for goods manufactured in England.

Captain John Smith, one of the founders of the Virginia colony, clearly understood the purpose of mercantilism. He viewed the colony as "a nurse for soldiers, a practice for mariners, [and] a trade for merchants."

Tobacco was Virginia's first great cash crop. Tobacco produced at manufactories as shown above ended England's need to import it from other countries. Thus, the colony contributed to a favorable trade balance.

him the men from the Roanoke colony had died during a war between two tribes near Jamestown shortly before 1607. Smith unsuccessfully searched for the colonists or some signs of their settlement.

Second, Africans arrived in Virginia in 1619 and provided badly needed labor. These Africans may have been **indentured servants**. Indentured servants agreed to work for someone for a set period of time (usually 4-7 years) in return for passage to the New World. At the end of that time, indentured servants were free to do anything they wished. As the seventeenth century wore on, Africans more and more were treated as slaves. **Slaves** had few rights and spent their entire lives in service to others.

Third, tobacco became Virginia's first great cash crop. John Rolfe, who married the Indian princess Pocahontas, planted the first crop in 1611. Ten years later, Virginians were exporting 40,000 pounds of tobacco. By 1630, shipments had risen to 1.5 million pounds.

Do You Remember?

1. Why did the Jamestown colony almost fail?
2. What is the difference between an indentured servant and a slave?
3. Why was the survival of the Jamestown colony important to North Carolina?

CAROLANA

With the tobacco boom, people became interested in the area south of Jamestown. Because tobacco quickly drains the nutrients from the soil, a field could only be used for about three crops of tobacco. Then it had to lie unused for several years. Farmers needed more land so they could grow tobacco in some fields while other fields lay idle. The English settlers spread quickly along the rich river bottoms in search of the best land. They also settled near **navigable** (passable by boat) rivers and streams, which made it easier to transport crops to market.

Since the streams of southeastern Virginia flow into the Albemarle Sound region, hunters and traders from Jamestown often visited the area. In 1622, John Pory, speaker of the first Virginia legislature and secretary of the colony, explored as far south as the Chowan River. He found a land perfect for both agriculture and trade.

THE HEATH PATENT

In 1625, King James died and was succeeded by his son, Charles I. In 1629, King Charles I gave his attorney general, Sir Robert Heath, a large piece of land in America. Charles gave Heath all the land between 31° and 36° north latitude, from sea to sea. This included all the land between Florida and the Albemarle Sound. Charles named the territory after him-

In 1629 King Charles I of England granted Sir Robert Heath a patent for all lands between Florida and the Albemarle Sound from sea to sea. Charles named the territory for himself, Carolana.

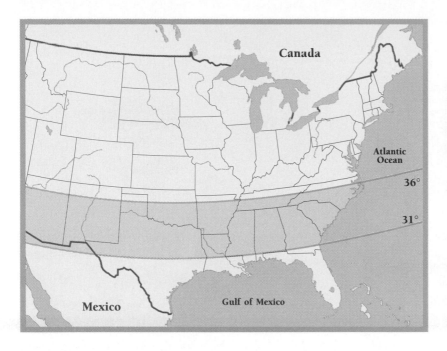

self, calling it *Carolana*. Charles hoped the Heath patent would extend "the Christian religion," enlarge England's "Empire," and increase "the trade & Commerce of this our kingdom."

Heath was not able to plant a colony in Carolana. He had hoped that French Huguenots and other European Protestants would find it a place safe from **persecution** (unjust treatment). In 1632, however, the king and Heath agreed that no foreign-born persons would be allowed into Carolana without permission. Settlers would also have to "submit and conforme" to the Church of England. In 1638, Heath gave the patent to Henry, Lord Maltravers. He too could not settle a colony in Carolana. During the 1640s and 1650s, unrest in England put a stop to colonizing efforts.

Sir Robert Heath (above) was not able to plant a colony in Carolana. In 1638, Heath gave the patent to Henry, Lord Maltravers. He too could not settle a colony in Carolana. During the 1640s and 1650s, unrest in England put a stop to colonizing efforts. The map (above, left) shows the location of the Heath Patent.

SETTLERS FROM THE NORTH

The push to colonize Carolana came from Virginia. In the mid-1600s, Virginia's population began to grow at a rapid rate. The early days of disease, hunger, and death had passed. Hundreds of indentured servants arrived each year. Most were men between the ages of fifteen and twenty-four who had been farmers and laborers in England. After their terms of service were over, the newly free servants wanted to make their fortunes in tobacco. For that, they needed land. At the same time, wealthy planters controlled more and more of the land. The result was a land shortage.

The hunger for land brought Virginians to the region north of the Albemarle Sound. Records show that Nathaniel Batts was the first permanent white settler in North Carolina. In 1655, at the western end of Albemarle Sound on Salmon Creek, Batts built a twenty-foot-square

The navigable rivers flowing southward from Virginia brought perhaps five hundred settlers to the area above the Albemarle Sound by the 1660s. Settlers sought additional lands on which to plant tobacco.

home. The two-room house also served as a trading post. Five years later, on September 24, 1660, Batts bought that land from the Weapemeoc Indians. That was the first recorded deed for North Carolina land.

Other settlers from Virginia quickly followed. They took up land along the Pasquotank, Perquimans, and Chowan rivers. Sometimes they bargained with the Native Americans for the right to settle on the land. But the Native Americans and the Europeans looked at the use of land differently. The Indians thought that the land belonged to the community. Anyone who had a use for the land could claim it. Once that use ended, others could claim the land. Europeans thought of land as something that could be bought and sold. They believed land transactions were permanent. The Indians believed they were temporary.

By the early 1660s, perhaps as many as five hundred settlers had moved into Virginia's southern frontier above Albemarle Sound. The region lacked order and any kind of regular government, but that was about to change.

Do You Remember?

1. How did tobacco increase interest in the area south of Jamestown?
2. Where was the first permanent white settlement in North Carolina?
3. How did the settlers and the Native Americans feel about the ownership of land?

THE LORDS PROPRIETORS

In the mid-1600s, England was ruled by Parliament and Oliver Cromwell, leader of Parliament's army. Parliament then decided to restore the monarchy. In 1660, Charles II, the son of King Charles I, became the king of England. Charles II wished to repay those who had helped him become king. On March 24, 1663, he granted the old Heath patent to eight of his supporters. These men became known as the **Lords Proprietors** of Carolina.

The Carolina Charter of 1663 guaranteed certain rights to the colonists. It was also the basis for representative government in North Carolina. Except in emergencies, any laws passed by the Proprietors had to be approved by the freemen of the colony or by their delegates. In time, the meeting of delegates became the **Assembly**. All laws passed by the Assembly had to be in agreement with the laws of England. Even though the Church of England was the established church in Carolina, the charter allowed the

The Carolina Charter of 1663 granted the old Heath patent to eight Lords Proprietors. Charles II, son of Charles I, made the grant to key supporters who had helped to restore the monarchy.

HOW MASSACHUSETTS CREATED THE FIRST BICAMERAL LEGISLATURE

In 1640, about twenty thousand English colonists scratched out a living in New England. They lived in twelve scattered communities, the largest of which was Massachusetts Bay Colony.

The Bay Colony was founded by religious dissenters known as Puritans, who tried to govern the colony by religious principles. Many settlers, however, demanded rule by law. The battle for a government of laws came to a head in the colony's General Court (legislature), which consisted of eight magistrates and twenty deputies. The magistrates served as assistants to the governor. The deputies represented the towns, each of which sent two representatives.

A disagreement over a pig turned into a challenge of the magistrates' power. The pig was claimed by both a wealthy, unpopular merchant and a widow who ran a boardinghouse. The deputies sided with the widow. The magistrates, who could veto the deputies' decisions, sided with the merchant. The issue of who owned the pig was lost in the political struggle that followed. The deputies protested the right of a few magistrates to overturn the decisions of the people's representatives.

A 1644 law resolved the matter. Deputies and magistrates would sit as separate bodies. To pass any measure, both bodies had to agree. Thus, a dispute over a pig led to the establishment of the first bicameral legislature.

practice of other religions. The Proprietors could grant "indulgencies and dispensations" to those who had other beliefs. Under the 1663 charter, the Proprietors had broad powers. They could establish counties, towns, and courts; collect fees and taxes; make grants of land; raise a **militia** (a citizen army); and wage war.

In 1664, the Proprietors created three counties along the coast of Carolina: Albemarle, Clarendon, and Craven. Albemarle County lay in the northeastern part of what is now North Carolina. In 1665, King Charles II issued a second charter to the Lords Proprietors. This charter gave the Proprietors all the land up to the present Virginia-North Carolina border. The Albemarle settlements were now under the Lords Proprietors' rule.

At first, Sir William Berkeley, governor of Virginia and one of the Proprietors, kept an eye on the area. In 1664, however, William Drummond, a Scot living in Virginia, was named the first **governor** of Albemarle County. The governor was the person named by the Proprietors to rule a colony.

To encourage settlement in Albemarle, the Proprietors drew up "The Fundamental Constitutions of Carolina." This 1669 document had several purposes. First, the Proprietors wanted to support the monarchy and avoid a democracy in Carolina. The Fundamental Constitutions, therefore, gave more power to the governor (who was named by the Proprietors) and less to the elected delegates.

Second, the Proprietors wanted to protect their property rights. The Fundamental Constitutions, therefore, gave two-thirds of the land in Carolina to the Proprietors and only one-third of the land to settlers.

The Fundamental Constitutions never worked. Still, the outlines of a modern system of government could be seen in Albemarle County. The Proprietors chose the governor. The governor appointed a **council**, which eventually had ten members. The council helped and advised the governor. For a while, it also acted as the colony's court. The Assembly was the only elected branch of government. Over the years, each branch's role became clearer. At first, the council and Assembly sat as a **unicameral** (one-house) legislature, over which the governor presided. Around 1700, the legislature became **bicameral**, that is, it had two houses. The council became the "upper" house. The Assembly, the "lower house," elected its own speaker and had power over money matters, including the governor's salary, taxes, and paper currency. At about the same time, a general court was created.

During the early years of the colony, its form of government had not yet taken shape. Albemarle County was a raw, often lawless frontier. Its early years were filled with dissension, disorder, and armed conflict.

Do You Remember?

1. Who were the Lords Proprietors?
2. What was the importance of the Carolina Charter of 1663?
3. What were the three branches of government that grew out of the Fundamental Constitutions?

CULPEPER'S REBELLION

The colony's land policies added to its troubles. To attract settlers to Albemarle, the Proprietors lowered taxes on land, even excusing taxes for the first year. **Taxes** are the money given to the government to pay for services the government provides. Land grants were limited to 660 acres. A **land grant** was a piece of land given to a settler who agreed to move onto it. The Assembly even protected settlers for five years from lawsuits arising from debts or crimes committed elsewhere. Soon, Virginians were calling Albemarle a "rogue's harbor," a place where thieves, debtors, runaway slaves, and pirates were safe.

Relations between Virginia and Albemarle got worse. Virginia would not recognize the borders set by the 1665 charter. Albemarle colonists accused Virginia of stirring up the Meherrin and Nottoway Indians, who attacked the southern settlements. In 1679, Virginia even refused to ship Albemarle tobacco from Virginia ports.

In the midst of all these problems, **Culpeper's Rebellion** broke out. The uprising came about when the Proprietors tried to enforce the Navigation Acts of 1651, 1660, and 1673. Those acts required that the colonies only use English vessels for their shipments. Some trade goods,

In 1664 the Lords Proprietors appointed William Drummond of Virginia as the first governor of Albemarle County. Drummond was described as "a sober Scotch gentlemen of good repute."

Anthony Ashley Cooper, Earl of Shaftesbury, feared that disorders in Albemarle County might endanger the Lords Proprietors' charter. For that reason he defended John Culpeper against charges of treason.

including tobacco, had to be shipped directly to England. Much of Albemarle's trade was with New England. The Plantation Duty Act of 1673 placed a tax on this trade. For example, if the colonists did not send their tobacco directly to England on English ships, they had to pay a tax of a penny a pound.

Settlers who had come to Albemarle before 1663, such as George Durant and John Jenkins, ignored the Navigation Acts. A newcomer to Albemarle, John Culpeper sided with Durant and Jenkins. Thomas Eastchurch, who was speaker of the Assembly, and Thomas Miller sided with the Proprietors. Using his powers as acting governor, Jenkins tried to dissolve (break up) the Assembly. The Assembly then removed him from office.

Eastchurch and Miller went to England to talk to the Proprietors. In 1676, the Proprietors named Eastchurch as the new governor and he and Miller set off for Carolina. Eastchurch was delayed in the West Indies and sent Miller ahead to serve as acting governor. The title apparently went to his head. Miller increased taxes, seized goods he said had been brought into the colony illegally, imposed heavy fines, and jailed several people who opposed him.

The colonists had had enough. In December 1677, a band of forty men surrounded Miller's house, jailed him, and took the tobacco and customs records he held. The "rebels" set up their own Assembly, which met at George Durant's house.

Miller later escaped from jail and went to England to seek the Proprietors' help. Culpeper followed to present the rebels' side of the story. When Culpeper arrived, however, he was arrested and tried for treason. Fearing that the Proprietors might lose their charter over this, Anthony Ashley Cooper, Earl of Shaftesbury and one of the Proprietors, defended Culpeper. Shaftesbury argued that Miller had no authority to serve as acting governor. The Proprietors agreed and Culpeper was acquitted.

Peace returned to Albemarle for a short time. Taxes were collected, and those who had opposed the Proprietors escaped serious punishment. The arrival of a new governor, however, brought on a new crisis.

UNREST IN ALBEMARLE

In 1678, the Proprietors named Seth Sothel governor of Albemarle. Sothel's governorship was doomed from the start. On the voyage to America, he was captured by Turkish pirates. He did not reach Albemarle until 1683.

When he finally took office, Sothel proved to be even worse than Thomas Miller. He jailed opponents without a trial; took over estates; and seized cattle, slaves, and personal goods. He even accepted bribes. In 1689, the colonists rose against him. Sothel was tried before the Assembly, found guilty, and banished from Albemarle. He made his way to Charles Town, South Carolina, claimed the governorship there, and continued his corrupt activities.

The Proprietors then named Philip Ludwell governor. This appointment, however, did not end the troubles. John Gibbs challenged the appointment and proclaimed himself governor. Apparently Gibbs believed he had a right to be governor because he was a relative of the Proprietor George Monck, Duke of Albemarle. Monck held one of the titles to nobility established under the Fundamental Constitutions. Both Gibbs and Ludwell went to England to present their claims to the Proprietors. The Proprietors chose Ludwell.

Ludwell's appointment was important for another reason. In their 1689 instructions, the Proprietors made Ludwell governor "of our province of Carolina that lyes north and east of Cape feare." The County of Albemarle was soon to become "North Carolina."

NORTH CAROLINA'S FIRST TOWNS

Between 1675 and 1715, the colony grew from about 4,000 people to 11,000. After 1690, the colony's government was fairly stable. More and more settlers arrived from Virginia. Some of them moved as far south as the Pamlico River. To extend government to them, Bath County was formed in 1696. The county included all the land from Albemarle Sound to Cape Fear.

John Lawson was the surveyor general of the colony. Along the Pamlico River, he staked off a village that in 1706 became Bath, the first town in North Carolina. By 1709, Bath had about a dozen houses and a public library.

At about the same time, a group of French Huguenots from Virginia began to settle along the Neuse and Trent rivers. In 1710, a party of German, Swiss, and English settlers came to the same region and founded the town of New Bern. The new settlement was largely the result of the efforts of Baron Christoph von Graffenried.

Von Graffenried was the leader of a group of German and Swiss Protestants who wanted to escape religious persecution in Europe. In England, he persuaded Queen Anne to pay for moving a colony of one hundred poor German families to America. He also talked with John Lawson about settling his colony in Carolina. Lawson was in London to publish his book *A New Voyage to Carolina*. Lawson told von Graffenried that his people would be free to practice their religion in Carolina. After hearing this, von Graffenried bought nearly 20,000 acres of land on the Neuse and Trent rivers. Lawson chose the site for the town of New Bern and laid it out in the form of a cross.

George Monck, Duke of Albemarle, was one the Lords Proprietors. At one time he had been a general in Oliver Cromwell's army. But he switched sides to help restore the monarchy and bring King Charles II to the throne.

Bath, established in 1706, is the oldest town in North Carolina. Two of the oldest buildings in Bath are St. Thomas Church (1734, top) and the Van der Veer House (mid-eighteenth century, above).

The colony, however, got off to a terrible start. During the stormy thirteen-week voyage to America, about one-half of the settlers died. A French privateer attacked and looted one of the ships as it neared Virginia. When the colonists finally reached New Bern, they had no food or shelter. As Von Graffenried said, "the colony was shattered before it was settled." Nevertheless, Von Graffenried began to organize the colony, build houses, and erect a water mill. The colony survived. Within eighteen months, it was doing very well.

Do You Remember?

1. Why did Albemarle come to be called a "rogue's harbor"?
2. What caused the relationship between Virginia and Albemarle to worsen?
3. What were the Navigation Acts?
4. Why was Seth Sothel unsuccessful as a governor?
5. What difficulty did Philip Ludwell have as governor?
6. Why did Von Graffenried and the German settlers want to come to Carolina?

CARY'S REBELLION

The Church of England was the "established" church of Carolina. Except for the 1632 agreement between Sir Robert Heath and King Charles I, however, the crown, Proprietors, and governors had been very tolerant of "dissenters." **Dissenters** were all non-Anglicans, that is, people who did not belong to the Church of England.

Among the colonists moving into Albemarle during the 1600s was a religious group known as **Quakers**. The Quakers were a very tolerant religious group who did not believe in churches or ceremonies and would not fight for any reason. They dressed very plainly. The Quakers came to Carolina looking for a place where they could practice their religion freely. Many of them settled along the Pasquotank and Perquimans rivers. By the turn of the century, the Quakers had a great deal of influence in the colony and held many elected positions.

In 1701, the Assembly passed a Vestry Act to lay out Anglican parishes, build churches, and pay clergymen (ministers). To pay for this, a tax would be collected. Quakers, Presbyterians, and some Anglicans protested the tax. The Proprietors would not approve of the law because it gave too much power to the church. The law was never enforced.

In 1703, however, the Assembly passed another Vestry Act. This new law struck directly at Quaker beliefs. It stated that all members of the Assembly must be followers of the Church of England and that they must *swear* an oath of allegiance to Queen Anne. The Quakers' religious beliefs would not allow them to swear. In the past, they had *affirmed* rather than sworn an oath.

The new governor, Thomas Cary, strictly enforced the law. Quakers could not take their seats in the Assembly. To hold any office without swearing an oath, they had to pay a fine. The Quakers were so upset they sent John Porter to London to talk to the Proprietors, one of whom, John Archdale, was a Quaker. Porter returned with an order allowing Quakers to *affirm* oaths. The order also removed Cary as governor.

William Glover, president of the council, became acting governor. The Quakers soon found him to be even worse than Cary. The Quakers then joined forces with Cary, who by now had changed sides. Together, they forced Glover to flee to Virginia. Cary then became governor, serving from 1708 to 1711.

To complicate an already confusing situation, the Proprietors appointed Edward Hyde governor of North Carolina. The settlements around Albemarle and Pamlico sounds and at Charles Town had grown large enough to need separate governors. By sending a governor to each area in 1712, the Proprietors divided Carolina into North Carolina and South Carolina.

The Lords Proprietors divided Carolina into North Carolina and South Carolina with the appointment of Edward Hyde (above) as governor of North Carolina in 1712. He died of yellow fever less than two years after arriving in the colony.

Hyde actually arrived in the colony and met with the Assembly in March 1711. That Assembly overturned many of the laws passed during Cary's term. It also pledged to enforce "all laws made for the establishment of the Church."

Cary could contain himself no longer. In the words of Von Graffenried, Cary "became an open and declared rebel." Trying to overthrow Governor Hyde, Cary sailed up Albemarle Sound until he was opposite Thomas Pollock's house. Hyde, his advisers, and perhaps forty supporters were meeting there. Cary fired cannonballs at the house, but the attack fizzled and the rebellion ended. Cary was later arrested and taken to stand trial in England. However, he was released for lack of evidence.

Despite Von Graffenried's description, Cary's Rebellion involved more than the Anglican-Quaker struggle or the anger of a supposedly drunken mob. The rebellion was also a sign of the tensions between Bath and Albemarle counties. Most of the rebel leaders came from Bath. Bath was very involved in the Indian trade for animal skins, but it did not have a major voice in the colony's political life. As the older settlement, Albemarle held most of the political power in the colony. Its prosperity depended heavily on tobacco. These regional tensions would surface again.

Do You Remember?
1. How did the Vestry Act strike at Quaker beliefs?
2. What resulted from the appointment of one governor for the settlements around Albemarle and Pamlico sounds and one governor for the settlements around Charles Town?
3. Why were there tensions between Bath and Albemarle?

THE TUSCARORA WAR

Relations between Albemarle colonists and Native Americans had never been entirely peaceful. There were hostilities, but no large-scale fighting had broken out. The smaller Algonquian tribes moved away. West of them, however, lived the Tuscarora, a powerful Iroquoian tribe. They lived in about fifteen villages along the Pamlico and Neuse rivers. Their presence there probably stopped the whites from moving westward during much of the seventeenth century. But pressures were building.

CONFLICTS BETWEEN THE INDIANS AND THE SETTLERS
The Tuscarora had three main complaints against settlers. First, white traders often cheated the Indians. The Tuscarora were middlemen in a trade route between Europeans on the coast and Siouan tribes to the west. They exchanged European goods for deerskins, furs, and Indian slaves.

Second, the Indian slave trade began to include the Tuscarora themselves. At first, the Indian slaves were captives from enemy tribes. But

Uneasy relations between the colonists and Native Americans exploded into warfare in 1711. The uprising by Tuscarora nearly destroyed the colony.

the Europeans made no distinction between tribes or captives. Many Tuscarora ended up among the Indian slaves shipped from Charles Town, South Carolina, to the West Indies. Slaves were also sent to other American colonies like Pennsylvania. In 1705, however, the Pennsylvania council, fearing an uprising, voted not to accept Indian slaves from Carolina.

Third, the number of settlers on Indian land was increasing. The settlers did not want the Native Americans to hunt near their farms. Using that excuse, they even took away the Indians' game, arms, and ammunition. The settlement of New Bern in 1710 took even more of the Indian lands. Desperate, the Tuscarora tried to move to Pennsylvania, but authorities there would not allow it.

THE OUTBREAK OF WAR

In September 1711, the Tuscarora captured Baron Von Graffenried and John Lawson, who were exploring along the Neuse River. They let Von Graffenried go but burned John Lawson at the stake. Before Von Graffenried could warn anyone, about 500 well-armed Tuscarora attacked settlements along the Neuse and Pamlico rivers. The Indians struck at

The Tuscarora War began in 1711 with the capture of John Lawson and Baron Christoph Von Graffenried, who were exploring the Neuse River.

dawn on September 22. Houses were burned, crops destroyed, and animals killed or run off. In just two hours, 130 people died. The whole region lay "totally wasted and ruined," in the words of one observer.

The Albemarle area was spared. The Tuscarora ruler in that region, Tom Blunt, remained neutral. Still, the entire colony was in danger. For the first time in the colony's history, the Assembly issued £4,000 in paper money and drafted all men between the ages of sixteen and sixty. Governor Hyde also asked for help from Virginia and South Carolina.

South Carolina sent £4,000 and an army of 30 settlers and about 500 friendly Indians, chiefly Yamasees. Colonel John Barnwell, nicknamed "Tuscarora Jack," led the force. Barnwell defeated the Tuscarora in two battles near New Bern in January 1712. In April, with North Carolina militia, Barnwell attacked the Tuscarora fort held by King Hancock in what is now Greene County. After ten days, Barnwell and the Tuscarora agreed to a peace treaty. The Tuscarora agreed to release all their hostages and to move out of the area between the Neuse and Cape Fear rivers.

The peace treaty did not hold, however. Before returning to South Carolina, Barnwell killed some 40 or 50 Tuscarora men. He also carried off nearly 200 of their women and children and sold them into slavery. His actions led to more Indian raids in the summer and fall of 1712. In March 1713, Colonel James Moore arrived from South Carolina with 33 whites and about 1,000 friendly Indians. At Fort Nehucke on Catechna Creek, Moore finally crushed the Tuscarora.

By the end of the war, as many as 1,000 Tuscarora had been captured and enslaved. Perhaps another 1,400 were dead. During 1712 and 1713, many of the Tuscarora left Carolina to settle in the Iroquois Confederacy in New York and Canada. King Hancock was captured by Tom Blunt and turned over to colonial officials, who apparently murdered him on the spot. As a reward for not joining the fighting, Tom Blunt's people received a reservation on the Roanoke River in Bertie County.

THE EFFECTS OF THE WAR

One important result of the war was to open up North Carolina for settlement. However, the Tuscarora War left the colony deeply in debt. Many lives were lost and the property damage was severe and widespread. Yet out of these grim conditions came several positive steps to rebuild the colony. The Assembly of 1715 revised all of the old laws and passed about sixty new ones. The new laws clearly set out the duties and powers of government officials. A new Vestry Act was passed, and the right of Quakers and other dissenters to practice their religions and hold office was protected. Other laws established procedures for building and maintaining roads, bridges, and ferries. Pilots at Roanoke and Ocracoke were told to find and mark channels through the shallow waters of the sounds.

Baron Christoph von Graffenried was captured by the Tuscarora in 1711 but released. Before he could warn other settlers, however, the Tuscarora struck.

To encourage growth, the Assembly gave all **borough towns** (towns with sixty or more families) representation in the legislature. Edenton was incorporated in 1722. That same year, Beaufort was made a port of entry. One problem, however, continued—piracy.

Do You Remember?

1. What were the three main complaints the Tuscarora had against the settlers?
2. What were the effects of the war on the Tuscarora tribe?

CAROLINA PIRATES

The period between 1689 and 1718 has been called the "Golden Age of Piracy." English trade laws were never popular in the colonies; both merchants and sailors did everything they could to evade them. **Smuggling** (bringing goods into the colony illegally) was common. With England at war for much of this time, it was hard to tell the difference between legal privateering and illegal piracy. As long as the pirates attacked French and Spanish ships, they were doing their patriotic duty. Unfortunately, they also attacked English and colonial ships.

The North Carolina coast offered many good hiding places for pirates. They could hide in the shallow sounds of the Outer Banks and then dart out to sea to capture rich cargoes.

The two most famous Carolina pirates were Edward Teach, known as "Blackbeard," and Major Stede Bonnet. Blackbeard was a very ferocious-looking man with long black hair and an unkempt beard. To look even more savage, he put bits of smoldering rope in his hair.

In contrast to Blackbeard, Bonnet was known as "the Gentleman Pirate." A respectable army officer and planter in Barbados, Bonnet turned to piracy without any warning.

Blackbeard made his headquarters at Bath, where he claimed he was welcome in any home. He may have been telling the truth. Many people approved of pirates, because they provided some protection against the Spanish and because they brought captured goods into the colony. Tobias Knight, acting chief justice of the colony, stored some of Blackbeard's loot in his barn.

In the end, it was South Carolina and Virginia that stopped the piracy in North Carolina waters. In September 1718, Governor Robert Johnson of South Carolina sent Colonel William Rhett to put an end to Stede Bonnet. Rhett found Bonnet at the mouth of the Cape Fear River. After a five-hour battle, the South Carolinians captured Bonnet and took him to Charles Town. He was tried, convicted, and hanged. Forty-nine other pirates were hanged in Charles Town that November and December.

Edward Teach, known as Blackbeard, was a brutal pirate. He made his headquarters at Bath and enjoyed the confidence of some of the colony's leading officials.

THE SEARCH FOR
QUEEN ANNE'S REVENGE

In November 1996, Intersal, Inc., a private research organization working under a permit from the state of North Carolina, discovered an early eighteenth-century shipwreck in Beaufort Inlet little more than a mile from

Fort Macon. The discovery sent a thrill through the archaeological community in North Carolina and indeed the world. Researchers believed that divers had found the *Queen Anne's Revenge*, the flagship of the notorious pirate Blackbeard.

In 1717, Edward Teach, also known as Blackbeard, captured the *Queen Anne's Revenge*, which was once a French slave ship named the *Concorde*. He used the vessel to raid shipping in the Caribbean and along the eastern seaboard of North America. In June 1718, a fleet of four ships under Blackbeard's command approached Beaufort Inlet after a week of plundering Charleston, South Carolina. Unfortunately, the *Queen Anne's Revenge* ran aground in Beaufort Inlet and sank. When one of Blackbeard's other ships, the *Adventure*, tried to save the stranded vessel, it too sank.

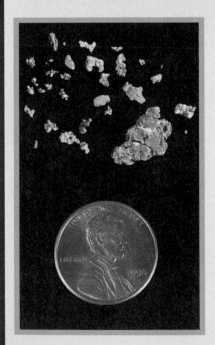

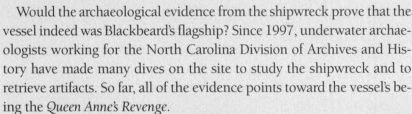

Would the archaeological evidence from the shipwreck prove that the vessel indeed was Blackbeard's flagship? Since 1997, underwater archaeologists working for the North Carolina Division of Archives and History have made many dives on the site to study the shipwreck and to retrieve artifacts. So far, all of the evidence points toward the vessel's being the *Queen Anne's Revenge*.

One of the first artifacts recovered was a bell with the date "1709" inscribed on it. Other artifacts include the barrel of a blunderbuss, pewter plates, scientific instruments, wine bottles, and even gold dust. All of the artifacts date from the late seventeenth or early eighteenth century.

The shipwreck may include the largest collection of cannons in the world. The *Queen Anne's Revenge* was a large vessel, perhaps 100 feet long and weighing 250 tons. Contemporary accounts stated that Blackbeard had armed the ship with forty cannons. At least twenty-two cannons have been identified in the shipwreck. Six have been recovered, and four of

those were still loaded. One loaded cannon included rope, paper wrappings, a cartridge, the cannon ball, and powder. Another cannon contained spikes, which were used to damage rigging and injure sailors. When one cannon was opened, a puff of air came out. Scientists hope to study any trapped air from the eighteenth century that is still present in other cannons that are recovered.

The cannons came from more than one country, and those multiple origins suggest that the vessel was a pirate ship. Cannons from at least three countries have been identified so far: Sweden, France, and England. The bell with the 1709 inscription appears to be Spanish. Although the pirates of myth and legend were always looking for gold and treasure, they were really opportunists. They seized whatever valuables a ship contained, including trade goods, weapons, instruments, and agricultural products.

The search for *Queen Anne's Revenge* will continue. Underwater archaeologists plan to continue excavating the shipwreck and to recover other artifacts that may demonstrate once and for all the ship's identity. In the meantime, visitors to the North Carolina Maritime Museum in Beaufort can see exhibits of numerous artifacts from the shipwreck.

Above: Crew members aboard the R/V Dan Moore *untie the first cannon recovered in 1997 from the likely* Queen Anne's Revenge *shipwreck near Beaufort. Nearly ten feet long, it is still undergoing conservation to remove concretions (encrusted shells and mud) and to stabilize the iron.* **Opposite page, above:** *Nautical archaeologist David Moore, cutting on a ship hull timber at the shipwreck site in preparation for raising it for conservation.* **Opposite page, below:** *Gold dust recovered from the shipwreck believed to be* Queen Anne's Revenge.

Above left: Governor Alexander Spotswood of Virginia sent out two ships under the command of Lieutenant Robert Maynard to find Blackbeard. Above right: Maynard killed Blackbeard in hand-to-hand combat near Ocracoke Inlet.

Meanwhile, Governor Alexander Spotswood of Virginia sent out two ships under the command of Lieutenant Robert Maynard of the Royal Navy. Maynard's mission was to find Blackbeard. On November 22, 1718, the Virginians found Blackbeard's ship, the *Adventure*, near Ocracoke Inlet. In a hand-to-hand fight, Maynard killed Blackbeard and cut off his head. Attaching it to the bow of the ship, Maynard sailed into Bath so all the people could see. Half of Blackbeard's crew were killed in the fighting. The remaining nine were taken to Virginia, where they were tried, convicted, and hanged. This ended the "golden age of piracy."

SETTLING THE CAPE FEAR REGION

By the 1720s, some peace had finally come to North Carolina. The Indian threat east of the Fall Line had largely been ended. The defeat of the pirates and a more orderly government brought on a period of expansion and new settlement. In 1724-1725 alone, about one thousand families moved to North Carolina. Between 1722 and 1729, four new counties were formed: Bertie (1722), Carteret (1722), Tyrrell (1729), and New Hanover (1729).

People had tried to settle in the lower Cape Fear valley since the 1660s. One group came from New England but left by April 1663. An expedition from Barbados in August 1663 led to the establishment of Clarendon County in May 1664. The Barbadians established Charles Town on the western bank of the Cape Fear River. That colony failed in 1667.

During the Tuscarora War, James Moore, Maurice Moore, and other South Carolinians had marched through the Cape Fear region. After the war, they decided to return and colonize it. By 1723, settlers began to take up land along the Cape Fear River, even though they did not hold title to it. Without the permission of the Proprietors, Governor George Burrington opened a land office and issued land grants.

More settlers soon followed. In 1725, Maurice Moore laid out the town of Brunswick fourteen miles above the mouth of the Cape Fear River. Eight years later, Wilmington was established sixteen miles farther up the river. North Carolina now had direct access to the Atlantic Ocean.

THE END OF THE PROPRIETORSHIP

The English government became more and more unhappy with the colonies it had chartered to private persons or corporations. (Rhode Island and Connecticut were the only corporate colonies.) In particular, the crown did not believe the colonies had obeyed the trade laws or contributed enough to England's defense. It soon began to take back those colonies. In 1719, South Carolina came under royal rule.

At first, the Proprietors resisted. But in January 1728, seven of the eight Proprietors agreed to sell their interests to the king. Only the Carteret share, later to become the Granville District, was not included in the sale.

The sale of Carolina for £17,500 became effective on July 25, 1729. From 1729 until the American Revolution, North Carolina was a **royal colony**, directly governed by the crown.

The Carteret County Courthouse (1796) in Beaufort, is the oldest public building in Carteret County. Beaufort is the third oldest town in North Carolina, surveyed in 1713 and incorporated in 1722.

Do You Remember?

1. Why was the North Carolina coast such a good place for pirates to operate?
2. Who finally eliminated piracy from the North Carolina coast?
3. What two new towns were founded in the Cape Fear area by settlers from South Carolina?
4. Why was the English government unhappy with the colonies it had chartered to private persons or corporations?

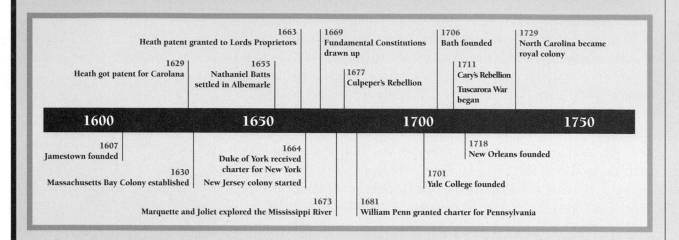

1600	1650	1700	1750

1663 Heath patent granted to Lords Proprietors

1669 Fundamental Constitutions drawn up

1706 Bath founded

1729 North Carolina became royal colony

1629 Heath got patent for Carolana

1655 Nathaniel Batts settled in Albemarle

1677 Culpeper's Rebellion

1711 Cary's Rebellion

Tuscarora War began

1607 Jamestown founded

1664 Duke of York received charter for New York

1718 New Orleans founded

1630 Massachusetts Bay Colony established

New Jersey colony started

1701 Yale College founded

1673 Marquette and Joliet explored the Mississippi River

1681 William Penn granted charter for Pennsylvania

Reviewing People, Places, and Terms

On a separate sheet of paper, write the word or words that best complete the sentences that follow.

- Assembly
- governor
- indentured servants
- Jamestown
- joint-stock company
- Lords Proprietors
- persecution
- Quakers
- royal colony
- slaves

1. The Virginia Company, a _____, established the first permanent English settlement in the New World at _____.
2. Shortages of laborers in the New World were filled first by _____ and then by _____.
3. Many groups, such as the _____, came to the New World to escape religious and political _____.
4. The "owners" of Carolina were known as the _____.
5. The _____ oversaw the operations of the colony; the law-making body of Albemarle County was known as the _____.
6. In 1729, North Carolina became a(n) _____.

Understanding the Facts

1. Where did the Virginia Company first try to establish a colony? Why did it fail?
2. What was the rumor about the Lost Colony that Captain John Smith heard from the Indians?
3. When and under what circumstances did Africans first arrive in Jamestown?
4. Why did farmers need so much land to grow tobacco?
5. What where the first three counties established in Carolina?
6. What was the Fundamental Constitutions of Carolina? How successful was it?
7. What was the basic reason for Culpeper's Rebellion?
8. In what year was Carolina divided into North and South Carolina? Why was the area divided?
9. Why was the establishment of the towns of Brunswick and Wilmington important to North Carolina?

Developing Critical Thinking

1. Why do you think someone would have volunteered to become an indentured servant in return for passage to the New World?
2. The First Amendment of the U.S. Constitution (1791) states, "Congress shall make no law re-

specting an establishment of religion, or prohibiting the free exercise thereof. . . ." Compare this statement with the religious rights granted by the Carolina Charter of 1663. How do these differ?

3. Why do you think it was eventually left to officials in South Carolina and Virginia to eliminate the piracy in North Carolina waters?

Applying Your Skills

1. In 1629, Sir Robert Heath was given all North American lands between 31° and 36° north latitude from the Atlantic Ocean to the Pacific Ocean. Using a modern map of the United States, determine what states today lie entirely or in part within the territory that was once known as *Carolana*.

2. The Lords Proprietors originally hoped to establish a European feudal system in Carolina. Prepare a report that explains what a "feudal system" is and how it might have operated in Carolina.

3. Using an outline map of the state, locate North Carolina's first towns: Bath, New Bern, Beaufort, Edenton, Currituck, Brunswick, and Wilmington.

4. Many legends exist about pirates. Prepare a report for the class on some of the legends surrounding Blackbeard or other pirates who operated around North Carolina.

Making Connections

1. Are countries still worried about their "balance of trade"?

2. The United States has become the world's largest debtor nation. What does this mean, and how do you suppose this happened?

3. The bicameral legislature that developed in the Massachusetts Bay Colony was an attempt to balance the power of two opposing groups. Can you think of other ways that power is balanced in our national government today?

BUILDING SKILLS: FINDING INFORMATION

As you continue your study of the history of North Carolina, your teacher may assign topics for you to research. In addition to looking in the card catalogue of your school media center, there are a number of other reference books in your media center available to help you complete these assignments. These include:

Almanacs: Contain facts and general information on important events, politics, geography, and so on

Atlases: Give map and place information and major travel routes

Biographical books: Provide general information about notable individuals

Dictionaries: Give meanings, spellings, and pronunciations of words

Encyclopedias: Summarize information on a wide variety of topics; usually arranged alphabetically by subject or topic

Newspapers/magazines: Contain information (sometimes opinionated) on current as well as featured topics

Read the following descriptions of information needed and determine which reference source is most appropriate to use. Some information can be found in more than one reference source or in reference sources not contained in the above list.

1. The distance between Asheville and Charlotte
2. The date North Carolina became a state
3. The yearly average rainfall in North Carolina
4. The capital of North Carolina
5. The definition of "goober peas"
6. An explanation of how to grow tobacco
7. The correct pronunciation of *poultry*
8. The location of Grandfather Mountain
9. Another word for *liberty*
10. A map showing the counties of North Carolina
11. A list of the major works of Thomas Wolfe
12. A list of the ten largest cities in North Carolina

UNIT 3

COLONIAL NORTH CAROLINA

DURING THE PERIOD that North Carolina was a royal colony, English, African, Scotch-Irish, German, Highland Scots, and Welsh peoples settled the land and pushed the frontier westward. Many made their living from farming or from lumber and naval stores. Towns were established along the coast. The colonists, however, became involved in the increasing tensions between Great Btitain and France.

Right: From 1725 to 1750 North Carolina's population doubled as settlers poured into the backcountry, as seen in this re-enactment. **Above:** *Moravians from Pennsylvania established Salem in 1766 and built the Single Brothers Workshop, which is at the far right in the photograph .*

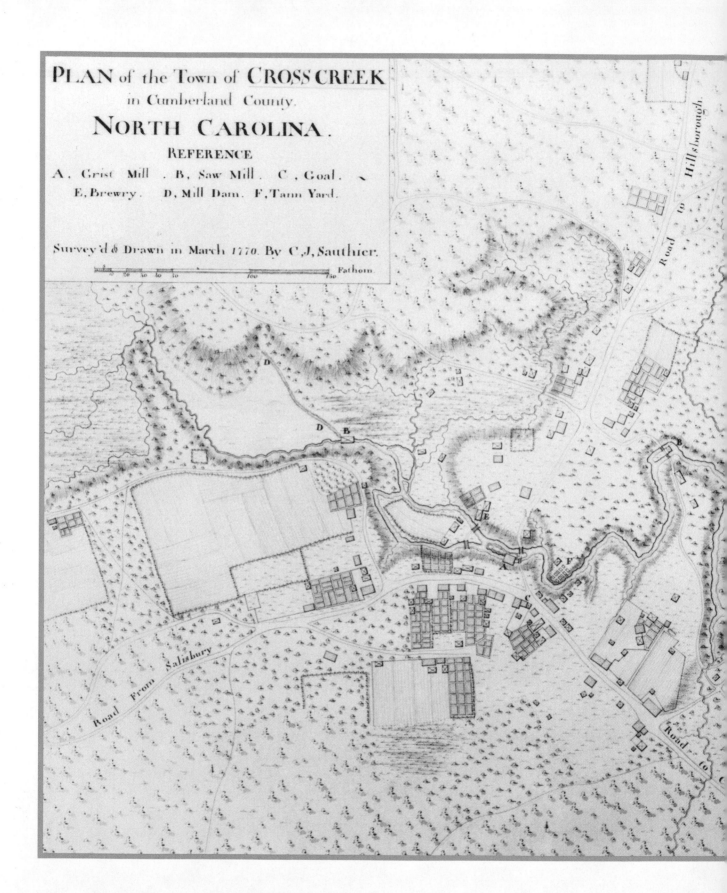

PLAN of the Town of CROSS CREEK
in Cumberland County.

NORTH CAROLINA.

REFERENCE

A, Grist Mill . B, Saw Mill . C , Goal .
E, Brewry . D, Mill Dam. F, Tann Yard.

Survey'd & Drawn in March 1770. By C,J, Sauthier.

CHAPTER SIX

THE SETTLEMENT OF NORTH CAROLINA

The Highlanders are mostly settled about [Cross Creek], each has a plantation of his own on the river side & live as happy as princes, they have liberty & property & no Excise, no dread of their being turned out of their lands by Tyrants....

—Alexander Campbell

UNTIL THE 1720S, MOST OF THE SETTLERS who came to North Carolina were English. Other groups had settled in the colony: French Huguenots, Swiss, Welsh, and Germans. Africans—against their will—had also been brought to North Carolina. During the next fifty years, the colony would grow dramatically.

In 1730, North Carolina had an estimated population of 35,000, about 6,000 of whom were slaves. By 1755, the colony's population had doubled. By 1775, some 345,000 people lived in North Carolina, 80,000 of them slaves. Only Virginia, Pennsylvania, and Massachusetts had more people.

THE GREAT WAGON ROAD

With its dangerous coast, North Carolina was not an easy colony to reach. Most new settlers came overland, first from Virginia and later from South Carolina. Before the 1720s, nearly all settlers stayed along the Coastal Plain. Most of the settlements were in the Albemarle region; the Neuse, Trent, and Pamlico river basins; and the lower Cape Fear River valley. Between 1730 and 1775, the Piedmont and upper Cape Fear River valley became home to thousands of settlers. It was during this time that

The Highland Scots came directly from Scotland to settle the upper Cape Fear River valley. C.J. Sauthier drew this map of Cross Creek in 1770.

North Carolina's **backcountry**—the region west of the Fall Line—began to fill up with new settlers.

Because of the many rivers and streams and the poor roads, east-west travel in North Carolina was difficult. By the mid-1700s, however, a new trail had been blazed into the backcountry. Settlers made their way south through the Shenandoah Valley of Virginia and along the eastern edge of the Blue Ridge Mountains until they reached the North Carolina Piedmont. The road eventually stretched 735 miles, all the way from Philadelphia, Pennsylvania, to Savannah, Georgia. This route came to be known as the **Great Wagon Road**.

Along this trail streamed thousands of Scotch-Irish and German settlers. Most came from Pennsylvania, but they also came from Maryland, Virginia, and New Jersey. Recognizing this expansion, the North Carolina Assembly created five new counties between 1746 and 1753: Johnston and Granville (1746), Anson (1750), Orange (1752), and Rowan (1753). Mecklenburg County was organized in 1763.

THE NEW IMMIGRANTS

In 1752, Bishop August Spangenberg described North Carolina in this way: "There is . . . a good deal of barren land, it would probably be correct to say that the tract is one half good, one quarter poor, and one quarter medium." Nevertheless, settlers poured into the unspoiled land during the 1700s. They came to live in freedom and to build farms on which their families could grow and prosper. From whatever colony or country they came, they arrived determined to make a better life. Only Afri-

The Great Wagon Road ran from Philadelphia, Pennsylvania, to Savannah, Georgia. Along that path streamed thousands of settlers to fill up the backcountry.

THE GREAT WAGON ROAD

Philadelphia
N.J.
MD.
DEL.
WEST VIRGINIA
KENTUCKY
VIRGINIA
Salem
Salisbury
Charlotte
NORTH CAROLINA
TENNESSEE
SOUTH CAROLINA
Augusta
ALABAMA
GEORGIA
Savannah

cans could not enjoy the fullness of this new land.

Four groups of people accounted for most of the population explosion: Scotch-Irish, Germans, Highland Scots, and Africans.

THE SCOTCH-IRISH AND THE GERMANS

The families of many of the Scotch-Irish had been in America for some time. The Scotch-Irish

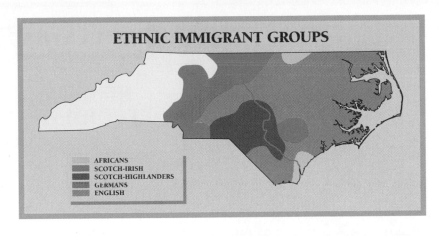

began moving into the Piedmont as early as 1735. This group was not really Irish but rather lowland Scots. In the 1600s, the English rulers sent the Scots to Northern Ireland hoping to drive out the Catholic Irish, whom the English regarded as savages. The Scotch-Irish were said to be stubborn, ferocious in war, independent, and casual about farming. For example, most farmers would cut down trees and then pull the stumps to clear the land. The Scotch-Irish farmers *girdled* trees; that is, they cut away the bark in a ring around the trunk. The trees would die and fall to the ground. The Scotch-Irish farmers then planted crops among the fallen trees and stumps.

The Germans had left Europe to escape poverty, war, and religious persecution. By 1775, perhaps one-third of the population in Pennsylvania was German, the so-called Pennsylvania Dutch (from the German word *Deutsch*, meaning "German"). Following the Great Wagon Road, German settlers arrived in Rowan County as early as 1747. They soon spread throughout the Piedmont.

Scotch-Irish farmers often girdled trees rather than cutting them down and removing the stumps.

In most parts of the backcountry, the Scotch-Irish and the Germans settled in groups close to family, kin, or congregation. One member of the family often went ahead of the rest to find a good place to settle. For example, shortly before he was born in 1767, Andrew Jackson's family left Northern Ireland to settle in the Waxhaw region along the North Carolina-South Carolina border. Close by were friends and family the Jacksons had known in Ireland.

The Scotch-Irish were Presbyterians. The Germans were usually Lutheran or German Reformed. Both groups tried to preserve their cultures in the New World. The Germans, for example, set up their own schools and churches. Their European background showed in the way they cared for their animals and built their barns. The Scotch-Irish believed in education, especially among the clergy. All Presbyterians were expected to read and interpret the Bible.

At first, the Scotch-Irish, the English, and the Germans did not mix. Nor did people marry outside their own ethnic group. Over time, however,

HENRY VIII, THE PROTESTANT REFORMATION, AND THE SEARCH FOR RELIGIOUS FREEDOM

During the 1500s, the Catholic Church was under attack from many quarters. Martin Luther began the Protestant Reformation with his demands for reform. His reforms became established beliefs in almost all Protestant religions.

In England, however, Luther's views met with stern disapproval in *Defense of the Seven Sacraments*, written by King Henry VIII. Henry had studied theology, and no one questioned his strong religious views. In gratitude, the pope named Henry "Defender of the Faith."

Unfortunately, Henry had no male heir. Henry asked the pope in 1527 to annul his marriage to Catherine of Aragon. When the pope refused, Henry pressured English church officials to grant him an annulment. They did, and Henry married Anne Boleyn. Their daughter became Queen Elizabeth I.

Henry VIII's break with the Catholic Church was completed in 1534 with the Act of Supremacy, which made the king the head of the Church of England. Henry's actions made it possible for even more radical forms of Protestantism to enter England and to find even freer expression in the New World. Thus the Protestant Reformation helped to unsettle the Old World and to feed colonists searching for religious liberty to the New World.

In the early 1500s, King Henry VIII of England broke with the Catholic Church and established the Church of England.

cultural differences broke down. But for most of the eighteenth century, settlement of the backcountry looked like a patchwork quilt of different peoples and cultures.

THE HIGHLAND SCOTS

Scottish Highlanders began to arrive in North Carolina as early as 1732. Unlike many of the other settlers, the Highlanders came directly to Carolina. Then they made their way up the Cape Fear River to settle around what is today Fayetteville. A colony of Highland Scots, led by Neill McNeill, arrived in 1739 from Argyll, Scotland.

Governor Gabriel Johnston, himself a Scot, encouraged his countrymen to **immigrate** (to move into and settle in a country of which one is not a native). In 1740, he persuaded the Assembly to excuse new settlers from all public or county taxes for ten years.

In Scotland, the English defeat of rebellious Highlanders in the bloody battle of Culloden in April 1746 convinced even more Scots to immigrate. After the defeat, Parliament punished the Scottish clans. Clan chiefs lost their power. Lands once used by the Scots for farming were given to English officers for pasture. Rent for land was higher than the Highlanders could pay. Hearing reports of cheap land in North Carolina, many Scots chose to leave their homeland.

Perhaps as many as 10,000 Highland Scots came to North Carolina before 1775. They settled in the upper Cape Fear River valley in, among others, Cumberland, Anson, Bladen, Robeson, Moore, and Richmond counties. So many Scots came that North Carolina was celebrated in dance and song. One dance, titled "America," showed, in the words of one observer, "how emigration catches till all are set afloat." One song was titled "going to seek a fortune in North Carolina."

According to Hugh McAden, a clergyman who preached among them, many of the Highlanders spoke only Gaelic, their native tongue. In fact, they continued to speak Gaelic well into the nineteenth century. Some slaves even spoke it. John Macrae, a Highlander who settled in North Carolina in 1774, composed perhaps the first Gaelic poem written in America. It was a lullaby for his daughter. This lullaby is still sung in Scotland and Nova Scotia.

Bishop August Spangenberg carefully chose a large tract of land in the northwest Piedmont for a Moravian settlement. The Moravians called it Wachovia.

> *Sleep sweetly, sleep peacefully, puppy beloved,*
> *You're cradled at last in a country that's new,*
> *Young men will be coming with honor and riches,*
> *And if you are good there will be one for you.*

When the American Revolution broke out, many Highland Scots remained loyal to England, including John Macrae.

THE MORAVIANS

Perhaps the most unusual settlement in North Carolina was founded by the Moravians. The Moravians, a German Protestant group also known as the United Brethren, had been persecuted for centuries for their religious beliefs. The Moravians were **pacifists**; that is, they did not believe in war and would not bear arms against others. Trying to escape the wars of central Europe and to find religious freedom, the Moravians settled in Georgia and Pennsylvania. The Georgia colony was short-lived, but the one in Pennsylvania did well.

In 1752, Moravian Bishop August Gottlieb Spangenberg explored North Carolina from Edenton to the Blue Ridge Mountains. He was looking for a new home for the Pennsylvania Brethren and for others coming from Europe. He decided on a tract (piece) of land in what is now Forsyth

Top: Each member of the Moravian community had a specific role to perform. Here, men are shown beating flax. Above: A child rolls a hoop on the commons in Old Salem.

County. The Moravians bought the 98,985-acre tract from Lord Granville for £500. They named it *Wachovia*, meaning "meadow valley." The first group of Moravian settlers arrived from Pennyslvania in November 1753. Moravian towns quickly sprang up: Bethabara in 1753, Bethania in 1759, and Salem in 1766.

Wachovia was a planned community with two purposes: (1) to earn profits through trade and (2) to set the Brethren apart from "worldly influences." The Brethren placed spiritual values and the needs of the community above the needs of individuals. Three groups made decisions for the community: the Elders' Conference, the Board of Overseers, and the Congregation Council. The church assigned land. Each man and woman had a specific role to perform.

Most Brethren owned their homes, businesses, and personal possessions. The profits from some businesses, however, went into a community account. Proceeds from the tavern, tannery, pottery, and retail businesses helped pay for such community services as waterworks on the central square of Salem, street maintenance, and fire protection. The Moravian society did not forbid ownership of property and business, but it did try to regulate it for the benefit of all.

The Moravians were thought of as being industrious, hard-working, and thrifty. They were among the best farmers in the colony, and their craftsmen produced fine tools and other goods. Unlike other groups that settled in North Carolina, the Moravians used little slave labor.

Moravians practiced domestic skills such as baking (left) as well as practical skills as represented by the tinker's shop (below).

THE AFRICANS

Africans were, of course, unwilling immigrants. The first slaves were brought from West Africa, which the Europeans called Guinea. Most Africans sold into slavery in America were war captives, criminals, or those being punished because they could not pay their debts. Some Africans were kidnapped and made slaves. West African kings protected the European slave traders, who set up posts to export slaves to the New World. Those Africans caught in the slave traders' net went through the so-called Middle Passage between Africa and America. Crammed body to body in ships' cargo holds, many Africans died.

The northern region of Guinea was influenced by Islamic culture. A few slaves continued to practice the Muslim religion in America. Slave owners valued Muslim slaves because they were more educated. On plantations, they often held positions of trust, such as managers or drivers. Perhaps the best-known Muslim slave in North Carolina was Omar ibn Said, owned by the brother of Governor John Owen. Ibn Said learned English and translated the Bible into his native language.

Most Africans in lower Guinea practiced religions that centered around agriculture and the need for good harvests. Guinea was a land of small farms. Rice was an important crop in Guinea as it was in South Carolina and the lower Cape Fear area. The Africans were also herdsmen and fishermen. All of these skills made them valuable workers when Europeans began to colonize Carolina.

In North Carolina, slavery did not play an important part in the state's economic and social life until after the 1720s. The Fundamental Constitutions of 1669 made slavery legal in Carolina, and slaves were being imported into Albemarle County as early as the 1680s. But until 1715, there were probably fewer than 1,000 slaves in North Carolina. The biggest increase in the slave population came between 1750 and 1800. In fact, just between 1765 and 1790, the number of slaves soared from about 40,000 to more than 100,000.

Most slaves entered North Carolina overland from Virginia or South Carolina, but some arrived by sea.

Do You Remember?

1. Why was it so difficult to travel from east to west in the colony?
2. Describe the path of the Great Wagon Road.
3. What four groups accounted for most of the rapid growth in population during the mid-1700s?
4. How did the German settlers try to preserve their culture?
5. What were the reasons the Highland Scots left their homes in Scotland to come to North Carolina?
6. What were two purposes of the planned communities of the Moravians?
7. Why could it be said that the Africans were "unwilling immigrants"?

THE EARLY SOCIAL ORDER

There were sharp social distinctions in colonial North Carolina. A **gentry** class made up of planters, public officials, and professionals such as lawyers, doctors, and clergy was the highest class. These people often had family ties with the upper classes of Great Britain.

The gentry's wealth was based on land and slaves. Some members of the gentry owned thousands of acres and more than one hundred slaves. In 1765, Governor William Tryon noted that "A Plantation with Seventy Slaves on it, is esteemed a good property." A planter who gave his daughter away in marriage "never talks of the fortune in Money but 20, 30 or 40 Slaves in her Portion."

Under English law and custom, women gave up many rights to their husbands when they married. In most cases, a married woman was considered legally one person with her husband. She could not sue or be sued, make contracts, buy or sell property, or draft a will. All property she owned before her marriage became her husband's. Divorces were almost impossible to get. Even educated women had few choices in colonial society. A few widows or never-married women ran their own businesses. In North Carolina, there were a number of women lawyers.

Artisans and small farmers made up the largest class of North Carolinians. **Artisans** were craftspeople who made needed products for farmers, townspeople, and sailors. The colony depended on the skills of blacksmiths, coopers (barrel makers), carpenters, and others. These skilled workers made, built, or repaired tools, buildings, and wharves.

Small farmers, also known as **yeomen**, raised just enough crops to feed their families and perhaps their livestock. Livestock were often allowed to roam free in the woods. In that way, cattle and hogs could feed themselves. Even a farmer who owned a good deal of land rarely had more than fifteen or twenty acres of "improved" land; that is, land that had been cleared to plant crops. These small farmers were very independent. If they had extra crops, the yeomen traded them for finished goods or supplies, such as salt and iron, which they could not easily make themselves. If they did raise a cash crop, such as tobacco, they always made sure that they grew enough food for their families.

Indentured servants followed farmers and artisans on the social scale. These people exchanged their labor for passage to America. At the end of their term, they received "freedom dues." The dues consisted of clothes, tools, training in a trade, and (before 1715) fifty acres of land.

Apprentices were in the same class as indentured servants. Apprentices went to live with a "master" to learn a trade or skill. Children needed the permission of their parents to become an apprentice. Laws were passed to provide such training for orphans. Girls were apprenticed until age

Omar ibn Said (1770-1864), born in Senegal, attended Muslim schools as a youth. Sold into slavery, he escaped a cruel South Carolina slave owner in 1810. The Owen family purchased him, and he lived the rest of his life in North Carolina.

eighteen and boys until age twenty-one. Boys learned such trades as blacksmith, carpenter, cooper, weaver, mariner, and tailor. Girls were taught to weave, spin, sew, and cook.

At the bottom of the social scale were Africans. In the 1700s, the Assembly passed laws that sharply limited blacks' freedom. Slaves could not leave their **plantations** (large farms or estates) without a pass from their masters. They could not gather in meetings, even to worship. Slaves could not vote or marry whites. Masters could not free their slaves except for "meritorious services" judged so by a county court. Above all, whites feared that the slaves might revolt. To prevent this, a 1741 law would not allow slaves to hunt or go "armed with Gun, Sword, Club or other Weapon." In 1753, patrols were started to watch the slaves' movements and activities.

A tiny number of blacks in North Carolina were free, perhaps 2,000 in 1767. Most free blacks had won their freedom legally. Children took on the status of their mothers. So a **mulatto** child (one with a black and a white parent) born to a white mother was free. Free blacks did enjoy a few rights in North Carolina. They could vote and serve in the militia. Along the coast, free black pilots competed with white pilots to guide ships through the sounds.

There were still Native Americans in the eastern part of the colony. These Indians, however, had adopted many of the traits and customs of white culture. Tribally organized Indians, such as the Cherokee, had removed themselves to the western frontier area.

Apprentices lived with a "master" to learn a trade. Shown here is an apprentice carpenter in Old Salem.

SMALLPOX INOCULATIONS

Native Americans suffered horribly from diseases such as smallpox against which they had no immunity. But smallpox could also be devastating to European Americans. In the early 1700s, a New England minister undertook the first experiment in the colonies to inoculate individuals against the disease. To *inoculate* someone is to infect the person deliberately with a mild case of the disease. The body then develops antibodies that enable it to fight off the disease.

The Reverend Cotton Mather came from a leading New England family of ministers. Mather was also a member of England's Royal Society, a group devoted to expanding scientific knowledge. He read in one of the Society's publications about how inoculation could prevent smallpox. When Boston suffered a major smallpox epidemic in 1720 and 1721, Mather and a doctor who supported the theory of inoculation urged people to be inoculated. Many people, including Boston's leading physician, opposed the idea.

However, when the epidemic ended, only 3 percent of those inoculated had died while 15 percent of those who had refused inoculation perished. Mather was proved correct. It would be midcentury before inoculation became widely accepted, but colonial Americans now had a defense against the most dreaded disease.

Reverend Cotton Mather used inoculations to protect Bostonians against smallpox.

Do You Remember?
1. What were four major classes of society in colonial North Carolina?
2. What were some ways in which the freedom of slaves was limited?
3. What rights did free blacks have in the colony?

THE COLONIAL ECONOMY

Most North Carolinians, of whatever class, engaged in agriculture. The most important food crops were corn, peas, wheat, and beans. The colony's first **cash crop** (a crop grown to sell) was tobacco. Tobacco was grown mainly in a line of counties stretching west from the Albemarle Sound. Rice and indigo, in smaller quantities, were grown along the lower Cape Fear River. Growing tobacco and rice required a great deal of labor. Slavery, therefore, was common in areas where these crops were raised.

Livestock was an important part of North Carolina's agricultural economy. Horses, mules, and oxen pulled plows and wagons. Farmers raised cattle, hogs, sheep, chickens, and other animals for market. Hogs and cattle were taken on long drives to markets as far away as Virginia, Maryland, and New Jersey.

Forest products were a large part of the North Carolina economy. Before the American Revolution, about 60 percent of all naval stores exported from the colonies came from North Carolina. **Naval stores** included tar, pitch, rosin, and turpentine. Sailors relied on these products to preserve the wood and ropes of their ships. Most of the naval stores were made in the lower Cape Fear valley, where the longleaf pine forests were. Skilled slaves took part in the production of the naval stores. An observer in 1765 said that "one Negro" could tend 3,000 trees. Those trees could produce about 100 barrels of turpentine. North Carolina's nickname—the Tar Heel State—refers to this industry.

North Carolina's forests produced other products. Casks and barrels were in demand for shipping both liquid and dry goods. Colonists in the West Indies had stripped those islands of almost all trees. Countless numbers of planks from North Carolina sawmills were shipped there. Northern colonies and even Great Britain depended on North Carolina lumber for their building needs. Cypress trees also made excellent shingles. Before the American Revolution, millions of shingles were exported from North Carolina each year.

Women also engaged in a "hidden" economy in which they exchanged goods or services among themselves or with merchants. For example, in the eighteenth century, a "spinster" was not an unmarried woman but rather an artisan, one who spun cloth for her family and others. She might be paid in cash, but more often she received other necessary items or services in exchange for her spun cloth. Most women artisans (spinsters, weavers, seamstresses) worked within their homes and used their earnings to support their households. Because they did not operate visible businesses, their role in the economy often has been overlooked.

Early settlers lived in log cabins made of local wood, clay, and stone. The dirt-floor dwellings rarely had more than one or two rooms.

Do You Remember?

1. What were some products, crops, and livestock produced for sale in the colony?
2. Why was slavery common in some areas and not in others?
3. Why were the forests so important to the colony's economy?

DAILY LIFE

The roles men and women performed in colonial America were sharply divided. In an agricultural society, men worked mostly outdoors. They planted and tended crops, chopped wood for the fireplace, cared for livestock, and butchered meat. Women generally worked indoors. They

prepared the food, cleaned the house, laundered dirty clothes, wove cloth, spun thread, and sewed.

Both men and women raised the children. Women cared for infants and toddlers, but men played active roles with the older children. Children were always needed to help in the hard work of farming. Fathers taught their sons farming, how to care for livestock, fishing, and crafts such as blacksmithing.

LIVING CONDITIONS

During the colonial period, most houses in North Carolina were poorly made. Local materials—wood, clay, and stone—were used to build simple one- and two-room homes. In two southeastern counties, "the first

Above: *Around the time of the Revolution, brick structures, such as this one at Old Salem, began to appear.* ***Above left:*** *The Francis McNairy House in Greensboro began as a log house in 1762; later a second story was added. It served as a hospital during the Battle of Guilford Court House.*

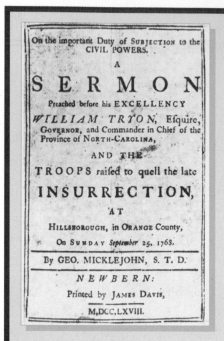

James Davis published this sermon given before Governor Tryon at Hillsborough during the Regulator insurrection. He was the colony's first printer.

JAMES DAVIS AND THE FIRST PRINTING PRESS

Today, we take for granted the many types of reading material available to us. An endless variety of information is found in books, magazines, and newspapers. In colonial North Carolina and well into the 1800s, printed material was scarce, and a book was a cherished possession.

For much of North Carolina's early history, all public and private publications had to be printed outside the colony. There were no printing presses or bookmakers in the colony. Not until 1749 did North Carolina have its first printer. In that year, James Davis of Williamsburg came to North Carolina and set up a print shop in New Bern. He was immediately hired by the government to print its paper money. Later, the colony appointed him "Public Printer," a position he held for thirty-three years.

During his time as public printer, Davis printed nearly all of the publications or "imprints" issued by first the colonial government and then the state government. These publications included the official laws and proceedings of the General Assembly, the governors' proclamations and messages, military records, and court documents. Davis also printed small books, sermons, and other private publications. In 1751, he published the colony's first newspaper, the *North Carolina Gazette*.

inhabitants of Duplin and Sampson Counties built and lived in log Cabbins, and as they became more Wealthy, some of them Built framed Clapboard Houses with Clay Chimneys." The log houses had dirt floors, board roofs, mud and stick chimneys, and wooden shutters. When the Moravians arrived in the Piedmont, they described the dwellings they saw as "poorly built wooden houses."

By the time of the American Revolution, sturdier brick buildings began to appear in the eastern counties. Visitors to the colony were impressed by the governor's residence and the seat of government in New Bern. Built between 1767 and 1770, Tryon Palace was described as "elegant" and the "finest building of all." One traveler called New Bern "a pretty little town" that contained "several exceeding good and even elegant houses."

COMMUNICATION AND TRANSPORTATION

Farms in colonial North Carolina were often far apart. As a result, farm families took every opportunity to socialize. Men came from miles around to attend court, gather with the militia, or grind grain at a mill. Women socialized around such ordinary chores as husking corn, making quilts, or spinning thread. Women also gathered to help at childbirth.

Religious services often became great social events. The Reverend Charles Woodmason was an Anglican missionary who traveled through the Carolina backcountry during the 1760s. He complained that, at the end of one of his sermons, the audience "went to Reveling Drinking Singing [and] Dancing . . . and most of Company were drunk before I quitted the Spot."

In 1728, Colonel William Byrd of Virginia helped lay out the boundary between Virginia and North Carolina. In his *History of the Dividing Line,* Byrd made many unflattering remarks about North Carolinians. He called the colony a "Lubberland," a paradise of idlers. Byrd said the climate was so mild that with little effort men could raise a large crop of corn to support a family. Meat was also plentiful since the livestock ranged through the woods. He thought only North Carolina women worked hard.

Obviously, Byrd was mistaken. Carving farms out of a wilderness was hard, back-breaking work. As late as the 1790s, travelers still regarded North Carolina as a "new Settlement," with farms "slowly cleared" of trees and land "still more slowly brought into cultivation." The sheer size of the land awed visitors. A German traveler in the 1780s described North Carolina "as a continuous, measureless forest, an ocean of trees, in which only here and there are cultivated spots."

Because of the great forests and many rivers, North Carolina's roads were no better than trading paths. Roads were poorly marked and poorly maintained. Travelers often became lost. After a heavy rain, the roads clogged with mud and the rivers became impossible to cross. One traveler wrote to himself: "Take no more short Cuts in North Carolina. Had to cross two Mill Dams & met with great Difficulty. Road through a very gloomy Cypress Swamp: lost my way."

The poor roads hurt trade. Nevertheless, several important trading routes developed. One ran from the Moravian settlements around Salem to the Cape Fear River at present-day Fayetteville. Another ran from Virginia to South Carolina and passed through Edenton, Bath, Wilmington, and Brunswick. The so-called Great Trading Path crossed North Carolina east to west, from the Albemarle Sound to the mountains. Along this road, such towns as Hillsborough, Salisbury, and Charlotte grew up. However, the road was not heavily used. Most of the trade in the Piedmont ran north to Virginia and Pennsylvania or south to Charles Town, South Carolina.

Do You Remember?

1. How was the daily work performed in the farm family in colonial North Carolina?
2. What were some of the social activities of colonial farm families?
3. What were the conditions of the roads in colonial North Carolina?

Colonel William Byrd, a member of the Virginia gentry, belittled North Carolina. He failed to appreciate the frontier conditions in which most North Carolinians lived.

CHAPTER REVIEW

1732 Highland Scots arrived in the colony	1735 Scotch-Irish began arriving in the colony	1747 Germans arrived in Rowan County		1767 Tryon Palace started
			1753 Moravians arrived	

1710	1720	1730	1740	1750	1760	1770

| | | | 1747 Ohio Company organized | | 1757 First street lights in a colonial city installed in Philadelphia | |
| 1718 New Orleans founded by French | | 1732 Colony of Georgia founded | 1734 Daniel Boone born | | 1754 Albany Congress proposed plan for uniting colonies | |

Reviewing People, Places, and Terms

On a separate sheet of paper, write the term from the list that could replace the underlined words in each of the following statements.

artisans
backcountry
cash crop
gentry
Great Wagon Road
immigrated
naval stores
yeomen

1. The road that stretched from Philadelphia to Savannah enabled thousands of settlers to pour into North Carolina's region west of the Fall Line.
2. Several groups moved into and settled in to North Carolina in the mid-1700s including the Scotch-Irish, Germans, Highland Scots, and Moravians.
3. The highest "class" of settlers in colonial North Carolina was the group made up of planters, public officials, and professionals.
4. Craftspeople and small farmers made up the largest class in colonial North Carolina.
5. Tobacco was North Carolina's first crop grown to sell and earn a profit.

6. Sailors relied upon the tar, pitch, rosin, and turpentine produced in North Carolina to preserve the wood and ropes on ships.

Understanding the Facts

1. How did the type of people who settled in North Carolina after it became a royal colony differ from those who had settled here earlier?
2. In what way was the arrival of the Highland Scots different from the arrival of the Scotch-Irish or the Germans?
3. From what part of Africa did most African slaves come?
4. Who were the artisans in the colony? Why were they important?
5. Describe the legal status of married women in colonial society.
6. People from North Carolina are often called "Tar Heels." How did the state's nickname develop?

Developing Critical Thinking

1. If you were a European settler arriving in North Carolina in the mid-1700s, where would you prefer to settle? What were some of the advantages of settling farther west? Some of the disadvantages?

2. The Moravians believed in working for "the common good." What do you think this means?

Applying Your Skills

1. Interview older members of your own family about their cultural roots. Are your ancestors Native American? African? European? Hispanic? Oriental? Discuss among your family what foods, music, and other fashions your ancestors may have contributed to the culture of our country. Compare your information with that of your classmates.

2. Prepare a report on the lives of the various social classes mentioned in the chapter. Describe, for example, what a person of the gentry class might do, how he or she might dress, what her or his leisure activities might be, and so on.

Making Connections

1. Ask your grandparents or an older person what they remember about the "polio season" that was so frightening to people in the 1940s and 1950s.

2. What comparisons can you see between the fear of smallpox in early New England and the fear of AIDS today? Do you believe that a vaccine for AIDS will be discovered?

3. Think about the freedom of religion enjoyed in this country today. Think also about the large number of religious denominations. What do you think might be the condition of religion in this country today had Henry VIII not severed England's ties with the Catholic Church?

Tar Heel Trivia

- Nearly all of the settlers who came to English North America were Protestants.

BUILDING SKILLS: USING GRAPHS

There are many ways to visually present statistics, which are facts using numbers. Charts, graphs, and tables all may be used to make it easier to see what is happening over a certain period of time.

Choosing the best type of graph to illustrate the relationships between two sets of numbers is important. *Bar graphs* are a good choice when comparing two sets of numbers over time. *Circle graphs* help illustrate data when comparing a part of a group to the whole group. *Line graphs* show change in data over a period of time.

Making a graph involves collecting the data, choosing the correct scale, and then drawing the graph. Once you have collected the data, it is helpful to organize the information in the form of a chart before you decide on the type of graph and the scale for the graph.

Choosing the correct scale is important when designing a bar or line graph. The scale chosen should allow the reader to make comparisons easily. Once you have chosen a scale, sketch your graph to make certain your scale is a good one. You are now ready to draw

the final version of your graph. The information in the next paragraph can be used to try these ideas.

In 1730, North Carolina had a population of 35,000, of which 6,000 were slaves. By 1775, the population of North Carolina had reached 345,000, of which 80,000 were slaves. A chart of the data might be as follows.

Year	Total Population	Slave Population
1730	35,000	6,000
1775	345,000	80,000

Try This!

1. Design a bar graph that illustrates the population figures given above.

2. Now make a circle graph for each year using the same information. You will want to express the population figures as percentages for these graphs.

3. Draw a line graph using the same information.

4. Which of the graphs best illustrates the data? Why?

CHAPTER SEVEN

NORTH CAROLINA AS A ROYAL COLONY

If I am to say how I find things in North Carolina I must admit that there is much confusion. There is discord between the Counties, which has greatly weakened the authority of the Legislature, and interferes with the administration of justice. . . . So in some respects anarchy reigns in these older Counties. . . . Land matters in North Carolina are also in unbelievable confusion. . . . A man settles on a piece of land and does a good deal of work on it (from the Carolina standpoint), then another comes and drives him out, —and who is to definitely settle the matter?

—August Gottlieb Spangenberg

CHAPTER PREVIEW

Terms: specie, barter, squatters, headright, French and Indian War, frontier, treaty

People: George Burrington, Gabriel Johnston, Lord Granville, Arthur Dobbs, Major Hugh Waddell, Colonel Archibald Montgomerie, Colonel James Grant, Attakullakulla

Places: Granville District, Fort Duquesne, Fort Dobbs

WHEN NORTH CAROLINA became a royal colony in 1729, its government changed very little. The governor, council, Assembly, and courts had the same powers and duties. The colony's leaders, however, now reported to the crown. Two kings sat on the British throne between 1729 and 1776. George II ruled until his death in 1760. His grandson George III ruled until 1820.

The crown began to tighten its control over North Carolina and the other royal colonies. The crown, for example, sent the governors detailed instructions on how to handle the colony's affairs. At the same time, North Carolinians were determined to protect their rights. North Carolina also became more and more involved in England's plan to create an "empire." That involvement came to a head in the Seven Years' War, known in America as the French and Indian War.

Opposite page: George II was king of England when North Carolina became a royal colony in 1729. He ruled until 1760.

THE FIRST ROYAL GOVERNORS

The first men to serve as royal governors of North Carolina were all different. But they all tried to carry out the wishes of the crown.

George Burrington was the most controversial. He had been governor under the Lords Proprietors in 1724-1725. Burrington was a violent and

JOHN PETER ZENGER AND FREEDOM OF THE PRESS

Born in Germany in 1697, John Peter Zenger settled in New York in 1710. Until 1719, he was indentured to the colony's leading printer, William Bradford.

In 1732, William Crosby became the royal governor of New York. He immediately sparked controversy by dismissing chief justice Lewis Morris. William Bradford defended the governor in the *New York Gazette*.

Opponents of the governor asked Zenger to edit and publish the *New York Weekly Journal*. Zenger's *Weekly Journal* vigorously attacked the governor's actions and opinions. The governor's supporters seized issues of Zenger's newspaper and burned them, and the governor ordered Zenger's arrest.

After ten months in jail, Zenger came to trial in August 1735. He was charged with seditious libel, publishing false stories for the purpose of overthrowing the government. Andrew Hamilton, Zenger's attorney, argued that Zenger was not guilty because the stories were true and that free speech was a basic right. The judge instructed the jury that mere publication was enough to convict Zenger of libel. The jury disagreed; they found Zenger not guilty.

The Zenger case helped establish freedom of the press. Thereafter, Zenger's name was linked with a person's right to discuss and criticize the government publicly.

quarrelsome man, and during his brief term he made many enemies. In spite of this, the crown named Burrington to the governorship once more in 1730. Again he angered many of the leaders of North Carolina. He had heated arguments with the council and Assembly over land policies and taxes. He dissolved the Assembly three times when it would not follow the orders of the king. His rule ended in 1734 when Gabriel Johnston was named governor.

Gabriel Johnston was a well-educated Scot who had taught Hebrew at St. Andrews University in Scotland. An able and clever politician, Johnston served as governor for eighteen years, longer than anyone else. Unlike Burrington, Johnston was very good at dealing with opponents. This made him a much more effective governor than Burrington had been. When he did reach an agreement with an Assembly that was more and more difficult to work with, the crown sometimes overturned it.

DISAGREEMENTS OVER MONEY

The collection of taxes was always a sore point between the colony and the crown. The crown insisted on being paid in **specie**, that is, gold or silver. Specie was rare in North Carolina, as in other colonies, because the colony brought more goods into the colony than it was able to make and sell outside the colony. People did not want to give up what little specie they had. Many people used provincial money (money issued by the colonial government). And, as early as 1715, the Assembly "rated" commodities, as many as twenty-two, for use as money. Tobacco, corn, wheat, animal skins, whale oil, pork, beef, and other items could be **bartered** (traded) for other goods or services.

In 1739, there were no accurate records of who owned land and who owed taxes on them. Governor Johnston reached a compromise with the Assembly. The Assembly agreed to prepare a tax list and to limit where the taxes were collected. In return, the governor would recognize the titles to about 500,000 acres of land and would accept provincial or commodity money in payment of taxes. The crown, however, would not approve this compromise because it included commodity money. The crown's action showed that *it,* not the Assembly or the governor, was the final authority.

The royal governors were often at odds with the Assembly over money. The Assembly insisted that it had the "sole right" to decide how taxes were raised and spent. The royal governors wanted to control how the money was spent because they had to answer to the crown. Using its "power of the purse," the Assembly tried to force the governor and the council to do things its way. For example, the Assembly refused to pay Governor Johnston a salary. When he died in 1752, he had not received a salary in fourteen years. This conflict over the "power of the purse" continued until the American Revolution.

SECTIONAL TENSIONS

Perhaps the most serious problem facing Governor Johnston was a north-south conflict within the colony. The northern counties around Albemarle Sound held most of the political power in the colony. The

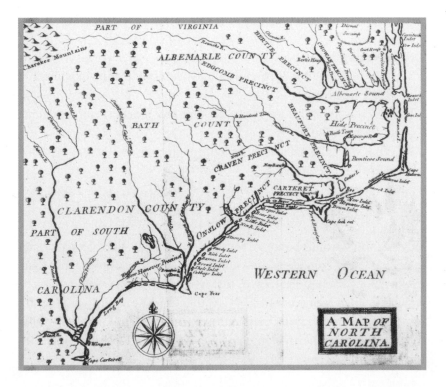

Above: Because of a shortage of specie, the Assembly permitted the use of commodities such as tobacco as money. **Left:** *John Brickell included this map of the colony in his* Natural History of North Carolina *(1737). Brickell's book, however, was largely copied from John Lawson's* New Voyage to Carolina *(1709).*

Lord Granville was the one Lords Proprietor who refused to sell his share of the colony to the crown. Instead he opened a land office in Edenton and sold nearly two million acres.

royal governor and the members of the council lived there. Chowan, Pasquotank, Perquimans, Currituck, Bertie, and Tyrrell counties had five delegates each in the Assembly. Each Cape Fear county elected only two delegates. As a result, the Albemarle counties easily won in the Assembly when there were disagreements.

Governor Johnston wanted to do something about this. In November 1746, Johnston called the Assembly into session in Wilmington. Because of a bad storm, only fifteen of the Assembly's fifty-four delegates could attend, none from Albemarle. That Assembly voted to move the seat of government to New Bern and to limit each Albemarle county to two delegates.

The Albemarle region was outraged. It refused to recognize the Assembly and called the new laws "trickery" and "fraud." In the elections held in February 1747, each of the northern counties returned its usual five delegates. The Assembly would not seat them. The two sides then asked the crown to settle the dispute. Governor Johnston refused to hold new elections until a decision was made. Meanwhile, Albemarle was ready to revolt. People refused to pay taxes, crimes went unpunished, and no delegates from Albemarle took part in the Assembly.

Seven years later, in 1754, the crown finally ruled in Albemarle's favor. The laws passed by the Wilmington Assembly were overturned. The crown ordered that new elections be held and that each of the Albemarle counties be allowed to elect five delegates. This ended the representation conflict. Soon, however, sectional tensions would shift from north-south to east-west as North Carolina's backcountry was settled.

Do You Remember?
1. How did Governor Burrington and Governor Johnston differ in their ability to govern?
2. Why was the collection of taxes such a problem between the colony and the crown?
3. What was unusual about the Wilmington Assembly that was held in November 1746?

LAND POLICIES

When North Carolina became a royal colony in 1729, Lord Carteret (later known as Lord Granville) would not sell his one-eighth proprietor's share in the colony back to the crown. Just what part of the colony was to be his was not determined until 1744. At that time, he determined that his share began at the Virginia border and extended south for seventy miles (to the latitude of Bath). Known as the *Granville District*, this included most of northern North Carolina.

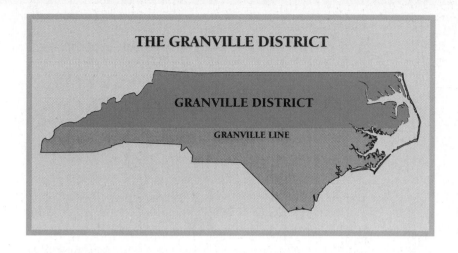

THE GRANVILLE DISTRICT

GRANVILLE DISTRICT

GRANVILLE LINE

This map of the Granville District shows how Lord Granville owned roughly the northern half of the colony.

THE GRANVILLE DISTRICT

The Granville District was owned by Lord Granville, not the crown. Within the district, Lord Granville could grant land previously ungranted and collect an annual land tax called a *quitrent*. In 1748, Lord Granville opened a land office in Edenton. Soon new settlers flocked into the district, attracted by the low land prices and quitrent. Between 1748 and 1763, the Granville land office sold almost 2 million acres, mostly in parcels of 300 to 500 acres.

Lord Granville's land agents, however, were not very responsible. Francis Corbin, who acted as Granville's agent for twelve years, seems to have been especially inefficient and corrupt. Between 1751 and 1756, Corbin sent £4,000 to Lord Granville, but nothing after that. Corbin admitted that he did not even know which lands in the Granville District had been granted and which had not. **Squatters**, people who settled on the land without a clear title to it, made a bad situation worse. Nobody knew who owned what land. Corbin's misconduct led to problems with the governor, the Assembly, and landowners. In 1759, a band of angry planters kidnapped Corbin in Edenton and took him to Enfield in Halifax County. There they made him promise to stand trial for collecting illegal fees and charging too much for rents and taxes.

During the last few years the office was open, Thomas Child was Granville's agent. Child was better organized and more honest than earlier agents. When Lord Granville died in 1763, however, the land office closed and never reopened.

ROYAL LAND GRANTS

Settlers could also get royal land grants, that is, grants in the king's portion of North Carolina. Governor Johnston opened a land office shortly after his appointment. When purchasing a land grant, a settler had to pay a fee and an annual quitrent to the crown. Within three

Royal Governor Arthur Dobbs encouraged settlement of the back-country and personally invested in western lands. He hoped to prevent French expansion into the Ohio and Mississippi river valleys.

ARTHUR DOBBS: GOVERNOR, SCIENTIST, ECONOMIST

North Carolina's royal governor Arthur Dobbs was not only an administrator. He was also a geographer with a passion for locating the Northwest Passage, an able economist, and a scientist—a man of many dimensions.

Dobbs left his Irish home and joined the army in 1711. After his father's death, he returned to Ireland and began his political career, eventually being elected to the Irish Parliament. It was during this time that he began writing. His first published work was a book on Irish economic history. He also wrote an unpublished work on how to prevent the counterfeiting of British and Irish coins.

Dobbs was also interested in Great Britain's colonies in the New World. He favored increased spending to defend the colonies, wanted the French out of Canada, and actively tried to find the Northwest Passage to the Pacific Ocean. In 1745 Dobbs bought several hundred thousand acres of land in the North Carolina colony, the majority of which was in present-day Mecklenburg and Cabarrus counties. As a condition of the purchase, Dobbs had to see to it that the land was settled. He immediately began to recruit settlers from Ireland and sent several hundred families to the area within a short time. Three years later,

years of receiving a royal land grant, a settler had to clear at least 3 acres out of every 100 acres for cultivation.

Settlers could acquire land by purchase or by headright. A grant by purchase meant a settler paid outright for the land. Under the **headright** method, a settler received land based on the number of persons in her or his family, including slaves. Normally, the head of a household received 100 acres plus 50 acres for each additional person. Grants by headright seem to have ended with the death of Governor Johnston in 1752.

By 1768, 11,000 proprietary and royal land grants had been issued in North Carolina, totaling 3 million acres.

A NEW ROYAL GOVERNOR

In 1754, Arthur Dobbs arrived in North Carolina to become the governor. Like Johnston, he was well educated. A native of County Antrim,

Dobbs invested in the Ohio Company of Virginia, which sought to settle the Ohio Valley.

Because of his interest in the settlement of the North American colonies in general and North Carolina in particular, Arthur Dobbs was appointed governor of North Carolina in April 1753. Dobbs concerned himself with many issues upon taking office: the problems caused by the war with France, the boundary disputes with South Carolina, the lack of currency and a postal system, and the establishment of a permanent capital within the colony. Dobbs favored a place called Tower Hill on the Neuse River at Kingston (now Kinston). He also was concerned about the increasing tensions in the Piedmont settlements between colonial officials and settlers.

While governor, Dobbs made his home at his estate near Brunswick named "Russellborough." It was here that Dobbs busied himself with writing. One of his writings was "An Account of North Carolina." Included in his correspondence with an English botanist is a description of the Venus flytrap. This correspondence is considered by historians to be the first recorded description of this rare plant found only in southeastern North Carolina.

Dobbs also brought considerable attention to himself in 1762 when, at the age of seventy-three, he married fifteen-year-old Justina Davis. Several months later, Dobbs suffered a paralyzing stroke but recovered enough to continue his term as governor until his death in 1765.

Fort Dobbs, named in honor of Governor Arthur Dobbs, was built in 1756 to protect settlers on the western frontier. Archaeologists have excavated the site, which is near Statesville.

Northern Ireland, Dobbs had written many articles about the economic policies he thought would benefit Ireland, Britain, and the North American colonies. Even before becoming royal governor, Dobbs had bought land in North Carolina, mainly in present-day Mecklenburg and Cabarrus counties. He encouraged people to settle in the backcountry, especially the Scotch-Irish, French Protestants, and Moravians. Perhaps more than any other royal governor, Dobbs understood precisely the threat France posed to Britain's plans in North America.

Do You Remember?
1. How did the Granville District come into being?
2. What problems arose in the Granville District?
3. Describe the two ways in which settlers could get royal land grants.
4. About how much land was sold by the Granville land office between 1748 and 1763?
5. Why was Arthur Dobbs especially able to govern the colony?

The **French and Indian War**, as the conflict was known in North America, began in 1754. A twenty-two-year-old Virginia military officer named George Washington led a small band of Virginia militia into the Ohio country to drive out the French. The Virginians were defeated at Great Meadows, Pennsylvania. Thus began a war for which North Carolina was totally unprepared.

Governor Dobbs reported to the king that many of the men in the North Carolina militia were unarmed or had inferior (poor quality) weapons. Nowhere in the colony had gunpowder been stockpiled. Still, North Carolina was expected to contribute its share to the war effort. The colony sent three hundred troops under Major Hugh Waddell to serve with British General John Forbes. Waddell and Sergeant John Rogers played a key role in the British capture of Fort Duquesne. Disguising themselves as Indians, Waddell and Rogers seized a Native American who had just been in the fort. With the information the Indian gave them, the British were able to take the fort in November 1758 without firing a shot.

After the fall of Fort Duquesne, North Carolina turned most of its attention to its western **frontier** (a region just beyond or at the edge of a settled area). In fact, in 1757 Lord Loudoun, the commander of British forces in North America, told the governors that they should prepare to defend their own borders. The French were stirring up the Native Americans and encouraging them to attack the settlements.

Hugh Waddell played crucial roles in the capture of Fort Duquesne and the defense of Fort Dobbs.

CHEROKEE ATTACKS

Before the war, the Cherokee had been friendly to the British. But when Virginia settlers killed a number of Cherokee, tensions on the frontier exploded. In the spring of 1759, reports of Cherokee and Creek attacks sent alarms across the southern frontier. At the Moravian town of Bethabara, the Brethren recorded several such attacks along the Yadkin and Catawba rivers. The Native Americans destroyed crops, slaughtered livestock, burned houses and barns, and killed white settlers.

To protect the settlers on the western frontier, the Assembly told Hugh Waddell to build a fort near present-day Statesville. In February 1760, Cherokee surrounded Fort Dobbs, which had been named after the royal governor. Waddell wrote Governor Dobbs this dramatic report:

. . . for several days I observed That a small party of Indians were constantly about the fort. . . . I took out . . . [a] party made up of ten: We had not marched 300 yds from the fort when we were attacked by at least 60

THE TENSIONS BETWEEN FRANCE AND GREAT BRITAIN

Throughout the 1700s, the European nations struggled for power and for control of North America. While Great Britain and Spain did clash, most of Great Britain's conflicts were with France. The French king wanted to increase France's power and territory. Great Britain, of course, didn't want that to happen. Between 1689 and 1763, Great Britain and France fought a series of four wars. The first three were fought mainly in Europe. The fourth, known in Europe as the Seven Years' War (1756-1763), began in North America.

Both France and Great Britain laid claim to the Ohio and Mississippi river valleys. In 1747, a group of Virginia colonists formed a company to settle the lands in the Ohio River valley and control the fur trade. In 1749, King George II gave the Ohio Land Company, as it was called, a grant of 500,000 acres. To strengthen its claims and slow down British expeditions into the area, France built forts at key points in the Ohio country, especially at river junctions. For example, the French built Fort Duquesne at the junction of the Allegheny and Monongahela rivers, which form the Ohio River.

North Carolina provided three hundred troops in the campaign against Fort Duquesne, which the French had built in western Pennsylvania. The British captured the fort in 1758 without firing a shot.

The growing tensions between the two countries and the bloody resolution determined whether France or Great Britain would control the western territories.

or 70 Indians. . . . We [received] the Indian's fire . . . I ordered my party to fire which We did not further than 12 Steps each loaded with a Bullet and 7 Buck shot . . . They found the fire hot . . . I then ordered my party to retreat, as I found the Instant our skirmish began another party had attacked the fort, upon our reinforcing the Garrison the Indians were soon repulsed. . . .

Right: George Washington, an officer in the Virginia militia, was defeated by the French at Great Meadows in 1754. That clash ignited a war in both America and Europe. **Above:** *Colonel Archibald Montgomerie suffered a crushing defeat at the hands of the Cherokee near present-day Franklin in 1760.*

Finally, the British sent a military expedition into the heart of Cherokee country. On June 27, 1760, a group led by Colonel Archibald Montgomerie met the Cherokee at Echoe near the present town of Franklin in Macon County. The Cherokee defeated Montgomerie's force of 1,600 Highland Scots. The following year, Colonel James Grant marched a force of more than 2,000 into the Cherokee towns. Grant's army included militia from Virginia, North Carolina, and South Carolina as well as Scottish Highlanders and Chickasaw and Catawba Indians. On June 10, 1761, Grant defeated the Cherokee within two miles of where the Highlanders had lost just a year earlier.

Grant's campaign had a devastating effect on the Cherokee. He destroyed fifteen Indian towns, burned their stores of grain, ruined their fields, and drove them further into the mountains. In August 1761, Grant met with Attakullakulla (Little Carpenter), one of the most respected Cherokee leaders. It was a sad meeting. Attakullakulla had always been friendly with the British. As a young man he had even traveled to England. He hoped to bring peace to his people and the frontier. Attakullakulla said many Cherokee were "Dying, Naked, & Starving." The "white people," he stated, were "too many" for the Cherokee.

THE CONGRESS OF AUGUSTA

Peace did come to the frontier. The governors of Georgia, South Carolina, North Carolina, and Virginia and John Stuart, Britain's Indian superintendent, met with more than twenty-five Indian leaders and seven hundred warriors. Governor Dobbs represented North Carolina at the Congress of Augusta (Georgia) in November 1763. The Native Americans included Chickasaw, Choctaw, Creek, and Cherokee.

As John Stuart explained, the Native Americans were to consider the four colonies as speaking with the single voice of the "Great King." In the same way, he wanted the four Indian nations to speak as one people. Stuart said such a meeting would end "Falsehoods" circulated by the "cruel French." The Indian chiefs promised to live in peace and brotherhood even as they were forced to give up more land to the whites. Only Attakullakulla spoke bluntly about continued expansion of white settlements into Indian lands. The "White People . . . must proceed no farther," he insisted.

On November 10, 1763, the peacemakers signed a treaty. A **treaty** is a formal agreement between two or more nations. This treaty covered four points. First, the Native Americans and the colonial governors agreed "That a Perfect and perpetual Peace and sincere Friendship shall be continued." Past crimes and injuries were forgiven. Second, traders would be able to visit Indian towns without fear of harm or trouble. Third, both sides agreed to punish offenders who stole horses, killed cattle, or murdered people, thus breaking the peace. Fourth, the Creek Indians gave up vast areas of land in Georgia (about 2.5 million acres). The Catawba received a small reservation in South Carolina. The British promised not to "settle upon or disturb the Indians in the Grounds or Lands to the Westward of the lines herein before described. . . ."

Thus ended the French and Indian War in the southern colonies. Across the Atlantic, the European powers ended the war by signing the Treaty of Paris in 1763. Spain (who had sided with France) gave up Florida. France gave up all her territory in North America. The victory left Britain in control of all the land east of the Mississippi River.

Archibald Montgomerie's second in command, Colonel James Grant, returned the following year to avenge the loss at Echoe. Colonel Grant's army included militia from Virginia, North Carolina, and South Carolina as well as Scottish Highlanders and Chickasaw and Catawba Indians.

Do You Remember?

1. How did North Carolinians help capture Fort Duquesne?
2. Describe two major battles between the colonists and Cherokee.
3. What were the results of the Congress of Augusta?

CHAPTER · REVIEW

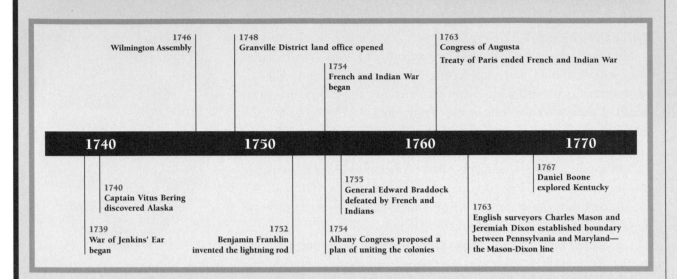

| 1740 | 1750 | 1760 | 1770 |

1746 Wilmington Assembly

1748 Granville District land office opened

1754 French and Indian War began

1763 Congress of Augusta
Treaty of Paris ended French and Indian War

1740 Captain Vitus Bering discovered Alaska

1739 War of Jenkins' Ear began

1752 Benjamin Franklin invented the lightning rod

1755 General Edward Braddock defeated by French and Indians

1754 Albany Congress proposed a plan of uniting the colonies

1767 Daniel Boone explored Kentucky

1763 English surveyors Charles Mason and Jeremiah Dixon established boundary between Pennsylvania and Maryland—the Mason-Dixon line

Reviewing People, Places, and Terms

Match each of the following words with the definitions that follow.

barter
French and Indian War
frontier
Granville District
headright
specie
treaty

1. A method of determining how much land settlers were granted that depended upon the number of family members
2. A formal agreement between two or more nations
3. To trade one item for another
4. Gold and silver
5. The war fought between France and Great Britain in America between 1754 and 1763
6. That part of North Carolina that was taken by one of the proprietors as his share
7. The area on the edge of or just beyond a settled area

Understanding the Facts

1. Who were the two kings on the British throne during the period that North Carolina was a royal colony?
2. With coins and paper currencies in short supply in the colonies, commodities were often used as money. What were some of the commodities that were used?
3. Roughly, where was the Granville District?
4. Why were colonists so eager to settle in the Granville District?
5. What two countries fought over control of North America in the mid-1700s?
6. How did the French and Indian War affect the Cherokee in North Carolina?

Developing Critical Thinking

1. During much of the royal period in North Carolina, the northeastern counties around Albemarle Sound held most of the political power in the colony. Why?
2. Why do you suppose that the colonists did not want to give up what specie they had to pay taxes they owed?

3. What do you think Attakullakulla felt about the future of the Cherokee when he said that there were "too many" white people?

Applying Your Skills

1. On a map of the United States, trace the Ohio and Mississippi rivers. Why do you think both Great Britain and France wanted control of these waterways?
2. Study pictures or diagrams of Fort Dobbs. Using popsicle sticks and other materials, construct a model of this fort. Why do you think the fort was designed and constructed the way it was?

Making Connections

1. What is "freedom of the press"?

2. Today, this country enjoys freedom of the press. But do you think that the press has too much freedom? Can you think of ways in which the press has "gone too far" in criticizing public figures?
3. How did Britain and France try to gain control of the Ohio and Mississippi river valleys?
4. Can you think of any examples of conflicting land claims that have recently led to war?

Tar Heel Trivia

- A tombstone in the Thyatira churchyard in Rowan County bears the inscription: "In memory of Richard King kild by Indians Feby 6, 1760 ageed 19 years."
- Indians on the eastern seaboard used clamshell beads, called "Roanoke," as money.

BUILDING SKILLS: FINDING CAUSES

When you read about a subject, you want to know what the facts are and why they are true. Listed below are two facts that appear in the chapter. Each fact is followed by three statements. Each of the statements is true, but only one explains why the *fact* is true. Look at each fact and the three statements provided. Choose the letter of the statement that gives the reason why the fact is true.

1. When North Carolina became a royal colony in 1792, its government changed very little.
   a. The governor, council, Assembly, and courts had the same powers and duties.
   b. Two kings sat on the British throne between 1729 and 1776.
   c. George II ruled until the Revolutionary War.
2. Grant's campaign had a devastating effect on the Cherokee.
   a. In August 1761, Grant met Attakullakulla, a respected Cherokee leader.
   b. Grant destroyed fifteen Indian towns, burned their grain, ruined their fields, and drove them further into the mountains.

c. As a young man, Attakullakulla had traveled to England to meet King George III.

In activities, tests, or conversations, you are often asked to use a fact and the reason it is true to answer a question about what you have read. For example: Why did North Carolina's government change very little when it became a royal colony? Using the first example above, you might answer that the government, council, Assembly, and courts had the same powers and duties.

The following questions are about facts given in the chapter. Answer each question with a complete sentence that gives the reason why the fact is true. The page number indicates where the fact is given.

1. Why was Gabriel Johnston a more effective governor of the royal colony than George Burrington? (page 148)
2. How did squatters make matters worse in the Granville District? (page 151)
3. Why was it said that the North Carolina colony was unprepared for the French and Indian War? (page 154)

UNIT 4

NORTH CAROLINA FROM COLONY TO STATE

ETWEEN 1765 AND 1776, North Carolina changed from a colony of Great Britain to an independent state. This came about because Parliament began to tighten its control over the colonies. It imposed new taxes that the colonists considered illegal. In response to colonial protests against taxes, British rule became harsher. War broke out.

North Carolina was the first state to urge independence from Great Britain. It also drafted its first state constitution and went through a painful civil war. The Revolutionary War resulted in an American victory and a new era for the state.

Above: Though Lord Cornwallis held the field at the Battle of Guilford Court House on March 15, 1781, British troops suffered such heavy losses that they never recovered. American forces under Nathaniel Greene may have carried a flag similar to this one. **Right:** The first capitol of North Carolina was completed in 1796.

By his EXCELLENCY

WILLIAM TRYON, Esquire,

Captain General, and Governor in Chief in and over the Province of *New-York*, and the Territories depending thereon in *America*, Chancellor and Vice Admiral of the same.

A PROCLAMATION.

WHEREAS I have received His Majesty's Royal Proclamation, given at the Court at *St. James*'s, the Twenty-third Day of *August* last, in the Words following:

BY THE KING,
A· Proclamation,

For suppressing REBELLION and SEDITION.

GEORGE R.

WHEREAS many of our Subjects in divers Parts of our Colonies and Plantations in *North-America*, misled by dangerous and ill designing Men, and forgetting the Allegiance which they owe to the Power that has protected and sustained them, after various disorderly Acts committed in disturbance of the public Peace, to the Obstruction of lawful Commerce, and to the Oppression of our loyal Subjects carrying on the same, have at length proceeded to an open and avowed Rebellion, by arraying themselves in hostile Manner, to withstand the Execution of the Law, and traitorously preparing, ordering and levying War against us: And whereas there is Reason to apprehend that such Rebellion hath been much promoted and encouraged by the traitorous Correspondence, Counsels, and Comfort of divers wicked and desperate Persons within this Realm:---To the End therefore that none of our Subjects may neglect or violate their Duty through Ignorance thereof, or through any Doubt of the Protection which the Law will afford to their Loyalty and Zeal; we have thought fit, by and with the Advice of our Privy Council, to issue this our Royal Proclamation, hereby declaring, that not only all our Officers Civil and Military, are obliged to exert their utmost Endeavours to suppress such Rebellion, and to bring the Traitors to Justice; but that all our Subjects of this Realm and the Dominions thereunto belonging, are bound by Law to be aiding and assisting in the Suppression of such Rebellion, and to disclose and make known all traitorous Conspiracies and Attempts against us, our Crown and Dignity; And we do accordingly strictly charge and command all our Officers, as well Civil as Military, and all other our obedient and loyal Subjects, to use their utmost Endeavours to withstand and suppress such Rebellion, and to disclose and make known all Treasons and traitorous Conspiracies which they shall know to be against us, our Crown and Dignity; and for that Purpose, that they transmit to one of our principal Secretaries of State, or other proper Officer, due and full Information of all Persons who shall be found carrying on Correspondence with, or in any Manner or Degree aiding or abetting the Persons now in open Arms and Rebellion against our Government within any of our Colonies and Plantations in *North-America*, in order to bring to condign Punishment the Authors, Perpetrators, and Abettors of such traitorous Designs.

Given at our Court at St. James's the Twenty-third Day of August, One Thousand Seven Hundred and Seventy-five, in the Fifteenth Year of our Reign.

In Obedience therefore to his Majesty's Commands to me given, I do hereby publish and make known his Majesty's most gracious Proclamation above recited; earnestly exhorting and requiring all his Majesty's loyal and faithful Subjects within this Province, as they value their Allegiance due to the best of Sovereigns, their Dependance on and Protection from their Parent State, and the Blessings of a mild, free, and happy Constitution; and as they would shun the fatal Calamities which are the inevitable Consequences of Sedition and Rebellion, to pay all due Obedience to the Laws of their Country, seriously to attend to his Majesty's said Proclamation, and govern themselves accordingly.

Given under my Hand and Seal at Arms, in the City of New-York, the Fortieth Day of November, One Thousand Seven Hundred and Seventy-five,
in the Sixteenth Year of the Reign of our Sovereign Lord GEORGE the Third, by the Grace of God of Great-Britain, France and Ireland, King, Defender
of the Faith, and so forth.

WM. TRYON.

By his Excellency's Command,
SAMUEL BAYARD, Jun. D. Secry.

GOD SAVE THE KING.

CHAPTER EIGHT

FROM REGULATION TO REVOLUTION

Well, Gentlemen, it is not our mode, or form of Government, nor yet the body of our laws, that we are quarrelling with, but with the malpractices of the Officers of our County Court, and the abuses which we suffer by those empowered to manage our public affairs. . . .

—Schoolmaster George Sims

I N 1765, GOVERNOR ARTHUR DOBBS DIED. Replacing him was perhaps North Carolina's most dynamic royal governor: William Tryon. In the six short years Tryon was governor, he would leave a lasting mark on the colony.

During his brief governorship (1765-1771), North Carolina faced two **crises** (serious situations or turning points). The first, the Regulator movement, grew out of problems inside the colony that caused thousands of North Carolinians to oppose the colonial government. The second arose when Britain tried to force new taxes on the colonies through the Stamp Act. The Stamp Act crisis sowed the seeds for the American Revolution. North Carolina's last royal governor, Josiah Martin, had to deal with the outgrowth.

UNREST IN THE BACKCOUNTRY

The movement known as the Regulation began in 1766, but it had its roots in earlier protests. When angry farmers kidnapped Francis Corbin, Lord Granville's land agent, and carried him to Enfield in 1759, they revealed the discontent in the backcountry. Settlers moving into the Piedmont area found that sheriffs, clerks, lawyers, and land agents charged fees that were much too high. Taxes had to be paid in gold or silver, which poor farmers rarely had. If a farmer could not pay the fees, the sheriff could take the farmer's property and sell it to pay the fees. Much of the money from taxes and fees was never turned over to the government.

Opposite page: An energetic royal governor, William Tryon put down the Regulation in North Carolina. Faced with an even larger rebellion in New York in 1775, he issued this proclamation. *Previous spread:* Though Lord Cornwallis held the field at the Battle of Guilford Court House on March 15, 1781, British troops suffered such heavy losses that they never recovered. American forces under Nathanael Greene may have carried a flag similar to this one.

In 1765 George Sims, a Granville County schoolmaster, issued his "Nutbush Address." In it, he protested the seizure of a person's property and the dishonest practices of the public officials. The westerners asked the Assembly for help, but their request was ignored.

The huge amounts of land owned by Lord Granville, Henry McCulloh, and the Selwyn family led to further unrest. Twice in 1765, bands of angry farmers attacked and beat surveyors working on the McCulloh and Selwyn lands in Mecklenburg County. These protests were part of the War of Sugar Creek.

THE REGULATOR MOVEMENT

The first meeting of the Regulators took place in Orange County in 1766. The **Regulators** were westerners who wanted better regulation (control) of government. They wanted help against corrupt government officials and illegal taxes and fees. They published a pamphlet later known as "Regulator Advertisement Number 1" urging the "sons of Liberty" to end "unjust Oppression in our own Province."

Between 1766 and 1768, the Regulator movement was peaceful. The Regulators sent their protests to Governor Tryon, who promised to look into them. When the Assembly approved new taxes to pay for the governor's palace in New Bern, however, backcountry farmers exploded in anger.

THE SPREAD OF THE REGULATORS

Until the 1760s, North Carolina had no set **capital** (official seat of government). Governor Tryon persuaded the Assembly to locate the capital in New Bern. The Assembly set aside £15,000 to construct a building that would serve as the governor's home and a meeting place for the council. Work on the building began in 1767.

Westerners were especially angry over the tax that the Assembly approved to pay for Tryon Palace, which few westerners would ever see. Orange County farmers told the sheriff they would not pay the tax for the next three years. In 1768, in their fourth pamphlet, the Regulators stated that they would pay no more taxes or fees that were higher than the legal amount. They went on to say that county officials were public servants and would be kept "under a better and honester regulation than they have been for some time past."

Violence broke out in April 1768. The sheriff of Orange County seized a Regulator's horse, saddle, and bridle for nonpayment of taxes. Sixty or seventy Regulators gathered and then rode into Hillsborough, where they took back the farmer's property. They also fired several shots into the home of Edmund Fanning. A graduate of Yale, Fanning held several offices,

To the Regulators, Edmund Fanning represented the corruption and unfairness of government. In 1770, they beat him severely and wrecked his house.

including member of the Assembly, register of deeds, colonel in the militia, and superior court judge. The Regulators hated Fanning, who was wealthy, powerful, cruel, and corrupt.

Fanning then helped the sheriff of Orange County arrest Herman Husband and William Butler, two of the leaders of the Regulation. Husband and Butler were taken to Hillsborough and charged with starting a riot. When the Regulators marched on Hillsborough, officials released the two men. Regulator protests spread to Anson, Cumberland, Johnston, and Rowan counties. In Rowan County, some three hundred Regulators burned the Salisbury jail.

In the fall of 1768, Husband and Butler went on trial for the riot charge. Fanning was also put on trial. To protect the Orange County superior court, Governor Tryon called out 1,500 of the militia and personally led them to Hillsborough. A force of 3,700 Regulators gathered nearby. Tryon ordered the Regulators to disband, demanded payment of taxes, and warned public officials against charging illegal fees. Husband was acquitted on the charges. Butler and two other Regulators were convicted but were given a pardon. Fanning was found guilty of charging excessive fees. He was fined only one penny and court costs. He did resign his position as register of deeds.

In the fall of 1768, Governor Tryon confronted the Regulators at Hillsborough. He ordered them to disband, demanded payment of taxes, and warned public officials against charging illegal fees.

THE RECONSTRUCTION OF TRYON PALACE

Located in New Bern, Tryon Palace was not only the governor's residence. This 38-room mansion also served as the meeting place for the colonial Assembly and for the legislature in the early years of North Carolina's statehood. Compared to English mansions of the eighteenth century, Tryon Palace was a modest brick structure. But compared to the simple buildings of colonial North Carolina, the two-story, Georgian-style house was "the most beautiful building in the Colonial Americas."

After Raleigh was established as the new state capital, state representatives held their last session in New Bern in 1794. Tryon Palace, already "hastening to Ruins," lost its official function. For the next several years, rooms in the former governor's residence were rented to individuals, to a private school, and to a local Masonic Lodge. In the winter of 1798, the main house was destroyed by fire.

During the 1950s, the Tryon Palace complex was painstakingly reconstructed. The home was furnished with rare antiques like those in the original building. Refurnishing the restored palace was made easier when, in 1952, a list of Governor Tryon's possessions was found in England. This detailed listing included descriptions of the governor's furniture, carpets, framed pictures, and many other items. The inventory also included the titles of hundreds of Tryon's books, which made it possible to recreate the governor's library.

One of the things visitors to Tryon Palace will see is a royal coat of arms over the central doorway of the main house. This coat of arms recalls Governor Tryon's duty to the British monarch, King George III. It includes the motto *Dieu et mon droit*, meaning "God and my right."

Between 1767 and 1770, John Hawks planned and built the original structure (right) for the colony's seat of government. It burned in 1798. During the 1950s, Tryon Palace (opposite page) was restored on the same foundation. The front gate (top) and kitchen (above) are shown here.

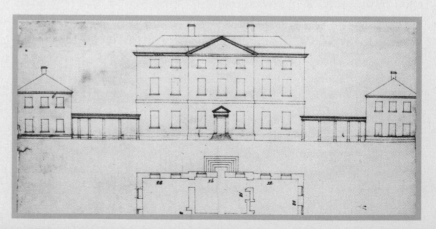

Tryon tried to help the Regulators, but the growing crisis between Britain and its colonies over taxation demanded his attention. In 1769, Tryon dissolved the Assembly and called for new elections. Orange, Anson, Granville, and Halifax counties elected Regulators. Before they could enact reforms, however, Tryon dissolved the Assembly once more.

The Regulators then took matters into their own hands. At the September 1770 term of the superior court in Hillsborough, a group of about 150 Regulators started a riot. They disrupted the court proceedings, attacked judges and lawyers, brutally beat Fanning, and held their own mock court. They also entered and wrecked Fanning's house. A Virginia newspaper, reporting on the events in Orange County, called the Regulators "desperate and cruel banditi."

Governor Tryon and the Assembly agreed. At its December 1770 session, the Assembly was going to consider reforms to help the westerners. But there were several rumors that the Regulators were marching on New Bern. Herman Husband, though elected to the Assembly, was denied a seat. Instead of passing the reforms, the Assembly enacted the Johnston Riot Act. Introduced by Samuel Johnston of Edenton, the law allowed the attorney general to move cases involving riots from the county in which they took place to any county in the colony. Persons who ignored a court summons could be declared outlaws and shot on sight. Finally, the governor could call out the militia to enforce the Johnston Riot Act.

Samuel Johnston of Edenton tried to crush the Regulation with a strict new law against rioting.

THE BATTLE OF ALAMANCE

The Regulators continued to oppose the governor and the Assembly. They refused to pay any taxes and threatened to kill Edmund Fanning on sight. Governor Tryon, who had agreed to become governor of New York, was determined to clear up the Regulator problem before he left North Carolina.

In the spring of 1771, Tryon called out the militia and marched west to Hillsborough. With nearly 1,500 men, he camped on the banks of Alamance Creek. At the same time, Hugh Waddell, hero of the French and Indian War, led a group of Cape Fear militia toward Salisbury, trying to surround the Regulators' army. A band of Regulators from Mecklenburg County, however, stopped Waddell.

On May 16, 1771, two thousand Regulators met Governor Tryon and his militia. When the Regulators asked to talk, Tryon demanded that they lay down their arms and disband. The Regulators refused, and the two-hour Battle of Alamance began. Tryon, who was also a British army officer, soundly defeated the poorly armed and poorly led Regulators. Nine of his men were killed and sixty-one wounded. The number of Regulators killed is unknown but may have been as

high as one hundred. James Few, a Regulator from the Hillsborough area, was captured and hanged without a trial. Fourteen other Regulators stood trial in Hillsborough in June. Twelve were found guilty. Six were pardoned; the other six were hanged on a hillside east of town as hundreds looked on.

After the Battle of Alamance, Governor Tryon offered to pardon any Regulator who laid down arms and swore allegiance to the government. Four Regulators, including Herman Husband, were denied a pardon. They fled the colony. Within six weeks, more than 6,000 Regulators took advantage of Tryon's offer. Many others fled over the mountains to the Watauga and Holston settlements, to Kentucky, and as far away as the Mississippi River. Thus ended the Regulation.

The Regulators were not without their defenders. In 1772, Josiah Martin, who followed Tryon as royal governor, toured the backcountry and looked into the Regulators' complaints. He reported that "I now see most clearly that they have been provoked by . . . tricking Attornies, Clerks and other little Officers. . . . " The Regulators, as well as northern newspapers, had also pointed out that the people who passed the Johnston Riot Act and crushed the Regulation at Alamance were also those who opposed British taxation. The Regulators demanded the protection of their rights and property against the corrupt colonial and local governments. The colonial leaders were demanding the same protection against Britain's imperial policies and taxation.

The Battle of Alamance took place on May 16, 1771. Tryon led a force of 1,500 militiamen. As many as 2,000 Regulators opposed him.

Do You Remember?
1. What was the "Nutbush Address"?
2. Why were the Regulators unhappy with the news about construction of the governor's home?
3. What were the provisions of the Johnson Riot Act?
4. Who was defeated at the Battle of Alamance?

BRITAIN'S TIGHTENING CONTROL

France's defeat in the French and Indian War presented Britain with many problems. To manage its enlarged empire, Britain adopted a new colonial policy. In a series of acts and proclamations (official announcements), Britain tried to protect the lands it had gotten in the war, maintain peace with Native Americans, pay off war debts, enforce the trade laws, and bring the American colonies under better control. In the colonies, Britain's new policies proved very unpopular.

At first, North Carolina was not really affected by the new policies. The Royal Proclamation of 1763 set the western boundary for settlement at the watershed line of the mountains. In other words, any land whose streams drained into the Atlantic Ocean was open to settlement. Lands beyond were reserved for Native Americans. North Carolina settlers had not yet reached that far west. The Sugar Act of 1764 was a minor nuisance to North Carolinians. Designed to raise money to defend the colonies, the Sugar Act taxed such imports as sugar, molasses, coffee, wine, and silk. **Imports** are goods brought into a country. Nevertheless, North Carolina showed that it would not bow to Britain's actions. In 1764, the Assembly warned Governor Dobbs that it alone had the right of taxation.

As a warning to those who might import tea, Boston patriots tarred and feathered tax collector John Malcolm, forced him to drink tea, and threatened to hang him.

THE STAMP ACT

The **Stamp Act**, passed by Parliament in 1765, shattered North Carolina's peace. This act required stamps or stamped paper to be used on all kinds of documents. The items that had to be stamped (taxed) included legal documents, pamphlets, newspapers, and playing cards. The cost of the stamps ranged from a half-penny to £10. Britain promised to use the tax money to defend the American colonies.

From New England to Georgia, colonists protested the new tax. They believed that it violated their rights as British subjects. "No taxation without representation" became a common cry. Many people began to **boycott** (refuse to buy) any goods from Great Britain. In North Carolina, Maurice Moore wrote a pamphlet attacking the Stamp Act. In it,

MAKING A REVOLUTION

To carry out the American Revolution, the patriots had to organize their local communities and colonies to oppose the political and military might of Great Britain. In the years leading up to the outbreak of war, patriots organized crowds to practice "out-of-door" politics. Viewed as unruly mobs by the British, they really acted purposefully. The Stamp Act riots of 1765-1766 brought that tax to an abrupt end. Probably the most famous "mob" was the one that took part in the Boston Tea Party. To protest the tax on tea, about sixty patriots disguised as Indians threw 342 chests of tea, valued at £10,000, into Boston Harbor.

Crowds, however, could not govern. The patriots therefore established extralegal government groups. Provincial congresses took the place of colonial assemblies and chose delegates to the Continental Congress. The Continental Congress in turn called for committees in every city, town, and county of America to enforce an economic boycott of Great Britain.

Patriots at the Boston Tea Party in December 1773 crudely disguised themselves as Native Americans. In fact, they were farmers, merchants, artisans, and apprentices.

The men democratically chosen as delegates and committeemen were often local officeholders. Many obscure patriots rose to positions of influence and leadership. Thus, as colonial Americans moved into open defiance of the crown, they created democratic institutions that became the foundation of a new nation.

he insisted that the people's "consent" to be taxed was "one of the most essential" rights. The colonists felt that only their elected legislatures, not Parliament, had the right to impose new taxes.

In North Carolina, the most violent protests against the Stamp Act took place in the lower Cape Fear region. In October 1765, a group of as many as five hundred people came together in Wilmington and forced Dr. William Houston, the stamp agent, to resign. Business and trade in the colony came to a stop at the end of November when John Ashe and

Maurice Moore wrote a pamphlet titled The Justice and Policy of Taxing the American Colonies *(1765). He argued that only the colonial legislatures could enact taxes, not the British Parliament.*

Hugh Waddell would not allow the stamps to be landed at Brunswick. In return, Governor Tryon closed down the courts.

Matters became tense in February 1766. At Brunswick, the British ship *Viper* had seized two ships because their clearance papers had not been stamped. An armed group of protestors, called the Sons of Liberty, broke into the customs office and took the ships' papers. Then they boarded the *Viper* and forced the captain to release the two ships. Cornelius Harnett then led the protestors to Governor Tryon's residence. There they forced the governor to turn over William Pennington, the customs collector. Pennington went to the center of town, promised not to enforce the Stamp Act, and resigned.

THE TOWNSHEND ACTS

Stunned by the reaction of the colonists, Parliament **repealed** (officially withdrew) the Stamp Act in 1766. At the same time, it passed the Declaratory Act, which proclaimed that Parliament *did* have the authority to tax the colonies. To prove its point, Parliament passed the **Townshend Acts** in 1767. These acts placed **duties** (taxes) on wine, tea, paper, glass, and lead brought into the colonies. The revenues from these duties were to pay the salaries of colonial governors and judges.

Despite efforts by Speaker John Harvey, the North Carolina Assembly would not take any action against the new taxes. Instead, the Assembly sent a message to the king in 1768. In it, the Assembly expressed their loyalty to the king and asked him to persuade Parliament to repeal the Townshend Acts. The legislators declared, "Free men cannot legally be taxed but by themselves or their representatives. . . ."

A year later, with the Townshend Acts still in force, John Harvey presented a Virginia proposal to form a "non-importation association." In other words, the colonies would agree not to import any of the items on which a duty had to be paid. The Assembly passed the proposal without a single no vote. When Governor Tryon angrily dissolved the Assembly, Speaker Harvey called the former legislators together at the courthouse in New Bern. There they formally signed a document supporting the non-importation association.

This opposition forced Parliament to back down once again. In 1770, all the taxes except the one on tea were repealed. North Carolina had taken an important part in the unified response to Britain's colonial policies.

Do You Remember?

1. What was important about the "watershed line"?
2. What did the Stamp Act require?
3. Why were the colonists so strongly opposed to the Stamp Act and the Townshend Acts?

SPREADING THE REVOLUTION

During the Revolutionary period, orators and pamphleteers gave purpose and reason to the Revolution. Many people could not read or write. They depended on political debates to *hear* about important issues. The most famous orator of the day was probably Patrick Henry of Virginia. In 1775, he stirred patriotic blood with his famous declaration "I know not what course others may take, but as for me, give me liberty or give me death."

The Revolutionary period was also a great age of pamphlets. Short, inexpensive to produce, and full of passion and opinion, pamphlets spread the agitation for liberty from house to house, town to town, and colony to colony. Most pamphlets, however, were written by lawyers for educated readers.

In January 1776, a new pamphlet appeared in Philadelphia. In *Common Sense*, Thomas Paine urged America to separate from Great Britain in language all people could understand. The pamphlet was a sensation and sold 120,000 copies in less than three months. Paine quickly followed *Common Sense* with a series of pamphlets called *The Crisis*. The first opened with these inspiring words: "These are the times that try men's souls. The summer soldier and sunshine patriot will, in this crisis, shrink from the service of their country; but he that stands it now, deserves the love and thanks of man and woman."

Thomas Paine had been in America just 14 months when he anonymously published his Common Sense.

TEA PARTIES AND CONGRESSES

In the 1770s, **committees of correspondence** were formed throughout the colonies. These groups were set up to keep each colony informed of British actions and other information. North Carolina's committee of correspondence included such leaders as John Harvey, Robert Howe, Richard Caswell, Joseph Hewes, and Samuel Johnston.

The committees played a key role in the crisis that set the colonies on the road to independence in 1774. In December 1773, the Boston Tea Party took place. Massachusetts patriots dumped 340 chests of tea into Boston harbor to protest the East India Company's monopoly on the tea trade. **Patriots** were colonists who resisted the tighter controls imposed by the British. Parliament responded with the so-called Coercive Acts, which the colonists called the Intolerable Acts. Among other things, the

North Carolina too had its own tea party. Penelope Barker (above) organized an "Association" of fifty-one women who pledged not to drink tea. A British cartoonist drew this unflattering picture of the Edenton Tea Party (right).

acts closed the port of Boston. The committees of correspondence quickly spread the news and asked all of the colonies to join in a general congress (meeting). At a mass meeting in Wilmington in July 1774, William Hooper, Cornelius Harnett, and others called for a "provincial congress independent of the governor."

Governor Martin expressed his displeasure at the idea in no uncertain terms. However, the First Provincial Congress took place on August 25, 1774. Seventy-one delegates elected from thirty of thirty-six counties and four of six borough towns met for three days in New Bern. Chaired by John Harvey, the congress condemned Parliament's tax policies, approved a general congress and a boycott of British goods, and pledged support for Boston. William Hooper, Richard Caswell, and Joseph Hewes were named delegates to the First Continental Congress.

The Continental Congress met in Philadelphia in September and October of 1774. Twelve of the thirteen colonies were represented. (Georgia had no delegates present.) The Congress agreed to stop all trade with Britain and urged each colony to set up *committees of safety*. These committees would enforce the boycott. Because its actions would have been called treason by the crown, the Congress carried on its work in secret. Nonetheless, Richard Caswell may have played an important role. John Adams of Massachusetts, later the second President of the United States, recalled that Caswell was a "model man and true patriot."

The women of North Carolina also showed their support for the patriot cause. Penelope Barker organized the event that became known as the Edenton Tea Party. On October 25, 1774, fifty-one women signed an "Association" in Edenton at the home of Elizabeth King. The women agreed not to drink any more tea nor wear any more British cloth. In Wilmington in March 1775, another group of women burned their tea.

Do You Remember?
1. What purpose did the committees of correspondence serve?
2. What actions did the First Provincial Congress take?
3. What role did women play in resisting unfair British policies?

THE ROAD TO WAR

As tensions between Britain and her colonies increased, Governor Martin became more angry and frustrated. When John Harvey called for a Second Provincial Congress, Martin tried to stop it by calling the Assembly into session at the same time. Instead, the two bodies, whose members were almost the same, united. On April 8, 1775, Martin dissolved the last royal Assembly to meet in North Carolina.

The minutemen were local militia members who had to be ready to fight "at a minute's notice."

Eleven days later the "shot heard round the world" was fired on Lexington green. Resistance to British authority had turned into rebellion. Massachusetts minutemen (militia who held themselves ready for service on short notice) fought British troops at Lexington and Concord, and the Revolutionary War began.

NORTH CAROLINA RESPONDS

Word of the battles at Lexington and Concord did not reach North Carolina until mid-May. When it did, North Carolina patriots reacted quickly. The most famous response was the **Mecklenburg Resolves** of May 31, 1775. At a meeting in Charlotte, patriots proclaimed "that all laws and commissions confirmed by or derived from the authority of the King and Parliament are annulled and vacated and the former civil constitution of these colonies for the present wholly suspended." The Mecklenburg Resolves also stated that "all legislative and executive powers" now rested with the Provincial Congress of each colony. In the Mecklenburg Resolves, North Carolinians made a bold statement in favor of independence.

On the same day that the patriots in Charlotte drew up the resolves, Governor Martin left New Bern with his family. Amid rumors that the patriots might seize the governor's palace, Martin went aboard the British ship *Cruizer* off the coast of North Carolina. He was the first royal governor in the colonies to flee his office.

North Carolina's patriots took part in their first military action in July 1775. Led by Cornelius Harnett, John Ashe, and Robert Howe, some five hundred minutemen captured Fort Johnston on the lower Cape Fear River. To prevent the British from using it, the patriots burned the fort to the ground.

In August 1775, the Third Provincial Congress met in Hillsborough. Samuel Johnston became the presiding officer of the congress after John Harvey's death in May. A total of 184 delegates represented every county and town. The congress established a new provisional government and readied the colony for war. It ordered that two regiments of five hundred men each be formed right away to join a Continental Army. The congress also divided North Carolina into six military districts, each with five hundred minutemen.

INTERNAL CONCERNS

Not everyone in North Carolina favored independence. Some still supported the crown. These people were known as **Loyalists** or Tories. Highland Scots, for example, had only recently moved to North Carolina. Many had sworn oaths of loyalty to the crown in order to receive land grants. Former Regulators recognized that the same men who had crushed their

The Battle of Concord on April 19, 1775, came only hours after the first battle of the Revolutionary War at Lexington, Massachusetts, five miles away. At Concord the first British blood was shed. Three men were killed and nine wounded.

movement were now numbered among the patriots. The Regulators had little reason to believe that independence would lead to badly needed reforms. As a result, many chose to remain loyal. The Moravians and Quakers as well as many German settlers in the Piedmont were pacifists or neutral.

Yet another concern to North Carolinians was the large slave population. Janet Schaw, a Scottish woman visiting the lower Cape Fear in 1775, declared flatly that the "Negroes will revolt." Rumors of a slave rebellion kept Wilmington in turmoil. Patriots charged that the British encouraged slaves to run away and that they had promised freedom to runaway slaves. In July 1775, a slave uprising did occur in Beaufort, Pitt, and Craven counties. The uprising was brutally put down. At least forty slaves were jailed. Several received eighty lashes and had their ears cropped.

In November 1775, Lord Dunmore, royal governor of Virginia, promised freedom to all slaves and indentured servants who fled their masters and joined His Majesty's Troops. When Robert Howe led a Continental force from Edenton to Norfolk, Virginia, in December 1775, the North Carolinians fought scores of blacks in the Battle of Great Bridge.

THE BATTLE OF MOORE'S CREEK BRIDGE

Fears of infighting in North Carolina were not groundless. Indeed, in the first major battle in the colony, North Carolinian fought North Carolinian. Determined to restore royal authority to the colony, Governor Josiah Martin convinced the crown to send a military expedition to North Carolina. In January 1776, Martin issued a proclamation calling upon the king's faithful subjects to rise up against the patriots. The British sent General Donald MacDonald to the backcountry to raise troops. The patriots, in turn, called out the militia and mobilized one of the North Carolina Continental regiments. The men were under the command of Colonel James Moore.

War was not long in coming. Led by General MacDonald, an army of 1,600 Loyalists (mostly Highland Scots plus about 200 former Regulators) left Cross Creek and headed toward Wilmington. On February 27, 1776, 1,100 minutemen under the command of Colonels Richard Caswell and Alexander Lillington met the Loyalists at the bridge over Widow Moore's Creek.

The patriots had removed many of the planks from the bridge and had greased those that remained. As the Loyalists tried to cross the slippery bridge, they were mowed down by gunfire. The battle ended quickly with a complete rout of the Loyalists. Moore estimated that at least 50 Loyalists were killed or wounded. The patriots suffered 1 dead

Robert Howe was North Carolina's highest ranking Continental officer during the Revolutionary War. He commanded the Southern Department for almost two years.

and 1 wounded. More than 850 Loyalists, including General Mac-
Donald, were captured.

When British forces arrived off the coast of North Carolina in May
1776, they found no Loyalist force to welcome them. The Battle of
Moore's Creek Bridge left North Carolina free from invasion for four
years. Without a Loyalist army to help them, the British went south
to Charles Town, or Charleston, as it came to be spelled. The patriots
drove back the British there in June 1776. The British would not try
to conquer the South again until 1778.

This diorama shows the Battle of Moore's Creek Bridge, which kept North Carolina free from British invasion for four years.

Do You Remember?

1. How did the Mecklenburg Resolves make a bold statement in favor
   of independence?
2. What groups in North Carolina did not favor independence from
   Great Britain?
3. Why was the patriot victory at Moore's Creek Bridge so important
   to their cause?

CHAPTER REVIEW

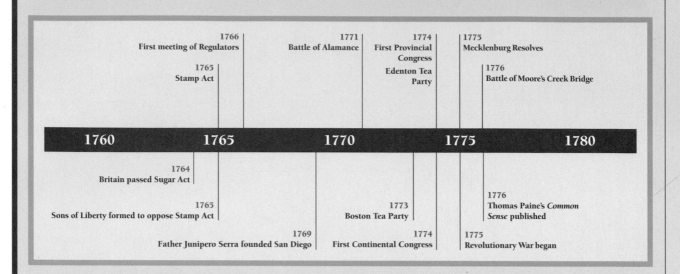

1760	1765	1770	1775	1780

1766 First meeting of Regulators
1765 Stamp Act
1771 Battle of Alamance
1774 First Provincial Congress / Edenton Tea Party
1775 Mecklenburg Resolves
1776 Battle of Moore's Creek Bridge

1764 Britain passed Sugar Act
1765 Sons of Liberty formed to oppose Stamp Act
1769 Father Junipero Serra founded San Diego
1773 Boston Tea Party
1774 First Continental Congress
1776 Thomas Paine's *Common Sense* published
1775 Revolutionary War began

Reviewing People, Places, and Terms

Use each of the following words in a sentence that focuses on the growing tensions between the colonists and the British government.

boycott
committee of correspondence
duty
import
Mecklenburg Resolves
patriot
repeal
Stamp Act

Understanding the Facts

1. What were the major reasons for the westerners' discontent that resulted in the Regulator Movement?
2. North Carolina had no established capital until the 1760s. Where did the Assembly locate the colony's first capital?
3. What did the Regulators do to be called "desperate and cruel banditi"?
4. Why was Governor Tryon unable to help the Regulators?

5. In what ways were the Regulators and the legislators who passed the Johnston Riot Act alike in their concerns?
6. What did Britain want to achieve by the new colonial policy it adopted after 1763?
7. Where did the first military action against the colonial government by the North Carolina patriots take place?
8. Who were the Tories?
9. For how many years after the battle of Moore's Creek Bridge was North Carolina free from British invasion?

Developing Critical Thinking

1. The Regulators were angry over the tax imposed to pay for Tryon Palace, which they considered extravagant and unnecessary. Can you name any government expenditures today that some may think extravagant and unnecessary?
2. What do you think American colonists meant when they opposed British policies by saying "no taxation without representation"?
3. What can citizens in this country do about taxes that have been imposed but that they do not agree with?

4. Do you think the American revolution against British rule could have been avoided? Why or why not?

Applying Your Skills

1. Imagine you and your classmates are Regulators and are writing to Governor William Tryon. Together, write a petition (a list of your complaints) about your colonial government. Describe the problems you are experiencing with taxes and royal officials.

2. William Hooper, Richard Caswell, and Joseph Hewes were delegates to the First Continental Congress, which was held in Philadelphia, Pennsylvania. On a modern-day map of the eastern United States, trace a route from New Bern to Philadelphia and determine the number of miles. Research what routes were available to those men in 1774.

3. Obtain a copy of "The Midnight Ride of Paul Revere," a poem from *Tales of the Wayside Inn* by Henry Wadsworth Longfellow. With several of your classmates, read the poem to the rest of the class.

Making Connections

1. Where do you think most Americans today get their information about political or economic issues?

2. Write a one-page "Common Sense" pamphlet calling for students to avoid drugs, stop smoking, start recycling, or some other good cause.

3. What were some of the methods the colonists used to oppose British policies?

4. Suppose that you were very strongly opposed to a law recently enacted by the state legislature. How would you go about voicing your opposition and rallying support for that law's repeal?

Tar Heel Trivia

- The Chowan County Courthouse, which was built in 1767, is the oldest structure still in use in the state.
- Although the British Parliament enacted the Stamp Act in 1765, there were no tax stamps sold in North Carolina.
- Mrs. Penelope Barker, organizer of the Edenton Tea Party, was the wife of Thomas Barker, North Carolina's agent in Great Britain.

BUILDING SKILLS: ANALYZING ILLUSTRATIONS

The illustrations—drawings, paintings, photographs—that appear in this book can tell you many things about the history of North Carolina and America. Sometimes illustrations are better than words because they *show* you something. Pictures can give you information about the houses people lived in, the tools they used, the clothes they wore, the work they did, and the communities and governments they built. Illustrations can put a face with a name, identify the focus of the chapter, and generally make the book more interesting.

As you go through this textbook, use the following steps to analyzing each illustration.

- Look at the illustration to get a general sense of what the subject is about.

- If there is one, read the caption that goes with the illustration.
- Try to determine whether the illustration was created during the time period it represents or whether it was created at a later time.
- Try to determine whether the illustration is posed or unposed and whether it is being used as a form of propaganda.
- Consider how the figures in the picture support the chapter topic.

Try This! Study the picture on page 171. As you study the picture, consider the following questions.

1. Why might the patriots have dressed up as Indians?
2. How do you know that the citizens supported those who were dumping tea in the harbor?

CHAPTER NINE

NORTH CAROLINA IN THE REVOLUTIONARY WAR

2. That you shall endeavor to establish a free government under the authority of the people of the State of North Carolina and that the Government be a simple Democracy or as near it as possible.
3. That in fixing the fundamental principles of Government you shall oppose everything that leans to aristocracy or power in the hands of the rich and chief men exercised to the oppression of the poor.

—Instructions to the Mecklenburg Delegates, Fifth Provincial Congress

A FTER THE BATTLE OF MOORE'S CREEK BRIDGE IN February 1776, North Carolina moved quickly toward independence. Before the Treaty of Paris was signed in 1783, ending the Revolutionary War, North Carolina would see seven long years of strife and suffering. In those years, North Carolina would draft its first state constitution, turn back an Indian threat from the west, become a battleground in the closing years of the war, and go through a painful civil war.

Opposite page: General Nathanael Greene drew Lord Cornwallis deep into the North Carolina Piedmont before turning on him at the Battle of Guilford Court House in March 1781.

THE FOURTH PROVINCIAL CONGRESS

When the Fourth Provincial Congress met in Halifax in April 1776, **Whigs** (patriots) were nearly unanimous in their support of independence. Robert Howe said he knew "not one dissenting voice." A committee of seven, headed by Cornelius Harnett, was formed to consider the "usurpations and violences attempted and committed by the King and Parliament." They also considered measures for the "better defence of this Province."

On April 12, 1776, Harnett's committee issued a report that was accepted unanimously. The report was known as the **Halifax Resolves**. In one part of the Resolves, the provincial congress urged the colonies to declare their independence.

That the delegates for this Colony in the Continental Congress be impowered to concur with the delegates of the other Colonies in declaring Independency, and forming foreign alliances, reserving to this Colony sole and exclusive right of forming a Constitution and laws for this Colony. . . .

Delegates from other colonies cheered the Halifax Resolves when the news reached the Continental Congress in Philadelphia. On June 7, 1776, Richard Henry Lee of Virginia offered a motion "that these United Colonies are and of right ought to be free and independent States. . . ." The Continental Congress passed that resolution on July 2. Two days later, it approved the **Declaration of Independence** as written by Thomas Jefferson with the help of Benjamin Franklin and John Adams. The three North Carolina delegates to the Continental Congress who signed the document were William Hooper, Joseph Hewes, and John Penn.

Before North Carolina's provincial congress adjourned in May 1776, it tried to draft a state constitution. When the delegates could not agree on its form, they adopted a temporary form of government—the Council of Safety. Cornelius Harnett from New Hanover County headed the nine-member council, which met continuously. Its chief functions were military and financial. Soon the council found itself having to take measures against Native Americans on the western frontier.

Do You Remember?

1. Who were the Whigs?
2. Who wrote the Declaration of Independence?
3. What body was chosen by the provincial congress in May 1776 to temporarily run the state government?

THE CHEROKEE

Two of North Carolina's three signers of the Declaration of Independence were William Hooper (top) and John Penn (above).

Officially, John Stuart, British Superintendent of Indian Affairs for the Southern Department, asked the tribes to remain neutral during the war. So did the Continental Congress. Some of the tribes in eastern North Carolina, those who were more a part of the white culture, fought in the Revolution against the British. Some Native Americans, however, saw the war as an opportunity to regain some of their lands. During the spring and summer of 1776, the Cherokee and Creek attacked along the western frontiers of Virginia, North Carolina, South Carolina, and Georgia. The Cherokee were led by Dragging Canoe, who promised an end to white expansion and a chance to settle old scores.

THE DECLARATION OF INDEPENDENCE

Left: The Continental Congress formally signed the Declaration of Independence on July 4, 1776. Below: Joseph Hewes of Edenton was one of North Carolina's leading patriots. He also was one of the state's three signers of the Declaration of Independence. His personal copy of the John Dunlap broadside, discovered in the 1970s, sold at auction for $412,500 in 1983.

On the night of July 4, 1776, John Dunlap printed an unknown number of copies of the Declaration of Independence. Each document was about 14 inches by 18 inches, and the legend "Philadelphia: Printed by John Dunlap" appeared at the bottom of each sheet. Only two dozen of those copies are known to exist.

On July 19, 1776, the Continental Congress ordered another printer, Timothy Matlack, to *engross* (print in final, legal form) the Declaration of Independence. Members of Congress who were present in Philadelphia signed the engrossed copy on August 2, 1776. Other members of Congress signed later. The signed, engrossed copy of the Declaration of Independence, which is 24 ½ inches by 29 ¾ inches, is on permanent exhibit at the National Archives in Washington, D.C.

In the 1970s, a copy of the John Dunlap *broadside* (a printed sheet) was discovered in Edenton, North Carolina. It was the personal copy of Joseph Hewes, one of North Carolina's three signers of the Declaration of Independence. At that time, it was the twenty-second known copy of the Dunlap document. In 1983, Williams College in Massachusetts bought the Hewes copy at auction for $412,500. A twenty-fourth copy later sold for $2.4 million.

The four colonies sent expeditions into Indian territory. General Griffith Rutherford of Rowan County led the North Carolina troops. Rutherford mercilessly destroyed thirty-six Cherokee towns throughout the mountains. The Indians turned once more to their best diplomat, the now elderly

Attakullakulla. On July 20, 1777, the Cherokee signed the Treaty of Long Island (in the Holston River) with Virginia and North Carolina. The Cherokee gave up all lands east of the Blue Ridge Mountains and the lands along the Watauga, Nolichucky, Upper Holston, and New rivers.

The Cherokee and the Creek never really recovered from the devastation of the Revolutionary War. Already settlers were pushing through the mountains into present-day Kentucky and Tennessee. In a 1791 report to the king of England, William A. Bowles, representing an alliance of Creek and Cherokee, described the impact of the war on those tribes.

Dragging Canoe led Cherokee attacks on the western fringes of the southern colonies in the spring and summer of 1776. The Indians hoped to stop further white expansion into their lands.

> *If your Majesty had been present at the ceremony dismissing the Indians from your service, had seen them hang their heads in dispondency, . . . you would have seen a picture of human distress, that cannot easily be imagined by those who are acquainted only with the state of society in Europe. . . . The people of the United States told us with Taunts, that our Father, the King of Great Britain, was conquered, and had yielded us and our lands to them; that we were now their people, & their subjects, and that we were to submit, as a conquered Nation. . . . they [Cherokees and Creeks] will not suffer the people of the United States to approach further into their country. . . . the ancient limits shall be preserved. . . . they will support the Same policy with their last blood.*

Despite such brave words, the "Trail of Tears"—the forced removal of the Cherokee to west of the Mississippi River—had its roots in the American Revolution.

Do You Remember?
1. Describe the military action against the Cherokee and Creek tribes in 1776.
2. Who was the leader of this military action?

CREATING A NEW STATE GOVERNMENT

Word of the Declaration of Independence reached North Carolina on July 22, 1776. In August, the Council of Safety called for elections to be held on October 15 to choose delegates to the Fifth Provincial Congress. That congress would draft North Carolina's first state constitution.

The election revealed sharp divisions over what form the government should take. One group, the Conservatives, was led by William Hooper, Samuel Johnston, and James Iredell. The **Conservatives** feared too much democracy. They believed that men of wealth, property, and social standing were better able to govern. Another group, the Radicals, included Willie (pronounced "Wiley") Jones, Griffith Rutherford, and Thomas Person, a former Regulator. The **Radicals**, who were mostly small farmers and westerners, wanted a "simple democracy." The campaign turned bitter. Samuel Johnston, who was defeated, blamed his defeat on "a set of men without reading, experience, or principles to govern them."

ADOPTING THE STATE CONSTITUTION

Beginning on November 12, 1776, the Fifth Provincial Congress met in Halifax for six weeks. On December 17, 1776, the congress adopted a **Declaration of Rights**. In twenty-five articles, the congress set out the rights that people had. Among those rights were freedom to worship, freedom to bear arms to defend the state, freedom to hold frequent elections, freedom to assemble, freedom to give their consent to any tax, and freedom to maintain a free press.

The following day—December 18, 1776—the congress enacted a constitution. A **constitution** sets out the rules under which a government will operate. The constitution reflected more than North Carolina's colonial experience. Instructions from the people of Halifax, Mecklenburg, and Rowan counties to their delegates influenced parts of the constitution. It also borrowed heavily from the new constitutions of states such as Virginia, Pennsylvania, Delaware, and New Jersey.

The news of the Declaration of Independence reached North Carolina on July 22, 1776. Cornelius Harnett read it publicly to a crowd in Halifax on August 1.

The constitution provided for three branches of government: a governor, a bicameral legislature, and courts. Each branch had certain powers and responsibilities. The legislature was called the General Assembly; its upper house was the Senate and its lower house the House of Commons. Members of the General Assembly would be chosen in annual elections. Each county would elect two members of the House of Commons and one senator. Only those men who owned at least 50 acres of land could vote for state senator. Free men, black or white, could vote for members of the House of Commons if they owned land or paid public taxes. Active clergymen could not serve in the General Assembly. To serve in the Senate, a man had to own at least 300 acres; to serve in the House, a person had to own at least 100 acres.

Only legislators were elected directly by the people. The General Assembly elected the governor and other members of the executive branch each year. The governor could hold office for only three out of any six consecutive years. The General Assembly also chose judges for the state supreme court and delegates to the Continental Congress.

The constitution kept the existing local government. The General Assembly, however, set the election, terms, and duties of such officials as sheriffs and constables. State offices could only be held by Protestants, which left out atheists, Roman Catholics, and Jews. Under the new constitution, there was no state church. All people were "at liberty to exercise their own mode of worship."

The constitution clearly gave more power to the legislature than to the governor. The governor could not call elections, summon or dissolve the General Assembly, or stop the passage of legislation. The weakness of the governorship would cause problems for the state during the war that followed. Not having a way to **amend** (change) the constitution would create problems for the next sixty years.

THE FIRST STATE GOVERNOR

The Fifth Provincial Congress named Richard Caswell, the president of the congress, to serve as governor until the first General Assembly could be elected. When the new Assembly met in April 1777, it unanimously (without a single "no" vote) elected Caswell the first state governor of North Carolina. He would hold that office for three years— years filled with conflict and danger.

The General Assembly elected Richard Caswell the state's first governor in April 1777. As a militia officer, he also took part in military campaigns such as Moore's Creek (1776) and Camden (1780).

Do You Remember?
1. What two groups had different ideas on the form the state government should take in 1776?
2. What were the three branches of government established by the first North Carolina constitution?

THE LOYALIST PROBLEM

One of the first problems Governor Caswell and the new state legislature faced was what to do about the Loyalists. The Whigs' victory at Moore's Creek Bridge had quieted, at least for the moment, any Loyalist thoughts of armed rebellion. Still, many North Carolinians did not like the idea of revolution and waited for the moment they could rise up and restore the king's authority.

One such group in Martin, Bertie, Edgecombe, and other eastern counties was led by a man named John Llewelyn. In 1777, Llewelyn and others met to plan the overthrow of the Whig government. Llewelyn and his supporters were good Anglicans; they did not like the fact that the new state government no longer supported the Church of England. Llewelyn's plans were discovered, and he and several of his followers stood trial. After this incident, Whig leaders kept a close eye on the Loyalists.

In one action, the legislature required everyone to take an oath of allegiance. If they did not take the oath, they had to leave the state. The legislature also set out penalties (punishments) for those who failed to take the oath of allegiance, pay taxes, or serve in the militia. One penalty was that a person's property and land could be seized. For not serving in the militia, pacifists such as the Quakers and Moravians had to pay three times as much in taxes as others.

FLORA MACDONALD

Although she lived in North Carolina for but four years, Flora MacDonald was probably one of North Carolina's most famous residents during the colonial period. Flora was born in Scotland in 1722. The Highland Scots supported the claim of Charles Edward, a Stuart, to the throne of Scotland. "Bonnie Prince Charlie" led a rebellion in Scotland that was crushed by the British at the Battle of Culloden in 1746. Charles Edward escaped and then set about to leave Scotland for France. Flora soon played an important part in his escape. Flora obtained passes for herself and "Betty Bourke, a stout Irish woman" to travel to the Isle of Skye. "Betty Bourke" was, of course, none other than Charles Edward. Shortly after their arrival at Skye, the "Bonnie Prince" escaped to France.

The British government was outraged. Flora was arrested, transported to London, and made a prisoner in the Tower of London. While in prison, she was presented with a silver tea set by an admirer. When King George II asked her why she had helped an enemy of the crown, she replied, "I only did what I would do for your Majesty in the same condition—relieved distress." She was set free in 1747 and returned to Scotland where she married Allan MacDonald in 1750.

After the Battle of Culloden, many Scots left from their homeland. Of these, almost one-fourth moved to the colony of North Carolina and settled at Cross Creek (present-day Fayetteville). Flora and her husband emigrated to North Carolina in 1775.

Flora and her husband lived in Cross Creek for a short time and then purchased land in Anson County. There they built a home on Mountain Creek and named it "Killegray." But life did not get easier for Flora and the other Highland Scots. Tensions were increasing between the colonies and England. When it appeared that war would break out, Flora's husband Allan joined the Loyalist forces, and Flora encouraged her Highland Scots neighbors to support King George. Flora was forced to flee Killegray. In 1779, her husband persuaded her to return to Scotland. To pay for her passage, Flora was forced to sell one of her few remaining possessions—the silver tea set. She returned to Kingsborough, her family home, and was joined by her husband later. Flora died on March 6, 1790, and the sheets that "Bonnie Prince Charlie" had slept on during his escape were used as her burial shroud. She had carried them with her throughout her entire life.

Flora MacDonald, famed for helping "Bonnie Prince Charlie" escape his pursuers, lived for a time in Cross Creek.

All able-bodied men 16 years of age and older were required to serve in the militia. Under the Whigs, the militia enforced the state government's authority. It was the militia that sometimes had to punish neighbors who failed to take the oath of allegiance or to pay taxes. But the militia also abused its powers. Members of the militia did not always follow the law or respect people's rights and property. Sometimes they accused people of being Loyalists as an excuse to seize their property. Many people turned against the Whigs because they were badly treated by the militia.

Such activities set the stage for brutal fighting among North Carolinians later. In the meantime, the British army, unable to gain a military advantage over George Washington and the Continental army in the North, turned its attention to the South.

Do You Remember?
1. What measures did the legislature take to keep the Loyalists under control?
2. What problems did the militia cause during this time?

WAR IN THE CAROLINAS

North Carolina's military forces consisted of troops in the Continental Line, the state militia, and independent bands called **partisans**. Five to seven thousand North Carolinians served in the Continental Line during the Revolutionary War. Many more served in the militia. William R. Davie and William Lee Davidson were two of the partisan leaders in the

Above: George Washington served as commander-in-chief of the Continental army. He stubbornly held the army together despite numerous defeats and shortages of food, supplies, and pay. **Right:** With little fuel, meager medical supplies, and almost no food, 2,500 soldiers died at Valley Forge.

state. Although they were officers in the Continental army, they led companies of irregulars (troops that were not part of the organized forces). The Loyalists also had militia forces and irregulars.

NORTH CAROLINA IN THE EARLY FIGHTING

During 1775 and 1776, North Carolina troops took part in the first battles of the Revolutionary War in South Carolina, North Carolina, and Virginia. When the British troops then turned northward, North Carolina's troops did also. Between 1777 and 1780, North Carolinians served under General Washington in New York, Pennsylvania, and New Jersey. More than a thousand North Carolinians spent the frigid winter of 1777-1778 at Valley Forge. A number of the North Carolinians at Valley Forge were slaves or free blacks. John Day, described as a "man of colour" from Granville County, died at Valley Forge. So did Frederick, a drummer. A muster of Continental troops at White Plains, New York, in August 1778 showed fifty-eight blacks in the North Carolina Line. North Carolina's most famous black soldier of the Revolution was John Chavis. A veteran

One of the pivotal points in the Battle of Germantown, Pennsylvania, on October 4, 1777, was the inability of the colonial forces to remove the British from this house owned by Benjamin Chew. This delay gave the British time to call up reinforcements and drive Washington from the field.

of the Fifth Virginia Regiment, Chavis was a highly respected teacher of black and white students in Raleigh. In 1832, he wrote United States Senator Willie P. Mangum: "Tell them that if I am Black I am free born American & a revolutionary soldier & therefore ought not to be thrown intirely out of the scale of notice."

North Carolina's highest-ranking soldier was Major General Robert Howe. He commanded the Southern Department of the Continental Line until the surrender of Savannah. There were some 7,000 troops in the Southern Department of the Continental army, of whom about 2,000 were North Carolinians. General Francis Nash led a brigade of North Carolinians in the battles of Brandywine and Germantown in Pennsylvania in 1777. They suffered heavy losses at Germantown, including Nash himself. North Carolina troops also served with distinction at the battle of Monmouth in New Jersey in 1778. However, North Carolina's bloodiest fighting came in the closing years of the war.

THE BRITISH TURN SOUTH

In 1778, the British shifted the war to the South. In December 1778, they took Savannah, Georgia. With the fall of Savannah, British troops swept through Georgia and invaded South Carolina. At Charleston, South Carolina, in May 1780, the British crushed the Continental forces. Over 800 North Carolina Continental soldiers and 600 militiamen were taken

The "over-mountain men" dealt the British a stunning defeat at Kings Mountain. Patrick Ferguson, an overconfident British officer, was killed, and his entire force of 1,000 Loyalists was killed or captured.

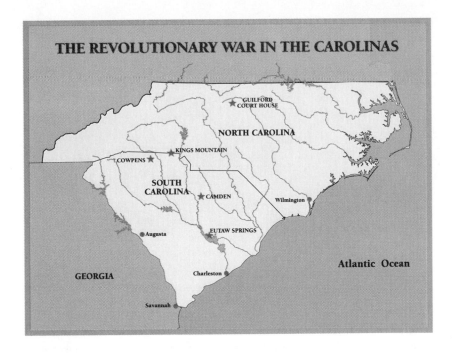

THE REVOLUTIONARY WAR IN THE CAROLINAS

GUILFORD COURT HOUSE

NORTH CAROLINA

KINGS MOUNTAIN

COWPENS

SOUTH CAROLINA

CAMDEN

Wilmington

Augusta

EUTAW SPRINGS

Atlantic Ocean

GEORGIA

Charleston

Savannah

Left: This map highlights the major battles of the Revolutionary War fought in the Carolinas.
Below: *When the British captured Charleston, South Carolina, in May 1780, Lord Cornwallis turned his attention to invading North Carolina and Virginia.*

prisoner. Lord Cornwallis, commander of the British troops, was now ready to invade North Carolina and Virginia.

In August 1780, American General Horatio Gates decided to face Cornwallis before he reached North Carolina. The two armies met at Camden, South Carolina. Out of Gates's force of 3,000, more than 800 were killed and 1,000 captured by the British. About one-half of the dead were North Carolinians. The defeat left North Carolina completely defenseless against Cornwallis. In September, accompanied by Josiah Martin (the royal governor), Cornwallis started toward Charlotte. The partisans, under Davie and Davidson, made sure that Cornwallis's march was not an easy one. They broke up his lines of communication and harassed British troops looking for food. When he arrived in Charlotte, Cornwallis found that the village was a "Hornet's Nest" of rebellion.

To the west, another battle was taking shape. When Cornwallis left Camden, he sent Patrick Ferguson into the Ninety-Six district of South Carolina to protect his left flank (side), to stir up the Loyalists, and to quiet the patriots in the area. Many of these patriots were "over-mountain men," people who lived on the other side of the Appalachian Mountains. At Gilbert Town in Rutherford County, Ferguson declared that he would destroy their homes and hang their leaders unless the patriots laid down their arms. Rising to the challenge, the patriots (led by John Sevier, Joseph and Charles McDowell, and Isaac Shelby) met Ferguson and his force of Loyalists at King's Mountain in October 1780. The battle lasted about an hour. It ended with the patriots dealing the Loyalists a crippling defeat. Ferguson was killed. In the wake of this disaster, Cornwallis returned to South Carolina.

THE BEGINNING OF THE END

While Cornwallis regrouped, Washington sent General Nathanael Greene to Charlotte to take command of the Southern Department. Greene knew that he did not have enough men to meet Cornwallis directly. He therefore decided upon a risky course. Greene divided his army into two groups; one would operate in the eastern areas of the Carolinas and one in the western areas. Greene went with the eastern troops, while General Daniel Morgan commanded the western wing.

Cornwallis followed Greene's example and divided his own troops. He sent Colonel Banastre Tarleton after Morgan. Morgan's army numbered 1,000, of whom 300 were North Carolinians. In January 1781, at Cowpens, South Carolina, Morgan trapped Tarleton and handed the British another stinging defeat. Furious that two of his best officers had been soundly defeated, Cornwallis began to chase Morgan across the Carolina Piedmont. He never seemed to be able to get any closer than 25 miles. At Ramsour's Mill, Cornwallis even left behind extra baggage, wagons, tents, and other supplies, hoping to speed his advance. Bad weather hit both armies. A cold, relentless rain fell, rivers overflowed their banks, and the clay soil of the Piedmont became a sea of red mud.

Greene's plans now paid off. He drew Cornwallis deep into North Carolina, far away from the British general's lines of supply. Although appearing to be in retreat, Greene united his two armies and waited for the best time and place to turn on Cornwallis. That place was Guilford Court House on March 15, 1781. By that time, Greene's army had grown to more than 4,000 troops, while Cornwallis's had fallen to less than 3,000.

The battle of Guilford Court House was ferocious. The North Carolina militia formed the first two lines of defense against the British. Greene turned back two British attacks and then withdrew from the battlefield.

General Nathanael Greene (above) made a daring decision to split his army and force Cornwallis to chase him across the Piedmont. At the Battle of Guilford Court House (top), Greene turned back two assaults by the British.

Cornwallis claimed victory, but as one British statesman concluded, "Another such victory would destroy the British army." More than one-quarter of Cornwallis's army lay dead or wounded.

His troops and his supplies exhausted, Cornwallis limped to Wilmington, which Major James Craig had captured in January 1781. Cornwallis arrived in April 1781. He remained only a few weeks before deciding to invade Virginia. So it was that Cornwallis found himself hemmed in by Continental troops and the French fleet at Yorktown, Virginia. On October 19, 1781, he surrendered.

THE TORY WAR

The approach of the British army in 1780 set off a partisan war in the Carolinas. The **Tory War** was a bloody civil war between Whigs and Tories (Loyalists) that raged until 1782. Bands of Whigs and Tories fought each other for control of their homes and communities. One of the most important of these engagements occurred at Ramsour's Mill in Lincoln County in June 1780. Since neither side had uniforms, the Whigs identified themselves by putting pieces of paper in their hats while the Tories wore sprigs of green. The Whigs won an important victory, preventing the Loyalists from joining forces with Lord Cornwallis.

Both the Whigs and the Loyalists were guilty of murder, plunder, arson, and attacks on women during these years. Many Loyalists took their revenge for years of violence directed at them by the Whigs. Wives and children of Loyalists were turned out of their homes and told to seek protection from the British. Years later, one Whig veteran recalled that, after the British left Wilmington in November 1781, he had been ordered "with a few soldiers to collect wives and children of the tories and carry them to Wilmington; that he found the execution of this duty so disagreeable that he resolved to desist from it at all hazards."

The most notorious Loyalist partisan leader was David Fanning. On September 12, 1781, he led an attack of 950 Tories on Hillsborough. Fanning took 200 prisoners, including Governor Thomas Burke, his council, members of the legislature, a number of army officers, and 71 Continental soldiers. On Christmas Day 1781, acting governor Alexander Martin offered to pardon all Loyalists except those guilty of murder, robbery, and arson. Fanning responded, "There never was a man who has been in Arms on either side but what is guilty of some of the above mentioned crimes, especially on the rebel side." Fanning continued to harass, murder, and rob Whigs until the spring of 1782, when he fled North Carolina.

With Fanning's departure, the vicious war ended. Hundreds of Tories left North Carolina. Many settled in Nova Scotia and New Brunswick, Canada. In 1783, the General Assembly passed an "Act of Pardon and Oblivion," accepting Tories back into the community. Those who did

David Fanning (top) struck fear in the hearts of patriots with his daring raids. In 1781 he even captured Governor Thomas Burke. After Burke's capture, Alexander Martin (above), acting governor, offered to pardon all Loyalists who had not committed murder, robbery, or arson. David Fanning doubted the sincerity of Martin's offer.

Governor Abner Nash faced a grave crisis with the British invasion of 1780-1781. Having to divide his powers with a Board of War frustrated him.

return often found that their property had been confiscated and that other laws stopped them from recovering it.

With the signing of the Treaty of Paris in 1783, the Revolutionary War officially ended. Peace had come, but the revolution continued. Creating a free state and federal union would challenge the patriots who had led the movement for independence from Great Britain.

Bitter feelings continued after the war. At least two former Tories elected to the General Assembly from Anson and Montgomery counties in the mid-1780s were not seated because of their military and political roles in the Revolution. The Loyalist problem, however, had largely been settled by the war's outcome. Other problems were not so easily solved.

Do You Remember?

1. What three groups made up the North Carolina military forces?
2. How did the partisans try to slow Cornwallis's march?

NORTH CAROLINA'S INTERNAL PROBLEMS

The war caused the tensions between the Whigs and Loyalists to erupt into violence. Other problems surfaced during this period.

BLACKS IN NORTH CAROLINA

Throughout the Carolinas, slaves greeted the British army as liberators. North Carolina slaveholders even accused the British of "carrying off large droves of . . . Slaves." In truth, the slaves needed little encouragement to flee to freedom.

Some runaway slaves did fight on the British side during the war. The British army used black refugees to perform duties other than combat. For example, blacks who were with Cornwallis as he marched through North Carolina seized food and property from locals. Blacks also took care of livestock and horses and performed nursing and engineering tasks.

At the end of the war, the British felt that those slaves who had worked for them should have their freedom. In the opinion of one officer, "These Negroes have undoubtedly been of the greatest use." American leaders tried to prevent blacks from leaving, without success. When the British left Charleston, South Carolina, in 1782, 5,000 blacks went with them. In 1783, 3,000 blacks left New York with the British.

WEAKNESS OF THE GOVERNORSHIP

The state constitution adopted in 1776 gave little power to the governor. During the war, that lack of power caused many problems for Governors Richard Caswell, Abner Nash, and Thomas Burke. For instance, the

MONEY, THE WAR, AND THE NEW STATE

The Revolutionary War brought financial chaos to North Carolina. To conduct the war, the Continental Congress and the states issued paper currency (money), which soon became nearly worthless. Between 1775 and 1783, North Carolina issued some $8 million in paper currency. Prices of all types of goods soared. By 1780, corn sold for £100 a bushel, beef for £48 a pound, and cornmeal for £120 a bushel.

The Moravians admitted that "as it [the state's paper currency] was in circulation it had to be accepted, though each man passed it on as quickly as possible." Others cursed the "Liberty money and them that made it for it was good for nothing."

Desperately in need of supplies for the army, William R. Davie noted, "our *money* and promissory *notes* are called *state tricks* and will no longer be receiv'd, so that I have been obligated to procure the necessary supplies by impressment and contribution."

The General Assembly adopted various tax plans to raise money for state government and to support the paper currency's value, but they all failed. In 1780, the state even went to a "tax-in-kind." Almost anything that could be used for the army—arms, ammunition, food, clothing—was accepted. But the way the tax was collected—often outright seizure—created resentment and anger.

William R. Davie, who led a band of irregulars during the war, struggled to find and pay for supplies for his men.

governors could do little to fill the state's quota (share) of soldiers for the Continental Line. North Carolina was never able to supply the number of soldiers asked for by the Continental Congress.

During the British invasion of 1780-1781, the governors could not deal effectively with the military crisis. The governor had few powers and only served a one-year term. The legislature had to create a three-member Board of War to handle wartime activities. That drained even more power from the governor, as Nash heatedly pointed out. As a result of these factors, state government ground to a halt.

Do You Remember?

1. What was the British attitude toward the slaves who had helped them in the war?
2. What problems during the war were caused by the governor's lack of power?

CHAPTER · REVIEW

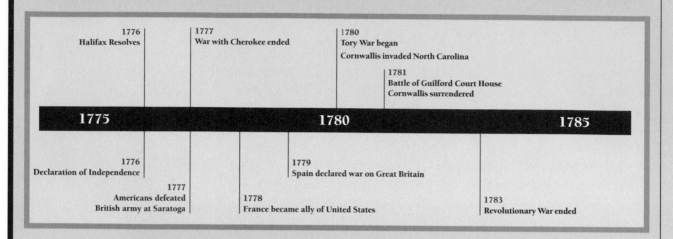

1776	1777	1780
Halifax Resolves	War with Cherokee ended	Tory War began
		Cornwallis invaded North Carolina

1781
Battle of Guilford Court House
Cornwallis surrendered

1775   **1780**   **1785**

1776
Declaration of Independence

1777
Americans defeated
British army at Saratoga

1779
Spain declared war on Great Britain

1778
France became ally of United States

1783
Revolutionary War ended

Reviewing People, Places, and Terms

Explain why each of the following terms appears in a chapter on the Revolutionary War.

constitution
Declaration of Independence
Declaration of Rights
Guilford Court House
Halifax Resolves
King's Mountain
partisans
Tory War

Understanding the Facts

1. How many years did the Revolutionary War last?
2. North Carolina was the first colony to instruct its representatives at the Continental Congress to do what?
3. Who were the three North Carolinians who signed the Declaration of Independence?
4. What was the first major problem that the Council of Safety faced?
5. Why did the Native Americans get involved in the Revolutionary War?
6. What were the results of the Treaty of Long Island signed by the Cherokee?

7. Under North Carolina's first constitution, who elected the members of the legislative branch? Who elected the governor?
8. What was the battle in North Carolina that might have been a turning point in the Revolutionary War?
9. What was the name of the treaty that ended the Revolutionary War?

Developing Critical Thinking

1. If you had been a Cherokee when the Treaty of Long Island was signed, how do you think you would have felt about your future?
2. It is said the victory by Lord Cornwallis at Guilford Court House contributed to the British army's later defeat at Yorktown. Do you agree or disagree? Why?
3. Why do you suppose the 1776 state constitution gave so little power to the governor?

Applying Your Skills

1. A number of different flags and banners were carried during the American Revolution. One popular flag included the warning "Don't tread on Me" written beneath a coiled snake. Think about the symbols that could represent North

Carolina. Design and draw a Revolutionary War flag for the state.

2. On a map of the eastern United States, trace the route of Cornwallis's army through the Carolinas and into Virginia.

3. Write a short essay on what might have happened if General Greene's forces had not opposed Cornwallis's army at Guilford Court House.

Making Connections

1. What financial problems in North Carolina were brought on by the Revolutionary War?

2. Why did prices soar when North Carolina issued currency during the Revolutionary War? What is this situation called?

3. Why do you think the Declaration of Independence was necessary?

4. Write a simple "declaration of independence" from procrastination, worry, debt, or some other similar problem you might have.

Tar Heel Trivia

- To reward the victorious officers at the Battle of Kings Mountain, the General Assembly in 1781 gave each one "an elegant mounted sword."
- The colonists often cut up coins on the spot to make change. A half coin was *four bits*; a quarter coin was *two bits*.
- Guilford Court House National Military Park was the first battleground in the nation to be designated a national military park.
- Sergeant Thomas Peters, a former slave from the lower Cape Fear region, joined the British forces in 1776 and served throughout the war. He settled in Canada for a while, but then led 1,200 black immigrants to the British colony of Sierra Leone in Africa. Those black immigrants formed the basis of a modern African state.
- When Flora McDonald and her husband arrived in Wilmington in 1775, she was welcomed with a huge ball.

BUILDING SKILLS: USING MILEAGE CHARTS

When planning a trip, it is important to determine the mileage from one place to another in order to calculate how long the trip will take, how much gas will be used, and which route will be the most convenient.

Many road maps provide a mileage chart similar to the one that follows. To find the mileage between two points, find the city that is your starting point on either the left or the top of the chart. Then find your destination city on the other side of the chart. Read down and across the chart to the point where the two cities intersect. The box at that point gives the number of miles between the two cities. For example, the distance from Asheville to Raleigh is 236 miles.

Determine the mileage for each of the following trips.

1. Asheville to New Bern
2. Charlotte to Raleigh
3. New Bern to Winston-Salem
4. Hickory to Asheville
5. Greensboro to Raleigh to Elizabeth City

	Asheville	Charlotte	Jacksonville	Raleigh	Winston-Salem
Boone	92	106	302	192	87
Charlotte	143		141	153	80
Elizabeth City	395	296	157	160	263
Greensboro	162	91	187	74	26
Hickory	75	64	290	177	72
New Bern	348	249	36	111	214
Raleigh	236	153	113		104
Wilmington	314	206	56	134	208

6. Charlotte to Wilmington to Jacksonville
7. Boone to Asheville to Charlotte
8. Hickory to Winston-Salem to Raleigh
9. Raleigh to New Bern to Jacksonville
10. Wilmington to Elizabeth City

CHAPTER TEN

NORTH CAROLINA AND THE FEDERAL UNION

It is my decided opinion (& no man is better acquainted with the public mind) that nine tenths of the people of this State are opposed to the adoption of the New System, without considerable Amendments & I might without incurring any great hazard to err, assure you that very Considerable numbers conceive an idea of a General Government on this extension impracticable & dangerous.

—Thomas Person

T THE END OF THE REVOLUTIONARY WAR, North Carolina was very weak. The war ruined the state's economy and divided its people. The war also showed that the state government was poorly equipped to deal with its problems. Frederic William Marshall, a Moravian leader at Salem, compared North Carolina in the early 1780s to a patient in need of medicine and care. He noted that the "the land itself, the people of property, commerce, public and private credit, the currency in circulation all are laid waste and ruined."

Opposite page: James Madison has been called the "father of the Constitution." He proposed a system of checks and balances among three branches of government. Above: North Carolina adopted its first state seal in 1779. The seal was replaced in 1794.

NORTH CAROLINA AFTER THE WAR

No newspaper was published in the state from 1778 to 1783. Private schools and academies that closed during the war remained closed afterward. Membership in North Carolina's churches declined. When the state constitution of 1776 failed to support it, the Church of England collapsed. One visitor from the North noted that many North Carolinians "cannot properly be classed with any sect of christians, having never made any profession of christianity and are literally, as to religion, nothingarians ….There is very little *external* appearance of religion among the people in general."

From these terrible conditions, North Carolina moved to improve its economic and social life.

REBUILDING THE ECONOMY

In 1789, a legislative committee reported that the state was almost $3.5 million in debt. The state had far more bills to pay than it collected in taxes. In 1786, for example, North Carolina collected only $86,000 in taxes. By today's standards, taxes were low. Legislators, however, did not want to make things harder for citizens by increasing taxes.

During the war, the legislature issued paper currency. As more and more currency entered the economy, it became less and less valuable. By the end of the war, the state's money was nearly worthless. The General Assembly tried to correct this but ended up issuing even more paper money in 1783 and 1785.

To pay off the state's debt and prop up the paper currency, the General Assembly imposed **tariffs** (taxes) on such imported goods as sugar, coffee, wine, and pepper. The legislature refused to tax any American-made goods.

Trade began to get better in the mid-1780s. By 1790, North Carolina's total trade was about double the 1769 mark. Before the Revolution, about two-thirds of North Carolina's exports went to Great Britain and the British West Indies. After the war, only about one-tenth of North Carolina's exports went to Great Britain. About one-half flowed to the West Indies and two-fifths to other American states. Naval stores remained the state's largest export, but most of those went to New England. Exports of corn, lumber, and tobacco also reached new heights by the end of the 1780s.

To help the state's economic recovery, the General Assembly passed laws to clear up the confusion over titles to property; to open a land office; and to build roads, ferries, and bridges. The lawmakers also passed a state law giving debtors (people who owe money to others) an extra year to settle with creditors (those to whom money is owed).

BAYARD V. SINGLETON

During the war, the state had **confiscated** (taken over) the lands of Loyalists and sold them to get money. This practice was later forbidden by the Treaty of Paris. North Carolina, however, used the Confiscation Acts of 1777 and 1779 to continue to seize and sell Loyalists' land during the 1780s. By 1790, the state had received more than £850,000 by selling Loyalists' property. In 1785, the General Assembly passed a law forbidding Loyalists from filing lawsuits in state courts to recover their property. This 1785 law laid the groundwork for one of the most famous legal cases in North Carolina history.

Mrs. Elizabeth Bayard was the daughter of Samuel Cornell, a Tory merchant. In 1786, she brought a lawsuit against Spyers Singleton, who had purchased property confiscated from her father. Mrs. Bayard's lawyers argued that no law could deprive a citizen of her or his property without

a jury trial. The judges agreed. Samuel Ashe, Samuel Spencer, and John Williams, judges of the superior court, ruled that the 1785 law passed by the General Assembly was, therefore, unconstitutional. The decision in *Bayard v. Singleton* (1787) set an important precedent (an example or rule to follow). It was the first time a law was declared unconstitutional.

The export of tobacco after the Revolutionary War reached new heights in the 1780s. Slave labor played an important part in the state's economic recovery.

EDUCATION

There were few formal schools in the state. Those that did exist were usually run by the Church of England or other religious groups. Wealthy citizens who could afford to do so educated their children privately.

There was no institution of higher learning (college) in the state. The 1776 state constitution, however, promised to extend education to all citizens. Article 41 stated: "That a School or Schools shall be established by the Legislature for the convenient Instruction of Youth . . . and all useful Learning shall be duly encouraged and promoted in one or more Universities."

However, the legislature did not establish "public" schools, those funded by tax money. The legislature did charter over forty private academies between 1777 and 1780, mostly just for boys. William R. Davie

NOAH WEBSTER AND THE BLUE-BACKED SPELLER

Noah Webster, who put together the first American dictionary, believed that "a national language is a bond of national union."

Noah Webster came from an average colonial family in Connecticut. His father farmed and worked as a weaver; his mother worked at home.

Webster loved learning, so his parents sent him to Yale, Connecticut's only college. He graduated in 1778, taught school, and studied law. Webster had some rather strong opinions about American schools. He disliked the crowded one-room schoolhouses, the untrained teachers, and the textbooks that had been published in Great Britain.

In 1783, Webster wrote the first of three textbooks, *The American Spelling Book.* Because of its blue cover, it became known as the "Blue-Backed Speller." For one hundred years, American children learned to read, spell, and pronounce words using Webster's textbook. It was the most popular book of its time; by 1850 more than 15 million copies had been sold.

Webster also prepared the first American dictionary. He labored twenty-seven years to publish the 70,000-word, 2-volume dictionary in 1828. A passionate nationalist, Webster used his dictionary to introduce American spellings and words. For example, Webster included American spellings such as *color* instead of the English *colour* and *music* instead of *musick.* He added American words such as *skunk* and *squash,* which were not in English dictionaries.

More than any other person, Noah Webster shaped modern American usage of the English language.

led the effort to establish the first state university in America. In 1789, the General Assembly chartered the University of North Carolina. The university opened at Chapel Hill in 1795, and its first student was Hinton James.

ESTABLISHING A NEW CAPITAL

The problem of where the capital of North Carolina should be located arose in the colonial period. At the start of the Revolutionary War, New Bern had been the capital for about ten years. But New Bern could be invaded from the sea. In addition, some legislators wanted to move the capital to a more "central" location. Many towns wanted the honor of being the seat of government, especially Fayetteville, Tarboro, and Hillsborough. Between 1778 and 1794, the General Assembly met in seven different towns: Hillsborough, Halifax, Smithfield, Fayetteville, New Bern, Tarboro, and Wake Court House.

Unable to agree on where to place the capital, the General Assembly turned the problem over to the Hillsborough Convention of 1788, which had been called to vote on the U.S. Constitution. The convention decided to locate the capital within ten miles of Isaac Hunter's tavern in Wake County. In 1792, the state bought Joel Lane's plantation of 1,000 acres and laid out the new capital, named "Raleigh." The legislature met for the first time in Raleigh in 1794. Richard Dobbs Spaight was the first governor to take his place in the new capitol, which was completed in 1796.

All of these developments helped restore North Carolina's social and economic order in the 1780s. But a much larger issue dominated the decade. That issue was what form the new national government would take. Until that issue was settled, the state's—and the nation's—future remained uncertain.

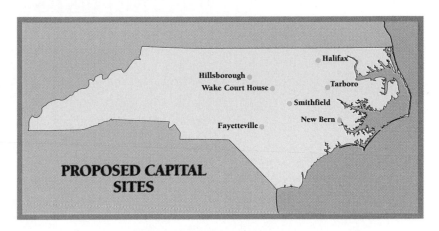

PROPOSED CAPITAL SITES

This map shows the various sites under consideration as the state capital. Which would you have chosen?

Do You Remember?
1. What efforts did the General Assembly take to try to pay off the state debt?
2. How did the General Assembly help debtors?
3. Who led the effort to establish the University of North Carolina?
4. Why wasn't it an easy task to select the site for the capital?

THE ARTICLES OF CONFEDERATION

During the Revolutionary War, the Continental Congress adopted the country's first constitution, called the **Articles of Confederation**. Each state had to **ratify** (approve) the Articles, a slow process. North Carolina ratified the Articles in 1778. But it was not until 1781 that Maryland became the last state to ratify them.

The Articles of Confederation provided for the states to enter "into a firm league of friendship with each other, for their common defense, the security of their liberties, and their mutual and general welfare." The Articles created a one-house legislature—Congress—in which each state had one vote. Delegates from nine states had to approve any important decision the Confederation Congress made. The Articles could only be amended with the approval of all thirteen states. Sometimes states, including North Carolina, did not even send representatives to the Confederation Congress.

THE FIRST STATE UNIVERSITY

The University of North Carolina at Chapel Hill is the nation's oldest state university. Although chartered by the state legislature in December 1789, the university did not officially open until over five years later.

The school was located in the woods of Orange County. The campus consisted of a single, plain brick structure, known today as Old East Building. Its first student, 18-year-old Hinton James, was said to have "trudged manfully" the 150 miles to Chapel Hill from his home near Wilmington. He arrived on February 12, 1795, and was greeted by the university's one teacher, Dr. David Ker, an Irishman. For two weeks after arriving at the university, Hinton James was the only student. Soon, however, other classmates began to trickle into the university. By the end of

The University of North Carolina was the first state university to open its doors. This 1797 drawing shows the University's first building, Old East.

the first school term, there were forty-one students in Chapel Hill. James was among seven students in the University of North Carolina's first graduating class. On July 4, 1798,—Independence Day—he was awarded an engineering degree.

During the 1800s, the university grew very slowly. By 1896, a century after the university opened, total enrollment was still only 388 students. In the 1900s, however, the university's size increased dramatically, especially in the decades after World War II. Today, the university at Chapel Hill has over 24,000 students and is referred to as the "flagship" of an expanded University of North Carolina system. This system extends throughout the state and includes fifteen other institutions.

The University of North Carolina remained the only institution of higher learning in the state until the 1830s. Today the university at Chapel Hill has over 24,000 students.

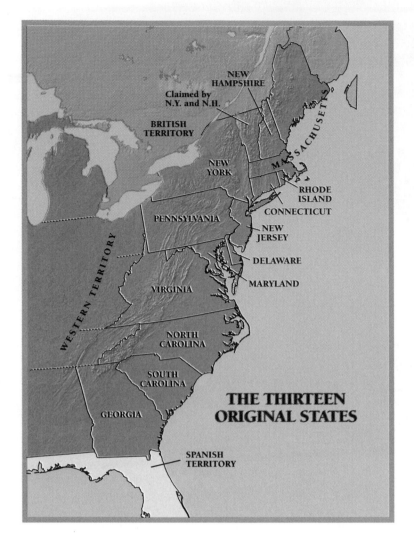

THE THIRTEEN
ORIGINAL STATES

Those who had fought to free the colonies from Great Britain now worked to mold thirteen separate states into one Union.

The young nation had no president or **judiciary** (court system). The national government had only limited powers to tax or to regulate commerce. Congress could ask the states for money to pay expenses, but had no power to force them to do so.

The Articles created a loose union where each state retained "its sovereignty, freedom, and independence." Any power not clearly given to the Congress belonged to the states. This em-phasis on **states' rights** weakened the Confederation from the start. North Carolina's delegates to Congress, however, strongly supported the states' rights idea. Thomas Burke even opposed the Articles of Confederation because it seemed to place too much power in the hands of the national government. Cornelius Harnett, however, believed that the Articles created "the best Confederacy that could be formed," considering the number of states and their different interests and customs.

One of the biggest problems facing the Confederation was what to do about the western lands. Several states, including North Carolina, claimed large areas of land west of the Appalachian Mountains. States that had no western claims (such as Maryland, New Jersey, and Delaware) were afraid they would stay much smaller and much weaker than their larger neighbors. They wanted those states with western lands to turn over the land to the national government. In 1780, Congress asked Georgia, North Carolina, and Virginia to give up their western lands. The following year Virginia agreed to do so. North Carolina, however, held back.

North Carolinians had different ideas about what to do with the land. Many people east of the mountains did not want to turn over the lands to the central government. They wanted the state to sell the lands to pay off the state's debts. Some easterners did not want to pay for the cost of maintaining government west of the mountains. They believed the national government should take that responsibility. Most people who lived in the Piedmont and beyond the mountains favored cession (turning the land over). The ongoing tension between east and west was behind some of that. Westerners disliked the power easterners had in state government and complained that state government did not pay enough attention to western interests. For example, there were no courts west of Morganton in Burke County. Nor did the state help protect the westerners against the Cherokee. The westerners believed the national government would do a better job of looking out for their interests and protecting their trade. They believed, for example, that only the national government could force Spain to reopen New Orleans, which was where they shipped most of their goods, to American trade.

In the spring of 1784, the General Assembly agreed to turn over North Carolina's western lands to the national government—but with several conditions. Land set aside for North Carolina's veterans of the Revolutionary War must be honored. Neither the lands nor the settlers in the territory could be counted when calculating North Carolina's share of the national debt. Finally, as a "benefit" for all the states, the lands were to be used to create at least one other state.

This Cession Act was not popular. William R. Davie and thirty-six other state legislators voted against it because it did not reduce the state debt. Even Hugh Williamson, the delegate chosen to present the act to Congress, opposed it. In October 1784, the General Assembly repealed the Cession Act. The timing of the repeal could not have been worse. Across the mountains, the westerners were about to launch their own independent state.

THE STATE OF FRANKLIN

By 1783, North Carolina had set up several counties west of the mountains, in what is today the state of Tennessee. Settlers in those counties had often talked about separating themselves from the rest of North Carolina. The Cession Act of 1784 provided what little encouragement the westerners needed.

Led by John Sevier, a convention of delegates from the counties west of the mountains met in Jonesborough in August 1784. The convention criticized North Carolina for ignoring westerners' interests and asked Congress to accept the Cession Act. Reacting to the criticism, the North Carolina General Assembly set up a judicial district and a military district in the western counties. John Sevier was named brigadier general.

These actions deeply divided those who lived in the western lands. One group, led by John Sevier, still wanted to form its own state. Another group, led by John Tipton, wanted to remain part of North Carolina. North Carolina's repeal of the Cession Act helped tip the scales in Sevier's favor. In December 1784, those who favored separation (Sevier's group) held another convention. At this convention, the delegates wrote a

William R. Davie and thirty-six other state legislators voted against the Cession Act of 1784 because it did not reduce the state debt.

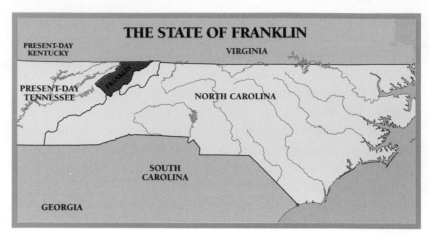

THE STATE OF FRANKLIN

PRESENT-DAY KENTUCKY

VIRGINIA

PRESENT-DAY TENNESSEE

FRANKLIN

NORTH CAROLINA

SOUTH CAROLINA

GEORGIA

Right: Western settlers were unhappy and proposed the creation of a new state, which they named "Franklin." Below: John Sevier briefly served as governor of the "State of Franklin." In 1780, he had helped lead the overmountain men to victory at King's Mountain.

state constitution, which was modeled after North Carolina's, and elected an assembly. In March 1785, delegates to the western assembly elected John Sevier governor of the "State of Franklin." However, they continued to send representatives to North Carolina's General Assembly.

The state of Franklin did not receive a hearty welcome. North Carolina Governor Alexander Martin was outraged. He issued a "Manifesto" in which he threatened to use force to bring down the "mock government." The Confederation Congress refused to recognize the new state.

The state of Franklin began to fall apart almost as soon as it was formed. Fighting broke out between the Sevier and Tipton groups. Some western counties elected two sets of officials who then disrupted each other's court sessions. When Sevier's term as the governor of Franklin ran out in 1788, there was no longer an assembly to choose a successor. Sevier's election to the North Carolina Senate in 1789 signaled the end of the state of Franklin.

In 1789, North Carolina finally turned its western lands over to the United States. In 1796, those lands became part of the much larger state of Tennessee. Tennessee's North Carolina roots could be seen in the lives of three men who later became president. Andrew Jackson, James K. Polk, and Andrew Johnson all spent their early lives in North Carolina but achieved fame in Tennessee.

Even more important decisions about government were occurring in Maryland and Pennsylvania.

Do You Remember?

1. Why were states with no western land claims so concerned about those that had claims?
2. Why did the settlers in western North Carolina want to form an independent government?
3. What finally happened to North Carolina's western lands?

THE RISE OF NATIONALISM AND REPUBLICANISM

The American Revolution gave rise to several important political realities. Patriotism was not limited to male colonists. Women actively supported the Revolution while their men were away serving. Some women actually fought, the most famous probably being "Molly Pitcher." These women expected to benefit under the resulting democracy. In fact, Abigail Adams, wife of John Adams, reminded her husband to "remember the Ladies." Unfortunately, the early legislatures did not.

Another important political lesson was nationalism. Disastrous British policies forced nationalism on thirteen separate colonies. Men from the different colonies served together in congresses, in the army. They worked for a common goal—independence—and took pride in their sacrifices and accomplishments. That forced them to think as a *nation*.

Republicanism was a major result of the Revolution. A republic rests solely on the consent and participation of the people. Revolutionary leaders believed that a "natural aristocracy" would rise to the top to govern society. But above all, they believed that the survival of the republic depended on the virtue of its citizens. In other words, they believed that the frugality, self-sacrifice, and responsibility of the people would ensure that government power would not corrupt those who held it. In the words of Philadelphia physician Benjamin Rush, "Virtue, Virtue alone . . . is the basis of a republic."

Left: *Mary Hays carried water to thirsty soldiers and then joined the fighting at the battle of Monmouth, earning her the nickname "Molly Pitcher."* **Above:** *Benjamin Rush was one of the most noted physicians in the early United States and was also a social reformer.*

THE CONSTITUTIONAL CONVENTION

Upset because Congress was not able to handle trade among the states, Virginia invited the other states to a convention at Annapolis, Maryland, in 1786. Only five states sent delegates to discuss trade and the problems of the Confederation. Governor Richard Caswell named five delegates from North Carolina. Only Hugh Williamson made an effort to attend, and he arrived too late. Nevertheless, the Annapolis Convention called for another convention to be held in Philadelphia in 1787 to consider revising the "constitution of the federal government."

THE MEETING IN PHILADELPHIA

In May 1787, fifty-five men representing all the states except Rhode Island met in Philadelphia. The plan was to give the government increased powers and authority to solve the nation's problems. Most of the men were wealthy and well thought of in their states. Merchants, planters, physicians, generals, governors, and especially lawyers (twenty-three in all) made up the convention.

North Carolina's General Assembly elected as delegates William R. Davie, Richard Dobbs Spaight, Governor Richard Caswell, Alexander Martin, and Willie Jones. Jones refused to serve, and Governor Caswell appointed Hugh Williamson in his place. When ill health forced Governor Caswell to withdraw, he chose as his successor William Blount. North Carolina's delegates were well-educated planters, businessmen, and lawyers. They were also fairly young. All five had served in civil or military roles during the Revolutionary War. Except for Williamson, all were slave owners. Four of the five were from eastern North Carolina. Only Martin came from as far west as the Piedmont. None could be said to represent the interests of the state's small farmers, who made up most of North Carolina's population.

The delegates soon decided that the Articles of Confederation could not be revised. An entirely new plan of government had to be created. The convention agreed that this national government should have three branches: legislative, judicial, and executive. This so-called *Virginia Plan* reflected the thinking of James Madison, known as the "father of the Constitution." Madison had prepared for the convention by studying more than two hundred books on history and government. He proposed a system of checks and balances among the three branches so that no one branch would be able to control the entire government. Madison believed that a large country like the United States was made up of people with many different interests. A stable, strong government would come from the compromises that would have to be made among these different interests.

This mural of the signing of the United States Constitution can be seen in the Capitol in Washington, D.C. William Blount, Hugh Williamson, and Richard Dobbs Spaight signed for North Carolina.

The delegates themselves had to make several compromises during that hot Philadelphia summer. A **compromise** is a way to settle disagreements in which each side gives way a little in its demands. According to the Virginia Plan, Congress would be divided into two houses. The members of the lower house would be elected by the people. The larger a state's population, the more representatives it would have. Members of the upper house would be elected by the lower house. But the smaller states feared that the larger states would control the legislative branch if the number of representatives were based only on population. They proposed the *New Jersey Plan* by which each state would send the same number of representatives to Congress. Those representatives would be elected by the state legislatures.

The delegates agreed that representation in the lower house of Congress (called the **House of Representatives**) would be based on population. They also agreed that state legislatures would elect members of the upper house (the **Senate**). But the smaller states wanted each state to have the same number of representatives in the Senate. The convention remained deadlocked on that issue for weeks. Finally, it reached a compromise. The delegates agreed that the states would have equal representation in the Senate. A state's two senators, however, could vote as individuals rather than as a unit. And all bills that involved providing money for the government must begin in the lower house. North Carolina supported what was called "The Great Compromise."

OTHER COMPROMISES

Another issue divided the convention along north-south lines. Delegates from southern states with large slave populations wanted representation in the House determined by the total population—both black and white. Delegates from northern states with no or few slaves wanted only free people counted. The matter was decided by counting five slaves as three instead of five persons. That decision became known as the *three-fifths compromise.*

The three-fifths compromise gave the South greater representation in Congress. It also gave the South a greater voice in the selection of the president since the size of each state's congressional delegation determined the number of its electoral votes. Slavery was never specifically mentioned in the **U.S. Constitution**; nevertheless, it was protected. The Constitution would not allow Congress to stop the "importation of such persons as any of the states should think proper to admit" (slaves) for twenty years. The fugitive workers clause ordered that runaway slaves be returned to their masters.

The convention made the president commander-in-chief of the armed forces and responsible for relations with other countries. The president was also given the power to appoint judges and other federal officials. North Carolina, however, was suspicious of presidential powers. Its delegates opposed a presidential veto but favored a long term of office. A **veto** is the power to refuse to approve something, in this case, bills passed by Congress. When the convention settled on a four-year term for the president and the possibility of re-election, North Carolina cast the only "no" vote.

Hugh Williamson, one of North Carolina's three signers of the U.S. Constitution, took an active part in the debates on the document. He did all he could to promote the nation's westward expansion.

North Carolina's delegates did not play leading parts in the convention. In fact, most of them were nearly invisible. Only Hugh Williamson took an active role. He made seventy-three speeches, served on five committees, and offered numerous motions. Williamson made two important recommendations for the presidency. First, Williamson introduced the idea of impeachment of the president for not carrying out the duties of the office. **Impeachment** is the act of charging a public official with wrongdoing while that official is still in office. Second, he suggested that a two-thirds majority be necessary to override a presidential veto. Both of these recommendations were adopted.

On September 17, 1787, thirty-nine of the forty-two members of the convention still present signed the completed Constitution. William Blount (with coaxing from Benjamin Franklin), Hugh Williamson, and Richard Dobbs Spaight signed for North Carolina. (Davie and Martin had left Philadelphia several weeks earlier.) Later that month, the Confederation Congress sent the Constitution to the states for approval. For the Constitution to go into effect, special conventions in nine of the states had to approve it. Qualified voters were to elect delegates to these state conventions. Unlike the Articles of Confederation, this new Constitution would be decided on by the people. The stage was set for a ferocious battle to ratify the Constitution.

William Blount also signed the U.S. Constitution for North Carolina. He played a key role in the early history of Tennessee as a governor and United States senator.

THE STRUGGLE FOR RATIFICATION

Arguments over the Constitution occurred throughout the nation. Minor differences in the convention became major differences as each state discussed the new "plan of Government." This new government would be stronger because it had certain powers that the Confederation government had not had. A government in which the states are united under a strong central government is called a *federal system*. **Federalists** (those who favored the Constitution) and **Antifederalists** (those who opposed it) carried on a sharp debate in newspapers and pamphlets.

The Federalists' strength lay in the towns and plantation areas of eastern North Carolina. Large slaveholding planters, merchants, and professional men wanted a stronger federal (national) government. Hugh Williamson, James Iredell, and William R. Davie were among those. The Antifederalists' strength lay in the backcountry, where small farmers felt that a strong government would destroy states' rights and threaten individual liberties. Willie Jones, Thomas Person, and Timothy Bloodworth were the leaders of the Antifederalists in North Carolina. Bloodworth warned that the proposed system of government would restore a monarchy. Person described the U.S. Constitution as "impracticable & dangerous."

THE HILLSBOROUGH CONVENTION

The campaign to choose delegates to the state's ratification convention was bitter and sometimes violent. In Kinston, the Federalists attacked election officials and stole the ballot box.

When the ratification convention gathered at Hillsborough in July 1788, the Antifederalists held a huge majority. Ten states—one more than necessary—had already ratified the Constitution when the convention began. Within days, New York became the eleventh state to ratify it. Only North Carolina and Rhode Island remained outside the Union.

For eleven days, the delegates at the Hillsborough convention debated the Constitution. As Willie Jones observed, however, "all the delegates knew how they were going to vote." Samuel Spencer led the Antifederalist attack, while James Iredell defended the Constitution. Iredell, an Edenton lawyer, argued that the "disordered and distracted" conditions in the country required a "united, vigorous government." The Antifederalists feared Congress's power to levy taxes and resented distant federal officials who would be far removed from the voters. Above all, the Antifederalists objected that there was no bill of rights such as the one included in the state's constitution.

In the end, the convention voted 184 to 83 *not* to ratify the Constitution. But the delegates did send Congress a "Declaration of Rights" composed of twenty separate articles. The convention demanded that Congress amend the Constitution to include a bill of rights before North Carolina would ratify it.

NORTH CAROLINA JOINS THE UNION

North Carolina's refusal to ratify the Constitution was a bold and brave act. But North Carolina did not remain out of the Union long. In November 1789, a second ratification convention met in Fayetteville. This time, the convention voted 194 to 77 to ratify the U.S. Constitution.

No one has ever fully explained how the vote was turned completely around in little more than a year. Politically, North Carolina had little choice. James Madison had introduced in Congress the **Bill of Rights**, the first ten amendments to the U.S. Constitution. No state had yet ratified them by November 1789; that would come in 1791. The election of George Washington as the first president of the United States no doubt made many North Carolinians proud. North Carolina clearly expected to become part of the Union. When Governor Samuel Johnston and the Council of State sent their congratulations to the newly elected president in 1789, they told Washington:

Though this state be not yet a member of the union under the new form of government, we look forward with the pleasing hope of its shortly becom-

*Top: Federalist James Iredell fought hard for the ratification of the Constitution in North Carolina. President George Washington appointed him to the United States Supreme Court in 1790. **Above:** Antifederalist Willie Jones opposed the Constitution. Even after its ratification, Jones believed too much power rested in the hands of President Washington.*

ing such; and in the mean time consider ourselves bound in a common interest and affection with the other states, waiting only for the happy event of such alterations being proposed as will remove the apprehensions of many of the good citizens of this state, for those liberties for which they have fought and suffered in common with others.

In 1789 North Carolina's second ratification convention met in this building, called the "State House," in Fayetteville. The General Assembly also met there several times in the 1780s.

In reply, Washington told North Carolina that its concerns were being addressed. Washington declared that free men, driven "by an equally laudable and sacred regard for the liberties of their country," could not be faulted for "a difference of opinion on political points." North Carolina's stand against ratification of the Constitution without a bill of rights impressed Washington. His gracious response showed that North Carolina's concerns were reasonable and serious. The vote for ratification at Fayetteville was not unexpected. The exchange between North Carolina officials and President Washington had smoothed the way. With Rhode Island's ratification in 1790, all thirteen states belonged to the Union.

Do You Remember?
1. What was the purpose of the convention in Philadelphia in 1787?
2. Why did James Madison propose a system of checks and balances among the three branches of the government?
3. How was the disagreement about representation in Congress resolved?
4. How was the question of counting slaves for representation settled?
5. What two important recommendations on the presidency did Hugh Williamson make?
6. How did the Federalists and the Antifederalists differ?

CHAPTER · REVIEW

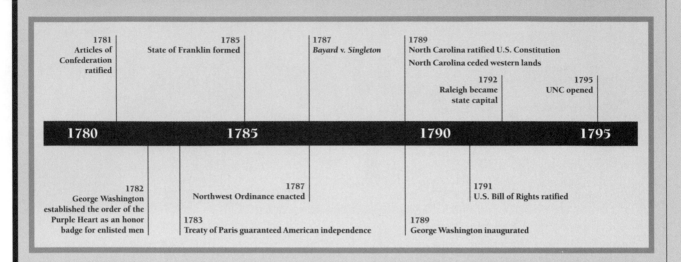

| 1781 Articles of Confederation ratified | 1785 State of Franklin formed | 1787 *Bayard v. Singleton* | 1789 North Carolina ratified U.S. Constitution / North Carolina ceded western lands | | |
| | | | 1792 Raleigh became state capital | 1795 UNC opened | |

1780 **1785** **1790** **1795**

| 1782 George Washington established the order of the Purple Heart as an honor badge for enlisted men | 1787 Northwest Ordinance enacted | 1791 U.S. Bill of Rights ratified |
| | 1783 Treaty of Paris guaranteed American independence | 1789 George Washington inaugurated |

Reviewing People, Places, and Terms

Use each of the following terms in a sentence.

Antifederalists
Articles of Confederation
Bill of Rights
compromise
Federalists
states' rights
U.S. Constitution

Understanding the Facts

1. How did the American Revolution affect North Carolina's economy?
2. Why was the decision in *Bayard v. Singleton* so important?
3. Where and when did the first state university in the United States open?
4. Why was there tension between westerners and easterners in North Carolina?
5. What were some of the problems with the Articles of Confederation?
6. Why didn't the state of Franklin succeed?
7. Which of North Carolina's five delegates was the most active at the Constitutional Convention?
8. Three men from North Carolina's delegation signed the U.S. Constitution. Who were they?
9. What was the final decision of the Hillsborough Convention?
10. What was the outcome of the ratification convention in Fayetteville?

Developing Critical Thinking

1. Why do you think the smaller states were politically afraid of states with more land?
2. Why do you think large slave holders and people in towns were generally in favor of a strong federal government?
3. In July 1788, North Carolina voted not to ratify the U.S. Constitution. A little over a year later, the vote was reversed. Why do you think the change of heart took place?
4. What do you think the impact on history might have been if the U.S. Constitution had forbidden the importation of slaves in 1787?

Applying Your Skills

1. Raleigh was chosen as the state capital because it was a more central location. Determine how far your hometown is from Raleigh.

2. North Carolina's modern state flag has several dates on it. Research the significance of those dates and prepare a report on your findings. Using fabric or a large sheet of paper, construct a copy of our state flag.

3. Prepare a report on the U.S. Constitution's first ten amendments—the Bill of Rights. Discuss how those ten rights affect our society's everyday life.

4. Assume that you are a citizen of North Carolina in 1787. Write a "letter to the editor" of a local newspaper telling why you believe North Carolina should, or should not, ratify the new federal Constitution.

Making Connections

1. Our language is constantly changing. Make a list of at least twenty-five words that have been added to our language over the past ten years.

2. How did Noah Webster's Blue-Backed Speller contribute to the growth of nationalism in the United States?

3. How do we exhibit nationalism today? Give five examples.

4. Patriot leaders who thought that citizens could govern themselves and not abuse public privileges for private gain were considered "radicals." Why do you think that was so?

Tar Heel Trivia

- The new capital of the state of North Carolina was named for Sir Walter Raleigh.

- None of the towns that served as the state capital before 1794 had adequate facilities for the General Assembly. In 1780, so few legislators showed up that there was no quorum.

- In her court case, Mrs. Elizabeth Bayard was represented by Samuel Johnston, William R. Davie, and James Iredell.

- Before North Carolina ceded its western lands, the General Assembly set up seven counties there. The county seat of one of those counties was named Nashville, in honor of General Francis Nash.

- Benjamin Latrobe, who designed the first capitol of North Carolina, also designed the U.S. Capitol in Washington.

⚬ BUILDING SKILLS: REACHING COMPROMISES ⚬

Americans have always had a knack for compromising between tough choices and almost impossible deadlocks between opposing points of view. The alternatives to not being able to reach a compromise can be lack of progress, indecision, and, in some cases, violent action.

America has sometimes been referred to as a "great melting pot" containing nationalities, social and political viewpoints, and religions from around the world. Certainly, the ability and willingness of Americans to reach compromises have helped our country survive and grow.

This chapter contains several references to several compromises that took place at the Constitutional Convention in 1787. Review how the differing viewpoints were resolved through compromise at the convention. Did any of the compromises cause a problem?

What might have happened without compromise? Do compromises ever leave basic problems unresolved?

As citizens of the United States, we all must make compromises. Almost daily, we must give-and-take with our fellow citizens in order to coexist. It is important, though, that we recognize that there are some areas of our lives—our basic values—that cannot be compromised. As citizens, we realize that there are parts of our constitutional democracy that we cannot compromise. What issues are not open to compromise in our society? What types of compromises are necessary for us to be able to exist in society? Would life as we know it be possible without compromise? Are there times when compromise is just not possible? Why are respect, open-mindedness, tolerance, and patience important qualities to have when making compromises?

CHAPTER ELEVEN

NORTH CAROLINA IN THE NEW NATION

The first ship to be named USS North Carolina *was built in Philadelphia. Launched in 1820, it remained in service until 1839.*

If Congress can make canals they can with more propriety emancipate. Be not deceived, I speak soberly in the fear of God, and the love of the constitution. Let not love of improvement, or a thirst for glory blind that sound common sense, with which the Lord has blessed you...your error in this, will injure if not destroy our beloved mother N. Carolina and all the South country. [A]dd not to the constitution nor take therefrom.

—Nathaniel Macon

NORTH CAROLINA JOINED THE UNION RELUCTANTLY. Although suspicious of a strong central government, North Carolinians were willing to give Washington's administration a try. However, they soon found themselves at odds with the policies (official plans) of the new federal government. North Carolinians turned away from federalism and returned to the more comfortable and familiar belief in small, decentralized national government.

By doing so, North Carolina paid an ecomomic and social price. The state did not keep up with the economic, social, and political advances taking place elsewhere in the nation. In the early 1800s, North Carolina was known as the "Rip Van Winkle" state. In those same decades, however, voices of reform began to be heard.

THE FIRST PARTY SYSTEM

President Washington had two strong men in his **cabinet** (group of advisors). Around these men two political parties formed. Alexander Hamilton of New York was the secretary of the treasury. Thomas Jefferson of Virginia was secretary of state.

Terms: cabinet, Republicans, Whiskey Rebellion, embargo, War Hawks, Rip Van Winkle state, internal improvements, illiterate, census, Great Revival

People: Alexander Hamilton, Thomas Jefferson, Nathaniel Macon, the Prophet, Archibald DeBow Murphey

Alexander Hamilton believed in a strong central government. Around his policies the Federalist party took shape.

DIFFERENT VIEWS, DIFFERENT PARTIES

Brilliant and ambitious, Hamilton was born in the British West Indies. As a result, he was not a supporter of states' rights. His loyalties were to the nation and to Washington, whom he looked up to like a father. As secretary of the treasury, Hamilton developed policies to strengthen the national government, often at the expense of the states. For example, he wished to set up a national bank, the Bank of the United States. This bank would lend money to the federal government and issue paper currency. It would also make the government stronger. The Constitution did not expressly (definitely) give the federal government the power to do this. But Hamilton argued that since the Constitution gave Congress the power to regulate the supply of money, it had the power to establish the bank.

Thomas Jefferson, however, believed that the Constitution must be strictly interpreted. Jefferson was, of course, the main author of the Declaration of Independence. He believed in individual rights and a weak central government. Any powers not clearly given to the federal government, he insisted, belonged to the states.

In the case of the national bank, Hamilton's views won out. In 1791, Congress chartered the Bank of the United States. But the lines had been drawn between Federalists, led by Washington and Hamilton, and **Republicans** led by Jefferson and James Madison. This political division established the nation's first two-party system.

The split between Federalists and Republicans was not just a difference of opinion over how strong the central government should be. Jefferson and Madison had, in fact, favored ratification of the Constitution. The Republicans were strong in the middle and southern states. In the South, slaveholding planters supported the Republicans, but so did yeoman farmers and artisans. Republicans were in favor of opening western lands to settlers and wanted more people to take part in government. When war broke out between France and Great Britain in 1793, the Republicans leaned toward supporting France, where the French Revolution had begun in 1789.

The Federalists were concentrated mostly in New England. They wished to restore ties with Great Britain, hated France and the French Revolution, and wanted to increase the power of the United States abroad. Believing in order, regularity, and authority in politics, the Federalists had little interest in democracy. They did not want to involve ordinary people in government.

NORTH CAROLINA POLITICS

North Carolina's political parties followed the same patterns. Republicans were strong everywhere in the state, especially in a line of counties along the Virginia border where there were many slaveholders and

BENJAMIN BANNEKER

Benjamin Banneker was born in 1731 in Baltimore County, Maryland, the son and grandson of free blacks. His maternal grandmother, Molly Welsh, was a white English indentured servant who taught him how to read.

While still in his early twenties, Banneker constructed a unique wooden striking clock even though he had never before seen one. While making a living as a tobacco farmer, Banneker taught himself mathematics and experimented with mechanical devices. He was past the age of forty when a Quaker neighbor lent him several instruments and books on astronomy. Turning his attention from the soil to the heavens, Banneker taught himself astronomy.

In 1789, his skills as a mathematician won him attention and a position on the three-man commission that surveyed the District of Columbia. That commission laid out the boundaries and the streets for the nation's new capital.

Meanwhile Banneker continued his mathematical calculations for an almanac bearing his name. Banneker's first almanac appeared in 1791, and five others followed. The almanacs received wide distribution. Aside from his astronomical calculations, Banneker commented on social issues and on bees and locusts. He correctly predicted a seventeen-year cycle for plagues of locusts.

Banneker sent his first almanac to then-Secretary of State Thomas Jefferson, with a letter denouncing slavery. Jefferson, a slaveholder, failed to appreciate Banneker's self-taught mathematical skills. Banneker overcame difficult obstacles to earn distinction as a mathematician and astronomer.

Benjamin Banneker's
PENNSYLVANIA, DELAWARE, MARY-
LAND, AND VIRGINIA
ALMANAC,
FOR THE
YEAR of our LORD 1795;
Being the Third after Leap-Year.

PHILADELPHIA:
Printed for WILLIAM GIBBONS, Cherry Street

A free black, Benjamin Banneker gained recognition as a farmer, mathematician, astronomer, and surveyor. He also published a well-known almanac.

plantations. Federalists were strong in towns and commercial areas of North Carolina. Until the end of the War of 1812, Fayetteville, Salisbury, and New Bern often elected Federalist congressmen.

The leading Federalists in North Carolina were James Iredell and William R. Davie. In 1790, President Washington appointed Iredell to the Supreme Court. Iredell served as an associate justice for nine years until his death in 1799. He is best remembered for his dissenting (disagreeing) opinion in the case of *Chisholm v. Georgia* (1793). Iredell argued that individual citizens could not sue a state in a federal court. That principle became the Eleventh Amendment to the U.S. Constitution in 1798.

When farmers bitterly protested a tax on whiskey, the Whiskey Rebellion broke out in Pennsylvania. North Carolina farmers also resisted the tax.

THE WHISKEY REBELLION

North Carolinians soon began to change their minds about federalism. This was clearly seen in the new nation's first great domestic crisis. In 1791, Congress passed a tax, called an *excise*, on whiskey made in the United States. The excise tax was one way Alexander Hamilton hoped to raise money for the government. Farmers were outraged and refused to pay the tax. Their protest became known as the **Whiskey Rebellion**. Farmers objected to the tax because they used whiskey as an article of barter. In frontier areas, especially the backcountry and mountains, it was easier to turn grain into whiskey than to get it to market over bad roads. Farmers, of course, didn't want to be taxed for making their whiskey. The farmers in western Pennsylvania resisted the tax. President Washington had to send federal troops in 1794 to put down the rebellion.

North Carolinians also resisted the tax. At one point, Secretary Hamilton even thought about sending federal troops to North Carolina to enforce the tax. In 1792, it was reported: "Some Riots have prevailed in the country during the Summer & Autumn, occasioned by the Excise law, which the Citizens dislike very much & are determined in many places to resist collection . . . ." In another incident, angry farmers threatened to grind off one tax collector's nose.

In 1802, at the request of President Thomas Jefferson, Congress repealed all excise taxes. But the damage had already been done to the Federalist party in North Carolina. The whiskey tax drove many North Carolina Federalists out of office. Others changed parties and became Republicans. Richard Hugg King had been the excise officer for the western part of North Carolina. When he tried to run for the legislature as a Federalist, he was humiliated and called names.

FROM FEDERALIST TO REPUBLICAN

The Federalists' problems in foreign policy (the government's plan of action toward other countries) also led to the party's decline in North Carolina. In 1794, the United States and Great Britain signed Jay's Treaty, which for a time lowered the tensions between the two countries. Unfortunately, it did not prevent the British navy from stopping and searching American ships it thought were bound for France.

Jay's Treaty did cause problems with France. An undeclared war on the high seas broke out between France and the United States in 1798. President John Adams appointed William R. Davie to a three-man commission to talk to Napoleon and end the conflict. In 1800, the United States and France signed the Convention of 1800, which ended the alliance held with France since 1778. France, however, refused to pay damages for the 2,300 American ships it had seized.

During the undeclared war with France, the Federalists were briefly in power in the legislature. Federalists also gained the governorship with the election of William R. Davie in 1798 and Benjamin Williams in 1799. However, after that time, Republicans dominated state government. North Carolinians disliked taxes and they disliked a strong central government. Republicans believed in cutting government spending. They interpreted the Constitution very narrowly and favored states' rights over federal power.

No politician better stood for the Republican beliefs than Warren County's Nathaniel Macon. He was elected to the House of Representatives in 1791 and to the U. S. Senate in 1815. In all, he served thirty-seven years in Congress, including the key post of Speaker of the House from 1801 to 1807.

Though a tobacco planter with seventy slaves, Macon lived a simple, plain life. He distrusted banks and an economy based on money, which he felt led to gambling. Macon believed in living debt-free, personally and as a nation: "Whoever is much in debt can hardly be perfectly free, he is dependent on his indebtors: and a nation in debt always has its strong arm of defense tied fast...." A friend of farmers and an agrarian (farm) way of life, he questioned whether the United States could become a manufacturing nation under the Constitution.

Macon predicted that the national urge to expand would lead to ruin. He also feared science and technology and the improvements they made possible: steam power, canals, and so on. Quite simply, he hated change. He believed that anything the government did to promote internal improvements or industrialization would weaken states' rights and threaten slavery. He interpreted the Constitution so strictly that he even opposed Republican presidents Jefferson and Madison. Macon favored a weak, decentralized federal government with few powers.

Macon's greatest influence nationally was before the War of 1812. After that war, however, the nation started on a new course, one that Macon

Top: Benjamin Williams served as governor of the state from 1799 to 1802 and from 1807 to 1808. His mild federalism made it acceptable for Republicans to support him. ***Above:*** Nathaniel Macon of Warren County believed in a narrow interpretation of the Constitution. His views reflected North Carolina's strict Republican values.

THE LOUISIANA PURCHASE

THE LOUISIANA PURCHASE

By 1800, the United States was bursting its boundaries. Hundreds of thousands of Americans had poured into western territories in search of rich lands and fresh opportunities. The Ohio and Mississippi rivers became highways of commerce as farmers floated their produce to the port of New Orleans.

Whoever owned Louisiana controlled the destiny of the United States. In 1763, Spain had received Louisiana from France. Spain's transfer of Louisiana back to France in 1802 greatly alarmed Americans. France's leader, Napoleon, wanted to spread French influence throughout Europe. Would he also try to re-establish the French empire in the New World?

In 1803, President Thomas Jefferson sent James Monroe to France to join the negotiations to purchase New Orleans. When Monroe arrived, he learned to his astonishment that France was ready to sell *all* of Louisiana (827,000 square miles) to the United States for $15 million. Monroe and Robert Livingston signed a treaty for a vast uncharted region stretching from the Gulf of Mexico to present-day Minnesota.

The Louisiana Purchase doubled the size of the United States and opened the way for westward expansion across the continent. Ironically, the Constitution contained no clear language about acquiring new territory and attaching it to the nation. Jefferson, who had argued for a strict interpretation of the Constitution, now took a broader view. He said that he had exercised the president's implied powers to safeguard the nation.

feared. In the meantime, the United States found itself fighting a second war of independence.

Do You Remember?

1. What principle did James Iredell support as a Supreme Court justice that later became part of the U.S. Constitution?
2. What were two reasons North Carolinians seemed to favor the Republicans during this time?

WAR OF 1812

In 1801, President Thomas Jefferson declared in his first inaugural speech: "Peace, commerce, and honest friendship with all nations, entangling alliances with none." Unfortunately, the United States found it very difficult to remain neutral while much of the world was at war.

INCREASING TENSIONS

The undeclared naval war with France was only one of the problems that tested the young nation's ability to survive. Between 1793 and 1815, France and Great Britain were almost always at war. American merchants were caught in the middle as both France and Great Britain tried to block the United States from trading with the other. Great Britain, which had the world's largest navy, even "impressed" American sailors; that is, it took the sailors off of American ships and made them serve in the Royal navy. Finally, in 1807, President Jefferson began an **embargo**, which stopped all trade with foreign countries. President Jefferson hoped to stop Great Britain and France from seizing American ships. However, the embargo was very unpopular and, in the end, it was ignored.

Americans were angrier at Great Britain than at France. The Royal navy controlled the Atlantic Ocean. Americans also believed that Great Britain was stirring up the tribes in the new states and territories beyond the Appalachian Mountains. In Congress, a group of land-hungry southerners and westerners known as the **War Hawks** wanted the United States to declare war on Great Britain. They hoped to capture Canada and to eliminate the British and Indian menace in the West.

Finally, in June 1812, President James Madison asked Congress to declare war on Great Britain. By a narrow vote, Congress agreed. It was not a good decision, for the nation was poorly prepared for war. Fortunately, the war had more skirmishes (minor fights) than battles.

Captain Johnston Blakeley won fame for his naval victories over the British in the War of 1812. Blakeley disappeared with his ship, the Wasp.

NORTH CAROLINA IN THE WAR

North Carolina was deeply divided about the war. Federalists, such as Congressman William Gaston of New Bern, spoke out against the war. Two of the state's Republican congressmen, Richard Stanford and William Kennedy, also opposed the war. North Carolina, however, was not really involved in the conflict. Few North Carolinians took part in any fighting.

The state's defenseless coast was the biggest worry. In July 1813, a British naval party landed at Ocracoke and Portsmouth but left after four days. About 7,000 men volunteered for the state militia. They were organized into eight regiments and divided evenly to defend the lower Cape Fear counties and the port at Beaufort. In 1814, when President Madison asked for 7,000 more men, they were sent to aid other states.

In 1814, the British burned much of Washington, including the Capitol and the White House. The cost in damages reached an estimated $1.5 million.

Though North Carolina remained largely on the edges of the war, several North Carolinians are remembered for their actions. Lieutenant Colonel Benjamin Forsyth of Stokes County took part in a number of battles along the Canadian border. In February 1813, using sleighs to cross snow and frozen rivers, Forsyth led a raid against Elizabethtown in Canada. He took 51 prisoners and captured more than 100 weapons without losing a man. He was killed at the battle of Odelltown in Canada in 1814. Captain Johnston Blakeley commanded the ships *Enterprise* and *Wasp*. The *Wasp*, which carried 22 guns and 173 men, raided British shipping in the English Channel and won major victories over two British warships. On the way back to the United States with a prize cargo, however, the *Wasp* mysteriously disappeared. Otway Burns, an Onslow County ship captain and shipbuilder, made a fortune as a privateer. He stopped British merchant ships from Newfoundland to South America and brought back valuable supplies for the war.

Two other North Carolinians played important roles during the War of 1812. In 1814, the British entered Washington and burned the Capitol and the White House, the president's residence. Dolley Payne Madison of Guilford County was the president's wife. She saved a portrait of George Washington and other valuable items before the British arrived. Andrew Jackson, born along the North Carolina-South Carolina border, was the hero of the Battle of New Orleans. Oddly, the battle was fought in January 1815, two weeks *after* a peace treaty was signed. Nevertheless, Jackson became a national hero.

THE EFFECTS OF THE WAR

The Treaty of Ghent, signed in Belgium in December 1814, ended the War of 1812. However, it settled none of the main issues of the war. The treaty restored everything to what it had been before the war. Although the United States did not gain anything, it did show that it was willing to fight for its independence. The experience also convinced the United States to stay away from European politics.

Again, the war was very hard on Native Americans. In 1813, at the Battle of Horseshoe Bend in present-day Alabama, Andrew Jackson and his Tennessee and Cherokee volunteers defeated the Creek nation. That victory opened the Mississippi Territory to white settlement. In the Old Northwest Territory above the Ohio River, two Shawnee chiefs and brothers, the Prophet and Tecumseh, tried to organize Indian resistance to white expansion. That resistance fell apart when the Prophet was beaten at Tippecanoe. Tecumseh then chose to fight on the side of the British and was killed in the Battle of the Thames (Moraviantown).

The Federalist party was perhaps the war's biggest loser. The New England Federalists had always opposed "Mr. Madison's war." In December 1814, they met in Hartford, Connecticut, to discuss making changes in the Constitution and perhaps withdrawing from the Union. Such talk disgraced the Federalists when word of the Treaty of Ghent and Jackson's victory arrived. The party never recovered.

Other results of the war were harder to see. The war started a change in the economy. When Americans could not get goods from abroad during the war, they were forced to make them. This increasing emphasis on manufacturing would have far-reaching effects on industry, transportation, and the economy—everywhere, that is, except in North Carolina.

Two North Carolinians played heroic roles in the War of 1812. Dolley Madison (top) saved many valuable items before the British set fire to the White House. Andrew Jackson (above) and his troops won the Battle of New Orleans.

Do You Remember?

1. What were some reasons that Americans were angry at Great Britain during this period?
2. Why was the decision to declare war on Great Britain probably not a good one?

THE RIP VAN WINKLE STATE

In the early 1800s, North Carolina earned a reputation as the **Rip Van Winkle state**. (Rip Van Winkle, a character in a story by Washington Irving, fell asleep for twenty years.) During the early 1800s, the state "fell asleep" and fell behind the rest of the nation in agriculture, transportation, manufacturing, and education. And few North Carolinians seemed interested in improving the state's social and economic conditions.

In 1835, a Raleigh newspaper included a funny story about a fictional character named Squire Oldway. No one could persuade the squire that an improved transportation system would be good for the state. "The fact is," said the squire, "I am perfectly satisfied with things as they are; and why do you want to make me any happier?" Concluded the squire, "No, no, give me the *oldways* yet."

Nathaniel Macon had said almost the same thing in a Senate debate in 1820: "why depart from the good old way, which has kept us in quiet, peace, and harmony...? Why leave the road of experience, which has satisfied all, and made all happy...?"

RESISTING CHANGE

These attitudes were a result of North Carolina's agrarian way of life. The state was controlled by eastern planters who depended on slave labor and who had already developed good markets for their crops in Virginia and South Carolina. Because representation in the state legislature was the same for all counties, no matter what size or population, the easterners kept firm control over state government. Even though the legislature created many new counties, more than half remained in the east. This was plainly unfair to the west, which by 1830 had more people.

Top: North Carolina's bad roads made it difficult for farmers to get their crops to market. ***Above:*** Governor John Motley Morehead understood that better roads and transportation, including railroads, would be necessary to improve economic conditions for all North Carolinians.

The east was able to block every effort by the west to reform state government or to make internal improvements. **Internal improvements** meant better roads, canals to transport agricultural products and other goods, better navigation of the state's rivers and shallow sounds, and eventually railroads.

In the Piedmont and the Mountains, farmers were largely able to take care of their own needs. They tended small farms without slave labor. But these western farmers were landlocked. They couldn't use the rivers because they were not completely navigable; there were too many rapids. Raising cash crops was impractical because it was difficult to get them to market. In 1842, Governor John Motley Morehead observed that it cost a farmer one-half the value of his crop just to transport the other half to market.

Industry was little better. In 1815, the state had only one cotton mill, three paper mills, and twenty-three iron works. To expand manufacturing meant more money was needed for new factories. The state had water power and raw materials, but there were few people willing to take the risk. As the growing of cotton spread in the eastern and southern counties, a few spinning mills appeared in Lincoln County, Rocky Mount, Greensboro, Salem, and Alamance Creek. By 1840, twenty-five cotton mills were operating in twelve counties. But the mills made cloth for local use. It was too difficult to reach larger markets.

The state could do little to help. Some revenue was collected in taxes. But North Carolinians were against taxes for any purpose. They paid very low poll and land taxes. In 1834, Governor David L. Swain noted that the cost of running the General Assembly was more than the combined costs of all other departments of state government. There were no funds left over for roads, public improvements, or schools.

In 1840, one-third of all white adults in North Carolina were **illiterate**; that is, they could not read or write. Education was considered a private matter, one the state should not get involved in. Even the University of North Carolina educated less than one hundred students a year. The

Above: Governor David L Swain, a westerner, realized that few improvements in education and transportation could be made until North Carolinians were willing to pay more taxes. *Left:* This map of North Carolina in 1830 shows how eastern counties outnumbered western ones. That meant eastern politicians held most of the power in the state.

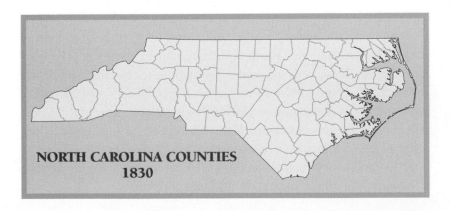

NORTH CAROLINA COUNTIES 1830

By 1840 about twenty-five cotton mills operated in North Carolina. Shown here is the Schenck-Warlick cotton factory near Lincolnton.

president of the university, Joseph Caldwell, sadly noted that North Carolina's "habits of legislation" had long neglected the education of its people. Even more disturbing to Caldwell, people sometimes boasted of their ignorance.

MOVING TO GREENER PASTURES

Life in North Carolina held little promise for many people. Thousands left. Many moved to new territories in the West where they could enjoy a more democratic government and economic opportunity. Many anti-slavery Quakers migrated north of the Ohio River. Tennessee, Georgia, Alabama, and Indiana were popular destinations for North Carolinians.

The decade of the 1830s saw the heaviest migration. North Carolina's population grew only 2 percent during that decade, compared to 15 percent in other decades. According to the 1850 census, about 300,000 free, native North Carolinians lived elsewhere in the United States. The 1860 census revealed more than 400,000 North Carolinians living elsewhere. (A **census** is an official, actual count of the population.)

Fifty years after the American Revolution, North Carolina remained rural, isolated, conservative, and poor. Worse, the people did not seem to have the energy or the vision to improve conditions for themselves or their children. A legislative committee reported in 1830 that North Carolina was

> a State without foreign commerce, for want of seaports, or a staple; without internal communication by rivers, roads, or canals; without a cash market for any article of agricultural product; without manufactures; in short without any object to which native industry and active enterprise could be directed.

Do You Remember?
1. Why was North Carolina called the Rip Van Winkle state?
2. How was the eastern part of the state able to control the state government during this time?
3. Why did people begin to move away from North Carolina?

VOICES OF REFORM

Not everyone was satisfied with the conditions in North Carolina. Two voices tried to wake the Rip Van Winkle state from its slumber. One was the voice of religion calling for spiritual renewal.

THE GREAT REVIVAL

During the 1700s, travelers had often commented on the lack of religion in North Carolina. In the early 1800s, however, evangelical Protestantism swept through the South. That burst of highly personal, highly emotional religious activity was known as the **Great Revival**. It began in the lowest ranks of society and bubbled upward.

The roots of the Great Revival went back to the 1700s. Baptists first brought revivalism to North Carolina in the 1750s. After 1784, Methodist circuit riders (clergymen with regular routes) fanned out across the South to bring religion to isolated settlements. The most famous of those roving preachers was Francis Asbury. Presbyterians also adopted revivalism to bring in new members.

Huge camp meetings gathered to hear preachers rail against the pleasure-seeking, luxury-loving, corrupt, and irreligious upper classes. Evangelicalism gave people a sense of community and self-esteem. The democratic nature of evangelicalism challenged the power of the upper class. This was most evident in its approach to blacks. Slaves were caught up in the religious intensity of the revivals. Baptists and Methodists preached about the brotherhood of man, regardless of race or social class.

Francis Asbury, the most famous of the roving Methodist ministers, visited North Carolina seventy-two times between 1780 and 1816. His antislavery views disturbed many slave owners.

In 1780 Francis Asbury preached to a congregation of about 200 people at William Courtney's "Yellow House" in Hillsborough.

In its early years, Methodism was openly antislavery. Together, blacks and whites worshiped, were converted, and even listened to black preachers.

By the 1820s, evangelicalism was well established in North Carolina. But sectional loyalties also began to reappear. More and more, religion in the South was used to defend and justify slavery. The antislavery stand in the early years of the Great Revival gave way to proslavery beliefs.

THE MURPHEY PROGRAM

The second voice calling for reform came from a small group of upper-class planters, politicians, and educators who wished to put the state on a new course. Archibald DeBow Murphey, a state senator from Orange County, belonged in that group.

In 1815, Murphey prepared a series of reports on North Carolina's problems for the General Assembly. In those reports, Murphey also laid out a plan of reform. Murphey insisted that government must play a leading role in the development of the state. He called for a program of internal improvements, public education, constitutional reform, and drainage of swamplands.

Murphey believed the state's most pressing need was for internal improvements. The state needed a system of land and water transportation that would bring both domestic and foreign trade to North Carolina's towns and ports. He suggested that the inlets at Ocracoke and Beaufort be deepened. Major rivers such as the Roanoke, Tar, Neuse, Cape Fear, Yadkin, Catawba, and French Broad should be cleared to make them more navigable. Canals should be built to connect Wilmington with the state's major rivers in the Coastal Plain and Piedmont. A new road system was needed to tie all of these together. Improved roads would allow farmers to bring their produce to towns on navigable rivers. Draining swamps in the east would provide more rich farmlands. Agriculture would flourish and towns would prosper. Murphey believed the state government had to coordinate this program because individuals, private companies, and county governments could not.

Murphey also called for public education for all white children. Under his plan, each county would have two or more primary schools. Those schools would teach three years of reading, writing, and arithmetic. Ten regional academies would teach classical languages, mathematics, geography, and history to prepare young men for the university. Both state and local funds would be used to support the schools. Poor children would attend for free, while others would pay tuition. Though Murphey's plan discriminated against (was unfair to) white girls and black children, it recognized the importance of education in a democratic society. In Murphey's words, "In a government, therefore, which rests upon the public virtue, no efforts should be spared to diffuse public instruction. . . ."

Murphey's plan for reform included revising the state constitution. He called for a convention that would address the problems in the state constitution. In particular, he believed that the unequal representation in the General Assembly had to be changed.

North Carolina adopted some parts of Murphey's program. The state did hire an engineer, Hamilton Fulton. Between 1819 and 1825, Fulton made a number of surveys for internal improvements. When the state did nothing about his reports, he resigned. In 1825, North Carolina established a Literary Fund, which was to create "common schools" for the education of white children. The fund, however, was too small, and the state treasurer often used the money in the fund to pay other expenses. The General Assembly did little to promote public education.

When Archibald DeBow Murphey died in 1832, he probably felt that his plans and labors had failed. His grand vision nevertheless had given North Carolina a blueprint for progress.

Archibald D. Murphey was the leading voice of reform in the state. His broad program for internal improvements gave the state a blueprint for the future.

Do You Remember?

1. What were the two voices of reform that tried to improve conditions in North Carolina?
2. What stand on slavery eventually came out of the Great Revival?
3. What four areas of improvement did the Murphey program call for?

PROMETHEUS: NORTH CAROLINA'S FIRST STEAMBOAT

The Prometheus *was the first steamship built in North Carolina. It operated out of Wilmington, seen here in the background.*

Otway Burns, a hero and privateer during the War of 1812, was also a shipbuilder. In early 1818, at his Swansboro shipyard, he began construction of the first steamboat to be built in North Carolina. It would be called the *Prometheus*, after the Titan who befriended mankind. The *Prometheus* was to operate on the Cape Fear River between Wilmington and Smithville (present-day Southport).

The citizens of North Carolina eagerly awaited this "first" for the state, and newspapers carried progress reports on its construction. Although steam-powered craft were relatively new, many people believed that they would soon ply the rivers of North Carolina — bringing prosperity along with them. In fact, there were already a few steamboats operating in North Carolina, but none had been built within the state.

The *Prometheus* was completed and arrived in Wilmington on June 10, 1818. It was a gala occasion, with the entire shoreline along the Wilmington waterfront crowded with citizens eager to catch a glimpse of the vessel. Burns was proudly standing on deck, smartly dressed in his naval uniform. As the *Prometheus* arrived, bells rang out, cannons were fired, and the crowd cheered wildly. Reports stated that celebrations lasted well into the evening.

On June 15, the *Prometheus* began its regular service on the Cape Fear River. Round-trip passage from Wilmington to Smithville cost passengers $2.00, weather permitting. Because she was underpowered, the vessel cruised at a speed of just 4 miles an hour, taking the better part of a day to reach Smithville from Wilmington.

In 1819, the *Prometheus* had its most famous passengers: President James Monroe and his Secretary of War John C. Calhoun. On April 12, the two men steamed down the Cape Fear River aboard the *Prometheus* on their way to inspect Fort Johnson the next day.

The *Prometheus* continued to ply the waters of the Cape Fear until sometime in 1825. No record exists of her fate. Was she scrapped? Did she sink? Or did she rot along the Wilmington or Smithville waterfront? What is certain is that no record exists of her activity after that year.

Otway Burns's popularity was great after the building of the vessel. He was elected to the North Carolina House of Commons in 1821 and to the Senate in 1828. He was so popular in the western portion of the state that the town of Burnsville, in Yancey County is named for him.

During the War of 1812, Otway Burns (left) commanded The Snapdragon. *He is buried in the Old Burying Ground in Beaufort. A cannon from* The Snapdragon *marks his grave (above).*

C H A P T E R · R E V I E W

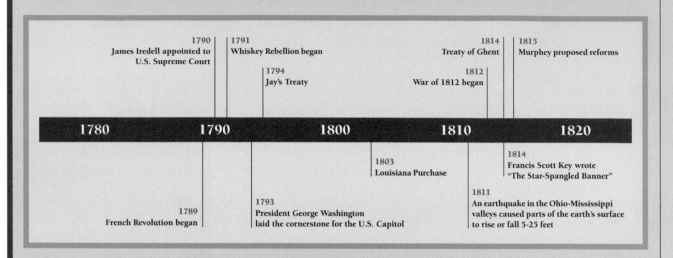

1790 James Iredell appointed to U.S. Supreme Court	1791 Whiskey Rebellion began		1814 Treaty of Ghent	1815 Murphey proposed reforms
	1794 Jay's Treaty		1812 War of 1812 began	

1780   1790   1800   1810   1820

1803 Louisiana Purchase

1814 Francis Scott Key wrote "The Star-Spangled Banner"

1811 An earthquake in the Ohio-Mississippi valleys caused parts of the earth's surface to rise or fall 5-25 feet

1789 French Revolution began

1793 President George Washington laid the cornerstone for the U.S. Capitol

Reviewing People, Places, and Terms

Match each word or phrase with the correct definition below.

cabinet
census
embargo
illiterate
Republicans
War Hawks

1. To stop all trade with a particular country
2. Group that wished to declare war on Great Britain in the early 1800s in order to seize Canada
3. An official, actual count of the population
4. Those who wished to open western lands to settlement and to involve more people in government
5. A group of advisors to the president
6. To be unable to read or write

Understanding the Facts

1. Who were the two strong leaders in President Washington's cabinet?
2. In what regions of the country did the Federalists and the Republicans have their greatest political support?
3. Who were the two early national leaders of the Republicans?
4. What early tax conflict damaged Federalist political power in North Carolina?
5. What North Carolinian was part of the commission that spoke with Napoleon and attempted to end the undeclared war between France and the United States?
6. The War Hawks who favored war with Great Britain were said to be "land hungry." What land did they want to add to the United States?
7. What was the basic result of the Treaty of Ghent?
8. When and why did Dolley Payne Madison, a North Carolinian and wife of President James Madison, save many historic items from being destroyed?
9. What effect did the War of 1812 have on Native Americans?
10. What was the purpose of the Literary Fund? How successful was it?

Developing Critical Thinking

1. Why do you think the Federalists "did not want to involve ordinary people in government"?

2. In what ways do you think Great Britain's ongoing war with France between 1793 and 1815 affected North Carolina?
3. What changes do you think were needed to awaken North Carolina from its Rip Van Winkle "sleep"?

Applying Your Skills

1. Read the Washington Irving story of "Rip Van Winkle." Compare that story to the conditions that existed in North Carolina during this period.
2. The treaty that formally ended the War of 1812 was signed in Ghent (or *Gent*). Locate Ghent on a world map.
3. An *excise tax* is a tax that is levied on the production, sale, or consumption of certain products. Research the products on which the government (state or national) currently collects an excise tax.
4. Many early cotton mills, grist mills, and factories relied on water power for energy to operate their machinery. Using books from your library, draw a diagram, construct a model, or prepare a short report that describes how water provided the power for early industry in North Carolina.

Making Connections

1. How did Benjamin Banneker's knowledge of mathematics help him lay out the District of Columbia?
2. Assume that you are a newspaper reporter in 1790. Write a brief news article about the accomplishments of Benjamin Banneker.
3. Which states came in total or in part from the Louisiana Purchase territory?
4. President Jefferson paid $15 million for the Louisiana territory, which was about 827,000 square miles. How much did he pay per square mile?

Tar Heel Trivia

- Forsythe County, created in 1849, was named for Benjamin Forsyth, a hero of the War of 1812.
- The Old Burying Ground in Beaufort contains the grave of War of 1812 naval hero Otway Burns.

BUILDING SKILLS: TRAVELING THROUGH TIME

You have the following task: For your vacation, you want to visit as many of the state's historic sites as you possibly can. There are, however, two important limits on your plans: time and money. As a result, you have determined that you can travel no more than 550 miles *round-trip* on your vacation.

Use a list of state historic sites and a North Carolina highway map to help you design your route. A student living in Jacksonville might, for instance, decide to begin the trip as follows:

Leave Jacksonville via US 258 and travel to Kinston to visit the Caswell Memorial and the *CSS Neuse* (41 miles). Leave Kinston on NC 55 and travel to Newton Grove (42 miles) to Bentonville Battleground.

Begin your trip from your starting point (your hometown or school). Visit as many sites as possible until you have used your allotted mileage. Remember—your mileage to return home must be included in your plans.

Present your vacation trip to the class by marking your route on a state highway map. After completing your trip plan, consider the following questions:

1. What parts of North Carolina history will you visit on your trip?
2. Were you able to see all the sites you wanted to see?
3. Did your starting point limit the number of sites you could include? If so, how?
4. Why do you think the state chose to make the sites you visited historic sites?
5. Is there a local site that you would like to nominate as a historic site? Why do you think it would make a good historic site?

UNIT 5

ANTEBELLUM
NORTH CAROLINA

THE ANTEBELLUM PERIOD (the years before the Civil War) was a period of prosperity and purpose in North Carolina. Guided by the ideas of Archibald D. Murphey, the state amended its constitution, making government more democratic and representative. The state also began to establish public schools, build railroads, and care for the unfortunate. Agriculture prospered, particularly cotton and tobacco. Crops were usually tended by slaves. Slaves' lives were harsh, but some laws did protect them.

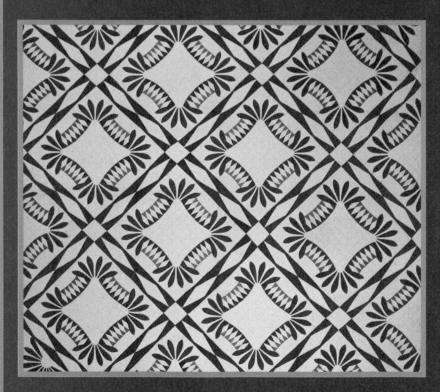

Right: One of the few grand mansions in antebellum North Carolina was Orton Plantation near Wilmington. Above: More typical of the state's small farmers was this quilt design celebrating the Whigs' defeat in 1852.

CHAPTER TWELVE

AN AGE OF REFORM

No more will [people] have to spend two days tugging through mud and over hills to visit our Capital; no more will our farmers have to endure the toil and exposure of wagoning, and expend all their profits in getting their produce to a market. The Iron Horse is now at their service, and time and space are almost annihilated. A brighter day, we trust, is dawning upon us.

—Hillsborough *Recorder*

I N THE MID-1830s, THE RIP VAN WINKLE STATE AWOKE. The Constitutional Convention of 1835 marked the beginning of an age of remarkable progress and reform. During the next quarter century, North Carolina moved toward becoming a state in which all of its citizens could share in its economic progress and its political democracy. Unfortunately, not all North Carolinians shared in the advances of those years. In particular, Native Americans, free blacks, and slaves experienced setbacks.

For many, the 1830s were an age of bright promise. The rise of a new political party set the stage for the changes that were to come.

THE EMERGENCE OF THE WHIG PARTY

After the War of 1812, the Federalist party collapsed. That left the Republicans in control of the political system. The Republicans were in power during the "Era of Good Feelings," the period of James Monroe's two terms as president (1817-1825). That era ended, however, with the presidential election of 1824.

THE ELECTION OF 1824

There were five candidates for president in 1824: Secretary of the Treasury William H. Crawford of Georgia, Secretary of State John Quincy Adams of Massachusetts, Secretary of War John C. Calhoun of South Carolina, Speaker of the House Henry Clay of Kentucky, and Senator Andrew Jackson of Tennessee. Calhoun later withdrew to run for vice

The stump speaker was a familiar sight in antebellum politics. Both the newly formed Whig party and the Democratic party tried to appeal to the common man.

THE MONROE DOCTRINE

Between 1808 and 1822, various colonies in Latin America, including Chile, Peru, Columbia, and Mexico, declared their independence from Spain. Many people in the United States wanted to recognize the independence of these former colonies, because they believed that Latin American patriots were carrying on the revolutionary traditions begun by the founding of the United States in 1776.

President James Monroe and Secretary of State John Quincy Adams were sympathetic but moved slowly. They distrusted Spanish, French, British, and Russian intentions in the New World. In 1822, the United States recognized the newly independent Latin American nations. To block European ambitions in the New World, Adams crafted the so-called Monroe Doctrine.

President Monroe presented the doctrine named after him to Congress on December 2, 1823. The doctrine had three principles. First, no European nation could establish colonies in the Western Hemisphere. The principle blocked Spain in Latin America and Russia on the West Coast. Second, no European nation could intervene in the affairs of independent nations of the New World. Third, Monroe promised that the United States would not interfere in European affairs, including any colonies Europe still owned in the New World.

The Monroe Doctrine became the foundation of American foreign policy in the Western Hemisphere. Americans viewed it as an assertion of their nationalism. In reality, it matched Great Britain's policies. The Royal Navy, not Monroe's words, gave force to the policy.

In a warning to European nations, President James Monroe stated that the American continents were closed to "future colonization by any European powers."

president. The four-way race divided the Republican party in North Carolina as it did elsewhere in the nation.

Each candidate represented his part of the country. Jackson won the popular vote in North Carolina. He was also the only candidate who had some support outside his region. Jackson received more votes than any of the other three candidates. But he did not have a **majority** (one more than half) of the electoral votes. As a result, the election was decided by the United States House of Representatives, as provided by the Constitution. The House was to choose a president from among the three candidates with the most votes. With the support of Speaker of the House Henry Clay, the House elected John Quincy Adams as president.

Jackson and his supporters were very upset. They believed Clay gave his support to Adams in return for an appointment as secretary of state. Furious over this "corrupt bargain," Jackson vowed to run for president again.

Jackson did run for president in 1828 against John Quincy Adams. This time he won easily.

In North Carolina, Jackson's strength lay in the eastern counties. Planters liked his emphasis on economy in government, his position against internal improvements, and his opposition toward banks, especially the Bank of the United States. Jackson also had North Carolina support because he chose John Branch of Halifax County to serve as his secretary of the navy.

The old hero of New Orleans also made many enemies. One of Jackson's most controversial policies was the Indian removal.

THE TRAIL OF TEARS

In his last annual message in 1824, President Monroe recommended that all Native Americans east of the Mississippi River be removed to the West. Southern tribes such as the Cherokee and Creek refused to go. Between 1789 and 1825, the southern tribes had entered into some thirty treaties with the United States. They wished to remain on their ancestral lands (lands that had belonged to their ancestors).

Most of these two tribes lived in Georgia, where pressure began to mount. Many Cherokee had adopted the lifestyle and ways of whites. To defend

CHAPTER PREVIEW

Terms: majority, Trail of Tears, Whig party, Democratic party, suffrage, referendum, free suffrage, plank road, antebellum, bright leaf tobacco, mint

People: Andrew Jackson, David L. Swain, William Gaston, Edward B. Dudley, William W. Holden, David S. Reid, Calvin H. Wiley, Mary Bayard Clarke, George Moses Horton

Places: Gold Hill

This map shows the routes the Cherokee took along what came to be known as the "Trail of Tears."

THE TRAIL OF TEARS

MISSOURI

KENTUCKY

TENNESSEE

NORTH CAROLINA

INDIAN TERRITORY

Arkansas River

Ohio River

Mississippi River

Tennessee River

ARKANSAS

CHEROKEE NATION

SOUTH CAROLINA

GEORGIA

Atlantic Ocean

ALABAMA

MISSISSIPPI

River Route
Land Route

themselves from Georgia's seizure of their land, the Cherokee under Chief John Ross turned to the federal courts. In two court decisions in 1831 and 1832, Chief Justice John Marshall ruled that Georgia could not remove the Cherokee from their land. President Jackson, however, ignored the Supreme Court's ruling. Using the Indian Removal Act of 1830, Jackson forced Native Americans living in the eastern United States to move west of the Mississippi River. Thus began the Cherokee **Trail of Tears**.

In the winter of 1831-1832, the first tribe was removed. It was the Choctaw of Alabama and Mississippi. When the time came for the Cherokee to leave in 1838, they refused. President Martin Van Buren sent federal troops to round them up. One soldier who took part in the removal recalled:

> *Men working in the fields were arrested and driven to stockades. Women were dragged from their homes by soldiers whose language they could not understand. Children were often separated from their parents and driven into the stockades with the sky for a blanket and the earth for a pillow. And often the old and infirm were prodded with bayonets to hasten them to the stockades.*

About 20,000 Cherokee were removed and marched, under military escort, to present-day Oklahoma. Nearly one-quarter of them died from

President Monroe recommended the removal of all Native Americans to west of the Mississippi River. Andrew Jackson carried out the policy, resulting in the Trail of Tears.

THE QUALLA BOUNDARY

Today, many North Carolinians forget that the Cherokee are the second largest tribe in the United States and that 7,000 Cherokee live on the Qualla Boundary in the Great Smoky Mountains. The Cherokee Nation is located mainly in two places: in Oklahoma, home of the Western Band of the Cherokee, and in North Carolina, home of the Eastern Band of the Cherokee.

Most members of the Eastern Band live on the 57,000-acre Qualla Boundary in Jackson and Swain counties. These Cherokee are largely the descendants of those who refused to relocate to Oklahoma in the 1830s. That relocation resulted in the infamous Trail of Tears.

In the 1990s, the Qualla Boundary went through marked changes. In 1997, the Eastern Band opened a large casino, which offers video gambling. The casino employs over a thousand people and has become a major tourist attraction. Its profits are shared with members of the tribe, helping to raise their standard of living. While some Cherokee welcome the year-round employment, others fear that gambling may corrupt their community.

Despite the economic success of the casino, the Cherokee still confront many problems. They continue to struggle to preserve their language, traditions, and culture. This is difficult to do in a predominantly white society. However, the reservation schools, the Museum of the Cherokee Indian in Cherokee, and the annual fair are important aspects of Cherokee culture. The Eastern Band has also bought the nearby land on which the ancient village of Kituwah was located. Kituwah is an important center of Cherokee native religion.

The outdoor drama Unto These Hills *tells the story of the estimated 1,100 North Carolina Cherokee who managed to escape into the mountains of western North Carolina. The escapees and others known as the Qualla Indians formed the Eastern Band of Cherokee, which exists to this day.*

disease and exhaustion along the way. An estimated 1,100 North Carolina Cherokee managed to escape into the mountains of western North Carolina. About 700 of them lived in the area around Quallatown near present-day Cherokee. The escapees and others known as the Qualla Indians formed the Eastern Band of Cherokee, which exists to this day.

OPPOSITION TO JACKSON

Jackson's determination to remove the Indians in the face of the Supreme Court's ruling was an example of "Old Hickory's" worst traits. Opponents called him "King Andrew." They also did not like his refusal to support internal improvements. By Jackson's second term, western North Carolina and the Albemarle Sound region were in political revolt against his administration.

To oppose Jackson, the **Whig party** was created in 1834. The Whigs took their name from a group of British politicians who had challenged the king's power in the eighteenth century. In North Carolina, the Whigs' greatest strength lay in the western counties and in commercial areas of the east. Many of the Whigs were once Federalists, including easterners William Gaston of Craven County, Edward Stanly of Beaufort County, and Edward B. Dudley of New Hanover County. Governor David L. Swain of Buncombe County led those westerners who had never liked Jackson.

The Whig party in North Carolina supported Henry Clay's program of internal improvements, a national bank, and a tariff on foreign goods to protect American manufacturers. The plantation areas of the east still supported Jackson and what they then called the Democratic party. The **Democratic party** took the place of the old Jeffersonian Republicans. The Democrats supported states' rights, strict interpretation of the Constitution, and a fairly weak federal government.

In North Carolina, the Whig-Democratic rivalry was close and intense. Between 1835 and 1852, neither party could gain firm control of state government. Often, only a few votes separated the two parties in the General Assembly. The Whigs, however, held the governorship until 1850. They were determined to deal with the state's problems. The first reform sought by the Whigs, the one upon which all others depended, was constitutional reform.

Governor David L. Swain, a founder of the Whig party in North Carolina, promoted the Constitutional Convention of 1835. He afterward became president of the University of North Carolina.

Do You Remember?

1. Why did Andrew Jackson not win the election of 1824 if he got the most popular votes?
2. Why did the Cherokee and Creek tribes refuse to be removed to Indian Territory?
3. Name some of the reasons for the opposition to Andrew Jackson.

THE CONSTITUTIONAL CONVENTION OF 1835

For many years the western part of the state had suffered under the undemocratic features of the state constitution of 1776. Each county, regardless of its size or population, had the same number of representatives in the House of Commons (2) and in the Senate (1). Between 1776 and 1833, eighteen new counties were created in the west and fifteen in the east, which allowed eastern planters to keep control of the state. The 1830 census showed that, for the first time, the west's population was higher than the east's. But the west's unequal representation in the General Assembly defeated any plans for reform or for internal improvements.

In 1834-1835, the cry for a constitutional convention to address the defects in the 1776 constitution was finally heard. A small number of eastern legislators voted with westerners to make a convention possible. Governor David L. Swain was also helpful in bringing about the constitutional convention. He was highly respected and made a strong case for a convention to the General Assembly.

In a very close vote in January 1835, the Assembly agreed to put the question of a convention to North Carolina's voters. The results of that vote indicated how deep the sectional differences in the state ran. North Carolinians voted 27,550 to 21,694 for the convention, but only 2,701 westerners voted against it and only 3,611 easterners voted for it.

One hundred thirty delegates to the constitutional convention met in Raleigh in June 1835. Seventy-eight-year-old Nathaniel Macon, now retired from the United States Senate, was elected president. The two strongest voices at the convention, however, were Governor Swain and William Gaston. Swain led the group favoring reform. Gaston, a justice of the state supreme court and a Roman Catholic, led the fight to overturn the state constitution's thirty-second article. That article would not allow Catholics, Jews, and atheists (those who do not believe in God) to hold state office. Judge Gaston gave a two-day address in which he argued against religious tests for office-holding. In a compromise amendment, the language in the constitution was changed from "Protestant" to "Christian." This removed the restriction against Roman Catholics, but Jews and nonbelievers could still not hold office.

Other amendments also resulted from similar compromises between the forces of reform and the forces of conservatism. **Suffrage** (the right to vote) was taken away from free blacks and acculturated Indians such as the Lumbees. (*Acculturated* refers to Indians who had taken on the cultural traits of white society.) The convention agreed upon two ways of amending the constitution, a provision missing from the 1776 document. The governor's term was increased to two years. More importantly, adult male taxpayers rather than the legislature would elect the governor.

At the Constitutional Convention of 1835, William Gaston, a Roman Catholic, fought to end religious tests for office-holding. He was a justice on the state supreme court.

The direct election of a governor by the people occurred for the first time in 1836. Whig candidate Edward B. Dudley of Wilmington was the winner.

The most important change, of course, concerned representation in the General Assembly. The convention agreed that the state Senate would have 50 members, elected from districts drawn up according to the amount of taxes citizens paid. The House of Commons would have 120 members, elected from the counties. The number of representatives from each county would be based on the federal census. By this compromise, the wealthier eastern counties would retain control of the state Senate; the more populated western counties would hold a majority in the House of Commons. The convention, however, kept the 50-acre requirement to vote for state senator.

The work of the convention was approved by a statewide **referendum** (vote of the people). The amendments to the constitution did pass by a vote of 26,771 to 21,606. However, the vote was again divided along sectional lines. Only 2,327 easterners supported the convention's work and only 3,280 westerners rejected it.

Despite all its compromises, the Constitutional Convention of 1835 still signaled a victory for political democracy. All white men who paid taxes could vote for the governor. The General Assembly would have more equal representation, a clear victory for the west. Sectionalism had not been wiped out, but it had been weakened. A path to reform now lay open for the west and for the Whig party.

Do You Remember?
1. What changes in the constitution did William Gaston favor?
2. What was the requirement to be able to vote for state senator?
3. Explain how the Constitutional Convention of 1835 was a victory for political democracy.

NORTH CAROLINA UNDER THE WHIGS

In 1836, the people of North Carolina directly elected a governor for the first time. They chose Edward B. Dudley, a Whig from New Hanover County. Other Whig governors followed: John Motley Morehead, William A. Graham, and Charles Manly. The Whigs pushed through a program of internal improvements, public education, and social reform that met Archibald Murphey's vision of a progressive state. The spirit of Nathaniel Macon had finally been laid to rest.

THE NORTH CAROLINA RAILROAD

The Whigs' top priority was better transportation, more specifically, railroads. The first railroad engine was built in England in 1825. By the 1830s, the call for trains was heard everywhere in America. There were not enough private *investors* (people who would risk their own money

THE TRANSPORTATION REVOLUTION

Between 1800 and 1860, the economies of the North, South, and West developed differently. Industry, trade, and banking became centered in the North. Plantations and subsistence farming took root in the South. Family farms, businesses devoted to processing agricultural products, and manufacturing arose in the West.

New types of transportation made these economic changes possible. Canal fever swept the nation in the 1820s. The 363-mile-long Erie Canal, completed in 1825, linked the Hudson River to Lake Erie. The canal carried easterners to new lands in the West. Western grain flowed back into eastern markets.

In the 1830s, railroad fever replaced canal fever. Technical problems, however, plagued early railroads. Iron rails replaced wooden tracks, and gravel beds created a firm foundation for ties. But without a standard track gauge (width), independent railroads could not link up. To travel from Philadelphia to Charleston, South Carolina, for instance, required eight changes in gauge.

Water transportation also improved. Steamships could carry bulk cargo more cheaply than railroads. On the Hudson River, Robert Fulton introduced the first successful steamboat, the *Clermont*, in 1807. In 1815, the *Enterprise* became the first steamboat to carry cargo up the Mississippi and Ohio rivers. Steamships also plied the high seas. By the 1850s, steamships had reduced travel time between New York and Liverpool, England, by more than half.

Better transportation tied the nation together and created markets for crops and manufactured goods.

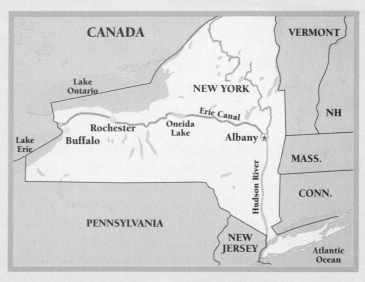

The opening of the 363-mile-long Erie Canal (top, under construction) in 1825 provided a water route from the Atlantic Ocean to ports on Lake Erie (map).

on a project) in North Carolina to take on the huge task of railroad building. So, in 1837, the Whigs committed the state to helping with the construction of railroads.

The state's first experience with railroads was not very successful. The state provided a great deal of money to build and operate the Wilmington

The North Carolina Railroad, approved by the General Assembly in 1849, began operation in 1856. The 223-mile line between Goldsboro and Charlotte opened up the Piedmont to commercial agriculture. Pictured is a North Carolina Railroad stock certificate issued in 1854.

and Weldon Railroad and the Raleigh and Gaston Railroad. Both railroads lost money in their early years of operation. But by the 1850s, they had become profitable; that is, they earned more money than they paid out in expenses.

The state's greatest success with railroads was with the North Carolina Railroad. In 1849, the General Assembly voted to provide two-thirds of the money needed to build the $3 million railroad. Eventually, the cost of building the North Carolina Railroad rose to $4 million, of which the state provided $3 million. Construction on the railroad began in 1852 and was completed in 1856. The 223-mile railroad connected Goldsboro with Charlotte along what came to be known as the Piedmont Crescent. At the dedication in 1856, John W. Ellis (soon to become governor) predicted that the railroad would encourage the growth of communities, business, and industry.

Ellis was correct. The North Carolina Railroad was an amazing success. It opened up the Piedmont to commercial agriculture, spurred the growth of towns and factories, and made people proud of their state. Railroad freight rates were cut in half. Farmers could raise crops and get them to market more easily and quickly. People could move easily from one part of the state to another. The railroad brought the state together and lessened isolation and sectionalism.

EDUCATION AND SOCIAL REFORMS

The Whigs passed a public school law in 1839. According to that law, the state would furnish $40 from the Literary Fund for every school district that supplied a school building and $20 in taxes. With $60, a school district could hire a teacher for two or three months. The first public school in the state opened in January 1840 in Rockingham County. By 1846, every county in the state had at least one school. By 1850, more than 100,000 white schoolchildren were enrolled in more than 2,500 schools. The schools were free; no one paid tuition.

Advances in higher education also took place during this time. In 1834, the Baptists founded Wake Forest College. Three years later, the Presbyterians opened Davidson College. In 1841, the Methodists chartered a school that was the forerunner of Trinity College and later Duke University. The Quakers chartered New Garden Boarding School in 1833; it was renamed Guilford College in 1889. From the beginning, this school was *coeducational*; that is, it had students of both sexes. But boys and girls recited lessons in separate classrooms. Schools for women that had their roots in this period included the Moravians' Salem Female Academy (1802), which later became Salem College; the Methodists' Greensboro Female College (1838) and Louisburg College (1857); and the Episcopalians' Saint Mary's School (1842).

With the passage of a public school law in 1839, free public schools began to replace the "old field schools" (top), which had depended on subscribers. The Baptists founded Wake Forest College (above) in 1834.

Governors Morehead and Graham also suggested reforms in the state's treatment of the mentally ill. In 1848, Dorothea L. Dix of Massachusetts presented a report to the General Assembly on the shocking treatment of patients she had found. Construction of a hospital for the mentally ill began in Raleigh in 1849; it opened in 1856. In 1852, legislators also established a school for those who could not hear, speak, or see.

Other reforms that took place during this period affected the rights of women and criminal laws. An 1848 law gave married women more (but still limited) protection for their property. No longer could a husband sell or rent without her approval real estate that was his wife's at the time of their marriage. The number of capital crimes (those punishable by death) was reduced from twenty-eight to seventeen and then to twelve. Capital crimes included murder, arson, burglary, dueling, stealing a slave, and stealing a horse. In general, however, North Carolina's legal system imposed harsh punishments for crimes. Lawbreakers could be hanged, mutilated, jailed, branded, flogged, and placed in pillories and stocks.

To carry out their program of reforms, the Whigs had to find new sources of revenue. The state's land and poll taxes were very low. (A poll tax was paid by a person who wished to vote.) North Carolinians only paid 6 cents for each $100 worth of land owned and 20 cents on each poll. Between 1835 and 1850, however, state tax revenues nearly doubled. In the late 1840s, the General Assembly passed new taxes on inheritances, incomes, licenses, and luxuries.

THE DECLINE OF THE WHIGS

During the 1830s and 1840s, the Whigs overcame the sectional differences in North Carolina by letting government take the lead in solving

Dorothea Dix (above) convinced North Carolina legislators that the state must take better care of its mentally ill. The legislature also incorporated the North Carolina Institute for the Deaf, Dumb, and Blind (below) in 1852.

North Carolina's antebellum legal system dealt harshly with lawbreakers. This early Carteret County jail dates from 1829.

the state's problems. However, a small group of powerful men identified with Hillsborough and especially Raleigh controlled the party. When they did not name a fair share of easterners and westerners to state and national offices, discontent arose. Also, by 1850, the Whigs' commitment to internal improvements and public education had begun to change. The party's shaky alliance between east and west began to come apart as new leaders in the Democratic party urged Democrats to adopt more forward-looking policies.

The Whig party also was breaking up at the national level. The Whigs opposed Democratic President James K. Polk's war against Mexico (1846-1848), which made them appear disloyal. The slavery issue also divided the party deeply. The South hoped to increase its power if slavery could be extended into Texas and California. Many northern Whigs, however, led the antislavery attack on the South. More and more, southerners came to believe that the Democratic party would better watch out for the region's interests. In North Carolina, all the Democrats needed was a popular issue with which to excite the voters.

Do You Remember?
1. Who was the first governor directly elected by the people?
2. What types of programs did the Whigs support?
3. What was the Whig party's top priority?
4. What changes did the North Carolina Railroad bring?

Two men in particular accounted for the Democratic party's return to power in North Carolina. The first was a newspaper editor named William W. Holden. Originally a Whig, Holden changed parties in 1843 to edit the *North Carolina Standard* of Raleigh. This newspaper soon became the most influential political paper in the state. In 1848, Holden boldly announced that the Democratic party should support state aid to internal improvements. He declared, "Let the voice of party, as to this question, at least, be silent; and let us all resolve, happen what may, that some plan shall be fixed upon and the work begun."

The other key Democratic figure was David S. Reid of Rockingham County. Reid and Holden supported a constitutional reform known as **free suffrage**. This reform would do away with the 50-acre requirement to vote for state senator. Reid ran for governor in 1848 on a campaign promise of free suffrage. He lost to Whig Charles Manly by only 854 votes. But in 1850, the free suffrage issue helped Reid gain the governorship

Above: William W. Holden turned *the* North Carolina Standard *into the most powerful newspaper in the state. Holden urged the Democratic party to adopt more progressive policies.* **Right:** *David S. Reid regained the governorship for the Democrats in 1850 by promising free suffrage for all voters.*

and helped the Democrats win control of both houses of the legislature. The Whigs delayed the free suffrage amendment until 1857. But when the amendment was finally approved, an estimated 125,000 voters received the right to vote for their state senators.

THE DEMOCRATIC RECORD

Once in power, the Democrats continued the Whigs' programs of internal improvements and public education. Under Democratic governors (Reid, Warren Winslow, Thomas Bragg, and John W. Ellis) and a Democratic-controlled General Assembly, the state voted money for railroads, navigation companies, and plank roads. During the 1850s, another 641 miles of railway were built. By 1860, North Carolina had a railroad system of almost 900 miles.

It was also during the 1850s that North Carolina built more than 500 miles of **plank roads**. These roads were usually eight feet wide. Large pine planks were laid very close together at right angles to the line of the road. Once the planks were in place, the road was covered with sand. The plank roads were an improvement over dirt roads, especially in bad weather. The longest plank road ever built ran from Fayetteville to High Point, Salem, and Bethania. The companies that built the plank roads charged tolls, but many people avoided the tolls by going around. The plank roads never became the "farmers' railroads" as some had hoped. They were costly and hard to maintain, and they could not compete with the railroad system then being built. With the coming of the Civil War, the plank roads disappeared.

Under the Democrats, public education made important gains. In 1852, the General Assembly created the office of state superintendent of common schools. In 1853, Calvin H. Wiley became superintendent, a position he held until 1865. A lawyer and Presbyterian minister, Wiley was an outstanding educational leader. In 1851, he wrote *The North Carolina Reader*, a mixture of history, geography, economics, and so on.

Wiley set up programs and institutes for training and licensing teachers, established teachers' conventions, and edited the *North Carolina Journal of Education*. His reforms resulted in graded schools; school libraries; and better textbooks on such subjects as math, spelling, reading, and natural sciences. In 1860, North Carolina had the best school system in the South. Nearly 120,000 students attended more than 3,000 schools staffed by more than 2,700 licensed teachers.

Do You Remember?
1. What election requirement did free suffrage change?
2. Why did the plank roads disappear from the scene?
3. What were some of Calvin Wiley's reforms?

Charles Manly was the last Whig elected governor of North Carolina. He won by only 854 votes in the 1848 election.

During the **antebellum** period (the years before the Civil War), North Carolina at last awoke from its Rip Van Winkle sleep. Political reform had created the conditions for economic and social progress.

With the discovery of a new curing process by a Caswell County slave, tobacco production nearly tripled in the 1850s.

AGRICULTURE

By the 1850s, North Carolina had two chief crops: tobacco and cotton. In Caswell County, Abisha Slade's slave Stephen accidentally discovered a process for curing tobacco leaves to a bright yellow color. The charcoal he burned in the tobacco barn produced a hotter, more even temperature. That and the thin, poor soil along the Virginia border were the secrets for producing **bright leaf tobacco**. Tobacco production rose from 12 million pounds in 1850 to 33 million pounds in 1860.

Cotton production nearly doubled from 1850 to 1860, reaching more than 145,000 five-hundred-pound bales. Two areas of the state grew cotton. One area lay in the eastern part of the state roughly within a triangle formed by the towns of Halifax, Washington, and Goldsboro. The second area lay in a line of counties along the South Carolina border from Robeson to Mecklenburg.

North Carolina farmers also continued to raise other crops, especially wheat and corn. A little rice was grown in Brunswick County. Most North Carolina farms were small. In 1860, over two-thirds of the farms in North Carolina had fewer than one hundred acres.

YEOMAN FARMERS

With the coming of the North Carolina Railroad in the 1850s, nonslaveholding farmers in the Piedmont cautiously began to grow cash crops such as tobacco and cotton. (A cash crop is one that is raised to be sold for a profit.) Given their small farms and limited labor, they were reluctant to abandon food crops since their first responsibility was to feed their families. Even so, in the counties along the path of the North Carolina Railroad, the amount of cash crops grown climbed markedly between 1850 and 1860.

For the most part, nonslaveholding families continued the traditional division between outdoor work for men and indoor work for women. But such a division was not always rigid. During times of sickness or pregnancy, men might take on household duties such as cooking, washing, and cleaning. Women occasionally helped in the field, following behind the plow and sowing seeds. Women also helped gather fodder to feed livestock and pack hay into haystacks.

Life on a typical North Carolina farm was hard. People enjoyed few luxuries. With little cash in circulation, they swapped skills, tools, labor, and crops to settle debts with stores and neighbors. They endured by sharing work, laughter, and faith in family, friends, and church. Quiltings, corn shuckings, and religious camp meetings became great social occasions where people gathered to work, play, worship, and forge the bonds of a community.

MINING

North Carolina was at the center of North America's first gold rush. In 1799, the children of John Reed of Cabarrus County discovered gold but didn't realize what it was. In the 1820s, a farmer discovered gold on his property and the rush was on. The first miners were simple farmers. In 1825, one farmer was described as having "determined to abandon the plough and the hoe, and shoulder the mattock and frying-pan, and dig and wash the earth for its mineral riches rather than cultivate it for its vegetable bounties." Gold mining companies sprang up to mine the precious metal in ten Piedmont counties, including Mecklenburg, Cabarrus, Montgomery, and Rowan. One nugget weighing 28 pounds was found at the Reed Gold Mine.

By 1848, gold mining was a major industry in North Carolina. At Gold Hill in Rowan County, 1,000 workers toiled in the mines. Many of the miners came all the way from Europe.

Because of North Carolina's importance in the gold industry, the federal government opened the United States Mint at Charlotte in 1837. A **mint** is a place where coins are made. An estimated $16 million in gold coins were minted in North Carolina before 1860. A private mint, owned by Christopher and Augustus Bechtler of Rutherford County, produced gold jewelry and more than $3.6 million in gold coins between 1831 and 1857. By the Civil War, gold mining was decreasing in North Carolina. Gold could no longer be easily found and mined. The discovery of gold in California drew many miners west.

Iron ore was also mined in North Carolina in the decades before the Civil War, especially in Lincoln County along the Catawba River valley. However, because of the poor transportation available, North Carolina's iron industry could not compete on a national level. Iron makers had to send

A private mint, owned by Christopher and Augustus Bechtler, produced gold coins valued at $3.6 million. The first Bechtler gold dollar is pictured here on a piece of gold-bearing quartz ore.

The "Alamance plaids" factory of Edwin Michael Holt produced a popular colored cotton fabric. In 1860, North Carolina had more textile mills than any other southern state.

their products overland by wagon to Camden, South Carolina. There, iron goods could be sold or loaded aboard boats for shipment to the coast.

MANUFACTURING

North Carolina's textile industry had not yet gained the importance it would have after the Civil War. Nevertheless, by 1860 there were thirty-nine mills in North Carolina, more than in any other southern state. Edwin Michael Holt was one of those textile manufacturers who got their start in North Carolina before the Civil War. In 1853, his mill became the first in the South to manufacture colored cotton fabric. His "Alamance plaids" were very popular in places as far away as Philadelphia.

As in the colonial period, turpentine remained North Carolina's leading manufactured item. The Tar Heel State produced about two-thirds of all the turpentine made in the United States. The longleaf pine forests in the counties around the Cape Fear River accounted for North Carolina's leadership in that area.

The progress in industry could not hide the fact that North Carolina was still a very rural state. According to the 1860 census, only 2 percent of the state's people lived in twenty-five towns. Wilmington was the largest town, with a population of just 9,552 in 1860. It was also the state's leading seaport and the end point of a major railroad. New Bern had just over 5,000 people; Fayetteville and Raleigh had around 4,000 each. Salisbury and Charlotte totalled about 2,000 residents each.

LITERARY AWAKENING

North Carolina's distinguished literary tradition had its roots in the antebellum era. Several histories of the state were published before the Civil War. In 1839, Robert Strange of Fayetteville wrote *Eoneguski,* a romance about pioneers and the Cherokee. It was the first novel to use North Carolina as a setting. Calvin H. Wiley, the great educator, published *Alamance* (1847) and *Roanoke* (1849), two other historical novels. George H. Throop, a northern tutor, wrote two novels about his experiences on a plantation in eastern North Carolina. They were titled *Nag's Head* (1850) and *Bertie* (1851). Hamilton C. Jones, H.E. Taliaferro, and Johnson Jones Hooper produced the best of the state's humorous writing.

Three poets deserve mention. Mary Bayard Clarke published *Wood-Notes* in 1854. It was a two-volume collection of 180 poems written by sixty authors. One of the poems included was "The Old North State," written by Judge William Gaston. This poem later became the state song.

Perhaps North Carolina's most famous antebellum poet was George Moses Horton, a slave. The black poet published three books during his lifetime. Horton lived in Chatham County, but often traveled to Chapel Hill. There he sold his poems to young men at the University of North Carolina who used them to court young women. Horton specialized in *acrostics,* verses in which the first letters of each line form a word. After the Civil War, he moved to Philadelphia. Horton left no doubt about how he felt about slavery. He wrote:

> *How long have I in bondage lain,*
> *And languished to be free!*
> *Alas! and I still complain*
> *Deprived of liberty.*

Horton's cry for freedom gave voice to the hopes of one-third of North Carolina's population. Despite North Carolina's advances, slavery kept all but a tiny minority of her black inhabitants in bondage.

Do You Remember?

1. What important tobacco process was discovered during this period?
2. Name two important items manufactured during this period.
3. Who was considered to be the most famous North Carolina poet during this period?

Two early literary figures in antebellum North Carolina were poet Mary Bayard Clarke (top), and humorist Hamilton C. Jones (above).

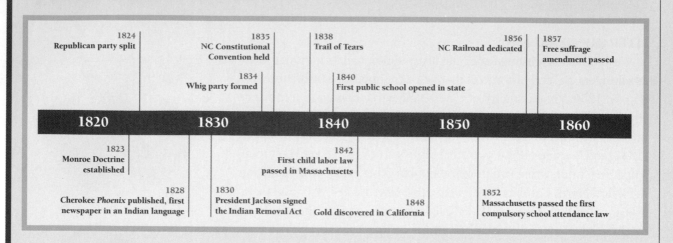

Timeline:

- 1824 Republican party split
- 1835 NC Constitutional Convention held
- 1838 Trail of Tears
- 1856 NC Railroad dedicated
- 1857 Free suffrage amendment passed
- 1834 Whig party formed
- 1840 First public school opened in state

1820   1830   1840   1850   1860

- 1823 Monroe Doctrine established
- 1842 First child labor law passed in Massachusetts
- 1828 Cherokee *Phoenix* published, first newspaper in an Indian language
- 1830 President Jackson signed the Indian Removal Act
- 1848 Gold discovered in California
- 1852 Massachusetts passed the first compulsory school attendance law

Reviewing People, Places, and Terms

Match each word or phrase with the correct definition below.

antebellum
Democratic party
majority
mint
referendum
suffrage
Whig party

1. A place where coins are made
2. The period before the Civil War
3. The political party formed to oppose President Andrew Jackson
4. One more than half
5. The political party formed in the early 1800s that supported states' rights and a fairly weak federal government
6. The right to vote
7. A vote of the people on a particular law before it can be put into effect

Understanding the Facts

1. In what part of North Carolina did those Cherokee who avoided the Trail of Tears settle?

2. What political party formed in opposition to President Andrew Jackson and his policies?
3. Why did people from the western part of the state say that the state constitution of 1776 had undemocratic features?
4. What were some of the important changes made in the state constitution in 1835?
5. Why did the Whig party begin to fade in North Carolina?
6. What were the two main crops in the antebellum period?
7. What two minerals were found in some abundance in North Carolina during the antebellum period?

Developing Critical Thinking

1. Why do you think people in eastern North Carolina opposed internal improvements for the western part of the state?
2. The Constitution of 1835 prohibited Jews and nonbelievers from holding office. Why is this prohibition not possible today?
3. In 1941-1942 at the outbreak of World War II, Japanese Americans were rounded up and placed in internment camps. What similarities do you see between their treatment and that of the Cherokee?

4. How did the North Carolina Railroad bring the state together and lessen sectionalism? What modern developments have brought North Carolinians even closer together?

Applying Your Skills

1. On a detailed map, locate the route of a railroad in your county or in a nearby county. List all of the towns, large and small, that are situated along its route.
2. Research and present a report on Junaluska (1779-1858), the famous Cherokee chief. Include in your report a map showing the location of geographical features in North Carolina (lake, mountain, and so on) named for Junaluska.

Making Connections

1. Why couldn't canals compete with railroads in the shipping business?

2. Railroads were in turn replaced by cars, trucks, buses, and airplanes. Choose one of these four means of transportation and discuss its effect on business and society.
3. Would the Monroe Doctrine be called "isolationist" today?
4. Do you believe that the United States is too involved in the affairs of other nations today? Explain.

Tar Heel Trivia

- In 1821 and 1822, Sequoyah, a self-taught Cherokee, invented a Cherokee-language syllabary.
- A greater variety of minerals—more than 300—have been found in North Carolina than in any other state.
- Prior to 1829, the only source of gold for the Philadelphia Mint was the Reed Gold Mine in North Carolina.

BUILDING SKILLS: USING MATHEMATICS

Have you ever asked your mathematics teacher, "When will I ever use this?" There are many opportunities to use your mathematics skills in the study of history. Taking time to use some of the skills you have learned can make the study of history more meaningful.

You will find that the problem-solving skills you have learned in mathematics will be helpful when solving the following questions.

1. In the election of 1824, the four candidates received the following electoral votes: Jackson, 99; Adams, 84; Crawford, 41; Clay, 37. What percentage of the total electoral votes did each candidate win?
2. In January 1835, North Carolinians voted on whether to have a constitutional convention. The vote was 27,550 to 21,694 for the convention; only 2,701 westerners voted against it while only 3,611 easterns voted for it. (a) How many North Carolinians voted? (b) What was the margin (number of votes) of victory? (c) How many westerners voted to hold the convention? (d) How many easterners voted against holding the convention?

3. In 1849, the General Assembly voted to provide two-thirds of the money needed to build the $3 million North Carolina Railroad. Eventually, the project cost $4 million, with the state providing $3 million. How much more did the state provide than it had originally agreed to provide? Give your answer in a percentage.
4. The 223-mile North Carolina Railroad cost $4 million to build. Approximately how much did the railroad cost *per mile*?
5. In 1860, North Carolina produced more than 145,000 five-hundred-pound bales of cotton. Approximately how many tons of cotton did the state produce that year?
6. Gold and other precious metals are measured in troy weight, where 12 troy ounces equal 1 pound. How many troy ounces are in a 28-pound gold nugget?

CHAPTER THIRTEEN

ANTEBELLUM SLAVERY

Slaves prayed for freedom. . . . Slavery was a bad thing and freedom, of the kind we got with nothing to live on was bad. Two snakes full of poison. One lyin' with his head pointin' north, the other with his head pointin' south. Their names was slavery and freedom. The snake called slavery lay with his head pointed south and the snake called freedom lay with his head pointed north. Both bit . . . and they was both bad.
— Patsy Mitchner, former slave from Wake County

NORTH CAROLINA NEVER DEVELOPED a plantation system like that of South Carolina or Virginia. Most North Carolinians who held slaves owned only a few. Still, slavery helped shape the economy and society of North Carolina. Slave ownership was a sign of wealth and prestige. The largest and wealthiest slaveholders had a great deal of power and authority in the state.

Slaves understood that it was their slavery, status as property, and labor that made the slave owners wealthy. Slaves resented the poor conditions under which they lived and their lack of freedom, and they looked for ways to resist. Knowing there were dangers in not giving blacks their freedom, whites took steps to keep slaves from rebelling. Antebellum North Carolina was far from a peaceful, harmonious society. Slavery brought out tensions that sometimes exploded into violence.

Opposite page: Slaves labored from sunup to sundown to produce such crops as cotton. Above: Ebenezer Pettigrew believed slaves should be managed carefully. He allowed his slaves to raise their own crops and trade them at a plantation store for needed items or a few luxuries.

SLAVERY IN NORTH CAROLINA

In 1790, there were 100,572 slaves in North Carolina, about 25 percent of the total population. In the antebellum period, the slave population reached and stayed at about one-third of the state's total population. In 1860, slaves numbered 331,059, whites 631,100, and free blacks 30,463.

In 1860, slaveholding families made up about 28 percent of the white population. Most slaveholders, however, owned only a few slaves. Only 3 percent of North Carolina's slave owners could be considered **planters,**

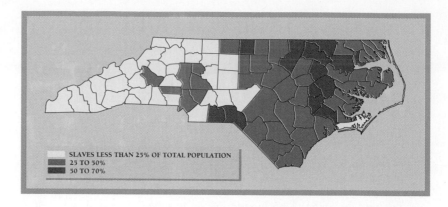

This map shows the percentage of slaves in the population of each North Carolina county in 1860.

SLAVES LESS THAN 25% OF TOTAL POPULATION
25 TO 50%
50 TO 70%

CHAPTER · PREVIEW

Terms: planter, slave code, driver, overseer, public works, discrimination, emancipate

People: David Walker, Nat Turner, Henry Evans, William Meredith, Thomas Day, Louis Sheridan, John Carruthers Stanly

slaveholders who owned twenty or more slaves. Only 2 percent owned more than fifty slaves. Among North Carolina slaveholders, nearly 71 percent owned fewer than ten slaves, and 53 percent owned five or fewer slaves.

During the 1720s, South Carolina planters brought slaves to the lower Cape Fear region to grow rice and to make naval stores. The spread of slavery followed the growth of agriculture. By 1860, slaveholding was concentrated in those counties of the Coastal Plain and Piedmont that produced cotton, tobacco, rice, and naval stores. Of the sixteen counties that had more slaves than whites, eleven were major cotton producers. In the other five counties, the principal cash crop was tobacco.

In the mountain counties, the number of slaves ranged from as few as 2 percent of the population to more than 25 percent. The black population in the southern Appalachian Mountains swelled in the summer months as owners brought their personal servants with them to the cooler mountain resort areas.

THE SLAVE TRADE

The U.S. Constitution ended the international slave trade to America in 1808. In 1795, however, North Carolina had stopped the importing of slaves from the West Indies. North Carolinians feared that the slave revolts in the Caribbean islands might spread to the mainland. Nevertheless, the illegal smuggling of Africans continued. An estimated 50,000 African slaves were brought to the United States between 1810 and the Civil War.

The slave trade among the states grew in the four decades before the Civil War. About 835,000 slaves from the upper South were sold and relocated in the lower South. North Carolina contributed to the lines of slaves marching south to meet the demand for labor in the newly opened lands of Alabama, Mississippi, Louisiana, and Texas. An antislavery Methodist minister who lived in Randolph County left the following description of the slave trade in 1853:

*It is heart Sickning to see the Poor Slaves Driven to Market like Brutes —
Parents Torn from their children without mercy and compeled to drag out
a miserable Existence In the Rice Swamps or on the Cotton Plantations
— In Passing to my appointment some time Since I saw a number of Poor
Slaves Marching Through a small Vilage with their driver[.] In the crowd
Some two or three of the slave Men were playing their Violins to keep up
the appearance of meriment but they would have looked but little Worse
I presume If they had been going to the gallows[.] Hundreds and Even
Thousands are Driven to Market[.]*

*Slave market auctions (sales) were
a time of fear and uncertainty
for slaves. Slave families were sometimes separated by these auctions.*

THE SLAVE CODE

The **slave code** defined the social, economic, and physical place of
slaves. The first slave code was written between 1715 and 1741. Later,
the code was changed slightly, but only to tighten controls over slaves.
In 1753, for example, slave patrols were begun. Very harsh laws were
passed between 1830 and 1833 after the publication of David Walker's
Appeal and Nat Turner's rebellion in Southampton County, Virginia.

David Walker was born in Wilmington, in 1785. Because his mother was a free black, Walker was also free. During the 1820s, Walker settled in Boston, Massachusetts. From there he argued for the immediate abolition (end) of slavery and urged slaves to revolt. In 1829, he published *An Appeal to the Coloured Citizens of the World.* Quoting directly from the Declaration of Independence, Walker asked whites to compare

Slave marriages were not recognized by law, but slaves still observed the union of couples with joyous celebrations.

> *your own language...with your cruelties and murders inflicted by your cruel and unmerciful fathers and yourselves on our fathers and on us.... Now Americans! I ask you candidly, was your sufferings under Great Britain, one hundredth part as cruel and tyran[n]ical as you have rendered ours under you?*

Shortly after the publication of his pamphlet, Walker was found dead, probably of foul play. The South tried to destroy copies of the pamphlet before they fell into the hands of slaves. Copies, however, showed up in Fayetteville, Wilmington, Chapel Hill, New Bern, and Hillsborough. Fearing the spread of Walker's *Appeal,* the General Assembly passed a law in 1830 forbidding anyone from teaching slaves to read or write. The lawmakers said that teaching slaves to read and write "has a tendency to excite dissatisfaction in their minds and to produce insurrection and rebellion to the manifest injury of the citizens of this state."

By 1855, the slave code prohibited certain actions by slaves: showing disrespect to white persons; trespassing on whites' property; marrying free blacks; running away; producing forged papers; hiring out their services themselves; raising horses, cattle, hogs, or sheep; selling alcohol; gambling; hunting with a gun; setting fire to woods; and selling articles of property without written permission.

At the same time, the legislature and courts began to recognize some limited protections for slaves. For example, in 1817, the courts ruled that it was a crime to murder a slave. Later, state supreme court rulings permitted a slave to defend his life if threatened by a master.

The entire white population of the South served as a giant militia to keep slaves in their place. Under such conditions, the slaves struggled to raise their families and create a community that would shelter them from the harshness of their lives.

Do You Remember?

1. What percent of the white population of North Carolina owned slaves?
2. What three crops led to the spread of slavery in the state?
3. What reason did the General Assembly give for forbidding anyone to teach slaves to read or write?
4. Name four actions that were prohibited by the slave code in 1855.

LIFE UNDER SLAVERY

Most observers agreed that slaves in North Carolina were poorly fed, housed, and clothed. In the 1780s, a German traveler stated that the largest planters were the worst offenders. They let blacks "run naked mostly or in rags, and accustom them as much as possible to hunger, but exact of them steady work."

ACQUIRING THE BASICS

Masters issued clothes twice a year, once in the spring and once in the autumn. Josiah Collins III, a fairly generous slaveholder, tried to make sure that his slaves were adequately clothed. He ordered

They are to have Two good Suits of—clothes one for Summer, and one of good woolen cloth for Winter—two pair of good double-soled shoes and one pair of woolen Stockings, one good wool hat [and] a Blanket not less than six feet long. A woman having one child is to have a Blanket for such child; when a woman has more than one child a Blanket is to be supplied for every two children.

Slave cabins were crude dwellings made out of timber and stone. The simple huts rarely had more than one window and one door.

Josiah Collins built Somerset Place on the shore of Lake Phelps. In 1786, he brought eighty slaves directly from Africa. The slaves spent three years digging a twenty-foot-wide canal from the lake to the Scuppernong River six miles away.

For rations (food supplies), slaves received meat, meal, molasses, potatoes, and corn. In 1853, the Raleigh *Farmer's Journal* recommended giving men five pounds of boneless pork and a peck of meal per week in the winter. Women were to receive four pounds of meat and a peck of meal. During summer months, these rations were increased by one pound of meat and a quart of molasses. In the winter of 1854-1855, a Brunswick County planter who owned 150 slaves slaughtered 150 hogs and as many cattle as needed to feed his slaves.

Slaves added to these rations by keeping their own gardens, hunting, and fishing. One former slave, Louisa Adams, recalled "My old daddy partly raised his children on game. He caught rabbits, coons, an' possums. He would work all day and hunt at night." On some plantations, masters encouraged slaves to grow extra crops or to raise their own livestock, even though the latter was against the law. Slaves kept vegetable gardens; produced butter, cheese, milk, and eggs; and raised chickens. They then sold these products to whites to earn money for items their masters could not or would not provide.

Most slave housing was poorly built with inferior materials or with timber and stone found nearby. The houses usually had stick-and-dirt chimneys, one door, and one window without glass. These slave huts were often "small, crowded, and smoky."

A few slaveholders built sturdy housing. The Pettigrew plantations in Washington County, for example, provided two-room houses for slaves. Along the Roanoke River, Henry and Thomas Burgwyn erected "good frame buildings" for their slaves. Paul Cameron of Orange County built solid one- and two-story frame houses for his slaves. Some of these houses are still standing on Stagville Plantation.

WORK ROUTINES

The jobs done by slaves varied in different parts of the state. Some slaves worked in their masters' homes. Most, however, worked out-of-doors. Rice was grown along the lower Cape Fear River. One eighteenth-century observer described rice growing as the "hardest work" that slaves did. Slaves worked long hours in flooded, swampy fields and were bent over for much of that time. Each slave was expected to produce four or five barrels of rice each season. (A barrel weighed about 500 pounds.) It took two acres of lowlands to produce the four or five barrels.

Cotton and tobacco were equally demanding crops. Slaves spent many hours in the hot summer sun "chopping cotton" to remove the never-ending weeds. From August to November, slaves had to pick the cotton by hand, stooping over each plant. Sometimes there were as many as six pickings, because the cotton ripened gradually instead of all at once.

Tobacco-growing seasons overlapped, so labor was continuous and hard. Tobacco was started in seedbeds. Each plant was then transplanted to the field. The tobacco plants were carefully tended to make the leaves grow larger, which increased their value. Slaves "primed" each plant by removing several leaves at its base, "topped" the plant by pinching off the top of the stalk, and "suckered" the plant by removing unneeded shoots that grew at the base of the leaves. This process went on for months. After working in the fields all day, slaves returned to the tobacco houses in the evening to strip leaves.

Planters wanted to keep their slaves busy at all times. The slaves usually worked in gangs under black drivers; some planters even had black overseers. The **drivers** and **overseers** made sure the slaves performed many different tasks. Without modern tools, clearing land was a huge, difficult job. One observer estimated that it would take one slave thirty days to clear one acre of farm land. The slaves cut down and sawed trees, rolled logs into heaps, cleared vines and underbrush, and rived staves and shingles. They also loaded crops on vessels, repaired ditches, and built dikes.

Slave women worked just as hard as slave men. When not working in the fields, they spent much of their time spinning, sewing, weaving, preparing food, and minding children. Even the children worked. One former slave recalled that, as a child, he "kept chickens out of the garden" and "fanned flies off the table." Other children carried water to

Paul Cameron of Orange County was the state's largest slave owner in 1860. His Stagville Plantation included sturdy one- and two-story frame houses for slaves.

An overseer on horseback watches over slaves working in a cotton field. Cotton was a demanding crop. To harvest cotton required more than one picking.

workers in the field, gathered nuts and berries, and collected kindling for fires.

In western North Carolina, where large-scale agriculture was impractical, slaves tended livestock. Slaves in the area also became involved in commercial, industrial, and manufacturing businesses. They worked in hotel resorts and mines, helped build railroads and **public works** (roads and courthouses), and made hats and cloth.

Some slaves had specialized skills: coachman, house servant, cook, blacksmith, carpenter. These skilled slaves were doubly valuable to owners. Each January 1, masters arranged to hire out their slaves. Slave craftsmen brought higher prices. Legally, slaves could not hire themselves out, but in Wilmington, New Bern, and other towns they usually did. Slave craftsmen often did not live with their masters. The slaves did, however, turn over most of their earnings to their masters. They kept the rest of their earnings for food and shelter. In 1857, however, white Wilmington mechanics rioted to protest the competition from slaves.

Slaves worked from sunup to sundown six days a week. This was not enough for some slaveholders. Charles Pettigrew admitted:

To manage negroes without the exercise of too much passion, is next to an impossibility. . . . They are slaves for life. They are not stimulated to care and industry as white people are, who labor for themselves. They do not feel themselves interested in what they do. . . .

His son Ebenezer agreed. "Negroes are a troublesome property, and unless well managed, an expensive one, but they are indispensable in this unhealthy and laborious country. . . ." For their part, slaves understood whites' motives. Andrew Boone, a one-time slave, noted that blacks "make the cotton and corn and the white folks get the money."

THE SLAVE COMMUNITY

Given the harshness of their lives, the black family proved remarkably strong. The slave community extended far beyond a particular plantation. Slaves who could not find marriage partners on their own plantations often found them on other plantations. Masters encouraged slave women to marry men on adjoining farms or plantations because any children that came from such a union became the property of the woman's master.

Women usually had their first children before the age of nineteen. Names given to slave children indicated strong family ties. For example, about 40 percent of the children on the Bennehan-Cameron plantations in Orange County were named after members of their families.

Unfortunately, the law did not recognize slave marriages. Even though many masters tried not to separate black families, that tragedy often happened. Changes in a master's life made slaves especially vulnerable. Marriage, death, or relocation in the slaveholder's family were the greatest threats to a slave family's stability. Planters often made presents of slaves to newly married children. In their wills, planters divided slaves among white family members. Slaves were also sold to pay off debts or to remove black troublemakers. When a master warned, "I'm going to put you in my pocket," the master was threatening to sell the slave.

Baptists and Moravians showed particular concern for the plight of slave families, but there was little they could do. In 1824, a Moravian minister who had been marrying slaves had to stop the practice. The Moravians observed, "It is not within the power of Negroes to promise that they will live together as married people, for it often happens that one or the other is sold by the owner. . . ." The Moravians decided that thereafter slave marriages would "simply be announced . . . and the blessing of God shall be wished for them."

Former slaves painfully recalled the breakup of slave families. Catherine Scales, a former slave from Rockingham County, remembered a slave woman with three children aged six, eight, and ten. When the mother learned she was being sold, she gathered her children between her knees

Charles Pettigrew, North Carolina's first Episcopal bishop, recognized that slaves found little satisfaction in working for masters instead of themselves.

SLAVE MUSIC

African musical traditions were kept alive in the slave communities. The fiddler was held in high esteem and many times his music was accompanied by the hand clapping, body slapping, and foot tapping known as "Jubba patting."

Music was an integral part of ceremonies and festivals in West African society. The music brought cheer to celebrations and to everyday life. Through slavery, African musical traditions reached the New World.

"Musicianers" played a key role in the slave community as teachers, entertainers, and preservers of African folk culture. Slave musicians played every instrument, and string instruments were prized the most. In the slave community, the fiddle was even more popular than the banjo, which was an African instrument. To be nicknamed "fiddler" was a high honor.

Slaveholders feared African drums and prohibited their use. They believed that drums might be used to signal a slave revolt, as, in fact, they were during the 1739 Stono Rebellion in South Carolina. To preserve the complex rhythms of West Africa, slaves resorted to "Jubba patting," which was hand clapping, body slapping, and foot tapping.

Slaves had many restraints on their freedom of expression and few outlets for their creativity or feelings. Slave songs provided both. The songs were also an "allowed" form of protest. "The songs of the slave," Frederick Douglass wrote, "represent the sorrows of his heart." Often, the songs conveyed images of broken families, the burden of work, and cruel treatment. But just as often they were filled with joy, deliverance, and the hope for a brighter future — even if that future lay in the next world.

and sang "Lord, Be with Us." Scales said the mother begged her children "Remember me/ Remember me/ Oh Lord, remember me. Then she cried! And they took her off, and the children never saw her no more." Viney Baker, another former slave, went to sleep one night and awoke to find her mother gone. "They had come and got my mammy without wakin' me up," she said. In later years, Viney felt "glad somehow that [she] was asleep" so that she did not see her mother taken off.

SLAVES AND RELIGION

Blacks took comfort in religion. During the Great Revival in the early 1800s, most blacks converted to Christianity. By 1810, separate black churches had been established in Wilmington, New Bern, Fayetteville, and Edenton. Henry Evans, a free black shoemaker, is credited with organizing the first Methodist church in Fayetteville during the 1790s.

Most slaves were members of white-controlled churches. White ministers gave sermons on the theme "Servants, obey your masters." But in the slave quarters, black preachers delivered a different message. In secret prayer meetings, they voiced a strong desire for freedom and justice. A few perhaps even pushed rebellion. In 1802, a slave preacher named Dr. Joe was accused of carrying a gun and stirring up a slave revolt in Pasquotank County. During the 1820s and 1830s, there were reports of black preachers who talked about abolishing slavery. Finally, in 1831, the General Assembly passed a law forbidding black preachers from speaking at worship meetings where there were slaves from different masters.

During the Great Revival, black preachers sometimes delivered sermons to mixed audiences. In that same period, separate black churches began to appear.

Do You Remember?

1. What were typical rations for a slave?
2. How did slaves add to the rations they received from their masters?
3. Why was it said that rice-growing was the hardest work that slaves had to do?
4. Why was it said that slave women worked just as hard as slave men?
5. What changes in the white master's life often caused separation in black families?
6. What religious movement brought many blacks to Christianity?

RESISTANCE TO SLAVERY

During the American Revolution, slave unrest frightened whites. After the Revolutionary War, the most serious threat of a slave rebellion in North Carolina occurred in 1802. Rumors of a revolt were heard along the Roanoke River from Virginia to Albemarle Sound. The discovery of a written message between slave conspirators (those involved in a scheme) in

Bertie County revealed the plot at the last moment. Hundreds of slaves in eastern North Carolina were rounded up for questioning. Many were placed on trial. In Bertie County alone, eleven blacks were executed. As many as another dozen were executed in other counties. Many slaves were punished by whipping.

In 1831, Nat Turner led the bloodiest slave revolt in American history. Turner was a slave preacher in a Virginia town along the North Carolina border. Between fifty-seven and sixty-five white men, women, and children were killed during the revolt. Panic spread through Virginia and North Carolina, but whites quickly put down the revolt. Turner was later captured by state and federal troops and put on trial. After being found guilty, he was hanged.

In North America, there were at least sixty-five slave revolts for which information exists. Armed revolts against slavery were never successful. Slaves, therefore, found other ways to resist slavery. They pretended to be sick, used various means to avoid work, fooled

In 1831 the bloodiest slave revolt in American history occurred in Southampton County, Virginia, along the North Carolina border. Nat Turner, a slave preacher, led the uprising before being captured.

whites verbally or with forged passes, and stole items from their masters, especially food. The slaves did not consider stealing food wrong, for they were simply making themselves stronger to perform their masters' work. Slaves, however, would not put up with theft by other slaves.

Slaves also stole themselves; that is, they ran away. Many ran away to states where slavery was illegal or tried to pass as free blacks. Their reasons for running away were understandable. Some were trying to get back together with family members from whom they had been separated. The cruelty of masters and overseers was also a reason for running away.

Notices for habitual runaways (slaves who ran away often) usually included descriptions of scars from whipping, branding, or marking. Samuel Johnston, the Revolutionary leader, described his runaway field hand Frank as "branded in the left Buttock with a P." Another slave owner reported that Bess was "branded in the breast." Another slave's back, according to his master, had "frequently undergone the Discipline of the Whip."

Some runaways formed their own communities, far away from whites. The Great Dismal Swamp was a perfect hideout for runaway slaves. One eighteenth-century observer noted that some runaways stayed there for as long as thirty years, living on corn, hogs, and fowl. The swamps were said to be so thick that local residents didn't enter them.

Tom Copper, one of the leaders of the failed 1802 slave revolt, had a camp in the swamps near Elizabeth City. And, in 1795, a band of runaway slaves boldly raided the area around Wilmington. In the end, however, they were all captured and executed.

Not all masters, of course, were harsh. But a slave's life had sharp limits. Slaves faced endless years of working for other people with few chances for freedom. A small number of blacks, nevertheless, managed to live as free men. A few even owned slaves.

FREE BLACKS

Before the American Revolution, there were few free blacks in any of the American colonies. At the North Carolina Constitutional Convention of 1835, William Gaston noted "that previous to the Revolution there were scarcely any emancipated Slaves in this State; and that the few free men of color that were here at that time, were chiefly Mulattoes, the children of white women." The mother's legal status—slave or free—determined her children's status.

The Revolution brought on an age of liberty. Many slaves fled to the British; others tried to pass as free. Some masters were moved by the ideals of the Revolution to free their slaves. North Carolina, however, continued to set limits on a slaveholder's ability to free slaves. By 1790, North Carolina was the only state where a master could not free slaves if he or she wished. Instead, a slaveholder had to show the county court that a slave deserved freedom for performing "meritorious services." And it was the county court that made the final decision on freedom for the slave.

THE ANTISLAVERY AND WOMEN'S RIGHTS MOVEMENTS

The religious revivals of the early 1800s led to a spirit of reform in the United States. Men and women increasingly began to address what they saw as the ills of society. In the 1830s, women became more involved with the antislavery movement. As they did, women realized the similarities between the oppression of slaves and the oppression of women.

Most men, however, would not accept women as equals in the movement, and women faced growing hostility for stepping out of their "place" in society. At the World Anti-Slavery Convention held in London in 1840, two American women delegates, Elizabeth Cady Stanton and Lucretia Mott, were refused permission to participate. Infuriated, they vowed to "form a society to advocate the rights of women" when they returned home.

Their vow resulted in the Seneca Falls Women's Rights Convention held in July 1848. A three-sentence announcement of the meeting to discuss "the social, civil, and religious rights of women" drew over three hundred people. Those attending adopted a 12-point Declaration of Sentiments, modeled after the Declaration of Independence. It detailed the injustices women had suffered; demanded the end of women's exclusion from trades, professions, and commerce; denounced educational discrimination and unequal legal rights, including the right to vote.

From this beginning, the women's rights movement spread across the country. However, after 1850, the country become more and more focused on the issue of slavery, and it wasn't until 1920 that women won the right to vote.

LUNSFORD LANE

Lunsford Lane earned enough money to arrange for a white family to buy his freedom. Forced to leave the state and separated from his family, Lane began making antislavery speeches in the North.

Lunsford Lane was born a slave in 1803. For many years, he served the wealthy Sherwood Haywood family of Raleigh. With a keen eye for business, Lane managed over time to earn money by performing odd jobs in what little spare time he had. At night he would cut wood and make tobacco pipes. He often sold the pipes and his "special smoking tobacco" to members of the state legislature.

Lane wanted to earn enough money to buy his freedom. Slowly, ever so slowly, he was able to save $1,000, the amount his owner agreed to accept to free him. According to state law, however, only the courts could free a slave. Lane, therefore, arranged for another white family to use his money to buy him and take him to New York. There, he received his freedom papers.

After gaining his freedom, Lunsford Lane returned to Raleigh, where his enslaved wife and children remained. He continued his firewood and tobacco businesses, hoping to save more money to buy and free his family. Unfortunately, Lane had to leave Raleigh in 1841 when officials told him that legally he was not allowed to return to North Carolina after being freed outside the state. Although he resisted and well-known white citizens tried to help him, Lane was forced to return to the North.

There he earned money for speaking at antislavery meetings. A year later, he traveled to North Carolina once again to buy his family. In Raleigh he was arrested because of his antislavery speeches. He was attacked by a mob of whites and almost hung. After being beaten and tarred and feathered, Lane escaped with the help of white friends. These friends arranged to get Lane and his family secretly aboard a northbound train. Lunsford Lane continued making antislavery speeches, but he never returned to North Carolina.

Free blacks worked as farmers, laborers, and tradesmen. Many free blacks moved to cities and towns. There they were more likely to find jobs and escape the constant attention of whites. Very few, however, became successful in business.

Most free blacks suffered under discrimination. **Discrimination** occurs when people are denied their rights because of prejudice. Until the Constitutional Convention of 1835, free blacks could vote. The convention took away that right. Free black women were taxed; white women were not. In 1785, the General Assembly passed a law requiring free blacks in Wilmington, Washington, Edenton, and Fayetteville to wear a "badge of cloth...on the left shoulder" marked with "the word FREE." Whites also tried to limit relations between slaves and free blacks. Free blacks could not entertain slaves in their houses on Sundays or at night, nor could they trade with slaves.

North Carolina produced a number of noted free blacks. John Chavis, a veteran of the Revolutionary War, was a highly respected teacher of both blacks and whites in Raleigh. Like Henry Evans of Fayetteville, William Meredith established a Methodist church in Wilmington that included 704 black members and 48 white members in 1812. Thomas Day of Milton in Caswell County was one of the most respected cabinetmakers in the state. In fact, the General Assembly set aside its laws forbidding free blacks to move into the state in order to allow Aquilla Wilson, Day's new wife, to join him. Louis Sheridan was a wealthy merchant and farmer and a resident of Elizabethtown in Bladen County. Sheridan became alarmed at the growing hostility of whites toward free blacks. In the 1830s, he freed his own slaves, left the country, and settled in Liberia.

Both Thomas Day and Louis Sheridan owned slaves. This was not unusual in the South and in North Carolina. In fact, the 1830 census included at least 192 free blacks in North Carolina who owned slaves. Of these, 92 held only 1 slave. Many free blacks owned their spouses children. Black slaveholders often asked the General Assembly to **emancipate** (set free) members of their family.

John Carruthers Stanly of New Bern was the largest black slaveholder in the entire South. Stanly was a barber who received his freedom in 1795. Within a decade, he was able to obtain the freedom of his slave wife and children. He then turned his attention to business interests that included a barbershop, farms, town property, and slaves. Most of the slaves Stanly owned were field hands, unskilled laborers, and children. In 1830, at the height of his success, Stanly owned around 160 slaves.

Stanly had the respect of the white community. He even owned a pew in the white First Presbyterian Church of New Bern. Even though he himself had been a slave, Stanly's treatment of his slaves differed little from that of white masters. Such were the ironies of what the South called its "peculiar institution."

Towns attracted free black craftsmen such as the carpenter shown here.

Do You Remember?
1. What determined the legal status of a child who had one white parent and one black parent?
2. Why did so many free blacks move to the cities and towns?
3. What were some instances of discrimination against free blacks during this period?

CHAPTER · REVIEW

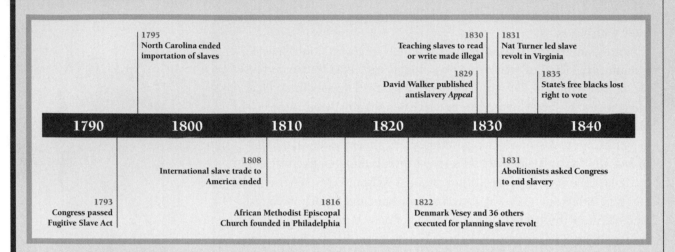

1795
North Carolina ended
importation of slaves

1830
Teaching slaves to read
or write made illegal

1831
Nat Turner led slave
revolt in Virginia

1829
David Walker published
antislavery *Appeal*

1835
State's free blacks lost
right to vote

| 1790 | 1800 | 1810 | 1820 | 1830 | 1840 |

1808
International slave trade to
America ended

1831
Abolitionists asked Congress
to end slavery

1793
Congress passed
Fugitive Slave Act

1816
African Methodist Episcopal
Church founded in Philadelphia

1822
Denmark Vesey and 36 others
executed for planning slave revolt

Reviewing People, Places, and Terms

Match each word or phrase with the correct definition below.

discrimination
driver
emancipate
overseer
planter
slave code

1. A person who was responsible for seeing that slaves performed the tasks assigned to them
2. Actions that deny people their rights because of prejudice
3. To set free
4. A slaveholder who owned twenty or more slaves
5. A set of laws that defined the social, economic, and physical rights of slaves
6. A slave placed in charge of a group of slaves

Understanding the Facts

1. How did North Carolina's slavery system differ from that in Virginia and South Carolina?
2. In what part of North Carolina's economy were slaves most often used?

3. Why was David Walker considered a free black when he was born?
4. From what famous document did David Walker quote in his *An Appeal to the Coloured Citizens of the World*?
5. What skills made some slaves especially valuable to their owners?
6. What did a slave owner mean when he or she said to a slave, "I'm going to put you in my pocket"?
7. Where and when did the most serious slave revolt take place? Who led the revolt?
8. Where would a slave most likely try to go when he or she ran away?
9. Could only whites own slaves?

Developing Critical Thinking

1. Why do you think the slave codes were so effective in keeping blacks enslaved?
2. If cotton and tobacco were so difficult for slaves to produce, why do you think slave owners wanted to grow these crops?
3. Why do you think the white population in the antebellum period was so fearful of allowing slaves to read and write?

4. In what ways might slaves have learned to read in spite of the restrictions that existed at the time?

5. What reactions do you think a slave might have had to the warning "I'm going to put you in my pocket"?

Applying Your Skills

1. Using the figures given at the beginning of the chapter, how many of the 1860 white population were slave owners?

2. Examples of Thomas Day's furniture and the arts and crafts of other African Americans are included in museums around our state. Black women and men continue to make pottery and quilts, paint, carve wood, weave baskets, compose music, and perform other activities that reflect African traditions and influences. Interview a local black craftsman or artist about her or his work.

3. Research the life of and prepare a short report on one of the free blacks mentioned in this chapter.

Making Connections

1. How did "slave music" make life more bearable for the slaves?

2. It was mentioned that slave songs were an "allowed" form of protest. Can you think of other ways in which music has been used as a form of protest?

3. What were the similarities between the oppression of slaves and the oppression of women?

Tar Heel Trivia

- In 1860, slaves made up 68 percent of the population of Warren County, the state's largest slaveholding county.
- A favorite slave dish was kush. Made of cornbread, it was cooked on a griddle in the fireplace and seasoned with onions and ham gravy.
- Slaves being moved from the upper South to the lower South were chained together in coffles.
- Just before the Civil War, there were 30,463 free blacks living in North Carolina.

● BUILDING SKILLS: USING MAPS ●

Knowing how to work with maps and read the information presented in them is an important skill — one that goes beyond this history class. For example, how many times have you seen maps on the nightly news or in newspaper and magazine articles? Maps show us landforms, countries and their boundaries, where places are, climate, natural resources, how to get somewhere, and all kinds of data that can be grouped geographically. Maps can be very detailed, such as those that show all the streets in a town and the elevation of a particular area, or general, such as one that shows the type of vegetation.

In the case of a general map, the *detail* may not be as important as the overall *impression*. The map on page 266 is a general map that shows the slave population in North Carolina in 1860. The map shows the outlines of the counties, but not the names of the individual counties. Data are often collected on a county basis, but for this map, the names of the counties are not important.

Whenever you look at a map, you should be able to draw some conclusions from the information presented. See if you can answer the following questions about the map on page 266.

1. In what part(s) of the state were there the least slaves? In what part(s) of the state were there the most slaves?

2. Why do you think slave ownership was concentrated in certain areas of the state?

3. Does the information gained from the map match what you read?

The next time you come to a map in your textbook, look at it before you read the surrounding text and see if you can draw some conclusions from what it presents. Then compare it with the information presented in the textbook.

NORTH CAROLINA IN WAR AND RECONSTRUCTION

THE NATION'S EXPANSION and the issue of slavery caused sharp political divisions between the North and the South. Lincoln's election as president in 1860 spurred many slave states to secede. North Carolina seceded and made great contributions to the Confederate war effort but could not prevent the Union Army from capturing much of its coast. Sherman's march into the state in 1865 brought defeat and the end of the war.

After the war, President Johnson and Congress worked to restore the former Confederate states to the Union. Reconstruction was harsh and many native whites resented the changes it brought. They used fraud and violence to regain control of state government from the Republican party.

Above: *Abraham Lincoln was inaugurated president on March 4, 1861, beneath the unfinished Capitol.* **Left:** *North Carolina's Fort Fisher is now a State Historic Site.*

CHAPTER FOURTEEN

MOVING TOWARD SECESSION

I hail dissolution with contentment...if the bonds of the union are to be maintained only to expose us to the taunts of fanatics and hypocrites. . . .
— Abraham W. Venable, North Carolina congressman

O N MAY 20, 1861, North Carolina seceded from the Union, the last state to do so. This withdrawal of the southern states from the Union is the only time the American political system has broken down. The factors leading up to this breakdown are not easy to identify and understand. Disunion was a result of many factors: the expansion of the nation, changes in northern and southern societies, the struggle of political parties for power, sectionalism, the conflict over slavery and the growing antislavery movement, and the issue of states' rights.

Nor would North Carolina have seceded had it not been for the breakdown of national institutions and the start of war. Indeed, a strong two-party system, with one party supporting the Union, kept the state in the Union as long as possible.

The most troubling issue to enter American politics in the 1800s, however, was the issue of slavery.

THE NATIONAL DIVISION OVER SLAVERY

In 1803, President Thomas Jefferson bought a vast area west of the Mississippi River from France. People pushed westward as the "Louisiana Purchase" area opened up for settlement. Eventually, the settlers organized into territories and began to call for statehood. In 1812, Congress admitted the slave state of Louisiana to the Union.

Opposite page: This lithograph, "News from the Mexican War Front," shows how interested people were in the war. This was a divisive war. Many people opposed it because they believed it would allow slavery to expand westward.

> ### CHAPTER · PREVIEW
>
> ***Terms:*** slave state, free state, Missouri Compromise, abolitionism, underground railroad, annex, Wilmot Proviso, secede, Compromise of 1850, popular sovereignty, Kansas-Nebraska Act, Republican party, extremist, platform, Confederate States of America
>
> ***People:*** William Lloyd Garrison, Theodore Dwight Weld, Levi Coffin, James K. Polk, Henry Clay, Stephen A. Douglas, Dred Scott, Hinton Rowan Helper, Abraham Lincoln, John W. Ellis, Jefferson Davis
>
> ***Places:*** Missouri, Texas, California, Kansas, Nebraska, Harpers Ferry, Fort Sumter

As the nation expanded, however, slavery became an important political issue. Thomas Jefferson called it "a fire bell in the night" that tolled the death of the Union.

THE MISSOURI COMPROMISE

By 1820, the United States had twenty-two states. Of these, eleven were **slave states** (states that permitted slavery) and eleven were **free states** (states that did not permit slavery). All of the slave states were located in the Southeast. All of the free states were located in the North and Northwest.

Up to this time, all of the presidents but one—John Adams—had come from a slave state, Virginia. In the U.S. Senate, there was an equal number of senators from slave states and from free states. In the House of Representatives, the slave states had fewer representatives than the free states, but the slave states had formed an alliance with the northwestern states. This alliance was threatened by the slavery issue.

In 1818, the Territory of Missouri, which had about 2,000 slaves, applied for admission to the Union. While the House of Representatives considered the bill to admit Missouri, New York representative James Tallmadge added an amendment requiring that Missouri abolish slavery. The House approved the bill with Tallmadge's amendment. The vote showed the free states voting for the amendment and the slave states voting against it. The Senate, where the votes of the free states and the slave states were equal, rejected the bill.

The disagreement over slavery became heated and pitted free states against slave states. Fortunately, in 1820, a compromise that both slave and free states could support was worked out. Missouri and Maine would

Above: Thomas Jefferson, himself a slave owner, called the issue of slavery "a fire bell in the night" that tolled the death of the Union. Right: The Missouri Compromise of 1820 cooled the heated rhetoric over slavery for a short time, but the issue arose again in the 1820s and the 1830s.

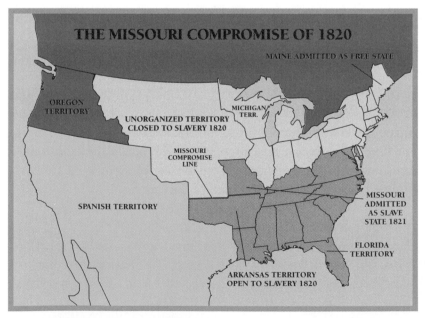

THE MISSOURI COMPROMISE OF 1820

MAINE ADMITTED AS FREE STATE

OREGON TERRITORY

MICHIGAN TERR.

UNORGANIZED TERRITORY CLOSED TO SLAVERY 1820

MISSOURI COMPROMISE LINE

SPANISH TERRITORY

MISSOURI ADMITTED AS SLAVE STATE 1821

FLORIDA TERRITORY

ARKANSAS TERRITORY OPEN TO SLAVERY 1820

enter the Union at the same time. Missouri would enter as a slave state and Maine as a free state. In addition, a line would be drawn from Missouri's southern border across the rest of the Louisiana territory. Slavery would not be permitted in states formed north of the line. States to the south would be permitted to have slavery. These provisions were called the **Missouri Compromise.**

Southern politicians learned several important facts from this compromise. First, the South could no longer depend on the alliance with the northwestern states to protect slavery and other economic interests. Second, the free states controlled the House of Representatives and the electoral votes for president. The presidency could shift at any time to northern politicians. Third, the South needed to keep the number of slave states and free states equal. This would give the slave states enough senators to block laws harmful to slavery.

THE GROWTH OF THE ANTISLAVERY MOVEMENT

Before the issue of slavery in the territories arose again, important changes occurred in northern and southern societies. In the 1820s and 1830s, evangelical revivals in New York and the Northeast led by the Reverend Charles G. Finney brought on a movement to reform American society. Finney believed that slavery was evil and he preached against it. At the same time, there was a movement in Great Britain to abolish slavery in its empire.

In 1833, William Lloyd Garrison founded the American Anti-Slavery Society. The society urged the immediate end to slavery, with no thought of how that would affect the South. The Reverend Theodore Dwight Weld carried the message of **abolitionism** (the movement to do away with slavery) across the free states at the cost of being ridiculed and stoned. The Society flooded Congress with petitions for the abolition of slavery. This led to many angry debates in Congress between the Whigs and the Democrats. The lasting impact of the Society, however, was to convince many people that slavery was morally evil and that slave owners were sinners. The abolitionists (those who wanted to end slavery) felt morally superior and launched bitter attacks on slavery and slave owners.

In the 1820s, antislavery groups did exist in the South, especially in North Carolina. The Quakers were opposed to slavery. They bought slaves, sent them to free states, and then set them free. One North Carolina Quaker, Levi Coffin, was a conductor on the **underground railroad.** This was a secret way to help slaves escape from the South. The American Colonization Society provided money for free blacks to return to Africa, especially to Liberia. By 1840, however, antislavery groups no longer operated in North Carolina. Southerners rejected abolitionism and would not tolerate abolitionists.

The Missouri Compromise (map, opposite page) suppressed the issue of slavery for a while, but William Lloyd Garrison (above) soon urged immediate abolition. This raised the issue again.

Levi Coffin, a Quaker from Guilford County, moved to Indiana in 1826 and headed the underground railroad in Cincinnati in the 1850s.

THE COFFINS OF NORTH CAROLINA

Although North Carolina was a slave state, there were a number of abolitionists who, at least for a time, resided there. Such was the case of the Coffin family — Levi and his cousin Addison. Both men had ancestors in the Massachusetts area, which was a hotbed of abolitionism in the nineteenth century. Their abolitionist beliefs, however, grew from the fact that they were members of the Society of Friends, also known as the Quakers.

Both Levi and Addison were born in Guilford County at New Garden, the site of Guilford College. As a young man, Levi joined a group that was interested in freeing the slaves. In 1821, he became involved in a school that was established to educate slaves. The slave school soon became very popular with the slaves but was as equally unpopular with local slaveholders. Levi moved to Indiana in 1826 and became active in the underground railroad. His home served as a depot on the underground railroad, and neighbors donated food and supplies to his cause. At night, he would personally lead runaways along the concealed routes and arrange further passage into Canada. In one instance, he helped a mother and her child who were being chased by men with dogs who wished to return the pair to slavery. The adventure was later described by Harriet Beecher Stowe in *Uncle Tom's Cabin*. It is estimated that Levi helped some 3,000 slaves escape to freedom.

Levi's cousin Addison was born in 1822. As a young man, Addison was greatly influenced by Levi and soon became involved in the abolition movement as well as groups favoring temperance and women's rights. In the 1840s, he attended the very first National Abolition Convention. During the War Between the States, he continued to work for the abolition of slavery and served as a conductor on the underground railroad. After the war, Addison remained busy arranging for the migration of thousands of freedmen out of the South to new opportunities in the Midwest. Through his efforts, other Quakers set up a model farm, schools for the freedmen, and teacher training schools in North Carolina.

Both Levi and Addison shared beliefs that were not popular in North Carolina and the rest of the South. Although both men left North Carolina early in life, they continued to work for the abolition of slavery and the freedom of slaves within the state.

Emigration to Liberia.

NOTICE.

THE *MANAGERS of the AMERICAN CO-LONIZATION SOCIETY* give NOTICE, that they are ready to receive applications for the conveyance of free people of colour to the Colony of Liberia.

In all cases, the age, sex and profession of the Applicants must be mentioned.

Application may be made in Baltimore to *Hon. Judge Brice, Charles Howard, John H. B. Latrobe, Esq. or Charles C. Harper, Esq.* Agents of the Society. June 25.

Although North Carolina was a slave state, many people opposed slavery. Some supported the emigration of free blacks to Liberia in Africa.

The antislavery movement also affected the Methodist and Baptist churches. At first, the Methodist Church in North Carolina was antislavery. But ministers who preached antislavery sermons saw their membership decrease. By the 1830s, the Methodists had become more proslavery.

The Methodists and the Baptists each had national organizations. At a national conference in 1844, northern antislavery Methodists insisted that a Georgia bishop free his slaves. The bishop's wife had inherited the slaves, and Georgia law would not let her free them. The bishop wanted to resign to keep peace in the church. Instead, the slave-state Methodists withdrew from the national organization and formed their own southern church.

A similar situation split the national Baptist organization. The Baptist Board of Foreign Missions was controlled by northern ministers. The Board forced a respected Indian missionary named John Bushyhead to resign because he owned slaves. The Board announced that it would not in any way show approval of slavery. The slave-state Baptists broke away and formed their own southern organization. The North-South split in these and other groups further loosened the social bonds that bound the nation together.

Do You Remember?

1. By 1820, how many slave states and how many free states were there? Where were they located?
2. Before the Civil War, was North Carolina *ever* a free state?
3. What impact did the American Anti-Slavery Society have on the attitudes toward slavery?
4. Did antislavery groups exist in North Carolina?

MANIFEST DESTINY

After the Revolution, the United States occupied an area bordered by Canada, Florida, the Atlantic Ocean, and the Mississippi River. By 1918, the nation had expanded across the continent and into Alaska, the Pacific, and the Caribbean.

The first territory was acquired in 1803 with the Louisiana Purchase, and in 1819, Spain sold Florida to the United States. In the 1830s, many Americans believed it was their "manifest destiny" to expand to the Pacific. Disliking the harsh rule of Mexico, Texans (mostly Americans) rebelled in 1836, won their independence, and then became a state in 1845. This led to a war with Mexico in 1846. After defeating Mexico, the United States got most of what became the southwestern part of the country.

In 1818, the United States and Great Britain had agreed to a joint occupation of the Oregon country. But an 1846 treaty gave the United States what became the northwestern part of the nation. The purchase of a small strip of land from Mexico in 1853 completed American expansion to the Pacific. In 1867, Russia sold Alaska to the United States, and the nation's continental expansion was complete.

A war with Spain in 1898 resulted in the acquisition of Puerto Rico, Guam, and the Philippine Islands. (The United States gave the Philippines its freedom in 1946.) In 1898, the United States annexed the Hawaiian Islands after a local uprising led by American planters. And in 1899, part of the Samoan Islands fell under American rule. A revolution in Panama in 1903 enabled the United States to complete the Panama Canal in 1914. The purchase of the Virgin Islands from Denmark in 1917 completed the territorial expansion of the United States.

President James Knox Polk, born in North Carolina, believed in the "manifest destiny" of the United States. He waged war with Mexico (1846-1848) in order to secure the Texas border and obtain New Mexico and California for the United States.

WAR WITH MEXICO

Another conflict over slavery and territorial expansion was waiting to erupt. Americans living in Texas, with support from some Mexicans, won their independence from Mexico. In 1837, Texas asked to be admitted to the Union as a slave state. Most of the North Carolina congressmen were in favor of admitting Texas. The Whigs and the Democrats, however, blocked the admission of Texas because of the feelings about slavery in the country.

In 1844, James K. Polk, a North Carolina native, ran for president on the Democratic ticket. He promised not only to **annex** (add) Texas but

also to acquire California and the Oregon territory. After his election, Polk made good on his promise. Texas was admitted as a slave state in 1845.

Mexico was very angry when the United States annexed Texas. It refused to sell California to the United States. President Polk, therefore, welcomed a clash that took place between Mexican and American troops along the disputed Texas border in April 1846. It gave him the excuse he needed to ask Congress to declare war on Mexico. Polk wanted to seize from Mexico the territory she would not sell and to set the Texas boundary at the Rio Grande River.

Unfortunately, the slavery issue arose again. Representative David Wilmot of Pennsylvania proposed that slavery be barred from any territory gained from Mexico. This **Wilmot Proviso** split the House of Representatives along sectional lines. Northern Democrats and Whigs supported the proviso while southern Democrats and Whigs opposed it. The proviso passed the House, but southern senators defeated it.

The United States won the war with Mexico, gaining the territory that now forms the southwestern part of the nation, including California. The issue of barring slavery from these lands was no longer just an idea, but a real political problem. Northern congressmen were still insisting that the Wilmot Proviso be passed.

Though seriously outnumbered, General Winfield Scott captured Chapultepec in the last battle of the Mexican War.

MILITARY SCIENCE AND THE MEXICAN WAR

Top: *The U.S. Navy successfully landed 10,000 troops at Vera Cruz in March 1847.* **Above:** *After six months of difficult fighting, General Winfield Scott and his troops entered Mexico City in September 1847.*

Military science, the study of the effective use of military force, studies past wars because you cannot start a war just to test new ideas. An important war still studied is the Mexican War, which took place 1846-1848. The American military learned a number of valuable lessons from it. One lesson was the importance of medical care. About 1,800 American men died from combat, but about 11,000 died from disease. Military doctors learned to focus on the prevention of disease. Another lesson was the importance of mobile field artillery, which stopped the excellent Mexican cavalry in several battles. Americans experimented with rockets, but they were not accurate. The U.S. Navy also learned to transport troops by ship and land them on a hostile shore at Vera Cruz. This was called an *amphibious* (land and water) operation.

Learning to command and use troops was an important lesson. General Winfield Scott raised the art of generalship with his campaign from Vera Cruz to Mexico City. Mexican General Santa Anna tried several times to force Scott to attack the front of his army, where he was strong. Instead, Scott attacked Santa Anna's sides, where he was weak, and in this way won many victories. Many of Scott's officers learned how to command troops. The great generals of the Civil War — Lee, Grant, Sherman, Meade, Jackson — developed their skills under Scott.

North Carolina opposed the proviso, but it did not feel the same outrage as did some Deep South states. In 1848, Democrats in the eastern slaveholding counties called it "an audacious outrage upon Southern Rights and destructive of the ends of our glorious Union." The Democratic state convention of 1848 also condemned the proviso. In the 1848-1849 legislature, the Democrats introduced bills calling for the state to **secede** (withdraw from the Union) if slavery were barred from the new territories.

The Whigs supported a plan to extend the Missouri Compromise line (set at 36° 30') to the Pacific Ocean. They also opposed abolishing slavery or the interstate slave trade in the District of Columbia, which northern congressmen were demanding. North Carolina voters showed how they felt about these issues in the 1849 congressional races. The Whigs, who strongly favored the Union, won six of nine congressional races.

Do You Remember?

1. Why did President Polk welcome a conflict with Mexico?
2. What was the major point of the Wilmot Proviso?
3. In the 1849 congressional elections, how did North Carolina voters show their feelings about the possibility of seceding from the Union?

THE COMPROMISE OF 1850

Senator John C. Calhoun of South Carolina was opposed to the Compromise of 1850. He wanted slavery protected in the territories. His death in 1850 helped make compromise possible.

By late 1849, several bills before Congress again threatened to divide the two parties along sectional lines. One bill proposed that California become a free state. This bill southern congressmen could not accept because the slave states would then be outnumbered in the Senate. Another bill proposed a stronger fugitive (runaway) slave law to replace the one free states were not enforcing. This northern congressmen could not accept. Another bill recommended that New Mexico and Utah be organized as free territories. This too was unacceptable to southerners.

Seeing that these hotly debated issues might disrupt the Union, Senator Henry Clay of Kentucky proposed a compromise bill in early 1850. Strong leaders on both sides opposed certain parts of this bill. Senator John C. Calhoun of South Carolina would not accept any limits on slavery. President Zachary Taylor would not sign any bill that tied California statehood to other issues. It looked like the compromise was dead and the Union in danger. Instead, death took both men, Calhoun in March and Taylor in July. The new president, Millard Fillmore, favored the compromise.

Clay's **Compromise of 1850** was thus passed by Congress. The free states got the admission of California as a free state and a ban on the slave trade in the District of Columbia. The slave states got a stronger fugitive slave law, which required people in the free states to help catch escaped slaves. In the new territories of New Mexico and Utah, the issue

Senator Henry Clay of Kentucky was a Senate leader in 1850. He urged the Senate to pass compromise legislation in order to preserve the Union.

of slavery would be decided locally. This was called **popular sovereignty.** Part of Texas was given to New Mexico. In return, the United States took over Texas's debts.

The admission of California to the Union upset the balance of slave and free states in the Senate. And, since no one expected slavery to develop in the dry lands of New Mexico and Utah, the slave states got much less than they gave. North Carolina congressmen voted strongly for the fugitive slave law. There were fewer votes for the other measures. Only two of North Carolina's congressmen, both Whigs, voted for the admission of California.

In North Carolina in 1850 and 1851, meetings of political conventions and the legislature accepted the Compromise of 1850 as a final settlement of the slavery issue. However, there was a condition—the faithful enforcement of the fugitive slave law. If it were not enforced, Whigs and Democrats both warned that the Union was in danger.

THE KANSAS-NEBRASKA ACT

In national politics, however, the slavery issue would not die. People moved into the grassy plains west of Missouri and Iowa and needed territorial government. In 1854, Senator Stephen A. Douglas of Illinois brought about passage of the **Kansas-Nebraska Act,** creating the territories of Kansas and Nebraska. Although both territories were north of the Missouri Compromise line, this act allowed the settlers to decide whether to have slavery or not. No one knows how this provision got in the bill. Perhaps it was to get southern support for its quick passage or for Douglas's bid for the presidency or to help the railroads. Whatever the reason, allowing popular sovereignty repealed the Missouri Compromise. Slavery could now move north of the Missouri Compromise line. While they had little hope that Kansas would become a slave state, southerners declared it their right to take slaves into all territories.

Abolitionists were outraged that another slave state might be created. They promised to send antislavery settlers with guns into Kansas so they could oppose slavery. Missouri proslavery people promised to send men across the border to fight for slavery.

The result was such violence between the proslavery and antislavery sides that the territory was called "Bleeding Kansas." In 1858, proslavery forces met at Lecompton and drafted a constitution that protected slavery. Antislavery representatives did not attend the meeting. The proslavery group then applied for statehood. President James Buchanan supported them in hopes of getting the state's votes in the election of 1860. Senator Douglas, however, opposed statehood because the Lecompton Constitution was not obtained properly. Congress rejected Kansas's bid to join the Union. Again, southerners realized that northern votes alone could keep slave states from the Union.

Do You Remember?

1. What were the provisions of the Compromise of 1850?
2. How did the war with Mexico lead to a new quarrel over slavery in the country?
3. Why was Kansas referred to as "Bleeding Kansas"?

POLITICS AND SLAVERY

The Kansas-Nebraska Act also had a great impact on political parties. Up to this time, the major parties had been national ones. But this was about to change. The Whig party began to break up after the election of 1852. The northern wing of the party had become more antislavery and was less willing to compromise with the southern wing to keep internal peace.

Senator Stephen A. Douglas of Illinois in 1854 secured a law to undo the Missouri Compromise. This law let the Kansas Territory settlers decide on slavery. Kansas became a battleground between antislavery and proslavery forces.

The result was the creation in 1854 of a new political party—one that existed only in the free states. This new party was called the **Republican party.** It grew quickly, drawing antislavery Whigs and Democrats as members. In 1856, the Republicans nominated John C. Frémont for president on a platform that opposed the spread of slavery. Democrat James Buchanan won the election, but Frémont managed to get 1.3 million votes.

North Carolina's reaction to the Republican party was typical of southern feeling. When Benjamin S. Hedrick, a Chapel Hill professor, announced that he would support Frémont, the University of North Carolina fired him and people ran him from the state. **Extremists** (those who will not compromise their views) warned that had Frémont won, they would have supported secession.

Because the Republican party did not exist in the slave states, the Democratic party was the only one binding the Union together. Southern extremists like Robert B. Rhett of South Carolina and William L. Yancey of Alabama wanted the slave states to secede. These "fire-eaters" worked to split up the Democratic party, believing that secession would follow.

INCREASING TENSIONS

Events from 1857 to 1860 helped the fire-eaters greatly. In 1857, the Supreme Court issued the Dred Scott decision. Dred Scott was a slave whose master took him from the slave state of Missouri to the free territories of Illinois and Wisconsin for five years. Scott asked the Court to free him because of the time he spent in the free territories. The Court did not free Scott, but it did rule that Congress could not forbid slavery in the territories. Republicans refused to accept this decision. They believed that they answered to a "higher law" in their fight against slavery. This position greatly angered southerners.

In 1859, the Republicans published parts of a document written by a North Carolinian. In 1857, Hinton Rowan Helper of Davie County had published *The Impending Crisis of the South: How to Meet It*. Helper compared the economic progress of the North with the backwardness of the South. Helper's answer to why the South lagged behind was slavery. Slavery "lies at the root of all shame, poverty, ignorance, tyranny and imbecility of the South," Helper wrote. "Slavery must be thoroughly eradicated; let this be done, and a glorious future will await us." What awaited Helper was the threat of death if he set foot in North Carolina again. A Methodist minister, the Reverend Daniel Worth, passed out copies of Helper's book in North Carolina. The state found him guilty of spreading "incendiary literature" and sentenced him to a year in prison. Worth fled the state rather than go to prison.

The most alarming event occurred in late 1859. John Brown, an abolitionist from Kansas, plotted to take over the federal arsenal (arms fac-

Hinton Rowan Helper of Davie County made southerners angry. His book, The Impending Crisis of the South *(1857), charged that slavery held back the economic progress of the South. The book was banned in North Carolina.*

tory) at Harpers Ferry, Virginia. He intended to arm nearby slaves so they could fight for their freedom. Brown and about twenty men seized the arsenal, but federal troops put an end to the raid. Wounded in the fight, Brown was jailed, tried, and hanged. Brown's death made him a martyr in the North. When southerners learned that leading Republicans had helped finance the raid and that northern opinion approved of it, they were enraged. These events encouraged extremists like Rhett and Yancey. People began to believe that it was impossible to stay in the Union if the Republican party won the presidency.

Left: John Brown led an attack on a U.S. arsenal at Harpers Ferry. He intended to arm nearby slaves so they could fight for their freedom. ***Above:*** A free black from Raleigh, John Anthony Copeland was one of Brown's small force. He was later hanged for his part in the raid.

THE ELECTION OF 1860

When the Democratic National Convention met at Charleston, South Carolina, in April 1860, a fight over the party platform brought matters to a head. (A **platform** is a statement of the principles and policies the party supports.) Stephen A. Douglas's supporters controlled the platform committee. They wanted a platform backing popular sovereignty. The extremists wanted a platform requiring Congress to protect slavery wherever it went. Douglas, the leading Democratic candidate, could not get northern votes if he ran on the extremist platform. Douglas's supporters convinced the committee to approve their platform. The Deep South delegates were so angry they walked out of the convention. The North Carolina delegates remained. Not enough delegates, however, were left to give a candidate the two-thirds' vote needed for the nomination.

This situation led to the nomination of four candidates for president. The Democrats who supported Douglas met in Baltimore and nominated him on a platform of popular sovereignty. The southern Democrats met separately in Baltimore and nominated John C. Breckinridge of Kentucky. Their platform called for Congress to protect slavery in all of the territories. The border-state Whigs met in Baltimore to form the Constitutional Union party. They supported the Union and nominated John Bell of Tennessee. The Republicans met in Chicago and nominated Abraham Lincoln of Illinois. The Republican platform was not just antislavery. It also supported a protective tariff, a plan to give free western land to settlers, and the construction of a transcontinental railroad with one end in the North. None of these measures would help the South.

Above: Abraham Lincoln's election as president in 1860 brought turmoil to the South. Many southerners believed his election justified secession. *Right:* The presidential election of 1860 split along sectional lines. Lincoln did not win any states south of the Ohio River.

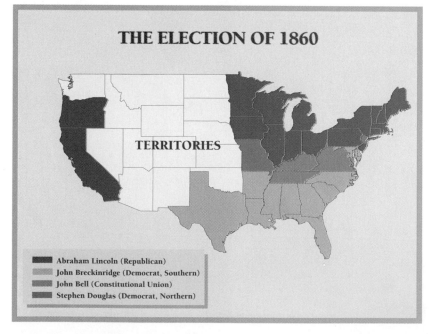

THE ELECTION OF 1860

TERRITORIES

■ Abraham Lincoln (Republican)
■ John Breckinridge (Democrat, Southern)
■ John Bell (Constitutional Union)
■ Stephen Douglas (Democrat, Northern)

The election amounted to a revolution in politics. For the first time, a party getting votes only from one section of the nation won the election. Abraham Lincoln received 1.9 million votes (a minority of the total votes cast) and was elected president. Almost all of Lincoln's votes were from the free states. Douglas had 1.4 million votes, while Breckinridge had 850,000 and Bell 590,000. Breckinridge barely carried North Carolina; he received 48,539 votes to 44,990 for Douglas and 2,701 for Bell.

Do You Remember?

1. What did the Supreme Court rule in the Dred Scott decision?
2. In his book *The Impending Crisis of the South: How to Meet It,* what did Hinton Rowan Helper say was the basic cause of the South's backwardness?
3. Who was John Brown and what did he attempt to do?
4. Who were the four candidates for president in the election of 1860? Who won the election?

THE PUSH FOR SECESSION

In North Carolina, the secessionists, led by Democratic governor John W. Ellis, considered the election of the "black Republican" Abraham Lincoln reason enough for secession. They had a long list of complaints against the Republican party. It was against slavery. Its abolitionist members could not be trusted to make national policy. Its control of the presidency and the Congress would endanger slavery. It supported laws in the free states that prevented enforcement of the Fugitive Slave Law of 1850. When southerners pointed out that the party's policies and actions violated the Constitution, the Republicans replied that they obeyed a "higher law." To protect slavery and southern economic interests, the secessionists believed they must withdraw and form a separate nation.

A political struggle between secessionists and unionists thus began in North Carolina in November 1860. The secessionists were mainly Democrats; the unionists were mainly ex-Whigs. Secessionists believed that the states could withdraw from the Union just as they had joined it—by the vote of a state convention representing the people. In addition, the Democratic secessionists had no hope of political appointments or influence under Lincoln. The Republican party did not exist in North Carolina, so Democrats could not expect to be appointed to federal offices. The future looked brighter in a southern Confederacy, where many positions would be open to them.

Unionists believed that the people had a right to overthrow a government when it became a tyranny and threatened life, liberty, and property. The unionists, however, did not believe that Lincoln and the

In the 1860 presidential election, John C. Breckinridge of Kentucky was the candidate of the southern Democrats.

Top: Senator John C. Crittenden of Kentucky introduced legislation in 1860 to permit slavery south of the Missouri Compromise line. *Above:* Congressman John A. Gilmer of Guilford County supported Crittenden's proposal. He tried to keep North Carolina in the Union. *Opposite page:* Governor John W. Ellis favored secession after Lincoln's election. He urged South Carolina to secede in hopes that North Carolina would follow.

Republicans had done anything to cause North Carolina to withdraw from the Union. The unionists wanted to wait until Lincoln and his party took direct action to harm slavery or the southern people. Then they would support revolution, not secession. It was "better to bear the ills we have, than fly to others we know not of," wrote unionist William W. Holden.

The unionists also saw a brighter political future for themselves within the Union. They no longer had a national party. These ex-Whigs could accept parts of the Republican platform if the Republicans would stop opposing slavery in the territories. The unionists thus thought they could join the Republican party.

When the legislature met in November 1860, Governor Ellis proposed a conference of all the southern states to consider secession. He also wanted the legislature to call a state convention to consider secession and to provide money for military preparedness. The unionists blocked these proposals until the Christmas recess.

ANOTHER STEP TOWARD SECESSION

Meanwhile, several important events took place outside the state. When Congress met in December 1860, Senator John J. Crittenden of Kentucky introduced legislation to settle the slavery issue. Basically, his legislation would permit slavery south of the Missouri Compromise line in the new territories and protect slavery where it existed. A majority of North Carolina's congressmen supported Crittenden's resolutions, including John A. Gilmer and Zebulon B. Vance. The amendments were voted down in the Senate committee, which had a majority of Republicans. Lincoln would not compromise on the question of extending slavery.

On December 20, South Carolina seceded. Governor Ellis had advised South Carolina to secede because he believed it would then be easier to convince North Carolinians to do the same. Following South Carolina out of the Union in January and February were Georgia and the Gulf states. The Union was broken.

On February 4, 1861, delegates from the seceding states met in Montgomery, Alabama. South Carolina, Georgia, Florida, Alabama, Mississippi, Louisiana, and Texas met to form a new government called the **Confederate States of America**. The delegates adopted a constitution closely modeled after the United States Constitution and elected Jefferson Davis of Mississippi president.

THE PEOPLE SPEAK

In North Carolina, the secessionists held meetings in unionist counties such as Wake, Moore, Chatham, and Buncombe to stir up support for secession. In those counties that already favored secession like

Mecklenburg, Anson, and Pitt, flag-raising ceremonies were held to keep secessionist feelings high.

On January 10, 1861, men from Wilmington and Smithville seized two federal forts near the mouth of the Cape Fear so federal troops would not reinforce them. One was Fort Caswell and the other was Fort Johnston. When the War Department promised not to send reinforcements, Governor Ellis ordered the men to leave the forts.

When the legislature met again on January 7, there was another call for a state convention to discuss secession. For three weeks, however, unionist legislators held up passage of the convention bill. In a compromise, the unionists agreed to pass the convention bill if the people could also vote on whether the convention should meet. The bill passed, and the election was to be held on February 28. Delegates to the convention were to be elected at the same time.

Both the secessionists and the unionists actively campaigned for the convention. The *North Carolina Standard* led the unionist fight. The unionists wanted the state to wait until Lincoln acted against the slave states. The *Raleigh State Journal* and the *Wilmington Journal* presented the secessionist side. The secessionists favored seceding immediately since the new Confederate government was ready to accept North Carolina.

The election results surprised both sides. The people voted 47,323 to 46,672 *not* to hold a convention. Had the convention met, unionists would have held 78 of 120 seats. The people of North Carolina thus voted to stay in the Union.

In late March, the secessionists renewed their efforts to push North Carolina into the Confederacy. They called a Southern Rights party convention to meet in Goldsboro. Over a thousand delegates from across the state met and elected Weldon N. Edwards president. They passed resolutions favoring the Confederacy and immediate secession. The delegates warned the federal government not to reinforce its forts on the coast. The delegates then disbanded to form county organizations to press for secession. They argued that the Confederacy was "waiting with open arms and willing hearts" to receive them.

THE ATTACK ON FORT SUMTER

Events in Charleston, South Carolina, soon put an end to any influence Tar Heel unionists had. Union troops still held Fort Sumter in Charleston harbor. South Carolina and the Confederacy wanted them to leave. On April 8, President Lincoln announced that he would send supplies to the fort. Southern leaders believed this meant Lincoln planned to hold onto the southern forts. On April 12, South Carolina and Confederate forces bombarded the fort. The next day, the Union troops surrendered. The war had begun.

The Southern Rights party elected Weldon N. Edwards president at their convention in Goldsboro.

President Lincoln then decided to use troops to force the rebellious states back into the Union. He asked the states to supply 75,000 troops, including two regiments from North Carolina. Governor Ellis immediately replied that "You can get no troops from North Carolina." He regarded this call for troops as a "wicked violation of the laws of the country" and a "war upon the liberties of a free people."

SECESSION

Governor Ellis prepared the state for secession. He ordered federal Forts Macon, Johnston, and Caswell and the federal arsenal at Fayetteville seized. Then he called a special session of the legislature for May 1.

The attack on Fort Sumter and Lincoln's call for troops silenced the unionists. They had been insisting that the Republicans had not harmed slavery or the South. Now war had come. The question was no longer whether North Carolina would fight, but on which side. The unionists gave up their fight to keep the state in the Union. Zebulon Vance best expressed their feelings.

Congressman Zebulon Baird Vance of Buncombe County opposed secession, but when war began he became a secessionist. He did so because he did not want the unionists and secessionists in the state fighting one another.

I was addressing a large and excited crowd, large numbers of whom were armed, and literally had my arm extended upward in pleading for peace and the Union of our Fathers, when the telegraphic news was announced of the firing on Sumter and the President's call for seventy-five thousand volunteers. When my hand came down from that impassioned gesticulation, it fell slowly and sadly by the side of a secessionist. I immediately with altered voice and manner, called upon the assembled multitude to volunteer, not to fight against, but for South Carolina.

On May 1, the legislature called for a convention to meet May 20 to discuss secession. At the convention, the delegates voted unanimously to secede from the Union by repealing the ordinance of 1789. This was the ordinance ratifying the United States Constitution. On May 21, President Davis proclaimed North Carolina a member of the Confederacy. For better or worse, the state had decided to fight where "blood was thicker than water."

Do You Remember?
1. What were the complaints of the secessionists in North Carolina against the Republican party?
2. What were the differences in the way secessionists and unionists in North Carolina looked at withdrawing from the Union?
3. What military action started the war?
4. What action did the legislature take at the May 20 convention?

CHAPTER · REVIEW

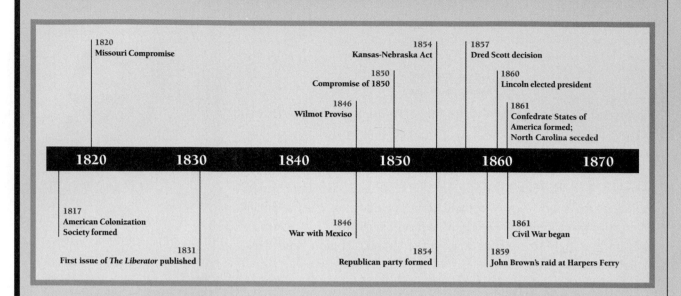

1820
Missouri Compromise

1854
Kansas-Nebraska Act

1857
Dred Scott decision

1850
Compromise of 1850

1860
Lincoln elected president

1846
Wilmot Proviso

1861
Confederate States of
America formed;
North Carolina seceded

| 1820 | 1830 | 1840 | 1850 | 1860 | 1870 |

1817
American Colonization
Society formed

1846
War with Mexico

1861
Civil War began

1831
First issue of *The Liberator* published

1854
Republican party formed

1859
John Brown's raid at Harpers Ferry

Reviewing People, Places, and Terms

Match each word or phrase with the correct definition below.

abolitionism
annex
Confederate States of America
popular sovereignty
secede
Wilmot Proviso

1. The government formed by the seven southern states who seceded in 1860-1861
2. To add to a larger area
3. The proposal that slavery not be permitted in any territory gained from Mexico
4. The right of the people who live within an area to decide upon an issue
5. The movement to do away with slavery
6. To withdraw from the Union

Understanding the Facts

1. Why was it important to the South that the number of slave states and free states be kept equal?

2. What were the provisions of the Missouri Compromise?
3. To which African country did many free blacks and freed slaves emigrate in the early 1800s?
4. Members of what religious group in North Carolina would often buy slaves so they could then set them free?
5. What happened to the Methodist and Baptist churches because of the slavery question?
6. President James K. Polk, a North Carolinian, supported the admission of what state as a slave state in 1845?
7. What did the Kansas-Nebraska Act allow that basically nullified the Missouri Compromise?
8. What seven states formed the Confederate States of America?
9. What did President Lincoln do that, in effect, forced North Carolina into the Confederacy?

Developing Critical Thinking

1. With the passage of the Missouri Compromise, it could be said that the United States government tried politically to "balance the scales" on

the issue of slavery in the country. Do you agree?

2. Why do you suppose most North Carolina congressmen were in favor of admitting Texas to the Union?

3. Do you think states should have the right to secede from the Union? Why or why not?

Applying Your Skills

1. Prepare a report on the history and operation of the underground railroad, which helped slaves escape to free states and Canada. As part of your report, plan an "escape" through your community or county.

2. Prepare a circle graph that depicts the results of the 1860 presidential election. Use the figures given on page 299.

3. What states were formed in total or in part from the territory acquired from Mexico after the Mexican War?

Making Connections

1. There are four different aspects to "military science." Find out what those four areas are.

2. What military tactics from the Mexican War are used in modern warfare?

3. Find out how much the United States paid for the Louisiana Purchase, Alaska, and the Gadsden Purchase.

4. What was meant by the idea of "manifest destiny" held by so many Americans in the 1830s?

Tar Heel Trivia

• When Harriet Beecher Stowe's antislavery novel, *Uncle Tom's Cabin*, was published in 1852, it sold more than one million copies in less than two years. Its publication helped increase the influence of the abolitionists and stir up sectional resentments.

• John Anthony Copeland was a North Carolina free black who was hung for his part in John Brown's raid upon the arsenal at Harpers Ferry.

BUILDING SKILLS: GENERALIZATIONS AND CONCLUSIONS

When you listen to what other people say or read what others have written, you usually draw a conclusion or make a generalization about what you have heard or read. When you do so, it is important to understand that the writer brings her or his own personal beliefs and feelings to what he or she writes. Some writers are fairly factual, others are trying to tell a story or make a point, some may try to convince others of the worthiness of their writings, and still others are trying to influence the beliefs of readers.

On a separate sheet of paper, write the numbers 1 to 9. Read the following statements, which might have been made during the period leading up to North Carolina's secession from the Union. Decide whether the person who might have made the statement was a secessionist or a unionist. Write the letter *S* next to the number on your paper if a secessionist would have made the statement. If a unionist would have made the statement, write the letter *U*.

1. We believe that the people have the right to overthrow a government when it becomes a tyranny and threatens life, liberty, and property.

2. To protect slavery and our economic interests, we must form a separate nation.

3. We must wait until Lincoln and his party take direct action to harm slavery or our people.

4. It is "better to bear the ills we have, than fly to others we know not of."

5. We will vote to hold a state convention to discuss secession if the people can first vote on whether such a convention should be held.

6. The federal government must not reinforce its forts along the North Carolina coast.

7. The *North Carolina Standard* editorials are right on the mark.

8. I certainly agree with the people who run the *Raleigh State Journal*.

9. We joined it, we can withdraw from it.

CHAPTER FIFTEEN

NORTH CAROLINA IN THE CIVIL WAR

. . . a brave people should carry the olive branch in one hand and the sword in the other.
> —James G. Ramsay, member of the Confederate Congress from Salisbury, North Carolina

THE CONFEDERATE STATE OF NORTH CAROLINA played an unusual role in the Civil War. It provided more troops than any other state in the Confederacy, yet it was the only state with an active peace movement. More men were drafted from North Carolina than from any other state, but more of its troops deserted from the army than from any other state. It opposed many of the policies of the Confederate government, yet fought until the end. North Carolina was also an important blockade-running state. Let's examine the reasons why North Carolina played such an unusual role in the war.

PREPARING FOR WAR

Once it seceded, North Carolina supported the major war aim of the Confederacy. That was to establish the Confederate States of America as a nation among nations.

The major goal of the United States was to restore the Union. Later, the Union adopted another war aim: the destruction of slavery. By the fall of 1862, President Abraham Lincoln found it necessary to free the slaves in the Confederate states. Lincoln's **Emancipation Proclamation** freed "all"

At Bentonville, General Joseph E. Johnston tried to destroy part of General William T. Sherman's army. It was the largest and bloodiest battle ever fought in North Carolina. This is a photograph of a re-enactment.

Terms: Emancipation Proclamation, strategy, blockade, ironclad, draft, writ of habeas corpus, Conservative party, blockade running, cavalry, deserter, draft resister, truce

People: General Robert E. Lee, General Walter Gwyn, General Benjamin F. Butler, General Ambrose Burnside, William W. Holden, Zebulon Baird Vance, James W. Cooke, General William T. Sherman, General Joseph E. Johnston, General George H. Stoneman

Places: Richmond, Bethel, Forts Clark and Hatteras, Fort Macon, Fort Fisher

persons held as slaves" as of January 1, 1863. He did this for many reasons. The Union Army was seizing many slaves, and some commanders were freeing them. Some Republicans were urging Lincoln to wage war against slavery and end the threat of future civil war. Lincoln also knew that Great Britain would support the United States if the war was being fought to end slavery.

ADVANTAGES AND DISADVANTAGES

If resources were the only thing that determined who would win a war, the Confederacy was at a great disadvantage. The Union's 19 million people greatly outnumbered the Confederacy's white population of 5.5 million. The Union could, therefore, supply more men for the armies and more laborers to produce supplies for the war.

The Union also had many more shipyards, iron mills, metal factories, textile mills, and arsenals than the Confederacy. Railroads were used to ship men and materials during the war. The Union had 22,000 miles of railroads to the Confederacy's 9,000 miles. In addition, the Union had a functioning government, able to put the nation on a war footing quickly. The Confederacy had to fight the war while putting together its national government.

The Confederacy did have some advantages. For the most part, the war was fought in the South. People fight harder when they are defending their homes. Also, they were fighting on "familiar" territory. Probably a higher percentage of southerners had some military training. And, the South had a number of strong military leaders including Robert E. Lee.

The Confederate States of America was formed by the eleven states highlighted on the map.

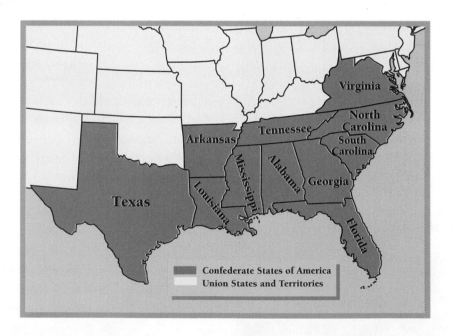

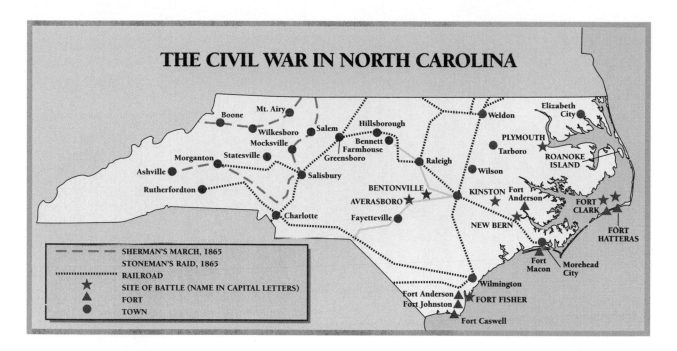

THE CIVIL WAR IN NORTH CAROLINA

Boone
Mt. Airy
Wilkesboro
Salem
Hillsborough
Weldon
Elizabeth City
Mocksville
Bennett Farmhouse
PLYMOUTH
Morganton
Statesville
Greensboro
Tarboro
ROANOKE ISLAND
Ashville
Salisbury
Raleigh
Wilson
Rutherfordton
BENTONVILLE
AVERASBORO
KINSTON Fort Anderson
FORT CLARK
Charlotte
Fayetteville
NEW BERN
FORT HATTERAS

Legend:
- - - SHERMAN'S MARCH, 1865
.... STONEMAN'S RAID, 1865
•••••••• RAILROAD
★ SITE OF BATTLE (NAME IN CAPITAL LETTERS)
▲ FORT
● TOWN

Fort Macon
Morehead City
Wilmington
Fort Anderson
Fort Johnston
FORT FISHER
Fort Caswell

UNION AND CONFEDERATE STRATEGY

Strategy is the overall plan for using military forces or for achieving a goal. The Union's strategy changed as the war progressed. At first, the Union strategy was to blockade all Confederate ports and seize the Mississippi River. A **blockade** (the use of naval forces to stop shipping) would prevent the Confederacy from selling cotton abroad and getting war supplies from other nations. Taking control of the Mississippi River would split the Confederacy in two, leaving Arkansas, Texas, and Louisiana stranded. This strategy was called the "Anaconda Plan" because it would squeeze the Confederacy to death, just as the giant anaconda snake does to its prey.

Lincoln's generals later decided that capturing the Confederate capital of Richmond could end the war. This strategy failed, however, because General Robert E. Lee was able to hold off Union armies from the doors of Richmond for several years. In 1864 and 1865, Union Generals Ulysses S. Grant and William T. Sherman came up with the strategy that brought victory. Their plan was to destroy Confederate armies and to lay waste the land so civilians would stop supporting the war.

The Union also had a political strategy: to stop European nations from recognizing the Confederacy. If Great Britain, for example, recognized the Confederacy, the Royal Navy might help break the blockade.

The Confederates also had military and political strategies. On land, they planned to "wear down" the invading Union armies. They hoped that rising casualties would cause northerners to tire of the war. At sea, the Confederacy wanted to make sure the Union blockade didn't work.

Top: This map shows important places and events in the state during the war. **Above:** *General Robert E. Lee was the ablest Confederate general. Most North Carolina troops served in his Army of Northern Virginia.*

Raw recruits in state regiments had to be trained for military service. Training occurred in camps all over the state.

The Confederate Navy used swift *raiders* (fast, lightly armed ships) to capture Union merchant ships and draw the Union Navy away from the blockade. In coastal waters, the Confederate navy used **ironclads** (armored vessels) and even a submarine to sink the Union's wooden ships and open the ports.

The Confederacy's political strategy was called "King Cotton Diplomacy." The Confederacy believed that British and French textile mills needed the South's cotton to keep running. If the Confederacy stopped selling cotton abroad for a time, it believed the French and British would be forced to help the Confederacy break the blockades to get the cotton they needed.

Do You Remember?

1. What advantages did the Confederacy have over the Union?
2. What was the Union's Anaconda Plan?
3. What was the Confederacy's "King Cotton Diplomacy" strategy?

THE EARLY DAYS OF THE WAR

North Carolina's most important job early in the war was to raise, train, and arm volunteer troops. North Carolina did this better than any other southern state. Although the state had only one-ninth of the Confederacy's population, it supplied one-sixth of all its troops. Some 125,000 Tar Heels served in the war.

To train them, the state opened thirteen camps in locations from Southport to Asheville. Arms were at first difficult to find. Some men trained with pointed sticks. But soon the men had rifled muskets from the captured Union arsenal at Fayetteville.

By the end of May 1861, the state rushed its first troops to Virginia to fight at Bethel. They left Raleigh singing "Dixie" and "The Girl I Left Behind Me." The troops' heroism "hallowed and marked every important battlefield."

WAR ON THE COAST

The coast of North Carolina was most vulnerable to Union attack. The Confederate Army, not the state, was in charge of its defense. General Walter Gwyn set up forts on the Outer Banks to guard the inlets into the sounds. At Hatteras Inlet, he raised two sand forts—Forts Clark and Hatteras. These forts, armed with 32-pound cannons taken from the Norfolk Navy Yard, protected the area while Confederate ships sailed out into the Atlantic to capture Union merchant ships.

The Union Navy wanted to capture the forts and stop the raids of the "mosquito fleet." In August 1861, Union General Benjamin F. Butler landed troops and captured Fort Clark but was unable to capture Fort Hatteras. Butler's ships then bombarded (fired cannonballs at) the fort, setting part of it on fire. The defenders surprisingly surrendered. The Union now had a foothold on the Outer Banks.

General Gwyn saw that he could not hold the other forts against a combined land and sea attack. He ordered the sand forts at Oregon and Ocracoke inlets to be abandoned. He moved their guns to Roanoke Island, hoping to prevent Union advances into Albemarle Sound.

BURNSIDE'S EXPEDITION

Butler's success at Hatteras Inlet led General George B. McClellan, who was now the commander of the Union Army, to plan further action in North Carolina. He knew that the Confederacy had only two major north-south railroads. One ran from Lynchburg, Virginia, to Chattanooga. The other ran from Richmond to Charleston and Augusta. The Wilmington and Weldon Railroad in North Carolina formed the part of this line nearest the coast. If Union troops occupied the mainland of North Carolina, they could cut the railroad and prevent supplies from reaching Lee's army in Virginia.

In February 1862, McClellan sent General Ambrose Burnside with 13,000 men and 76 ships to seize Roanoke Island and New Bern. Burnside quickly defeated the 1,500 Confederate troops he faced and destroyed 7 small Confederate gunboats. Burnside's victory opened the way to Albemarle Sound. Union troops quickly captured Elizabeth City and

General Ambrose Burnside commanded Union troops that seized Roanoke Island and New Bern. Men called his cheek whiskers "sideburns."

Above: General Burnside's troops drove out the outnumbered Confederate forces and captured New Bern on March 13. Union forces held North Carolina's second largest city for the remainder of the war. *Opposite page:* Confederate troops stationed at Fort Macon on Bogue Banks were bombarded by Union guns for eleven hours before they surrendered late in the day.

Edenton, blocked the Chesapeake and Albemarle Canal, burned Winton, and sacked Columbia.

With Albemarle Sound in Union hands, Burnside attacked New Bern in March 1862. His men easily drove out the Confederates, who set fire to the town before retreating. Next, Burnside captured Washington. He then sent his men south to capture Morehead City and Beaufort. Fort Macon guarded the entrance to the channel leading to Morehead City. Burnside's ships bombarded this brick fort while troops attacked it from the land side. Surrounded on land and water with no hope of relief, the fort surrendered in April. Burnside controlled the coast of North Carolina from Morehead City northward.

Do You Remember?

1. What was North Carolina's most important job during the early days of the war?
2. Why did the Union commanders feel it was important to occupy the mainland of North Carolina?

The Union conquest of the coastal area had an effect on the state election of 1862. Many people blamed the loss of eastern North Carolina not only upon the Confederate government in Richmond but also upon the secessionists who controlled the state government. The people were also angry over the Conscription Act of 1862. This act made men between the ages of 18 and 35 eligible to be **drafted** (forced to serve in the army). At the same time, it also permitted men who were drafted to hire substitutes. However, only the wealthy could afford substitutes.

People were also upset when the Confederacy suspended the **writ of habeas corpus.** A basic American protection, this court order releases imprisoned people if the authorities cannot show why they are being held. The Confederacy had begun to jail men who seemed to be disloyal—including some North Carolinians—without bringing charges against them.

People also had complaints against the state government, which was controlled by secessionists. Governors John W. Ellis and Henry T. Clark failed to appoint to government or military offices any men who had opposed secession. The secessionists thus failed to get the support of all classes of people for the war effort. They even began to persecute people who opposed the war effort.

THE ELECTION OF 1862

William W. Holden was the editor of the *North Carolina Standard.* Holden had helped lead the state Democratic party to victory in the 1850s. The Democrats, however, would not nominate him for governor or United States Senator in the 1850s, offices he felt he had earned. In 1860, Holden tried to keep the national Democratic party from splitting. After it did split, he supported the Union Democratic candidate for president, Stephen A. Douglas. Even after Governor Ellis proposed secession, Holden supported the Union.

As the war began, though, Holden voted for secession as a member of the convention. Still, he was politically on the outside looking in at the secessionists running the state government.

Holden was determined to restore two-party politics in the state. In 1862, the secessionists nominated William Johnston as Democratic candidate for governor. Johnston, an ex-Whig, was a railroad executive from Charlotte. Holden wanted a candidate who would appeal to the old unionists he hoped would join the new **Conservative party.** At a secret meeting, Conservatives decided to nominate a young ex-Whig, Zebulon Baird Vance. They then organized county meetings to nominate him, making him appear to be a popular choice.

Top: Henry T. Clark became governor after John W. Ellis's death in 1861. Opposite page: Zebulon B. Vance was elected governor in 1862. A Whig unionist, he opposed many of Jefferson Davis's policies. Above: Vance (right) with two of his fellow officers.

Vance was born on Reems Creek, Buncombe County, in this homeplace, now a state historic site.

Zebulon Vance was one of the most interesting and popular politicians in the state's history. He was born on Reems Creek in Buncombe County in 1830. After completing a one-year law course at the state university in 1852, Vance practiced law in Asheville. Finding law too dull, Vance entered politics, which became his life's work. He was elected county solicitor in 1852 and a state legislator in 1854. Using his powerful way of speaking and down-home ways, Vance was elected to the United States House of Representatives in 1859. There and at home, he worked to preserve the Union. When war came, though, he enlisted in the Confederate Army as a private. He quickly rose to the rank of colonel in the 26th North Carolina Regiment.

Neither Vance nor Johnston campaigned. The newspapers campaigned for them, the *North Carolina Standard* for Vance and the *Raleigh State Journal* for Johnston. The election results surprised everyone. Vance was elected governor by a vote of some 55,000 to 21,000. Conservative party candidates also won a majority of the seats in the legislature. Not only did this election restore the two-party system, but it also rejected secessionist and Confederate policies. In no other Confederate state did the old unionists gain control of the government. This situation led to conflict with the Confederate government.

CONFLICTS WITH THE CONFEDERACY

Governor Vance supported the war effort, but he was often at odds with the Confederate government. In part, he did this to keep the support of the Conservatives who had elected him. These Conservatives believed that the Confederate government of President Jefferson Davis was becoming a military dictatorship with little regard for the rights of individuals.

Vance's first task was to insist that the Confederacy bring an army to the North Carolina coast and push the Union Army out. Davis responded that the Confederacy did not have enough troops to do that. He did promise to build ironclads to destroy the Union Navy in the sounds if Vance would strip the railroads of iron for the ships. This Vance did, but the Confederacy used the iron for other purposes. Davis asked Vance to help build another north-south railroad line from Danville, Virginia, to Greensboro. Vance refused. He was afraid that, when this line opened, the Confederacy would no longer have a reason to defend the Wilmington and Weldon line. The railroad was "the lifeline of the Confederacy" by which men and supplies reached Lee's army. In early 1863 and later, Davis did send troops to defend the coastal plain, but they were only able to retake Plymouth.

Vance's next task was more difficult. Many Conservatives believed the Conscription Act was unconstitutional because it forced men to join the army against their will. Many conscripts (those forced to join the army) refused to report as ordered. Vance, however, supported the bill. He did look for more acceptable ways to enforce the law. Vance got the Confederacy to agree to let state militia officers collect the conscripts. In this way, the conscripts would avoid harsh treatment from Confederate soldiers. Still, the Confederacy sent troops into the state to enforce the law, violating its agreement with Vance.

The Conscription Act was not clear on hiring substitutes. One North Carolinian who had hired a substitute was ordered to report for service anyway. The man got a court order from a state judge stating that he did not have to report. The Confederate secretary of war, however, ordered conscription officers to ignore such court orders and to seize the man, which they did. Governor Vance ordered state militia officers to resist Confederate officers with force if they ignored state court orders. Tensions became so high that an armed clash seemed likely, but the Confederacy backed down. It agreed not to seize citizens freed by state court order.

At first, the Davis administration promised to allow conscripts to join regiments of their choice. But it violated that pledge as well. Despite these difficulties, the state supplied more conscripts to the Confederacy (over 21,000) than any other state.

Confederate President Jefferson Davis allowed the state to arm and clothe its troops. Still, people disliked some of his policies: the draft, suspension of the writ of habeas corpus, and the lack of coastal defense.

Above: Fort Fisher kept Union ships away from the mouth of the Cape Fear River so that blockade runners could enter and leave. Wilmington became the Confederacy's largest-blockade running port. **Opposite page, below:** *General W. G. Lewis's coat was typical of clothing the state made for its troops. Blockade runners imported enough cloth for 25,000 uniforms, many of which were never used.*

Another problem with the Confederacy arose over the appointment of officers. Compared to the number of troops supplied, there were fewer men from North Carolina appointed as general officers than from any other state. The Confederacy may have doubted Tar Heels' loyalty, since the state had supported the Union so strongly. The Confederate War Department also appointed officers from other states to command North Carolina regiments. Vance protested these policies but could not change them.

Governor Vance also fought the Confederacy for violating the civil rights of North Carolinians. In 1863, unionist civilians in Madison County raided Marshall, the county seat, and stole salt and clothing. They retreated to their stronghold in Shelton Laurel near the Tennessee line. The Confederate government ordered Colonel James A. Keith to punish them. He captured thirteen old men and boys, accused them of the raid, and executed them on the spot. Vance was furious because the accused raiders should have been turned over to civil courts for trial. Vance demanded that Keith be tried in a military court for murder. Instead, the Confederacy let Keith resign. He was never tried or punished.

BLOCKADE RUNNING

Early in the war, the Confederacy agreed to let the state clothe its troops because the Confederacy could not handle the task. This agreement worked to the state's advantage, for North Carolina had forty-six textile mills, more than any other state. These mills supplied all the cloth the troops needed. In late 1862, however, the Confederacy tried to end this arrangement, wanting to control all supplies itself. Governor Vance asked the Confederacy to let the state continue supplying clothing, and President Davis consented. But the mills then increased their prices, and the state could not afford to buy from them.

In 1863, Governor Vance came up with a plan to get clothing and other supplies from Great Britain by **blockade running** (using ships to sail through a blockade). With state funds, Vance bought cotton and a blockade-running steamship named the *Advance*. Purchased cheaply in the Confederacy, the cotton brought a high price in Europe. Vance also bought a one-fourth interest in four British ships, all used in running the blockade. These British ships carried cotton to Bermuda and returned with goods needed by the state.

THE AMERICAN CIVIL WAR AND GREAT BRITAIN

During the Civil War, the fate of the Union rested partly in the hands of Great Britain. The British used millions of bales of cotton, most of it imported from the South. If the British recognized the Confederacy as an independent nation, they could claim the right to trade with her. British ships would sweep aside the North's blockading ships to get the cotton. President Lincoln sent Charles Francis Adams to London. Adams worked very hard to prevent Great Britain from recognizing Confederate independence.

Two events threatened good relations between the United States and Great Britain. In November 1861, the U.S. Navy stopped the British steamer *Trent* and forcibly removed two Confederate diplomats. The British condemned the act and prepared for war. To end that crisis, President Lincoln released the diplomats.

The second event involved naval rams, which are armored steamships with 7-foot spikes jutting from the prow below the water line. Rams sink ships by punching holes in them below the water line. A British firm secretly began building rams for the Confederacy. Adams strongly protested, and the British government instead bought them.

In addition, poor wheat harvests in Europe meant the British needed northern wheat more than southern cotton. Great Britain was also strongly antislavery, having abolished slavery in 1833.

All of these factors prevented the British from becoming directly involved and thus contributed to Union victory.

In late 1863, the Confederacy started to require all blockade runners to rent one-third of their cargo space to the government (later increased to one-half). This was to help the government get the supplies it needed. Vance called these regulations "stupid & destructive," for they made blockade running too costly for him to continue. The Confederate Congress passed bills excusing state-owned ships from the regulations, but Davis vetoed them. Finally, in the summer of 1864, Vance got an exemption for the *Advance,* but Union ships captured her in September after her twelfth voyage. By this time, Vance had decided that the Union Navy would soon stop all blockade running, and he sold the state's interest in the ships.

In eighteen months of blockade running, the state's ships imported these goods: 250,000 pairs of shoes, 50,000 blankets, 2,000 rifles with ammunition, cloth for 250,000 uniforms, 50 tons of bacon, and many other items. As Lee's tattered and hungry army surrendered at Appomattox in 1865, state warehouses bulged with 100,000 uniforms and 75 tons of bacon. Vance's blockade running was very successful, more successful than Confederate attempts to push Union troops from the coastal area.

Do You Remember?

1. What did the suspension of the writ of habeas corpus allow?
2. Why were the Conservatives so successful in the 1862 election?
3. Name two problems that arose between Governor Vance and the Confederacy.
4. What was the purpose of blockade running?

WAR IN THE EAST

Confederate forces made no serious efforts to attack Union troops in eastern North Carolina until March 1863. At that time, General James Longstreet sent General Daniel Harvey Hill to divert the Union's attention at New Bern while Longstreet attacked Suffolk, Virginia. Hill moved his troops in a four-part attack on New Bern. But because two of Hill's commanders did not capture their objectives (one across the Neuse River to the north and the other across the Trent River to the south), Hill was forced to withdraw. Next, Hill surrounded the Union forces at Washington, North Carolina. But Union ships with reinforcements got past Hill. Hill was again forced to withdraw. His men did, however, collect badly needed supplies for Lee's army from nearby counties.

In February 1864, General George Pickett's 13,000 men launched a three-pronged attack against New Bern. To destroy Union ships in the Neuse, Pickett sent a group of sailors and marines down the river in boats. They were able to capture and burn one ship, but the Union positions north and south of New Bern were too strong. Pickett had to give up the attack. While Pickett was at New Bern, General James Martin attacked Newport Barracks at Beaufort to prevent Union reinforcements from reaching New Bern. His attack was very successful, and he captured large amounts of supplies that he could not remove and had to destroy.

The next major Confederate attack occurred at Plymouth on the Roanoke River. Union troops had strongly fortified the town, which was the key to holding Albemarle Sound. Early in 1863, upstream from Plymouth, the Confederate Navy started building an ironclad ram named the *Albemarle*. A ram is a ship that sinks other ships by running into them and making a big hole in their sides. The plan was for the *Albemarle* to steam downstream and sink the Union ships defending Plymouth while the army attacked the Union troops. In April 1864, the *Albemarle* started downstream although it was not completed.

At the same time, Confederate General Robert F. Hoke surrounded Plymouth and captured one of the Union forts defending it. He desperately needed the *Albemarle* to sink the two Union ships defending Plymouth. When the *Albemarle* arrived, it found a trap. The two Union ships faced upstream with chains stretched between them. They hoped to catch the *Albemarle* between them and sink it with their guns. Seeing the trap, *Albemarle's* commander, James W. Cooke of Beaufort, avoided it and rammed one ship, sending it to the bottom and chasing the other downstream. General Hoke then captured the 2,500 Union troops defending Plymouth and their supplies. Plymouth was in Confederate hands again. Union forces then left Washington so that they would not be trapped there.

Top: *Lieutenant General Daniel H. Hill was the state's highest ranking officer. He was unable to push Union troops from the coast.* ***Above:*** *North Carolina General Robert F. Hoke captured Plymouth from Union forces and chased them from Washington in 1864.*

These victories raised Confederate hopes of capturing New Bern and clearing the state of Union forces. General Hoke planned a combined land and water attack on New Bern, using the *Albemarle*. In early May 1864, Commander Cooke sailed for New Bern. At the head of Albemarle Sound, he found seven Union ships waiting for him. A battle began, but the Union ships' cannonballs bounced harmlessly off the *Albemarle's* two-inch iron plate. Next, a Union ship rammed the *Albemarle*, nearly sinking it. Commander Cooke had to retreat. General Hoke surrounded New Bern and planned to attack even without the *Albemarle*. However, General Lee was under attack in Virginia and ordered Hoke to join him. In October 1864, a daring Union raiding party caught the *Albemarle* at her berth in Plymouth and sank her. The Confederates made no further attempts to push Union troops out of eastern North Carolina, but they were more successful defending the mountains.

Do You Remember?

1. How was the *Albemarle* to be used on the Roanoke River?
2. Why did General Hoke have to change his plans to attack New Bern?
3. What finally happened to the *Albemarle*?

WAR IN THE MOUNTAINS

People in the mountains of North Carolina had little to fear from Union forces until the fall of 1863. At that time, Union armies moved into eastern Tennessee at Chattanooga and Knoxville. Fearing that these Union armies might march through the mountains and cut the railroads, the Confederacy placed troops to block the mountain gaps leading into the state. Some of these troops were Cherokee warriors under the command of Colonel William H. Thomas, a white chief of the Cherokee.

Meanwhile, General James Longstreet attacked Union forces at Knoxville. He asked the Confederacy to send troops from North Carolina to help him. General Robert Vance, the governor's brother, went to his aid. Vance and his troops, however, were captured near Newport. This left western North Carolina nearly undefended.

Union troops used this opportunity to raid the mountain area. In early 1864, **cavalry** (troops mounted on horseback) raided Cherokee County and Quallatown. That summer, Colonel George W. Kirk led infantry through the Toe and Linville river valleys to capture Camp Vance, an army training camp near Morganton. Then he burned the railroad facilities at

Above: The ironclad ram Albemarle *sank one Union ship at Plymouth. The other ship fled.* **Opposite page, top:** *Inside the* Albemarle's *armored casement during a battle.* **Opposite page, below:** *Commander James W. Cooke built the* Albemarle *and commanded it at Plymouth. In Albemarle Sound, he later fought the battle to a draw.*

Pro-Union sentiment and rugged terrain made the mountains a safe place for draft resisters and deserters from the Confederate Army.

Morganton and escaped on foot into Tennessee, taking many prisoners with him.

Many mountain people were strong unionists during the war. This Union sentiment and the rugged mountain terrain made the area a safe place for army deserters and draft resisters. A **deserter** is a soldier who leaves military service without permission. A **draft resister** is one who does not want to be forced to join the army. Unionists hid the deserters and helped Union prisoners escaping from the Salisbury prison find their way to Union lines in Tennessee. Some deserters and draft resisters banded together to avoid capture. One such band led by Montreval Ray raided Burnsville in the summer of 1864. The Confederacy was never able to get rid of these bands and gain complete control of the mountains.

THE HOME FRONT

Life on the home front became more difficult as the war went on. Living mainly on cornbread, molasses, and peas, people rarely ate meat. Salt, used in preserving meat, was scarce, although the state built a factory at Wilmington to get salt from sea water. Tea and coffee were not available. The army took the output of the textile mills. Cloth became scarce, and people patched their clothes over and over. Children went barefoot, even in winter. Women tore up sheets and curtains to make hospital bandages. Medicines were not available for civilians.

Worst off were women whose husbands and fathers went off to war. Women were left to tend children and do the hard farm labor. In the letters they wrote to their soldier-husbands, they wondered if they could survive. Many men deserted from the army to return home to feed and protect their families. More North Carolina troops deserted than from any other state. To help destitute families, the state bought food and sold it at cost. But this help was not always adequate.

Women living in the cities were better off. They found work in hospitals as nurses. They also worked in shops sewing uniforms for troops. They made $0.75 for sewing a pair of pants and $3.00 for a jacket. Other women voluntarily knitted socks and caps for soldiers.

As goods became scarce, prices rose. A barrel of flour costing $18.00 in 1862 cost $500.00 in 1865. In the same period, bacon went from $0.33 to $7.50 a pound, corn from $1.00 to $30.00 a bushel, and wheat from $3.00 to $50.00 a bushel. The rise in prices was caused in part by the type of money used. The Confederacy issued paper money with no backing. By war's end, the money was nearly worthless.

With their men gone to war, many families suffered. Here Southern women in an occupied area ask Union troops for food.

RICHARD JORDAN GATLING AND THE GATLING GUN

Richard Jordan Gatling was born in Hertford County in 1818, the son of a farmer and inventor. He received little formal education; most of what he knew he learned himself or was taught by his father. Gatling, however, displayed an endless curiosity and loved to tinker. He patented his first invention, a rice-seed planter, in 1839.

Gatling moved to Missouri in 1844 and then to Indiana. There he attended college and received a medical degree in 1850. Although trained as a physician, Gatling did not practice medicine. He continued to tinker and he invented and manufactured many agricultural tools, machines, and transportation devices.

The outbreak of the Civil War turned Gatling's inventiveness to weaponry. In 1862, he patented his best-known invention: the Gatling gun, an early crank-operated machine gun. Oddly, his purpose for developing his "Revolving Battery Gun" was not to increase casualties during battle but to *decrease* them. Early in the war, Gatling had visited northern army hospitals and the trains that brought the dead and wounded soldiers from battlefields. Shocked by the amount of suffering he saw, Gatling reasoned that a rapid-fire gun would give greater firepower to armies, which would then need fewer soldiers. Fewer men in battle meant, in Gatling's view, fewer deaths. He also believed that his gun's sheer destructive power would discourage warfare.

Top: Richard Jordan Gatling was an inventor and physician. Hoping to reduce casualties in war, he patented the first machine gun in 1862. This gun found much use in later wars. Above: This is an early model of the Gatling gun.

The gun that Gatling patented had six rotating barrels that were fed with bullets as the gunner turned a crank to fire the weapon. This early gun could fire more than 200 rounds or shots a minute. (For comparison, a Civil War soldier using a muzzle-loading musket usually could fire no more than two or three shots per minute.)

Gatling demonstrated his weapon for the United States Army, but the army's leadership decided not to adopt it. They believed its value in battle was far outweighed by what they thought to be its major weakness. The army thought the gun wasted too much ammunition. The army did, however, adopt it shortly after the war's end. Gatling continued to improve his weapon and later developed a model that fired over 3,000 rounds per minute. By the later 1800s, the Gatling gun was being used by armies all over the world.

William Woods Holden was a notable Democratic newspaper editor. He supported reforms to relieve human misery. Originally a secessionist, he became a unionist in 1860. In 1862 he helped organize the Conservative party that secured Vance's election as governor. Believing continuation of the war to be useless, he ran for governor in 1864 on a peace platform. He lost to Vance.

THE PEACE MOVEMENT

By 1863, many North Carolinians were upset by Union attacks on the coast and in the mountains and depressed by Union victories at Gettysburg, Vicksburg, and Chattanooga. They wanted peace. Their desire resulted in a peace movement that ended with the state election of 1864.

In mid-1863, William W. Holden became the leader of the peace movement. Using his newspaper, the *North Carolina Standard*, Holden blamed the Confederate government for a number of problems: conscription, imprisonment of North Carolinians who opposed the war, food shortages, raids by bands of deserters, Union occupation of the eastern part of the state, and high prices. Holden called the war "a rich man's war and a

The failure of Confederates to win at Vicksburg helped produce the peace movement in the state.

poor man's fight." He called for Union and Confederate peace talks to end the war.

Holden's peace movement reflected the feelings of many people and caused sharp divisions within the state. Secessionists urged Governor Vance to suppress this "reckless politician" because he encouraged deserters and caused a feeling of defeat. President Davis called Vance to Richmond and urged him to charge Holden with treason. Believing in freedom of the press and afraid of splitting his party, Vance refused. He did, however, issue a statement asking North Carolinians to obey the laws of the Confederacy and discouraging peace meetings.

In the fall of 1863 elections, North Carolina elected six Confederate congressmen who supported peace. Three of the six were Conservatives (Holden's party) and one was a secessionist. Holden then asked the legislature to call a convention to take action for peace. Holden did not make it clear whether he wanted North Carolina to secede from the Confederacy or rejoin the Union. Either action threatened internal civil war.

In the election of 1864, both Vance and Holden ran for the governorship. Vance stole Holden's issues by arguing that he was really the peace candidate and Holden the war candidate. Vance argued that the way to peace was to support the Confederacy and see the war through. In this way, Davis could get a peace settlement that would recognize the independence of the Confederacy. Vance also argued that Holden's proposals would result in internal civil war, causing even more bloodshed. The people overwhelmingly elected Vance, by a vote of about 72,000 to 14,000. North Carolina thus supported the Confederacy and the war to the end.

Do You Remember?

1. Why were the mountains such a safe place for army deserters and draft resisters?
2. How well did North Carolinians eat during the war?
3. Why did Vance believe North Carolina should continue to support the Confederacy?
4. Why did many North Carolinians want peace by 1863?

THE BEGINNING OF THE END

The end was near as Union forces moved toward the state. A Union force of troops and ships planned to attack Wilmington and close the last major blockade-running port in the Confederacy. The key to Wilmington's defense was Fort Fisher, some twenty-eight miles downriver.

THE FALL OF FORT FISHER

Fort Fisher lay on a narrow spit of land between the ocean and the Cape Fear River. Its forty-eight long-range guns guarded the entrance to the river. The fort was shaped like an L, with the angle facing toward the sea. The walls were of sand piled two stories high and twenty-five feet thick. They stretched a mile along the beach and over a half mile across the neck of the peninsula.

The first Union attack came on Christmas Eve 1864. General Benjamin F. Butler exploded a ship loaded with gunpowder near the walls of the

The first Union attack on Fort Fisher in December 1864 failed. The second attack in January 1865 resulted in the capture of the fort.

Fort Fisher's guns kept the Union's blockading ships away from the mouth of the Cape Fear River. Now it is a state park.

fort, but it had little effect. Next, Admiral David D. Porter's fifty ships fired their six hundred guns so that shot and shell "fell like rain." But the shells exploded in the soft sand and did little damage. On Christmas Day, Butler landed 3,000 men and attacked the north side of the fort. He withdrew to the ships, however, when darkness and bad weather threatened to cut him off.

The second attack came on January 13, 1865. General Alfred H. Terry landed 8,000 men. Some 2,000 sailors and marines attacked the northeast point of Fort Fisher but were driven back. Meanwhile, army troops broke into the fort near the river. Confederate General Braxton Bragg, with 6,000 of Lee's best troops, was three miles north of the fort ready to help. However, two brigades of black Union troops held him there. Inside the fort, 1,500 Confederate troops fought the invaders in six hours of hand-to-hand combat before they surrendered. Wilmington fell in February, and a greater danger threatened to the south.

SHERMAN'S INVASION

In January 1865, General William T. Sherman left Savannah, Georgia, with an army of 60,000 men. He had two objectives: (1) to make civilians suffer and turn against the war and (2) to unite with General Grant's army in Virginia. Grant had Lee's army pinned down between Richmond and Petersburg. Sherman's objectives along the way were Columbia, Fayetteville, Goldsboro, and the rear of Lee's army. He did not expect to meet any opposition before reaching Virginia.

Sherman left a trail of destruction on his route north. He entered North Carolina in early March. He told his men not to be as destructive as in South Carolina because the people of North Carolina had shown some Union support. Still, his men destroyed much property in Monroe, Wadesboro, Rockingham, and Fayetteville and set fire to the large pine forests. After picking up supplies in Fayetteville, Sherman set out for Goldsboro. He split his army into two wings, traveling on parallel roads.

Meanwhile, General Lee realized that his only hope for survival was to organize an army in North Carolina to stop or delay Sherman. He appointed General Joseph E. Johnston as commander of an army to be gathered from all over the Southeast. Johnston rushed troops to North

Above: *General William Sherman led his army into North Carolina in March 1865.* **Below:** *General Joseph E. Johnston's troops failed to defeat Sherman's army at the Battle of Bentonville, the last major pitched battle of the Civil War.*

Above: During the Battle of Bentonville, the Harper House served as a hospital. The lower floor was restored to the way it was in 1865. **Right:** This is the exterior of the Harper House, now a state historic site.

Carolina from as far away as Mississippi. Since General Johnston did not know Sherman's objective, he sent most of the men to Smithfield, half way between Goldsboro and Raleigh. He also ordered General Wade Hampton's cavalry to stay in front of Sherman's troops and report their positions.

In mid-March, Hampton decided to attack Sherman's left wing near Averasboro on the Cape Fear River. In the skirmish, Sherman lost about 700 troops. More importantly, the skirmish delayed the advance of the left wing. This delay separated the left wing from the right wing by a day's march.

Although more men were arriving every day, Johnston's army numbered only about 20,000 men. He could not hope to defeat Sherman's army except by attacking smaller units that separated from the main force. When Sherman's left and right wings became separated after Averasboro, Hampton suggested that Johnston attack Sherman's left wing at Bentonville, south of Smithfield. Johnston's men surprised Sherman's left wing on March 19. The battle lasted for two days. For a hastily organized army, the Confederate troops fought well. But Sherman soon brought his whole army into the battle. Johnston, fearing that he might be surrounded, retreated toward Raleigh. Losses on each side were about 2,000 troops. Sherman then moved his troops on to the town of Goldsboro. Meanwhile, another danger came from the west.

Union General George Stoneman fought his way to the Salisbury prison to release Union prisoners, but they had been removed.

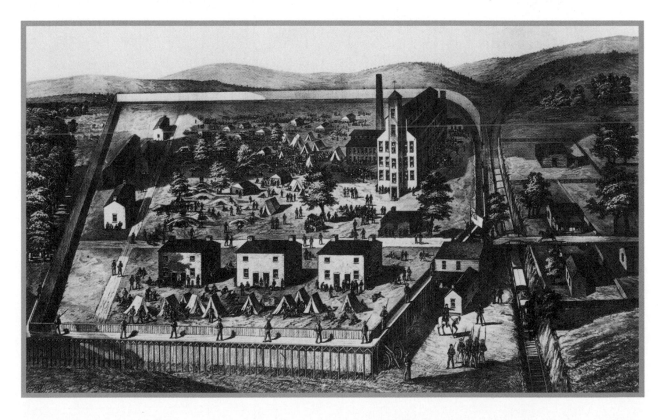

STONEMAN'S RAID

A week after the Battle of Bentonville, Union General George H. Stoneman entered North Carolina from Tennessee with 4,000 cavalry. General Grant had ordered Stoneman to destroy the railroad west of Lynchburg, Virginia, so Lee could not use it to escape into the mountains. Stoneman also planned to destroy the railroads south of Danville and to release Union prisoners thought to be in the Salisbury prison.

From March 28 through April 11, Stoneman did just that. Moving through Boone, Wilkesboro, and Mount Airy, his men destroyed sixty miles of railroad west of Lynchburg. Then they moved south, cutting the railroad above and below Greensboro and destroying a cotton mill at Salem. At Greensboro, his cavalry narrowly missed capturing President Davis and his cabinet, who were retreating to Charlotte. At Salisbury, they found a Confederate storehouse, which they burned, but there were no prisoners. Next, Stoneman's force cut the railroads north, south, and west of Charlotte. By late April, they captured Asheville, after occupying Lenoir and Morganton.

*Right: Stoneman and his staff ordered the destruction of property along his route of march from Boone to Mount Airy and from Greensboro to Asheville. **Above:** After Lee's surrender, General Joseph E. Johnston had no choice but to surrender to Sherman.*

JOHNSTON'S SURRENDER

By mid-April, General Johnston knew that it was useless to resist. Lee had surrendered on April 9 at Appomattox, leaving Grant's army free to move south against him. Sherman was advancing on Raleigh with an army of 80,000 men. Stoneman had cut the railroads to the west and destroyed the supply base at Salisbury. On April 14, Johnston asked Sherman for a **truce** (a suspension of fighting) and the start of peace talks. The two men met at the Bennett farmhouse near Durham. Johnston surrendered on April 26.

The war was over for North Carolina except for a small skirmish near Waynesville in early May. The state lost some 20,000 men in battle during the war. This was over one-fourth of all Confederate battle deaths. Another 21,000 died of disease. North Carolina troops were, nevertheless, proud of being "First at Bethel, farthest at Gettysburg, and last at Appomattox."

After several meetings at the Bennett farmhouse near Durham in late April 1865, Johnston surrendered his army to Sherman.

Do You Remember?
1. Why was Wilmington important?
2. What were Sherman's two objectives in his march north?

PHOTOGRAPHY IN THE CIVIL WAR

The Civil War was the first major national event to be photographed. In 1839, a Frenchman named Daguerre developed a process to take a picture using a copper plate coated with silver. Samuel F. B. Morse (inventor of the telegraph) happened to be in Paris then and learned the process. Back in New York, Morse opened a studio, and the photography craze soon swept America.

When the Civil War came, some 3,154 Americans listed their occupations as photographers. At least 1,500 of them took war photographs, and practically all of these worked with Union forces. The Union blockade made it difficult for southern photographers to get the chemicals needed to coat the copper plates and develop them.

Photographers mainly reached the battlefields after the battles were over. And because exposure times were long, photographers took pictures of

still scenes: dead people and animals, splintered trees, destroyed buildings, and the debris of war. The most popular pictures were those of individual soldiers. Illustrated newspapers bought photographs from which they made wood engravings. Important photographers included Mathew Brady, Edward and Henry Anthony, Alexander Gardner, George Barnard, Timothy O'Sullivan, and Henry P. Moore.

Artists argued about whether photographs were art. Some people regarded them as depictions of reality. Others argued that the photographer posed his subjects, determined the light, and thus took pictures that had the elements of art. Art or not, the nation is fortunate to have an extensive pictorial record of the Civil War.

Mathew Brady (opposite page above) took this photograph (opposite page below) at the Battle of Chancellorsville on May 3, 1863. This George Barnard photograph (above) of Union artillery men before the Battle of Fair Oaks was taken in 1862.

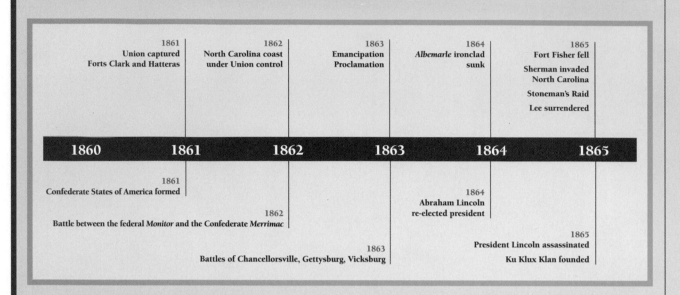

1860	1861	1862	1863	1864	1865

Above timeline:
- 1861 — Union captured Forts Clark and Hatteras
- 1862 — North Carolina coast under Union control
- 1863 — Emancipation Proclamation
- 1864 — *Albemarle* ironclad sunk
- 1865 — Fort Fisher fell; Sherman invaded North Carolina; Stoneman's Raid; Lee surrendered

Below timeline:
- 1861 — Confederate States of America formed
- 1862 — Battle between the federal *Monitor* and the Confederate *Merrimac*
- 1863 — Battles of Chancellorsville, Gettysburg, Vicksburg
- 1864 — Abraham Lincoln re-elected president
- 1865 — President Lincoln assassinated; Ku Klux Klan founded

Reviewing People, Places, and Terms

Define, identify, or explain the importance of the following.

1. blockade running
2. Conservative party
3. deserter
4. draft
5, strategy
6. Zebulon Baird Vance
7. writ of habeas corpus

Understanding the Facts

1. What were the reasons behind President Lincoln's Emancipation Proclamation?
2. What transportation link in eastern Carolina did Union forces want to capture?
3. What was so significant about the 1862 gubernatorial race in North Carolina?
4. Why were North Carolinians so upset over the Conscription Act of 1862?
5. Early in the war, North Carolina was able to clothe its soldiers better than other Confederate states. Why?

6. To what destinations did North Carolina's blockade runners usually sail?
7. In what part of the state was pro-Union sentiment strongest?
8. Who was the leader of North Carolina's peace movement? How did he fare in the 1864 governor's race against Zebulon Vance?
9. How many men did the state lose in the Civil War?

Developing Critical Thinking

1. Why did William Woods Holden call the war "a rich man's war and a poor man's fight"?
2. What do you think was the greatest factor in the Confederacy's defeat?
3. How did the use of ironclads change the history of naval warfare?
4. Was Sherman's "seared earth" policy really necessary? What did it accomplish?

Applying Your Skills

1. On a map of the United States, highlight using different colors (a) the Union states, (b) the

Confederate states, and (c) the border states that did not secede.

2. Choose one of the years 1861 to 1865 and prepare an expanded timeline that includes events mentioned in this chapter.

3. Zebulon Vance won the governor's election of 1864. Using the figures given on page 328, calculate the percentages of total votes cast that were won by Vance and Holden.

Making Connections

1. From the library or other reference source, find a photograph taken during the Civil War that you find particularly moving.

2. Have photographic images affected people's impressions of or reactions to wars or fighting in recent times? Explain.

3. What factors led Great Britain to support the Union against the Confederacy in the Civil War?

4. Do you think the outcome of the war would have been different if the South's "King Cotton Diplomacy" had worked and Great Britain had recognized the independence of the Confederate States of America?

Tar Heel Trivia

- Secretary of the Confederate Treasury Christopher Gustavus Memminger tried to persuade Jefferson Davis to relocate the Confederate capital from Richmond, Virginia, to Flat Rock.

- In the course of the Civil War, General Bryan Grimes of Grimesville had six horses shot from under him.

- Experts believe one of the finest examples of nineteenth-century military architecture is represented in Fort Macon.

- The world's largest painting, a cyclorama of the Battle of Gettysburg, is stored in Winston-Salem.

◦ BUILDING SKILLS: UNDERSTANDING CAUSE AND EFFECT ◦

Everything that happens does so because something makes it happen. What happens is the *effect*. The person, condition, or event that makes the thing happen is the *cause*. The connection between what happens and what makes it happen is known as the cause-effect relationship.

Not all cause-effect relationships are clear-cut. And sometimes an event may have more than one effect, and an effect may have more than one cause. At other times, an effect may not appear for a long time after the cause. The following guidelines will help you identify cause-effect relationships in written material.

1. Often statements contain "clue words" that alert you to cause and effect. Be aware of and look for words or phrases such as *because, led to, brought about, produced, as a result of, so that, thus, since, outcome, as a consequence, resulted in, gave rise to,* and *therefore*. This example appeared in Chapter 14: *In the 1820s and 1830s, evangelical revivals in New York and the Northeast led by the Reverend Charles G. Finney brought on a movement to reform American society.*

2. There may not be any "clue words." In their place, may be the word *and* or a comma. This example is from Chapter 13: *Slaves resented the poor conditions under which they lived and their lack of freedom, and they looked for ways to resist.*

3. Usually it takes more than one sentence or paragraph to describe a cause-effect relationship. If you're not sure whether a description illustrates a cause-effect relationship, ask yourself if economics, geography, religion, or technology is involved in the event or condition being studied. These are major forces in history that make things happen.

Try This! Write out three examples of the cause-effect relationship that appear in this chapter. Draw a single rule under the part of the sentence or paragraph that illustrates the cause. Draw a double rule under the part that illustrates the effect. Circle any clue words that point out these relationships.

CHAPTER SIXTEEN

NORTH CAROLINA AND RECONSTRUCTION

The time has arrived when we can strike one blow to secure those rights of Freemen that have been so long withheld from us.
— Wilmington *Herald*, 1865

W HEN THE CIVIL WAR ENDED, the people of North Carolina were afraid of what the conquering Union forces might do to them. Would they be punished for their war against the Union? Would their property be taken away from them? Would they lose their rights as citizens? Much to their relief, President Andrew Johnson (who succeeded Lincoln) had a lenient (easy) program to restore the state to the Union in 1865. The state did all that he required. But when Congress met in late 1865, it refused to seat the congressmen elected from North Carolina.

Congress did not believe that President Johnson's program was strong enough. Congress placed North Carolina under military rule and forced the state to meet other requirements before it would be considered fully restored to the Union. Only then did Congress seat the state's congressmen. Congress's program left its mark on the state because it brought about political and social revolution.

THE AFTERMATH OF THE WAR

A number of questions had to be answered at the end of the war. What could be done to prevent another civil war? How could the bonds of affection that had tied the southern states to the Union be restored? What should be done with the four million **freedmen** (freed slaves)? What should be done about the sectional political parties that had helped cause the war?

During the war, President Lincoln and Congress had discussed these questions but had not come up with any firm answers. Lincoln wanted

> **CHAPTER • PREVIEW**
>
> **Terms:** freedmen, Reconstruction, nullify, Black Code, Freedmen's Bureau, Reconstruction Act, carpetbaggers, scalawags, Union League, universal manhood suffrage
>
> **People:** President Andrew Johnson, Jonathan Worth, Reverend James W. Hood

Opposite page: Andrew Johnson succeeded to the presidency in 1865 when Abraham Lincoln was assassinated.

PUNISHMENT OF EX-CONFEDERATES

After the war, those who took up arms against the United States could have been charged with treason and, if found guilty, executed. Presidents Abraham Lincoln and Andrew Johnson, however, favored lenient treatment. They believed leniency would make it easier to restore the Union in spirit.

In 1865, President Johnson issued a proclamation that pardoned all Confederates who had supported the war except those in fourteen classifications. The classes generally included Confederate leaders and wealthy southerners. These people could personally apply to the president for pardons, and thousands did. Johnson pardoned some 13,500 people.

Still, scores of Confederate leaders were imprisoned until Johnson could decide what to do with them. Chief among them was Jefferson Davis, who was imprisoned for two years at Fortress Monroe. He was charged with treason, but in 1867 the federal government decided not to prosecute him. He was freed but never pardoned.

The ratification of the Fourteenth Amendment in 1868 created new problems for ex-Confederates. It prohibited them from holding office until pardoned by a two-thirds vote of Congress. Those who were elected to office in 1868 as Republicans were easily pardoned. By 1877, Congress had pardoned all but about 500 ex-Confederate leaders. In 1898, Congress finally passed an act of general amnesty.

Overall, the United States government was most lenient and forgiving of ex-Confederate leaders. It thus secured their loyalty and the loyalty of the South.

to treat southern leaders leniently. The execution or imprisonment of hundreds of southerners would only produce martyrs and ill will toward the Union. During the war, Lincoln believed that men in Louisiana, Arkansas, and Tennessee who were willing to swear their loyalty should be allowed to elect state and local governments. He also wanted a constitutional amendment to abolish slavery, but did not support black suffrage. The Thirteenth Amendment to the United States Constitution, which abolished slavery, went into effect in December 1865.

Congress expressed its views in a bill passed in 1864. According to this bill, only men who could swear they had never voluntarily opposed the Union would be able to vote and hold office in the South. All others would be considered disloyal. A few radical congressmen wanted southern leaders punished. Many congressmen believed that blacks were the only ones in the South who were truly loyal. They felt blacks should receive the right to vote to keep the southern states loyal in the future.

Lincoln had seen that sectional political parties helped cause the war. The Republican party (renamed the Union party during the war) had existed only in the free and border states. After the war, it was still a sectional political party. The Democratic party had a better chance of becoming a national party. Although it had existed in both the North and South, its southern members had supported secession and disunion. Lincoln saw that it would be necessary to create a new national party, one that men from both the North and the South could join and support.

JOHNSON'S RECONSTRUCTION PLAN

President Lincoln was assassinated on April 14, 1865. This brought Andrew Johnson to the presidency. Born in Raleigh, North Carolina, Johnson had been apprenticed to a tailor he did not like. He ran away to the state of Tennessee, settling in Greeneville. There he married, and his wife taught him to read and write. Although not as able a politician as Lincoln, Johnson was a good debater in the rough and tumble of state politics. By 1861, he had risen to the position of U.S. Senator. A strong Union Democrat, Johnson refused to leave Congress when his state seceded. When Union troops invaded Tennessee, Lincoln appointed Johnson wartime governor. In 1864, Lincoln needed a vice presidential running mate who would attract the votes of Union Democrats. He chose Johnson (a Democrat). With Lincoln's death, Johnson became president. Johnson also became head of the Union party, which consisted mainly of Republicans.

Advised by Lincoln's cabinet, Johnson developed a plan to restore the southern states to the Union. He hoped to have all the states back in the Union before Congress met in December 1865. In May 1865, Johnson issued two proclamations to start the process. One proclamation pardoned southerners, except for those in certain classes, who would swear an oath to protect and defend the Constitution.

The second proclamation appointed William W. Holden provisional governor of North Carolina. Johnson selected Holden because he was well known in the North for leading the state's peace movement in 1864. Holden was to call a state convention that would take the necessary steps to restore the state to the Union. Only men who had voted before the war and who had been pardoned could vote for and become delegates to this convention. Holden was to arrange for the election of a loyal state government and congressmen. The state would then be restored to the Union.

President Johnson began his reconstruction plan without consulting Congress. **Reconstruction** refers to the steps taken to restore the southern states to the Union and rebuild the South. Johnson knew that some congressmen wanted to punish the South and would oppose his plan. He wanted to be able to tell Congress in December that the southern states already had loyal governments.

To accomplish the plan, Johnson and Holden paid careful attention to northern public opinion. They tried to shape what North Carolina did according to what northerners wanted. In that way, they hoped the public and Congress would approve the president's plan.

Do You Remember?
1. Why did Lincoln think it necessary to create a new political party?
2. How did Andrew Johnson come to be president?

Andrew Johnson was born in 1808 in this house in Raleigh.

A Quaker and unionist, Jonathan Worth served as Governor Vance's treasurer. In 1865 the people elected him governor instead of Holden.

Unfortunately, Holden met strong opposition at home. The Conservative party disliked Holden because of his lowly birth, his flip-flopping on political issues, and his great desire to be governor. A delegation of Conservatives met with President Johnson in May in an unsuccessful attempt to block Holden's appointment as provisional governor.

Later, Holden refused to recommend pardons for Conservatives who disagreed with him. To some Conservatives, it seemed that Holden recommended pardons only for those men who would support him for the governorship. The Conservatives, therefore, determined to oppose him. This opposition surfaced in the state convention that was held in October.

THE CONVENTION OF 1865

By October 1865, northern public opinion indicated that the state should nullify the secession ordinance of 1861 and abolish slavery. Some delegates just wanted to repeal the ordinance of secession. To repeal the secession ordinance meant that passing it in the first place was legal. But to **nullify** the ordinance meant that the act of secession was never legal. The convention did finally nullify the secession ordinance. When it came to the vote on the abolition of slavery, some delegates wanted to include a statement that the federal government was forcing them to vote for abolition. But in the end, the convention simply abolished slavery.

While the convention was in session, northern papers began demanding that the southern states declare the Confederate war debt void. The northerners believed paying off the debt would seem like a reward for those who had supported secession. Holden therefore instructed the convention to set aside the war debt. Some delegates opposed Holden simply for political reasons. But to the northerners following the convention closely, the delegates opposing Holden did not seem loyal or sorry for their actions. The delegates, however, believed that voiding the war debt would harm the state. Widows, banks, and the Literary Fund had bought the bonds the Confederacy sold to finance the war. (The Literary Fund was a state fund used to pay public school teachers.) Declaring the bonds worthless would close banks and schools and deprive widows of income. Holden became concerned that the delegates might refuse to act on the war debt. He asked the president to step in. President Johnson sent the convention a telegram saying the debt must be voided. The convention then did so.

THE ELECTION OF 1865

Further problems came up during the state elections in November. Fifty-three of the convention delegates endorsed Holden for governor. He thought he would be the only candidate. But the Conservatives per-

THE BALLAD OF TOM DULA

A *ballad* is a song made up by various singers. It usually has some foundation in real events, but it is based on oral tradition. As the ballad passes from one singer to another, the facts become twisted and turn into folklore. Such is the case with the ballad about Tom Dula.

After fighting in the Civil War, Tom Dula returned home to Wilkes County. In early 1866, he began a love affair with Laura Foster of nearby Caldwell County. While courting Laura, Tom was also having an affair with her married sister, Ann Foster Melton. On May 25, 1866, Laura disappeared. By June, evidence indicated that Tom was involved in her disappearance. He fled to Watauga County and then Tennessee. The community searched for Laura and in late summer found her body in a shallow grave. She had been stabbed in the chest.

The sheriff sent men to Tennessee to bring Dula back for trial. Upon his return, Dula was charged with murder and Ann Melton was charged with being his accomplice. The case received national attention. Zebulon B. Vance defended Dula, but Dula was found guilty and hanged in Statesville on May 1, 1868. Ann Melton was acquitted.

There are many versions of the ballad about Tom Dula. The best known is "Tom Dooley," recorded by the Kingston Trio.

Tom Dula is buried in Wilkes County.

suaded Jonathan Worth, Holden's state treasurer, to run for governor also. Worth was an ex-Whig who had supported the Union until war broke out. During the war, he served as Governor Vance's treasurer. He sided with the peace movement, but did not take part in it. Holden's supporters claimed that the state would not be restored to the Union if Worth were elected. Nevertheless, Worth defeated Holden by about 6,000 of the 60,000 votes cast. So shocked was Holden at his loss that he stayed in bed for three weeks. He was well enough, however, to ask President Johnson to send another telegram. "The results of the recent elections in North Carolina have greatly damaged the prospects of the State in the restoration of its governmental relations," wrote Johnson.

The other results of the election were mixed. A majority of the newly elected legislators supported Holden, as did four of the seven congressmen. Still, only one of the congressmen could take the "iron-clad" oath desired by Congress (the oath that a person had never willingly supported secession and war). Of the seven congressmen elected, four had served in the Confederate Congress. When the legislature met, it ratified the

Blacks in Asheville voted for delegates to the state constitutional convention in the fall of 1867. Free blacks had voted before 1835.

Thirteenth Amendment and elected William A. Graham and John Pool as U.S. senators. Graham had not yet received his pardon. When Congress met in December, it refused to seat the congressmen elected from North Carolina or any other southern state because they did not appear to be loyal.

THE BLACK CODE

Before seating any southern congressmen, Congress wanted to be sure that the South was loyal and that freedmen were truly free. Congress therefore appointed a joint committee on reconstruction to look into conditions in the South. The committee hearings went on into 1866. Congress decided to wait and think about what to do before seating southern congressmen.

In the fall of 1865, a convention of freedmen met in Raleigh. The leader was a black man from Pennsylvania, the Reverend James W. Hood. Hood had grown up black and free in the North. Life there, however, was not easy. There were no schools for black children; blacks could not ride the streetcars in Philadelphia nor get a hotel room. The religious beliefs of his parents influenced him to enter the ministry. After serving as a missionary to blacks in Nova Scotia, he went to North Carolina in 1865 to start black Methodist churches. When he found that black people needed a spokesman, he turned to politics.

Hood and other black leaders at this convention prepared several resolutions, which they sent to the state convention. By an 1838 court decision, the freedmen already had state citizenship. Although the freedmen wanted the right to vote, they did not believe that the state would grant

it. Instead, their resolutions asked for state protection and educational opportunities. They also called for laws that applied equally to whites and blacks. (Before the war, North Carolina had passed many laws that applied only to free blacks.) When the state convention met in October, the delegates decided to let the legislature act upon the resolutions.

In January 1866, the legislature finally met, but it ignored the freedmen's requests. Instead, the legislature passed a set of laws called the **Black Code.** The Black Code applied only to freedmen and recognized the rights that free blacks had before the war. These included the right to own property, to have a jury trial, and to sue in the courts. The Code legalized slave marriages and permitted blacks to testify against whites only with the whites' consent. It also applied criminal law equally to both whites and blacks, except for attacks on white women for which blacks could get the death penalty. The law of apprenticeship gave former masters first claim on the services of their former slaves. Overall, the North Carolina Black Code was much more lenient than those in other states. Still, the idea that one set of laws applied to blacks and another to whites angered Congress.

Congress created the Freedmen's Bureau to help feed, clothe, and educate destitute freedmen. They lined up at Bureau offices all over the state to get help.

Do You Remember?

1. What did the state convention of 1865 do about the secession ordinance of 1861 and slavery?
2. Why were delegates to the convention of 1865 reluctant to void the Confederate war debt?
3. What did Congress want to be sure of before they would seat southern congressmen?

JAMES CITY

Once the Union seized control of eastern North Carolina, black refugees flocked to the Union lines and several all-black communities were established. One such community was James City, located just outside New Bern.

The Reverend Horace James was appointed Superintendent of Negro Affairs for North Carolina, and he immediately began to set up freedmen's camps in occupied portions of North Carolina. James selected an area about two miles from where the Trent and Neuse rivers converged as the site for the freedmen's camp in the New Bern area. Streets and lots were laid out over the 30-acre site, and by 1864 almost 3,000 freedmen lived there. As the war drew to a close, shacks were replaced with more permanent structures. The community also had a school, blacksmith shop, hospital, and churches. The settlement soon became known as James City in honor of Horace James. There was, however, one problem: that land was privately owned by the Peter Evans family of New Bern.

After the war, freedmen began moving out of the settlement to take jobs as tenant farmers with local landowners. The population fell to about

1,700 persons. In 1867, the federal government returned ownership of the James City property to the Evans family. Those who remained in James City were to pay rent to the Evans family. By the end of 1868, all federal aid to the residents of James City was ended.

Despite this, the residents continued to emphasize education and hard work. During the period between 1880 and 1890, three black teachers taught at the local school. By 1900, more than half of the residents could read and write. Many of the people in the community supplemented their income by selling fish, and some grew small plots of cash crops such as tobacco and cotton.

In 1880, the Evans family sold the James City land to the Bryan family of New Bern. By 1893, the Bryan family had grown tired of being landlords, and they tried to have the residents evicted. When the residents refused to leave, it fell to the local sheriff to evict them. The sheriff eventually appealed for help to Governor Elias Carr, who sent in the national guard. Violence seemed imminent. But the governor met with James City representatives, who agreed to pay rent to the Bryan family if allowed to remain. A violent showdown was avoided. The only casualty was a militia colonel who died after being thrown from his horse during a parade in New Bern to celebrate the peaceful resolution of the crisis.

Today, about 700 people live in an area near the original James City, which is still owned by the Bryan heirs.

Below: Freedmen established a settlement across the Trent River from New Bern. They called it James City after a Massachusetts regimental chaplain, Horace James, who helped them. **Opposite page above:** *The Reverend Hurley Gaines was the minister at Mt. Shiloh Baptist Church at James City. Churches were important social and political centers.*

Andrew Johnson looks very much like the fighter he was when it came to his battles with Congress over Reconstruction policies. His disagreements with Congress led to impeachment proceedings against him.

CONFLICT BETWEEN THE PRESIDENT AND CONGRESS

President Johnson might have continued to direct Reconstruction had he and Congress agreed on the basic issues. Congress, however, passed two bills that President Johnson vetoed. The president's vetoes caused great conflict with Congress.

PRESIDENTIAL VETOES

The first bill that Congress passed continued the work of the Freedmen's Bureau. The **Freedmen's Bureau** was a government agency created in 1865 to provide food, clothing, shelter, and education for the former slaves in the South. The Bureau helped over 300,000 freedmen in North Carolina alone. It established hospitals and supported an orphanage. Blacks eager to learn to read and write flocked to some four hundred schools organized by the Bureau.

Many white leaders disliked the Bureau for a number of reasons. Bureau agents, many of them army officers, did not believe that whites would treat the freedmen fairly. As a result, the agents helped black laborers get favorable contracts with plantation owners. The agents also removed criminal cases against blacks from the state courts and tried them in Bureau courts. Since the state had no prison, state courts ordered that convicted blacks be whipped. The Bureau courts used other, less degrading punishments. Worst of all, however, was the fact that Bureau schools taught blacks about government and politics and the equality of all people before the law. This teaching enraged white leaders, who wanted to establish a postwar society dominated by whites.

Congress also passed a Civil Rights Bill in early 1866. The purpose of this law was to strike down the Black Codes and ensure that there was one set of laws for both blacks and whites. The bill proposed to make the freedmen citizens of the United States and the states in which they lived and to provide them with "equal benefit of all laws and proceedings for the security of person and property as is enjoyed by white citizens." Leading whites in North Carolina disliked the bill because it would make blacks and whites equal before the law.

President Johnson vetoed both bills in early 1866. In his veto messages, he explained that he felt parts of the bills were unconstitutional and that the bills gave too much power to the federal government. He believed that the states should control the relations between the races. Johnson pointed out that the eleven states with the greatest black populations were not represented in Congress and were, therefore, not consulted on the bills. He did not believe it was right for one section of the nation to dictate terms to another. The vetoes marked the beginning of a break between President Johnson and Congress over Reconstruction policies.

The president and Congress also clashed over party politics. In December 1865, leading Republicans in Congress met with the president to talk about the national political parties. Many Republicans favored Lincoln's plan to create a new Constitutional Union party. But many Republicans were afraid that President Johnson's Reconstruction policy was strengthening the Democratic party in the South. A strong, national Democratic party would be a serious threat to the Republican party, which did not exist in the old Confederate states. President Johnson would not tell the Republican leaders what he planned to do about political parties. Since it appeared to the Republicans that the president might be moving into the Democratic camp, they began to oppose him.

The Republicans were determined to overturn President Johnson's vetoes. To do this, they needed two-thirds of the votes in each house of Congress. They were short one vote in the Senate. To get that one vote, Congress took another look at a disputed Senate election from New Jersey. Earlier, Congress had decided to seat the Democrat. Now, they removed the Democrat and seated his Republican opponent. This gave the Republicans the vote they needed to override the president's two vetoes. Congress was on a collision course with the president.

Scores of Northern teachers sailed to North Carolina in 1865 to teach freedmen. One of the early schools operated at James City, south of New Bern.

CONGRESS TAKES CHARGE

The next action came from Congress. The Joint Committee on Reconstruction reported that conditions in the South were terrible. Witnesses from North Carolina, for example, testified that freedmen were in

John Pool of Pasquotank County was elected U.S. Senator in 1865. A strong Union man, he had refused to support the war effort. After his election in 1865 he told people of his anti-war feeling and they shunned him. He then became a Republican and was elected to the U.S. Senate in 1868. There he strongly opposed the Ku Klux Klan.

danger of being re-enslaved and that northerners and unionists were not safe in the state. They also indicated that the men running the state government were disloyal.

Congress therefore approved the Fourteenth Amendment to the Constitution. This amendment was similar to the vetoed Civil Rights Bill. The amendment proposed to protect the freedmen by making them citizens of the United States and of the states where they lived. As a result, states could not deny them equal protection under state laws or deprive them of life, liberty, or property without due process of law. The amendment also: (1) set out terms for reducing the number of a state's representatives in Congress if that state did not permit blacks to vote; (2) gave Congress (rather than the president) the power to grant pardons; and (3) voided all of the debts of the Confederacy.

This amendment needed the approval of three-fourths of the state legislatures before it could become a part of the Constitution. Congress required each southern state to ratify the amendment before it could be restored to the Union. Only one southern state did so. When Tennessee ratified the amendment in mid-1866, its congressmen were seated.

In North Carolina, ratification became the main issue in the fall elections. Governor Jonathan Worth ran for re-election opposing ratification, believing that the amendment was degrading (insulting). Alfred Dockery ran for governor favoring ratification. William W. Holden supported Dockery. Holden and Dockery believed that if the state did not ratify the amendment Congress would impose even harsher conditions. Worth won easily, and a majority of the legislators elected at the same time opposed ratification. North Carolina thus rejected the Fourteenth Amendment.

Elsewhere in the fall of 1866, the states elected all of the members of the United States House of Representatives and about one-third of the senators. President Johnson campaigned in the North for those congressmen who supported his Reconstruction plan. He attacked Republican congressmen who opposed him.

The election resulted in a victory for the Republicans. Northerners apparently approved of the policies of the Republicans toward the South. The Republicans won enough seats to give them a two-thirds majority in both houses of Congress. The Republican Congress could now put into effect its *own* program of Reconstruction for the South. If the president vetoed its program, Congress had the votes to override his veto.

Do You Remember?

1. What was the purpose of the Freedmen's Bureau?
2. Besides making blacks citizens of the United States and of the states where they lived, what else did the Fourteenth Amendment do?
3. What was the main issue in the statewide elections of 1866?

CONGRESSIONAL RECONSTRUCTION

When Congress met in December, the Republican leaders began considering new legislation for the Reconstruction of the South. North Carolinians sped to Washington in December to try to influence that law. William Holden met with Thaddeus Stevens, a radical Republican congressman from Pennsylvania, and proposed a law for North Carolina that had been drafted by John Pool. Their proposal called for a constitutional convention to revise the state constitution. Blacks who owned property and were able to read and write could vote for delegates to the constitutional convention.

Although Congress considered Holden's proposal, what it passed was quite different. The **Reconstruction Act** of March 2, 1867, placed all southern states except Tennessee under military rule. The ten southern states were divided into five military districts, each district under the control of a general from the Union Army. (North Carolina was in the 2nd military district, under the command of Daniel E. Sickles.) The general was responsible for registering voters to elect delegates to a constitutional convention. Adult black males could vote and could also become delegates. Whites who had sworn to uphold the United States Constitution and who had then helped the Confederacy could not vote or hold office. Nor would they be able to do so until Congress pardoned them. The convention had to revise the state constitution to permit all adult males—including blacks—to vote. The new state legislature then had to ratify the Fourteenth Amendment. Only then would Congress restore the state to the Union and seat its representatives.

Before the war William A. Graham of Hillsborough had served as legislator, governor, Secretary of the Navy, and U.S. Senator. During the war he was a Confederate Senator. Elected U.S. Senator again in 1865, Congress would not seat him. He strongly opposed black suffrage and helped organize the Conservative party.

THE REPUBLICAN PARTY IN NORTH CAROLINA

The Reconstruction Act gave William Holden's supporters the opportunity to elect Holden governor and gain control of the state government. To give them the organization to do so, they formed a statewide Republican party in February 1867. The organization of the statewide party was the first step in creating a national Republican party. Members of the Republican party in North Carolina included native whites, blacks, and northerners who had moved into the state to help carry out Congress's Reconstruction plan. The northerners were called **carpetbaggers** because they supposedly arrived in the South with all their belongings packed in cheap luggage made from carpet. The native whites who supported the Republican party were called **scalawags,** after thin, mangy cattle.

The new state Republican party supported the vote for black males, passage of the Reconstruction Act, and ratification of the Fourteenth Amendment. The party believed that whites neither could nor should control the blacks. The Republicans believed that whites and blacks

Thomas S. Ashe of Wadesboro was a lawyer and legislator. A strong unionist, he supported secession only after war began. He served in the Confederate Congress as representative and senator. He was the Conservative candidate for governor in 1868, but Holden defeated him.

should create a new society of mutual trust and respect. Although the party appealed to blacks and poor whites, it also attracted men with money. These wealthy men believed that the state had many business opportunities but needed northern capital to develop them. They favored remaking southern society to be more like the North in order to attract this capital.

One issue nearly split the newly formed party. This issue was whether the state should confiscate the lands of Confederate leaders and distribute those lands among freedmen. A small group of Republicans believed that, without land, the freedmen could not become independent and protect their freedom and new rights. The majority of Republicans, however, opposed this scheme. They pointed out that confiscating the land would drive white men from the party and make martyrs of the Confederate leaders.

The Republicans used new techniques to organize their supporters across the state. Most effective for organizing blacks was the **Union League.** Using secret signs and passwords, the League promoted loyalty to the Union and to the Republican party. Freedmen's Bureau agents and northern schoolteachers also brought blacks into the party. Among whites in western counties, a secret group called the Heroes of America was effective in organizing the party.

Opposing the Republicans were two groups: the Conservatives, mainly ex-Whigs who had elected Vance and Worth, and the Democrats. Before the war, these two groups were bitter opponents. Although they took the name Conservative-Democrats to show that they had come together into one party, they found cooperation difficult. Later, when they found that the only national party they could join was the Democratic party, they all became Democrats. This party resented the northern values and legal equality for blacks forced upon the state. The Conservative-Democrats opposed Congressional reconstruction, the black vote, and a more democratic government.

In the fall of 1867, these parties faced each other over the election of delegates to the state constitutional convention. Major General Daniel E. Sickles, the military commander, had registered about 180,000 loyal voters, some 73,000 of them blacks. Loyal voters had to swear to uphold the U.S. Constitution. Because many of their supporters were unable to take the oath and register to vote, the Conservative-Democrats were not really a force in the election. The Republicans won overwhelmingly, electing 107 Republican delegates to the Conservative-Democrats' 13. Among the Republican delegates were 18 carpetbaggers and 15 blacks, many of them able leaders. The remaining 74 Republicans were native North Carolinians whom the Conservative-Democrats called "false to their mother and leagued with her enemies."

A NEW STATE CONSTITUTION

When the delegates assembled in the state constitutional convention in Raleigh in January 1868, they had to draft a new constitution that would satisfy Congress. The new constitution they drew up was liberal and democratic and is the basic constitution still in effect today. It provided for **universal manhood suffrage,** meaning that all men—including blacks—could vote. The governor's term was increased to four years. Property qualifications for the governor and legislators were abolished. The offices of lieutenant governor, superintendent of public works, and auditor were created. Judges and solicitors (prosecuting attorneys) would be elected by the people. The administration of county affairs was placed in the hands of elective county commissioners. The constitution also set up a system of tax-supported schools open to all races.

The next step in Reconstruction was the ratification of the new constitution by the voters and the election of new state officers. The Republicans nominated William W. Holden for governor and the Conservative-Democrats nominated Thomas S. Ashe. Living in Anson County, Ashe served in the Confederate House and Senate during the war.

The campaign was bitter. In the end, voters ratified the constitution and elected Holden governor. The vote for the constitution was about 93,000 to 74,000; Holden won by a vote of about 92,000 to 74,000. Conservative-Democrats won only one congressional seat and one judgeship. The Republicans won all other elective positions. However, over one-half of the newly elected legislators and local officers could not take their offices until Congress pardoned them. In late June, Congress approved the state constitution and pardoned about 700 people, almost all of them Republicans. On June 30, the military governor ordered the newly elected state officers to take their positions the next day, thus removing Governor Worth from office. "I regard all of you as in effect appointees of the military power of the United States," Governor Worth wrote Holden, "and not deriving your powers from the consent of those you claim to govern."

The final step was the ratification of the Fourteenth Amendment by the new government. On July 2, the legislature met and ratified the amendment. By July 20, 1868, Congress seated all of the state's congressmen. Congressional Reconstruction was complete. But the bitter struggle for political control of the state was just beginning.

John Adams Hyman was born a slave in Warrenton. A farmer and grocer, he helped organize the state Republican party in 1867. He served in the Constitutional Convention of 1868 and later was elected state senator for six years. In 1874 he became the state's first African American representative in Congress.

Do You Remember?

1. What did the Reconstruction Act require the state constitutional convention to do?
2. Which party was the overwhelming winner in the state election of delegates to the constitutional convention of 1867?

CHAPTER · REVIEW

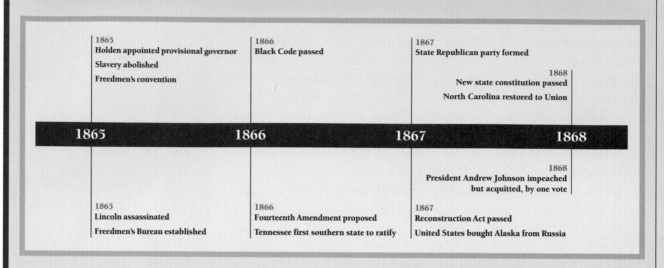

1865	1866	1867
Holden appointed provisional governor	Black Code passed	State Republican party formed
Slavery abolished		
Freedmen's convention		

		1868
		New state constitution passed
		North Carolina restored to Union

1865   1866   1867   1868

		1868
		President Andrew Johnson impeached but acquitted, by one vote

1865	1866	1867
Lincoln assassinated	Fourteenth Amendment proposed	Reconstruction Act passed
Freedmen's Bureau established	Tennessee first southern state to ratify	United States bought Alaska from Russia

Reviewing People, Places, and Terms

Use the following terms in a paragraph describing North Carolina after the Civil War.

Black Code
carpetbaggers
freedmen
Andrew Johnson
Reconstruction
scalawags

Understanding the Facts

1. Why did many congressmen believe that blacks should receive the right to vote?
2. Who was the North Carolina native who became president of the United States after the assassination of Abraham Lincoln in 1865?
3. Why was William W. Holden chosen as provisional governor of North Carolina?
4. Did the Black Code specify that blacks and whites were to be treated equally?
5. What was the purpose of the Civil Rights Bill of 1866?
6. When the Republican party was organized in North Carolina, what three groups did the party include?

7. Name three major provisions of the 1868 state constitution.
8. What was the final step in Congressional Reconstruction of the state?

Developing Critical Thinking

1. Why did congressional leaders distrust President Johnson and his Reconstruction plan?
2. Why do you think radical congressmen wanted southern leaders punished?
3. After the Civil War, what kind of "social revolution" did Reconstruction impose on North Carolina, the South, and, in a sense, the entire nation?

Applying Your Skills

1. Prepare a chart comparing the plans for Reconstruction put forth by President Johnson and by Congress. Which was the fairest? Why?
2. Assume you are a young person living in North Carolina in 1868. Write a letter to an acquaintance in another state describing changes that have taken place during Reconstruction.
3. Choose one of the following people and write a short report on that person's life: (a) Andrew Johnson, (b) Jonathan Worth, (c) John Pool, (d)

Reverend James W. Hood, (e) Alfred Dockery, (f) Thomas S. Ashe.

Making Connections

1. Find a copy of one version of "The Ballad of Tom Dula." Discuss the meaning of the various verses.
2. Make a list of at least three other ballads or folk songs that are based in part upon actual events. Share these songs with your classmates.
3. Jefferson Davis was never pardoned for his participation in the Confederacy. Prepare a short report on why this was so.
4. The victorious side in a war often charges those on the losing side with "war crimes." What are "war crimes"? Give examples of this practice in the twentieth century.

Tar Heel Trivia

- During the Civil War, two black regiments of troops were organized from Union-controlled North Carolina.

BUILDING SKILLS:
• STUDYING HISTORIC DOCUMENTS •

The night President Abraham Lincoln was assassinated by John Wilkes Booth, he was attending a performance of "Our American Cousin" at Ford's Theatre in Washington, D.C. Pictured here is Lincoln's original program; notice the blood stains. Read the program, then see if you can answer the following questions.

1. What was the date of Lincoln's assassination? What day of the week was it?
2. What was the name of the patriotic song and chorus?
3. Who was the featured actress for the performance of "Our American Cousin"?
4. When you attend a movie today, you are shown "coming attractions." What was the coming attraction at Ford's Theatre?
5. Who was the star of the coming attraction?

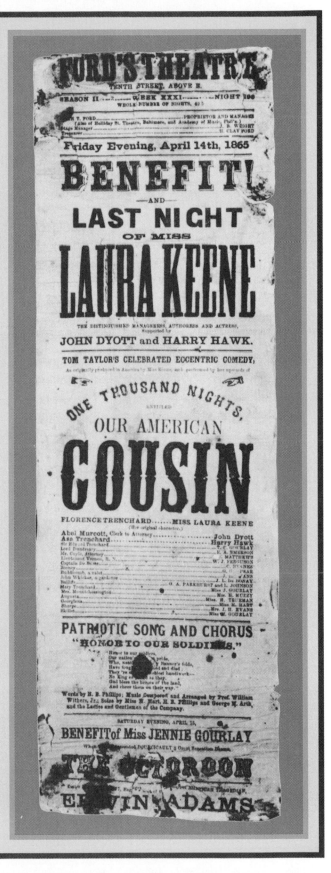

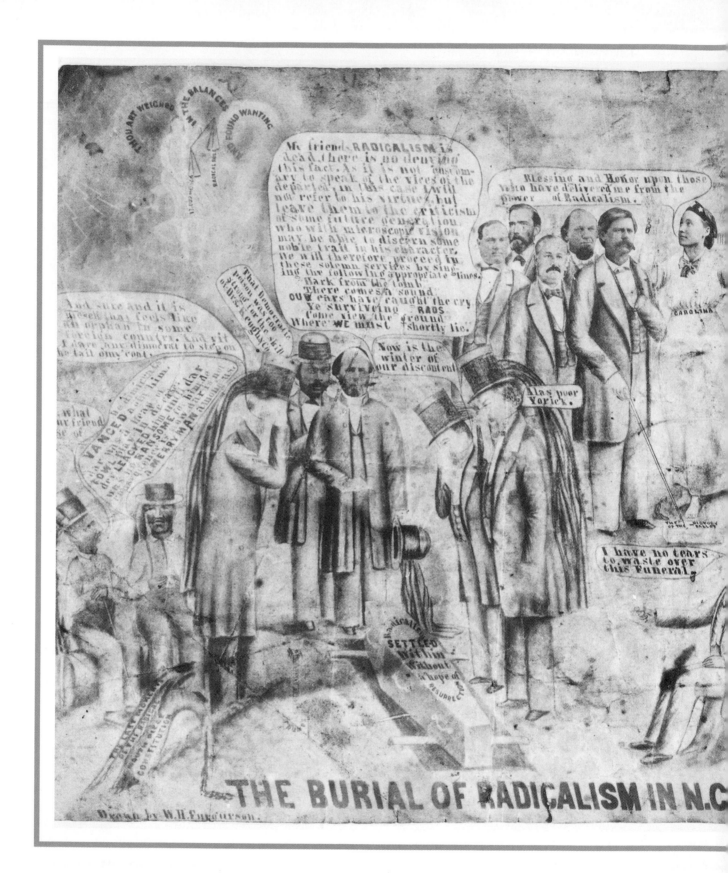

CHAPTER SEVENTEEN

RECONSTRUCTION UNDER ATTACK

And as the scriptures regards no man on account of the color of his skin, we encourage all men to do likewise.
— Roanoke [Black] Missionary Baptist Association

ALTHOUGH CONGRESSIONAL RECONSTRUCTION was a success in North Carolina, the Republican party could not hold onto the changes it brought. Suffrage and civil rights for blacks, a more democratic government, and Republican control of the state government all came under attack. The Conservative-Democrats resented the changes forced upon the state and vowed to restore the state to native white rule. The Conservative-Democrats used violence, threats, fraud, and changes in the law to regain power. By 1877, they controlled state government and undid many of the changes brought about by Reconstruction. The bitter political conflicts left their imprint on the state for decades.

THE CHANGING FACE OF THE STATE

An ever-present reminder of the social revolution brought about by Reconstruction was the changed status of blacks. Under slavery, a host of customs reminded African Americans—both slaves and free blacks—of their low position in society. Blacks were forbidden to go to the front door of a white's house; they had to go to the back door. On sidewalks, blacks had to step off to let whites pass. Black males had to remove their hats when talking to whites, especially women. At wells, blacks had to let whites drink first. In churches, blacks sat apart from whites, usually in a balcony, and took communion after whites. Blacks could not eat with whites, stay in white hotels, or eat in white restaurants. Not following any of these customs could bring a whipping or even death. Unfortunately, the end of slavery did not bring an end to these customs.

This is an 1876 cartoon of the burial of radicalism in North Carolina. What was radicalism? What caused its death? Who was Yorick?

CHAPTER • PREVIEW

Terms: bond, white supremacy, Ku Klux Klan, martial law, Kirk-Holden War

People: Samuel S. Ashley, George W. Swepson, General Milton S. Littlefield, John W. Stephens, Colonel George W. Kirk, Josiah Turner, Tod R. Caldwell

Places: Jones County, Alamance County, Caswell County

In the first rush of freedom during the war, the freedmen flocked to the Union Army. At Roanoke Island, Beaufort, New Bern, and Wilmington, they lived by the thousands on handouts from the army and the Freedmen's Bureau. After the war ended, even more gathered in the towns, and thousands wandered the countryside testing their freedom. Most African Americans, however, had no land; federal promises of "40 acres and a mule" never came to pass. And many freedmen no longer wanted to work under conditions that were still much like slavery.

Many whites wanted to keep African Americans working at the lowliest jobs. Positions such as field hand, cook, and servant belonged by custom to blacks. Whites felt that the economy would decline without blacks to perform these tasks. Especially hurt would be the planters who depended on blacks to plant, tend, and harvest their crops.

At the urging of Freedmen's Bureau agents, many freedmen returned to the plantations of their old masters. But there was now a difference. Bureau agents made sure the freedmen were fed and clothed. The freedmen now received wages under the terms of a written contract, which most of them could not even read. They could no longer be ordered about or whipped for disobedience or discourtesy. Former masters who abused or cheated their freed workers could be charged and tried in a Bureau court.

Another area of changed relations was religion. Before the war, slaves could not worship together without a white supervisor present because whites feared uprisings. Slaves generally worshiped in white churches. In these white churches, however, slaves could not hold church office, sit with white congregations, or take communion with them.

When freedom came, the freedmen thought that these practices would change. They did not. The only difference was that freedmen no longer needed a white supervisor present when they worshiped. As a result, the freedmen began to establish their own churches. Northern ministers, white and black, came to help and to train their ministers. New black churches sprang up across the countryside. By 1875, the withdrawal of blacks from white churches was almost complete.

These new churches became centers of social activities. They instilled religious beliefs and taught children and adults to read and write. The black churches also provided opportunities to learn public speaking and leadership skills. When blacks received the vote in 1867, their churches guided them toward the Union League and the Republican party.

The idea that the freedmen had rights that the planters had to observe enraged many plantation owners. They resented Freedmen's Bureau agents and the changed relationships with their former slaves. Whites also resented the northern ministers and the "new" ideas they taught blacks. Many native whites even entered religious work in order to regain control. Some white women, for example, taught Sunday school for blacks. To both former slaves and former owners, it seemed that freedom might tear apart the fabric of social custom that separated the races.

Above: In April 1866, President Johnson sent Generals Joseph S. Fullerton and James B. Steedman south to investigate abuses in the Freedmen's Bureau. They spoke in a black church near New Bern.
Opposite page: The freedmen at James City had a blacksmith and wheelwright shop. It took skilled workers to operate this shop. Most freedmen were not skilled.

Do You Remember?
1. Give three examples of the customs that reminded blacks of their low social standing after the end of slavery.
2. Why did many whites want to keep blacks working at the lowliest jobs?

The Republicans were in power in North Carolina from 1868 to 1870. When the Republican legislature met in Raleigh in 1868, it proposed many programs. One of their most important programs concerned education.

EDUCATION

In 1840, North Carolina established one of the best common school systems in the South, but it was open only to white children. It was illegal to teach slaves to read and write. In 1866, the legislature voted not to reopen the public schools for fear that the army or the Freedmen's Bureau would force the state to educate black and white children together.

*Right: In April 1862, Vincent Colyer established the state's first public school for freedmen at New Bern. Union troops were occupying the town at the time. **Above:** A freedmen's school at James City. By 1867, northern groups had established 170 such schools in North Carolina.*

The state did have private schools for blacks, however. During the war, northern religious organizations sent teachers southward to teach in freedmen's schools on Roanoke Island and at New Bern and Beaufort. When the war ended, the American Missionary Association sent a minister named Samuel S. Ashley to Wilmington to establish schools for freedmen. As quickly as he got teachers, black or white, he sent them to schools in Southport, Fayetteville, Lumberton, and Goldsboro. By 1867, northern groups, supported by the Freedmen's Bureau, had established over 170 freedmen's schools in the state. Every town with a sizable black population had at least one such school.

Whites generally hated these schools. They believed that, once educated, blacks would no longer be satisfied with lowly jobs. Even more, they feared that northern teachers would teach black children and adults their ideas of political and social equality. As a result, native whites shunned and mistreated northern teachers. Ashley himself constantly felt in danger.

By 1867, however, whites began to change their minds about education for freedmen. Plantation owners discovered that their field hands badly wanted an education. These hands would leave their jobs on the plantation if a black school opened nearby. To attract workers, some planters set up schools on the plantations for them.

Acting upon this changing sentiment, religious groups began to found colleges to train black teachers, ministers, and homemakers. The Episcopal Church founded St. Augustine's College in Raleigh. Northern Baptists established Shaw University in Raleigh. Northern Presbyterians founded Biddle Memorial Institute in Charlotte, which later became Johnson C. Smith University. The Presbyterians also organized Scotia

TOURGÉE'S *A FOOL'S ERRAND*

The literature of a period often reveals much about the attitudes, fears, and experiences of the people of that period. One such novel is *A Fool's Errand*, a fictional story drawn from Albion W. Tourgée's experience as a carpetbagger in North Carolina. Here is a summary of one part of the book:

By the light of a full moon, Lily Servosse calmed her horse in the shadows at a crossroads. She was on a desperate twenty-mile ride to save the life of her father and a judge. News that the Ku Klux Klan planned to kill them prompted her dash. As the Klan indicated the road they would take, she spurred her horse out of the woods and past a guard, firing her pistol at him. Although her bullet broke his arm, he gave chase, his pistol drawn. But he stopped in surprise and let her go when he recognized Lily as the woman he hoped to marry.

The hero of the novel is Colonel Comfort Servosse, a Michigan carpetbagger who went south after the Civil War. Servosse supported the "wise men" in Congress, although he thought them wrong to impose military and black rule on the South. Servosse believed that the Republicans imposed harsh rule to increase their power, not to heal the nation's wounds. Servosse predicted that such a policy would fail, and, when it did, he regarded his work in the South as "a fool's errand."

Top: Episcopalians, with northern support, established St. Augustine's College in Raleigh, mainly to educate black ministers. This is an 1889 view. Above: Mrs. Ellen Noyes Storey graduated from St. Augustine's in 1896. She taught school in Wilmington many years.

Seminary in Concord to train young women to become Christian home-makers. A similar purpose moved northern Methodists to found Bennett College in Greensboro. One black group, the African Methodist Episcopal Zion Church, established its own college at Salisbury to train ministers. Unable to raise enough money locally to keep it open, its president traveled to England to look for funds. To thank their English donors, the trustees renamed the school Livingstone College, in honor of the famed English missionary to Africa.

The constitution of 1868 left to the townships of a county the decision about whether to build and open public schools. The constitution also required that schools be open to *all* children age six to twenty-one—black and white. To pay teachers, the state levied taxes. State taxes for education were something new. Before the war, the state used the interest from the Literary Fund to pay teachers. The state's voiding of the war debt, however, nearly destroyed the fund.

The task of establishing the first tax-supported public school system for all races fell to the first elected state superintendent of public instruction, Samuel S. Ashley. Ashley appointed the Reverend James W. Hood as his assistant to establish black schools. Ashley worked hard to develop a school law, which the legislature passed in 1869. This law set out how the school system would operate and how it would be funded. The new schools began opening their doors in 1870 to some 49,000 children, about half of them black. This was not a good beginning, since the state had about 330,000 school-age children. The biggest problem was a lack of money to operate the schools. Taxes brought in much less money than expected. The lack of public support also hurt the effort.

In 1870, the Conservative-Democrats gained control of the legislature. They hated Ashley and were determined to run him from office. The legislature cut his salary and took over control of the school fund. Ashley resigned rather than see the legislature destroy the schools he had established. The schools, however, did not do much better under the Conservative-Democrats. The school term was only ten weeks each year, and the schools in 1874 reached less than half the 357,000 children of school age. It is little wonder that North Carolina had one of the highest illiteracy rates in the nation during this period.

THE RAILROAD BOND SCANDAL

When the war ended, the people were poverty-stricken. But some men had visions of the great wealth that could be made. Coal deposits in Chatham, timber in Buncombe, iron ore in Lincoln, feldspar in Mitchell, and granite in Surry—all waited to be developed. The major need was for railroads to move this potential wealth to market. Then the state could become prosperous.

State leaders recognized the need for a better transportation system even before the war. They urged the state to supply the funds to build the railroads. By 1860, the state had about 900 miles of railroads, many of them built with state aid.

When the war ended, the state needed money not only to build new railroads, but to repair the old ones. The Conservative-Democrats voted $3 million for this purpose in 1866. The Republican-controlled constitutional convention of 1868 added another $2.2 million. The money was raised by selling bonds to the public. A **bond** is actually an IOU. People

Capitalists desired to exploit the state's natural resources after the war. The natural resource at Cranberry Iron Mine in Avery County was iron ore.

lend money to the state, and the state promises to repay the borrowed money over a certain period of time. During the repayment period, bond owners receive yearly interest payments.

Governor Holden and the Republican legislature of 1868-1869 believed that more railroads would bring prosperity to the state. A dishonest group of men called the "railroad ring" took advantage of this belief. The leaders of this ring were George W. Swepson, a Raleigh banker, and General Milton S. Littlefield, formerly of the Union Army and a leading Republican.

Swepson pictured himself as the head of a great railroad empire. He planned to steal bonds from the state and use them to buy controlling interest in other railroads. His first task was to win the governor's and the legislators' confidence so he could convince the legislature to issue millions of dollars in bonds. As the first step in this plan, the railroad ring bought Governor Holden's newspaper, the Raleigh *Standard,* for $15,000 cash. Next, Littlefield spent $200,000 bribing leading legislators to issue some $28 million in railroad bonds. Swepson even offered to give Holden $25,000 in state bonds, but Holden did not accept them.

Holden did agree to divide the state-owned Western North Carolina Railroad into an eastern division and a western division. Swepson got himself elected president of the western division. In order to get control of $6.4 million in state bonds, he told the governor that he had issued construction contracts for the western division. He had not. When the governor released the bonds, Swepson used them to get control of other railroads, even one in Florida. The railroad ring, and others, stole millions of dollars in state bonds using such schemes.

By late 1869, everyone knew that the state was in financial trouble. State taxes brought in only about $450,000, just enough to pay the inter-

Another natural resource was granite, quarried in Surry County. Here, blocks of granite await shipment by railroad.

est on the railroad bonds. There was no money left to meet other state expenses. The bonds then became almost worthless. The state could not raise money by issuing more bonds because no one would buy them. Investors knew that the state could barely pay the interest, much less the principal (the original amount borrowed).

Altogether, the legislature authorized the issue of about $28 million in bonds. Holden was able to get back about $4 million of the $18 million that had actually been issued. The railroad ring thus stole nearly $14 million from the state. All the state got was about 72 miles of track and many miles of prepared roadbed.

This scandal nearly split the Republican party. It did delay for about fifteen years the building of the western division of the railroad and the economic development of the mountains.

Do You Remember?
1. Why did the legislature vote not to reopen the public schools?
2. Why did whites generally hate the freedmen's schools in the state?
3. Why was the development of a railroad system so important to the state?
4. What resulted from the railroad scandal?

THE RISE OF THE CONSERVATIVE-DEMOCRATS

The railroad scandal helped the Conservative-Democrats gain control of the legislature in 1870. They charged the Republicans with being the party of wasteful spending and robbery. The Conservative-Democrats used two other means to regain control of the legislature: the white supremacy issue and violence.

White supremacy is the belief that the white race is superior to the black race, or any other race. The Conservative-Democrats hoped to use the issue of white supremacy to split the Republican party. About half of the party's members were white and half were black. The Conservative-Democrats argued that state government should be by and for white people. They believed blacks were too ignorant and inferior to vote and hold office. They also charged that whites who associated with blacks were traitors to their race. This tactic (plan) did draw some whites into the Conservative-Democratic party.

KU KLUX KLAN
Violence was an even more effective tool for intimidating (frightening) Republican voters. The **Ku Klux Klan** carried on much of that violence. Starting as a social organization of Confederate veterans in Tennessee in 1866, the Klan became a secret, racist organization whose

Starting as a social group, the Ku Klux Klan became a secret political terrorist organization. It tried to stop Republicans, mostly blacks, from voting. The costume above was typical of KKK dress.

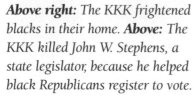

purpose was to restore political and social control to whites. By 1868, the Klan had spread into North Carolina.

The Klan used violence and threats to help Conservative-Democrats win elections. It was most active in the Piedmont counties where the change of a few votes could mean a victory for the Conservative-Democrats. First appearing in Jones and Lenoir counties in 1869, the Klan took four blacks from a Kinston jail and killed them. It also killed the Republican sheriff of Jones County and murdered another Republican leader from the North. Later, in Moore County, the Klan murdered a black woman and her five children and then burned their house.

The Klan was strongest and most persistent in Alamance County. In one instance, it tortured a black man, Caswell Holt, to force him to confess to stealing. Holt was able to identify twelve of his torturers and swore out warrants for their arrest. However, the county prosecutor released the men because it was their word against that of a black man. Later, the Klan returned, shot and wounded Holt, and beat his daughters.

The Alamance Klan also attacked Republican leaders. Wyatt Outlaw, a black leader of the Union League, lived in Graham. The Klan first fired shots into his house and later hanged him. In return, blacks began burning the barns of suspected Klansmen. The Klan ran from the county a white Quaker who taught a school for blacks. When the Klan threatened to kill state senator T. M. Shoffner for sponsoring a law against the Klan, he fled to Indiana.

One state senator who was unable to flee was John W. Stephens of Caswell County. Stephens was from a poor white family. The Klan disliked him because he treated blacks as equals. In May 1870, Stephens attended the Conservative-Democratic party convention at the courthouse in Yanceyville as an observer. A friend lured him into a basement room where waiting Klansmen stabbed him to death. The Klan planned to move his body and claim that blacks had killed him. However, several black men noticed that Stephens did not come out of the meeting. They stood guard around the building until Stephens' body was found.

As governor, William Holden was the state's chief law enforcement officer. But he did not know how to put down the Klan. At first, he simply asked the people not to support it, but that did not work. Next, he sent detectives and the militia into Jones and Lenoir counties. The Klan stopped its killings there. Holden then asked the Union Army commander to send troops to Alamance and Caswell counties. The commander insisted that Holden use the state militia first. This Holden could not do because the militia was sympathetic to the Klan. Desperate for help, Holden went to Washington and appealed to President Ulysses S. Grant. Grant refused to help on the grounds that this was a state matter. Congress promised to pass a law against the Klan, but it did not do so until 1871, too late to help Holden.

Josiah Turner was the leading Conservative editor in the state. His paper, the Raleigh Sentinel, *attacked Governor Holden and the Republican party.*

THE KIRK-HOLDEN WAR

In 1870, after the murders of Outlaw and Stephens, Holden decided to declare martial law in Caswell and Alamance counties. **Martial law** occurs when military forces are used to keep order in an emergency or when civilian forces cannot. The Shoffner Act, passed in 1869, gave the governor the right to do this. Holden hoped to use the military to break the Klan. He placed Colonel George W. Kirk, a man "notorious for his desperate and brutal character," in charge. After raising a force of over six hundred men in the mountains, Kirk arrived in the area and arrested about one hundred suspects in Alamance and Caswell counties.

Meanwhile, Holden threatened to arrest Josiah Turner, editor of the Raleigh *Sentinel*, for being a leader in the Klan. Turner, who was a supporter of the Klan, challenged Holden in his paper: "Gov. Holden: You say you will handle me in due time. You white-livered miscreant, do it now. You dared me to resist you; I dare you to arrest me." Holden then ordered Colonel Kirk to arrest Turner in Orange County, where there was no martial law. Kirk jailed Turner in the Yanceyville courthouse room where Stephens was murdered.

Turner's lawyers then tried to get Turner and the other prisoners released. They applied to the state courts for writs of habeas corpus. These writs required the state to release the men unless it brought specific charges against

The 1871 General Assembly impeached and convicted Governor Holden. He was the first governor ever to be impeached and removed from office.

them. When the state courts refused to grant the writs, the lawyers turned to a federal judge in Salisbury, who did issue them. Holden appealed to President Grant, but Grant advised him to obey the federal judge. Holden had to release the prisoners, most of whom were never tried. Turner swore out a warrant for the arrest of Holden for assault and battery, but the sheriff of Wake County refused to serve it.

Meanwhile, Klan activity decreased rapidly. Many of the Klan's leaders were from the state's wealthiest families. They had begun to hate the Klan's brutality. But they could not just drop out for fear of being killed as accessories to murder. Holden's attack on the Klan gave its leaders the chance to urge that it be disbanded.

This so-called **Kirk-Holden War** was just one of the issues Conservative-Democrats used against the Republicans in the election of 1870. The result was an overwhelming victory for the Conservative-Democrats. Both houses of the state legislature came under their control, the senate by a two-thirds majority. Six Conservative-Democrats were also elected to the United States House of Representatives.

Do You Remember?

1. In addition to the railroad scandal, what helped the Conservative-Democrats regain control of the legislature?
2. What was the chief weapon of the Ku Klux Klan in intimidating voters?

THE IMPEACHMENT OF GOVERNOR HOLDEN

As soon as the election was over, Conservative-Democratic newspapers began calling for the impeachment of Governor Holden because he had imposed martial law. Holden tried to explain his actions in his address to the new legislature. It did no good, however. The house of representatives impeached him "for high crimes and misdemeanors in office." Having been charged with committing nine illegal acts by the house, Holden was tried before the state senate. Chief Justice Richmond Pearson presided over the impeachment hearings. The senate found Holden guilty of unlawfully arresting Josiah Turner and others and of refusing to obey a writ of habeas corpus. It also found him guilty of raising troops without legal authority and unlawfully paying them. Holden was removed from office and replaced by Lieutenant Governor Tod R. Caldwell. Holden thus became the first governor in the United States to be impeached and removed from office. Holden went to Washington, D.C., before the senate's verdict was announced because he was afraid he would be arrested. He stayed out of North Carolina for about a year, editing the Washington *Chronicle* for part of that time.

THE CONSERVATIVE-DEMOCRATS TAKE CONTROL

After the impeachment of Holden, the Conservative-Democrats looked forward to a victory in the election of 1872. The Republicans nominated Tod R. Caldwell for governor. The Conservative-Democrats nominated an Asheville lawyer, Augustus S. Merrimon. They were delighted when Liberal Republicans broke away from the Republican party. These Liberals hated the corruption in the party, especially the railroad scandals. They supported Merrimon and other Conservative-Democratic candidates. Merrimon seemed sure to be elected.

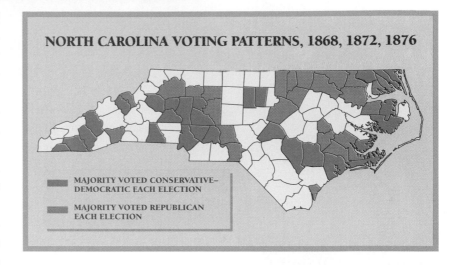

The election, however, showed that the Republican party was still very much alive in North Carolina. Republican Caldwell defeated Merrimon by a vote of about 98,000 to 96,000, one of the closest races in state history. Although Caldwell won the governorship, the Conservative-Democrats still controlled the legislature.

The Conservative-Democrats used this control to undo much of the Republican Reconstruction. After reducing state expenditures and lowering taxes, the legislature called a constitutional convention in 1875 to change parts of the Constitution of 1868 that the Conservative-Democrats didn't like. The bill calling for the convention would not allow the convention to change some parts of the constitution, especially rights granted to blacks, women, and working people. President Grant also told the legislature that he would not overturn the changes made by the convention.

The election of delegates greatly surprised the Conservative-Democrats, who were again overconfident. The people elected fifty-eight Conservative-Democrats, fifty-eight Republicans, and three Independents. Since the Conservative-Democrats had controlled the legislature since 1870, this vote showed the strength of the Republican party.

The convention proposed some thirty amendments to the constitution, all of which were ratified in the popular election. Most of the amendments had the support of both parties. Secret political societies like the Union League and the Ku Klux Klan were outlawed, as was carrying concealed weapons. Marriage between blacks and whites and the racial integration of schools were forbidden.

Top: This map shows which North Carolina counties voted consistently Conservative-Democratic or Republican during Reconstruction. *Above:* Lieutenant Governor Tod R. Caldwell of Burke County became governor when Holden was removed. Caldwell was also elected governor in 1872.

THE REPUBLICAN PARTY AND RECONSTRUCTION

During the years 1865-1870, the Republican Congress secured the passage and ratification of amendments to the U.S. Constitution that abolished slavery, made freedmen citizens, guaranteed their equal treatment under state law, and assured their right to vote. But by 1877 the Republican party had abandoned black citizens to the mercy of southern Democrats.

Moderate Republicans needed the support of whites to build Republican parties in the southern and border states. Yet, the Congressional Republicans did things that drove whites away from the party. The South needed national banks, levees along the Mississippi, and free southern land for homesteads. Congress did little to help the South. They levied a cotton tax (the only one on an agricultural product), gave no aid to build railroads or improve harbors in the South, and prohibited ex-Confederates from holding office. Besides, many Republicans were stirring up emotions against the South in order to win votes.

The rise of liberal Republicans in 1872 split the party and undermined support for black rights. The Liberal Republicans opposed using military force to uphold corrupt southern state governments. When Grant was re-elected president, he reduced military forces in the South. As a result, state governments fell back under Democratic control. The deal struck for 1876 Republican presidential candidate Rutherford B. Hayes was the final blow. When Hayes was elected, federal troops were removed from the South, and white Democrats regained control of every southern state. The rights of African Americans were no longer secure.

In the 1876 presidential election, Rutherford B. Hayes promised to withdraw federal troops from the South in return for the votes from three southern states.

Some changes worked to benefit the Conservative-Democratic party. For example, one amendment gave the legislature the power to elect all justices of the peace, who in turn elected county commissioners. The Conservative-Democrats resented the election of blacks to county office in those counties with black majorities. This amendment ensured that only white Conservative-Democrats would be elected to local offices. Another amendment gave the legislature control of the judicial system, apparently to prevent the election of Republican judges. The residence requirement for voting was raised from sixty to ninety days. This made it more difficult for the Republicans to bring in blacks from other states to vote in elections, as had sometimes been done.

THE END OF RECONSTRUCTION

After the constitutional changes, both parties expected a victory in the election of 1876. At the urging of President Grant, the Republicans nominated Judge Thomas Settle for governor. Conservative-Democrats, now calling themselves Democrats, nominated former governor Zebulon B. Vance. Vance hit hard at Republican corruption at the state and national levels, while Settle charged Vance with bringing war and destruction upon the people.

The Democratic victory was overwhelming. The governor's race was close, with Vance winning After eight years, the Democrats finally won control of the governorship. In the General Assembly, the Democrats won by a landslide. They elected all but one congressman.

The presidential election of 1876 resulted in a different kind of victory. Rutherford B. Hayes of Ohio was the Republican nominee, while Samuel J. Tilden of New York ran as a Democrat. When the election returns came in, neither man had a majority of the votes. The returns in three southern states, however, were disputed (Florida, Louisiana, and South Carolina). Hayes was awarded all of these disputed electoral votes and won the election. To get those votes, the Republicans made some promises. They promised to withdraw the military from the South. This meant that Hayes and the Republicans would no longer support Republican state governments and give federal protection to blacks.

The election of 1876 thus ended Reconstruction in North Carolina. But it did not end the long-term effects of the bitter partisan struggles. It is true that blacks made great gains during Reconstruction: the abolition of slavery, citizenship, equality under state law, protection from arbitrary state actions, and the right to vote. But Reconstruction did not give blacks the power or the property needed to hold onto those rights. Reconstruction thus left blacks with freedom, but little else.

The Democrats adopted the white supremacy issue and resolved to make state government a white man's government. Because Republicans depended upon the black vote, the result was decades of bad race relations in the state. Reconstruction also showed Democrats how effective violence was in winning elections.

The bitterness of Reconstruction helped to make North Carolina a one-party state for nearly a century. Between 1876 and 1972, the Republicans won the governorship only once, in 1896.

Top: *After Reconstruction, Zebulon Vance served the state as governor and U.S. Senator.* *Above:* *Rockingham County native Thomas Settle was defeated for governor in 1876 by Vance. Settle was a former Democrat, a judge, a Confederate veteran, and a founder of the Republican party in North Carolina.*

Do You Remember?
1. Of what charges was Governor Holden found guilty ?
2. What were some gains blacks made during Reconstruction?
3. What lasting effect did Reconstruction have on politics in the state?

(left sidebar image: poster reading "THE SWAMP OUTLAWS, OR THE LOWERY BANDITS OF NORTH CAROLINA")

Top: *Henry Berry Lowry led a band of outlaw Indians in Robeson County from 1865 to 1872. No one knows what became of him.* **Right:** *This is a rendering of the Lowry band in the Lumber River swamp.*

HENRY BERRY LOWRY

In the final months of the Civil War and during the years that followed, an outlaw "Indian gang" led by Henry Berry Lowry roamed throughout southeastern North Carolina. Born in Robeson County, Lowry was of Native American and Scottish ancestry. His exploits, daring escapes from jail, and armed conflicts with state and local officials made him a folk hero, especially to the state's Indian, black, and poor white populations. He gained a "Robin Hood-like" reputation as a man who robbed from wealthier white planters to support his band and who often shared his stolen foodstuffs with the poor. He was viewed as a sincere, but perhaps misguided, crusader against the racial and economic injustice of his day.

During the war, the Lowry gang resisted efforts by Confederate officials to force them and other local Indians to build forts in the Cape Fear region. Hiding out in the swamps, the Lowry family and other Indians fought against Confederate authorities, often using hit-and-run tactics. Several of Lowry's cousins were killed, and in 1865 his father and brother were captured and executed by white officials.

These events only increased Lowry's resistance to the government and his hatred for his pursuers. He was jailed twice, but escaped with the help of friends. The state legislature finally offered a $25,000 reward for his recapture, dead or alive.

Lowry's band was slowly cut down by white authorities and bounty hunters. Lowry himself managed to avoid being recaptured. In 1872, he mysteriously disappeared. No one knows whether Lowry died of natural causes, was killed, or left the state. One Lumbee Indian remarked about his disappearance: "It doesn't matter how he died, or when he died, or where his body lies, for it's dust; it's his spirit that counts."

Top: Thomas Lowry, Henry's brother, joined Henry's band. In 1872 bounty hunters ambushed and killed Thomas, collecting $6,200 for the deed. Above: George Applewhite, a former slave, joined Lowry's band. He was a mason and plasterer from Wayne County.

CHAPTER • REVIEW

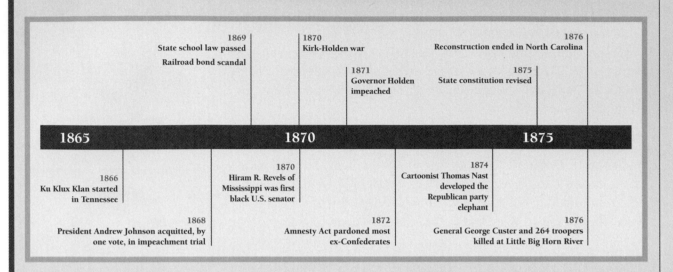

1869	1870	1876
State school law passed	Kirk-Holden war	Reconstruction ended in North Carolina
Railroad bond scandal		

	1871	1875
	Governor Holden impeached	State constitution revised

1865 · 1870 · 1875

1866	1870	1874
Ku Klux Klan started in Tennessee	Hiram R. Revels of Mississippi was first black U.S. senator	Cartoonist Thomas Nast developed the Republican party elephant

1868	1872	1876
President Andrew Johnson acquitted, by one vote, in impeachment trial	Amnesty Act pardoned most ex-Confederates	General George Custer and 264 troopers killed at Little Big Horn River

Reviewing People, Places, and Terms

Explain why each of the following terms or phrases appears in this chapter on the decline and end of Reconstruction.

1. bond
2. Kirk-Holden War
3. Ku Klux Klan
4. martial law
5. white supremacy

Understanding the Facts

1. How were relations between freedmen and planters different after the Civil War?
2. Before the Civil War, why did blacks generally worship in white churches rather than in their own?
3. Name three colleges established by religious groups soon after the war to train black teachers, ministers, and homemakers.
4. During the 1870s, how long was the school term for students attending North Carolina public schools?
5. How did the state plan to finance the repair and construction of railroads?

6. What was the major factor that delayed the construction and expansion of railroads in western North Carolina after the Civil War?
7. What actions did Governor Holden take against the violence and intimidation of the Ku Klux Klan?
8. Who was the first state governor in the United States to be impeached and removed from office?
9. What did the election of 1872 and the election of delegates to the 1875 constitutional convention show about the Republican party?

Developing Critical Thinking

1. What improvements did early black churches make to black society?
2. Why do you think Governor Holden was impeached? If this had not been the Reconstruction period, do you think he still would have been impeached?
3. In what ways do you think Reconstruction was successful? Unsuccessful?
4. What did blacks *not* gain during Reconstruction? Explain your answer.

1. Many churches are involved in activities for both their members and members of their communities. Talk to a local minister, rabbi, or priest to learn of the programs or services offered by that church. Share your findings with the class.

2. The railroad ring stole nearly $14 million from the state. All the state had to show was about 72 miles of railroad (plus many miles of prepared roadbed). How much did it cost *per mile* to build those 72 miles of railroad?

3. States, counties, cities, and towns issue bonds to raise the money needed for large projects, such as highways or water and sewer systems. Find out whether your city or town has issued bonds. If so, determine how many bonds were issued, for what purpose, when they must be repaid, and what the interest rate was.

Making Connections

1. The words *carpetbagger* and *scalawag* were often spoken by southerners with a tone of bitterness. What did the words symbolize to the South?

2. Albion Tourgée based his novel on his experiences as a carpetbagger and judge in North Carolina. Write a short story based on your experiences as a student in North Carolina.

3. Why were moderate Republicans unable to get white support in the South?

4. If the Republican party was the party of Lincoln and Reconstruction, why do you think most African Americans today belong to the Democratic party?

Tar Heel Trivia

- Albion W. Tourgée was North Carolina's best-known Republican carpetbagger. After a distinguished, if troubled, career as a lawyer and superior court judge, he left North Carolina and won national literary fame as a novelist writing about his experiences during Reconstruction. His most popular novels were *A Fool's Errand* and *Bricks Without Straw*.

- John H. Smythe, a black member of the 1875 constitutional convention from New Hanover County, served as U.S. Minister to Liberia from 1878 to 1885.

- The outdoor drama *Strike at the Wind* is based on Henry Berry Lowry's exploits.

• BUILDING SKILLS: CONDUCTING INTERVIEWS •

Throughout your study of North Carolina history, and in other courses, you may be given assignments to interview a person to collect specific information. To make the interview go more smoothly and to help ensure that you get the information you want or need, follow these steps.

1. Before you schedule the interview, call or visit the person to get permission for the interview.

2. Plan and then write out the questions you will ask. You might start with *who*, *what*, and *where* questions.

3. Either write out or tape-record the person's answers, after asking and receiving permission to do so.

4. Thank the person for the information.

5. Soon after the interview, go over your notes or listen to the tape recording. You may remember another point that was not included.

Try This! As is true in every time period, many people make contributions at the local level but never receive national or statewide acclaim for their efforts. Interview relatives or other responsible adults who have lived in your area for some time. Ask them for information about local citizens who have made contributions of note. Record the names and achievements of those individuals. Be sure to find out the essential information about the individual's achievements (time period, motives, obstacles faced, people who benefitted, and so on). Bring the information to class to share.

NORTH CAROLINA AT THE END OF THE CENTURY

AFTER RECONSTRUCTION, the state experienced great economic growth. Textiles, furniture-making, and tobacco prospered. The railroads expanded. Farmers, however, faced low prices and other problems. When the Democratic party ignored their needs, farmers organized the Farmers' Alliance and later the Populist party. The Populists joined forces with the Republicans to take control of state government in the 1890s. The Democrats returned to the use of fraud and violence to regain control of the legislature. The Democratic campaigns led to the disfranchisement of African Americans and the beginning of segregation.

Right: The last decades of the nineteenth century were difficult ones for the state's farmers. *Above:* Their economic problems led to a political revolution at the ballot box. Shown here is an 1884 election scene in Swain County.

CHAPTER EIGHTEEN

NORTH CAROLINA IN THE NEW SOUTH

Out of our political defeat we must work out a glorious material and industrial triumph. We must have less politics and more work, fewer stump speakers and more stump pullers, less tinsel and show and boast, and more hard earnest work. . . . Teach the boys and girls to work and teach them to be proud of it. Demand a better and more liberal system of public education, and if need be, demand increased taxation to obtain it. . . . Work for the material and educational advancement of North Carolina, and in this, and not in politics, will be found her refuge and her strength.

— Raleigh *News and Observer*

WHEN THE CIVIL WAR ENDED, many people wondered about the "New South" that would arise from the ashes of war. Would the New South remain a land devoted to agriculture? Would it try to be more like the industrial North and build factories and businesses?

An overwhelmingly rural state, North Carolina could be expected to depend heavily on agriculture. Yet, by the end of the nineteenth century, North Carolina had started on a course toward **industrialization** (manufacturing).

Between 1880 and 1900, the roots of modern North Carolina were planted deeply. Its abundant raw materials enabled North Carolina to become the industrial leader of the New South. As industry began to boom, however, agriculture declined.

The state's largest port, Wilmington, was also the largest city until 1910. That year Charlotte gained the distinction of being North Carolina's largest city.

THE GROWTH OF CITIES AND TOWNS

In 1860, only about 20,000 people, 2 percent of North Carolina's total population of around 1 million persons, lived in urban areas (towns and cities). Over the next forty years, the population of North Carolina and its urban areas increased steadily. In 1880, North Carolina's population of approximately 1.4 million included about 55,000 urban residents (3.9 percent). In 1900, there were nearly 1.9 million North Carolinians, of whom 187,000 (9.8 percent) lived in towns and cities.

Wilmington had been the state's largest city since the 1830s. In 1879, it was the only North Carolina town with more than 10,000 residents. By 1900, five other towns had reached a population of 10,000: Charlotte, Asheville, Winston, Raleigh, and Greensboro. Wilmington remained the state's largest town until 1910, when Charlotte passed it.

North Carolina's increasing industrialization spurred the growth of the urban middle class. The rapid growth could especially be seen in the Piedmont and Mountains sections of the state. People moved to towns and villages to work in the mills and factories. The towns, in turn, needed the services and businesses that middle-class professionals, trades people, and managers provided.

To attract manufacturers and businesses, **municipalities** (cities and towns organized to govern local affairs) had to concern themselves with such issues as sewers, water supplies, electric power, transportation, parks, and paved roads. Before 1900, most of these developments were still in their infancy in most North Carolina towns. For example, electric trolley cars first appeared in Asheville in 1889. Two years later, Charlotte and Raleigh began operating electric streetcar systems.

RAILROADS

In North Carolina, railroads were both a cause and an effect of industrialization. After the Civil War, the railroads expanded slowly because of the bond scandals and inadequate funding. The Western North Carolina Railroad, a key extension of the North Carolina Railroad, was finally completed from Salisbury to within seven miles of Asheville in 1880. Elsewhere, other lines were completed from Charlotte to Shelby and from Raleigh to Hamlet.

Between 1880 and 1900, the state's various railroads were consolidated into three major systems owned or controlled by interests outside North Carolina. The state leased the North Carolina Railroad to the Richmond and Danville Railroad in 1871 and then signed a ninety-nine-year lease with the newly formed Southern Railway Company in 1895. The Seaboard Airline Railway and the Atlantic Coast Line Railroad were the other two major systems in the state. Unlike the nineteenth-century dream of a major east-west railroad crossing the state, these three systems generally ran north-south.

The Piedmont Crescent—the industrial, urban corridor slicing across central North Carolina—was originally located parallel to the North Carolina Railroad. In recent years, Interstate 85 has been built to provide

CHAPTER PREVIEW

Terms: industrialization, municipality, tobacco industry, textile industry, furniture industry, tenancy system, credit, sharecropper, Farmers' Alliance

People: R. J. Reynolds, Washington Duke, James B. "Buck" Duke, David A. and William E. White, Ernest Ansel Snow, John H. Tate, Thomas F. Wrenn, Leonidas Lafayette Polk

Places: Piedmont Crescent, Winston, Durham, High Point

PUBLIC HEALTH

The movement for public health grew out of the Civil War experience. Before the war, most Americans lived in dirt and grime. In caring for the sick and wounded during the war, reformers realized that there was a connection between cleanliness and good health.

In the decades after the war, urban areas became the centers of the public health movement. Because urban areas were crowded, smelly, dirty, and noisy, disease spread quickly. The most feared diseases were cholera, typhoid, and yellow fever. Cholera outbreaks in the United States occurred in 1832, 1849, and 1866. Yellow fever visited nearly every year. The 1878 epidemic killed 8,100 people in New Orleans and 5,100 in Memphis.

To halt these epidemics, health boards were created and took steps to cleanse cities, quarantine (isolate) the sick, protect water supplies, and remove garbage and waste. Physicians made house-to-house visits. Volunteers distributed circulars giving advice on personal hygiene. Diseased areas received large doses of disinfectant.

By 1900, nearly every major city and state had a health department. Cities began to install running water and sewers. Ordinances prevented businesses and private citizens from simply dumping waste and debris in the streets. Where public health was concerned, Americans learned that they had to be their "brothers' keepers."

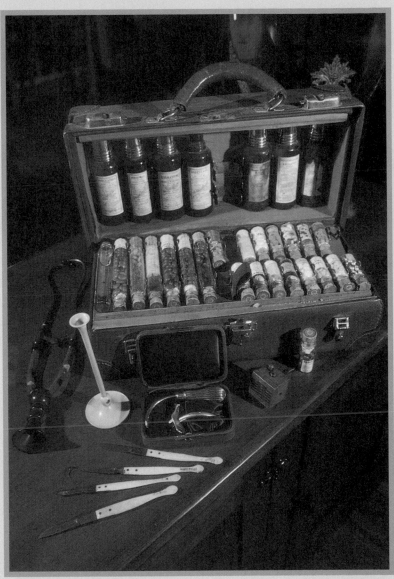

An example of a turn-of-the-century physician's medicine case and tools from an exhibit at the Country Doctors Museum in Bailey, North Carolina.

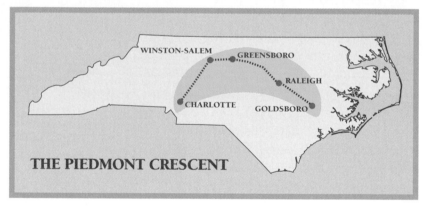

THE PIEDMONT CRESCENT

WINSTON-SALEM
GREENSBORO
RALEIGH
CHARLOTTE
GOLDSBORO

Above: In 1871 the Richmond and Danville Railroad (locomotive #12 is seen here) leased the North Carolina Railroad from the state. *Right:* This map shows the Piedmont Crescent where cities and industry grew up along the route of the North Carolina Railroad. *Opposite page:* Washington Duke and his family began manufacturing smoking tobacco at their home in Durham (top). At the same time, Richard Joshua Reynolds (below) started a tobacco factory in Winston.

modern roads for the Crescent's chain of cities. The Crescent, however, had its beginnings in the decades just before the turn of the century. Three major industries grew up along the Piedmont Crescent: tobacco, textiles, and furniture.

Do You Remember?

1. What were the six largest towns in North Carolina in 1900?
2. What caused people to move to the towns?
3. What issues did municipalities have to deal with to attract manufacturers and businesses?
4. What were the three major systems that owned or controlled North Carolina's railroads in 1900?

THE TOBACCO INDUSTRY

After the discovery of the bright-leaf curing process before the Civil War, the popularity of that lemon-yellow, fragrant tobacco increased steadily. It was first used as a wrapper for chewing tobacco, then for pipe smoking, and finally for cigarettes. The 1870s and 1880s were important years in the development of the **tobacco industry.**

In 1874, Richard Joshua Reynolds, a native of Virginia, arrived in the small town of Winston. Reynolds knew tobacco, having grown up on a tobacco farm. He had also sold homemade chewing tobacco in the mountains of Kentucky and Tennessee. Reynolds set up a tobacco factory in Winston that grew and prospered.

Winston and Durham were important to the development of tobacco manufacturing in North Carolina. By 1880, there were 126 tobacco factories in the state, most of them in Winston and Durham. Durham, for example, was home to W. T. Blackwell and Company, a tobacco manufacturer that won worldwide fame with its Bull Durham smoking tobacco. Blackwell and his partner Julian Shakespeare Carr were pioneers in the use of advertising. They placed advertisements in newspapers and offered buyers prizes and premiums. Perhaps their boldest stunt was to paint a huge sign of the Durham Bull on the pyramids in Egypt!

In the early years of the tobacco industry, many small manufacturers challenged the position of Bull Durham smoking tobacco. However, it

The Duke home and factory (top) expanded into the American Tobacco Company. Washington Duke (above) began as a yeoman farmer in Orange County. His son James B. "Buck" Duke was the driving force behind the family's business success.

was Washington Duke and his three sons Brodie, Benjamin, and James who were destined to dominate the tobacco industry.

The same year that R. J. Reynolds arrived in Winston, Washington Duke and his family moved to Durham. Washington Duke had been a yeoman farmer in Orange County before the Civil War. After moving to Durham, he manufactured smoking tobacco, which he then sold in eastern North Carolina. In the early 1880s, the Dukes and Blackwell and his partners decided to produce hand-rolled cigarettes. They brought Russian Jewish "rollers" to North Carolina to prepare the cigarettes. In 1885, W. Duke Sons and Company gambled on machine-made cigarettes. The company was so successful that it became the largest maker of cigarettes in the nation. James B. "Buck" Duke was the family's business genius. In 1890, he formed the American Tobacco Company. Through intense, even ruthless, business practices, he expanded the company into a giant that controlled three-fourths of the tobacco industry in the United States.

Tobacco was very important to the industrialization of North Carolina, but the textile industry was perhaps even more important. It represented the hope of future prosperity.

Do You Remember?

1. What curing process led to the growth of the tobacco industry in North Carolina?
2. Name three families that were leaders in the development of the tobacco industry in North Carolina.
3. What "gamble" helped the Duke family become a tobacco giant?

THE TEXTILE INDUSTRY

The **textile industry** was the focus of the New South movement. It was to be the salvation of poor, honest farmers who desperately needed employment. In the words of one mill owner,

This was not a business but a social enterprise. Any profit that might accrue to the originators of the mills was but incidental; the main thing was the salvation of the decaying community, and especially the poor whites, who were in danger of being submerged altogether. The record of these days is filled with a moral fervor that is astounding. People were urged to take stock in the mills for the town's sake, for the South's sake, literally for God's sake.

Before 1895, textile manufacturing was largely a homegrown industry. Up until the 1880s, many of the same families that operated mills in the 1830s and 1840s were still operating them. Names such as Battle, Morehead, Fries, and Holt ruled the industry. In 1884, there were eighty-eight textile mills in North Carolina. In the 1870s alone, the value of the textiles manufactured increased from $8 million to $13 million.

Between 1880 and 1900, the textile industry grew at an extraordinary pace. New men with textile or business backgrounds entered the industry. Daniel Tompkins of Charlotte, for example, brought an engineer's training to the industry as well as important contacts with New England machinists who helped modernize the industry. Names like Cannon,

The textile industry was considered the salvation of poor farmers who could no longer make a living in agriculture. Seen here (top) is a cotton mill near Charlotte. New men like Daniel Tompkins (above) brought engineering know-how to the industry in the 1880s and 1890s.

Women made up over one-third of the labor force in the cotton mills. Wages were very low.

Gray, Love, Lineberger, Stowe, Erwin, and Cone became well known in textile manufacturing.

By 1900, there were 177 textile mills in North Carolina employing more than 30,000 workers. About 90 percent of the mills were located in the Piedmont. Originally, these mills depended on the water power from the region's fast-flowing rivers. But the development of less costly steam power allowed mills to leave the banks of the rivers and spread across the countryside. By 1900, nearly two-thirds of the textile mills used steam power.

One North Carolina businessman, Richard H. Wright of Durham, estimated that mill owners made an annual profit of 25 to 30 percent on their capital investment. He believed there were several reasons for the high profits: cotton for the mills was grown nearby, railroad transportation was easily available, and labor was cheap.

Labor in the mills was indeed cheap. *Annual* wages in the textile industry in 1900 averaged $216 for men, $157 for women, and $103 for

IMMIGRATION

Immigration helped create modern America. In the nineteenth and twentieth centuries, immigrants arrived in two waves. The first wave began in the 1840s and reached a climax in the 1880s. These immigrants were mainly from western Europe. The second wave surged in the first decade of the twentieth century, from 1900 to 1910, and brought large numbers of people from southern and eastern Europe.

Between 1870 and 1920, 26 million European immigrants entered the United States. Most settled in cities. Soon southern blacks joined the mass movement to the cities, especially after 1915. As the nation became more urban-

After the Civil War, millions of immigrants poured into the United States. Most settled in the Northeast and Midwest.

ized, modern American culture flourished. That culture came to include African-American jazz, Jewish theater and music, Irish comedy, Italian food, and American folk music and literature. Newcomers changed society as much as it changed them.

Even so, Americans whose families had settled in the New World before the Revolution feared the arrival of so many foreigners with their "different" religions and cultures. During the 1920s, Congress passed various acts to restrict immigration. The National Origins Act of 1924 set quotas for each nationality, favoring immigrants from northern and western Europe and limiting immigration from southern and eastern Europe. The laws virtually excluded people of Asian ancestry. The laws, however, did not restrict immigrants from the Western Hemisphere. As a result, Mexicans and Puerto Ricans soon became the largest groups of newcomers.

children. Mill workers put in from 63 to 75 hours per week. Men made up only 42 percent of the labor force in the mills in 1900. Women accounted for 34 percent and children 24 percent of the workers. Textile jobs, however, were only for whites. In contrast, African Americans made up two-thirds of the work force in the tobacco industry.

Villages, often built by the mill owners, sprang up around the textile factories. The mill villages have been compared to "industrial plantations." Mill owners controlled outright when, where, for how long, and for what wages their laborers worked. They also had a great deal of influence over where workers lived, shopped, studied, played, and worshiped. Such tight control usually discouraged unions' efforts to organize the mills.

Both tobacco and cotton had roots in antebellum North Carolina. But a third industry, furniture, was born after the war.

THE FURNITURE INDUSTRY

The **furniture industry** began much like the tobacco industry. Craftsmen in small shops built furniture largely for a local market. In 1881, brothers David A. and William E. White opened a factory in Mebane that grew into a major plant. Until it closed in the early 1990s, the White Furniture Company was the oldest furniture manufacturer in North Carolina.

High Point became the center of the state's furniture industry. Three men played important roles in establishing the industry: Ernest Ansel Snow, John H. Tate, and Thomas F. Wrenn. In 1889, these three businessmen formed the High Point Furniture Manufacturing Company. During its first year, the company sold $75,000 worth of furniture. In its second year, it doubled that figure. By 1900, there were forty-four furniture factories employing some 2,000 workers.

The furniture industry grew up along the North Carolina Railroad and its feeder lines. The railroad offered easy transportation of both raw materials (lumber) and finished goods (bedsteads, sideboards, chairs, and so on). Durham anchored the industry in the east and Asheville in the west. In between were such furniture-producing towns as Thomasville, Lexington, Statesville, Morganton, Hickory, Mount Airy, and Lenoir.

The rise of the tobacco, textile, and furniture industries in the closing decades of the nineteenth century took place when agriculture in the state fell upon hard times. Indeed, poor and landless farmers provided much of the cheap labor for the tobacco and textile factories.

Unlike the tobacco and cotton industries, which had antebellum roots, the furniture industry emerged after the Civil War. Sawmills provided plentiful lumber to manufacture finished goods.

AGRICULTURE

In the years following the Civil War, most North Carolinians continued to make their living on the farm. Farmers seemed to recover well from the war's devastation. They concentrated on the two great staple crops: cotton and tobacco. Between 1860 and 1900, farmers more than tripled production of those two crops. During the same period, the number of farms increased from 75,000 to 225,000. However, the average number of acres per farm decreased, from 316 in 1860 to 101 in 1900.

Looking at such statistics, you might think that large farms had been broken up. Unfortunately, that was not the case. In fact, fewer and fewer people actually owned the land. The reason for this was the **tenancy system.** After the Civil War, credit was tight. **Credit** is the ability to buy something now and pay for it later. Not much money circulated in the South. Large landowners could not pay wages, and poor farmers could not afford to buy land or the necessary equipment, seed, and fertilizer to operate their farms. The tenancy system gave landowners the labor they lacked and poor farmers the credit they needed.

The tenancy system worked in two ways. First, a farmer could simply rent farmland at an agreed-upon price. More often, however, a poor farmer needed credit to purchase seed, livestock, tools, and such household needs as food and clothing. Merchants, who often were landowners too, extended credit to a landless farmer in exchange for a share of the farmer's crop. These farmers became known as **sharecroppers.**

Usually, a sharecropper agreed to give the merchant one-third of the crop to pay for all the items bought on credit over many months. The "furnishing merchant" usually charged much higher prices for goods bought on credit. As a result, the sharecropper was always in debt. The furnishing merchant also usually decided what crops the sharecropper would raise. Since tobacco and cotton would not spoil and usually brought the best profits, they were the crops the merchant most often wanted.

The sharecropper's problems were made even worse by the low prices farmers got for their crops. For example, cotton that sold for 25 cents per pound in the late 1860s fell to 12 cents during the 1870s. It hit rock bottom at 5 cents per pound in 1893. This decline lasted for more than twenty years and wiped out an entire generation of independent farmers.

The state's farmers fell on hard times in the 1890s. Shown here is a farm from that period in the Great Smoky Mountains National Park.

Both black and white farmers became tenants. Blacks had little choice. In order to survive, they traded their labor for a plot of land, a place to live, and a share of the crop. White tenants always outnumbered black tenants, but a higher percentage of black farmers were tenants. By 1900, more than 40 percent of the state's farmers were tenants, and another 33 percent owned less than one hundred acres. In 1899, nearly one-half of the state's cotton crop was produced by tenant labor. Farmers began to search for ways to escape the endless cycle of debt and poverty.

FARMERS' ORGANIZATIONS

To get relief from their economic problems, farmers began to organize. In 1873, the Patrons of Husbandry, better known as the Grange, established its first local chapter at McLeansville in Guilford County. At the height of its popularity in North Carolina, the Grange had more than 500 chapters (local groups) and 15,000 members, many of them women. But the purpose of the Grange was mainly social. Its popularity declined because it did not address the farmers' economic needs.

The most successful farm organization in North Carolina was the **Farmers' Alliance.** Reaching the state in the late 1880s, the Alliance was concerned with critical economic issues. Leonidas Lafayette Polk, editor of the *Progressive Farmer* and former state agricultural commissioner, became national president of the Alliance. By 1890, the Alliance claimed more than 2,000 chapters and 90,000 members in North Carolina. Like the Grange, many of the Alliance's members were women.

The Alliance did not endorse either of the two major political parties. It did, however, favor political action to solve farmers' problems. The Alliance wanted to change the federal government's money policies. The federal government had followed a "tight" money policy since the Civil War. That is, it limited the amount of money in circulation and measured that money against the value of gold. The Alliance believed this policy caused prices for crops and other goods to fall. It also led to the limited amount of credit available to farmers. The Alliance's solution called for the federal government to issue more paper money (as it had during the Civil War). It also wanted the government to make and circulate silver coins again. By increasing the amount of money in circulation, the Alliance reasoned, prices would rise and ease the farmers' debt burden.

The Alliance wanted other reforms as well. The farmers depended on the nation's railroads to get their produce to market, yet the railroads often charged unfairly high rates. The Alliance wanted the federal government to regulate the railroads because they were "public highways." They also wanted to break up the trusts or combines that controlled the prices of fertilizers, machinery, and cotton bagging.

The Farmers' Alliance tried to ease farmers' economic problems by creating cooperative stores. Shown here is an advertisement for a tobacco product made by the Farmers' Alliance.

One of the reforms the Alliance suggested was the establishment of cooperative stores and state farm agencies. This plan would enable farmers to sell their crops when prices were highest and buy farm supplies at lower rates. The plan would have helped farmers escape sharecropping and the cycle of debt. Unfortunately, the cooperatives were short-lived. Hostility from merchants, bankers, and manufacturers who refused to sell goods to the Alliance ended the cooperative store movement.

The Alliance filled a need for farmers much like the Agricultural Extension Service does today. It sponsored speakers to discuss farming techniques, fertilizers, crop rotation, and numerous other issues. It held institutes and agricultural fairs. In many respects, the Alliance was a grassroots democratic movement to aid farmers when the government, political parties, banking institutions, railroads, and industry seemed to be against them.

Indeed, the political and economic leaders of the state seemed to be against any reforms that might help the laboring masses of North Carolina. A newspaper editor in Raleigh had a special name for those leaders.

Railroads charged unfairly high rates to ship farmers' produce. Shown here are bales of cotton at the Kinston railroad station.

Do You Remember?

1. Why were the textile mill owners able to make such high profits on their investments?
2. Why did the furniture industry grow up along the North Carolina Railroad system?
3. Why was the Farmers' Alliance more successful than the Grange as a farm organization?
4. What were three areas of reform the Farmers' Alliance worked for?
5. What caused the cooperative movement to fail?

THE "MUMMIES"

In the 1880s, Walter Hines Page was the editor of the *State Chronicle*. Later, he was an editor and publisher in New York City, and, during World War I, he was President Woodrow Wilson's ambassador to Great Britain. But before Page left North Carolina, he wrote articles attacking the conservative Democratic leaders who opposed any kind of social or intellectual progress. He called these leaders "mummies" because they had not entertained a new idea since ancient Egypt had crumbled.

Page's description especially applied to education. Between 1870 and 1880, illiteracy actually increased in North Carolina. As late as 1900, almost one-fifth of the whites and nearly one-half of the blacks could not read and write. Attitudes toward public education ranged from indifference to open hostility.

The public school system that Calvin Wiley had carefully built up during the 1850s collapsed during Reconstruction. During the brief time they held power in the late 1860s, the Republicans showed a strong interest in education. But when the Democrats returned to office, public education almost died from a lack of funding and strong leadership. Local governments could levy taxes for schools, but few chose to do so.

Poverty, North Carolinians' well-known hatred for taxes, and a general apathy (a feeling of not caring) toward education reduced the state's school system to an average term of nine weeks in 1880. Only about 30 percent of the state's school-age children even attended. By 1900 that figure had risen to 58 percent, but the school term was still only twelve weeks.

Only in the area of higher education did North Carolina seem willing to support schools, particularly those that trained teachers. Between 1877 and 1891, the state established five new schools of higher education.

At Governor Zebulon B. Vance's urging, the General Assembly of 1877 approved two schools to instruct future teachers. The University of North Carolina would train white teachers and the newly established Fayetteville Colored Normal School (present-day Fayetteville State University) would

Walter Hines Page attacked the state's conservative Democratic leaders for failing to promote social and intellectual progress. He called them "mummies."

train black teachers. During the 1880s, agricultural and industrial leaders like Leonidas Lafayette Polk led a movement to establish a state agricultural and mechanical college. The General Assembly chartered what became North Carolina State University in 1887. The school opened its doors in 1889.

To satisfy other needs, the state authorized three more institutions of higher education in 1891. Through the efforts of Charles D. McIver, reform-minded teachers, and the Farmers' Alliance, the State Normal and Industrial School for white women in Greensboro (the present-day University of North Carolina at Greensboro) was chartered. The General Assembly also founded two new schools for blacks: the North Carolina Agricultural and Mechanical College for the Colored Race at Greensboro (present-day North Carolina Agricultural and Technical State University) and Elizabeth City Colored Normal School (present-day Elizabeth City State University).

In 1891 the state chartered the State Normal and Industrial School for white women in Greensboro. Charles D. McIver (holding stick), the first president, is shown here with the faculty.

THE FIRST INTERCOLLEGIATE FOOTBALL GAME IN NORTH CAROLINA

The first intercollegiate football game in North Carolina was played in Raleigh in 1888. Wake Forest defeated the University of North Carolina 6 to 4. Shown here is the University of North Carolina football team of 1892.

The popularity of sports grew dramatically in the decades after the Civil War. Much of that popularity was a result of the establishment and growth of colleges and universities. These institutions encouraged the playing of team sports such as baseball and football. Athletic competition or "challenges" between rival schools quickly became the fashion.

The American game of football—a mixture of soccer and the English sport of rugby—was introduced in colleges in the mid-1800s. At that time, football had few rules and was a far rougher game than it is today. Players on the team kicked, punched, and gouged their way down the playing field to score a goal, which counted two points. Teams did not have captains or co-captains like teams today. Instead, players elected presidents, vice presidents, and secretaries for their teams.

On October 18, 1888, on a warm Thursday afternoon, the first intercollegiate football game in North Carolina was played in Raleigh. The site was the state fairgrounds, and the contest was between students of Wake Forest and the University of North Carolina at Chapel Hill. Each team fielded fifteen players. The game was played before what a local newspaper reported to be a "tremendous crowd."

As the players collided, bumps and bruises abounded. Early in the game, one UNC lineman, Charles Mangum, was knocked unconscious and had to be dragged off the field. Along the sidelines, nearby Saint Mary's College set up a small first-aid station.

In private education, Baptists and Methodists continued to support church colleges. The Baptist State Convention opened Meredith College in 1899. Trinity College, a Methodist school and forerunner of Duke University, moved from Randolph County to Durham in 1892. Meanwhile, Davidson College (Presbyterian) and Wake Forest College (Baptist), church schools that traced their roots to the 1830s, opened again after closing during the Civil War.

North Carolina's relatively generous support for higher education came at the same time it neglected the very real needs of public education. It would happen again in the decades that followed.

The "mummies" about whom Walter Hines Page wrote practiced policies that tended to protect the economic interests of the upper classes but harmed most North Carolinians. The reign of the "mummies" was challenged by hard-pressed farmers, but the Farmers' Alliance could not solve agriculture's deep-seated economic problems. It had shown, however, that the state was ripe for a political revolt.

The legislature also chartered the North Carolina Agricultural and Mechanical College for the Colored Race in 1891. It was one of two black institutions of higher education established that year.

Do You Remember?

1. What three factors led to the poor condition of education in North Carolina in 1880?
2. For what area of education did the citizens of the state show more support?

CHAPTER · REVIEW

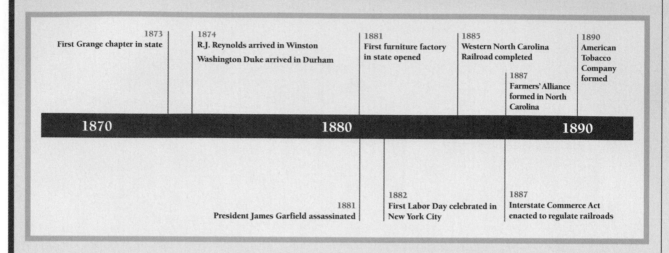

1873	1874	1881	1885	1890
First Grange chapter in state	R.J. Reynolds arrived in Winston Washington Duke arrived in Durham	First furniture factory in state opened	Western North Carolina Railroad completed	American Tobacco Company formed
			1887 Farmers' Alliance formed in North Carolina	

| **1870** | | **1880** | | **1890** |

| | 1881 | 1882 | 1887 |
| | President James Garfield assassinated | First Labor Day celebrated in New York City | Interstate Commerce Act enacted to regulate railroads |

Reviewing People, Places, and Terms

Use the following terms in a paragraph that describes North Carolina's economy at the end of the nineteenth century.

1. Farmers' Alliance
2. furniture industry
3. industrialization
4. tenancy system
5. textile industry
6. tobacco industry

Understanding the Facts

1. What was North Carolina's largest city throughout the 1800s?
2. What three major industries developed along North Carolina's Piedmont Crescent?
3. What two cities became centers for tobacco manufacturing in the decades after the Civil War?
4. What North Carolina family established and controlled the giant American Tobacco Company?
5. What development allowed textile mills to locate away from rivers in the late 1800s?
6. Describe the work force of North Carolina's early textile industry. How did that compare to the work force in the tobacco industry?

7. What North Carolina city became the center of the state's furniture industry?
8. What led to the "endless cycle of debt and poverty" for farmers?
9. What policies did the "mummies" generally practice?

Developing Critical Thinking

1. What is meant by the statement "Railroads were both a cause and an effect of industrialization."
2. Why was there a high percentage of African-American workers in the tobacco industry and a low percentage in the textile industry?
3. Why do you think North Carolinians did not support taxes for the state's school system during this period?

Applying Your Skills

1. *Annual* wages in the textile industry in 1900 averaged $216 for men, $157 for women, and $103 for children. If a worker worked 60 hours a week, 50 weeks a year, what was the hourly pay for a man? a woman? a child? Draw a bar graph to compare the annual wages of men, women, and children.

2. It is likely that much of the furniture in your school and in your home was made in North Carolina. With permission, *carefully* inspect one or two different pieces of furniture for any tags or stamps that identify the manufacturer. Make a list of the manufacturers and report your findings to the rest of the class.

3. Prepare a short report (1-2 pages) on any one of the colleges or universities mentioned in this chapter.

Making Connections

1. Prepare a table that lists the deadly diseases smallpox, cholera, typhoid, yellow fever, influenza, tuberculosis, and polio. For each disease, indicate (a) the average number of deaths per year in the United States, (b) the highest number of deaths in a 1-year period, (c) the year in which that happened, and (d) the current status (eradicated, under control, and so on).

2. Prepare a report on what your local board of health does to protect the public health. Are there any other organizations in your area that work to protect the public health?

3. Prepare a chart or graph that depicts immigration to the United States. Use the period 1890-1990 and report your findings in 10-year increments. Have the numbers of immigrants increased or decreased in recent years?

4. Do you favor unlimited immigration into the United States? Explain your position in a one-page report.

BUILDING SKILLS: DISTINGUISHING FACT FROM OPINION

Not everything you read in a book, newspaper, or magazine is a fact. A *fact* can be proven by examining it against other information or by your own observations or research. For example, "Eighteen-year-old U.S. citizens have the right to vote" is a statement of fact. This can be proven by reading the Twenty-sixth Amendment to the U.S. Constitution.

An *opinion* is something a person thinks, believes, or feels is true. For example, "A person should not be allowed to vote until she or he is twenty-one years old" is a statement of opinion. Sometimes an opinion is based on facts, but it is the writer's personal interpretation of the facts. It is up to you to decide whether you agree with that opinion.

Some opinions are based on inaccurate information or illogical arguments. For example, "No eighteen-year-old has the experience necessary to make a logical decision in a voting booth." This statement too is an opinion, but the argument is illogical. You would probably not agree with this opinion.

Understanding the difference between facts and opinions will help you become a more critical reader or listener.

Examine the following statements carefully, then decide which of the statements are fact and which are opinion.

1. R. J. Reynolds was a great man.
2. The Piedmont Crescent brought prosperity to North Carolina.
3. The textile industry proved to be the salvation of North Carolina's farmers in the late 1800s.
4. Women made up over one-third of the employees in the textile mills.
5. Mill owners profited from the work of their mill employees.
6. The tenancy system caused widespread suffering among both whites and blacks.
7. Farmers who bought supplies on credit paid higher prices than those who bought supplies with cash.
8. Sharecropping was an evil that merely replaced slavery.
9. The Farmers' Alliance was very successful in North Carolina.
10. The "mummies" reflected the opinions of North Carolina's upper classes.

CHAPTER NINETEEN

THE POPULIST REVOLT

Their [the Democrats'] *plan does not mean argument or discussion, it means riot, slander, abuse, physical violence and general anarchy. Their plan now is to red-shirt every town in the State, and to terrorize voters through the means of such characters as can be hired to wear red-shirts, drink mean whiskey and raise commotion generally.*

— Hal W. Ayer, Populist state auditor

CHAPTER · PREVIEW

Terms: coalition, home rule, Populist, Fusionist, partisan politics, propaganda, segregation, corporation commission, disfranchise, grandfather clause

People: Elias Carr, Marion Butler, Jeter C. Pritchard, Daniel L. Russell, Furnifold M. Simmons, Charles B. Aycock

Places: Wilmington

A T THE END OF THE NINETEENTH CENTURY, North Carolina underwent a political revolution. Farmers, unhappy over the inability of the Farmers' Alliance to bring about economic reform, organized their own political party. To gain some political power, the People's party formed an alliance with the Republican party. Their **coalition** (association) ended twenty years of Democratic rule.

To regain power, the Democratic party turned to a tactic that had been successful earlier. The white supremacy campaigns that the Democrats launched in 1898 and 1900 resulted in violence, riots, disfranchisement, and the formal beginnings of segregation. The People's party never recovered, and the Republicans were pushed out of power for decades. The 1890s marked an important turning point in the state's history.

THE BOURBON DEMOCRATS

The Democratic party governed the state from 1877 to 1894, although the Republican party still had some power during this period. Between 1880 and 1896, the Republicans got as much as 46 percent of the vote in the gubernatorial elections (elections for governor). But in other respects, the Democrats had firm control of the legislature and the state.

Beginning in 1877, for example, the Democratic legislature passed laws giving it the power to elect justices of the peace. Justices of the peace had the power to hear and decide local disagreements. Now they were given the power to elect county commissioners. This change ensured that local

Opposite page: Marion Butler helped forge the political alliance between the Populist and Republican parties. He served in the U.S. Senate from 1895 to 1901.

Democrat Elias Carr was elected governor in 1892. In 1895 he leased the North Carolina Railroad to the Southern Railway for ninety-nine years.

finances would be controlled by people whom the legislature considered "safe" (such as white Democrats). The other county offices (sheriff, clerk of superior court, register of deeds, and so on) were still chosen by popular election. Democrats claimed they were protecting whites from African American "rule" in those counties with black majorities. But this move also took **home rule** (local self-government) away from the western counties.

The legislature also passed election laws that allowed Democratic registrars to disqualify (bar) voters for the slightest reason. Many who would probably have voted Republican, especially blacks and illiterate whites, were disqualified. When legal measures did not work to win elections, the Democrats turned to other, "less legal" practices. These practices included dishonest vote counting, ballot-box stuffing, and vote buying.

Because of their policies, the Democrats came to be called "Bourbons." (Walter Page had called them "mummies.") Like the French Bourbon kings, the Democrats opposed change. They cared little about helping farmers or laborers, providing public education, or making internal improvements. Instead, they protected the interests of industries, banks, and railroads and opposed any social or economic reforms, saying such measures would require higher taxes.

The Bourbon Democrats' policies could be seen in their treatment of the railroads. The antebellum policy of state aid for the railroads ended. The state leased most of its railroad properties to private corporations. Meanwhile, the legislature excused railroads from taxes and regulation. In return, legislators and party leaders enjoyed "favors" from the railroads in the form of free passes, rebates (the return of part of a payment), and appointments as railroad lobbyists and attorneys. Many legislators owned stock in the railroads.

The railroads prospered (did well). By 1900, the state had 3,800 miles of railroad lines. But at the same time, the railroads charged rates that some said were unfair, in spite of the creation of a regulatory Railroad Commission in 1891. If reforms were to come, they would not come from the Democrats.

Do You Remember?

1. What reason did the Democrats give for having the legislature elect justices of the peace?
2. What "favors" did the railroads give to legislators and party leaders for their support?

THE EMERGENCE OF THE POPULIST PARTY

In 1892, the Farmers' Alliance realized that the Democrats would not support the reforms the Alliance believed would help the farmers get out of debt. A group led by Leonidas L. Polk broke away from the Democratic party and formed the People's party. Supporters of that party were known as **Populists.** Many people believed Polk would be the Populist candidate for president in 1892, but his sudden death in June ended that dream. Marion Butler, a dynamic Sampson County legislator and newspaper editor, succeeded Polk as leader of the North Carolina Populists.

In the 1892 elections, the Democrats nominated former Alliance president Elias Carr for governor. The Populists nominated W. P. Exum. The Populists' platform demanded tax and election reforms, called for a 10-hour workday for laborers, and urged a 6 percent limit on interest rates for loans. Carr won the election, but he did not get a majority of the votes. The combined Populist-Republican vote was nearly 52 percent of the total votes cast for governor. This turned out to be a sign of future events.

After the election, the Populists became even more displeased with the Democrats. Farm prices continued to fall and the Panic of 1893 ruined many farmers. In 1894, the Populists made an agreement with the Republicans. The two parties agreed to support a single ticket that had candidates from both parties. This arrangement was known as "fusion" and members of the two parties were called **Fusionists.** At the national level, the Populists and Republicans had very different views about the economy. But at the state level, the two parties found much to agree on. Both wanted to return home rule to the counties. Both demanded free elections and a fair count of the ballots. Both favored increased spending on public education. And both wanted to remove partisan politics from the state supreme court, which for too many years had handed down decisions that supported and strengthened the Democratic party. **Partisan politics** refers to actions that are biased in support of a single political party or cause.

In the 1894 elections, the Fusionists won an overwhelming victory. They swept nearly all of the state and congressional offices and held a huge majority in the General Assembly. The stage was set for a political revolution in the state.

Leonidas L. Polk helped launch the People's party in North Carolina. Had he not died, he might have become the Populist candidate for president in 1892.

FUSIONIST REFORMS

With firm control of the General Assembly in 1895, the Fusionists began their reform program. Self-government was restored to the counties. Voters could directly elect justices of the peace and three county commissioners. The Fusionists also passed a new election law, perhaps the fairest and most democratic in the post-Reconstruction South. This law called for one election judge from each party to be present when ballots were counted. The law also made it harder for registrars to disqualify voters without reason and established colored ballots with party symbols to help illiterate voters. The Fusionists also set the legal rate of interest at 6 percent, increased spending for public schools, and seemed willing to raise taxes on businesses and railroads. Finally, the General Assembly of 1895 elected Populist Marion Butler and Republican Jeter C. Pritchard to the United States Senate.

In 1896, the Populists and Republicans again joined forces to retain control of the General Assembly. Fusionists won all major statewide offices except the state supreme court. Republican Daniel L. Russell of Brunswick County was elected governor. The number of votes cast in the election was the largest ever recorded. And the increase of more than 50,000 votes over 1892 showed how effective the Fusionists' electoral reforms had been. Unfortunately, the cooperation between the Populists and Republicans was about to end.

Two major issues facing the General Assembly of 1897 divided the Fusionists. First was the re-election of Republican Jeter C. Pritchard to the United States Senate. The Populists did not like Pritchard's stand on monetary reforms at the national level and wanted to name their own candidate. Some Populists, however, joined the Republicans to re-elect Pritchard. This move led to increasing problems between the parties.

The second issue involved the railroads. In 1895, Governor Carr leased the North Carolina Railroad to the Southern Railway for ninety-nine years. The North Carolina Railroad was an important part of the Southern Railway's network of lines to the lower South. These lines transported much freight and tied southern agricultural and manufacturing areas to the deepwater port at Norfolk, Virginia.

The North Carolina Railroad was the state's most valuable piece of property. The long-term lease, however, gave control of the railroad to a large business monopoly. In the minds of Governor Russell, his Populist allies, and a few Democrats, the ninety-nine year lease was a symbol of the corruption that existed between government and big business.

In the General Assembly of 1897, Governor Russell tried to cancel the lease, provide stricter regulation of out-of-state corporations, increase taxes on railroads, and reduce passenger fares and freight rates. Russell's attack on the railroads was too much for the Republicans. Most of the Republican legislators turned away from the governor. They voted with the Democrats against Governor Russell's reforms. The Republicans' action weakened the already shaky fusion agreement with the Populists, most of whom supported Russell's fight with the Southern Railway Company.

In 1896 Republican Daniel L. Russell was elected governor. He was the last Republican to be elected to that office until 1972.

THE BIRTH OF MASS CULTURE

Until the late 1800s, Americans had little leisure time. But as the work week and the workday shortened, people found themselves with more free time and turned to leisurely pursuits.

Baseball, primarily an urban game, was the first and most popular sport. The Cincinnati Red Stockings became the first professional club in 1869. With the formation of the National League in 1876, baseball became a big business.

In the 1890s, bicycling was almost as popular. Both men and women rode bicycles. In order to ride, women had to give up the formal Victorian fashions of the period. Informal bicycling clothing eventually gave women the freedom to wear more casual attire.

American show business appealed to all classes of people. Musical comedies featured song, humor, and dance. George M. Cohan set the standard with such popular songs as "Yankee Doodle Dandy." Vaudeville was probably the most popular form of entertainment at the beginning of the twentieth century. Shows included song, dance, magic, ethnic humor, and animal acts.

Thomas Edison's invention of moving pictures in the late 1880s grew into the most popular art form of the twentieth century. The most famous movie of the period was D. W. Griffith's *The Birth of a Nation*. Although flawed by its racism and glorified treatment of the Ku Klux Klan the film showed the power and influence of the movies.

Technology—photography, phonographs, and movies—put mass entertainment within the reach of all Americans.

These two women riding bicycles indicated a changing culture as people found time available for leisurely pursuits.

The reforms proposed by Russell and the Populists had frightened the state's business community. Bankers, mill owners, businessmen, and, of course, the Democrats were determined to remove the Populists from state politics. However, they weren't sure that they could win the 1898 elections using just economic issues. Instead, they turned to a more inflammatory issue—race.

Do You Remember?
1. On what issues did Populists and Republicans agree?
2. How did the Fusionists improve election practices?
3. In what ways did Governor Russell "attack" the Southern Railway?

THE CAMPAIGN OF 1898

The success of the Populist-Republican fusion rested in large measure on black voters. Fusionist reforms increased African American participation in politics both as voters and as officeholders. An estimated 87 percent of the eligible black voters went to the polls in 1896, an increase of 23 percent over 1892. Eleven African American legislators served in the General Assembly of 1897, the most since the 1880s. The General Assembly of 1895 named three hundred African American justices of the peace in such counties as New Hanover, Edgecombe, Halifax, Craven, Bertie, and Granville. African Americans also served as county commissioners, registers of deeds, school committeemen, aldermen, and policemen. Even though they held many local offices, at no time did blacks ever enjoy representation equal to their numbers nor did "Negro rule" ever exist in North Carolina.

Nevertheless, the Democrats used the race issue to frighten voters and regain power. Furnifold M. Simmons, a New Bern lawyer and former congressman, ran the Democrats' 1898 campaign. Simmons had former governor Thomas J. Jarvis talk to businessmen and manufacturers and promise that the Democrats would not raise taxes. Simmons also told the church colleges that the Democrats would not increase spending for state institutions of higher learning. In return, Jarvis and Simmons collected all the campaign funds they needed. By August 1898, Simmons was ready to launch the Democrats' campaign.

THE WHITE SUPREMACY ISSUE

Simmons organized White Government Unions in the eastern counties to draw white voters back to the Democratic party. He also set up a speakers' bureau to send white supremacy spokesmen across the state. Many Democrats who became well known in the twentieth century took part in the 1898 campaign. Future governors Robert B. Glenn, William W. Kitchin, Locke Craig, Cameron Morrison, Clyde Hoey, and especially Charles B. Aycock carried the white supremacy message to voters. They promised to "restore the state to the white people." They claimed that "fusion laws and fusion legislation" had been placed under the control of blacks, and they pledged to end "Negro domination."

Newspapers played an important role in the election. In that period, newspapers were known for taking sides on an issue; they did not even try to provide even-handed coverage. The Democrats dominated the press. The Raleigh *News and Observer*, the *Charlotte Observer*, and the Wilmington *Messenger* in particular took an active part in the campaign. The Fusionists had no daily newspapers in which they could speak out against the racist propaganda that appeared in these three news-

Furnifold M. Simmons (left), a former congressman, was the mastermind of the Democrats' 1898 campaign. At Simmons's instruction, former governor Thomas J. Jarvis (above) promised businessmen that the Democrats would not raise taxes.

PLESSY V. FERGUSON

Justice John Marshall Harlan of Kentucky served 34 years on the U.S. Supreme Court. He cast the lone dissenting vote in the Plessy v. Ferguson *case.*

In 1892, Homer Plessy bought a train ticket from New Orleans to Covington, Louisiana. Because he was seven-eighths white and one-eighth black, he took a seat in the "whites only" car. When he refused to move, he was arrested under the "Jim Crow Car Act of 1890," which required separate-but-equal accommodations for whites and blacks on railroad cars.

Plessy staged the incident to test the constitutionality of the 1890 law. In 1896, the U.S. Supreme Court heard the case and, by a 7-1 vote, upheld the law. A southerner, Justice John Marshall Harlan, cast the single dissenting vote. Harlan argued: "Our Consitution is colorblind, and neither knows nor tolerates classes among citizens. In respect of civil rights, all citizens are equal before the law."

Plessy v. Ferguson gave states the right to control social discrimination and to promote segregation of the races. Throughout the South, numerous laws forced blacks to use separate facilities such as schools, parks, and public transportation. Those facilities were almost never equal to ones available to whites.

Not until *Brown v. Board of Education* (1954) did the Supreme Court reverse itself. In that landmark decision, the Court determined that separate educational facilities were "inherently unequal" and harmful to black students' self-esteem. The *Brown* case led to the end of legal segregation.

papers. **Propaganda** consists of ideas, facts, or rumors spread to help a cause or to hurt an opposing cause.

One African American newspaper, the Wilmington *Daily Record*, created a sensation that the Democrats used to their advantage. On August 18, 1898, Alex Manly, the black editor of the paper, published an editorial defending his race against lynching. His comments about relations between blacks and whites were seen as an insult to white women. Democratic newspapers used the editorial to increase racial tensions.

In the following weeks, bands of men calling themselves "Red Shirts" and "Rough Riders" appeared in southeastern counties. Riding horses, wearing red shirts, and carrying guns, these Democratic ruffians broke up Fusionist political rallies, disrupted black church meetings, whipped outspoken blacks, and drove black voters from the polls when they tried to register. In late October, Governor Russell issued a warning against the use of such tactics. Russell's warnings, however, went unheeded.

THE 1898 ELECTION

In the election, the Democrats won an overwhelming majority in the General Assembly. Many members of the Populist party, fearing for their lives and property, suddenly became Democrats. Many black Republican voters either were too afraid to vote or were kept from the polls by the Red Shirts.

Two days after the election, on November 10, the so-called Wilmington race riot took place. Actually, the riot was the Democrats overthrowing Wilmington's Republican government. Alfred Moore Waddell, a former Confederate officer and congressman, led the rioters. The rioters dragged white and black Republicans to the railroad depot—some with ropes around their necks—planning to run them out of town. Black and white officials in the city government resigned, and a new Democratic administration was sworn in with Waddell as mayor. Rioting whites burned the office and press of Manly's *Daily Record* and attacked African American neighborhoods. Between eleven and thirty blacks were killed; only two or three whites were injured.

Once they had gained control of the legislature, the Democrats took steps to make sure they stayed in power. In particular, they wanted to eliminate any further threat of a political coalition between blacks and poor whites.

During the Wilmington race riot of 1898, a white mob burned the office and press of Alex Manly's newspaper and attacked black neighborhoods. Between eleven and thirty blacks were killed.

Do You Remember?

1. In what ways did the Fusionist reforms increase African American participation in politics?
2. What violent tactics did the Red Shirts and Rough Riders use against African Americans?
3. What happened in Wilmington after the 1898 election?

THE DEMOCRATIC COUNTERREVOLUTION

The General Assembly of 1899 set about undoing the Fusionists' reforms. It re-established legislative control of county government by making most county offices appointive rather than elective. To put even more power into the hands of the legislature, the Democrats passed an election law that required all voters to reregister. The General Assembly also appointed a new state board of elections, which selected county boards of election. It was the responsibility of the county boards of election to name local election officials.

The Democrats passed a number of other important pieces of legislation in 1899. The first law formally enforcing separate accommodations for blacks and whites on steamboats and railroads was passed. In practice, North Carolina railroads had provided "second-class" cars for blacks since before the Civil War. But strict **segregation** (separation of the races) had not always been followed. First-class tickets held by African American passengers had been honored on occasion. After 1899, however, that was no longer possible.

The legislature abolished the Railroad Commission and replaced it with a **corporation commission** . The new commission, the first of its kind in the nation, had the power to regulate railroads, banks, telephone and telegraph companies, street railways, and express companies. In time, its duties expanded. The legislature also repealed the 1869 school law, but did provide $100,000 for public schools.

However, the most significant action by the General Assembly was to create an amendment to the state constitution that effectively disfranchised blacks and illiterate whites. To **disfranchise** means to take the right to vote away from an individual or group. Furnifold M. Simmons, the Democrats' state party chairman, had promised during the 1898 campaign that no man would lose his right to vote. That pledge was forgotten once the election was over.

The Democrats' suffrage amendment was carefully written so as not to violate the Fifteenth Amendment. (The Fifteenth Amendment to the United States Constitution protected blacks' voting rights.) First, anyone registering to vote must have paid a poll tax. Second, a voter must be able to read and write any section of the state constitution. Finally, the amendment contained a so-called grandfather clause. The **grandfather clause** allowed any man to register to vote before December 1, 1908, without passing the literacy test if he, his father, or his grandfather had voted before January 1, 1867. The grandfather clause naturally helped illiterate whites. Few African Americans, however, qualified to vote under the grandfather clause. You will remember that the Constitutional Convention of 1835 had disfranchised free blacks, and the Fifteenth Amendment was not ratified until 1870.

THE WHITE SUPREMACY CAMPAIGN OF 1900

The suffrage amendment was put to a vote of the people in August 1900. The Democrats were not sure that North Carolina's voters would support it. They were afraid that voters in western North Carolina, an area that had fewer blacks and many illiterate whites, would oppose the amendment.

The Populists and Republicans were in chaos. Even though Populist Senator Marion Butler and Republican Senator Jeter C. Pritchard condemned the suffrage amendment, both parties were deeply divided by the issue. Many whites in both parties actually favored the disfranchisement of black voters. Since the Fusionists' success had depended so much

Democrat Charles B. Aycock was elected governor in 1900. He ran on a platform of white supremacy, disfranchisement, and public education.

on black votes, however, the two parties treated the issue carefully. The Republicans denounced the suffrage amendment in their platform but did little to encourage blacks to take part in the election. The Populists refused to oppose the amendment in their platform.

Two tactics helped the Democrats win in 1900. First, they used the same white-supremacy strategy that had worked so well in 1898. White Government Unions and Red Shirts once more dominated the political process. Second, they nominated Charles B. Aycock for governor. Aycock was a lawyer and had served as United States Attorney for eastern North Carolina from 1893 to 1897. Aycock had been interested in public education since the 1880s. He turned his campaign into a crusade for public education so that no white man would be disfranchised when the grandfather clause ran out in 1908.

In the days leading up to the August 1900 election, the Red Shirts were very visible. They rode about the countryside warning opponents of the suffrage amendment not to vote, firing rifles, and whipping blacks. In Smithfield, they tore down a platform to prevent a Populist from speaking. In Moore County on election day, Red Shirts surrounded the polling places to frighten voters.

These tactics worked. Charles Aycock was elected governor and the suffrage amendment passed by more than 50,000 votes. There were some curious results in the balloting. All of the eighteen counties with black majorities voted for the amendment. In New Hanover County, scene of the Wilmington race riot of 1898, there were only two votes against the amendment and only three votes for the Republican gubernatorial candidate. The effects of disfranchisement were seen immediately. Less than 50 percent of the adult males went to the polls in 1904 compared with 85 percent in 1896.

The Democrats had won overwhelmingly. Fusion was dead. Blacks and poor whites were effectively removed from politics. One-party politics would dominate the state until the 1970s. But along the way the Democrats had learned an important lesson. The reforms begun by the Fusionists could not be ignored. The Democrats, therefore, supported programs that improved public health care, emphasized education, and built roads in the early twentieth century. North Carolina thus became one of the South's most progressive states.

George H. White served two terms (1897-1901) in the United States Congress. White was the last African American to sit in Congress until 1929 and the last from North Carolina until 1995.

Do You Remember?

1. What was the most significant action by the General Assembly of 1899?
2. What three provisions of the suffrage amendment were meant to avoid conflict with the Fifteenth Amendment to the United States Constitution?

BILTMORE HOUSE

Richard Morris Hunt (above) was the architect of Biltmore House. The grounds of the estate, by Frederick Law Olmstead, include this outdoor sculpture (below).

Nestled in the mountains of western North Carolina near Asheville is what is considered to be the largest home in the United States—Biltmore.

George Washington Vanderbilt was a frequent visitor to the Asheville area. He was taken with the views and decided to build a home on one of the mountains. He began purchasing land and by 1890 owned an estate of 125,000 acres. Vanderbilt was impressed with a chateau in the Loire Valley of France and felt that such a home would fit well into the North Carolina mountains. He hired two of America's best known architects, Richard Morris Hunt and Frederick Law Olmstead, to design and construct the house and the gardens and parks that were to surround it.

Construction began in 1890. Hundreds of workers and artisans were employed; brick kilns, woodworking shops, and a railroad spur to the property were constructed to aid in the building of the house. Biltmore was to be a state-of-the-art home having plumbing, refrigeration, central heat, electricity, and elevators. It is believed that some of Thomas Edison's first light bulbs were used at Biltmore. The house has 250 rooms and

4 acres of floor space! Within the house are 34 master bedrooms, 43 bathrooms, 3 kitchens, and 65 fireplaces. It also contains a swimming pool, a gymnasium, a bowling alley, a banquet hall with a 75-foot ceiling, and living quarters for the 80 or so servants. A man of many tastes and interests, Vanderbilt filled his home with art, books, and fine furnishings. When completed in 1895, it was as much a museum as it was a home.

Vanderbilt also financed research and work on the estate. Land that had been nonproductive was turned into rich farmland through proper plowing, drainage, and the use of fertilizer. Imported livestock was used to improve existing stock. Vanderbilt's wife, Edith, became very involved in the preservation of mountain crafts. As a result, many shops opened nearby to sell the carvings, weaving, ironwork, and sewing that was done in the surrounding area. Gifford Pinchot and Dr. Carl Schenck operated the nation's first school of forest management on the estate. After Vanderbilt's death in 1914, Edith deeded the land that was to become Pisgah National Forest to the federal government.

Biltmore later became the residence of Vanderbilt's daughter Cornelia and her husband John Cecil. In 1930, it opened to the public for house and garden tours. Thousands of people visit this truly beautiful and unique home every year. In the 1970s, a winery was built on the grounds. Biltmore has also become somewhat of a movie star. Many films, including *Richie Rich*, have been filmed in and around the home.

The Biltmore Mansion (top) was built in the late 1800s by George Washington Vanderbilt. The interior of the home was lavishly decorated (above).

CHAPTER REVIEW

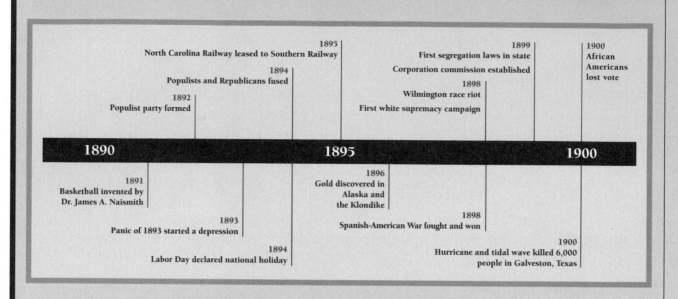

1890		1895		1900

Above the timeline:

1895
North Carolina Railway leased to Southern Railway

1894
Populists and Republicans fused

1892
Populist party formed

1899
First segregation laws in state
Corporation commission established

1898
Wilmington race riot
First white supremacy campaign

1900
African Americans lost vote

Below the timeline:

1891
Basketball invented by
Dr. James A. Naismith

1893
Panic of 1893 started a depression

1894
Labor Day declared national holiday

1896
Gold discovered in
Alaska and
the Klondike

1898
Spanish-American War fought and won

1900
Hurricane and tidal wave killed 6,000
people in Galveston, Texas

Reviewing People, Places, and Terms

Use each of the following terms in a sentence that describes the political climate of North Carolina in the 1890s.

1. coalition
2. disfranchise
3. Fusionist
4. grandfather clause
5. home rule
6. Populists
7. propaganda
8. segregation

Understanding the Facts

1. Who were the "Bourbon" Democrats? What policies did they support and oppose?
2. Why was the People's party formed?
3. What two political parties formed an alliance in 1894 to oppose the Democrats?
4. What two issues led to the breakdown of the fusion agreement?
5. Which political party did the railroads support and why?

6. Why were newspapers such an effective weapon in promoting the white supremacy issue?
7. What political tactics did the Democratic party use in the 1898 and 1900 elections? Were these tactics generally successful or unsuccessful?
8. What was one result of disfranchisement?

Developing Critical Thinking

1. Why do you think that the Democrats opposed social change?
2. What journalistic attitudes did the newspapers of the day have? How are those different from newspapers today?
3. How was the grandfather clause blatantly discriminatory? How did it contribute to the white supremacy movement?
4. What long-term effects did the Democratic victories of 1898 and 1900 have on North Carolina's political history?

Applying Your Skills

1. The Grange and the Farmers' Alliance were two national groups organized to help farmers in the

later 1800s. Today, many young people belong to a 4-H Club or the Future Farmers of America. Prepare a report on the activities of one of these two groups.

2. The People's party was considered to be a "third" or minor political party. Prepare a short report on the existence of third parties in our country's history. What issues might be the basis for a third party today?

3. In the 1890s, the Fusionists set the legal rate of interest on loans at 6 percent. Survey the lending institutions in your community to determine the current interest rate(s) charged on unsecured loans.

Making Connections

1. Why was the doctrine of "separate but equal" an impossibility from the start?

2. Research another Supreme Court decision that has greatly affected Americans either politically, economically, or socially. Prepare a short report to share with your classmates.

3. List five inventions that you believe have been the most instrumental in giving Americans more leisure time.

4. Today there are arguments over whether entertainment reflects our culture or whether culture reflects our entertainment. What do you think about this issue?

Tar Heel Trivia

- In 1893, a group of settlers from northern Italy bought 3,000 acres in the Blue Ridge Mountains. These settlers, called Waldensians, established the town of Valdese. Their story is told in the outdoor drama "From This Day Forward."

BUILDING SKILLS: RECOGNIZING PROPAGANDA

After reading about the political campaign of 1898, you probably thought, "Nothing has changed in the past century." The use of propaganda to persuade people to make certain decisions has been a part of political life since political parties were organized. What we sometimes forget is that these same techniques are used today in advertising.

Bandwagon approach. You've probably used this technique on your parents to try to convince them to let you do something or go somewhere because "everybody else is." You hope your parents will think it's all right since other parents are allowing their sons and daughters to go.

Testimonial. With this technique, a well-known person—an athlete or a movie star, for example—describes how great a particular product or brand (of motor oil, athletic shoes, sport drink, and so on) is. This technique is also used when movie stars campaign for political candidates. When an influential person is shown with another person or thing, it is an attempt to *transfer* honor and respect from one individual to another. Think of all the television commercials that try to transfer the good feeling about an athlete to a particular product. Has this technique ever influenced your decision about buying a product?

Repetition. Watch television one evening and you'll see that many short commercials are repeated several times during a particular show. Advertisers use repetition to drive home a particular message. They're hoping that if you see the message often enough, you'll remember it.

Cause-effect relationship. A misleading cause-effect relationship is often used to persuade. "Twenty students in the class who used computer X to write their history reports got an A." The implication here is that those twenty students only got an A because they used computer X. Would this persuade you to go buy computer X if you got a poor grade? Why or why not?

Try This! Write an ad for a newspaper or television station for a product or a political candidate using one or more of the above techniques.

NORTH CAROLINA MOVES INTO THE TWENTIETH CENTURY

THE EARLY TWENTIETH CENTURY was a time of rapid change. Industries and towns grew. North Carolina built roads, improved public education, limited child labor, prohibited the sale of liquor, and tried to make government more democratic. Thousands of young men fought in World War I. Women got the right to vote. Attracted by better jobs, African Americans migrated to the North. Electricity made life easier.

Depression and war dominated the 1930s and 1940s. The 1929 stock market crash brought on a depression that lasted more than ten years. The "New Deal" provided some relief, but the depression did not end until the start of World War II. The United States entered this war in 1941, and North Carolina made many contributions to the war effort.

Right: *This soaring granite monument at Kill Devil Hill is the Wright Brothers Memorial. At the foot of the memorial, which is shaped a little like a bird's wing, you will feel the winds that brought the Wrights to this place.* **Above:** *Flight of all kinds is still popular at Kitty Hawk.*

CHAPTER TWENTY

NORTH CAROLINA AND THE PROGRESSIVE ERA

I would have the strong to bear the burdens of the weak and to lift up the weak and make them strong—teaching men everywhere that real strength consists not in serving ourselves but in doing for others.
— Governor Charles B. Aycock

T HE DISFRANCHISEMENT OF African Americans at the turn of the century ensured that the Democratic party continued to hold political power in the state. Both the Democrats and the Republicans became conservative, but that was soon to change.

The rapid growth of industry and cities in North Carolina in the early twentieth century created great wealth. But it also brought problems. Progressive reformers in both parties tried to correct some of the poor social and working conditions that existed. They had some success in improving education, banning alcohol, abolishing child labor, reforming prisons, and making the political process more democratic. The progressives also made some headway in regulating corporations.

The state responded to the call to serve in World War I and made valuable contributions to the war effort.

NORTH CAROLINA POLITICS

After African Americans were disfranchised in 1900, the Republicans lost members and power in the state. By 1912, the Republican party was for whites only. Called a "lily-white" party, the Republicans never elected more than a few legislators between 1900 and 1920. The Republican party, however, dominated national politics. North Carolina Republicans, since they could not get elected to state government, were often appointed to jobs with the federal government.

CHAPTER PREVIEW

Terms: progressive movement, Women's Christian Temperance Union, Anti-Saloon League, prohibition, chain gang, corporation, labor union, trust, primary, city commission, arbitrator, neutral, World War I, ration, armistice

People: Sallie Southall Cotten, Helen Morris Lewis, Woodrow Wilson, Josephus Daniels, Walter Hines Page, Angus W. McLean, Walter Clark

Opposite page: Charles B. Aycock was governor from 1901 to 1905. He supported better public schools for all races.

While the Democrats controlled the state government, they themselves were divided between conservatives and liberals. The conservatives favored business and were led by Senator Furnifold M. Simmons. Simmons organized a strong Democratic political organization, which his enemies called the "Simmons machine." Lawyer Aubrey Lee Brooks said that this machine "was perfected, integrated and abundantly financed by the railroads, trusts, liquor interests and other big business." Business leaders helped develop the policies of the Simmons organization. Senator Simmons himself often handpicked the Democratic candidate for governor.

Opposing Simmons was the liberal or progressive group in the party. These Democrats wanted to continue the reforms that had been started by the Fusionists. Well-known Democratic progressives included Chief Justice Walter Clark; Josephus Daniels, editor of the Raleigh *News and Observer*; and Governors Robert B. Glenn, William W. Kitchin, and Thomas W. Bickett. Oddly, it was Governor Locke Craig of Asheville, one of Simmons's men, who was responsible for the most significant reforms in this period.

Do You Remember?

1. Why was the Republican party referred to as the "lily-white" party?
2. What were the two divisions of the Democratic party?

THE PROGRESSIVE MOVEMENT

The **progressive movement** cut across both political parties. Actually, this reform movement was not a single movement, but a series of movements. Progressives believed government—local, state, and national—was best equipped to correct the ills of society. They had faith in the idea of *progress*, the belief that humans could keep improving their society to make it better and better.

Progressives worked to reform society in three main ways. First, progressives wanted government to fight poverty and improve the living conditions of its citizens. Progressives worked hard to improve schools, outlaw alcohol, end child labor, and reform prisons. Second, they wanted to break up large corporations and regulate business. They hoped to decrease corporations' voice in government. Third, they wanted voters to have more influence in government. Progressives had great faith in the people's ability to improve society; they believed that the people needed only a greater voice. Strangely, progressives also justified the disfranchisement of African Americans on the ground that the black vote could be bought.

CHARLES DARWIN AND SOCIETY

In 1859, British scientist Charles Darwin published *On the Origin of Species by Means of Natural Selection, or the Preservation of Favoured Races in the Struggle for Life*. This work created great controversy because it argued that plants and animals "evolved" or changed gradually over thousands of years by a process called "natural selection." Darwin believed that some species were able to adapt to their natural environment and thrive; species that were unable to adapt died out.

Darwin's ideas had a great impact on ideas about society. Englishman Herbert Spencer and American William Graham Sumner argued that Darwin's theory applied to society. Natural selection caused some societies to live on and others to die out; they called this "survival of the fittest." Sumner argued that, through competition, the strongest individuals would rise to the top of society. Government therefore should not regulate business nor help the poor. Its main role was to protect property, especially the great fortunes being made by industrialists.

Other thinkers used Darwin's ideas to *promote* government's reform of society. An American sociologist named Lester Ward noted that humans had used their intelligence to breed the best species of plants and animals. In like manner, humans should apply their intelligence to make society stronger and better. By 1910, Ward's ideas were winning out with the American public.

Charles Darwin faced considerable criticism when he published his On the Origin of Species.

EDUCATION

The first priority of progressives was to improve the state's public schools. Governor Charles B. Aycock led the fight for better schools for both races. Aycock grew up in a poor farm family near Goldsboro. His father served in the legislature, but his mother could not read or write. Aycock thus had a personal reason for improving the schools.

Soon after Aycock became governor in 1901, he faced a difficult test in the legislature. Whites in many counties with large black populations resented paying taxes to support black schools. Two bills in the 1901 legislature would require taxes paid by whites to be used only to support white schools. If passed, these bills would make black schools even worse. Aycock threatened to resign if the bills passed. The bills were withdrawn, but black schools still got much less than their fair share of local taxes.

Opposite page, top: *Justice Walter Clark supported progressive reforms like woman's suffrage and the abolition of child labor.*
Opposite page bottom: *Senator Furnifold M. Simmons established a Democratic political machine aligned with business interests.*

North Carolina had a higher proportion of people who were illiterate than any other state. About one in five whites and one of two blacks were illiterate. Aycock wanted to improve education so that, after 1908, all adult males would be literate and could register to vote. (According to the suffrage amendment, after 1908 all men would be required to pass a literacy test in order to vote.)

North Carolina's public schools badly needed money and attention. In 1900, only three of five school-age children were enrolled in school. Of these, only half attended school, meaning that the schools reached less than one-third of the state's school-age children. Short school terms also hurt education. Although the state constitution called for a four-month school term, the state averaged less than that. In 1900, for example, Swain County schools met only twenty days during the year. Schools were poorly built, and many were log cabins with dirt floors. Teacher pay was low, only about $25 a month. Because most money to support schools came from local taxes, poor counties had poor schools and wealthy urban counties had good schools. The poorest schools were always the black schools.

This log school in the mountains shows the condition of public schools about 1900.

Governor Aycock first worked to build public support for education, hoping to put pressure on local politicians. Using money from the Southern Education Board, he had Charles D. McIver and others conduct a campaign for education in over seventy counties in 1902 and 1903. This campaign was so effective that the legislature doubled its annual appropriation to $200,000. Local governments nearly doubled their tax support for schools.

Public school reform continued under later governors. In 1907, the legislature gave rural areas the authority to organize high schools, something only towns had been able to afford until then. Within a year, there were 157 rural high schools. In 1913, the legislature passed laws requiring children to attend school until age 14 and establishing a special fund to help poor school districts. In 1918, the people approved a constitutional amendment for a six-month school term. By 1920, some 3,000 new schools had been built. These educational reforms were effective. In 1920, only one of twelve whites and one of four blacks were illiterate. However, other states had also made progress, and North Carolina was still near the bottom in literacy.

Progressives next turned their efforts to the abuse of alcoholic beverages.

Whites did not like to pay taxes to support black schools. This is the classroom of a black school in Edgecombe County.

Do You Remember?

1. Over what issue did Governor Aycock threaten to resign in 1901?
2. What was one result of the educational reforms?

The illegal manufacture of whiskey increased during prohibition. Here, the Surry County sheriff poses with a confiscated bootleg distillery.

PROHIBITION

Public drunkenness was a major problem. In 1900, the state had over 400 distilleries (places where alcoholic beverages are made). They sold their products to saloons, which existed in almost every town.

A number of groups had already organized to oppose the sale of liquor. The **Women's Christian Temperance Union** (WCTU) believed that drunken men were a threat to women and the home. They opposed saloons as centers of drunkenness, gambling, and corrupt politics. In 1902, representatives of five Protestant churches organized the **Anti-Saloon League** (ASL) in Raleigh. They demanded the closing of all saloons. The ASL won a victory in 1902 when Cumberland County voted to prohibit the sale of liquor.

This victory helped convince the Democratic party to back **prohibition** (forbidding by law the making or selling of alcoholic beverages). The Democrats also discovered that prohibition was an issue they could use against the Republicans. Many Republicans served as federal revenue agents for the distilleries. Closing down the distilleries would put these agents out of work and hurt the Republican party.

The Democrats therefore supported a bill sponsored by A. D. Watts of Iredell County in 1903. The Watts Act prohibited the manufacture and sale of liquor everywhere in the state except in incorporated towns of more than 1,000 people. Lawmakers reasoned that lawlessness was common around rural distilleries and saloons where there were no police officers. This law reduced the number of distilleries from 428 to 283 and the number of saloons from 1,185 to 817.

The prohibitionists then worked to ban the sale of liquor in towns. By 1907, voters in Statesville, Wilson, Charlotte, Greensboro, and many small textile towns had chosen prohibition. In the mountains, every county but Haywood voted to become "dry." Still not satisfied, the antiliquor forces demanded statewide prohibition. They pointed out that the Watts Act was not working. Liquor dealers simply moved to the larger towns and flooded the surrounding dry counties with alcohol. From Salisbury, for example, boys traveled by train to deliver black satchels of liquor to nearby dry towns.

The public demand for statewide prohibition became so strong that the politicians could not resist it. In 1908, Governor Robert B. Glenn called a special session of the legislature to authorize a referendum (popular vote) on statewide prohibition. In the election, 60 percent of the voters approved prohibition. As Governor Glenn signed his proclamation of prohibition on January 1, 1909, the audience sang "Praise God from Whom All Blessings Flow." North Carolina was the first state to become dry by popular vote.

In 1909, the legislature authorized private "social clubs" to sell liquor to members. The law also permitted beer halls, called "blind tigers," to sell beer with a low alcohol content. The prohibitionists set to work and repealed this law in 1911. A federal law prohibited the sale of liquor by mail in 1913. In 1919, when the Eighteenth Amendment to the Constitution proposed to prohibit the manufacture, sale, or use of liquor after 1920, North Carolina became the twenty-eighth state to ratify it.

Carrie Nation of Kansas, famous for smashing bar rooms with her hatchet after her husband had died of alcoholism, spoke for prohibition in Salisbury.

CHILD LABOR

The textile industry was the largest employer of children in North Carolina. In 1900, about one of every four textile workers was a child between the ages of 10 and 16. These children worked long hours, usually 66 to 75 hours a week. Their pay for this often dangerous work was low, as little as 60 cents a week. Because they could not attend school, many were illiterate. Uneducated, these children could look forward to little more in life than the drudgery of the mills.

Many voices demanded an end to child labor. The textile workers themselves wanted better lives for their children. Wages were so low, however, that whole families sometimes had to work just to eke out a living. Labor unions opposed child labor because it drove down wages. Well-known North Carolinians such as newspaper editors Josephus Daniels and Josiah W. Bailey also favored reform. The most effective worker for children's rights was the Reverend Alexander J. McKelway, editor of the

Top: *Nearly a fourth of the state's textile mill workers in 1900 were children.* **Above:** *Newspaper editor Josiah W. Bailey favored reform of the child labor laws.*

Presbyterian Standard in Charlotte. Reverend McKelway helped persuade Governor Aycock to oppose child labor.

Aycock urged the legislature to abolish child labor in industry and "protect small children against labor which dwarfs them physically, mentally, and morally." Before the legislature could act in 1901, 125 of the 212 textile mill owners promised not to hire children under the age of 10 and not to hire children under the age of 12 when school was in session. When the mill owners did not keep their promise, the legislature passed the state's first child labor law. Passed in 1903, the law prohibited children under age 12 from working in industry. Children between the ages of 12 and 18 could work no more than 66 hours a week. Unfortunately, there was no way to enforce the law, so the mill owners regularly ignored it.

Finally, in 1919, the legislature passed a law that could be enforced. It raised the minimum age for child laborers to 14. A new child welfare commission was formed to enforce the law. In 1920, this commission made 4,000 inspections and found 738 violations of the law. The progressives had taken the first steps to protect their children's future.

Do You Remember?

1. What was the purpose of prohibition?
2. Why wasn't the state's first child labor law successful?

PRISON REFORM

The progressives also worked for prison reform. North Carolina established the first state prison in Raleigh in the 1880s. To save money, however, the state leased six of every ten prisoners to industry. Prisoners in this "convict lease system" usually performed the dirtiest, most dangerous work. Industry fed prisoners as cheaply as possible. Living conditions were terrible. Railroads sometimes housed prisoners in wire cages with slab board roofs. Guards could and did whip or shoot prisoners for little reason.

Also common was the county **chain gang,** so called because, while they were working, prisoners had their legs chained to prevent their escape. By 1908, over forty counties in North Carolina used chain gangs, mainly to maintain county roads. This system was also sometimes cruel and inhumane, depending on the prison officers.

Progressives wanted prisoners to be paid for their work, flogging (beating) of prisoners to be stopped, and boys to be separated from hardened criminals. Governor Aycock asked the legislature to establish a boys' reformatory. The legislature agreed and, in 1907, the Stonewall Jackson Training School for white boys opened. In the 1920s, the legislature created the Morrison Training School for young black men. A 1917 law provided for state regulation of chain gangs, which improved the treatment prisoners received.

The state leased convicts to corporations as laborers. Convicts helped build the Western North Carolina Railroad near Asheville.

Another reform was the regulation of corporations. A **corporation** is a business, owned by a group of investors, that has a life of its own apart from its founders.

CORPORATION COMMISSION

Industry expanded rapidly during the first part of the new century. From 1900 to 1920, the value of products manufactured in the state increased tenfold—to $944 million. By 1920, the value of manufactured products was double the value of the state's agricultural products. The number of industrial workers more than doubled to 158,000. By 1920, North Carolina was the leading industrial state in the Southeast.

Industrial growth made many people very wealthy. For example, an investment of $60,000 in a textile mill brought an average profit of $18,000 a year. One Durham mill owner made a profit of over 50 percent a year. The wealth, however, did not extend to the workers. Adult textile workers averaged $2.40 to $4.50 for a 63- to 75-hour work week. A child's pay was much less, 60 to 90 cents a week.

Many workers felt that they had lost control of their lives. Workers had to endure long hours, low wages, and working conditions that threatened their health. If they joined a labor union to bargain for better hours and pay, they were fired. A **labor union** is an organization of workers formed to improve wages, benefits, and working conditions.

The growing wealth of corporations made them very powerful. By 1920, most of the state's small railroad lines had become part of four large systems. These were the Southern Railway Company in the Piedmont and Mountains, the Atlantic Coast Line Railroad in the Coastal Plain, and the Seaboard Air Line Railway and the Norfolk and Southern in the Piedmont and Coastal Plain. The Southern Railway was especially active in politics. It hired well-known lawyers to keep them pro-railroad, gave free rides to politicians and editors, and paid certain newspapers to present its viewpoint.

Above: The Southern Railway bought out smaller lines, like the Western North Carolina Railroad, shown here crossing Grant's Creek at Salisbury. *Left:* Railroads formed the state's first good transportation system and linked major cities.

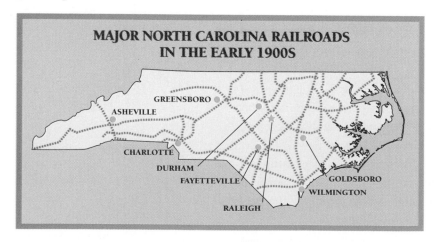

MAJOR NORTH CAROLINA RAILROADS IN THE EARLY 1900S

GREENSBORO

ASHEVILLE

CHARLOTTE

DURHAM

FAYETTEVILLE

GOLDSBORO

WILMINGTON

RALEIGH

Top: In 1890, James Buchanan Duke organized the nation's largest tobacco trust, the American Tobacco Company. In 1911, the U.S. Supreme Court ordered it broken up into four companies. *Above:* Robert B. Glenn, governor from 1905 to 1909, favored prohibition, tried to restrain big business, and opposed the lynching of blacks.

The tobacco industry also had much political influence. In 1890, James "Buck" Duke organized the American Tobacco Company. By 1904, Duke had taken over so many smaller tobacco companies that he controlled about 80 percent of the nation's tobacco business. He also controlled about 95 percent of the cigarette manufacturing business. The American Tobacco Company became known as the "tobacco trust." A **trust** is a group of firms that controls all or nearly all business in an industry so that there is little, if any, competition. In 1903 and again in 1907, tobacco farmers charged that the trust paid them much less than they should have received for their crops.

In 1891, the state had created a railroad commission, mainly to regulate the rates charged by the railroads within the state. The state soon found that other corporations needed regulating. In 1899, the Democratic legislature created the corporation commission. Its three members were appointed by the governor.

The railroads fought the state over the regulation issue. In 1899, the corporation commission raised the assessed value of all railroad property. This meant that the railroads would have to pay more taxes. The four major lines refused to pay their taxes in 1900 and 1901. The state was forced to back down and lower the railroads' taxes.

Because the conservative Democrats who served on the corporation commission favored corporations, the commission did a poor job of regulation. As a result, Governor Glenn turned to the legislature in 1907. He asked the legislature to join with other states in an effort to reduce railroad passenger rates to $2\frac{1}{4}$ cents a mile. The railroads took the states to federal court. North Carolina agreed to compromise on a rate of 2 cents a mile. From 1897 to 1911, the commission heard over 4,000 complaints about overcharges and rate discrimination. Clearly, regulation was a difficult task.

For years, the state legislature tried to pass an antitrust law to make corporations' unfair practices illegal. Buck Duke had enough influence with the legislature to block passage of an effective law. In 1911, however, the federal government used the Sherman Anti-Trust Act to break up the American Tobacco Company. The Sherman Anti-Trust Act made illegal any "conspiracy in restraint of trade." The American Tobacco Company was split into four companies: American, Liggett and Myers, P. Lorillard, and R. J. Reynolds.

Do You Remember?

1. What was a chain gang?
2. What is the purpose of a labor union?
3. What federal law did authorities use to break up the American Tobacco Company?

POLITICAL REFORMS

Progressives believed that government should be more democratic. That is, they believed that if more people took part in government, corporations and special interest groups would have less influence. Progressives, therefore, worked to reform state and local government and extend the right to vote to more citizens.

Statewide Primary

Up to this time, candidates for statewide office were nominated at a political party's convention, which was attended by hundreds of party delegates. Corporations or politicians needed only to influence a few hundred delegates to ensure the nomination of their candidate. Progressives favored the statewide **primary** method of nominating candidates. Progressives believed it would be more difficult to buy or rig a nomination if all the party's members across the state voted.

In 1907, the legislature passed a law permitting counties to hold primaries if they chose. Democratic party leaders, however, chose not to use it. In 1915, at the urging of Governor Locke Craig, the legislature passed a statewide primary law. In 1916, progressive Thomas W. Bickett was chosen as the Democratic candidate for governor in the primary. (Republicans rarely held statewide primaries since there were few Republican candidates.)

City Government

From 1900 to 1920, the rapid growth of cities and towns continued. By 1920, some 490,000 people lived in cities and towns (1 in every 5 people). This growth was due in part to the new factories and mills, which drew workers from the countryside. Towns also extended their boundaries to take in more territory. North Carolina was still a rural, agricultural state, but its cities were expanding rapidly.

The rapid growth of the towns created many problems. People needed schools, paved streets, lights, water, police and fire protection, sanitation, and recreation. The alderman-mayor system of city government was not able to meet these growing needs. (An alderman is an elected city official.) Aldermen made decisions and carried them out as a group. When things went wrong, it was impossible to say who was responsible.

Under this system, graft (the dishonest use of one's position to gain money or other advantages, such as power) and corruption were common. In Asheville, the mayor used the police to intimidate voters. In Raleigh, the saloon owners gave money to the aldermen. In return, the aldermen promised not to regulate them.

To make city government more responsive to the people, progressives asked for a new type of city government—the **city commission** form.

Top: *Although a "machine" candidate, Governor Locke Craig of Buncombe County supported reforms, including better roads and direct primaries.* **Above:** *Governor Thomas W. Bickett, 1917-1921, was the first candidate for governor nominated by the direct primary.*

Cities began to grow quickly in the early twentieth century. What items in this picture of Raleigh in 1913 can you see that helped the city grow?

Each elected commissioner was responsible for a particular department in city government, such as streets. If the streets were not repaired, for example, the people could vote the street commissioner out of office. In the 1910s, the city commission form spread to Asheville, Greensboro, Raleigh, and Charlotte.

The Woman's Suffrage Movement

In 1900, many people believed that women were guardians of good morals and the home. Because politics was "dirty" and women were morally "pure," they believed that women should stay out of politics. Many progressives, however, believed that women's votes could help clean up politics and enact reforms. Many women felt the same way.

Women's organizations—church mission groups, teachers' organizations, and women's clubs—arose and taught women leadership skills and how to become active in politics. In 1902, Sallie Southall Cotten of Edgecombe County persuaded local women's clubs to form a state federation. Among other things, the North Carolina Federation of Women's Clubs worked for city sanitation, cleaner school buildings, and compulsory school attendance. Other women's groups worked for prison reform, an end to child labor, aid to the poor, and improved education. Women wanted many of the same reforms progressive men did, but they lacked the vote to get them enacted.

The woman's suffrage movement in North Carolina began in the 1890s. In 1894, Helen Morris Lewis of Asheville called a meeting at the courthouse. Out of this meeting Lewis and others formed the North Carolina Equal Suffrage Association. As president, Lewis spoke out for woman's suffrage, saying that women were denied the vote because of "prejudice and superstition." Soon Senator J. L. Hyatt of nearby Yancey County

Gertrude Weil of Goldsboro, on the left, headed the North Carolina Equal Suffrage Association to secure woman's suffrage. Her efforts were in vain. The legislature did not pass a woman's suffrage law.

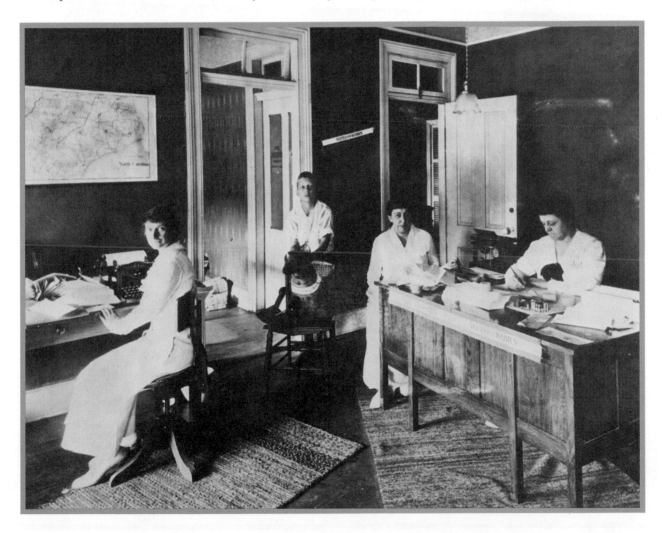

GEORGIA "TINY" BROADWICK

On June 21, 1913, an 80-pound, 20-year-old woman sat in a flimsy wooden seat attached to the underside of the wing of an airplane. Two thousand feet below, an excited crowd gazed upward from a parking lot at Griffith Field, just outside Los Angeles, California. The plane's pilot tapped the young woman on the shoulder, signaling her that it was time to jump. A lever released a latch, the seat's trapdoor fell, and the woman dropped into the sky. Moments later, her parachute opened, and she drifted downward, rocking slowly from side to side. She finally landed in a meadow. This young daredevil, the first woman to parachute from an airplane, was a native of North Carolina. Her name was Georgia "Tiny" Broadwick.

Tiny was born in 1893 on a farm near Henderson. She married, became a mother, and was widowed at a very young age. She struggled to support herself and her baby by working 12-hour shifts in a nearby cotton mill. To earn more money—and for sheer adventure—she decided in 1908 to join a carnival, where she began her career as a parachutist. She made her first jump from a hot-air balloon at the state fair. Tiny used a homemade parachute, one made of heavy cotton muslin rather than silk.

Two months after her feat in Los Angeles, Tiny Broadwick parachuted into the cold waters of Lake Michigan. She thus became the first person—male or female—to parachute into water from a seaplane. In 1914, she demonstrated the use of the parachute or "airplane life preserver" to officers in our country's young air force.

For years, Tiny Broadwick traveled throughout the United States and Canada performing her daring jumps in air shows. In 1922, at the age of twenty-nine, she made her last jump, explaining that "I was getting old." Tiny Broadwick was credited with making over 1,000 jumps from balloons and airplanes and is recognized today as a pioneer in parachuting.

Georgia "Tiny" Broadwick (top) was welcomed as a celebrity in St. Louis (above). She is seen above Los Angeles (opposite page), just prior to making her first jump.

introduced a bill in the 1897 legislature to allow women to vote. To show what he thought of the bill, the leader of the senate referred it to the committee on asylums for the insane, where it died.

The suffragists were quiet until 1913. At that time, they formed the Equal Suffrage League in Charlotte. This group organized local clubs and called for the 1915 legislature to pass a suffrage bill. However, the legislature voted down all attempts to give women the vote at this session and later ones.

In 1920, Governor Thomas W. Bickett called a special session of the legislature to vote on the ratification of the Nineteenth Amendment to the United States Constitution. This amendment extended the right to vote to women. Many Republicans and Democrats favored woman's suffrage. Gertrude Weil, president of the Equal Suffrage League, worked

Above: *Sallie S. Cotten helped establish women's clubs where women could learn public speaking and leadership.* **Right:** *Senator Lee S. Overman of Salisbury was opposed to ratification of the Nineteenth Amendment.*

hard to have North Carolina be the 36th state to ratify the amendment, which would have made it law. Unfortunately, Senators Simmons and Lee S. Overman opposed ratification. They convinced the legislature to reject the amendment. The amendment was ratified the next day, however, when Tennessee approved it. Women voted for the first time in 1920.

NORTH CAROLINIANS IN NATIONAL POLITICS

The election in 1912 of Woodrow Wilson as president of the United States delighted North Carolinians. The son of a Presbyterian minister, President Wilson had once lived in Wilmington and attended Davidson College. He was only the second Democratic president elected since the Civil War. To reward friends in North Carolina who had helped elect him, Wilson appointed four Tar Heels to high office.

Josephus Daniels, editor of the Raleigh *News and Observer*, was named Secretary of the Navy. Daniels's assistant was Franklin D. Roosevelt, who later became president. On their shoulders fell the task of preparing the Navy for the coming war.

Wilson appointed Walter Hines Page as U.S. ambassador to Great Britain. A native of Cary, Page started his publishing career as editor of the *State Chronicle* in Raleigh. Page then went to New York where he edited the *Forum*, the *Atlantic Monthly*, and *World's Work*. He was also a partner in a publishing firm. While serving as ambassador to Great Britain, Page supported the British in the war and worked to obtain American support for them.

Angus W. McLean was a Lumberton banker and textile mill owner. He directed the War Finance Corporation, a government agency that loaned money to war industries. Chief Justice Walter Clark served as an **arbitrator** (one who settles differences between two parties) on the War Labor Board. He helped to settle labor disputes so they did not stop war production.

Angus W. McLean of Robeson County headed the national War Finance Corporation, which borrowed money to keep war industries operating. He later became governor.

Do You Remember?
1. Why did progressives favor the use of a statewide primary system to nominate candidates?
2. Why would the city commission form of government be more responsive to the people?
3. What was one reason many people believed women should stay out of politics?
4. Which amendment gave women the right to vote?
5. Name three North Carolinians appointed to positions in the federal government by President Wilson.

NORTH CAROLINA AND WORLD WAR I

War broke out in Europe in August 1914. President Wilson declared America a **neutral** nation. In other words, the United States would not take sides between the Central Powers led by Germany and Austria-Hungary and the Allied Powers led by France, Great Britain, and Russia.

Some North Carolinians did take sides. They volunteered to fight for the French and British, serving as aviators, soldiers, ambulance drivers, and nurses. Kiffin Y. Rockwell of Asheville organized the Lafayette Escadrille, a squadron of American aviators who fought for France. When Rockwell was killed in battle, French airplanes overflew his funeral and scattered flowers. James McConnell of Carthage also flew in the squadron.

Although President Wilson wanted to remain neutral, he asked Congress to declare war against Germany in April 1917. When President Wilson spoke to Congress, he asked Americans to fight a war "to make the world safe for democracy." This war has come to be known as **World War I.**

North Carolinians responded to his noble war aim. Nearly half a million men, blacks and whites, registered to fight. Some 86,000 men and women served in the military, one-fourth of them black. Cherokees also answered the call to serve.

Above: The largest army training base in the state was Camp Greene, near Charlotte. ***Opposite page below:*** *Josephus Daniels, editor of the Raleigh* News and Observer, *was appointed Secretary of the Navy by President Wilson. His assistant was Franklin D. Roosevelt of New York, later to become president.* **Left:** *The 30th "Old Hickory" Division with German prisoners of war.*

Two Army divisions had the largest number of Tar Heel troops. They were the 30th "Old Hickory" Division and the 81st "Wildcat" Division. Each division contained about 15,000 men. The 30th Division trained at Camp Sevier near Greenville, South Carolina. The division left Boston in 1918 bound for Liverpool, England, where they faced a German zeppelin (airship) bombing raid. The unit later took up battle stations with the British troops in Belgium. In September 1918, the division fought near Ypres and Verdun.

THE UNITED STATES AND WORLD WAR I

When World War I began in Europe in 1914, the United States remained neutral. By international law, the United States could trade with both warring sides. This was called "freedom of the seas." The British tried to stop neutrals' trade with Germany by mining the North Sea with explosives. Germany hoped to use its submarines to sink ships trading with the British.

In May 1915, a German submarine sank the British ocean liner *Lusitania* off the coast of Ireland. Among the hundreds killed were 128 Americans. President Wilson warned Germany of dire results if it continued to violate international law requiring warships to provide for

the safety of passengers and crews of trading ships they sank. Germany apologized and stopped the submarine warfare for a time lest the United States enter the war.

Meanwhile the United States became more committed to the Allies, who depended on the United States for food and war supplies. The British bombarded America with anti-German propaganda. Americans believed the propaganda, especially after German spies tried to sabotage American industry. Congress began preparing for war.

In early 1917, Germany resumed submarine attacks, and in March 1917 its submarines sank several American ships. Meanwhile the British intercepted and decoded a secret radio message from Germany to Mexico. In this "Zimmermann Telegram," Germany urged Mexico to attack the United States in return for getting the southwestern United States. This was the final blow. President Wilson asked Congress to declare war.

Opposite page, top: The conning tower of a German U-boat rises out of the water. The U-boats were a major threat to Allied shipping. ***Opposite page, bottom:*** *French schoolchildren wave as American troops march past. Thousands of Americans served in France and Belgium during the war.* ***Above:*** *American machinegunners in World War I. "The Great War," as it was called, was marked by the misery of trench warfare.*

Overall, Tar Heel casualties in the war were light. Some 833 troops died in battle or from wounds. Another 1,542 died from disease.

Three military training camps were located in North Carolina: Camp Greene near Charlotte, Camp Polk near Raleigh, and Camp Bragg near Fayetteville. The largest was Camp Greene where 65,000 men at one time trained. Artillerymen (those who handled large guns) trained at Camp Bragg and the tank corps at Camp Polk.

Citizens joined volunteer groups to help the war effort. The Red Cross raised about $2 million, made surgical dressings and hospital clothing, and provided refreshments for traveling soldiers. The War Camp Community Service entertained and provided a homey atmosphere for soldiers at the training camps.

Two hundred North Carolina firms manufactured materials used in the war effort. Ships were built in the Wilmington, Morehead City, and Elizabeth City shipyards. Textile mills made tents, uniforms, blankets, sheets, and socks. Other war goods made in the state included aluminum, chromium, airplane propellers, explosives, and wagon wheels.

People helped in other ways. In 1918, North Carolinians planted over 56,000 "victory" gardens to raise more food for themselves. This released commercial crops to be used by the American troops and the Allies. To save food, families observed wheatless, meatless, and porkless days. There was no shortage of food, but sugar was **rationed** (given out in limited amounts).

The Central Powers were defeated and the war ended on November 11, 1918, when both sides signed an **armistice** (an agreement to stop fighting). For years afterward, North Carolinians rang church bells on November 11 to commemorate victory and peace.

Do You Remember?

1. Who was president in 1917?
2. Which war did the United States enter in 1917? What did the president ask Americans to do?
3. How did people in North Carolina help to provide food for the troops and the allies?

Opposite page, above: Kiffin Rockwell of Asheville (second from left) and James R. McConnell of Carthage (far right) served in the French Lafayette Escadrille before the U.S. entered the war.
*Opposite page, below: Red Cross volunteers gave food and drink to troops. **Above:** The Raleigh Iron Works made explosive shell casings for artillery.*

CHAPTER · REVIEW

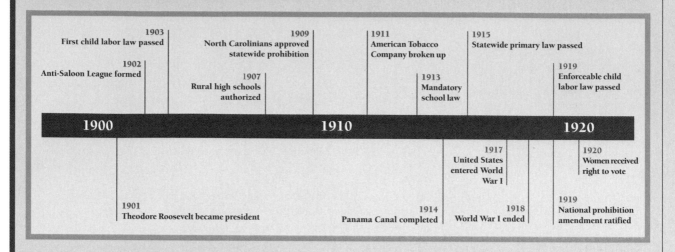

1903 First child labor law passed

1902 Anti-Saloon League formed

1909 North Carolinians approved statewide prohibition

1907 Rural high schools authorized

1911 American Tobacco Company broken up

1913 Mandatory school law

1915 Statewide primary law passed

1919 Enforceable child labor law passed

1900   **1910**   **1920**

1917 United States entered World War I

1920 Women received right to vote

1901 Theodore Roosevelt became president

1914 Panama Canal completed

1918 World War I ended

1919 National prohibition amendment ratified

Reviewing People, Places, and Terms

Explain why each of the following terms appears in a chapter on North Carolina and the Progressive Era.

1. armistice
2. chain gang
3. city commission
4. primary
5. prohibition
6. trust
7. Women's Christian Temperance Union

Understanding the Facts

1. How did the Republican party change after 1900?
2. In what three ways did the progressives work to reform society?
3. Give three reasons for the poor quality of education in North Carolina in the early 1900s.
4. What amendment to the U.S. Constitution enacted nationwide prohibition?
5. What were the provisions of North Carolina's first child labor law?
6. What was the "convict lease system"?
7. What reforms did progressives initiate in state and local government?

8. When did women receive the right to vote?
9. Name three war materials that were manufactured in North Carolina.

Developing Critical Thinking

1. How would you describe a "political machine"?
2. What impact do you think child labor had on the economy?
3. The practice of using prisoners to maintain roads or to do other maintenance work has recently been reinstituted in some areas of the country. Do you think this is a good policy? Why or why not?
4. Why do you think women were kept from voting for so long?

Applying Your Skills

1. In 1900, about one in five whites and one of two blacks were illiterate. By 1920, the figures were one in twelve whites and one of four blacks. Convert these figures to percentages and compare the decrease in illiteracy between white and black North Carolinians during this time.
2. At the beginning of the twentieth century, the number of corporations in the country increased

rapidly. Research how a corporation is formed. Try to find out whether any businesses in your city or town are organized as corporations.

3. If by 1920, some 490,000 people lived in cities or towns (1 in 5), about how many people lived in North Carolina in 1920?

4. Susan B. Anthony and Elizabeth Cady Stanton were leaders in the national woman's suffrage movement. Prepare a report on one of them.

Making Connections

1. Which elements of society were most likely to support Herbert Spencer's ideas? Why?

2. Do you think that Darwin's ideas still have an impact on society today? In what ways?

3. Research international law and marine warfare. How did submarines violate international law?

4. World War I was fought to make the world "safe for democracy." Do you think it did that? Why or why not?

Tar Heel Trivia

- Mount Mitchell State Park, the first state park in North Carolina, opened in 1915. Mount Mitchell is the highest peak east of the Mississippi River.
- The Clinchfield Railroad, completed in 1908 and running between Marion and Erwin, Tennessee, is considered to be the curviest section of line in the eastern United States.
- In 1900, North Carolina had 177 cotton mills.

BUILDING SKILLS: NOTETAKING

In your school career, you have no doubt found that it is impossible to remember all of the information you need for assignments or when studying for tests. One of the best ways to remember something is to write it down. *Notetaking*—writing down information in a brief and orderly manner—will not only help you remember information but also make studying easier.

Notetaking only works if you use it and can understand the notes you have taken. Your system for notetaking may be different from the student next to you, but there are some general guidelines that everyone should find helpful.

- Take a sheet of plain or lined notebook paper and draw a vertical line down the page about 6 inches from the left edge. Draw a horizontal line across the page about 2 inches up from the bottom of the page.
- Identify the subject by writing it at the top of the sheet. You might, for example, write "The Progressive Movement" at the top of the page for the notes you take on this chapter.
- Write your notes in the wide, left-hand column. Periodically, write down key words or key ideas in the narrow, right-hand column.

- Don't try to write down everything. Listen carefully to what your teacher says. If your teacher stresses or repeats something or spends a good deal of time on a topic, that is a clue to its importance. If you are doing research, you might want to write down topic sentences or key words or phrases.
- Learn to *paraphrase*, or write down the information in your own words. This will help you think about what was said or written.
- Make sure your notes are legible and neat so that you can understand them when you read them again.
- At the bottom of each sheet of notes, write out several questions that could be answered by the notes on the page. You might want to work with a classmate and practice answering the questions.

These guidelines on taking notes work equally well if you are gathering information from various reference sources.

Try This! Practice your notetaking skills by completing Activity 4 under the Applying Your Skills head. Use the notes you take to help you prepare the report.

GROWTH AND CHANGE IN NORTH CAROLINA

Opposite page: The Wright brothers, Wilbur (left) and Orville (right), made the first powered flight in 1903 at Kitty Hawk on North Carolina's Outer Banks.

Nothing will do more to banish ignorance and to encourage that spirit of charity that makes the whole world kin than a system of highways....

— Frank Page, chairman of the Highway Commission

THE EARLY TWENTIETH CENTURY was a time of remarkable economic growth and social and cultural devel-opment in the state. The growing use of automobiles, the building of roads, and the expanding electrical power industry contributed to the state's economic growth.

Among cultural developments, the evolution controversy and the migration of blacks left their marks. Literary figures also grew in importance. People's demands for more services led to the growth and increased efficiency of state government. Women began to play more prominent roles in government.

ECONOMIC GROWTH

By the early 1900s, textiles, tobacco, and furniture manufacturing had become the state's major industries. Developments in transportation and energy contributed directly to this growth.

One of the most remarkable developments in the twentieth century took place in North Carolina.

THE FIRST FLIGHT

In the early 1900s, two bicycle makers from Dayton, Ohio, became interested in flight. They were brothers Wilbur and Orville Wright. For several years, the two had built and experimented with gliders. But they needed a windy place from which to launch their gliders. After checking with the Weather Bureau in Washington, D.C., they chose Kitty Hawk,

BERNOULLI'S THEOREM

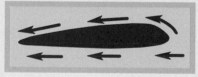

The Wright brothers made use of the theorem on the flow of fluids developed by Daniel Bernoulli (top) to design the wings used in the first powered flights at Kitty Hawk on December 17, 1903 (above). The cross section diagram shows how a curved wing creates unequal air pressure above and below the wing, causing it to lift.

The Wright brothers used science to design their gliders and airplanes. One scientist whose work helped them was Daniel Bernoulli. Born in 1700 in Switzerland, Bernoulli was a mathematician, physicist, and philosopher. In 1738, Bernoulli published (in Latin) an important work called "Hydrodynamica" ("The Dynamics of Water"), which contained his theorem (or principle) on the flow of fluids. Bernoulli's theorem states that the pressure of a fluid decreases as the speed of the fluid increases.

If you think of air as a "fluid," the theorem can be applied to aircraft design. Look at this cross section of an aircraft wing. Because the air moving over the top of the wing moves faster than the air moving across the bottom, the air pressure on the top is less. Since the air pressure on the bottom is more, the air pushes *up* on the wing and lifts the whole airplane.

The Wright brothers built a small wind tunnel to test Bernoulli's principle on different wing shapes. They used the data they gathered to build new and larger wings, Finally, they were ready to add power to their glider. And the rest is history.

North Carolina. On the Outer Banks between Currituck Sound and the ocean, they made hundreds of glider flights from Kill Devil Hill.

Finally, they decided to try their theories of flight with a motor-driven flying machine. In 1903, they built an airplane that had a gasoline motor and two propellers. Camped at the bottom of Kill Devil Hill in a rough shack, they waited from September to December for just the right wind conditions. Finally, on December 17, conditions were right. Orville won the toss of the coin and got to pilot the first try. The airplane buzzed into the air and flew 120 feet in 12 seconds. They made three more flights that day, the longest 852 feet. The aviation age had arrived—just behind the start of the automobile age.

THE GOOD ROADS STATE

No one knows when the first automobile came to North Carolina. About 1880, Peregrine Cook of Sampson County invented a steam-propelled vehicle. Around 1900, Gilbert Waters of New Bern built a gasoline-powered "Buggymobile." At about the same time, a bicycle merchant in Asheville, Eugene Sawyer, built a gasoline-powered vehicle on four bicycle wheels. The first automobile manufacturer in the state was the Corbitt Automobile Company of Henderson. Founded by Richard J. Corbitt, the company produced its first "Motor Buggy" in 1907.

The first automobiles were handmade and so expensive only wealthy people could afford them. In 1910, only 3,220 automobiles were registered in the state. But by 1919, Tar Heels were driving some 109,017 cars. This amazing increase was mainly due to Henry Ford. In 1908, the first

North Carolina's first automobile manufacturer was the Corbitt Automobile Company of Henderson, producing its first car in 1907. This parade of Corbitts in Henderson took place in 1909.

Automobiles gave rise to many new businesses like this Chevrolet garage in Sanford in 1916.

mass-produced Model T automobile rolled off the assembly line at Ford's factory in Michigan. **Mass production** is the manufacture of great quantities of an item through the assembly of interchangeable parts. This new concept so reduced the cost of making cars that Ford was soon able to sell the Model T for less than $400. The Model T was produced for some 18 years and put a whole generation on wheels. By 1928, North Carolinians drove some 474,000 motor vehicles.

In the 1920s, motor vehicles brought many changes to people's lives, especially those who lived in rural areas. Farmers were able to bypass high-priced country stores and drive to less expensive stores in town. Libraries used "bookmobiles" to lend books in rural areas. Fire trucks extended fire protection to larger areas. Medical doctors made their rounds in the country faster, and patients got to hospitals quicker. Free dental and health clinics made their way into rural areas to improve health care. School buses made it possible for rural students to attend high schools and consolidated primary schools. Automobiles gave owners a feeling of freedom and independence.

THE "MOTHER OF GOOD ROADS" IN NORTH CAROLINA

Harriet Morehead Berry was born in Hillsborough, Orange County, in 1877. Harriet, or "Hattie" as she was known, became involved in civic and political projects and issues at a time when women's views were often disregarded. She was, among other things, an educator, a conservationist, a women's rights advocate, and a newspaper editor. She was also a very effective lobbyist in the state legislature long before women even had the constitutional right to vote.

After graduating with honors from what is now the University of North Carolina at Greensboro, Hattie Berry briefly taught at a home for orphans in Oxford. In 1901, she began work in Chapel Hill with the North Carolina Geological and Economic Survey. It was here that Berry became interested in conservation and road construction. She also became involved in the North Carolina Good Roads Association.

As a leader of the movement to expand and improve the state's poor road system in the early 1900s, Berry is given much credit for pulling North Carolina "out of the mud." Berry and her supporters had to contend with many powerful individuals who believed that the counties, not the state, should build and care for roads. Undeterred, Berry helped draft legislation in 1915 that created a state highway commission. She gathered public support for the state-funded highway system by writing letters and editorials, making speeches, and traveling throughout the state (with much difficulty due to the poor roads). Between 1919 and 1921, she spoke in eighty-nine of the state's one hundred counties. With

the increased support, Berry successfully guided the road law of 1921 through the legislature, committing the state to an ongoing road-building program.

In 1962, twenty-two years after her death, a bronze plaque was unveiled in the state Highway Commission Building. The plaque honored Harriet Berry as "the mother of good roads in North Carolina."

Top: As director of the state Geologic and Economic Survey, Harriet Morehead Berry lobbied for a state system of paved roads. ***Above:*** This section of I-40 near Durham is named in honor of Hattie Berry.

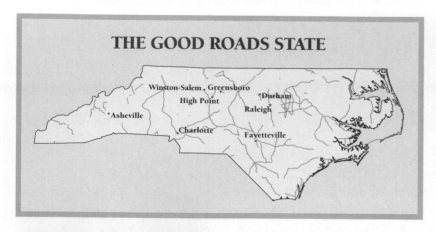

THE GOOD ROADS STATE

With the coming of the automobile came a need to build more and better roads. The Good Roads Movement was born. Before 1921, counties built and maintained all roads. The result was a patchwork system of roads, with not a single good paved road running across the state.

What was needed was a system of roads built by the state. In 1916, Congress agreed to provide federal money to build state roads if the states would match those funds. At first, North Carolina gave the federal money to the counties, which built the roads. A piecemeal road system was still the result. By 1920, however, several people became convinced that the state had to become more involved. Frank Page of Aberdeen, chairman of the highway commission, wanted the state to build and maintain 5,500 miles of roads connecting the county seats. T.L. Kirkpatrick of Charlotte wanted the state to borrow $50 million to build roads as soon as possible. Hattie M. Berry of Chapel Hill wanted the state, not the counties, to maintain the roads once they were built.

The leader who put all of these ideas together was Governor Cameron Morrison. In 1921, Governor Morrison convinced the legislature to pass a law making the state a roadbuilder. This law authorized the state to borrow $50 million to build the roads proposed by Page. Money collected for gasoline and vehicle license taxes was used to repay the loan. Once the roads were built, the state maintained them. By 1929, the state had borrowed $115 million for roads and gotten matching funds from the federal government. Throughout the 1920s, white ribbons of concrete began to stretch across the state. The state became known as the "Good Roads State" because it had the best roads in the South.

The combination of good roads and automobiles led to new economic activity. Automobile dealerships arose to sell cars. "Filling stations" popped up at city street corners and at country stores. Mechanics opened automobile repair garages. New stores opened to sell just automobile tires and accessories. The first bus lines made short runs between towns. In 1919, Charles H. Frederickson of Charlotte opened the first registered commercial trucking company in the state to cart freight.

Top: *This map shows the current system of state roads, a result of the Good Roads Movement.*
Above: *Frank Page, brother of Walter Hines Page, served as chairman of the state highway commission from 1919 to 1929.*

Do You Remember?

1. What happened at Kitty Hawk to change modern transportation?
2. What led to the huge increase in the number of cars owned by North Carolinians?

ELECTRIC POWER

By the early 1900s, business people realized they could make a profit selling electrical power. In the 1890s, Buck and Benjamin Duke had begun buying **hydroelectric** sites, planning to use electricity generated by water power to run their mills. In 1904, Buck Duke financed a hydroelectric dam in South Carolina. In 1905, Duke created the Southern Power Company to develop that project and other hydroelectric sites. He hoped the company would sell power to textile mills. However, many mill owners were very suspicious of electricity. One owner said, "You must be drunk or a . . . fool if you think I will bring electricity into my mill and kill my people." To show that electricity was safe and cheap, Duke installed electric lights and motors in his own mills. One textile leader, James W. Cannon, used Duke's power to build and operate a whole textile town at Kannapolis. By 1930, Southern Power, later called Duke Power, had electrical plants throughout the Piedmont of North Carolina.

Another large power company got started in a different manner. The General Electric Company of New York (GE) made and sold generators (machines that changed mechanical energy into electrical energy). Several small North Carolina power companies bought equipment from GE and

Electricity made many labor-saving devices possible, like this washing machine (above) and toaster (left).

By 1930, electric power companies developed many power sites. In 1929, the Carolina Power and Light Company completed the Waterville Dam on the Pigeon River in Haywood County.

then could not pay for it. GE took the companies over and, in 1908, created Carolina Power and Light Company.

At first, electrical power was sold to industry and to cities. However, it soon became popular for home use. Electricity was used first for lights, but products that ran on electricity soon became available. Refrigerators, irons, washing machines, vacuum cleaners, fans, heaters, ranges, and hot water heaters made life much easier for homemakers.

To meet increasing demands for electricity, power companies expanded. They found that the cheapest way to generate electricity was to build dams on the state's rivers. By 1930, major hydroelectric sites were in operation on the Cape Fear, Yadkin, Catawba, and Pigeon rivers. North Carolina was second in the nation (to New York) in generating hydroelectric power.

INDUSTRY

Between 1900 and 1930, industry in North Carolina grew at an amazing pace. By 1930, the value of the state's manufactured goods was $1,155 million, compared to $362 million for agricultural products. Textiles, tobacco products, and wooden furniture accounted for three-fourths of the value of manufactured goods.

The supply of abundant cotton and cheap labor helped the textile industry grow to importance in North Carolina. From 1900 to 1930, the value of textile products grew from $30 million to $450 million and the number of textile workers from about 30,000 to 125,000. With about 600 mills by 1930, North Carolina led the nation in producing cotton goods. It also led the South in knit goods—socks, hose, and underwear.

Abundant cotton and cheap labor helped increase the value of textile products fifteen-fold between 1900 and 1930.

Above: The major tobacco companies bought at public auction all the
bright leaf tobacco that farmers
produced. *Right:* The state's many
hydroelectric sites and cheap
electricity spurred the growth of
manufacturing plants.

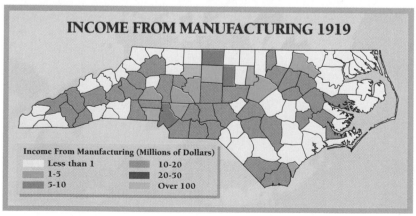

INCOME FROM MANUFACTURING 1919

Income From Manufacturing (Millions of Dollars)

Less than 1   10-20
1-5   20-50
5-10   Over 100

Left: The furniture industry used machines that made many pieces at the same time, thus saving on labor. Below: In early years the quality of furniture was not high. This 1909 kitchen cabinet made in Thomasville cost $9.

North Carolina boasted the world's largest mills for producing towels, denim, damask, and men's underwear.

Despite its great growth, the textile industry was in poor health. Overproduction of cotton goods caused a drop in prices and profits. The mills looked for ways to increase their income. In 1926, they created the Cotton Textile Institute to help regulate production and marketing, but it was not very successful. Next, the industry cut wages and started the "stretch-out." The stretch-out required workers to tend more machines at a faster rate. The lower wages and faster work was more than many workers could bear. In Marion and Gastonia, workers went out on strike in 1929. A **strike** occurs when workers refuse to work, in protest over some grievance. The strikes became violent, and a number of people were killed and wounded. Neither strike resulted in gains for workers.

The tobacco industry, meanwhile, expanded and became very profitable. Between 1900 and 1927, the value of tobacco products rose from $16 million to $413 million. The number of workers increased from 7,000 to 16,000. (This fairly small increase in workers is because the factories began to use machines to replace human labor.) The state became a national leader in producing tobacco products—cigarettes, pipe tobacco, chewing tobacco, snuff, and cigars. The industry was concentrated in the cities of Durham, Winston-Salem, and Reidsville.

The third industry in importance was furniture. Because of the abundance and variety of lumber, the industry grew rapidly. At the turn of the century, the value of North Carolina's furniture products was less than $2 million. By 1930, that amount had risen to $54 million. North Carolina led the nation in the production of wooden furniture. Leading furniture-making towns were High Point, Hickory, and Lenoir.

Despite the growing use of machines, it still took much hand labor to cultivate cotton. This photograph from the 1950s shows a scene little changed in a hundred years.

AGRICULTURE

Despite the rapid growth of industry, North Carolina remained a rural, agricultural state. The major cash crops continued to be cotton and tobacco. The most valuable crop was bright leaf tobacco, which was grown in the Coastal Plain and northern Piedmont counties. North Carolina was second only to Kentucky in tobacco production.

Farmers cured bright leaf tobacco in special, heated barns and sold it through auctioneers at tobacco warehouses. American cigarette companies bought about one-half of the crop. Export companies bought the other half, using it to make cheap cigarettes for sale in Asia. An **export** is a product sent or sold to another country.

The second most valuable crop was cotton, which was grown mainly in the Coastal Plain and southern Piedmont. The cleaner and longer the cotton fiber when picked, the higher price it brought. Most cotton grown in the state had fibers about an inch long and was called "middling" cotton. Some three-fifths of the crop was exported.

In the 1920s, an insect threatened to destroy the cotton crop. The small **boll weevil** bored into and killed the boll where the cotton fiber was formed. Entering Texas in 1892, the boll weevil had spread throughout North Carolina by 1923. At first the weevil did great damage, but farmers soon learned to poison it. By 1930, cotton production was again high. The boll weevil threat did encourage some farmers to plant other crops.

In spite of the value of cotton and tobacco, many North Carolina farmers faced economic problems in this period. By 1925, almost one-half of Tar Heel farmers were tenants or sharecroppers. This agricultural system made it very difficult for farmers to get out of debt. Many farm families lived in poverty, ignorance, and poor health. The tenancy system also led to an overproduction of cotton and tobacco, which in turn led to low crop prices.

The years from 1911 to 1919 had been very profitable for farmers. Cotton prices went as high as 40 cents a pound and tobacco prices as high as 44 cents. In 1920, however, those prices dropped to 14 cents and 21 cents, respectively. Prices rose a little from 1922 to 1924, but overall prices were low in the 1920s. Even small farmers who owned their own land struggled to feed their families.

Farmers and others tried to raise prices. In 1908, farmers organized the North Carolina Farmers' Union. This was part of the national **Farmers' Union,** started in Texas in 1902. Some 33,000 North Carolina farmers joined the Farmers' Union, about one-third of the national membership. The Union pushed for better schools, banking reform, and the breakup of trusts in the tobacco, fertilizer, and farm machinery industries. Their efforts may have helped, but they did not solve farm problems.

After reaching a high of 44 cents a pound, tobacco prices fell to less than half that in 1920. One of the causes was overproduction.

Some farmers believed that the few large tobacco companies were cooperating to keep tobacco prices low. About 80,000 tobacco farmers in the Carolinas and Virginia formed the Tri-State Association. This organization planned to collect its members' tobacco and sell it at times of *its* choosing. Tri-State planned to bypass the tobacco warehouses and get higher prices from the companies. This effort failed because of the opposition of tobacco companies and warehouses and the corrupt management of Tri-State.

Farmers eventually began to realize that overproduction was causing the low farm prices. Cotton and tobacco were largely export crops. Farmers in South America, Africa, and Asia were starting to compete with American farmers. The new fields caused a worldwide overproduction, which in turn caused prices to fall. To cut total American production of these crops would require the cooperation of all farmers. Such cooperation was not possible without government intervention. And, in the 1920s, farmers were not ready to let government tell them how much cotton and tobacco they could plant.

Do You Remember?
1. Who were the first users of electric power?
2. In 1930, what were the three most important industries in North Carolina?
3. What threatened the cotton crop in the 1920s?

THE GREAT MIGRATION

Many black families sent their young men to the North to get jobs to earn enough money for the rest of the family to migrate to the North. These young men found work in shipyards, meat-packing plants, and steel mills.

Between 1916 and 1930, one of the largest population movements inside the United States took place. Over 1 million African Americans moved from the South to the North and West. This movement came to be called the "Great Migration," and it continued well into the 1960s.

Overproduction in the 1920s created an agricultural depression, forcing tenants (many of them black) off farms. In the South, African Americans had few economic opportunities; most well-paying jobs went to whites. Better jobs and higher pay were available in the North. In fact, northern companies actively recruited African Americans for jobs.

There were other reasons for the migration. Few blacks could vote in the southern states, while the North offered the hope of full citizenship rights. Public schools for blacks were poor in the South but better in northern cities. Health care was better in the North. Segregation in the South kept blacks from hotels, restaurants, and recreation areas, but the North offered access to these facilities.

Because they usually did not have enough money to move everyone at once, black families first sent their young men to get jobs. Most were unskilled and found work in the meat-packing plants, shipyards, and steel mills. When the young men had saved enough money, they sent for the rest of their families.

Blacks generally improved their lives by moving north. But they were also crowded into segregated housing and faced prejudice.

THE EVOLUTION CONTROVERSY

The early twentieth century was also a time of great cultural and social change. Movies, radio, automobiles, urban growth, and World War I all caused changes in how people lived and the information that was available to them. While many people accepted new ideas, others did not.

The people most upset by these changes were Christian **fundamentalists**. The fundamentalists believe that the Bible is the source of all religious authority. They believe the Genesis creation story as written: that God created the world and all living things in six days and rested on the seventh. They also believe that man was the last and highest living being created.

Threatening the fundamentalists' beliefs was the changing science of biology. Many biologists had come to accept the ideas of English biologist Charles Darwin. In his book *On the Origin of Species*, Darwin wrote about the process of "natural selection." Darwin also believed in **evolution**, the theory that man evolved (developed) from earlier, simpler life forms. This idea was directly opposed to the Genesis creation story, which stated that man was divinely created apart from other living beings.

THE SCOPES TRIAL

The teaching of evolution was controversial throughout the southern states. In 1925, the state of Tennessee passed a law against the teaching of any theory that denied the creation of man as taught in the Bible. The American Civil Liberties Union (ACLU) offered to defend any teacher who was willing to test the law. John T. Scopes, a high school biology teacher in Dayton, Tennessee, agreed to put the law to a test. He was indicted (charged with a crime) and brought to trial.

National interest in this trial resulted from the fame of some of the people who took part in it. William Jennings Bryan volunteered to be the lawyer for the state. Bryan was an orator and politician and had run for the presidency in 1896, 1900, and 1908. Clarence Darrow, the most famous criminal lawyer of the time, volunteered to defend Scopes. The trial was heard by a judge with no jury. The judge refused to hear any testimony about whether Scopes had a *right* to teach evolution. The only issue was whether Scopes had or had not taught the theory of evolution in his classes.

Scopes was convicted, and the judge fined him $100. When appealed to the Tennessee Supreme Court, the decision was overturned on the ground that only a jury could impose a fine of more than $50.

RESISTANCE TO EVOLUTION IN NORTH CAROLINA

Fundamentalists opposed all teaching about Darwin and evolution in the state's public schools and colleges. They tried to have one college president removed. William L. Poteat, president of Wake Forest College,

In June 1925, John T. Scopes was convicted of teaching evolution in violation of Tennessee law. His trial in Dayton, Tennessee, helped weaken the anti-evolution appeal in North Carolina.

Did Not Come From HIM ☞
NEITHER DID YOU!
I May Look Like Him, But
I Refuse to Claim Kin
On This I Stand!
J. Sherwood Upchurch
They are Going to Talk About Him in the Next
LEGISLATURE
So They Say
I WANT TO BE THERE!

For House of Representatives
DEMOCRATIC PRIMARY
SATURDAY, JUNE 5TH

Right: In 1926, J. Sherwood Upchurch ran for the state legislature in opposition to teaching evolution; he lost. Below: William L. Poteat was a biology professor and president of Wake Forest College. Anti-evolutionist Baptists tried to have him fired for teaching evolution, but they failed.

taught biology. He taught Darwin's theory of evolution, but he also believed that God could have used evolution over millions of years to create the natural world described in Genesis. Poteat had many supporters, and fundamentalists were unable to have him removed.

Fundamentalists opposed evolution in other ways. In 1925, David S. Poole of Hoke County introduced a resolution in the state legislature. This resolution would not allow state-supported teachers to teach as a fact "Darwinism or any other evolutionary hypothesis that links man in blood relationship with any lower form of life." By a vote of 67-46, the state house of representatives rejected Poole's bill. When they could not prevent the teaching of evolution, the fundamentalists proposed that the public schools and colleges teach the Bible. Some city schools then offered Bible courses as electives (courses students could choose to take).

The last attack on evolution came in 1926-1927. Fundamentalists tried to elect legislators who would support a strong anti-evolution law, but they failed to gain control of the legislature. When the 1927 legislature met, Poole introduced another anti-evolution bill, but there was little support for it. The fundamentalists failed because many people favored academic freedom and the separation of church and state more than they opposed the teaching of evolution.

LITERATURE

The early twentieth century saw many North Carolina writers rise to literary prominence. These writers contributed to the national literature through novels, poems, short stories, and drama.

One North Carolinian who rose to fame was William Sydney Porter, better known as O. Henry. Born in Guilford County in 1862, Porter became the nation's best-known short story writer. His own life was as interesting as those of his characters. After getting a good private education, Porter moved to Texas at the age of 19. Problems in a banking job caused him to go to prison in Ohio. His most productive years were in New York where, in 1904 and 1905, he wrote a story a week for the *New York Sunday World*. Two of his best-known short stories are "The Ransom of Red Chief" and "The Gift of the Magi."

Another well-known literary figure from North Carolina was Thomas Wolfe, an Asheville native. Born into a large family in 1900, Wolfe was a quiet child who loved literature. While attending the University in Chapel Hill, Wolfe determined to become a dramatist (one who writes plays). While at Harvard he wrote a number of plays, but none publishers would accept. To make ends meet, he taught English in New York City.

During a 1926 trip to Europe, Wolfe began writing stories about his Asheville childhood. The result, published in 1929, was *Look Homeward, Angel: A Story of the Buried Life*. This book, a novel of a boy maturing to manhood, shocked Asheville because many characters in the book were identifiable as real people.

Another writer who gained fame was Charles W. Chesnutt from Fayetteville. In 1899, he published *The Conjure Woman*, a collection of folk tales. Chesnutt, an African American, wrote a series of novels about the problems blacks had in living in a white-dominated society. The novels included *The House Behind the Cedar*, *The Marrow of Tradition* (about the Wilmington race riot of 1898), and *The Colonel's Dream*.

On the opposite side of the racial issue stood Thomas Dixon of Cleveland County. Educated at Wake Forest College, Dixon turned from the law and ministry to write fiction. His famous novels of Reconstruction are *The Leopard's Spots* and *The Clansman*. The latter book was the basis for the movie "The Birth of a Nation." Dixon's books were popular because they reflected the white supremacy attitudes of the time and glorified the antebellum period.

The state's most famous poet at the turn of the century was John Charles McNeill of Wagram. Many of his poems first appeared in the *Charlotte Observer*, where he worked. A romantic, McNeill wrote in the black dialect and the language of country whites. *Songs, Merry and Sad* was his first book of poems. Others were *Lyrics from Cotton Land* and *Possums and Persimmons*.

The state's leading dramatist was Paul Green of Harnett County. In 1927, he published *In Abraham's Bosom*, the tragic story of a black educator, for which he won a Pulitzer Prize. Other plays with local settings were *The Last of the Lowries*, *The Field God*, and *The House of Connelly*. Green's most famous production is *The Lost Colony*. This outdoor drama has played every summer at Manteo since the 1930s.

*Top: Charles W. Chesnutt of Fayetteville was the state's best-known black writer at the turn of the twentieth century. **Above:** The nation's best-known writer of short stories at the turn of the century was William Sydney Porter (O. Henry) of Greensboro.*

Above: *Acclaimed as the state's greatest writer, Thomas Wolfe posed with his mother, Julia Westall Wolfe.* **Right:** *The fictional "Old Kentucky Home" of Eugene Gant in Look Homeward, Angel bears a sharp resemblance to Wolfe's own home in Asheville, now a state historic site.*

The best historical novelist of the period was James Boyd, editor of the Southern Pines *Pilot*. His best-known work was *Drums* (1925), the story of Johnny Fraser who turned from Loyalist to revolutionary. After sailing with John Paul Jones, Fraser returned to North Carolina and helped secure her independence. Boyd's novel *Marching On* continued the story of the Frasers in the Civil War.

Do You Remember?

1. Why did fundamentalists oppose the theory of evolution?
2. What was William Sydney Porter's pen name?
3. Why was Asheville shocked by Thomas Wolfe's book *Look Homeward, Angel*?

THE GROWTH OF STATE GOVERNMENT

During the early 1900s, people began to believe that government could become an agent for positive change in society. They wanted the state to provide more services, services they could not provide for themselves. As a result state expenditures increased. In 1915-1916, it cost $5 million to run state government. By 1930, the cost was $78 million. Most of this increase was due to increased spending on education and highways.

State government expanded by 1929 to include the highway patrol. At first patrolmen rode motorcycles, but by 1935 they drove cars.

The public school system expanded, and the state had to pay more and more of the cost. Rural high schools were opened. Compulsory school attendance increased both enrollments and expenses. In 1917, citizens voted to increase the school term from four to six months. Counties had to build more schools as they moved one-room schools into graded schools and began busing students. All of these changes cost more money. From 1901 to 1913, the state spent about $100,000 a year for schools. In 1929, the amount had risen to $5 million. Much of this money was obtained from an income tax started in 1921.

The state also took over the building and maintenance of roads. The counties continued to maintain local roads, but the state built and maintained about 10,000 miles of paved roads connecting all county seats and major towns. The counties paid for their roads with property taxes, while the state used gasoline and license taxes.

The state responded to the call for other services. In 1917, it created a welfare board to provide services for the insane, the deaf, the blind, children, and poor blacks. A department was established to regulate insurance companies and building and loan associations. A historical commission collected, preserved, and published the state's history. A library commission encouraged the establishment of local libraries and the circulation of books. A textbook commission prepared courses of study and approved textbooks for use in the schools.

To prevent local governments from going too deeply into debt, the state set up a local government commission. The state established **worker's compensation** to pay for accidental death or injuries in the workplace. To protect the public health and safety, the state examined and licensed certain professions. These professions included teachers, doctors, dentists, nurses, pharmacists, veterinarians, architects, accountants, embalmers, surveyors, and contractors. In 1929, the state created the highway patrol, mounted on motorcycles, to enforce motor vehicle laws. These developments attracted women into government.

WOMEN IN GOVERNMENT

For years, women had worked in government, but usually as clerks. In 1916, Minnie W. Leatherman managed the Library Commission and Daisy Denson the Board of Public Charities. As director of the North Carolina Geological and Economic Survey in 1917, Hattie M. Berry of Chapel Hill effectively lobbied for good roads. In 1920, Lillian Exum Clement Stafford, an Asheville lawyer, was the first woman elected to the legislature. In 1921, Kate Burr Johnson of Morganton directed the Board of Charities and Public Welfare. In 1925 and 1927, Julia Alexander and Carrie Lee McLean, both lawyers from Mecklenburg County, were elected to the state house of representatives. In 1930, Gertrude Dills McKee, a teacher and women's club leader from Sylva, was the first woman elected to the state senate. That same year, Lily Morehead Mebane, a cotton mill owner, was elected to the state house of representatives. By 1929, women were serving on about one-half of the boards and agencies of state government.

Lillian Exum Clement Stafford, a lawyer from Asheville, was, in 1920, the first woman elected to the General Assembly.

Do You Remember?
1. What accounted for most of the increased spending by state government in the early 1900s?
2. Name three new services that the government provided during the early 1900s.
3. In what year was the first woman elected to the state legislature? Who was she?

CHAPTER REVIEW

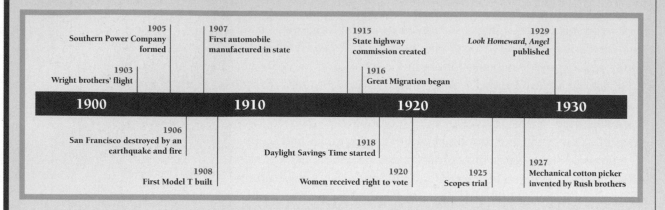

| 1905 Southern Power Company formed | 1907 First automobile manufactured in state | 1915 State highway commission created | 1929 *Look Homeward, Angel* published |
| 1903 Wright brothers' flight | | 1916 Great Migration began | |

1900   **1910**   **1920**   **1930**

1906 San Francisco destroyed by an earthquake and fire   1918 Daylight Savings Time started

1908 First Model T built   1920 Women received right to vote   1925 Scopes trial   1927 Mechanical cotton picker invented by Rush brothers

Reviewing People, Places, and Terms

Use each of the following terms in a sentence that describes some of the changes that took place in North Carolina in the early 1900s.

1. evolution
2. fundamentalist
3. hydroelectric
4. mass production
5. strike
6. Orville and Wilbur Wright

Understanding the Facts

1. How did the construction and improvement of roads and the increased use of motor vehicles help the education of children who lived in rural areas of the state?
2. What nickname was given to the state of North Carolina because of its road-building and road-improvement programs?
3. What new businesses developed as a result of the growing number of motor vehicles on the roads?
4. What was the "stretch-out" used in the textile mills?
5. In 1930, what were North Carolina's two major cash crops?
6. What led to the low farm prices in the 1920s?
7. Which science was directly affected by the theory of evolution?

8. List three well-known Tar Heel writers. For what is each best known?
9. How did the state finance the increased spending on education and highways in the 1920s?

Developing Critical Thinking

1. Why was the Wright brothers' first motor-powered flight at Kitty Hawk important?
2. How would your life be different without electric power?
3. The title of one of Thomas Wolfe's novels was *You Can't Go Home Again*. What do you suppose he meant by this?
4. "During the early 1900s, people began to believe that government could become an agent for positive change in society." Do you believe this has proven to be true? Why or why not?

Applying Your Skills

1. During the early 1900s, the value of North Carolina's tobacco products grew from $16 million to $413 million and the value of its furniture products grew from $2 million to $54 million. Which industry had the better growth rate?
2. In their first flight, the Wright brothers flew 120 feet in 12 seconds. What was the speed of the airplane in miles per hour?

3. Write a letter to your local power company requesting information about its hydroelectric plants. Then incorporate that information in a short report on the development and importance of these plants to North Carolina's economy. You might want to include the benefits of the lakes formed when the dams were built. Use maps, charts, and diagrams to help the reader better understand the information in your report.
4. O. Henry was known for his use of *irony*. Read one of O. Henry's short stories, such as "The Ransom of Red Chief" or "The Gift of the Magi." In what way is the story ironic?

Making Connections

1. Find out whether wind tunnels are used today. If so, how?

2. Cut a 2-inch-square piece of heavy paper. Put a straight pin through the center of the paper. Place a thread spool over the pin and paper. Hold the paper, pin, and spool in the palm of one hand. Blow through the top of the spool and see what happens. As you blow, take the supporting hand away. The paper should appear to stick to the spool the harder you blow. When you stop blowing, the paper and pin fall away. Why do you suppose this is so?
3. Give three reasons that led to the Great Migration.
4. What effects do you think the Great Migration had on North Carolina?

Tar Heel Trivia

- North Carolina's first radio station, WBT in Charlotte, began broadcasting in 1920. It was only the second radio station in the nation.

BUILDING SKILLS: USING ROAD MAPS

We are a mobile society. Most families own a motor vehicle of some sort, and some own more than one. We think nothing of getting in the car and going— to school or work, shopping, visiting, on vacation. We can probably navigate around our neighborhood or local area because we are so familiar with it. But if we are going to a new destination or just driving in unfamiliar territory, we might need some help.

Road maps provide information about the distances between specific locations, the types of highways, and connections to other roads. Travelers can purchase road maps at most bookstores, service stations, and convenience stores; they can sometimes get maps free of charge from tourist bureaus, chambers of commerce, and welcome centers.

Using a North Carolina highway map, plan a trip from your town or city to any one (or more) of the following destinations. Make sure that your destination is *at least* 3 hours or 150 miles away: Boone, Flat Rock, Mt. Gilead, Murfreesboro, Southport. Answer the following questions.

1. Which highways make up the shortest route to your destination?
2. What types of roads will you be traveling on (interstate highways, secondary roads, and so on)?
3. What is the distance in highway miles to your destination?
4. Assume that you travel to your destination at an average speed of 55 miles per hour. How long will the trip take if you do not make any stops? How long will the trip take if your average speed is 40 miles per hour?
5. If the trip requires more than 6 hours, where would you most likely spend the night after about 6 hours of driving time?
6. If your car averages 20 miles per gallon of gasoline, how many gallons will the trip require? What will be the cost of the gasoline if the average price is $1.10 per gallon?
7. List three kinds of information — other than route numbers and mileage indications — that you can find by looking at the map you are using.

CHAPTER TWENTY-TWO

NORTH CAROLINA IN DEPRESSION AND WAR

. . . the only thing we have to fear is fear itself—nameless, unreasoning, unjustified terror. . . .

— President Franklin D. Roosevelt

FROM 1929 TO 1945, NORTH CAROLINA experienced great suffering and change. The stock market crash of 1929 brought the worst economic depression the state had ever known. Agriculture and industry declined while unemployment was widespread. All levels of government tried to ease the suffering and bring about an economic recovery.

The nation had little success against the depression until Congress passed President Franklin D. Roosevelt's New Deal proposals. The New Deal gave people hope, but it did not end the depression. What ended it was America's entry into World War II.

THE GREAT DEPRESSION

From 1929 to 1942, the state and nation experienced a long and severe economic depression. A **depression** is a downturn in economic activity. Sales of goods and prices fall, manufacturing decreases, businesses close, banks fail, and people lose their jobs.

A SHAKY ECONOMY

Called "The Great Depression," it was the worst in the nation's history. There were several factors that combined to cause the Great Depression. Agriculture declined during the 1920s and weakened the economy. Farmers around the world grew too many products, which lowered the

Governor O. Max Gardner faced the worst problems of the depression in North Carolina from 1929 to 1933.

One cause of the depression was the rapidly increasing production of consumer goods that many people could not afford to buy.

prices farmers could get for them. Farmers had less money and could not pay their debts. When farmers could not repay their bank loans, the banks failed. Businesses that supplied goods to farmers had fewer sales; some could not continue to operate. Low farm prices, like the ripples on a pond, spread out to hurt others.

In the 1920s, the economy began producing more consumer goods. Before 1910, the economy mainly produced goods for industry, such as locomotives and machinery. After 1920, American industry began producing such items as cars, radios, and refrigerators. Workers, however, didn't earn enough to buy the products. For example, in North Carolina, the average weekly pay of textile workers was about $12. On those wages, they could not pay living expenses *and* buy a new car, the cheapest of which cost about $450. Some economists (specialists who study the economy) believe that this consumer economy grew too quickly. When it produced more consumer goods than people could buy, it had to cut back. This too had a ripple effect.

International trade (trade between countries) with the United States also declined in the 1920s. During World War I, the United States had loaned money to other nations. After the war, these nations began repaying the loans and, as a result, did not have the money to buy many American goods. In the 1920s, Congress also passed high tariffs. The tariffs made it difficult for foreign businesses to sell their products in America and thus get dollars with which to buy American products.

The American banking system was weak. Banking inspectors sometimes overlooked banking violations. Accounts were not insured. As a result, depositors could cause a "run" on a bank if they thought the bank might fail. A run took place when many depositors lined up to withdraw their money from the bank at the same time. A run could cause a bank to fail because banks rarely kept enough cash on hand to pay all their depositors at one time. Weak banks were allowed to continue their operations, which usually made them even weaker. When banks closed, the money in people's accounts was frozen, often for years.

The stock market was another weak part of the economy. A **stock market** is a place where the stock of corporations is bought and sold. The largest stock market was the New York Stock Exchange. Throughout the 1920s, millions of investors bought and sold stock. Investors usually bought stock at low prices, waited for the prices to rise, and then sold the stock at a profit. Stock prices went up and up. Westinghouse stock, for example, sold at $92 a share in March 1928. By September 1929, it sold at $313 a share.

On "Black Thursday," October 24, 1929, the stock market "crashed." On this day, stock prices plunged. A smaller crash occurred on October 29. By November 13, for example, that Westinghouse stock had fallen from $313 a share to $102 a share. Thousands of people lost money. Businesses began to cut back on production and employees. The Great Depression had begun.

October 24, 1929, was known as "Black Thursday" on Wall Street in New York City. There, stock prices dropped sharply and spread financial panic.

NORTH CAROLINA IN THE DEPRESSION

From 1929 to 1933, the depression got steadily worse in North Carolina. Agriculture was hardest hit. Cotton prices dropped from 17 to 6 cents a pound. Tobacco prices fell from 19 to 12 cents a pound. Total farm income in 1932 was less than half what it had been in 1929. Landowners pushed thousands of tenants from the land because farming was no longer profitable. Unable to make a living, many small farmers looked for work in nearby towns.

Industry declined. In the textile and furniture industries, for example, sales dropped by about one-half. Some factories were only open six months a year; others closed forever. Some industries cut production but remained profitable. The most profitable were the tobacco, electrical power, telephone, chemical, and paper companies.

As crop prices fell, land owners ejected many black tenant farmers from their farms.

The depression hit banks hard. From 1930 to 1933, over 190 North Carolina banks failed. Most of the failures were small, rural banks, which had loaned money mainly to farmers. Others closed because dishonest managers embezzled (stole) money. The worst bank failure in the state occurred in Asheville. The Central Bank and Trust Company had loaned money to investors to buy real estate. After the stock market crash, the bank was left holding titles to overpriced real estate. To try to save itself, the bank borrowed money from other banks. When Central Bank failed in 1930, eleven other banks failed also.

Many workers in the state lost their jobs. By 1932, over 144,000 workers in the state were unemployed. This caused great suffering and despair. Children of the unemployed did not go to school because they did not have shoes or proper clothes. Families went hungry. Many lived on a single food like rice or cornmeal for weeks.

EASING THE BURDEN

With earlier depressions, the economy had always begun to recover after a year or two. But this depression went on year after year.

President Herbert Hoover was the first president to use the power of the federal government to help the economy recover. One program, designed to help farmers, had the government buying large amounts of cotton, wheat, and other commodities. This would cause farm prices to rise. The government would then sell its commodities on the world market later, when prices rose. Unfortunately, the plan didn't work because the government bought too little of the commodities.

President Hoover approved a program that loaned federal money to needy businesses. He also supported public works projects, such as the building of post offices, parks, courthouses, and roads. These projects put many unemployed men back to work. Hoover also loaned money to the states for their own public works projects. North Carolina borrowed about $3 million to build highways, providing jobs for about 15,000 men. Hoover also used the government's stored wheat and cotton to provide flour and cloth for the needy. Hoover's programs helped but did not end the depression or provide adequate relief for the unemployed.

In North Carolina, falling revenues and the need to balance the budget limited what Governor O. Max Gardner could do. Like Hoover, Gardner believed that the state should not pay money to help the unemployed. He believed this was the responsibility of private agencies and local governments. Gardner also wanted the people to work for the **relief** (money and goods given to people in special need) they received. Governor Gardner thus tried to help without spending money. His Live-at-Home program encouraged farmers to grow gardens, can food, and raise the necessities they usually bought at the store. Home extension agents, led by Jane S. McKimmon, showed farm wives how to can food.

Many local agencies also helped. The most effective were the Red Cross and the Salvation Army. Hospitals provided free health care for the needy. Local governments paid men low wages to sweep streets, plant trees, drain swamps, cut firewood, and plant gardens. They also provided free lunches for needy children. Still, public and private relief efforts were not enough. What was needed was a program that coordinated efforts at all levels.

Jane S. McKimmon of Raleigh directed the state home demonstration service that taught farm women how to can food and thus feed their families.

Do You Remember?
1. What happens to the economy during a depression?
2. What is meant by a "run" on a bank?
3. What happened on "Black Thursday"?
4. What caused many banks in North Carolina to fail during the Great Depression?
5. What was Governor Gardner's Live-at-Home program?

THE NEW DEAL

In 1932, the people overwhelmingly elected Franklin D. Roosevelt president of the United States. Although he was from a wealthy family, Roosevelt had much sympathy for those less fortunate. President Roosevelt, who was unable to walk because of polio, projected an image of self-confidence and inspired Americans to overcome their problems.

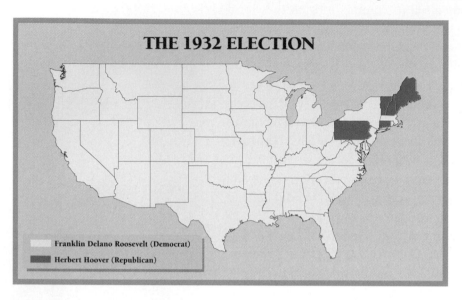

THE 1932 ELECTION

☐ Franklin Delano Roosevelt (Democrat)
■ Herbert Hoover (Republican)

The map above shows the overwhelming presidential victory Franklin D. Roosevelt, a Democrat, enjoyed in electoral votes when he ran against Herbert Hoover, a Republican, for president in 1932.

Roosevelt had no clear ideas about how to deal with the depression. At his urging, however, Congress passed a series of laws that came to be known as the **New Deal.** These laws were to bring about economic recovery, relieve the suffering of the unemployed, reform defects in the economy, and improve society.

ECONOMIC RECOVERY

The first objective of the New Deal was economic recovery—bringing the economy back to about the same level it had been in early 1929. The first need was to make sure the banking system was sound. On the day after his inauguration, President Roosevelt ordered all banks closed until government inspectors could examine them. In a few days, the banks that seemed sound reopened. The government loaned money to banks that were weak in order to make them stronger and prevent their failure.

Congress then passed a number of laws designed to help farmers. To increase farm prices, the government asked farmers to cut production. The Agricultural Adjustment Act (AAA) provided **price supports** (guaranteed higher prices) to farmers who agreed to cut back on their cotton and tobacco crops. In 1933, North Carolina's cotton farmers agreed, but world prices did not go higher than about one-half what they were before the depression.

At first, tobacco farmers did not want to cut production. But in the summer of 1933, tobacco prices were very low. The farmers met and agreed to cut production by 30 percent for the next two years. Tobacco prices rose from 1933 to 1935, and the farmers prospered. When the U.S. Supreme Court declared the AAA unconstitutional, Congress passed other laws to help farmers.

Congress also passed the National Industrial Recovery Act (NIRA). In North Carolina, the NIRA applied mainly to cotton textile manufacturers. To increase prices and profits, the law allowed them to regulate themselves by cutting production. The textile manufacturers agreed to reduce their hours of operation from 105 to 80 a week. They also promised workers a 40-hour week and a minimum wage of $12 a week. A **minimum wage** is the least amount an employer can pay an employee for a certain number of hours worked. Congress hoped this would put more people to work at higher wages. The law also permitted workers to organize themselves into labor unions, which would bargain collectively for higher wages. Workers joined the United Textile Workers of America union by the thousands.

The mill owners, however, did not treat workers fairly. They turned to the stretch-out again and ignored workers' complaints. The mill owners also tried to destroy the unions. They fired union members and black-listed them (put out the word that they should not be hired). In September 1934, some 65,000 textile workers went out on strike. They wanted the owners to recognize the union, to rehire fired union members, and to reduce the workweek to 30 hours.

As Franklin D. Roosevelt campaigned in 1932, he spread a feeling of optimism that times would get better.

FDR'S FIRESIDE CHATS

President Roosevelt's "fireside chats" did much to restore the morale of the American people.

Those who framed our government expected the House of Representatives to become the part of government closest to the people. After 1933, though, people expected the president to hear their pleas. This change occurred in part because President Franklin D. Roosevelt was an excellent communicator. In fact, he was so popular that the people elected him to four terms in office.

Roosevelt could attribute part of this popularity to his direct communication with the American people by radio. From 1933 to 1945, he spoke to the American people about thirty times. After the first program in 1933, a broadcaster called Roosevelt's talk a "fireside chat." The name stuck.

Why did these fireside chats resonate in the hearts of Americans? One reason is that Roosevelt referred to his listeners as "my friends," and he spoke like one friend to another. He used the simplest language and concrete examples. Roosevelt was personable, optimistic, and even charming. He instilled hope in the people. After calling attention to the opponents of his programs, he made references to American traditions. And, after every radio address, the national anthem was played. These techniques helped Roosevelt establish good rapport with the people and gained their support for his programs.

The strike eventually failed. The federal government was not willing to force the mills to recognize the union as the law required. Governor J. C. B. Ehringhaus called out the National Guard to intimidate the workers. The mill owners were willing to stay closed because they had more goods on hand than they could sell. The union, however, ran out of money and could not continue the strike.

Because the tobacco industry was very profitable, it did not want to go along with the NIRA. Just before the U. S. Supreme Court declared the NIRA unconstitutional, the tobacco industry owners agreed to a 40-hour workweek and a minimum wage of 30 to 35 cents an hour. Three-fourths of the tobacco workers were African Americans. The tobacco companies paid them the lower wage of 30 cents an hour.

To replace the NIRA, Congress quickly passed several laws to protect workers. The Wagner Act of 1935 guaranteed workers the right of **collective bargaining.** It also outlawed many unfair labor practices (such as firing union members) and set up a board to enforce the law. When workers asked for a union in a mill, the board oversaw the election. Congress hoped workers would organize and fight for higher wages. They could then buy more consumer goods and help the economy recover.

Farmers picking up their money after a tobacco auction in 1938. Federal controls on the production of tobacco made tobacco farming more profitable.

UNEMPLOYMENT IN THE GREAT DEPRESSION

Soup kitchens and breadlines provided help for thousands of unemployed people during the Depression.

The worst aspect of an economic depression is the suffering it causes the unemployed. Today, an unemployment rate of 5-6 percent is considered acceptable. In 1933, the worst year of the depression, the unemployment rate was 25 percent. African Americans experienced the greatest loss of jobs. By 1933, half of all black workers were unemployed. Many single women were fired so that their jobs could go to men or women with children to support.

People who lost their jobs for a long time suffered greatly. They lost their sense of personal worth, blamed themselves for their misfortune, and avoided friends. Those who accepted a handout felt ashamed and became indifferent. Families with children suffered more; many families went hungry and lacked adequate medical care. Children without clothes and shoes did not want to attend school.

Before 1932, people believed that families, churches, and private agencies like the Red Cross should help the jobless. If more help were needed, the unemployed should turn to local governments. People did not believe that the state or federal government should be involved. But so many people were unemployed and hungry that this idea changed — and brought a fundamental change in government. State and federal relief agencies were established to spend money on public projects, mainly to give work to the unemployed. Other safety nets to help the unfortunate in society include programs like Social Security, the Job Corps, Medicaid, and food stamps.

The Fair Labor Standards Act established the 40-hour workweek and a minimum wage of 25 cents an hour.

Unfortunately, these new laws did little to help workers get higher wages. The Tobacco Workers International Union, for example, was recognized by only two of the three tobacco companies. In 1937, the Congress of Industrial Organizations tried unsuccessfully to organize textile workers. By 1939, only about 4 percent of the state's industrial workers belonged to a union. As a result, North Carolina workers' wages were among the lowest.

Do You Remember?
1. What was the "New Deal"?
2. How did the government revive the banking system?
3. What did the Wagner Act do?

RELIEF

A number of New Deal measures were designed to help the unemployed. The Emergency Relief Administration gave money to the states to provide jobs, food, and clothes. North Carolina received about $41 million, providing jobs for 300,000 workers. The Public Works Administration (PWA) built useful public projects to help the economy recover. One of these projects was the Blue Ridge Parkway. The Civil Works Administration put 70,000 North Carolinians to work improving roads, repairing schoolhouses, and building sanitary facilities in rural areas. In 1935, Congress created the Works Progress Administration (WPA) to provide jobs for workers as quickly as possible. WPA projects included building school buildings, parks, roads, and airports. The WPA employed about 40,000 Tar Heels a month and spent some $174 million in the state by 1942.

In 1933, the Civilian Conservation Corps (CCC) was established. Run by the army, this agency established about 1,300 camps across the country for unemployed young men just out of high school. The CCC put some 2.5 million young men to work preserving the soil and purifying the water. It was very successful. In the Midwest, the CCC helped plant over 200

The WPA employed out-of-work playwrights and actors. In 1937 famous playwright Paul Green (seated center) worked with a WPA theater group.

Below: The Civilian Conservation Corps put thousands of unemployed young men to work on conservation projects. *Right:* Construction on the Blue Ridge Parkway provided jobs for many unemployed people. *Opposite page:* The completed Blue Ridge Parkway, a federal scenic highway, helped increase tourism in the mountains. It is still one of the most popular attractions in the area.

million trees to hold the soil. North Carolina had over a hundred CCC camps, many for blacks. Cherokee youth also served from their homes on the Qualla Reservation. A number of camps operated in the new Great Smoky Mountains National Park. Young men built trails and campsites where logging railroads and lumber mills had operated only a few years before.

These relief efforts did not reach those people who could not work—children, the blind, widows with small children, and the elderly. In addition, workers needed some protection against unemployment. To meet these needs, Congress passed the **Social Security Act** in 1935. The federal government would provide old-age insurance from taxes paid by both workers and employers. The states, helped by the federal government, would meet the other needs. By 1937, North Carolina passed the laws needed to provide unemployment insurance for workers and help for the needy.

ECONOMIC REFORMS

The New Deal also tried to correct weaknesses in the economy that may have added to the depression. One important reform was the creation of the Federal Deposit Insurance Corporation (FDIC). The FDIC insured depositors' accounts in banks. That is, if the bank failed, the FDIC would see to it that depositors would get their money back.

Congress also tried to reform the stock exchanges, where investigators found many abuses. One abuse was *insider trading.* People "inside" corporations or stock exchanges used information they knew about their companies to make fortunes or avoid losses. Another abuse was giving out false information about corporations in order to sell their stocks. Congress also discovered that investors bought too much stock with borrowed money. The Securities Exchange Act of 1934 was passed to eliminate these abuses.

Two leaders in the development of electricity for farms were E.C. Branson (above) and Clarence Poe (above right). Their work led to the establishment of the Rural Electrification Administration.

Another reform involved the regulation of electrical utility holding companies. Some thirteen holding companies controlled three-fourths of the power companies in the nation. Carolina Power and Light, for example, was controlled by a holding company. Investors in these holding companies took the power companies' profits out of the business. This left little money for expansion and led to higher rates for customers. Congress passed a law abolishing all electrical holding companies. The law also permitted the government to organize power companies into regional systems to provide power more cheaply and efficiently.

SOCIAL IMPROVEMENT

The New Deal went beyond trying to solve the problems of the depression. It also tried to improve people's lives.

Congress started a huge social improvement project when it created the **Tennessee Valley Authority** (TVA). The Tennessee River valley stretched through seven states. The TVA built a number of dams on the Tennessee River and its tributaries. The dams provided cheap electricity, improved the navigation of the river, attracted industry, controlled flooding, improved farming, and created recreational areas.

The TVA was also involved in **conservation** (the management of a natural resource to prevent its destruction). The "dust bowl" in Oklahoma showed what happened when drought and wind eroded the soil. People could no longer live on the land. The TVA built model farms to show farmers how to conserve the soil and restore its fertility.

The TVA helped North Carolina somewhat. It regulated the water flow from North Carolina reservoirs into the Tennessee River. To control the amount of silt in streams, the TVA helped farmers plant trees on eroded land. During World War II, the TVA built Fontana dam and lake, the highest dam and longest lake in the state. The dam generated power for a factory at Alcoa, Tennessee, that made aluminum for warplanes.

Another New Deal program involved **rural electrification.** In the 1920s, power companies ran lines mainly to towns and cities. Because the rural population was spread out, power lines were expensive to build and maintain. In 1935, 11 percent of the nation's farmers had electricity; but only 3 percent in North Carolina did.

Two Tar Heel farm leaders fought to bring electricity to farmers in the 1920s. E. C. Branson, a professor at the University of North Carolina, and Clarence Poe, editor of the *Progressive Farmer* in Raleigh, asked the power companies to run rural lines. When the companies refused, Branson and Poe urged farmers to form cooperatives to extend their own power lines and buy power wholesale. A **cooperative** is an organization owned by and operated for those using its services. One cooperative was created near Shelby. At the urging of Governor Ehringhaus, the 1935 legislature created a state agency to get power companies to extend power lines to rural areas or to help farmers create cooperatives. North Carolina was the first state to do this.

The largest TVA project in North Carolina was the construction of the Fontana Dam. The dam helped provide electricity, flood control, and recreation.

That same year, Congress created the Rural Electrification Authority (REA) for the same purposes. The REA loaned over $300 million to farmers' cooperatives across the country. By 1940, about 25 percent of the state's farmers had electricity. Electric water pumps, lights, milking machines, fences, and appliances made farm life much easier.

Do You Remember?

1. Name four government agencies established to put people to work during the Great Depression.
2. How did the government try to help those who could not work?
3. What good did the TVA do?

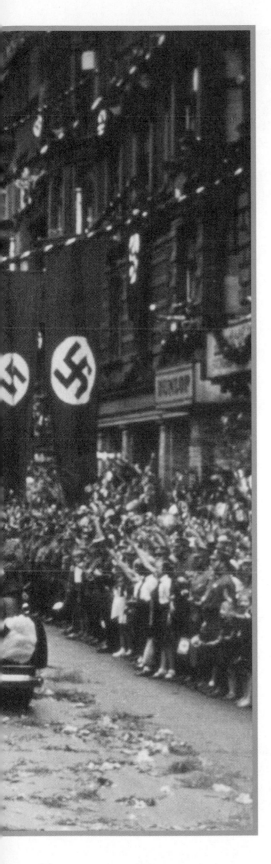

THE SECOND WORLD WAR

As the United States struggled with the problems of the Great Depression, international relations got worse. Four nations were trying to expand their power and territory. These nations were Japan, Italy, Germany, and the Soviet Union.

INCREASING TENSIONS IN THE FAR EAST AND EUROPE

Between 1931 and 1941, Japan's actions placed her on a collision course with the United States. In 1931, the Japanese Army took over Manchuria, a province of China. This violated the Open Door Policy, by which all nations were free to trade with China. In 1937, Japan seized most of the coastal area of China. Then, in 1938, the Japanese announced a "New Order in East Asia." Japan was an industrial nation, but lacked basic raw materials like coal and iron ore. She would now take them from China and not let other nations trade there. Japan slammed shut the Open Door and bolted it.

Under Benito Mussolini, Italy also wanted to expand its power and territory. In 1935, Mussolini invaded the African nation of Ethiopia and quickly defeated its poorly equipped army. In 1939, Italian troops sailed across the Adriatic Sea to conquer Albania. The nations of the world proved powerless to stop the aggression.

In 1933, Adolf Hitler came to power in Germany. He promised to make Germany a great nation again and to regain the territory it had lost after World War I. Hitler, however, was a **dictator** (a ruler who has complete control over a country). He and his followers (called Nazis) silenced all opponents.

Hitler's racial policies were especially hateful to Americans. Hitler believed that Aryans (white Indo-Europeans) were superior to all other races. Because he believed that German Jews were responsible for Germany's defeat in World War I, he began to persecute them. Hitler also hated the Slavic peoples of Eastern Europe and the Soviet Union. Millions of his political enemies, European Jews, and other so-called inferior people died in Hitler's concentration camps.

In Hitler's quest for power, he first tried to unite all of the Germanic people in Europe. In 1936, he seized the Rhineland (the area between Germany and France). Next, he forced the government of Austria to turn over power to the Austrian Nazi party. In 1938, Hitler threatened to seize a part of Czechoslovakia called the Sudetenland, where some 3 million

Adolf Hitler returned to Germany in triumph after France fell to the German army in June 1940. Many Germans saw Hitler as restoring the power and prestige lost after World War I.

In 1939 these German troops in a half-track helped seize Prague, Czechoslovakia, after Hitler promised not to do so.

Germans lived. Great Britain and France were alarmed. But they agreed to let Hitler have the Sudetenland on the condition that he seize no more territory. Hitler, however, took over the rest of Czechoslovakia in 1939.

Do You Remember?
1. What four nations were trying to expand their power in the 1930s?
2. Why did Japan feel the need to expand her territory?
3. What racist views did Hitler have?

THE WAR BEGINS

Hitler next turned against Poland. He charged that Poland was abusing Polish Germans and made plans to invade. He also made an agreement with the Soviet Union that neither would attack the other. At the same time, they secretly agreed to divide Poland between them.

Great Britain had a defensive alliance with Poland. On September 1, 1939, German troops invaded Poland. Shortly thereafter, Great Britain, France, Australia, New Zealand, Canada, and South Africa declared war on Germany. But before these countries could send troops, German and Soviet forces had divided Poland between them. The Soviet Army also took over Estonia, Latvia, and Lithuania and invaded Finland. **World War II** had begun.

From October 1939 to April 1940, little fighting took place in Europe. But Hitler struck again in April 1940. The German Army conquered Denmark and Norway in a month. In May and June, German troops overran Holland, Belgium, Luxembourg, and a large part of France. The British Army retreated from the continent across the English Channel, leaving their weapons behind. Hitler made plans to invade Great Britain. His air force heavily bombed British cities from August through December 1940. The Royal Air Force, however, was able to hold off the German bombers, and Great Britain was not invaded.

President Roosevelt watched with alarm as Japan, Italy, the Soviet Union, and Germany carved up the world. He felt he had to do all he could to save Great Britain from invasion. Only the British could stop Hitler from crossing the Atlantic Ocean.

Although Roosevelt had proclaimed America's neutrality in 1939, he looked for ways to help the British. He first, however, had to overcome strong antiwar feelings in America. In the 1930s, Congress passed neutrality acts to keep the United States out of another war. One of these acts would not allow the president to sell arms to any warring nation. In 1939, Roosevelt asked for and got a new law that allowed Great Britain and France to buy arms if they paid cash and carried them in their own ships.

In 1940 German troops captured France in about two months with a new kind of warfare called "blitzkrieg." These German troops were sightseeing in Paris.

In 1940, Roosevelt gave Great Britain old weapons and traded fifty destroyers for British bases in the Western Hemisphere.

In early 1941, when the British ran out of cash with which to buy American supplies, Congress authorized Roosevelt to lend or lease arms to them. After Germany turned on and invaded the Soviet Union in June 1941, Roosevelt gave lend-lease aid to the Soviets also. To make sure the supplies got to them, Roosevelt built air bases in Greenland and Iceland. Planes from these bases tracked German submarines. Roosevelt also ordered the U.S. Navy to convoy (escort) British ships part of the way across the Atlantic. In late 1941, German submarines sank an American destroyer. The United States was engaged in an undeclared war that was about to become a declared one.

AMERICA ENTERS THE WAR

Meanwhile, American-Japanese relations got worse. To protest Japanese aggression, the United States stopped exporting airplanes, metals, aircraft parts, and aviation gasoline to Japan. Roosevelt also revoked the trade treaty with Japan. After Japan invaded French Indochina in 1941, he seized all Japanese property in the United States.

Badly needing the oil that Roosevelt had cut off, Japan decided to invade the Dutch East Indies (now Indonesia) in late 1941. The only force that could stop her was the U.S. Navy stationed in Hawaii. The Japanese made a surprise attack on the fleet at Pearl Harbor on December 7, 1941, causing great damage. On December 8, the United States declared war on Japan and entered World War II. A few days later, Germany and Italy declared war on the United States.

NORTH CAROLINA IN WORLD WAR II

American participation in World War II lasted from December 1941 to September 1945. During that time, North Carolina made many contributions to the war effort.

In 1940, 450,000 Tar Heels registered for the nation's first peacetime draft. In all, about 362,000 North Carolinians served in the military. Some 258,000 people served in the Army; 90,000 in the Navy; 13,000 in the Marines; and 1,000 in the Coast Guard. About 7,000 women volunteered for military service. The war was costly. About 7,000 Tar Heels were killed in combat. Thousands more were wounded.

North Carolina was the site for several major military training bases. Fort Bragg was the largest artillery post in the world, housing about 100,000 troops by 1945. Camp Mackall near Hoffman specialized in

On December 7, 1941, Japanese warplanes launched from carriers attacked the U.S. naval base at Pearl Harbor on the Hawaiian island of Oahu.

During World War II, Governor J. Melville Broughton entertained servicemen and women at the governor's mansion in Raleigh.

airborne troop training. The 82nd, 101st, 11th, and 13th airborne divisions trained there. The Marines trained at Camp Lejeune, which opened in 1942 near Jacksonville. Cherry Point Marine Air Base trained aviators. Camps Battle, Butner, and Davis trained infantry for the Army while Camp Sutton trained engineers. Training for Air Force aviators was held at Seymour-Johnson, Pope, Laurinburg-Maxton, Knollwood, and Raleigh-Durham fields. The Navy trained aviators at Elizabeth City. Many colleges and universities had training programs for the military.

The military unit most closely associated with North Carolina was the 30th Division. Landing in France in June 1944, the 30th broke through German lines at St. Lo. It raced across France and Belgium and into Germany to meet Russian troops at the Elbe. Men of the 30th were heavily decorated for bravery. Many Tar Heels also served in the 4th and 80th divisions.

There was fear that important places in the state would be **sabotaged** (deliberately damaged or destroyed). Shipyards and military bases on the coast were heavily guarded. Across the state, guards stood watch at dams, power plants, textile mills, railroad freight yards, munitions factories, and other locations.

POW CAMPS IN NORTH CAROLINA

During World War II, American and Allied forces captured large numbers of enemy soldiers in Europe and in North Africa. Not all of these POWs (prisoners of war) were held in Europe. By 1943, tens of thousands of German and Italian POWs were being transported to the United States and put in over six hundred prison camps scattered throughout the country. The camps or compounds usually consisted of rows of tents surrounded by double barbed-wire fences. Armed American guards patroled outside the fences and stood watch in nearby wooden watchtowers.

Eighteen of these camps were located in North Carolina. Most of the prisoners in North Carolina's camps were Germans, over 10,000 of them. In fact, the first German

prisoners of war in the United States were the crew of a German submarine that sank off North Carolina's Outer Banks in the spring of 1942. These POWs were confined at Fort Bragg in Cumberland County. Other POW camps were located in Forsyth, Granville, Hertford, Martin, New Hanover, Onslow, Pender, Richmond, Scotland, and Union counties.

With the United States at war and with millions of American men away in the military, there was a serious civilian labor shortage in many places. Prisoners of war were paid 80 cents a day to work in jobs where these shortages existed. The POWs often planted and harvested farm crops. They also worked in forestry, fighting fires, planting trees, and cutting and clearing brush for roadways. After a day's work, the POWs would return to their camps. Compared to their military comrades imprisoned in Europe and to American POWs held in enemy camps, German and Italian prisoners were very well treated in the United States.

These German prisoners of war worked at Fort Bragg. After some submarines were sunk, the crews were captured and imprisoned in North Carolina. Prisoners of war were paid 80 cents a day for work where labor shortages existed.

Below: The state's industries helped produce war materials. The Wilmington shipyard built ships for the war effort. Over 300 ships were built in North Carolina shipyards. **Opposite page, above:** *The battleship* USS North Carolina *fought many battles against the Japanese Navy in the Pacific during World War II.* **Opposite page, below:** *U.S. Marines at Camp Lejeune practiced going over the side of a ship into a landing craft.*

From 1941 to 1943, German submarines operated freely off the North Carolina coast. By August 1942, they had sunk over twenty ships. So many ships were sunk off Cape Hatteras that it was called "Torpedo Junction." At night, people on shore could sometimes see burning tankers far out at sea. The military ordered "blackouts" (periods when no lights could be seen) along the coast so the submarines could not see the outlines of ships. The Coast Guard and the Civil Air Patrol searched for submarines along the coast, sinking or capturing a few.

North Carolina's textile mills turned out tents, uniforms, blankets, towels, socks, and cloth. Shipyards at Wilmington, New Bern, and Elizabeth City built over three hundred ships for the Navy and Merchant Marine. Lumber mills provided boards for the new military camps. Miners reopened old mines to supply one-half of the nation's mica, which was used in electronic parts. Olivine from the state became a source of magnesium, a lightweight metal. Other industries supplied parts for radios, radars, and airplanes.

Farmers in the state grew more of every crop. The state ranked third in the nation in the value of commodities produced. The value of her crops in 1944 was double what it had been in 1929. The shortage of farm work-

ers made it necessary to release high school students from classes to harvest the crops. Increased production in agriculture and industry ended the depression.

Because of the war effort, civilian goods were in short supply. Meat, butter, canned goods, sugar, coffee, shoes, gasoline, and tires were all rationed. Rationing limited purchases to one pair of shoes a year, 2.5 pounds of meat a week, and 5 gallons of gasoline a week. Hoarding (saving a supply for future use) was a serious offense. The government controlled prices of these scarce goods. The scarcity of food led people to plant "victory" gardens and raise their own livestock.

Do You Remember?

1. Why did President Roosevelt feel so strongly about helping the British?
2. In what ways did the United States protest Japanese aggression in the Far East?
3. What event finally led the United States to enter the war?
4. Name two contributions North Carolina made towards the war effort.
5. Why was the area off Cape Hatteras called "Torpedo Junction"?

CHAPTER · REVIEW

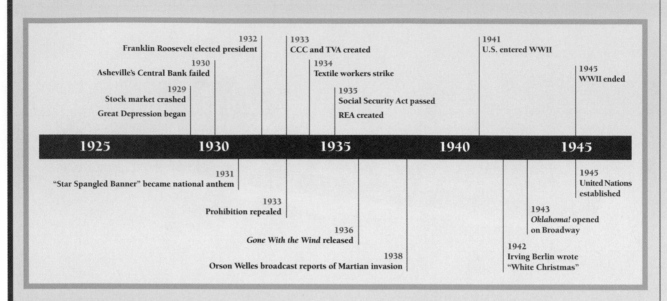

1932
Franklin Roosevelt elected president

1930
Asheville's Central Bank failed

1929
Stock market crashed
Great Depression began

1933
CCC and TVA created

1934
Textile workers strike

1935
Social Security Act passed
REA created

1941
U.S. entered WWII

1945
WWII ended

| 1925 | 1930 | 1935 | 1940 | 1945 |

1931
"Star Spangled Banner" became national anthem

1933
Prohibition repealed

1936
Gone With the Wind released

1938
Orson Welles broadcast reports of Martian invasion

1942
Irving Berlin wrote
"White Christmas"

1943
Oklahoma! opened
on Broadway

1945
United Nations
established

Reviewing People, Places, and Terms

Use the following terms in a paragraph describing the United States during the Great Depression and World War II.

1. depression
2. dictator
3. New Deal
4. ration
5. relief
6. Social Security Act
7. stock market

Understanding the Facts

1. Name three problems in the American economy that led to the Great Depression.
2. When did the great stock market "crash" occur? What happened to the economy when that crash occurred?
3. Name two ways in which President Hoover tried to help the economy recover.
4. When President Roosevelt took office, what parts of the economy did he try to stabilize (make sound) first?

5. What New Deal laws were intended to help the nation's workers?
6. When and by what government program were Fontana Dam and Fontana Lake built?
7. What event occurred on December 7, 1941?
8. What finally brought the United States out of the Great Depression?

Developing Critical Thinking

1. Do you believe that another "great depression" is possible in this country today? Why or why not?
2. Do you think a guaranteed minimum wage is a good policy? Why or why not?
3. What might have been the impact on history had the United States not entered World War II?
4. Why was rationing necessary in the United States during World War II?

Applying Your Skills

1. The number of shares of stock traded on the New York Stock Exchange for the years from 1920 to 1935 is as follows: 1920–227, 636,000; 1925–459,717,623; 1929–1,124,800,410; 1930–

810,632,546; and 1935-381,635,752. Prepare a line graph using this information. What does the graph suggest about the nation's attitude toward buying stock after the stock market crash?

2. Prepare a short report on one of the New Deal agencies or laws. Include information on when the law was passed or the agency created, its purpose, and its effectiveness.

3. Locate Tokyo, Japan; Rome, Italy; Berlin, Germany; and Moscow, Russia on a world map or globe. What are the coordinates (longitude and latitude) of these cities? Which is closest to Raleigh, North Carolina?

Making Connections

1. Why were President Roosevelt's fireside chats so important to the American people?

2. Recent presidents have continued the practice of "fireside chats" with the American people. Listen to one radio broadcast by the president. Prepare a short report that describes the topic, the president's presentation, and your reaction to the broadcast.

3. Ask someone you know who lived through the Great Depression what their most lingering memory of that period is. Share your findings with the class.

4. During the depression, many people turned down help because they were asked to "take charity." Do you think the attitude toward accepting public help is different today? Why or why not?

Tar Heel Trivia

- As late as 1945, only 5 percent of the farms in North Carolina had telephones.

⚬ BUILDING SKILLS: DETECTING BIAS ⚬

Everyone has certain opinions or ideas about certain topics or subjects. For this reason, written material is not always objective (free from the writer's personal opinions). Even though a writer may try hard to be objective, what he or she writes or says may show *bias*, a highly personal, and sometimes unreasonable, opinion about something or someone. Bias can be either for or against an idea or individual.

To be a good and thoughtful citizen, you need to learn how to detect bias in both written and oral materials and in materials from both the past and the present. Asking the following questions may help you.

- When and why was the material written or the statement made?
- Did the writer or speaker use certain phrases for emotional impact or try to play on your emotions rather than present facts?
- Does the writer or speaker tend to show one group as good and the other group as evil?

Try This! In the early 1930s, over 15 million men were out of work. Many who had lost everything took to the road in search of something better. Read the following statements and identify any bias you believe exists.

Why, it's the best education in the world for those boys, that traveling around! They get more experience in a few months than they would in years at school.
(Henry Ford)

They are the people whom our post offices label "address unknown," and whom we call transients. Every group in society is represented in their ranks. . . . We think of nomads of the desert—now we have nomads of the Depression.
(Newton D. Baker, reporter for the *New York Times*)

Many of those who are most boisterous now in clamor for work have either struck on the jobs they had or don't want to work at all, and are utilizing the occasion to swell the communistic chorus.
(John E. Edggerton, National Association of Manufacturers)

UNIT 9

NORTH CAROLINA AFTER 1945

A FTER WORLD WAR II, North Carolina became much more urban. It also became the most industrialized state in the nation. The state made major efforts to improve public and higher education. The arts flourished as the state supported a symphony, art and history museums, and numerous historic sites. Excellent literary works came from the pens of Tar Heel authors. Television and sports grabbed public attention.

The civil rights movement resulted in the integration of schools, colleges, sports, hotels, restaurants, and jobs. Sit-ins that young people staged in Greensboro helped open up public eating places to African Americans. Native Americans and women began their own civil rights movements.

A number of challenges face North Carolina as it enters a new century. North Carolinians, however, have a blueprint for the future and look forward to a better quality of life.

Left: As the Charlotte skyline indicates, the state has become more urban since 1945. **Above:** The University of North Carolina at Chapel Hill is symbolic of the rapid expansion of higher education in North Carolina since 1945.

CHAPTER TWENTY-THREE

NORTH CAROLINA IN THE POSTWAR PERIOD

I believe that government is charged with the duty of providing the means for the fulfillment of the human spirit and the fruitful use of all talents.
— Governor Terry Sanford

THE LAST HALF OF THE TWENTIETH CENTURY was a time of many changes. The state became more urban, as over half the people now live in towns and cities. The state improved the quality of public schools and created many community colleges. The state colleges merged into one university system

and first-rate private colleges arose. Support for the fine arts and literature became part of the growing urban culture. Popular culture became centered around television and sports.

The downtown buildings in Winston-Salem reflect the urban growth that such industries as tobacco and banking have brought to the city.

AN URBAN LAND

Until the 1970s, North Carolina was considered to be a rural state. Over half the people lived outside cities. By 1980, though, over half the people lived in cities. This change can be seen in the growth of the six largest cities. From 1940 to 2000, Charlotte's population grew from 100,000 to 541,000; Raleigh's from 47,000 to 276,000; Greensboro's from 60,000 to 224,000; Durham's from 60,000 to 187,000; and Winston-Salem's from 80,000 to 186,000. In those years, Fayetteville's population jumped from 17,000 to 121,000.

This urban growth has occurred largely in the Piedmont Crescent. It was made possible by good transportation and the growth of manufacturing and business. Yet the six largest cities contained less than one-fifth of the state's population in 2000. North Carolina is still a "small-town" state, and that fact helps explain its conservative values. Although Charlotte has become a national banking center, it is small compared to major cities in the South.

EXPANDING URBAN AREAS

The rapid growth of the cities began during World War II. Military training sites located near Fayetteville, Chapel Hill, Charlotte, Oxford, and Jacksonville caused those areas to grow. The federal government spent $2 billion producing war supplies in North Carolina. This greatly helped the state's economy and brought new types of industry to the cities. These new industries included food products, printing and publishing, chemicals, rubber and plastic products, and machinery.

After the war, the use of machines revolutionized agriculture. The tractor, cotton picker, combine, and other equipment made it possible for fewer farmers to do the work of many. In addition, as new **synthetic** (man-made) fibers replaced cotton for clothing, cotton acreage shrank. Mecklenburg County, for example, had 80,000 acres of cotton in 1946 but only 1,800 acres in 1966. Farmers left the farms for the towns and cities, seeking work.

Good roads, public transportation, and automobiles allowed people to live in the **suburbs** (residential areas outside city limits). The cities then annexed the suburbs to increase their revenues. From 1950 to 1999, Charlotte and Greensboro expanded greatly. Charlotte's land area grew from 30 to 240 square miles and Greensboro's from 18 to 109 square miles.

Improved transportation encouraged businesses to relocate in North Carolina's cities. Raleigh, Charlotte, and Greensboro built municipal airports in the 1920s, but it was not until after 1945 that air travel really boomed. In the early 1960s, jet travel made it possible to fly

Above: As Charlotte's urban population grew, more people moved to the suburbs. Top: Rayon manufacturing at Enka helped provide jobs for suburban workers.

from Asheville to Charlotte in 30 minutes and from Asheville to Raleigh in 60 minutes. Today, Charlotte, Greensboro, and Raleigh are regional hubs (centers) for major airlines.

The rise of trucking lines also brought North Carolina's cities "closer" to the rest of the country. Trucking companies provided dependable one-day service to New York or Miami. By the 1950s, North Carolina was an important base for trucking operations. Charlotte alone had seven major trucking lines. Also helping the trucking industry was the construction of interstate highways. **Interstate highways** are limited-access multilane highways that extend through more than one state and are,

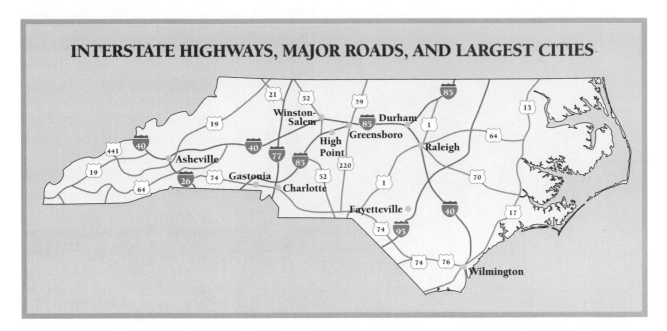

INTERSTATE HIGHWAYS, MAJOR ROADS, AND LARGEST CITIES

therefore, part of the federal highway system. Five interstates, built since the 1950s, link the major cities of the state with one another and with other states. Interstate 40 runs east-west, while Interstates 26, 95, and 77 run north-south. Interstate 85 runs through the Piedmont Crescent, connecting Charlotte and Durham.

Cities also began to build meeting places to attract out-of-town visitors. In the late 1940s, North Carolina State College in Raleigh built an enclosed coliseum (stadium) for sports and entertainment events. In 1955, the city of Charlotte opened an auditorium and a coliseum. These buildings have hosted sports events, merchandising shows, symphonies, circuses, and other events.

PROBLEMS IN THE CITIES

With the growth of the cities also came problems. One of the first was increased traffic. Vehicles crowded the city streets, and there was never enough parking. In the 1950s, cities built four-lane thoroughfares (main roads) to carry the increased traffic. Later, the state built bypasses and beltways (highways around cities and towns) to cut down on the traffic in town. These too have become crowded, especially as workers **commute** (go to and come from workplaces). Recently, cities have urged people to park outside town and use public transportation.

As the suburbs grew and traffic clogged the central city, businesses moved to the suburbs. **Shopping centers** (groups of retail stores with large parking areas) first appeared in the 1950s, malls arose in the 1970s. These shopping areas offered abundant free parking and close, one-stop shopping. As fewer people came to the downtown area, the central city

Top: This map depicts the transportation network that is part of the federal highway system.
Above: Both the state and federal governments built better highways to improve the flow of traffic and commerce. This photograph shows the paving of Interstate 95.

declined and crime increased. People no longer felt safe and moved to the suburbs, causing even more decline.

When people first moved into the cities, residential areas became racially segregated. Many of these neighborhoods were poor. In the 1950s and 1960s, the federal government gave money to cities to improve housing. From 1965 to 1968, for example, Charlotte used this money to tear down 3,300 run-down buildings, which housed mainly African Americans. However, the city built only 425 houses and apartments to replace them. The urban poor had to find housing where they could and to form new communities from scratch.

The cities tried to revitalize (give new life to) their downtown areas. Charlotte built a civic center, parking garages, and walkways between a new government center and businesses. It urged citizens to restore homes in certain areas. In Raleigh, the city closed the main business street and made it a pedestrian mall. Asheville turned hotels into apartments and got tourist-related businesses to move into vacant downtown buildings. Winston-Salem built a convention center downtown, while Greensboro built a coliseum.

President Lyndon Johnson's Great Society sought to eliminate slums, as in Charlotte (top), and to restore inner city housing, as in Charlotte's Fourth Ward (above).

Do You Remember?

1. What is the state's largest city?
2. Name one reason why the state's farm population decreased after World War II.
3. Why did businesses move to the suburbs?

THE DEFEAT OF POLIO

One of childhood's most devastating diseases is poliomyelitis. Polio, as it is known, is caused by a virus that attacks the nervous system, which in turn paralyzes muscles. When respiratory muscles are paralyzed, the result can be death. In 1921, Franklin D. Roosevelt, who later became president, contracted polio. His legs were paralyzed and he could walk only by using leg braces and crutches.

In 1935, research showed that immunization against the disease was possible. To direct the fight against polio, Roosevelt in 1938 founded the organization that would later become the March of Dimes. Scientists at Harvard found a way to grow large quantities of the polio virus, the first step toward producing antibodies. Dr. Jonas E. Salk was the first to develop a vaccine using an inactive virus. Salk's polio vaccine was field-tested in 1954, found to be effective, and mass inoculations began.

At the same time, a Russian immigrant named Albert B. Sabin developed an oral vaccine containing live viruses. Sabin's oral vaccine was successfully tested in 1957. These two vaccines are responsible for virtually eliminating the scourge of polio from children in the United States and most of the developed world.

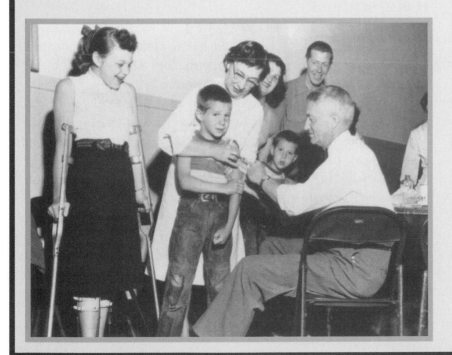

Above: After years of research, Dr. Jonas Salk developed a vaccine against poliomyelitis. *Left:* A San Diego boy receives a polio shot during the first mass inoculation following approval of the vaccine in 1955. The boy's sister, a polio victim, looks on as the inoculations take place.

The North Carolina School of the Arts was founded in Winston-Salem in 1963. Today the school has an enrollment of over one thousand students.

EDUCATION

Since World War II, great progress has been made in organizing and improving all levels of education in the state.

PUBLIC SCHOOLS

In 1945, the state's public schools were weak, racially segregated, and poorly funded. By many measures, including performance on national tests, the state's schools ranked near the bottom nationally. But by the end of the century, the schools had improved.

Since 1945, local governments have been combining several small one- and two-teacher schools into fewer, larger schools. These **consolidated schools** enabled communities to provide better programs and facilities for less money per student. Many of these larger schools hired special teachers for art, music, business, and other areas. Because they mainly taught one subject, these teachers knew their subject matter well.

A strong educational leader arose in 1960 when the people elected Terry Sanford governor and charged him with improving the schools. The popular support for education arose partly because of an achievement by the former Soviet Union. In 1957, the Soviets launched the world's first **satellite** (a man-made object that orbits Earth). It was called "Sputnik" and could be seen in North Carolina's skies. The Soviets' success hurt American pride and led to an interest in improving science education.

Governor Sanford broadened the sales tax to raise the money needed to improve education. At Winston-Salem, he established the summer Governor's School to encourage to high school students to attend college. Governor Sanford started kindergartens for the children of the poor so they could learn to count and write their ABCs. He insisted that students with special needs attend regular school where they could develop their potential and have contact with other children.

Governor Sanford also created the School of the Arts, which offers college-level programs to students gifted in the **fine arts** (art, music, dance, and theater). The legislature was unwilling to fund a school for "toe dancing" and "banjer picking." It did agree to create the school if private funds could be found. When Winston-Salem donated land and buildings, the school was located there.

In the 1960s, the federal government began to provide money for education. Schools used that money to hire teachers' aides, to purchase library books and equipment, and to set up special programs. For example, the Head Start program provided preschool classes for underprivileged children. In exchange for a free education, students in the Teacher Corps agreed to teach in schools that served the poor.

In the 1980s, the state tried to improve the quality of education. Teachers had to achieve higher scores on national teacher exams in order to be certified. Those teaching outside their subject areas were required to return to college for more preparation. To address the problem of teacher "burnout," Governor James Hunt established the North Carolina Center for the Advancement of Teaching in Cullowhee. This unique center offers a free week of intellectual enrichment for good teachers. The university system also helped by requiring that certain student teachers take more courses in subject areas.

Above: *Governor Terry Sanford brought about many educational reforms in the state.* **Left:** *North Carolina became the first state to establish a statewide high school for students talented in science and mathematics. It is located in Durham.*

To improve education even further, the state set up the Basic Education Program in 1985. This program raised teachers' salaries, reduced class sizes, and provided teachers with aides. Foreign language instruction was introduced in the elementary schools. Students were also required to pass more standardized tests. Students who did not pass were not promoted. To reinforce the Basic Education Program, the university system required incoming students to have taken courses in math, science, history, English, and a foreign language.

In 1981, Governor Hunt established the North Carolina School of Science and Mathematics in Durham, a free residential school for gifted high school students. Students take a full high school curriculum with special emphasis on math and the sciences. Many of the courses are college-level courses. This school has had more National Merit scholars than any other high school in the state.

In 1996, the legislature authorized local groups to establish state-supported charter schools. A **charter school** is an independent public school of choice exempted from many of the traditional rules and regulations that public schools must follow. The school operates under a charter from the local school district. Experimental in nature, charter schools are expected to develop new approaches that can help improve public schools. Their work is still being evaluated.

COMMUNITY COLLEGES

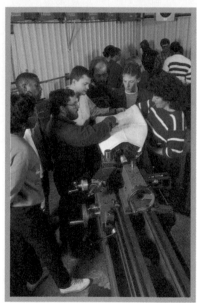

The state established over fifty technical and community colleges to teach practical subjects (above). The largest of these two-year schools is Central Piedmont Community College in Charlotte (top).

The state has established a number of community and technical colleges since 1945. These colleges offer special technical programs plus beginning-level college courses. Their students are those who wish to learn a technical or business skill, adults who want to re-enter the workforce, students who need to work while attending school, and those who want to attend a smaller, less costly college that is nearby.

In the 1950s, Governor Luther Hodges tried to attract new industries to the state. Industries, however, did not want to relocate to North Carolina because the state's workers were not well educated and had few skills. Governor Hodges encouraged local governments to establish industrial education centers to train workers needed by industry. The state supplied part of the funds for these schools. By 1963, there were twenty of these schools enrolling about 20,000 students. They offered programs to train carpenters, plumbers, brick masons, mechanics, technicians, practical nurses, and secretaries.

When Governor Sanford took office, the state supported twenty industrial education centers, five community colleges, and one technical institute. There was little planning among the schools for current or future needs. Sanford and the legislature created the Department of Community Colleges. Its purpose was to plan and coordinate the establishment of a system of community colleges and technical institutes. By 1978, the state supported fifty-eight of these two-year schools. The largest is Central Piedmont Community College in Charlotte.

HIGHER EDUCATION

By the 1990s, North Carolina was known for the high quality of its colleges and universities. The University of North Carolina at Chapel Hill and Duke University are usually rated among the top twenty-five universities in the nation. North Carolina State University at Raleigh, Wake Forest University, and Davidson College also have national reputations.

The increasing wealth of the state and gifts from private citizens made possible many good institutions. The Duke family used tobacco profits to endow (give money to) Trinity College and persuade it to move from Randolph County to Durham in 1892. In 1924, Trinity was renamed Duke University in honor of the Duke family. In the 1950s, money from the R. J. Reynolds family was used to build a new campus for Wake Forest College in Winston-Salem and raise it to university status. The University of North Carolina received large contributions from the Morehead, Kenan, Hill, Davis, and other families.

An important achievement has been the creation of a state university system. The first university system, created in 1931, included the University of North Carolina, North Carolina State College, and Women's College. Frank Porter Graham was the first president of the university system. Graham controlled the development of programs at all three institutions. For example, it was Graham who decided that engineering and agricultural programs would be located at North Carolina State College, thus making it the leading technical school.

By the mid-1950s, the state was expecting an increase in the number of students in the state's colleges. **Baby boomers**, those born right after 1945, would begin entering college in 1963. The state needed some way to coordinate the growth of its twelve senior colleges and five community colleges. To do this, the state created the Board of Higher Education. The board planned to raise the community colleges in Wilmington, Charlotte, and Asheville to university status. The supporters of Western Carolina, East Carolina, North Carolina Agricultural and Technical, and

Top: Frank P. Graham led the consolidated University of North Carolina to national prominence. ***Above:*** Governor Robert W. Scott established a state university system to promote educational quality and avoid waste.

The desire to grow by Western Carolina University at Cullowhee (above) and similar schools led to the creation of the statewide university system in 1971.

Appalachian bypassed the board and had the legislature declare them universities. Nearly a decade of controversy resulted.

By 1970, state-supported higher education was in chaos. The state did not have the money to develop high-quality universities at all the state schools. Even if it tried, programs would be duplicated and waste would result. The state seemed headed toward schools that were only average.

Elected in 1968, Governor Robert W. Scott was determined to bring order from the chaos. He said, "A halt must be called to the infighting, the maneuvering, the overlapping, the duplication" in higher education. No one, however, could agree how this could be done. A special session of the legislature in 1971 developed a system stronger than anyone thought possible. It created a Board of Governors over all sixteen state colleges and universities. The Board had the power to control, supervise, and manage all institutions. Each institution kept its own name and had a separate board of trustees that reported to the Board of Governors. The name of this new system was "The University of North Carolina."

Do You Remember?

1. What happened to one- and two-teacher schools after World War II?
2. What was the purpose of industrial education centers?
3. How many institutions are part of The University of North Carolina system?

CULTURAL DEVELOPMENTS

The increasing population and wealth of the state after World War II brought an interest in cultural activities and popular entertainment.

FINE ARTS AND HISTORY

State support for the fine arts has grown. Founded in the early 1930s, the North Carolina Symphony is supported in part by state monies and tours the state annually, bringing music to thousands of schoolchildren. The state was also among the first to support an art collection. After establishing a state art society and an art gallery, the 1947 legislature appropriated $1 million for the purchase of art. To display the collections of ancient to contemporary art, the state opened the North Carolina Museum of Art in 1956. The state also contributes to the North Carolina Civic Ballet Company and the School of the Arts in Winston-Salem.

Support for the fine arts is not limited to the state. Charlotte, Greensboro, and Asheville have organized local symphony orchestras and choral groups. Many cities have set up art galleries and museums. Two in particular are the Museum of Early Southern Decorative Arts in Winston-Salem and the Mint Museum in Charlotte.

The North Carolina Museum of Art in Raleigh houses the state's art collections.

DISCOVERY PLACE

Exhibits at Discovery Place in Charlotte (above and opposite page) are designed to involve visitors and increase their understanding and interest in science and technology.

In recent decades, the number of museums, historic sites, and organizations committed to preserving North Carolina's past has grown significantly. In small towns and in large cities, from the state's mountains to its coast, many North Carolinians are working to gather and preserve information about their local cultures and natural resources.

Today's museums are no longer facilities that simply display the remains or dusty fragments of our history. Many are educational extensions of our schools. They provide "hands-on" experiences for visitors and demonstrate the cultural diversity and natural wonders of our state and of the world. Generally, museums here and elsewhere are divided into three types: art, social history, and science.

One of the most popular science museums in North Carolina, and in the Southeast, is Discovery Place. Located in Charlotte, Discovery Place is an award-winning, hands-on museum that attracts hundreds of thousands of visitors each year. Inside this museum, visitors learn about science and technology through the senses, by actually doing, not just looking. Exhibits demonstrate the natural laws of motion, chemical reactions, or the intricate workings of the human body. Here visitors can generate their own electricity by peddling a bicycle, peer inside a giant kaleidoscope of mirrors, experiment with computers, or take part in any number of other activities.

A centerpiece in Discovery Place is the three-story reproduction of a tropical rain forest, complete with a waterfall, live exotic birds, and plants. Elsewhere, in a series of aquariums, visitors can use their hands to examine marine life in the "touch pool." One visitor dazzled by the museum's activities wrote, "Discovery Place offers something for every visitor, young and old. It is a perfect place for exploring and wondering and discovering . . . again and again and again."

The theater has also become more popular. Professional and amateur productions take place in many towns across the state. The summer Flat Rock Playhouse is a notable professional group. Other quality theater groups include the Carolina Playmakers at UNC-Chapel Hill, the Raleigh Little Theater, and the Southern Appalachian Repertory Theater. The Blowing Rock Stage Company also operates in the summer. North Caro-

lina has a number of outdoor dramas. In addition to *The Lost Colony* at Manteo, *Unto These Hills* has been produced in Cherokee every summer since 1950. The latter play is the story of the Cherokee in North Carolina about the time of their removal to Oklahoma. The outdoor drama *Horn in the West*, produced at Boone, tells the story of the frontier and Daniel Boone.

Above: *Some of the underground tunnels at the Reed Gold Mine have been restored and opened for tours.*
Right: *The Mint Museum of Art is housed in what was once the Charlotte branch of the U.S. Mint. One exhibit in the museum features gold coins minted in Charlotte.*

Since 1945, North Carolina has produced many outstanding writers and poets. Inglis Fletcher wrote a series of twelve novels on episodes from North Carolina's history. One of the better-known titles is *Lusty Wind for Carolina*. Legett Blythe's *Alexandriana* was set in the state's revolutionary years. The setting for Burke Davis's two historical novels (*The Ragged Ones* and *Yorktown*) is Lord Cornwallis's campaigns in the Carolinas and Virginia. John Ehle of Asheville found time not only to become educational adviser to Governor Sanford, but also to write a series of six novels about his native mountains.

Reynolds Price, a professor at Duke University, is considered to be a major American writer. His novel *Kate Varden* won national praise. Fred

Chappell is a professor at UNC-Greensboro and a native of Haywood County. Chappell has written both poetry and fiction. His factional account of adolescent years in the mountains is entitled *I Am One of You Forever*.

The state has benefited by the publication of several high-quality newspapers. The three daily newspapers with the highest circulations are the Raleigh *News and Observer*, the *Greensboro Daily News*, and the *Charlotte Observer*.

North Carolinians have also taken pains to preserve their past. The state's Division of Archives and History has a national reputation for excellence. Located in Raleigh, this agency has preserved state and local records, set up a historical museum, opened historic sites, and published records and histories about the state. Among its more popular historic sites are the Reed Gold Mine, an early English ship named the *Elizabeth II*, and Fort Fisher. Private agencies also operate historic sites. Old Salem, for example, is a restored Moravian settlement. New Bern is home to Tryon Palace, the first government building in North Carolina. Orton Plantation near Wilmington, an early rice plantation, also attracts many visitors. The Biltmore Estate near Asheville was the summer home of George Vanderbilt, heir to a railroad fortune.

ENTERTAINMENT

Sports have become very popular since 1945. Football and basketball teams from the "Big Four" universities—Wake Forest, Duke, North Carolina, and North Carolina State—attract thousands of spectators every year. The high quality of basketball competition is shown in the eight national championships won by Duke, North Carolina, and North Carolina State between 1957 and 2001. Demand for seats has been so great that these schools have enlarged their sports facilities.

North Carolina has its share of professional sports. Minor league baseball has long been widespread. Since the 1940s, stock car racing has become popular. Motor speedways near Charlotte and Rockingham hold national stock car races. Smaller race tracks around the state hold local races. As more people from the North move into the state, they bring their love of ice hockey and help develop teams. Fans can watch national competition in other sports. Charlotte has a professional football team. The annual golf tournament in Greensboro attracts golfers of national rank.

The offerings of radio and television have become part of popular culture. In 1920, ham radio operators in Charlotte experimented with voice communications. Their experiments resulted in the first commercial radio station in North Carolina—station WBT. Other radio stations soon operated in the larger cities. In the 1940s, people thrilled to such radio

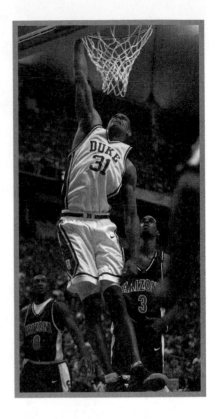

Duke's Blue Devils won the men's NCAA basketball championship in 2001.

North Carolina native Andy Griffith (left) starred in one of the most popular TV series of the 1960s, "The Andy Griffith Show," set in the fictional North Carolina town of Mayberry.

shows as "Inner Sanctum," "The Lone Ranger," and "Grand Ole Opry." Radio also brought news and sports into the home. By the 1950s, many small towns had radio stations and produced their own programs, usually music. FM (frequency modulation) brought static-free radio by the 1950s. Today, radio offers a wide range of musical programs, as well as news, talk, and sports programs.

Television was a more powerful instrument of popular culture. The state had barely a thousand receivers when station WBT-TV of Charlotte started broadcasting in 1949. This medium caught on quickly, drawing people away from radio and the movies. Shows like "Omnibus," "Gunsmoke," "The Jack Benny Show," "Bonanza," "The Twilight Zone," "Star Trek," "I Love Lucy," "All in the Family," and "Sixty Minutes" entertained viewers. Millions of children have grown up on the daily shows of "Captain Kangaroo" and "Sesame Street." An educational channel, WUNC-TV, began broadcasting in the 1950s from the University of North Carolina. North Carolinians who achieved national reputations in newscasting include Edward R. Murrow, David Brinkley, and Charles Kuralt.

Technical changes in television gave it even greater impact. At first, television pictures were black and white. In 1967, WBT-TV began broadcasting in color. Cable television soon came to urban areas. By the 1980s, satellites and dish antennas brought nationwide programming into the home. Viewers could select from channels that specialized in news, movies, sports, or educational programs. Television has truly brought the world into the living room.

Do You Remember?

1. What are some of the fine arts organizations for which the state legislature supplies funds?
2. Name three historic sites operated by state or private agencies.
3. What was the first television station in North Carolina?

THE COLD WAR

The "Cold War" was the name given to the unfriendly relations between the United States and the Soviet Union after World War II. This Cold War was fought not with bullets but with words, diplomatic moves, and proxies.

The hostility arose for several reasons. At the end of the war, the United States and the Soviet Union were the two most powerful countries in the world. The United States expected the Soviet Union to permit free elections in the East European countries it occupied. Instead, the Soviets held them in an iron grip. Former British Prime Minister Winston Churchill likened it to an "iron curtain."

The Soviets believed that communism would triumph over democracy and capitalism, and they supported communist revolutions in other nations. The United States thus feared for its security. The United States adopted a foreign policy called "containment," which was intended to prevent the Soviet Union from expanding its control over other nations. As part of this policy, the United States formed military alliances with nations on both sides of the Soviet Union. Containment led the United States into wars in Korea and Vietnam, a confrontation over nuclear weapons in Cuba, and the "arms race."

The Cold War ended with the breakup of the Soviet Union in the 1980s and Russia's movement toward democratic government. The fear of nuclear war was lessened, but regional conflicts are emerging all over the world.

For almost thirty years, the Berlin Wall was a symbol of the Cold War. In November 1989, East and West German citizens tore the wall down.

CHAPTER REVIEW

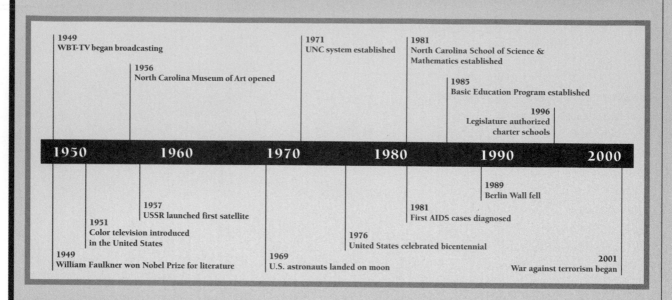

1949 WBT-TV began broadcasting		1971 UNC system established	1981 North Carolina School of Science & Mathematics established
1956 North Carolina Museum of Art opened			1985 Basic Education Program established
			1996 Legislature authorized charter schools

1950   1960   1970   1980   1990   2000

			1989 Berlin Wall fell
1957 USSR launched first satellite		1981 First AIDS cases diagnosed
1951 Color television introduced in the United States		1976 United States celebrated bicentennial
1949 William Faulkner won Nobel Prize for literature	1969 U.S. astronauts landed on moon	2001 War against terrorism began

Reviewing People, Places, and Terms

Use the following terms in a paragraph that describes the growth of North Carolina's cities after World War II.

commute
interstate highway
shopping center
suburb

Use the following terms in a paragraph that describes the improvements made to education in North Carolina in the postwar period.

baby boomers
charter schools
consolidated schools
fine arts

Understanding the Facts

1. Where can most of North Carolina's urban population be found?
2. What were some of the problems that accompanied the rapid growth of North Carolina's cities in the years after World War II?
3. In what ways have cities tried to revitalize their downtown areas?
4. What event led people to support improved education in the 1960s?
5. What is the purpose of the North Carolina School of Science and Mathematics?
6. In the early 1960s, what town donated land and buildings to establish North Carolina's School of the Arts?
7. What types of programs are offered by technical and community colleges?
8. Why did Trinity College change its name? What did it change its name to?
9. The outdoor drama *Horn in the West* tells the story of what famous frontiersman?
10. What are the state's "Big Four" universities? Where are they located?

Developing Critical Thinking

1. How do you think cars contributed to the decline of downtown areas in large cities? Do you think there is a way to reverse this situation? Why or why not?

2. What do you think are the major problems in inner cities today? What could be done to solve those problems?
3. What do you consider to be North Carolina's most important contribution to the nation?
4. Today, sporting events are a fixture on national television. Why do you think sports have become so popular in our society in recent years?
5. Do you believe that television has changed American life? If so, how?

Applying Your Skills

1. Using the information in this chapter and from other resources, make a list of the sixteen schools that make up the University of North Carolina system. Locate those schools on a state map.
2. Contact a local radio or television station. Find out when the station began operation and what type of programming it broadcasts. Share the information with your classmates.
3. Several public universities in the state were founded to serve certain groups of students, although today they serve students of all races. Prepare a report on the history of one of these schools: North Carolina Central University, Pembroke State University, or Elizabeth City State University. Include in your report a timeline that highlights the school's history.

4. Prepare a short report on one of the North Carolina writers mentioned in this chapter.

Making Connections

1. Find out which diseases have been virtually eliminated in the United States.
2. Interview someone who remembers the polio epidemics of the postwar period. What precautions did people take then?
3. Do you think the United States finally "won" the Cold War? Why or why not?
4. What problems have developed for the countries that once made up the Soviet Union?

Tar Heel Trivia

• While living in the Executive Mansion, Governor Robert W. Scott replaced a bed that had once been used by Governor Daniel Fowle, who died in office. Soon after replacing the bed, Governor Scott began to hear a strange knocking in his bedroom each night around 10 o'clock. He decided it was Governor Fowle's ghost looking for his bed!

• Eight North Carolina teams have won the men's NCAA basketball championship: The University of North Carolina at Chapel Hill (1957, 1982, 1993), North Carolina State University (1974, 1983), and Duke University (1991, 1992, 2001).

BUILDING SKILLS: DECISION MAKING

You will find it easier to make decisions if you follow a step-by-step process. The steps in the decision-making process are:
1. Identify the problem.
2. List the different alternatives for dealing with the problem.
3. Evaluate each alternative. That is, identify the pros and cons of each alternative.
4. Choose one alternative. In other words, make a decision.
5. Act on your decision.
6. Evaluate your decision.

Try This! Use the steps in the decision-making process to solve the following problem. Describe the actions you would take at each step.

Assume that you live in an area next to a city of 30,000 people. You attend the county schools. The adjoining city is thinking about annexing the area in which you live (adding your area to the city). Most of the residents of your area moved there because they wanted a more rural way of life, liked the schools, and were taxed less. If you get annexed, all that will change. What steps could you take to prevent the annexation of your area?

CHAPTER TWENTY-FOUR

THE CIVIL RIGHTS MOVEMENT

In the past we have had to swallow the insults, smile at the pain, and quench the spirit of human dignity throbbing in our breast. We had to act in some many ways as though we believe in our own inferiority in order to get along and survive. This day is over.

— Samuel Proctor, president of North Carolina Agricultural and Technical College

ALTHOUGH BLACKS BECAME CITIZENS of the United States in 1868, they did not enjoy the full rights of citizens. Beginning in the 1940s, African Americans made greater efforts to obtain the rights long denied to them. These efforts became the *civil rights movement*. Its leaders pressed for jobs, voting rights, admission to all-white schools, equal access to public transportation and accommodations, and an end to segregation in all areas of life.

The phrase *civil rights movement* can also be applied to the struggles by Native Americans and women.

THE BEGINNINGS OF THE CIVIL RIGHTS MOVEMENT

In 1868, the Fourteenth Amendment to the U.S. Constitution made blacks citizens of the United States. It also placed restrictions on the states to make sure they did not take away from blacks their rights as citizens. For example, a state could not have separate sets of laws for blacks and for whites. A state could not take away a person's life, liberty, or property without proper legal steps. In 1870, the Fifteenth Amendment ensured that blacks had the right to vote.

These rights of citizens are called **civil rights**. There is no complete list of them. However, most people include the following: free speech, freedom of religion, access to courts, trial by a jury of one's peers (equals),

The Jim Crow laws permitted separate but "equal" public facilities like the waiting room in this bus station. Veterans returning from the war were less willing to accept laws that segregated blacks and whites.

property ownership, voting if qualified, access to jobs, privacy, and the ability to travel wherever one wishes inside the country.

Despite the passage of the Fourteenth and Fifteenth amendments, African Americans were denied many of their rights in North Carolina and in other states. After years of slavery, many whites believed that blacks were inferior and should be kept separate. They did not want blacks mixing with them on an equal basis. Whites feared interracial marriage (marriage between members of different races), and the state constitution prohibited it.

A 1900 amendment to the state constitution denied qualified blacks the right to vote. The state required voters to pass a literacy test and pay a poll tax (a tax to be able to vote). North Carolina finally abolished the poll tax in 1923, but it kept the literacy test.

SEPARATE BUT EQUAL

The Fourteenth Amendment to the U.S. Constitution (1868) prohibited states from denying citizens the equal protection of the laws. But many states passed *Jim Crow laws* that required separate public facilities for each race. These facilities included restrooms, water fountains, railroad cars, waiting rooms, and schools. In 1896, the U.S. Supreme Court created the **separate-but-equal concept** with its ruling in *Plessy v. Ferguson* (see Chapter 19). States could require separate facilities for African Americans if they were equal to facilities used by whites.

While the states legislated separate facilities, they were rarely equal. This was especially true of schools, where African American students had much inferior buildings and equipment. Local governments also banned African Americans from swimming pools, golf courses, and recreation areas although their taxes helped support these facilities.

Private businesses were also segregated. White-owned restaurants and hotels would not accommodate black customers. They hired African Americans for only the lowliest jobs. Variety stores sold goods to all races but forbade black customers from eating at their lunch counters. Movie houses either refused African Americans admission or seated them in segregated balconies.

AFRICAN AMERICAN POLITICAL ORGANIZATIONS

In the early 1900s, African Americans began to organize to fight for their civil rights and to end America's segregated society. The best-known group was the National Association for the Advancement of Colored People (NAACP). One of the NAACP's tactics was to bring lawsuits against states and cities that had laws discriminating against blacks.

The Congress of Racial Equality (CORE) was founded in Chicago in 1942. Members of this organization believed in nonviolence. In 1943,

CORE staged sit-ins at restaurants in Chicago. A **sit-in** occurred when people entered a restaurant or other public facility and refused to leave until their demands were heard. In 1947, CORE staged the first "freedom ride" to protest the segregation of bus terminals. CORE later conducted voter registration drives in the South and in the urban ghettos of the North. A **ghetto** is a section of a city where members of a minority group live, usually because of social or economic reasons.

The Southern Christian Leadership Conference (SCLC) was an organization of churches serving African Americans. Founded in 1957, the group believed in confronting racial discrimination directly and peacefully. The founder and main leader of the SCLC was the Reverend Martin Luther King, Jr. Influenced by the ideas of Thoreau, Gandhi, and Jesus, Dr. King believed in reaching out in peace and love to oppressors of blacks.

Jim Crow laws governed the everyday activities of southern blacks. As seen here, there were separate water fountains for blacks and for whites.

Do You Remember?
1. List three rights of U.S. citizens.
2. Name three important civil rights organizations.

NORTH CAROLINA MUTUAL LIFE INSURANCE COMPANY

At one time, North Carolina Mutual Life Insurance Company of Durham was the largest black-owned, black-operated business in the world. Under its motto "Merciful to All," North Carolina Mutual was originally established to provide "relief to the widows and orphans, of the sick, to those injured by accident, and for the burial of the dead." The company began operating in 1899 with capital of $394. Today, it controls hundreds of millions of dollars in assets and manages billions of dollars in insurance coverage.

The company's high-rise headquarters in Durham stands as a monument to three African Americans who founded the business and were responsible for its early success. John Merrick, a former slave, is generally regarded as the founder of the company. Also instrumental in starting and managing the business were Dr. Aaron M. Moore and Charles Clinton Spaulding. Dr. Moore was Durham's first black physician and the founder of Lincoln Hospital. Spaulding became the leading figure in directing North Carolina Mutual's early development. A native of Columbus County, Spaulding was the president of the company from 1923 to 1952. He was also an enthusiastic supporter and promoter of African American enterprise, education, and the early civil rights movement.

In a time noted for its white supremacy campaigns, disfranchisement of black voters, and rigid segregation, the success of these men emphasized in the African American community a policy of "self-help, racial solidarity, and moral uplift."

Opposite page: John Merrick, right, was founder of North Carolina Mutual Life. Charles Clinton Spaulding, center, was president from 1923 to 1952. **Above:** Asa Timothy Spaulding, president from 1959 to 1967, in front of the company headquarters in Durham.

THE BLACK CABINET

Perhaps the most prominent person in Roosevelt's black cabinet was Mary McLeod Bethune, seen here with First Lady Eleanor Roosevelt. In 1936, Bethune was appointed to the Office of Minority Affairs in the National Youth Administration. She was also on the Advisory Committee to the Women's Army Corps.

From 1862 to 1932, African American voters largely supported the Republican party. In the twentieth century, however, the Republican party used black votes but gave black leaders few positions in government.

When Franklin D. Roosevelt became president in 1933, he wanted to attract African American voters to the Democratic party. During the 1930s, he appointed over one hundred African American leaders to significant government positions. These leaders were mainly professionals, not politicians. They included editors, lawyers, social workers, and educators. Two of the more influential were Mary McLeod Bethune, president of Bethune-Cookman College in Florida, and Robert C. Weaver, later the first African American cabinet member under President Lyndon Johnson.

Collectively, these scores of government officers became known as the "black cabinet." Appointed mainly as advisors to federal departments, they never met as a body. Only a few even talked to President Roosevelt. Yet the black cabinet played an important role in government. It gave African Americans sympathetic points of contact with their government. The members also helped African Americans secure better treatment: equal wages in the textile industry, admission to unions, aid to students, and more relief jobs. Their work also led to more African American workers being employed in the federal government and with federal contractors.

All of these activities helped lead to a historic shift of African American voters from the Republican to the Democratic party.

PRESIDENTIAL SUPPORT FOR CIVIL RIGHTS

Black political organizations first looked to the federal government for help. In the 1930s, President Franklin D. Roosevelt appointed a number of African Americans to high government positions to advise him on their needs. One of these was Lawrence Augustus Oxley from North Carolina. Oxley worked in the Department of Labor in Washington

During World War II, however, African Americans were placed in segregated military units. In southern training camps, black troops met much discrimination. Most war industry jobs went to whites. To protest this treatment, A. Philip Randolph, president of a black railroad workers'

union, planned a march on Washington for June 1941. To head off the march, President Roosevelt agreed to form a Fair Employment Practices Committee. The committee encouraged war industries to hire blacks. By the war's end, African Americans were working in every war industry.

The president also helped African Americans get better positions in the military. He had Benjamin O. Davis promoted to general, the first African American to reach that position. He ordered a flying school and officer training units established at a few black colleges, including North Carolina A&T.

In 1945, Harry S Truman became president when Roosevelt died. President Truman was determined to protect civil rights. He appointed a Committee on Civil Rights, which recommended ways in which the federal government could help secure rights for African Americans. In 1948, Truman ordered the federal government to disregard race when hiring people. He also ordered the military to abolish segregated units. By the time of the Korean War (1950-1953), blacks and whites served together in the same units.

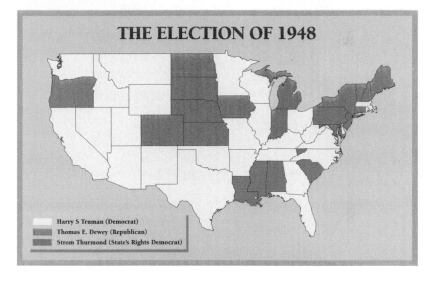

THE ELECTION OF 1948

Harry S Truman (Democrat)
Thomas E. Dewey (Republican)
Strom Thurmond (State's Rights Democrat)

*Top: President Truman surprised the press and won a very narrow victory in the 1948 election despite a southern backlash against some of his policies. Truman ordered the armed services integrated and supported fair employment for blacks. **Above:** This map shows the results of the electoral college vote in the 1948 election.*

Rosa Parks chose to submit to arrest and go to court rather than give up her seat on a bus.

Truman's actions, supported by the Democratic party, caused a political revolt. Southern Democrats, upset over Truman's support for civil rights, formed the States' Rights Democratic party. Everyone thought this split in the Democratic party would lead to Truman's defeat in the 1948 election. Instead, he won. African Americans overwhelmingly joined the Democratic party because of Truman's civil rights stand. The African American vote in three states helped give Truman the margin of victory.

Republican President Dwight D. Eisenhower, Truman's successor, also supported civil rights. During the 1950s, whites killed several civil rights protesters in the South. Alarmed, President Eisenhower asked Congress to pass a civil rights act, the first since 1875. Led by Lyndon B. Johnson of Texas, Congress did so. The Civil Rights Act of 1957 established a Civil Rights Commission, which looked into the condition of civil rights. The Act also created a federal government agency to act on civil rights violations. Last, it encouraged African Americans to vote.

EARLY PROTESTS AND DEMONSTRATIONS

Throughout most of the first half of this century, the inability of African Americans to use many public accommodations reminded them daily of their inferior place in society. During World War II, CORE **picketed** (protested outside) hotels and restaurants in major northern and western cities. Most of the places that were picketed opened their doors to African Americans. For example, by 1956, hotels and restaurants in Washington, D.C., were almost completely integrated. **Integration** is the process of bringing different groups (races) into society as equals.

This was not the case in most of the South. In 1955, in Montgomery, Alabama, when a tired Rosa Parks refused to give up her seat on a bus to a white person who was standing, she was arrested. Blacks came to her defense. She and others organized a boycott of the city's buses. The Reverend Martin Luther King, Jr., first came to national attention in this struggle. The boycott soon spread to Tallahassee, Florida. It ended when the U.S. Supreme Court ruled that segregation on buses was unconstitutional.

From left to right, Leroy Frasier, John Lewis Brandon, and Ralph Frasier of Durham were, in 1955, the first black undergraduates admitted to the University of North Carolina at Chapel Hill.

EDUCATION AND INTEGRATION

North Carolina's public schools and universities were completely segregated before 1950. Many university programs had no counterparts in black colleges. Qualified African American students who wanted a program not available in a black college could secure a tuition grant from the state to attend college in another state. The state had established a law school at the North Carolina College for Negroes in Durham to avoid integrating the law school in Chapel Hill. NAACP lawyers brought federal lawsuits to show that segregated colleges and schools were not equal.

Education and the Federal Courts

A case arose in North Carolina in 1950 when Floyd McKissick of Asheville applied for admission to the University of North Carolina law school in Chapel Hill. The university denied him admission, arguing that state law required him to attend the law school in Durham. McKissick appealed to a federal court,

THE NAACP AND THE FOURTEENTH AMENDMENT

These lawyers successfully argued the Brown case before the U.S. Supreme Court. Thurgood Marshall, in the middle, became a Supreme Court justice himself.

The Fourteenth Amendment to the U.S. Constitution required states to treat people equally under the law. But in 1896, the U.S. Supreme Court ruled in *Plessy v. Ferguson* (see page 410) that separate facilities could be provided for blacks if they were equal to those provided for whites. In a 1938 case (*Gaines v. Missouri*), the Court further ruled that states had to provide equal educational facilities for all citizens within the state.

By the late 1930s, the National Association for the Advancement of Colored People (NAACP) decided to use the Fourteenth Amendment to show that separate facilities were rarely equal. The NAACP determined that it would be easier to prove the inequality between all-black and all-white law schools. Thurgood Marshall led those efforts.

In 1950, the NAACP supported Herman Sweatt's application to the University of Texas law school. Texas had a separate law school for blacks, but the U.S. Supreme Court reasoned that the University of Texas law school had better facilities and a better faculty and would provide the opportunity for Sweatt to associate with influential whites. The Court ordered Sweatt admitted.

Similar reasoning was used to strike down segregated public schools. In the 1954 *Brown v. Board of Education* case, the Court ruled that segregated schools could never be equal. It reasoned that segregated schools caused black students to feel inferior, an argument advanced by NAACP lawyers. Thus did the NAACP use the courts to secure equal treatment in education for African Americans.

which ordered him admitted to the university law school in 1951. Following McKissick's lead twenty-four African Americans were admitted to professional programs in the university by 1954. Then, in 1955, the university began admitting black undergraduates.

Another federal court case arose in Kansas and other states that had great consequences for North Carolina. In 1951, Linda Brown's father tried to enroll her in a white-only school four blocks from her home. School authorities refused her admission, and the NAACP sued to have her admitted on the grounds that she was denied the equal protection of Kansas law. In the 1954 *Brown v. Board of Education* decision, the U.S. Supreme Court ruled the separate-but-equal concept of the *Plessy* case to be unconstitutional. The following year, the court ruled in *Brown II* that states should integrate their schools with "all deliberate speed."

The Pearsall Plan

The *Brown* decision caused great consternation in North Carolina. Governor Luther Hodges had segregationist feelings, and he believed that the *Brown* decision lacked the support of black citizens. Fearing violence from angry whites, Hodges sought a state policy on school integration to keep the peace.

State senator Thomas J. Pearsall developed a policy called the "Pearsall Plan." The plan had three parts. First, the responsibility for assigning pupils to schools was taken from the state and given to local schools boards. This would prevent the NAACP from filing one case that could integrate all schools at once. Second, African Americans were urged to accept segregation voluntarily to preserve the peace. Third, local school boards could abolish schools if parents objected to integration. The plan also authorized tuition grants so white parents could send their children to private, nonreligious schools.

Calling his plan "moderate," Governor Hodges hoped it would avoid integration and violence as long as possible. Although school boards knew the state would not push integration, some boards began the process. In 1957, Charlotte, Greensboro, and Winston-Salem picked certain black students to attend white schools. Even so, angry whites harassed them and their parents. By 1961, only eighty-nine black students statewide attended white schools. A federal court case in Charlotte helped speed integration.

School Integration

In 1965, Darius Swann, a black theology professor at Johnson C. Smith University, sued to have his son admitted to a neighboring white school. The school board gave parents freedom to choose among several schools in their attendance zone in order to achieve integration. The federal judge

Governor Luther H. Hodges wanted to delay school integration as long as possible.

Julius L. Chambers (standing, left), seen here as editor-in-chief of the North Carolina Law Review, later successfully argued the Swann case before the federal courts.

ruled against Swann because the white school he chose was not in his attendance zone.

In 1968, Swann and his lawyer, Julius L. Chambers, revived the case. They were encouraged by a U.S. Supreme Court ruling that stated freedom of choice was not adequate to achieve integration. Judge James McMillan of Charlotte therefore ordered the **busing** of Mecklenburg County students so that both races were enrolled in all schools. In the 1971 case of *Swann v. Charlotte-Mecklenburg Board of Education*, the U.S. Supreme Court approved busing to achieve more rapid integration. School boards then realized that they must develop workable plans for full integration lest federal courts intervene.

The state's colleges and universities also had to integrate. Over the years, North Carolina had established five black colleges at Fayetteville, Greensboro, Durham, Winston-Salem, and Elizabeth City. In 1957, the legislature abolished segregation in higher education. Still, by 1970, eleven of the schools in the university system were 98 percent white and five were almost 100 percent black. The federal government sued the state to end segregated higher education.

Although the university system agreed to do many things to encourage its sixteen colleges and universities to integrate, the federal government was not satisfied. In 1978, it threatened to cut off all federal funds unless the state improved buildings at black colleges and centralized some programs to encourage integration. For example, the federal government wanted a program like electrical engineering available at only one college so that black and white students would be forced to integrate the college. The state refused because these proposals would enable the federal government to control its budgets and programs. In 1978, the state sued to prevent federal funds being cut off. In 1981, the university system reached an agreement with the federal government. The system agreed to increase black enrollments at traditionally white schools and vice versa. It also agreed to improve the quality of buildings, programs, and faculty at traditionally black schools.

CIVIL RIGHTS IN THE SIXTIES

During the 1960s, changing attitudes, social unrest, political activism, and a willingness to fight for civil rights for all people brought about great changes in the civil rights movement.

THE GREENSBORO SIT-IN

In Greensboro, in February 1960, four freshman students at North Carolina Agricultural and Technical College decided to protest local discrimination. Blacks could buy goods at the Woolworth's but could not sit down and eat at the store's lunch counter. On February 1, the four students sat at Woolworth's lunch counter and waited. The waitress refused to serve them because they were black. They sat there until the store closed.

On February 1, 1960, Ezell Blair, Franklin McCain, David Richmond, and Joseph McNeil started a sit-in at the Greensboro Woolworth's to integrate the lunch counter.

Word of the sit-in spread quickly. In the following days, hundreds of students from North Carolina A&T and other schools volunteered to sit at the counter until served. They also sat in at the lunch counter of Kress's store. Soon angry crowds of whites gathered, and the police feared a riot. The managers of the two stores refused to serve anyone and closed their lunch counters. The stores were picketed until the summer. Then, in late July, both stores started serving all customers. African American college students elsewhere quickly adopted the sit-in. Slowly, they opened restaurants, motels, parks, beaches, movie houses, and other places to blacks.

The success of the student sit-ins led to a new organization. Black students at Shaw University in Raleigh in April 1960 organized the Student Non-Violent Coordinating Committee. It was abbreviated "SNCC" and pronounced "Snick." The first president was John Lewis.

PUBLIC PROTESTS AND DEMONSTRATIONS

In 1961, CORE gained national attention by sponsoring "freedom rides" from the North into the South. Blacks rode buses through Alabama and Mississippi to demonstrate against segregated bus terminals. In Alabama, the freedom riders were met by angry white crowds, who beat them up and burned one of their buses. When local police would not protect them, President John F. Kennedy sent in federal marshals. In 1961, the

Interstate Commerce Commission ruled that segregated bus terminals for interstate buses were illegal.

During the early 1960s, the Reverend Martin Luther King, Jr., emerged as a major leader in the civil rights movement. In August 1963, Dr. King organized what came to be called "the March on Washington." After the march, Dr. King delivered his "I Have a Dream" speech from the steps of the Lincoln Memorial. This speech was heard not only by some 250,000 people gathered at the Lincoln Memorial, but also by millions of people watching it on television.

Despite growing support for the civil rights movement, many people reacted violently to these demonstrations. Even in a supposedly liberal town like Chapel Hill, civil rights demonstrators met with determined resistance. In 1963 and 1964, local demonstrators led by university students marched, held sit-ins, blocked traffic, and used other means to get private businesses to open their doors to all races. Hundreds of demonstrators were arrested and a few served prison terms.

*Above: The Reverend Martin Luther King, Jr., gave his impassioned "I Have a Dream" speech before the Lincoln Memorial in Washington. **Opposite page, above:** John Lewis, seen here at a demonstration in Mississippi, organized the Student Non-Violent Coordinating Committee to enlarge the sit-in movement. **Opposite page, below:** Freedom riders trying to integrate buses and segregated waiting rooms had their bus burned in Alabama.*

As demonstrations continued all over the South, President Kennedy announced he would seek a civil rights act that would abolish segregated public accommodations. After Kennedy was killed in November 1963, President Lyndon B. Johnson carried on the task. Congress passed the **Civil Rights Act of 1964**. Any privately owned business involved in interstate commerce (trade between the states) had to open its doors to all races. The law also required school districts to avoid discrimination against minorities or lose federal funds for education. The barriers to equal treatment under the law were beginning to fall.

VOTER REGISTRATION DRIVES

Many black political groups were active in the effort to register African Americans to vote. Voter registration received help from President Kennedy in 1962. The Kennedy administration was alarmed by the violence in the South and persuaded blacks to try to change things through the ballot. The administration proposed a Voter Education Program for the South. In the summer of 1962, members of SNCC started teaching African Americans about the need to register and vote. If they met white resistance, they were to seek remedies through the courts, a slow process. In the summer of 1964, three student workers in Mississippi were brutally killed. President Johnson, however, refused to provide protection for the workers.

Dr. King decided to force the federal government to help register voters. In early 1965, he led a march on the Selma, Alabama, courthouse to help African Americans to register. King expected the sheriff to use violence to break up the march, but he did not. The SCLC then planned a march from Selma to Montgomery on March 7. Before the six hundred marchers could leave Selma, the sheriff and the highway patrol used tear gas and clubs to turn them back. Shown on national television, the events caused public outrage and a demand for a federal voting rights law.

In 1965, Congress passed the Voting Rights Act. The law did away with literacy tests and provided federal registrars in areas that had a low percentage of minorities registered. Federal registrars were sent to twenty-six counties in North Carolina, mainly in the northeast. The number of African Americans registered to vote increased greatly. In 1947, only 15 percent of voting-age blacks were registered in North Carolina. The Voter

The Reverend Martin Luther King, Jr., led the march from Selma to Montgomery to get federal protection for voter registration.

Education Program raised that percentage to 47 percent; by 1968, it was 55 percent. By 1984, some 60 percent of voting-age blacks in the state were registered.

The increased number of African American voters made it possible to elect blacks to office. In 1968, Henry Frye of Greensboro was the first black since the 1890s to be elected to the legislature. In 1983, he became a justice on the state supreme court. In 1969, Howard Lee became the mayor of Chapel Hill, and in 1973 Clarence Lightner was elected mayor of Raleigh. In 1990 and 1996, Harvey Gantt, former mayor of Charlotte, ran (unsuccessfully) against Jesse Helms for the U.S. Senate.

In the 1960s, only a few African Americans were elected to the General Assembly. But in 2001, twenty-three of them served in this body, six in the senate and seventeen in the house. By 2001, over eight hundred African Americans had been elected to state or local offices since the 1960s. Henry E. Frye was appointed chief justice of the state supreme court in 1999, but he failed to be re-elected in 2000.

Howard Lee was elected the first black mayor of Chapel Hill in 1969.

African Americans also elected two members of Congress in the 1990s. Under a provision of the Voting Rights Act of 1982, the federal government required states to create voting districts in which black voters held a majority. The North Carolina General Assembly created two such congressional districts in 1992. As a result, Mel Watt and Eva Clayton became the first African Americans elected to Congress from North Carolina since 1898. While voters have contested these districts before the U.S. Supreme Court, the court has let them stand because race was not the only factor in their creation.

Do You Remember?

1. Why did college students stage a sit-in in Greensboro?
2. Where did Reverend Martin Luther King, Jr., hold a huge demonstration in August 1963?
3. What was the Voter Education Program of the early 1960s?

Black Panthers caused white backlash by urging blacks to defend themselves with violent means.

THE DECLINE OF THE CIVIL RIGHTS MOVEMENT

The civil rights movement brought new laws and greater freedom for African Americans. But this progress did not erase their high unemployment, poor housing, and inadequate education. By the mid-1960s, discontent with these conditions led to violence in major cities around the country.

African Americans rioted and burned their own neighborhoods. One of the worst riots was in the Watts section of Los Angeles, where five days of unrest in August 1965 resulted in thirty-four deaths and $40 million in property damage. In the summer of 1967, there were riots in Detroit, Newark, and thirty other cities. Many people – white and black – feared a complete breakdown in law and order. The public began to withdraw its support from the civil rights movement.

BLACK POWER

The movement was also hurt when leaders who favored nonviolence were replaced by leaders who favored stronger measures, including violence. In 1966, SNCC replaced John Lewis with the more radical Stokely Carmichael. Carmichael began to speak of "black power." The **black power movement** hoped to bring about social equality through political power gained by uniting the black community.

CORE also changed leadership, electing Floyd McKissick as its national chairman. McKissick favored a "black revolution" to gain power. Under McKissick, CORE moved toward becoming an all-black group and removed the word *multiracial* from its membership description.

Black power attitudes were also reflected by the Black Muslim movement, centered in Chicago and New York. Many Black Muslims adopted Arabic names to show how they felt about white American culture. Following the teachings of Islam, Black Muslims were taught to be sulf-sufficient and to separate themselves from white society.

As head of SNCC, Stokely Carmichael (center, pointing finger) moved the organization from nonviolence to black power.

The Black Panther party accepted violence and was well-armed. Led by Bobby Seale and Huey P. Newton, the Black Panthers spread through urban ghettos. Many Black Panthers were killed in confrontations with federal authorities.

In the midst of this violence came the Vietnam War, In 1965, large numbers of combat troops were sent to Vietnam, at the peak of the civil rights movement. The fact that a higher percentage of blacks than whites was being drafted made the war even more unpopular. Black civil rights leaders did not support the war. Dr. King, in particular, was opposed to the war. When, by 1968, it appeared that the war was being lost, supporters of the war regarded African Americans as unpatriotic.

Dr. King was a victim of this feeling. On April 4, 1968, a white man shot and killed Dr. King in Memphis, Tennessee. News of his death caused rioting in over forty-five cities.

After the Reverend Martin Luther King, Jr.'s assassination in Memphis in 1968, people in Durham marched to show their feeling.

WHITE BLACKLASH

In national politics, African American voters supported the Democratic party, a defender of civil rights. Because of this fact, the Republican party seized an opportunity to increase its strength among southern whites. Segregationist George Wallace ran for president on the American Independent party ticket in 1968 and secured 14 percent of the popular vote. His support came largely from working class whites who resented black civil rights gains. Republicans developed a "southern strategy" to recruit white voters into their party. They treated the South as if the federal government had victimized it in the enforcement of civil rights. In 1972, Richard Nixon used this strategy to win southern votes, and it has increased Republican strength in the South.

White backlash could be seen in North Carolina. In 1969, Greensboro school officials refused to recognize the election of an African American as high school class president. African Americans protested strongly, and black power activists stirred up the community. The white community became afraid, leading the governor to call up the National Guard. The Guard invaded the North Carolina A & T campus, and an African American student was killed. The disorder was suppressed, as was the willingness of demonstrators to protest inequities.

In 1970 and 1971, the integration of Wilmington high schools resulted in racial tensions and violence. Fights broke out, and African American students boycotted classes. They demanded fair treatment, a black studies program, and the celebration of Martin Luther King's birthday. Bands of white extremists entered the black community and fired on bystanders and the church where students met. Score of people were wounded and several killed.

Local officials called on Ben Chavis of Oxford, a civil rights worker, to help end the conflict. Chavis asked the mayor for a curfew and protection for the African American community. When the mayor refused, African Americans armed themselves. They fired at police and firefighters trying to put out a fire, and two people were killed.

State officials then arrested Chavis and nine others, called the "Wilmington 10," and charged them with arson and being accessories to murder. They were convicted and sentenced to an average of twenty-eight years in prison. Appealing to federal courts, these ten defendants secured the overturn of their convictions in 1980.

Whites have dealt less harshly with busing as a means of integrating schools. In some cities, whites moved to the suburbs to avoid busing their children. This "white flight" has created some inner city schools with majorities of black students. The federal courts, the enforcers of busing, are inclined to accept this resegregation of schools if it is caused by residential patterns. The courts are currently deliberating whether busing in Charlotte should cease.

Busing was started in the late 1960s as a means of integrating the public schools.

Affirmative action in state university admissions is also under attack. This is a policy of treating racial minorities favorably in admission. The U.S. Supreme Court ruled in 1978 that public universities could not establish quotas for admitting black students. Recent court cases specify that universities cannot use race alone as a criterion for favored admission. But they may use race as one of several criteria in order to secure a diverse student body.

Do You Remember?
1. What was white backlash?
2. Who were the Wilmington 10?

THE NATIVE AMERICAN RIGHTS MOVEMENT

The civil rights movement had a counterpart among Native Americans. Although they were made U.S. citizens by an act of Congress in 1924, they did not secure full rights of citizenship. They especially wanted the ability to determine their own affairs.

Native Americans have long been considered wards (persons under protection) of the federal government. The government agency responsible for working with Native Americans is the Bureau of Indian Affairs (BIA), which was established in 1924. In law, the Native American tribes are dependent sovereign nations. In practice, they are forced to rely upon the government for food, education, medical care, and the daily regulation of their lives.

The policy of the federal government toward Native American tribes has varied in the twentieth century. Early in the century, the government hoped Native Americans would adopt white ways and become a part of white society. It tried to give Native Americans parcels of land from the reservations. However, this policy resulted in a great loss of reservation lands as individual tribe members sold their parcels to whites for badly needed money. Reservation land decreased from 138 million acres in 1887 to 48 million acres in 1934.

The government set up schools on the reservations in which only English was allowed. Native American children were not permitted to learn their own language or customs. Children caught speaking their native tongues were punished.

In 1934, however, the federal government changed its policy. Although the government encouraged Native Americans to restore their tribal government, the BIA had to approve everything that these tribal governments did. In the 1950s, the Eisenhower administration stopped supporting many tribes. The policy was called **termination**. Thousands of Native Americans lost government benefits and had to become self-supporting.

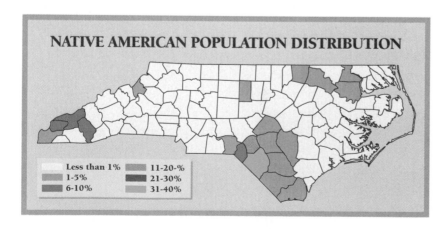

NATIVE AMERICAN POPULATION DISTRIBUTION

Less than 1%
1-5%
6-10%
11-20-%
21-30%
31-40%

Above: To show their displeasure with the treatment of Native Americans, members of the American Indian Movement forceably occupied Wounded Knee, South Dakota. *Left:* In 1990 the Indian population was highest among the Lumbee and Cherokee.

As a result, they moved to the large cities to find jobs. This meant the breakup of tribes, the loss of old customs and language, and movement into a strange society.

Well-educated, bright, young Native Americans began to protest the termination policy and to assert treaty and other rights. Young Native Americans founded the National Youth Indian Council in 1963. In 1968, the American Indian Movement (AIM) was founded in Minneapolis. AIM was a militant organization that demanded "Red Power," freedom from

BIA domination, and a return to traditional Native American culture. Rejecting the name "Indian," they called themselves "Native Americans."

The American Indian Movement demanded old treaty rights to fish in western rivers. In 1969, they seized Alcatraz Island in San Francisco harbor, site of an abandoned federal prison, to start a cultural center. In 1972, they staged a sit-in at the BIA headquarters to protest its policies. In 1973, AIM members occupied the historic village of Wounded Knee, South Dakota. This village is the site of the last major Indian battle where U.S. Army troops massacred about three hundred men, women, and children of the Sioux tribe in 1890.

These actions caught the attention of the nation. The federal government responded to the demands. It gave tribal governments more authority over funds. It gave the tribes more control over their schools, hired Native American teachers in reservation schools, and restored the teaching of tribal language and culture. The government also provided loans to attract businesses and jobs to the reservations.

All of these changes were reflected in the lives of the Eastern Band of Cherokee in North Carolina. The Lumbees identified more closely with Indian culture and protested discrimination against them in the communities where they lived. They sought recognition as a tribe by the BIA.

THE WOMEN'S RIGHTS MOVEMENT

The way men and women have related to one another has changed over time. In colonial America, women worked beside men in social and economic activities and were considered equal partners. Yet men were the heads of the households and the political and religious leaders, and women were regarded as being inferior to men.

As America changed from an agricultural to an industrial nation, the idea of separate "spheres" for men and women developed. Men's sphere was working in industry, while women's sphere was in the home. Women were expected to be morally pure and to maintain the home as a haven for their husbands and children. Motherhood was considered the highest status of women, and women were expected to pass on their "purity" to their children. These ideas were expressed in the phrase *true womanhood*.

By 1900, women began to reject the idea of true womanhood. They wanted to help solve the many social problems that harmed home and family. Through their clubs, women demanded better public education and health care, prisons for juvenile delinquents, prohibition, an end to child labor, and the right to vote. Men welcomed women's help in the effort to reform society, accepting women in a limited public sphere where home and family were affected. They helped women get the right to vote and get elected to office. This was the era of the "new woman" who began limited

Opposite page, above: In the 1970s, Cherokee High School began offering courses in the Cherokee language to its students as part of the emphasis on Indian culture. Opposite page, below: The Lumbees began emphasizing their culture as this boy indicates in his dress and musical instrument. Below: The two world wars offered women a chance to work at jobs traditionally reserved for men. These women helped the war effort by working in an aircraft factory during World War I.

public duties and worked outside the home in occupations considered woman's work.

World War II was another stage in changing gender roles. Millions of men went off to war, and their civilian jobs were filled by women. Demonstrating their ability to do "man's work," women gained confidence that they could do many things besides clerk, type, nurse, teach, and tend house and children. When the war ended, many women continued to work outside the home.

THE EQUAL RIGHTS MOVEMENT

By the 1960s, many women were unhappy with their lot. The Civil Rights Act of 1964 made it illegal to discriminate against women in hiring practices. Federal affirmative action programs opened even more work opportunities for women. Still, women were not being treated fairly at work. They were discriminated

People held many rallies, like this one at the state capitol in Raleigh, to get the legislature to ratify the Equal Rights Amendment, but they were unsuccessful.

against, and their pay was not equal to men's pay for the same work. Most working women held traditional women's jobs. Leadership positions in business and government were generally closed to them.

Women wanted equal acceptance into American society, and they organized to secure the treatment they felt they deserved. They joined the National Organization for Women (NOW), which worked for legal and institutional changes to benefit women. They also joined the National Women's Political Caucus to get more women into political office. These organizations and others supported a drive to add an Equal Rights Amendment (ERA) to the U.S. Constitution. This proposed amendment read: "Equality of rights under the law shall not be denied or abridged by the United States or by any State on account of sex." In 1970, Congress voted to send the proposed amendment to the states for ratification. Three-fourths of the state legislatures (38 of 50) had to approve the amendment before it would become law.

The North Carolina General Assembly voted on the amendment at almost every session from 1973 to 1982. Opponents of the ERA (who included many women) argued that equal rights would undermine the family, send women into combat, and require common restrooms for both sexes. Many people feared the social change the ERA might bring. The General Assembly never ratified the ERA. Nationally, the ERA failed by three state votes.

Despite the failure of the ERA, women have continued to make considerable economic and political gains in North Carolina.

WOMEN IN GOVERNMENT

Although women were active in state government before 1945, their numbers were small. Since then their presence has grown. In 1949, Susie Sharp became the first woman to serve as a superior court judge. Later she served on the state supreme court, becoming chief justice in 1974. In 1971, only two women were members of the General Assembly, but in 2001 twenty-seven women served there. The University of North Carolina board of governors selected Molly Broad the first woman president of the university system. Women have served as chancellors at several state universities. The state elections of 2000 were significant for women. The voters elected Beverly Perdue lieutenant governor, the first woman to hold the office. They also elected three women to the council of state.

Women have entered many occupations formerly closed to them, such as the construction industry.

Other women from North Carolina have won distinction by serving in the federal government. Ellen Winston became U.S. Commissioner of Public Welfare under President John F. Kennedy. In 1977, Juanita Kreps of Durham became secretary of commerce under President Jimmy Carter. President Ronald Reagan appointed Elizabeth Dole of Salisbury his secretary of transportation. She later served as secretary of labor under President George H. W. Bush.

Do You Remember?
1. What resulted from the Eisenhower administration's termination policy?
2. Name two Native American civil rights organizations formed during this period.
3. What two well-known women's organizations were involved in the women's movement?

CHAPTER REVIEW

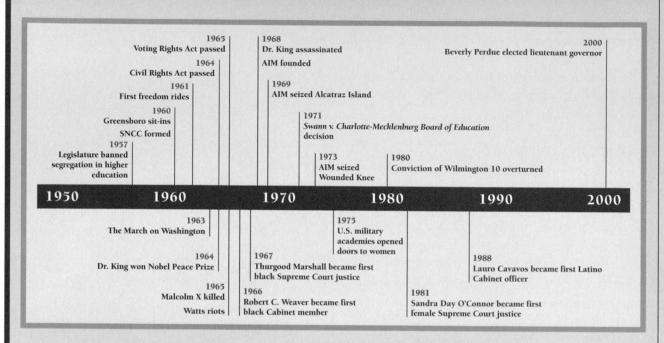

| 1950 | 1960 | 1970 | 1980 | 1990 | 2000 |

1965
Voting Rights Act passed

1964
Civil Rights Act passed

1961
First freedom rides

1960
Greensboro sit-ins
SNCC formed

1957
Legislature banned
segregation in higher
education

1968
Dr. King assassinated
AIM founded

1969
AIM seized Alcatraz Island

1971
Swann v. Charlotte-Mecklenburg Board of Education
decision

1973
AIM seized
Wounded Knee

1980
Conviction of Wilmington 10 overturned

2000
Beverly Perdue elected lieutenant governor

1963
The March on Washington

1964
Dr. King won Nobel Peace Prize

1965
Malcolm X killed
Watts riots

1966
Robert C. Weaver became first
black Cabinet member

1967
Thurgood Marshall became first
black Supreme Court justice

1975
U.S. military
academies opened
doors to women

1981
Sandra Day O'Connor became first
female Supreme Court justice

1988
Lauro Cavavos became first Latino
Cabinet officer

Reviewing People, Places, and Terms

Use the following in a paragraph describing the civil rights movement(s).

affirmative action
busing
civil rights
Reverend Martin Luther King, Jr.
integration
picket
separate-but-equal concept
sit-in

Understanding the Facts

1. What was the significance of the Fourteenth and Fifteenth amendments to the U.S. Constitution?
2. What practice did the U.S. Supreme Court's ruling in *Plessy v. Ferguson* establish?
3. What were Jim Crow laws?
4. Why did the southern Democrats form the States' Rights Democratic party in 1948?
5. What was the "Pearsall Plan"?

6. What were the freedom rides of the 1960s?
7. Why did the public turn away from the civil rights movement?
8. What government agency is responsible for working with Native Americans?
9. Why didn't the proposed Equal Rights Amendment become part of the U.S. Constitution?

Developing Critical Thinking

1. In what areas have you seen improvements in race relations in your lifetime?
2. What have been the positive effects of busing as a means of eliminating segregation in the schools? The negative effects?
3. Early in this century, the federal government established schools for Native American children. How did these government schools negatively affect Indian culture?
4. Affirmative action programs have come under increasing criticism in recent years. Many white males claim that they are a form of "reverse" dis-

crimination. What is reverse discrimination? Do you agree or disagree with the criticism of affirmative action?

Applying Your Skills

1. Get a copy of Reverend Martin Luther King's "I Have a Dream" speech. With at least one classmate, read Dr. King's speech to your class.
2. Many people and organizations important to the civil rights movements were mentioned in this chapter. Prepare a report on one group or person. Share your findings with the class.
3. Obtain a copy of the U.S. Constitution and the state constitution. Compile a list of the civil rights granted to citizens in each document. How do the two lists overlap? What are the differences?

Making Connections

1. Read the Fourteenth Amendment and then explain its intent in your own words.
2. Why was the decision in *Brown v. Board of Education* so important?

3. Today, are blacks associated more with the Democratic party or the Republican party?
4. How do cabinet members and other government leaders serve as role models?

Tar Heel Trivia

- The first North Carolina law formally segregating the railroads was passed in 1899. Segregation, however, was practiced on the North Carolina Railroad before the Civil War.
- Between 1913 and 1915, Clarence Poe, the editor of the Raleigh *Progressive Farmer*, launched a campaign to segregate rural land throughout the South. In 1915, the North Carolina senate defeated the plan.
- In 1947, Kenneth Williams, a minister in Winston-Salem, was elected to the board of aldermen. He was the first black city official to defeat a white opponent in the twentieth-century South.
- One of the Wilmington 10, Ben Chavis, went on to become head of the NAACP in 1993. He was removed from that office in 1995.

BUILDING SKILLS: READING NEWS ARTICLES

Newspapers are a good way for citizens to keep informed on a wide range of topics—local, national, or international. First, however, you must distinguish a news article from an editorial. Editorials mix facts and opinions and give a newspaper's opinion on an issue or event. A news article does not include opinions.

Newspaper articles usually follow a standard format. The *headline* is written in large, bold type with just a few key words. Its purpose is to capture the "heart" of the story and make you want to learn more. The size of the type often indicates the story's importance. The *byline* indicates who wrote the story, either an individual or a news service. The *dateline* includes the date and city where the story was filed. The *lead* is the first sentence of the article—the most important. It summarizes the main idea of the article and should tell you the five W's: *who, what, where, when,* and *why.* The *body* contains a more detailed account of the basic facts. The body often contains quotations and background facts. As you read through the article, you will find fewer and less important details.

Look at any daily newspaper and select one of the major stories on the front page. Answer the following questions.

1. From reading just the headline, can you tell why the editors chose to put the article on the front page?
2. Who wrote the story and where was it filed?
3. What are the *who, what, when, where,* and *why* of the story?
4. After reading the article, do you think the headline accurately represented the information in the article?

Try This! Reread this chapter and choose an issue on which to write a news article. Write the article first, then the headline.

CHAPTER TWENTY-FIVE

ECONOMIC AND SOCIAL DEVELOPMENTS SINCE 1945

North Carolina is a state of immense vitality, variation, and change. Hailed by many as a progressive symbol of the contemporary South's modernization and by others as being among the most conservative of Southern States, North Carolina provides an interesting contrast of forms and behaviors.

— North Carolina Focus

THE NATION AND THE STATE have seen much economic growth and change since the end of World War II. Technology has brought many new devices that have changed the way people live and work. North Carolina became the most industrialized state in the nation as the increasing use of farm machinery freed thousands of farmers to work in industry. To improve wages for workers, the state recruited new industry.

The increasing economic strength of the state has brought about many social improvements. As have the rest of us, religious groups have struggled to deal with a number of issues that have grown out of these social changes. Nevertheless, as people look to the future, they are optimistic about resolving the problems and issues that confront them.

TECHNOLOGY

The postwar period has brought remarkable technological change. **Technology** is the practical use of scientific knowledge, especially in business and industry. Technology refers to the inventions—including tools and

The Rosman dish antenna was used by the federal government for signals intelligence and tracking objects in space. It is now used for public research in radio astronomy.

Terms: technology, software, diversified, per capita income, microelectronics, right-to-work law, mediate, service sector, food stamps, Medicaid, Appalachian Regional Commission, denomination, Moral Majority

People: Billy Graham

Places: Research Triangle Park, Henderson, Appalachia, Montreat

techniques—that people make and use to survive and prosper. American technology has allowed us to explore the outer reaches of space and the depths of the oceans. Many of these activities would not have been possible without the aid of computers.

In the 1940s, a computer was large and bulky and required specialists to run it. Today silicon chips (the "brain" of a computer) are so small and powerful that some forms of computers will fit in the palm of your hand. Computers have revolutionized the way we live and work. Personal computers have changed the face of the work place—and where that work place is located.

Software programs provide the instructions that enable the computer to perform a variety of tasks. Using a word processing program, for example, a person can easily write, change, print, and store copy. Most word processing programs check spelling and grammar and suggest synonyms. Other software programs are used for accounting, recordkeeping, storing records, taking care of finances, solving difficult mathematical problems, designing buildings, aiding in research, and helping students learn. This book was written, edited, and typeset on a personal computer.

Computers can be programmed (instructed) to control the heating and air-conditioning for both large buildings and homes, to fly airplanes, to monitor the systems of automobile engines, to handle millions of telephone calls each day, to run the machines in factories, to play music, and to create awesome special effects for movies. Computers make possible video games, microwave ovens, cable television, and the Internet.

Technology has produced other inventions that have made modern life more exciting and pleasurable. With camcorders (video camera-recorders), you can make home videos and record them on magnetic tape. You can watch those home videos on a video cassette recorder (VCR). You can also record television programs and watch rented movies. A whole new industry arose around the VCR. With a digital camera, you can take a picture and "develop" it right on your computer. Technology has brought music lovers stereos, long-play records, cassette tapes, and compact discs (CDs) that operate using a laser beam.

In medicine, new technology has improved health care. Dialysis machines purify the blood of kidney patients. Doctors can "look" into the human body using laparoscopes (miniature TV cameras), ultrasound, CAT scans, and magnetic resonance imaging (MRI). New operating room equipment helps doctors transplant organs. Sound waves are used to break up kidney stones, thus avoiding surgery. Small electronic devices can be implanted in the body to regulate the heartbeat. Special optical scanners enable the visually impaired to read. Electronic hearing aids are almost unnoticeable.

Overall, technology has made our lives safer, healthier, and much more pleasurable.

THE AMERICAN ECONOMY AND THE INTERNET

In the 1970s, few people could have foreseen the impact the Internet would have on our economy. The Internet is a worldwide network of computer networks used to share information. Begun as a means of communication among the military and scientists and academics, it has greatly expanded since the 1970s. A common computer language (known as TCP/IP) has made it possible for almost anyone with a computer and a modem to use the Internet.

The Internet expanded in the 1990s with the creation of the World Wide Web. The Web, which is part of the Internet, is a set of programs and standards that make it easy to handle multimedia documents—those with text, pictures, and sounds. The Internet and the Web were opened to commercial usage in the 1990s. Today, most Americans, and others around the world, have access to the Internet. It has facilitated advertising, the buying and selling of goods, finding information, and communication.

Many corporations, known as "dot-coms," were formed just to profit from the Internet. Software companies sold computer programs to enable people to connect to the Internet. There is also software that makes it possible for users to perform tasks like banking, shopping, and making travel reservations on the Web. Other software allows users to send and receive electronic mail, more commonly called e-mail. Some companies created search engines, to look for information on the Internet. Many companies rely on the Internet to sell their products. It is possible to shop online for everything from automobiles to zinc.

The Internet has greatly stimulated the American economy to the tune of billions of dollars as more and more people have gone online. There is a downside to this dot-com economy, however. By 2000, the stock prices of companies dependent on the Internet had became greatly overpriced. The fall of these prices in 2000-2001 caused other stock prices to fall and thousands of people to be laid off from work. By 2001, the excitement over Internet company profits had subsided. Nevertheless, this new technology has become firmly embedded in the American economy. It is hard to imagine American business existing without it.

Amazon.com is one of the new breed of Internet companies. Customers can order books, CDs, videos, DVDs, toys and games, electronics, and other items online. The items are then shipped to the customer from one of Amazon's distribution centers.

ECONOMIC DEVELOPMENTS

Since World War II, technology has also spurred economic change. North Carolina has moved from an agricultural to an industrial and service economy. With the help of state aid, industry has also become more diversified, depending less on textiles and tobacco. In addition, jobs in the service sector have increased greatly.

AGRICULTURE

Remarkable changes have occurred in agriculture since 1945. Most noticeable has been the decline in the numbers of farms and farmers. In 1947, 40 out of every 100 jobs in the state were in agriculture. By 1992, only 2 of every 100 jobs were on the farm. There were many reasons for this change. As tractors replaced mules, farmers could plow four times the land in half the time. Machines were also invented to pick cotton, a job once done by hand. Tobacco farmers replaced old wood fireplace barns with automatic oil-fired furnaces. In 1939, only 19 percent of the state's farms had electricity; by 1971, 99 percent of them had it. While electrical equipment helped farmers become more efficient, the improved technology also meant that fewer farmers were needed.

A decline in cotton production also caused a decrease in the number of farmers. Synthetic fibers like rayon, nylon, orlon, dacron, and polyester became popular, replacing cotton. Because the demand for cotton was less, farmers produced less. In 1940, cotton sales brought $26 million to the state's farmers; but in 1967, sales were only $9 million. After years of decline, cotton has recently become more popular, and farmers are growing more cotton. Sales in 1999 were $793 million.

As the number of farmers decreased, the size of farms increased. In 1940, the average farm had 68 acres. In 2000, the state's 57,000 farms averaged 161 acres. With more and better machines, fewer farmers could tend more land. In addition, large businesses bought thousands of acres of farmland, thus increasing the average farm size.

Although the numbers of farms and farmers have declined, agriculture is still important to the state's economy. In 1940, farmers received $316 million for their products, In 1998, they got $6.7 billion. Livestock is now the leading farm product, mainly the result of more hog farms. In 1998, livestock was valued at $3.9 billion, while crops were second at $2.8 billion. Other leading farm products include poultry, tobacco, corn, and peanuts.

INDUSTRIAL GROWTH

In the 1980s, North Carolina became the most industrialized state in the nation. That means that the state had a greater proportion of its work-

Tobacco remains North Carolina's most valuable crop although tobacco manufacturing has declined.

ers employed in manufacturing than any other state. The number of industrial workers increased from 381,500 in 1947 to 851,900 in 1992. By
1999, though, the number of workers had fallen to 802,700, the result of
some industries moving to countries with cheaper labor.

Today, industry in the state is much more **diversified** than in 1947. That is, there are more types of industry. In 1947, the leading industries were (in order of value) textiles, tobacco, lumber and wood, and furniture. They employed 78 percent of all industrial workers. By 1997, the most important industries had changed. Textiles were no longer on top. Instead the chemical industry's products were of greatest value. The next three industries in order of value were textiles, computer and electronic products, and tobacco.

The value of tobacco products has been decreasing recently because of legal suits against the industry. In the 1990s, forty states sued the tobacco companies because tobacco products damage citizens' health. The two sides settled in court in 1996. The tobacco companies agreed to curtail advertising, especially to young people, and to pay billions of dollars to the states. North Carolina will use part of this money to help tobacco farmers.

The state has attracted new and diverse industries for many reasons. One reason is a large work force willing to work for lower wages. Another reason is weak labor unions. Cheap electricity, good transportation, sound government, and good higher education have also attracted industry. Finally, state government has worked hard to bring new businesses to North Carolina. Let us look at what the state has done.

Do You Remember?

1. What is a computer?
2. What has been the most noticeable change in agriculture since 1945?
3. What was the leading industry in the state in 1947? What was the leading industry in 1997?

STATE ECONOMIC DEVELOPMENT POLICY

In 1954, Governor Luther Hodges received a report that alarmed him. The report showed that North Carolina ranked 44th among the states in per capita income, the same rank it had held in 1929. (**Per capita income** is the average income earned per worker.) Governor Hodges was concerned because the state had made no progress in twenty-five years. The governor believed that the best way to raise per capita income was to recruit new industry.

Governor Hodges did many things to attract industry. First, he convinced the legislature to lower taxes on business. Then he traveled to several large American cities and abroad, telling industrial leaders about North Carolina. Hodges also improved the state-owned docks at Wilmington and Morehead City, resulting in better port facilities for industry. In six years, Governor Hodges and his staff brought into the state 1,000 new industries that created 80,000 new jobs.

*Opposite page: Textile manufacturing is still important to the state's economy, although it is no longer the largest industry. **Above:** North Carolina State University is developing its Centennial Campus to create a workplace where university, industry, and government can interact to solve contemporary problems.*

Governor Hodges's greatest long-term achievement in recruiting industry was the creation of the Research Triangle Park. Chapel Hill, Durham, and Raleigh form an urban triangle. Located in these towns are the state's three major research universities: the University of North Carolina at Chapel Hill, Duke University in Durham, and North Carolina State University in Raleigh. Governor Hodges believed that the universities' faculties and research facilities would attract even more industry. He wanted to establish a park where industrial research laboratories could locate.

GlaxoSmithKline is one of the largest employers in the Research Triangle Park.

Private funds were used to buy 5,000 acres of land for the park in 1957. It was not long before the park began to attract industry. By 2002, Research Triangle Park was home to over one hundred industries that employed about 45,000 workers. The park itself had grown to 7,000 acres. The park thus brought growth, better jobs, and increased population to the Triangle area.

Later governors followed Hodges's lead. Governors Sanford, Moore, Scott, Holshouser, Hunt, Martin, and Easley all worked to attract industry to the state. Unfortunately, problems developed. Governor Hodges wanted industries to locate mainly in rural areas so people could continue living on farms and in small towns. But the industries preferred to locate in large cities. To avoid traveling long distances to work, many rural people moved to the cities.

Another problem was caused by the kinds of new industries moving to the state. Most of the new plants were in textiles, furniture, and apparel. These industries required the least skilled workers and paid the lowest wages. Some higher-paying industries like electronics did try to move to North Carolina. But the lower-paying industries worked to keep them out for fear they would raise wages (and thus cut profits) or create a shortage of workers.

In the 1970s, Governor James B. Hunt, Jr., wanted to attract the "high tech" electronic industry. Also called **microelectronics**, this industry produces silicon chips, the "brains" of computers. Hunt wanted the state to develop its own "Silicon Valley" (the name given to the area south of San Francisco where many microelectronics companies had located). At

Hunt's urging, the 1980 legislature created the Microelectronics Center of North Carolina. This center has helped recruit high-wage businesses.

All governors, from Hodges to Easley, have encouraged international trade. That is, they have encouraged foreign businesses to locate in North Carolina and state businesses to sell goods abroad. By 1998, this encouragement was successful. Hundreds of foreign firms have established themselves in the state, and exports were over $12 billion in 1998. The state's leading export was industrial machinery and computers, with electric and electronic equipment being second. Canada and Mexico were the leading export markets.

The state has invested millions of dollars in the Microelectronics Center in order to attract new microelectronics firms.

ORGANIZED LABOR

The federal Wagner Act of 1935 gave workers the right to form labor unions. Once established, unions could bargain with management for better benefits, wages, and working conditions for employees.

North Carolina industries, and even some workers, did not like unions. The textile industry, the state's largest employer, was especially opposed to the unions. Textile mill owners treated their workers in a paternalistic (fatherly) manner. They resented their workers making demands on them through a union. Reflecting this attitude, the 1947 General Assembly passed a **right-to-work law**. The law permitted a worker to get and keep

Textile companies like J. P. Stevens long resisted unions. It took six years to unionize the workers at the Stevens plant in Roanoke Rapids.

a job without having to join a union. The right-to-work law made it even harder to form unions in the state.

The union's most effective weapon against management is the threat of a strike. However, strikes do not always help workers, as the Henderson strike of 1958-1959 showed. The workers' union contract with the Harriet-Henderson textile mill expired in 1958. When the managers and workers could not agree on a new contract, the workers struck and the mill closed.

In February 1959, mill president John Cooper reopened the mill to workers who wanted to return. Violence erupted. Within a month, there were sixteen bombings. Union leader Boyd Payton was beaten unconscious. Governor Hodges dispatched the highway patrol to keep order and twice tried unsuccessfully to mediate the strike. (**Mediate** means to get an agreement between two opposing sides.) Violence erupted again, and Hodges sent in the National Guard.

The strike failed after the state brought criminal charges against eight union members in 1959. Boyd Payton, three other union officers, and four workers were charged with conspiracy to dynamite the mill and its electric plant. They were convicted on the testimony of a police informer who had only talked to the defendants by telephone. The men appealed, but the conviction was upheld. In 1961, Governor Terry Sanford reduced the men's sentences, but the damage to the union had been done.

The union did succeed in organizing workers in the J. P. Stevens textile mills in Roanoke Rapids, but it took six years. The contract the union finally got in 1980 only brought wages up to the level of mills that had no unions. A version of the story of the union's organizing efforts was told in the movie *Norma Rae*.

Today, North Carolina has the second lowest percentage of workers belonging to unions. In 1996, only about 5 percent of the state's industrial workers belonged to unions. Only South Carolina was lower, at about 4 percent. Nationally, about 15 percent of industrial workers belong to labor unions.

THE NORTH CAROLINA ECONOMY

The economic changes occurring since 1945 have produced both good news and bad news. The good news is that, in 2000, the state's per capita income ranking had risen from 44th to 29th place. Governor Hodges's policy of attracting new industry to raise income worked. The bad news is that average industrial wages rank 46th among the 50 states. Higher paying industrial jobs are still needed.

The nature of the state's work force has also changed. In 1945, over half of all jobs were in industry. By 2000, however, about two-thirds of all jobs were in the **service sector**, that part of the economy where people provide services to others for a fee. Examples of services include medical care, car repair, preparing and serving food, teaching, and retailing. The service sector generally does not pay high salaries. These service jobs, added to the low-paying industrial jobs, help explain the state's rank in per capita income.

In recent years, the service sector of the economy has grown more rapidly than agriculture and manufacturing.

Tourism has become increasingly important to the North Carolina economy. People come to visit our beaches, our mountains, and our historic sites. In 2000, tourism brought in about $12 billion in business.

Do You Remember?
1. Research Triangle Park is located in an urban triangle formed by what cities?
2. How did Governor Hunt hope to attract the high tech electronics industry to North Carolina?
3. What is the most effective weapon that a labor union has against management?

NASCAR AND NORTH CAROLINA

During the colonial period, horse racing was a popular entertainment, and there were race tracks in several North Carolina towns, such as New Bern and Edenton. With the advent of the automobile, many Tar Heels and other southerners became interested in racing automobiles rather than horses.

Auto racing became popular in the South during the 1930s. Some farmers started to use the automobile to deliver crops to market. Often that "crop" was illegal liquor. To elude the federal revenue agents, or "revenooers," the drivers of these delivery vehicles modified their cars to make them faster and more maneuverable. Soon there were contests among the moonshiners to see who had the fastest cars.

After World War II, the National Association for Stock Car Racing (NASCAR) was organized to standardize rules for the cars and the operation of race tracks. In 1950, the first track for stock cars was built in Darlington, South Carolina. Today, races are held at tracks across the United States, but the Piedmont region of North Carolina contains the greatest number of tracks, races, and drivers' bases of operation. It is also home to such legendary drivers as Richard Petty and others.

Today North Carolina boasts tracks at Charlotte and Rockingham. Many of these tracks draw in excess of 200,000 spectators on race days. The Lowe's Motor Speedway in Charlotte, with a permanent seating capacity of well over 112,000, bills itself as the "Mecca of Motor Sports." Radio and television audiences in the millions are also part of the viewing public.

Drivers have become very recognizable, and some have been elevated to legend status. In fact, one of Richard Petty's race cars is in the North Carolina Museum of History. Large corporate sponsors pay enormous sums to have their products advertised on the cars. Auto makers are also interested in the sport. Racing has become big business throughout the South and the rest of the nation.

Auto racing has become a very popular spectator sport in recent years. The Charlotte Motor Speedway is one of two tracks in North Carolina.

The sport that started very informally with moonshiners and speed en-
thusiasts has today become the largest spectator sport in the United States.
Fan loyalty to drivers and manufacturers is some of the strongest in any
sport. The racing of stock cars has become so popular that a supertruck
series of races for pickup trucks was begun in 1994.

The changing economy of the state and nation has brought changes and improvements in society.

Above: President Lyndon Johnson visited a tenant farming family near Rocky Mount to emphasize his fight against poverty. ***Opposite page:*** Governor Sanford started a summer volunteer program for college students. Suzy Sterling worked as a volunteer in Rockingham in 1964. The program served as a model for VISTA.

THE WAR ON POVERTY

In 1962, Michael Harrington published a book entitled *The Other America.* In it, he declared that about a fifth of all Americans lived in poverty—a disgrace for the richest nation in the world. Poor people could be found across the nation, but the elderly, African Americans, ghetto dwellers, southerners, and southern mountaineers were more likely to be poor. Once in a "cycle of poverty," the poor found it difficult to escape.

Having experienced poverty himself as a child, President Lyndon Johnson declared war on poverty in 1964. He asked Congress to pass a number of laws to help the poor. Under these laws, the government gave income supplements (extra money or items) to the poor and provided training to help them get better jobs. Johnson hoped that these programs would help low-income people escape that cycle of poverty.

Many government income supplements were in the form of goods and services. Families below a certain income level could get **food stamps**. At grocery stores, families could exchange the stamps for food. The federal government then paid the stores for the stamps they collected. The **Medicaid** program provided free health care for people with very low incomes. (The *Medicare* program likewise provided low-cost health care for the elderly.) The government paid rent subsidies for poor families so they could afford better housing. Congress also provided grants and loans for cities to build public housing for low-income people. Nonworking, single mothers could get money to enable them to stay at home with small children.

President Johnson also wanted the poor to get better jobs through education and training. The neighborhood Youth Corps provided summer jobs for ghetto youth. The Job Corps provided job training and work experience for disadvantaged youth. Poor children attended preschool Head

Start classes to help them succeed in the first grade. The VISTA (Volunteers in Service to America) program sent people with special skills to work among the poor. High school students from low-income families could attend the Upward Bound program to prepare them for college.

The war on poverty had good results in North Carolina. In 1960, about 20 percent of the state's families lived in poverty. In the 1990s, only about 13 percent did. Poverty still hits African Americans harder than whites. About 9 percent of whites live in poverty while about 27 percent of black families do.

REGIONAL DEVELOPMENT

Regional development provided another way to defeat poverty. Before the war on poverty began, the nation realized that the southern Appalachian Mountain area was isolated and poor. The same was true of North Carolina's coastal region. In the mountains, corporations had mined the region's minerals and cut its timber. When the resources were gone, the corporations left, leaving the mountain people, with their small farms and low income, worse off than before.

The plight of the mountain people became known in various ways. Harry Caudill's *Night Comes to the Cumberlands* focused the nation's attention on Appalachian poverty. In 1946, people in the eleven westernmost North Carolina counties created the Western North Carolina Associated Communities. This organization sponsored *Unto These Hills*, an outdoor

APPALACHIAN REGIONAL COMMISSION

APPALACHIAN REGIONAL COMMISSION

Top: *Head Start classes, like this one in Boone in 1965, helped prepare children for the first grade.* **Above:** *The Appalachian Regional Commission served the westernmost counties.*

drama about the history of the Cherokee. One purpose of the drama was to increase tourism and thus help lift poverty. In 1954, the Western North Carolina Planning Commission was founded. It was the first regional planning agency in the state, covering seventeen mountain counties. The commission studied the economy and confirmed the region's poverty.

In 1961, the governors of the Appalachian states held a conference. Governor Terry Sanford was an active member. He urged the federal

government to help lift the mountain people from poverty. It was too big a task for any one state. In 1965, Congress did what Sanford and the other governors wanted. The **Applachian Regional Commission** (ARC) was created to coordinate state and federal help for Appalachia. The commission's goal was "to build the foundation for a vigorous, diversified, self-sustaining Appalachian economy that affords a wide range of social and economic opportunities for the people of the region."

The ARC believed that the building of good roads was the key to economic development. In 1965, western Carolina had only one good four-lane highway, part of Interstate 40. Traveling on most mountain roads was like "trying to ride a snake's back." The ARC poured millions of dollars into four new roads. One road connects Asheville to Johnson City, Tennessee; another connects Waynesville to Murphy; a third goes from Dillsboro toward Atlanta; and the fourth connects I-26 to Greenville, South Carolina. By 2001, these roads were nearly completed, The ARC also helped build hospitals, water and sewer systems, and vocational schools.

Much poverty also existed along the Atlantic coastal region from North Carolina through Georgia. In 1967, Congress created the Coastal Plains

Appalachian children wait for a school bus. Narrow, winding roads were considered a prime reason for Appalachia's lack of economic development.

Commission to coordinate state and federal help for the forty-five easternmost counties in North Carolina. The commission's proposals included plans to improve workers' skills and attract industry. The building of more highways, water routes, and better housing were also important. The commission wanted farmers to grow crops other than tobacco and fishermen to harvest seafood more effectively. It also worked to increase area tourism and protect the environment.

These efforts in regional development helped to lift the burden of poverty from many people. Both eastern and western regions became more attractive to tourists and industry. The number of jobs increased, young people found work closer to home, and the population grew. People became healthier, better educated, and more prosperous. The work is not yet finished though. The poorest people are still to be found in northeastern and far western North Carolina, and religious groups try to help them today.

Construction of the Home Moravian Church at Old Salem was begun in May 1798.

RELIGION IN A CHANGING WORLD

Religion has played an important part in the lives of North Carolinians. The dominant religion in the state is Christianity, which is based mainly on the New Testament teachings of the Bible. There are a number of different Christian **denominations** (groups). Over half of the Christians in the state are Baptists, about a fourth are Methodists, and about a tenth are Presbyterians. The remaining Christians are divided among the Episcopal, Lutheran, Moravian, Roman Catholic, and other denominations. People of other religious groups also live in the state, especially those of the Jewish faith. Peoples moving into the state from Asia have brought their religions—including Islam, Hinduism, and Buddhism—with them.

Social changes sweeping the state in recent years have affected religious groups. One change has been racial integration. For over a hundred years, African Americans have had their own churches in the state. The largest of these are the General Baptist and the African Methodist Episcopal Zion denominations. Black churches served not only as religious centers, but also as centers of social and political activities. As the integration of schools and other public facilities began, many white churches opened their doors to black members, especially in urban areas. In large part, though, churches remain segregated by race.

The women's movement has also affected religious groups. For centuries, churches have generally denied women positions as ministers, priests, and deacons. In recent years, women have moved into these positions, except in the Catholic Church. In almost all denominations, however, women have become much more active.

TELEVANGELISM

Another important development that has affected religion is the increasing use of radio and television. The federal government requires radio and television stations to give free air time for public service broadcasting. Because religious programs are considered public service in nature, religious groups were offered free air time. Public support of these programs encouraged them to expand.

In the 1970s, evangelical Christian groups began to buy air time or form their own networks. (Evangelical groups emphasize converting people to Christianity.) The most successful in doing this were the Reverends Pat Robertson, Jerry Falwell, Oral Roberts, Jim Bakker, and Jimmy Swaggert. Their viewers numbered in the millions each week and included many North Carolinians. In the early 1990s, though, some televangelists lost viewers and influence because of scandals. One televangelist went to prison for mail fraud.

In contrast, one evangelist has grown in respect and stature. He is William Franklin (Billy) Graham, Jr., of Charlotte and Montreat. Graham became a devout Christian after attending a Charlotte revival led by Billy Sunday, a former baseball player. Graham committed himself to becoming an evangelist after attending a Bible college in Florida. Nervous at first, Graham soon felt at ease speaking to large audiences. He came to national attention after he led a Los Angeles revival in 1949. Since then, he has led revivals in the United States and around the world, many of them televised. Graham has been a friend and adviser to every president since Harry Truman. In the 1990s, he founded a religious training center at "The Cove," near his home in Montreat.

The African Methodist Episcopal's Dickerson Chapel reflects the religious values of the people of North Carolina.

RELIGION AND POLITICS

The growing political conservatism in recent years has had an impact on religion, and vice versa. Since the 1970s, various Christian groups have become concerned with social problems. Of special concern to them were abortion, prayer in public schools (which the U.S. Supreme Court has prohibited), the proposed equal rights amendment, the use of drugs, and pornography.

In the 1970s, some Christian groups formed a group called the **Moral Majority**. Its purpose was to elect public officials who would oppose the ERA, restore prayer to the schools, and fight abortion and homosexual rights. The leaders of the Moral Majority were the Reverends Jerry Falwell and Pat Robertson, both of Virginia. They worked to defeat candidates who opposed their views and to elect Ronald Reagan as president in 1980.

The Moral Majority has waned since then, but Pat Robertson has revitalized the "Christian right" to influence local, state, and national politics. Conservative Christians have been especially active in Republican party politics. In the presidential campaigns of 1992, 1996, and 2000, they urged Republican candidates to support their positions. They also helped write the Republican platforms of 1996 and 2000.

Above: One of the nation's most honored religious leaders is the Reverend Billy Graham of Charlotte and Montreat. Opposite page: An important challenge for the future is the improvement of public education. Exposure to, and participation in, the fine arts, as shown in this photograph, is one element of that improvement.

CHALLENGES AND OPPORTUNITIES

As the people of North Carolina face the future, they are confronted with a number of challenges and opportunities.

The public school systems pose a most serious challenge. Violence, crime, and disorder have plagued schools in recent years, reflecting similar problems in society. Students' test scores indicate they are not performing well. About 6 percent of parents have chosen private schools or home schooling.

The state has tried to improve public schools. The Basic Education Program enacted by the General Assembly in 1985 employed more teachers and raised salaries. The Accountability Act of 1989 made each school accountable for reaching education goals. The main goal was improving student performance. Each year, schools receive "report cards" on how well students are performing. Student scores on standard national tests are improving, but they are still low.

A number of suggestions have been made to help schools improve further. Some people want the state to help pay for private education;

opponents say this would help private schools grow and eventually destroy public schools. Some people want to change the structure of the state educational system. The constitution requires the election of a state superintendent of public instruction. Yet, a state board of education sets educational policy. The board cannot force the superintendent to do its bidding. Some people want the governor to appoint the superintendent, thus making this office accountable to the board of education. To do this, however, the state constitution would have to be changed.

Crime and punishment also need attention. The rate of violent crime in North Carolina has more than doubled since 1972. For the same period, the national violent crime rate has increased only about 40 percent. People have demanded that the state decrease crime. One response by the state has been to build more prisons. Another action that may help reduce crime is the "truth-in-sentencing" law that took effect in 1995. It reserves prison mainly for violent and repeat offenders and eliminates the possibility of parole. These policies were somewhat successful. Violent crimes have decreased since 1990, while robbery and motor vehicle theft have increased.

Environmental conditions are of major concern also. In 1987, the state prohibited the sale of detergents containing phosphates. This helped reduce the growth of algae in rivers. The algae have been using up much of the oxygen, which resulted in fish kills. Another major problem is the pollution of the Neuse River and the sounds with all kinds of metals, oils, and fertilizers. This pollution, added to disease, has prevented fish and shellfish from reproducing. Fishermen are catching fewer fish, and the coastal economy is hurting. Oyster harvests, for example, are less than half what they were ten years ago. The rapid growth in the number of commercial hog farms is also increasing coastal pollution. Many of the hog waste lagoons break open or overflow in wet weather and pollute streams. People are demanding stricter controls on commercial hog farming.

Acid rain and air pollution are growing problems. Acid rain is killing mountaintop forests and trout streams. Air pollution, largely from automobiles, is hurting air quality in urban areas. The state is beginning to take action to reduce this air pollution. To solve these problems requires state and federal cooperation.

One pressing need of the future will be the solution of environmental problems like solid waste disposal. Recycling efforts like those shown above are reducing the materials put into landfills.

Do You Remember?
1. Which United States president declared a "war" on poverty in the 1960s?
2. What did the ARC believe was the key to the development of western North Carolina?
3. What is the largest religious group in North Carolina?

THE EFFECTS OF THE VIETNAM WAR

The Vietnam War was one of the most socially and politically divisive wars in American history. This was the first televised war. Americans could see what was happening on the evening news and compare that with what the government was telling them. The two were not always the same. Television coverage helped increase opposition to the war and distrust of government.

This distrust increased in the late 1960s and early 1970s as American casualties rose and there were revelations of Americans killing Vietnamese civilians. The distrust fueled antiwar sentiment and led federal and state governments to use heavy-handed methods to suppress the war's opponents. Belief that the war was necessary to contain communism waned.

The war caused great problems for the military. Civilian leaders would not let the military invade North Vietnam or Laos. They feared that China would enter the war. Military leaders believed that they were fighting at a disadvantage. Disrespect for the military increased as young men burned draft cards or fled to Canada. In 1973, Congress found it necessary to end the draft and depend on volunteers. Returning veterans were met with scorn and hostility.

The war led to a reluctance to use military force. People feared being drawn into another long and divisive war. It was not until the Persian Gulf War of 1991 that the American people again supported large-scale military action.

Vietnam turned out to be a "different kind of war." As the war dragged on, support decreased and eventually turned to opposition.

CHAPTER · REVIEW

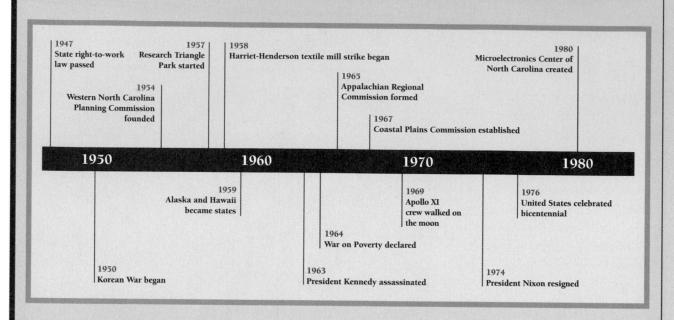

1947
State right-to-work law passed

1957
Research Triangle Park started

1958
Harriet-Henderson textile mill strike began

1980
Microelectronics Center of North Carolina created

1954
Western North Carolina Planning Commission founded

1965
Appalachian Regional Commission formed

1967
Coastal Plains Commission established

1950   **1960**   **1970**   **1980**

1959
Alaska and Hawaii became states

1969
Apollo XI crew walked on the moon

1976
United States celebrated bicentennial

1964
War on Poverty declared

1950
Korean War began

1963
President Kennedy assassinated

1974
President Nixon resigned

Reviewing People, Places, and Terms

Define, identify, or explain the importance of each of the following.

1. denomination
2. diversified
3. mediate
4. Moral Majority
5. per capita income
6. right-to-work law
7. service sector
8. software
9. technology

Understanding the Facts

1. Name three ways in which technology has affected people's lives.
2. After World War II, the number of farms declined but the size of the farms increased. Why?
3. Name five reasons why North Carolina has attracted so much new industry.
4. Name two problems that arose in attracting new industry to the state in the 1960s and 1970s.
5. Why was it difficult to unionize North Carolina workers?
6. Give three examples of jobs in the service sector.
7. According to Michael Harrington, which groups are more likely to be poor?
8. Who is Billy Graham?

Development Critical Thinking

1. Do you agree that there will eventually be no family-owned farms in America? Why or why not?
2. Why do you think such a small percentage of workers in the state belong to labor unions?
3. What do you consider to be the most critical social problem facing the state at this time?
4. Recent statistics point to an ever-widening gap between rich and poor. Ask five people of your parents' age or older if they see specific examples of this trend in their daily lives. Share your findings with classmates.
5. What can individuals do to slow down the damage to and destruction of the environment?

1. You have learned how North Carolina's economy has changed since World War II and how those changes have affected the state's citizens. Prepare a brief report on one of the following topics: (a) Life on a modern North Carolina farm, or (b) The change in North Carolina as it moved from a manufacturing economy to a service economy.
2. Do a survey of the manufacturing facilities in your community or in a community nearby. Categorize these facilities by the types of products they produce.
3. Identify an environmental problem in your neighborhood, school, or community. Investigate the causes of the problem and find out what individuals, authorities, or agencies are doing to solve the problem.
4. List potential tourist areas in your hometown or county. Make a brochure advertising these places to visit and listing what they have to offer.

Making Connections

1. Make a list of ten of your daily activities that are affected in some way by the computer. Compare your list with the lists of your classmates.
2. Write a one-page story entitled "The Day the Computers Shut Down." Share your story with your classmates.
3. Survey five adults who lived during the Vietnam War. Ask them whether they believe America should have been involved in the war. Share your findings with your classmates.
4. Interview a Vietnam veteran. Find out how he or she felt about American reaction to our participation in the war.

Tar Heel Trivia

- At no time during the postwar period have more than 10 percent of the state's workers belonged to labor unions.
- The Harriet-Henderson textile mill has had labor unions since 1944.

BUILDING SKILLS: COMPARING COSTS AND BENEFITS

One of the responsibilities state and local governments have assumed is to provide essential services for the people. Examples of these services include education, environmental protection, road construction and repair, and health services. None of these services is, of course, free, and one of the ways to raise revenue to pay for the services is by levying taxes. The property tax and sales tax are two taxes used by state and local governments.

While citizens are usually willing to accept increased services, the decision to raise taxes is often met with a fair amount of resistance. Lawmakers are increasingly being forced to choose between services they can provide with limited revenues. One way to decide is to compare the costs and benefits of each service. Generally, the benefits that a community expects to receive from a particular service should outweigh the costs to provide that service. This is not as easy as it sounds; not all benefits or costs can be measured in monetary terms.

Try This! Suppose you are a member of the governing body of your local community. Suppose too that your community provides the following services: police and fire protection; trash removal; schools; public libraries; parks and recreational facilities; road building, maintenance, and repairs; emergency management; licensing and inspection services. For this exercise, assume that the cost of each service is $1,000. Your community expects annual revenues to be $7,000 from the property tax this year. Which services would you cut? Why? You may wish to form a "committee" of several classmates to discuss your options.

Can you think of any services for which you would be willing to pay higher taxes? If so, list them and give your reasons.

CHAPTER TWENTY-SIX

GOVERNMENT AND POLITICS

We, the people of the State of North Carolina, grateful to Almighty God, the Sovereign Ruler of Nations, for the preservation of the American Union and the existence of our civil, political, and religious liberties, and acknowledging our dependence upon Him for the continuance of those blessings, to us and our posterity, do for the more certain security thereof and for the better government of this state, ordain and establish this Constitution.

— Preamble, North Carolina Constitution

IDEAS ABOUT NORTH CAROLINA government have changed greatly over the centuries. The Revolutionary generation believed that government existed to protect life, liberty, and property. This philosophy required only a small government. But today's generations believe that government should also provide education, build roads, relieve poverty, protect health, and make the economy grow. These activities require much larger state and local governments. Although government has grown and done different things, several basic principles have stayed the same since 1776.

PRINCIPLES OF GOVERNMENT

One of the most basic principles of American government is the idea of **sovereignty**. Before 1776, North Carolina was a British colony. In theory, the British king was the "sovereign," and all governmental power came from him. When the United States gained its freedom, the source of power shifted from the king to the people. The people are thus sovereign now. That is, the people are the source of authority in government. The people elect representatives to make the laws. This practice results in a *republican* form of government.

The North Carolina General Assembly enacts state laws in the Legislative Building in Raleigh.

Terms: sovereignty, constitutionalism, federal system, legislative branch, General Assembly, committee, bill, executive branch, budget, revenues, judicial branch, jurisdiction, appeal, supreme court, court of appeals, superior court, felony, jury, district court, misdemeanor, mayor-council form, council-manager form, caucus

People: president of the senate, president pro tempore, speaker of the house, lieutenant governor, secretary of state, treasurer, auditor, attorney general, superintendent of public instruction, commissioner of agriculture, commissioner of labor, commissioner of insurance, Kerr Scott, James Holshouser, Jesse Helms

Constitutionalism is another basic principle of American government. This means that a written constitution describes the rights of the people and the framework of government. By describing the framework of state government, the constitution *limits* government's powers. The state's constitution can, of course, be amended. Amendments can be proposed by either a convention of the people or a three-fifths' vote of each house of the legislature. The people must vote on any proposed amendment, either accepting or rejecting it.

Each of North Carolina's constitutions has had a *declaration of rights*. This declaration sets out certain principles of government and the rights of the citizens. You learned of these rights in Chapter 24. The listing of rights was a warning to government not to violate them.

The U.S. Constitution also contains another principle of state government. The principle of *comity* among the states means that a state must give "full faith and credit" to the acts of other states. For example, a driver's license issued by North Carolina is good for driving in any other state. A marriage performed in any other state is valid in North Carolina.

North Carolina colonists believed that individual liberty should be protected from the tyranny of government. They believed that the best way to do this was to have a *separation of powers*. In other words, the powers of the state government were divided among the three branches of government: legislative, executive, and judicial. And to prevent any one branch from becoming too powerful, the state constitution established a system of *checks and balances*. Each branch of government can use its powers to prevent another branch from abusing its powers.

When the U.S. Constitution was ratified in 1788, it established a **federal system** of government. A federal system is a form of government in which the national government and the state government exercise authority over the same territory and the same people. North Carolinians are state citizens, but they are also United States citizens. They are subject to both state and national laws. If there is a conflict between these laws, the national law is supreme. State officials must swear or affirm that they will uphold the U.S. Constitution and national laws over the state constitution and state laws when they are in conflict.

NORTH CAROLINA STATE GOVERNMENT

The forms and functions of today's state government are found mainly in the constitution and laws of the state. The last major revision of the state constitution was in 1971, but laws are made every year.

North Carolina's state government is composed of three branches: the legislative branch, the executive branch, and the judicial branch.

THE LEGISLATIVE BRANCH

The **legislative branch** is responsible for writing laws and appropriating (setting aside) the funds necessary to run the government. The law-making power is vested in the legislature, or **General Assembly**. The General Assembly has two houses: the senate and the house of representatives. All laws must be passed by both houses. The legislature also finances state government, investigates wrongdoing by government officials, impeaches and tries such officials when necessary, votes on amendments to the U.S. Constitution, and proposes amendments to the state constitution.

The legislature has what are called *plenary*, or full, powers. That is, it may exercise any legislative power that is not specifically denied by the

The North Carolina house of representatives has 120 members elected from 98 districts.

NORTH CAROLINA STATE SENATE DISTRICTS

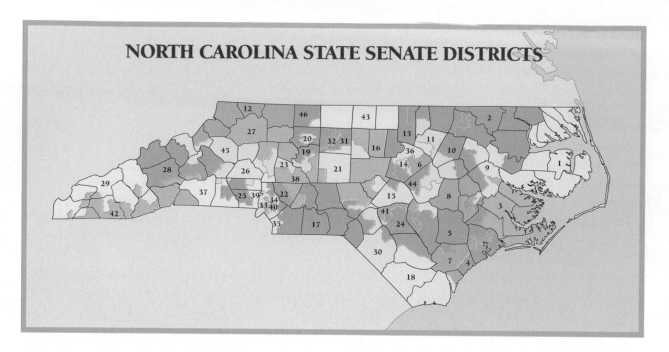

The North Carolina senate has 50 members elected from the 42 districts shown on the map above.

constitution. This is unlike the U.S. Congress, which has only those powers that the U.S. Constitution has given it. Some powers that the legislature may *not* exercise are the creation of long-term debt; the passage of certain local laws, like changing the names of cities; and specifying the death penalty for any crimes but the most serious ones.

Members of the General Assembly are elected every two years in November of even-numbered years. They are elected from districts that have populations as nearly equal as possible. However, the numbers and sizes of districts change as the population changes. The population figures used for redistricting are those from the federal census, which is taken every ten years (2000, 2010, and so on).

The constitution requires the General Assembly to meet every two years in odd-numbered years. These are called *biennial* (two-year) sessions. However, the General Assembly frequently meets in shorter sessions during even-numbered years. The governor may call the General Assembly into *extra session* to address a specific issue. Extra sessions were called in 1989, 1991, and 1994. The sessions dealt with hazardous waste disposal, the apportionment of legislative seats, and protection from criminals.

The Senate

The senate has fifty members elected from forty-two districts. To be elected, a senator must be at least 25 years old, a qualified voter, a state citizen for two years, and a resident of his or her election district for one year.

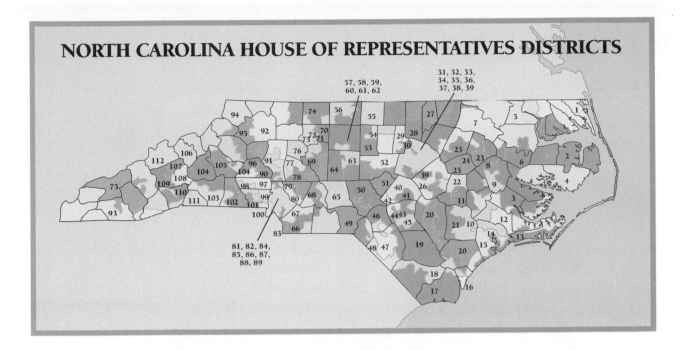

NORTH CAROLINA HOUSE OF REPRESENTATIVES DISTRICTS

57, 58, 59,
60, 61, 62

31, 32, 33,
34, 35, 36,
37, 38, 39

81, 82, 84,
85, 86, 87,
88, 89

The presiding officer of the senate is the lieutenant governor, whose title is *president of the senate*. The governor and the General Assembly may assign additional duties to the lieutenant governor. Because the lieutenant governor is not an elected member of the senate, he or she may not vote on any issues coming before the senate. Only when the senate has a tie vote may the lieutenant governor vote. The senate also elects a *president pro tempore* or "pro tem" (meaning "for a time") to preside when the lieutenant governor is absent.

The president pro tem appoints senators to serve on committees. A **committee** is a small group of senators (or representatives) that studies **bills** (proposed laws) on a particular subject and makes recommendations on those bills to the full senate (or house). Each committee specializes in a certain area such as education, finance, appropriations, health, or transportation. In this way, senators become specialists in certain areas of legislation.

The 98 North Carolina house of representatives districts are shown on the map above.

The House of Representatives

The house of representatives has 120 members elected from 98 districts. To be elected, a representative must be at least 21 years old, a qualified voter, and a resident of her or his election district for at least one year.

The representatives elect a *speaker of the house* who presides over the house of representatives. They also elect a speaker pro tem. As an elected member of the house, the speaker may vote on any issue before the house. The house of representatives also has committees, which function like those in the senate. Members of committees are appointed by the speaker.

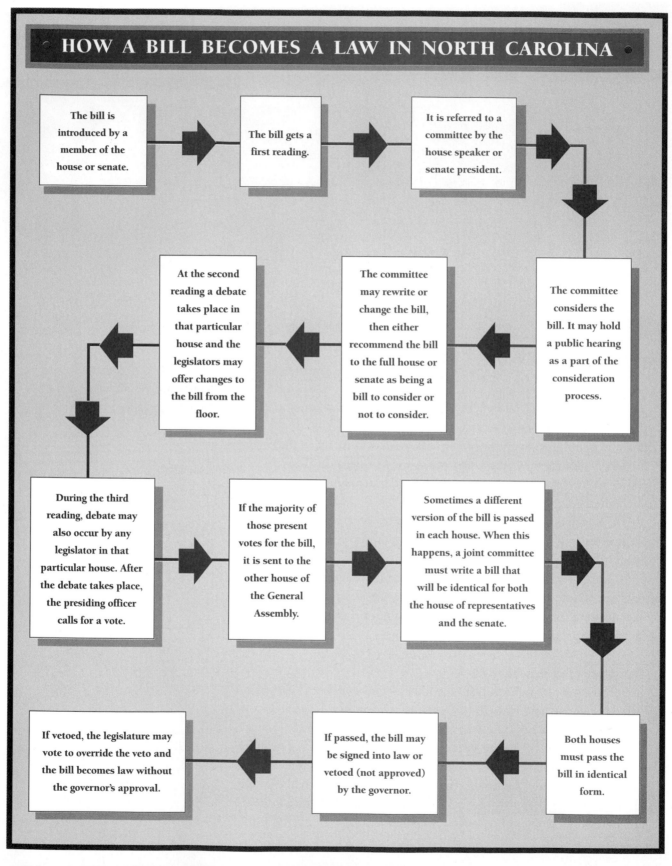

HOW A BILL BECOMES A LAW IN NORTH CAROLINA

The bill is introduced by a member of the house or senate.

The bill gets a first reading.

It is referred to a committee by the house speaker or senate president.

At the second reading a debate takes place in that particular house and the legislators may offer changes to the bill from the floor.

The committee may rewrite or change the bill, then either recommend the bill to the full house or senate as being a bill to consider or not to consider.

The committee considers the bill. It may hold a public hearing as a part of the consideration process.

During the third reading, debate may also occur by any legislator in that particular house. After the debate takes place, the presiding officer calls for a vote.

If the majority of those present votes for the bill, it is sent to the other house of the General Assembly.

Sometimes a different version of the bill is passed in each house. When this happens, a joint committee must write a bill that will be identical for both the house of representatives and the senate.

If vetoed, the legislature may vote to override the veto and the bill becomes law without the governor's approval.

If passed, the bill may be signed into law or vetoed (not approved) by the governor.

Both houses must pass the bill in identical form.

How a Bill Becomes Law

A bill may be introduced in either house of the General Assembly. Once introduced, the bill follows the same procedure in each house. Suppose, for example, that a bill is introduced in the state senate.

When a member introduces a bill, the clerk reads its title and assigned number. This is the first reading (the constitution requires three). The presiding officer assigns the bill to the appropriate committee for study. The committee may hold public hearings on the bill so interested persons and groups have the opportunity to tell the lawmakers what they think about it. The committee members then discuss and evaluate the bill; they may also choose to rewrite it. The bill is then returned to the senate with a favorable or unfavorable recommendation. An unfavorable recommendation usually means that the bill is dead. Occasionally, a bill dies in committee.

If the bill receives a favorable committee recommendation, it is read two more times. Both readings may take place on the same day, but revenue bills must be read on two separate days. Senators may debate or amend the bill after either reading. After the third reading, a vote is taken.

If a majority of senators votes against a bill, it dies. If a majority votes for a bill, it goes to the house of representatives, where the entire process is repeated. A bill must pass both houses in exactly the same form if it is to become law. If the house changes the bill, the senate must vote on the changed bill. If the senate disapproves the changed bill, it goes to a *conference committee* of members from both houses. There, senators and representatives work out differences between the two versions of the bill. The new version is then sent to both houses for another vote. If either house votes against the bill, it is dead. If both approve it, the bill becomes law.

Once the bill is ratified by the General Assembly, it is sent to the governor who may veto it or sign it into law. In 1996, the people approved a constitutional amendment that gave the governor veto power for the first time. If the governor signs the bill, the secretary of state publishes it as a law.

Lieutenant Governor Beverly Perdue is the presiding officer of the state senate. She may not vote on a bill unless there is a tie vote.

Do You Remember?

1. What is the source of power for the United States government and for each state government?
2. What is a federal system of government?
3. Who are the presiding officers in each house of the legislature?
4. What is a conference committee?

THE GOVERNOR'S MANSION

The governor's mansion on Blount Street in Raleigh is one of the best examples of Queen Anne/Victorian architecture in the state. Every person holding the office of governor since, and including, Daniel G. Fowle has called this 30-room mansion home.

Originally, the executive mansion was to have been built on the six-acre square named for Revolutionary War hero Thomas Burke. Instead, the legislature purchased a house on Fayetteville Street for the governor. In 1813, that residence was sold and the proceeds used to construct a new mansion.

The new governor's residence, located at the end of Fayetteville Street, was completed in 1816. After the Civil War, the mansion was left to deteriorate, and the governors rented homes in the capital.

In 1883, the General Assembly appropriated funds for a new mansion on Burke Square. Construction began under a strange collaboration with the work being done at the new state penitentiary. A decision was made to combine the two projects to save money on building materials and to use unskilled prison labor for both buildings. For the most part, native materials were used for the mansion: sandstone from Anson County, marble from Cherokee County, and native heart pine. Bricks were made from local clay by convicts. You can see the names of convicts written in some of the bricks along pathways surrounding the home.

Governor Thomas Jarvis pushed for the completion of the mansion. When construction lagged in 1887, the mansion was referred to as "Jarvis's Folly." Finally, in January 1891, Governor Daniel G. Fowle and his family moved into the new mansion. His residence, however, was short term. Governor Fowle died in April 1891. His ghost is supposed to haunt the second floor bedroom in which he died. The bed in which he died is still in the house.

Over the years, the mansion has been renovated and modernized, and the grounds surrounding the Blount Street mansion have been landscaped. The most extensive renovations were done during the governorship of James Holshouser in 1973. Today, the 30-room mansion is a source of pride for the state's citizens.

The governor resides in this Queen Anne-style mansion in Raleigh.

THE EXECUTIVE BRANCH

The **executive branch** enforces, executes, and administers the laws of the state. The head of the executive branch is the governor. To be elected, the governor must be at least 30 years old, a citizen of the United States for at least five years, and a citizen of North Carolina for at least two years. The governor is elected to a four-year term and may not serve more than two consecutive terms. Governor James Hunt is the only governor to be elected for more than two terms. He served from 1977 to 1985, stayed out of office for eight years, and was elected to two more terms in 1992 and 1996.

The governor has many duties. The most important is to enforce the laws of the state. An equally important duty is to prepare the annual **budget**, the state's plan for receiving and spending money. After the budget is approved by the General Assembly, the governor administers the budget to ensure that the state's money is spent properly. The state may not spend more money than it takes in. When **revenues** (income from taxes and other sources) fall short, the governor must cut spending. This is called keeping a *balanced budget*.

Michael F. Easley was elected governor in 2000. In this photograph, he and his wife Mary are on their way to his inauguration.

The governor is responsible for keeping the General Assembly informed about important state matters and may call extra sessions of the General Assembly when necessary. The governor is the commander-in-chief of the state National Guard and has the power to grant pardons and reprieves. As head of the executive branch, the governor appoints persons to certain state offices (with the approval of the senate) and oversees the operations of various departments. The governor also has the power to change the administrative structure of government to make it more efficient.

Assisting the governor are a number of officials elected to four-year terms. Besides presiding over the state senate, the *lieutenant governor* serves on various state boards and commissions. If the governor dies or leaves office before his or her term is up, the lieutenant governor becomes governor for the rest of the term.

The heads of several executive departments are also elected for four-year terms. The *secretary of state* is the keeper of all official state papers and records, including the laws passed by the General Assembly. The state *treasurer* receives state revenues and pays the state's bills. The state *auditor* makes sure that state funds are spent according to state law. Serving as the state's chief lawyer and head of the Department of Justice is the *attorney general*. The *superintendent of public instruction* oversees the state's

POLITICAL CARTOONS

A *political cartoon* is a drawing that makes a statement about a subject of public interest. It can be about a person, an event, or an important problem. Good cartoons deal with emotions and are a form of protest. They get their message across in a simple and humorous way, usually with few words.

Thomas Nast was one of the earliest and best known American political cartoonists. His cartoons were very dramatic and supportive of the Union during the Civil War. Abraham Lincoln called him the Union's best recruiting sergeant. Nast created several symbols that are used by political cartoonists today —the Republican elephant and the Democratic donkey.

Thomas Nast created this cartoon entitled "Who stole the money? Do tell. Twas he," criticizing political corruption in New York. He is also given credit for creating the image of Santa Claus as we know him today.

In 1884, Joseph Pulitzer's New York *World* became the first newspaper to hire a political cartoonist, Walt McDougall. One of McDougall's cartoons so increased the *World*'s circulation that Pulitzer hired him full time. Political cartooning as a profession was born.

One of the best known recent cartoonists was Herbert Block. A New Deal liberal supporting the newly rising middle class, Block used humor to lampoon or mock conservatives. He did not regard them as mean, but as daffy and dim-witted.

In recent years, the political cartoon profession has found able practitioners in people like Pat Oliphant, Jeff MacNelly, Bill Mauldin, and Bill Sanders. They deftly use humor to present a political point of view.

public school system, including teacher certification and textbook adoption. At the head of the Department of Agriculture is the *commissioner of agriculture*. This officer helps farmers and consumers of farm products. The *commissioner of labor* tries to ensure the health and safety of the state's workers. Enforcing the insurance laws is the *commissioner of insurance*. All of these individuals, plus the governor and the lieutenant governor, make up the *council of state*.

THE JUDICIAL BRANCH

The **judicial branch** of government consists of the state's courts. The major duty of the courts is to judge the actions of people in light of the laws of the state. Each court has its own area of **jurisdiction** (area of authority). The senate serves as a court for impeachment trials. The *General Court of Justice* consists of the state's appellate, superior, and district courts. The courts hear both civil cases and criminal cases. (*Civil cases* involve differences between persons.)

The appellate courts are the North Carolina supreme court and the court of appeals. To **appeal** means to take a case to a higher court for rehearing. The **supreme**

*Above: The North Carolina supreme court is made up of the chief justice and six associate justices. Each member of the court is elected by the state's voters to an eight-year term. **Opposite page:** These fine old county courthouses in Orange County (above) and Swain County (below) have been replaced by more modern buildings.*

court is the highest court in the state. It consists of a chief justice and six associate justices, who are elected for eight-year terms. The supreme court only hears cases on appeal from lower courts and from the Utilities Commission. It makes decisions based on points of law, not on issues of fact. The supreme court also oversees the General Court of Justice, setting up procedures for its operations.

Below the supreme court is the **court of appeals**, which consists of twelve judges elected to eight-year terms. A panel of at least three judges hears cases on appeal from the state's superior and district courts. Its jurisdiction is determined by the General Assembly.

The court of original jurisdiction is the **superior court**. Superior courts hear civil cases involving property worth more than $10,000 and criminal felony cases. A **felony** is a serious crime such as murder, arson, or burglary that is punishable by death or imprisonment for more than one year. Both criminal and civil cases are tried before a **jury**, a group of people chosen to hear evidence on a legal case and to make a decision based on the evidence provided. The General Assembly determines the number of superior court districts and judges. In 2001, there were 47 court districts and 127 judges. Judges are elected by the voters for eight-year terms; the governor may appoint judges to vacant or new positions.

District courts are trial courts that hear: (a) civil cases involving property worth less than $10,000, (b) family disputes, (c) juvenile cases, and (d) criminal misdemeanor cases. A **misdemeanor** is a crime that is less serious than a felony and is usually punishable by a jail term of less than one year. Judges hear the most cases in district courts, although the parties in civil cases may request a trial by jury. In 2001, there were 47 district courts and 262 judges. The voters elect district court judges for four-year terms.

Superior court judges may appoint *magistrates* to serve as officers of the district courts. The duties of magistrates, who serve two-year terms, are determined by the General Assembly, but the magistrates may determine probable cause of a crime being committed, issue warrants, and hear small civil claims cases.

The election of judges is not supported by all of the citizens in the state. Some people believe they should be appointed by the governor. They argue that judges do not participate in campaigning, and few voters know who they are or what they stand for. As a result, it is hard to vote intelligently for judges. Those who support appointment of judges argue that the governor would best know who the most qualified people are.

Do You Remember?
1. What is the state's plan for raising and spending money called?
2. What is the responsibility of the secretary of state?
3. What is the highest court in the state?

LOCAL GOVERNMENT

Counties and municipalities are created by the state to help the state govern. These local governments provide many services, including education, public safety, utilities, recreation, and waste disposal. The state has 100 counties and about 518 municipalities.

The voters in all counties and municipalities elect their own officials. The voters in counties elect *commissioners*, who may then appoint a manager to help run the county government. Many municipalities are *incorporated*, which means that they are self-governing. Most small towns have a mayor-council form of government, while large cities have the council-manager form. In the **mayor-council form** of government, the people elect both the mayor and the council members for two-year terms. The council governs the city, while the mayor performs certain arranged duties. In the **council-manager form** of government, the voters elect the council members, who set policy and pass ordinances. The council members elect a mayor. They also hire a professional city manager who is in charge of the day-to-day operations of the city government.

W. Kerr Scott appealed to the common people to win election as governor in 1948.

The North Carolina constitution does not mention political parties. Yet, they are essential to effective, democratic government. In North Carolina, as in other states, political parties listen to the state's citizens, determine the issues voters want addressed, and then work to elect their candidates to office. Once in office, members of political parties try to enact laws or policies that a majority of the voters want. Politicians thus try to do things that will keep them in office.

The governor is the leader of his or her party. As the leader, the governor selects the state party chairperson and can name party members to appointive state offices. The governor can also further the party's priorities by telling the General Assembly what laws he or she wants passed and by requesting from the General Assembly funds for favorite projects.

Political parties have great influence in the General Assembly. Each party's legislators hold **caucuses** (meetings) to elect the speaker of the house and the president pro tem of the senate. Party caucuses are also used to influence the appointment of committee chairpersons, the assignment of legislators to committees, and the laws that are passed.

The history of party politics in North Carolina since 1945 is very interesting.

TOWARD TWO-PARTY POLITICS

For much of the twentieth century, North Carolina was controlled by the Democratic party. In the 1970s, however, the Republican party began to gain ground.

When the Democratic party dominated state politics, the "real" election was the Democratic primary. In the primary, one Democrat's stand on issues was usually much like another's. Sometimes, though, the Democratic candidates were sharply divided on issues, and the people had real choices. In 1948, for example, *two* primaries were needed for Democrats to nominate Kerr Scott for governor over Charles Johnson. Johnson had the support of the state's wealthy, conservative interests. Scott appealed to the common people, whom he called the "branchhead boys." Under Scott, the Democratic party supported such "progressive" programs as paving secondary roads and improving education and public health.

Terry Sanford campaigned with presidential candidate John F. Kennedy in 1960.

In 1960, the lines between Democratic candidates for governor were again sharply drawn. Terry Sanford ran against segregationist I. Beverly Lake. Lake opposed school integration, while Sanford wanted to move ahead with it and spend more money on education. In the primary, the Democrats nominated Sanford over Lake. When Sanford became governor, he convinced the General Assembly to enact his program into law.

As new businesses and industries moved into the Piedmont, they brought with them executives and workers who were Republicans. These new arrivals strengthened the Republican party (also called the "Grand Old Party" or GOP). In 1952, they helped elect a Republican congressman, Charles R. Jonas of Lincolnton. Jonas, the highest-ranking Republican official elected since 1928, served in the U.S. House of Representatives until 1973.

Events in the 1960s and 1970s made it appear that society was coming apart: sit-ins, antiwar demonstrations, increasing violence, attacks on capitalism, illegal drugs, and the rejection of "traditional American values." Because of its support for civil rights and its antiwar stand in 1972, many people saw the national Democratic party as the source of much of

In 1972, James Holshouser became the first Republican elected governor since 1896.

the disruption in society. They began to turn away from Democratic candidates and to vote for Republicans. Republicans were able to attract independents and Democrats by supporting traditional values and appealing to the resentment against civil rights gains. These positions were part of the "southern strategy" that enabled President Richard Nixon to carry the state in 1972.

In 1972, the Republicans also won the governorship, a U.S. Senate seat, and about a third of the seats in the state legislature. James Holshouser of Boone became the first Republican governor elected since 1896. His policies, however, were not much different from those of conservative Democratic governors.

The new Republican U.S. Senator elected in 1972 was Jesse Helms of Monroe, who became the state's "most controversial politician of the twentieth century." Helms had been a well-known Raleigh television news commentator. He held strong conservative views and was not afraid to express them. He supported free enterprise, opposed government regulation (except for tobacco prices) and large government expenditures (except those for military spending), and supported Christian values in society. Helms appealed to people who had become alarmed over the erosion of traditional values and beliefs. He was re-elected in 1978, 1984, 1990, and 1996.

Republicans have had many victories since 1972. In 1980, conservative John East of Greenville was elected U.S. Senator. Lauch Faircloth switched from the Democratic to the Republican party to be elected U.S. Senator in 1994. In 1984 and 1988, Republican James G. Martin, a former Davidson College professor and representative in Congress, was elected governor. In 1988, Republican James Gardner was elected lieutenant governor. In 1994, voters elected 67 Republicans to the house of representatives, giving Republicans control of the house. The Republicans nearly gained control of the senate as well, electing 24 of 50 senators. In 2000, the people elected 58 Republicans and 62 Democrats to the house of representatives, giving the Democrats slight control. From 1968 to 2000, the state voted Republican in every presidential election except in

1976, when Jimmy Carter carried the state. North Carolina is thus becoming a two-party state where either party may win control of state government.

VOTING

North Carolina state law requires that a person register in order to vote. Every person who meets the following qualifications can register to vote.

1. A person must have been born in the United States or be a naturalized citizen.
2. A person must be at least eighteen years old.
3. A person must be a North Carolina resident for one year.
4. A person must be a resident of a particular voting district for thirty days.
5. A person must not have been convicted of a felony.

Statewide in 1992 about 73 percent of those persons qualified to vote actually registered. In statewide off-year elections from 1974 to 1994, only about 50 percent of registered voters on average bothered to vote. Voter turnout worsened in the 1994 and 1998 elections, when only 42 percent and 47 percent of registered voters voted. This figure is much higher during presidential elections, averaging 66 percent from 1972 to 1992. This means that, on average, less than half of the potential voters determine who is elected.

Low voter turnout at elections is a serious concern today. Many people fear that democratic government will not last if so few people are concerned enough about issues and individuals to vote. Some people fear that government will be taken over by wealthy interests who have only their self-interest at heart. Effective, democratic state government needs voters who are interested in the common good.

Jesse Helms, Republican from Monroe, was first elected to serve in the U.S. Senate in 1972. In November 2002, Republican Elizabeth Dole of Salisbury defeated Democrat Erskine Bowles for the Senate seat held by Helms, who retired. Dole is the first female U.S. senator in North Carolina history.

Do You Remember?

1. How many counties are there in North Carolina?
2. How do political parties influence the operation of the General Assembly?
3. Who is the state's "most controversial politician of the twentieth century"?

INTERNATIONAL TERRORISM COMES TO AMERICA

On September 11, 2001, with sudden and unexpected fury, international terrorism struck the United States. Nineteen Islamic fundamentalists hijacked four commercial jetliners. In a coordinated attack, they piloted two of the jets into the World Trade Center's twin towers in New York City. A third jet crashed into the Pentagon outside Washington, D.C. Hijackers evidently would have used a fourth jet to attack a similar target in Washington. Before they could do so, however, passengers learned on their cellular phones of the earlier attacks. A group of passengers heroically tried to overcome the hijackers. The jet plunged into the countryside of southern Pennsylvania, killing all aboard.

More than three thousand people died in the four attacks, including the citizens of more than eighty countries who worked in the World Trade Center. New York City fire fighters and police rushed to the site to rescue survivors. More than three hundred of the rescuers died when the more-than-100-story towers collapsed.

President George W. Bush immediately declared a national emergency and called upon Congress to give him warlike powers. The president reassured Muslim nations that the United States's war on terrorism was not a threat to Islam. Our focus was on those who commit acts of mass murder against civilized nations and innocent people in the name of Islam.

President Bush singled out Afghanistan for retaliation because it harbored Osama bin Laden, an exiled Saudi Arabian believed to have been behind the attacks on the United States. The president warned that no distinction would be made between terrorists and the nations that protected them. He demanded unconditionally that the Afghan government, ruled by extremist Muslim clergy, turn over bin Laden and other terrorists hiding in the country. After weeks of delicate diplomatic negotiations to secure the support of many other nations, to put economic sanctions in place, and to make military preparation, the United States launched air strikes on Afghanistan on October 7, 2001.

The attack on the World Trade Center (seen here) and the Pentagon shocked the nation. Rebuilding will take years.

President Bush cautioned Americans that the war on terrorism would last weeks, months, or even years. He called it "the first war of the twenty-first century" and pledged that the United States would not falter or fail in eliminating terrorism from the civilized world.

2002 Elections for: house of representatives senate local elections	**2004** Elections for: governor house of representatives senate superior courts appellate courts local elections	**2006** Elections for: house of representatives senate local elections	**2008** Elections for: governor house of representatives senate superior courts appellate courts local elections
2002	**2004**	**2006**	**2008**
2002 Elections for: U.S. House of Representatives U.S. Senate	**2004** Elections for: President U.S. House of Representatives U.S. Senate	**2006** Elections for: U.S. House of Representatives U.S. Senate	**2008** Elections for: President U.S. House of Representatives U.S. Senate

Reviewing People, Places, and Terms

Use the following terms in a paragraph describing the basic principles of democratic government.

constitutionalism
executive branch
federal system
judicial branch
legislative branch
separation of powers
sovereignty

Use the following terms in a paragraph that describes how laws are made in North Carolina.

bill
committee
conference committee

Understanding the Facts

1. If there is a conflict between a federal law and a state law, which law has precedence?
2. What are the three branches of state government?
3. What are the two houses of the General Assembly? Which has more members?
4. What do you think is the major function of the General Assembly?
5. Why are committees so important to the legislative process?
6. Who is the head of the executive branch of state government?
7. What is meant by a "balanced budget"?
8. What is the major duty of the state's courts?
9. What is an independent voter?
10. What are the qualifications to register to vote in North Carolina?
11. What is the difference between the mayor-council form of government and the council-manager form?

Developing Critical Thinking

1. Why is a constitution so valuable?
2. Why is it important in a democratic society to have a separation of powers in government?
3. Why is it important to have roughly the same number of people in each legislative district in the state?
4. Why was it said that the "real" election in the state for most of the twentieth century was the Democratic primary?
5. Is North Carolina a one-party or a two-party state? Explain your answer.

Applying Your Skills

1. Using the most recent population figures and a map showing the counties, try to apportion the state into fifty state senatorial districts.
2. Assume that a bill has been introduced in the North Carolina house of representatives. Prepare a flowchart that illustrates how that bill can become a law.
3. Contact the legislature and obtain a copy of a previously introduced bill. After examining the format, write your own bill.
4. Prepare a chart that shows
   a. the current officials in the executive branch (governor, lieutenant governor, and so on)
   b. your state senate district and your senator
   c. your state house district and your current representative
5. Get a copy of the most recent state budget. Determine the major source of revenue for that year and the percentage each source was of the original amount received.
6. Research your county and/or municipality. Find information about its history as well as its current officials. Determine its main sources of revenue and its major expenditures.

Making Connections

1. Collect three political cartoons from the newspaper. Write a brief interpretation of each cartoon.
2. Draw a political cartoon about a leading state or national politician or a political issue. Share the cartoon with classmates.
3. What kind of acts are considered terrorist acts? How do you think terrorists should be punished for their actions? Who should punish them?
4. Terrorists bombed the World Trade Center in 1993, and five people were killed. Why was the World Trade Center a target in each attack?

Tar Heel Trivia

- It is not easy to get laws passed. In 1993, legislators introduced 3,798 bills, but only 558 of them became laws.
- The laws passed at a session of the General Assembly are published in books called *Session Laws*. The laws that are current today are collected and published in volumes called *The General Statutes of North Carolina*.
- All judges must be qualified to practice law in the state.
- The smallest county is Chowan, which contains 173 square miles; the largest is Robeson County, which contains 949 square miles.
- Governor Hunt strengthened the modern governorship by leading two constitutional movements in the last quarter century: the succession amendment allowing a governor to serve two consecutive terms and the veto amendment.

BUILDING SKILLS: ANALYZING STATE INTERESTS

A *state* is a group of people living in the same area and under the same government. Each state is unique; for example, there is no other state like North Carolina.

Just as individuals look at things from their own personal viewpoint, a state tends to look at events and issues from its own viewpoint. A state has concerns about its political and economic well-being as well as the personal well-being of its citizens. And each state acts to promote its own interests. Those state interests may vary from year to year as the state's circumstances change from year to year.

1. Read a newspaper or listen to a news broadcast to identify current issues in North Carolina. Make a list of these issues.
2. Talk to family members, friends, and neighbors to find out what issues they believe are important in North Carolina. Add these to the list you made in #1.
3. Compile a list of laws passed by a recent session of the General Assembly.
4. Compare your two lists. How many of the laws address the issues you identified in #1 and #2?

APPENDIX ONE

NORTH CAROLINA STATE SYMBOLS

Beverage
MILK

Bird
CARDINAL

Colors
RED & BLUE

Dog
PLOTT HOUND

Fish
CHANNEL BASS

Flower
DOGWOOD

Historic Boat
SHAD BOAT

Insect
HONEY BEE

Mammal
GRAY SQUIRREL

Motto
"TO BE RATHER THAN
TO SEEM"

Nickname
THE TAR HEEL STATE,
THE OLD NORTH STATE

Precious Stone
EMERALD

Reptile
EASTERN BOX TURTLE

Rock
GRANITE

Shell
SCOTCH BONNET

Song
"THE OLD NORTH STATE"

Tree
LONGLEAF PINE

Vegetable
SWEET POTATO

NORTH CAROLINA COUNTIES

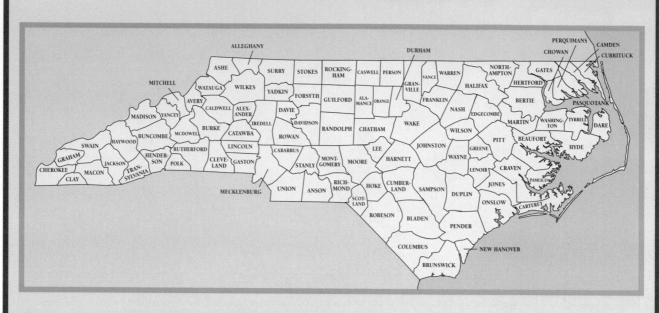

County	Date Founded	Current County Seat	Named For
Alamance	1849	Graham	Battle of Alamance Creek
Alexander	1847	Taylorsville	William Julius Alexander
Alleghany	1859	Sparta	Allegewi Indian word
Anson	1750	Wadesboro	George, Lord Anson
Ashe	1799	Jefferson	Samuel Ashe
Avery	1911	Newland	Waightstill Avery
Beaufort	1712	Washington	Henry Somerset IV, Duke of Beaufort
Bertie	1722	Windsor	James and Henry Bertie
Bladen	1734	Elizabethtown	Martin Bladen
Brunswick	1764	Bolivia	Town of Brunswick
Buncombe	1791	Asheville	Edward Buncombe
Burke	1777	Morganton	Thomas Burke

County	Year	County Seat	Named For
Cabarrus	1792	Concord	Stephen Cabarrus
Caldwell	1841	Lenoir	Joseph Caldwell
Camden	1777	Camden	Charles Pratt, Earl of Camden
Carteret	1722	Beaufort	John Carteret, Earl of Granville
Caswell	1777	Yanceyville	Richard Caswell
Catawba	1842	Newton	Catawba Indian tribe
Chatham	1771	Pittsboro	William Pitt, Earl of Chatham
Cherokee	1839	Murphy	Cherokee Indian tribe
Chowan	1670	Edenton	Chowan Indian tribe
Clay	1861	Hayesville	Henry Clay
Cleveland	1841	Shelby	Benjamin Cleveland
Columbus	1808	Whiteville	Christopher Columbus
Craven	1705	New Bern	William Craven, Earl of Craven
Cumberland	1754	Fayetteville	William Augustus, Duke of Cumberland
Currituck	1668	Currituck	Currituck Indian tribe
Dare	1870	Manteo	Virginia Dare
Davidson	1822	Lexington	William Lee Davidson
Davie	1836	Mocksville	William Richardson Davie
Duplin	1750	Kenansville	Thomas Hay, Lord Duplin
Durham	1881	Durham	Town of Durham and Dr. Bartlett Snipes Durham
Edgecombe	1741	Tarboro	Baron Richard Edgecumbe
Forsyth	1849	Winston-Salem	Benjamin Forsyth
Franklin	1779	Louisburg	Benjamin Franklin
Gaston	1846	Gastonia	William Gaston
Gates	1779	Gatesville	Horatio Gates
Graham	1872	Robbinsville	William Alexander Graham
Granville	1746	Oxford	John Carteret, Earl of Granville
Greene	1799	Snow Hill	Nathanael Greene
Guilford	1771	Greensboro	Francis North, Earl of Guilford
Halifax	1758	Halifax	George Montague, Earl of Halifax

Harnett	1855	Lillington	Cornelius Harnett
Haywood	1808	Waynesville	John Haywood
Henderson	1838	Hendersonville	Leonard Henderson
Hertford	1759	Winton	Francis Seymour Conway, Earl of Hertford
Hoke	1911	Raeford	Robert Frederick Hoke
Hyde	1712	Swan Quarter	Edward Hyde, proprietary governor
Iredell	1788	Statesville	James Iredell
Jackson	1851	Sylva	Andrew Jackson
Johnston	1746	Smithfield	Gabriel Johnston
Jones	1779	Trenton	Willie Jones
Lee	1907	Sanford	Robert E. Lee
Lenoir	1791	Kinston	William Lenoir
Lincoln	1779	Lincolnton	Benjamin Lincoln
Macon	1828	Franklin	Nathaniel Macon
Madison	1851	Marshall	James Madison
Martin	1774	Williamston	Josiah Martin
McDowell	1842	Marion	Joseph McDowell
Mecklenburg	1762	Charlotte	Charlotte Sophia of Mecklenburg-Strelitz
Mitchell	1861	Bakersville	Elisha Mitchell
Montgomery	1779	Troy	Richard Montgomery
Moore	1784	Carthage	Alfred Moore
Nash	1777	Nashville	Francis Nash
New Hanover	1729	Wilmington	The House of Hanover
Northampton	1741	Jackson	James Compton, Earl of Northampton
Onslow	1731	Jacksonville	Arthur Onslow
Orange	1752	Hillsborough	William V of House of Orange
Pamlico	1872	Bayboro	Pamlico Sound
Pasquotank	1668	Elizabeth City	Indian word
Pender	1875	Burgaw	William Dorsey Pender
Perquimans	1668	Hertford	Perquimans Indian tribe

Person	1791	Roxboro	Thomas Person
Pitt	1760	Greenville	William Pitt
Polk	1855	Columbus	William Polk
Randolph	1779	Asheboro	Peyton Randolph
Richmond	1779	Rockingham	Charles Lennox, Duke of Richmond
Robeson	1787	Lumberton	Thomas Robeson
Rockingham	1785	Wentworth	Charles Watson-Wentworth, Marquis of Rockingham
Rowan	1753	Salisbury	Matthew Rowan
Rutherford	1779	Rutherfordton	Griffith Rutherford
Sampson	1784	Clinton	John Sampson
Scotland	1899	Laurinburg	Scotland, Great Britain
Stanly	1841	Albemarle	John Stanly
Stokes	1789	Danbury	John Stokes
Surry	1771	Dobson	County of Surrey in England
Swain	1871	Bryson City	David Lowry Swain
Transylvania	1861	Brevard	Latin words meaning "across the woods"
Tyrrell	1729	Columbia	John Tyrrell
Union	1842	Monroe	Descriptive name
Vance	1881	Henderson	Zebulon Baird Vance
Wake	1771	Raleigh	Margaret Wake
Warren	1779	Warrenton	Joseph Warren
Washington	1799	Plymouth	George Washington
Watauga	1849	Boone	Watauga River
Wayne	1779	Goldsboro	Anthony Wayne
Wilkes	1777	Wilkesboro	John Wilkes
Wilson	1855	Wilson	Louis Dicken Wilson
Yadkin	1850	Yadkinville	Yadkin River
Yancey	1833	Burnsville	Bartlett Yancey

APPENDIX THREE

NORTH CAROLINA GOVERNORS

Lords Proprietors	Term
William Drummond	1664-1667
Samuel Stephens	1667-1669
Peter Carteret	1670-1672
John Jenkins	1672-1677
Thomas Eastchurch	1676-1678
Thomas Miller	1677
John Harvey	1679
John Jenkins	1679-1681
Philip Ludwell	1689-1691
Thomas Jarvis	1691-1694
John Archdale	1694-1696
Thomas Harvey	1696-1699
Henderson Walker	1699-1704
Robert Daniel	1704-1705
Thomas Cary	1705-1706
William Glover	1706-1708
Thomas Cary	1708-1711
Edward Hyde	1711-1712

Thomas Pollock	1712-1714
Charles Eden	1714-1722
Thomas Pollock	1722
William Reed	1722-1724
George Burrington	1724-1725
Richard Everard	1725-1731

Royal Governors	Term
George Burrington	1731-1734
Gabriel Johnston	1734-1752
Nathaniel Rice	1752-1753
Matthew Rowan	1753-1754
Arthur Dobbs	1754-1765
William Tryon	1765-1771
James Hasell	1771
Josiah Martin	1771-1775

Governor	Term
Richard Caswell	1776-1780
Abner Nash	1780-1781
Thomas Burke	1781-1782
Alexander Martin	1782-1784
Richard Caswell	1784-1787
Samuel Johnston	1787-1789
Alexander Martin	1789-1792

Richard Dobbs Spaight, Sr.	1792-1795
Samuel Ashe	1795-1798
William Richardson Davie	1798-1799
Benjamin Williams	1799-1802
James Turner	1802-1805
Nathaniel Alexander	1805-1807
Benjamin Williams	1807-1808
David Stone	1808-1810
Benjamin Smith	1810-1811
William Hawkins	1811-1814
William Miller	1814-1817
John Branch	1817-1820
Jesse Franklin	1820-1821
Gabriel Holmes	1821-1824
Hutchins Gordon Burton	1824-1827
James Iredell, Jr.	1827-1828
John Owen	1828-1830
Montfort Stokes	1830-1832
David Lowry Swain	1832-1835
Richard Dobbs Spaight, Jr.	1835-1836
Edward Dudley Bishop	1836-1841
John Motley Morehead	1841-1845
William Alexander Graham	1845-1849
Charles Manly	1849-1851

David Steele Reid	1851-1854
Warren Winslow	1854-1855
Thomas Bragg	1855-1859
John Willis Ellis	1859-1861
Henry Toole Clark	1861-1862
Zebulon Baird Vance	1862-1865
William Woods Holden	1865
Jonathan Worth	1865-1868
William Woods Holden	1868-1871
Tod Robinson Caldwell	1871-1874
Curtis Hooks Brogden	1874-1877
Zebulon Baird Vance	1877-1879
Thomas Jordan Jarvis	1879-1885
Alfred Moore Scales	1885-1889
Daniel Gould Fowle	1889-1891
Thomas Michael Holt	1891-1893
Elias Carr	1893-1897
Daniel Lindsay Russell	1897-1901
Charles Brantley Aycock	1901-1905
Robert Broadnax Glenn	1905-1909
William Walton Kitchin	1909-1913
Locke Craig	1913-1917
Thomas Walter Bickett	1917-1921
Cameron Morrison	1921-1925

Angus Wilton McLean 1925-1929

Oliver Max Gardner 1929-1933

John Christoph Blucher Ehringhaus 1933-1937

Clyde Roark Hoey 1937-1941

Joseph Melville Broughton 1941-1945

Robert Gregg Cherry 1945-1949

William Kerr Scott 1949-1953

William Bradley Umstead 1953-1954

Luther Hartwell Hodges 1954-1961

Terry Sanford 1961-1965

Daniel Killian Moore 1965-1969

Robert Walter Scott 1969-1973

James Eubert Holshouser, Jr. 1973-1977

James Baxter Hunt, Jr. 1977-1985

James G. Martin 1985-1993

James Baxter Hunt, Jr. 1993-2001

Michael F. Easley 2001-Present

NORTH CAROLINA ATLAS

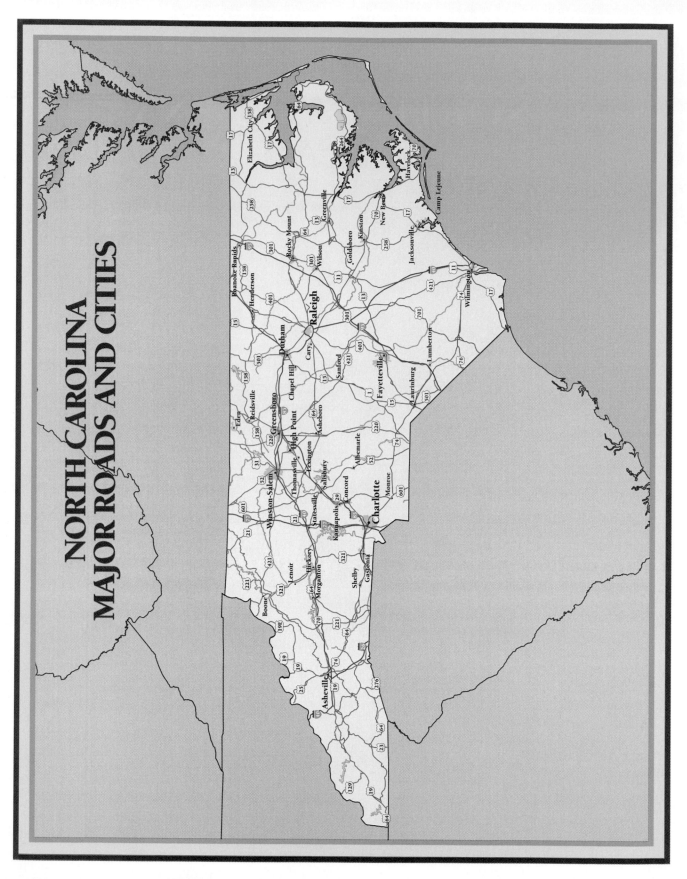

NORTH CAROLINA
MAJOR ROADS AND CITIES

Elizabeth City

Roanoke Rapids

Havelock

Camp Lejeune

Henderson

Greenville

New Bern

Rocky Mount

Wilson

Kinston

Jacksonville

Goldsboro

Raleigh

Reidsville

Eden

Durham

Cary

Wilmington

Greensboro

Chapel Hill

Sanford

Lumberton

High Point

Asheboro

Fayetteville

Thomasville

Lexington

Albemarle

Laurinburg

Winston-Salem

Salisbury

Concord

Monroe

Statesville

Kannapolis

Charlotte

Lenoir

Hickory

Shelby

Gastonia

Boone

Morganton

Asheville

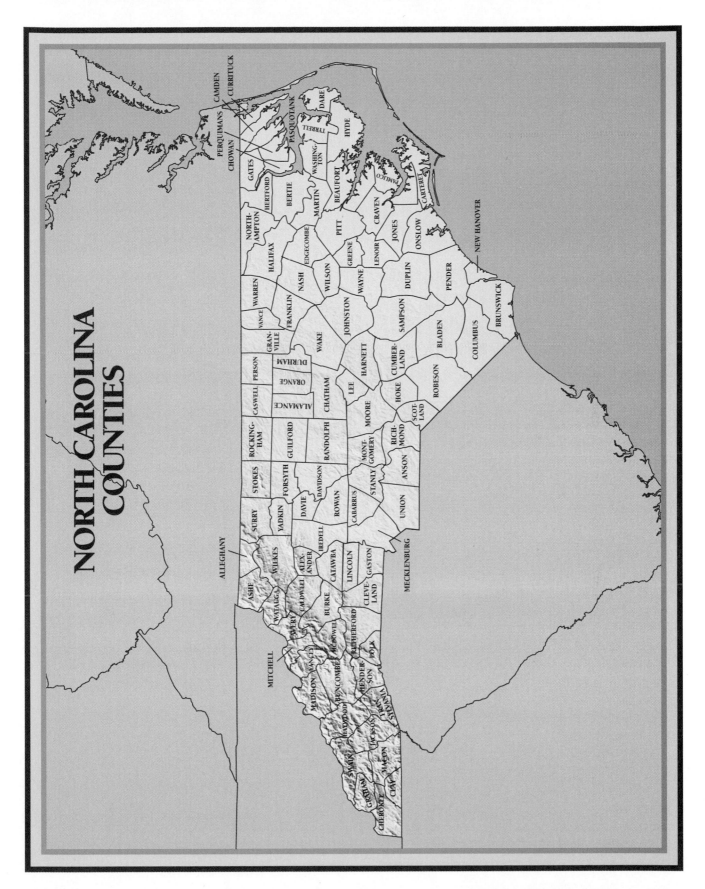

NORTH CAROLINA COUNTIES

CAMDEN
CURRITUCK
PERQUIMANS
CHOWAN
GATES
PASQUOTANK
DARE
TYRRELL
WASHINGTON
HYDE
HERTFORD
BERTIE
MARTIN
BEAUFORT
NORTHAMPTON
HALIFAX
PITT
CRAVEN
PAMLICO
CARTERET
EDGECOMBE
WILSON
GREENE
LENOIR
CRAVEN
JONES
ONSLOW
NEW HANOVER
WARREN
NASH
WAYNE
DUPLIN
PENDER
VANCE
FRANKLIN
JOHNSTON
SAMPSON
BLADEN
COLUMBUS
BRUNSWICK
GRANVILLE
WAKE
HARNETT
CUMBERLAND
ROBESON
PERSON
DURHAM
ORANGE
CHATHAM
LEE
HOKE
SCOTLAND
CASWELL
ALAMANCE
MOORE
RICHMOND
ROCKINGHAM
GUILFORD
RANDOLPH
MONTGOMERY
STANLY
ANSON
STOKES
FORSYTH
DAVIDSON
ROWAN
CABARRUS
UNION
SURRY
YADKIN
DAVIE
IREDELL
ALLEGHANY
WILKES
ALEXANDER
CATAWBA
LINCOLN
GASTON
CLEVELAND
MECKLENBURG
ASHE
WATAUGA
CALDWELL
BURKE
RUTHERFORD
POLK
MITCHELL
AVERY
McDOWELL
YANCEY
BUNCOMBE
HENDERSON
MADISON
HAYWOOD
TRANSYLVANIA
SWAIN
JACKSON
GRAHAM
MACON
CHEROKEE
CLAY

NORTH CAROLINA ATLAS   613

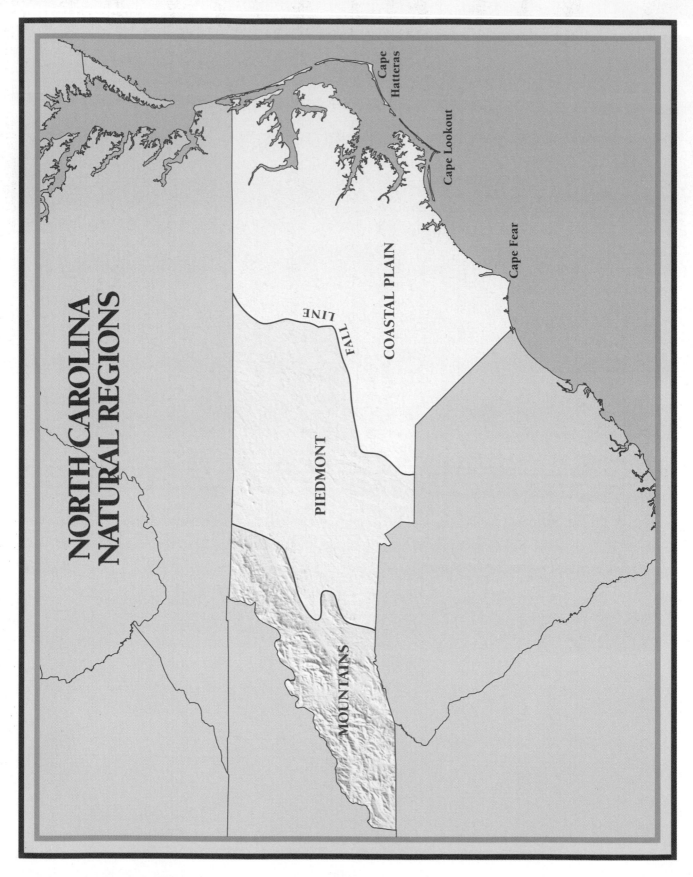

NORTH CAROLINA
NATURAL REGIONS

Cape Hatteras

Cape Lookout

Cape Fear

COASTAL PLAIN

FALL LINE

PIEDMONT

MOUNTAINS

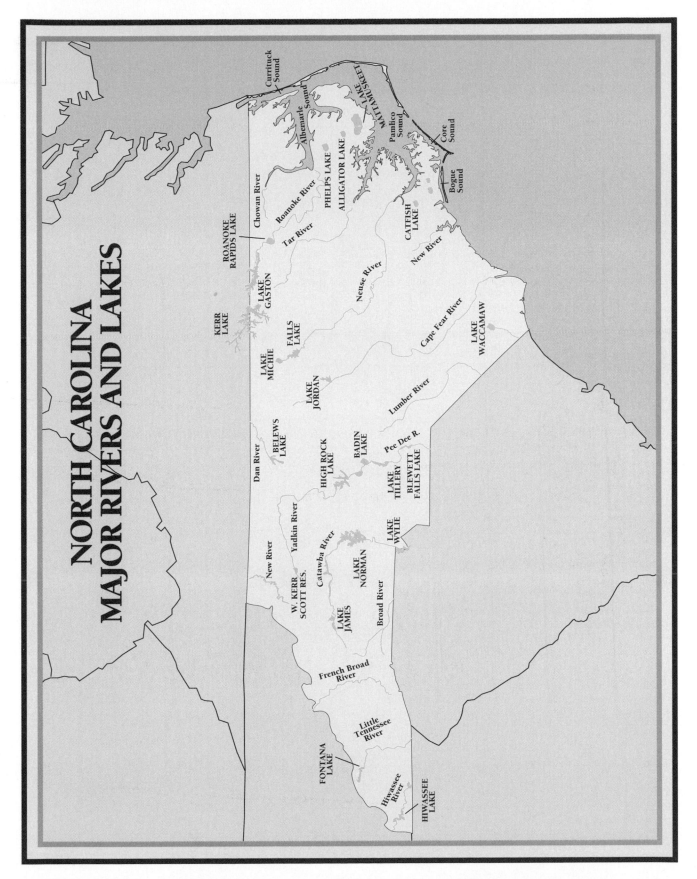

NORTH CAROLINA
MAJOR RIVERS AND LAKES

Currituck Sound

LAKE MATTAMUSKEET

Albemarle Sound

Pamlico Sound

Core Sound

Chowan River

Roanoke River

PHELPS LAKE

ALLIGATOR LAKE

Bogue Sound

ROANOKE RAPIDS LAKE

Tar River

CATFISH LAKE

KERR LAKE

LAKE GASTON

Neuse River

New River

FALLS LAKE

Cape Fear River

LAKE WACCAMAW

LAKE MICHIE

LAKE JORDAN

Lumber River

BELEWS LAKE

HIGH ROCK LAKE

BADIN LAKE

Pee Dee R.

Dan River

LAKE TILLERY

BLEWETT FALLS LAKE

Yadkin River

LAKE WYLIE

New River

Catawba River

W. KERR SCOTT RES.

LAKE NORMAN

Broad River

LAKE JAMES

French Broad River

Little Tennessee River

FONTANA LAKE

Hiwassee River

HIWASSEE LAKE

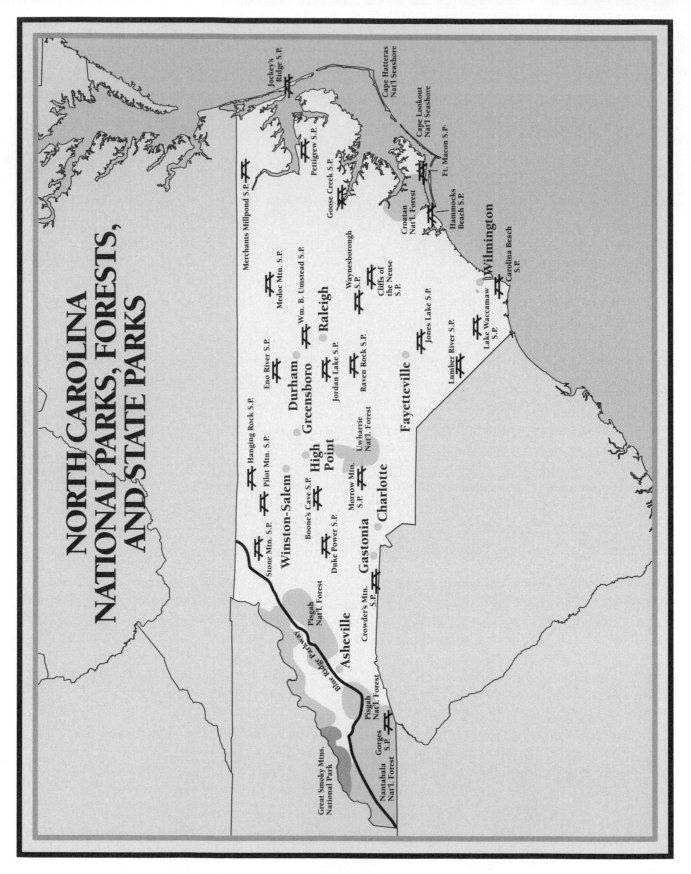

NORTH CAROLINA
NATIONAL PARKS, FORESTS,
AND STATE PARKS

Jockey's Ridge S.P.

Cape Hatteras Nat'l Seashore

Cape Lookout Nat'l Seashore

Ft. Macon S.P.

Merchants Millpond S.P.

Pettigrew S.P.

Goose Creek S.P.

Hammocks Beach S.P.

Croatan Nat'l Forest

Wilmington

Carolina Beach S.P.

Medoc Mtn. S.P.

Wm. B. Umstead S.P.

Waynesborough S.P.

Cliffs of the Neuse S.P.

Eno River S.P.

Raleigh

Durham

Greensboro

Jordan Lake S.P.

Raven Rock S.P.

Jones Lake S.P.

Lumber River S.P.

Lake Waccamaw S.P.

Hanging Rock S.P.

Pilot Mtn. S.P.

High Point

Uwharrie Nat'l Forest

Fayetteville

Stone Mtn. S.P.

Winston-Salem

Boone's Cave S.P.

Morrow Mtn. S.P.

Charlotte

Duke Power S.P.

Gastonia

Crowder's Mtn. S.P.

Pisgah Nat'l Forest

Asheville

Blue Ridge Parkway

Pisgah Nat'l Forest

Gorges S.P.

Great Smoky Mtns. National Park

Nantahala Nat'l Forest

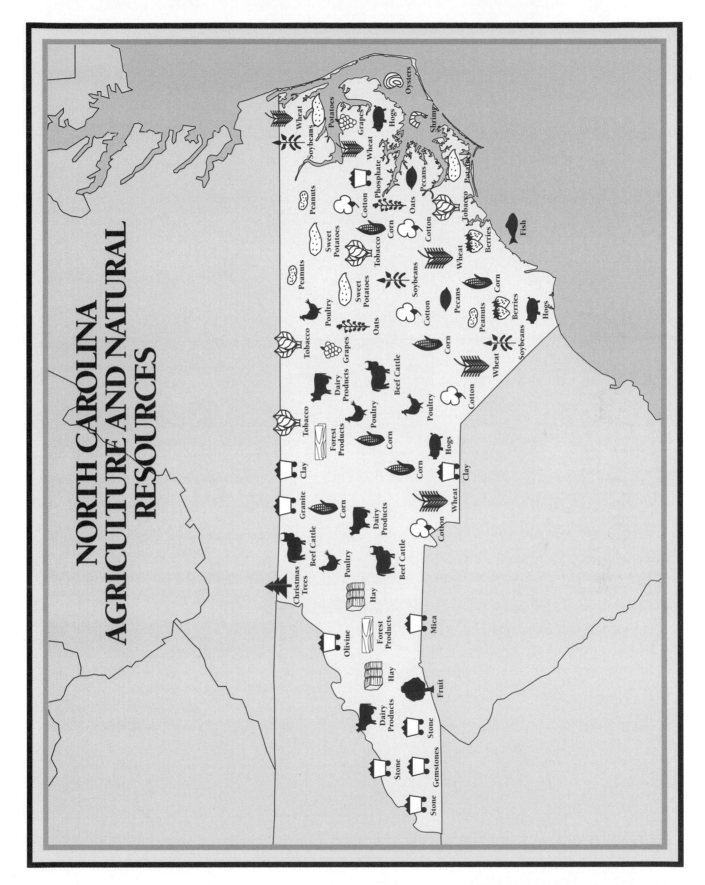

NORTH CAROLINA AGRICULTURE AND NATURAL RESOURCES

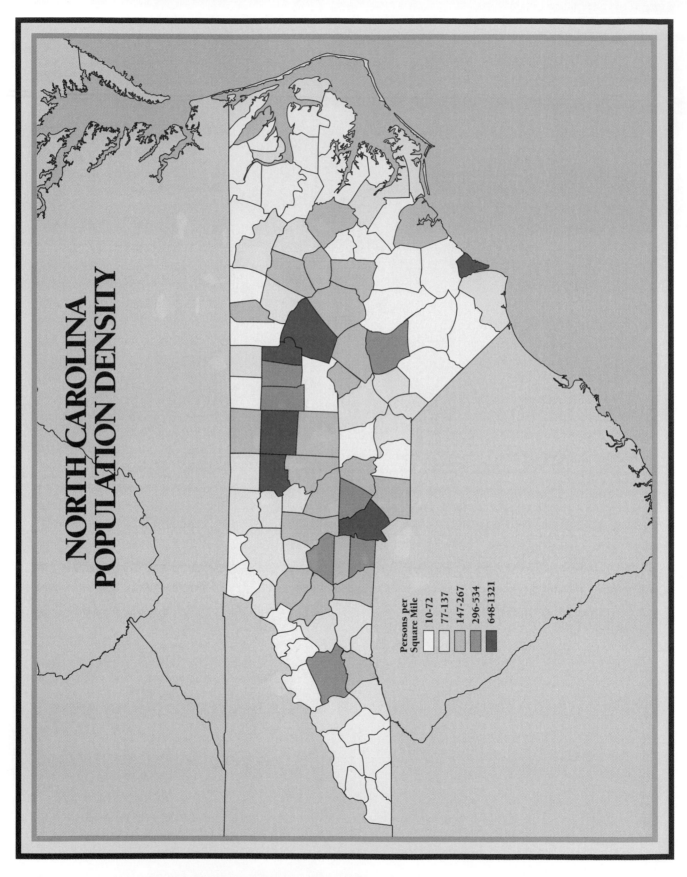

NORTH CAROLINA
POPULATION DENSITY

**Persons per
Square Mile**

10-72
77-137
147-267
296-534
648-1321

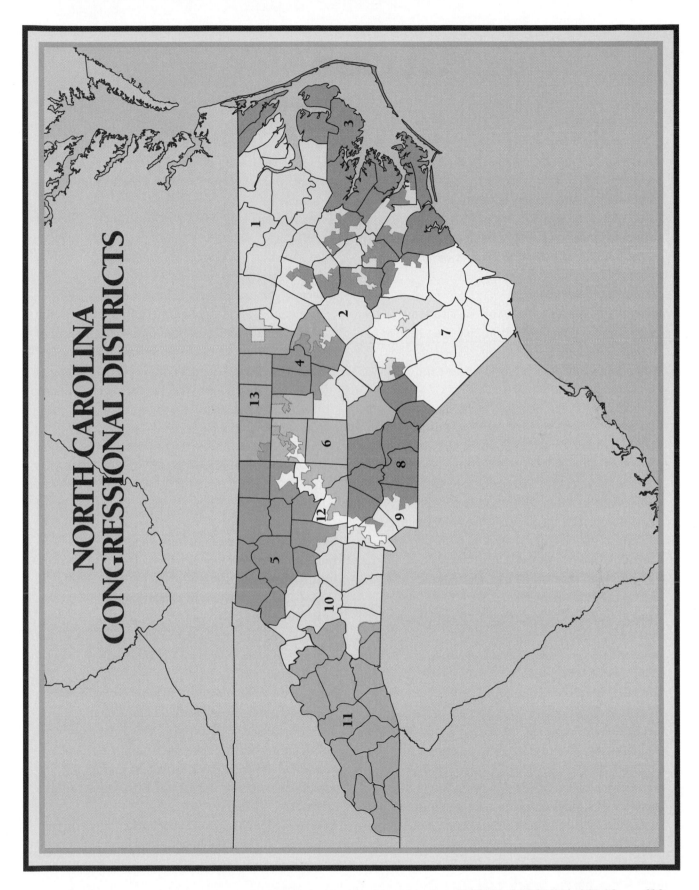

GLOSSARY

A

abolitionism the movement to do away with slavery (14)

acid raid a combination of moisture and gases that is harmful to growing things (1)

affirmative action programs designed to increase the number of women and minorities in the workplace (24)

agriculture farming (2)

amend to change, as a law or constitution (9)

ancestors people from whom one is descended (2)

annex to add to a larger area (14)

antebellum refers to the period before the Civil War (12)

anthropologist a scientist who studies human cultures (2)

Antifederalist one who opposed ratification of the U.S. Constitution (10)

Anti-Saloon League an organization formed by representatives of five Protestant churces that worked to stop the sale of alcoholic beverages in the state (20)

Appalachian Regional Commission a federal agency created in 1965 to coordinate state and federal help for Appalachia (25)

appeal to take a case to a higher court for rehearing (26)

apprentice one who is learning a trade or skill from a "master" (6)

arbitrator one who settles differences between two parties (20)

archaeologist a scientist who studies the items left behind by ancient peoples to determine how they lived (2)

armistice an agreement to stop fighting (20)

Articles of Confederation the first constitution of the United States; it created a loose union of states (10)

artifacts pieces of stone, bone, pottery, and tools left behind by ancient peoples (2)

artisan a craftsperson, such as a blacksmith or carpenter (6)

Assembly the law-making body during the colonial period (5)

atlatl a short stick used by pre-contact Indians to throw spears with more force (2)

attorney general an elected member of the executive branch of state government who serves as the state's chief lawyer and head of the Department of Justice (26)

auditor an elected member of the executive branch of state government who makes sure that state funds are spent according to state law (26)

B

baby boomers the name given to those born right after 1945 (23)

backcountry the region of North Carolina west of the Fall Line (6)

barter to trade one item for another (7)

bicameral two house, as a legislature (5)

bill a proposed law (26)

Bill of Rights the first ten amendments to the U.S. Constitution (10)

Black Code a set of laws enacted by many of the southern states after the Civil War that applied only to freedmen (16)

black power movement a movement by which blacks expected to bring about social equality through political power gained by uniting the black community rather than through integration (24)

blockade the use of naval forces to stop shipping (15)

blockade running using ships to sail through a blockade (15)

boll weevil an insect that attacks the boll of the cotton plant where the fibers are formed (21)

bond an IOU; a document serving as proof of a debt and requiring the repayment of the money borrowed plus interest (17)

borough town a colonial town with sixty or more families (5)

boycott to refuse to buy something (8)

bright leaf tobacco a type of tobacco whose leaves turn bright yellow when cured (12)

budget a plan for receiving and spending money (26)

busing transporting students to schools outside their neighborhood in order to achieve racial integration (24)

C

cabinet a group of advisors chosen by a president; they also head up major departments within the federal government (11)

capes parts of the barrier islands that jut far out into the Atlantic Ocean (1)

capital the seat of government for a state or a nation (8); money and property such as supplies and tools (5)

carpetbagger a northerner who moved into the South to help carry out Congress's Reconstruction plan after the Civil War (16)

cash crop a crop that is raised to be sold for a profit (6)

caucus a meeting of a small group of political party leaders to decide policy, elect party officials, and so on (26)

cavalry troops mounted on horseback (15)

census an official, actual count of the population (11)

century a period of one hundred years (3)

chain gang a group of prisoners chained together while working to prevent their escape (20)

charter school an independent school of choice that is exempt from many of the traditional rules and regulations that regular public schools must follow (23)

city commission a form of city government in which elected commissioners are responsible for particular departments (20)

civil rights the basic rights of citizens (24)

Civil Rights Act of 1964 federal legislation that required businesses involved in interstate commerce to open their doors to people of all races; it also required school districts to avoid discrimination against minorities (24)

clan a group of people who believe themselves related by blood (2)

coalition an association of different parties or groups with a common purpose or goal (19)

Coastal Plain that part of North Carolina located between the Atlantic Ocean and the Fall Line (1)

collective bargaining discussions between a union and an employer to determine such things as employees' wages, hours, working conditions, and benefits (22)

colony a group of people who settle in a distant land but who are still under the rule of their native land (3)

commerce trade (4)

commissioner of agriculture an elected member of the executive branch of state government who is head of the Department of Agriculture, which helps farmers and consumers of farm products (26)

commissioner of insurance an elected member of the executive branch of state government who is charged with enforcing the insurance laws (26)

commissioner of labor an elected member of the executive branch of state government who tries to ensure the health and safety of the state's workers (26)

committee a small group of senators (or representatives) who studies bills on a particular subject and makes recommendations on those bills to the full senate (or house) (26)

committees of correspondence groups formed by the patriots in the 1770s to keep the colonies informed of British actions and other events (8)

commodity a useful article or item of trade (4)

commute to go to and come from the workplace (23)

compromise a way to settle disagreements in which each side gives way a little in its demands (10)

Compromise of 1850 a proposal introduced in Congress by Henry Clay of Kentucky by which California was admitted as a free state, the slave trade was banned in the District of Columbia, the fugitive slave law was strengthened, and popular sovereignty was permitted in new territories (14)

Confederate States of America the name of the government formed by the southern states when they seceded from the Union in the early 1860s (14)

confiscate to take over or seize (10)

conquistador Spanish conqueror of the New World (3)

conservation the management of a natural resource to prevent its destruction (22)

Conservative party a short-lived political party formed by William W. Holden in 1862 and meant to appeal to unionists (15)

Conservatives a group of men in the late 1770s who believed that men of wealth, property, and social standing were better able to govern (9)

consolidated school a school formed by combining several smaller schools (23)

constitution a document that sets out the rules under which a government will operate (9)

constitutionalism the principle of having a written document that describes the rights of the people and the framework of government (26)

continental shelf an underwater plain extending out from a continent (1)

cooperative an organization owned by and operated for the benefit of those using its services (22)

corporation a business, owned by a group of investors, that has a life of its own apart from its founders (20)

corporation commission a state agency established in 1899 to regulate railroads, banks, telephone and telegraph companies, street railways, and express companies (19)

council a group in the colonial period who helped and advised the governor (5)

council-manager form a form of municipal government in which the voters elect the council members, who set policy and pass ordinances; the council members elect a mayor and hire a professional city manager who is in charge of the day-to-day operations of the city government (26)

court of appeals that part of the judicial branch that is just below the supreme court; its jurisdiction is determined by the General Assembly, but it generally hears cases on appeal from the state's superior and district courts (26)

credit the ability to buy something now and pay for it later (18)

crisis a serious situation or turning point (8)

Culpeper's Rebellion an uprising in 1677 to protest the enforcement of the Navigation Acts and the rule of Thomas Miller (5)

culture way of life (2)

current a flow of water within a larger body of water, such as the ocean (1)

D

Declaration of Independence the 1776 document by which the American colonies declared their independence from Great Britain (9)

Declaration of Rights a 1776 document prepared by the Fifth Provincial Congress that set out the rights that people have (9)

Democratic party a political party formed in the early 1800s from the old Jeffersonian Republicans; it supported states' rights, strict interpretation of the Constitution, and a fairly weak federal government (12)

denomination a religious group, such as Baptist, Methodist, or Roman Catholic (25)

depression a severe downturn in economic activity where sales and prices drop, manufacturing decreases, businesses close, banks fail, and people lose their jobs (22)

deserter a soldier who leaves military service without permission (15)

dialect a regional form of a language (2)

dictator a ruler who has complete control over a country (22)

discrimination actions that deny people their rights because of prejudice (13)

disfranchise to take away one's right to vote (19)

dissenters non-Anglicans; people who did not belong to the Church of England (5)

district court a trial court that hears civil cases involving property worth less than $10,000, family disputes, juvenile cases, and criminal misdemeanor cases (26)

diversified varied (25)

draft to force men to serve in the military (15)

draft resister one who opposed being forced to join the army (15)

driver a slave placed in charge of a group of slaves (13)

drought a long period of no rainfall (1)

duty a tax on goods brought in from another country (8)

E

elevation the height above sea level (1)

emancipate to set free (13)

Emancipation Proclamation the 1863 proclamation by which President Abraham Lincoln freed the slaves in the Confederate states (15)

embargo to stop all trade with a particular country or countries (11)

environment surroundings (1)

evolution the theory that man developed from earlier, simpler life forms (21)

executive branch that branch of government that enforces, executes, and administers the laws of the state (26)

expedition a journey for a specific purpose, such as exploration (4)

export a product sent or sold to another country (21)

extremist one who will not compromise her or his views (14)

F

Fall Line an imaginary line that runs from Richmond County to Halifax County through the places on rivers where falls become prominent (1)

Farmers' Alliance a farmers organization in the late 1800s that was concerned with economic issues; it wanted the government to issue silver coins, regulate railroads, and break up trusts; it encouraged the establishment of cooperative stores (18)

Farmers' Union a farmers' organization formed in the early 1900s that worked for better schools, banking reform, and the break up of trusts (21)

fauna animals (1)

Federalist one who supported the ratification of the U.S. Constitution (10)

federal system a form of government in which the national government and the state government exercise authority over the same territory and the same people (26)

felony a serious crime such as murder, arson, or burglary that is punishable by death or imprisonment for more than one year (26)

fine arts art, music, dance, and the theater (23)

flora plants (1)

food stamps stamps issued by the federal government that are accepted by grocery stores as payment for food items (25)

free state a state that did not permit slavery (14)

free suffrage a reform that did away with the requirement that a voter own property to vote for state senator (12)

freedmen freed slaves (16)

Freedmen's Bureau an agency of the federal government established in 1865 to provide food, clothing, shelter, and education for blacks in the South (16)

French and Indian War a war fought between France and England in America between 1754 and 1763 (7)

frontier a region just beyond or at the edge of a settled area (7)

fundamentalists members of religious groups who believe that the Bible is the source of all religious authority and who believe the Genesis creation story as written (21)

furniture industry the activities involved in producing furniture (18)

Fusionist a member of the People's or Republican party, which in 1894 agreed to cooperate to elect their members to statewide office in order to pass legislation they favored (19)

G

General Assembly the state legislature, made up of two houses—a senate and a house of representatives (26)

gentry a social class in colonial North Carolina composed of planters, public officials, and professionals (6)

geography the study of the physical features of Earth and the interaction of humans and the environment (1)

ghetto a section of a city where members of a minority group live, usually because of social or economic reasons (24)

governor one who rules a colony or state (5)

grandfather clause a clause added to the 1899 suffrage amendment that allowed a man to register to vote without taking a literacy test if he, his father, or his grandfather had voted before 1867 (19)

Great Revival a movement of evangelical Protestantism that swept the South in the early 1800s (11)

Great Wagon Road a route followed by settlers in the mid-1700s that extended from Philadelphia to Savannah (6)

H

Halifax Resolves a report issued in April 1776 by the Fourth Provincial Congress that, in one section, urged the colonies to declare their independence from Great Britain (9)

headright a method by which settlers received land based on the number of persons in the family (7)

home rule local self-government (19)

House of Representatives the lower house of Congress (10); the lower house of the General Assembly after 1867

hurricane a tropical storm that covers hundreds of square miles and whose winds measure more than 74 miles an hour (1)

hydroelectric using waterpower to generate electricity (21)

I

illiterate unable to read or write (11)

immigrate to move into and settle in another country (6)

immunity natural resistance to disease (3)

impeachment the act of charging a public official with wrongdoing while that official is still in office (10)

imports goods brought into a country to sell (8)

indentured servant one who agreed to work for another for a period of time (usually 4-7 years) in return for passage to the New World (5)

industrialization the process of changing to a manufacturing economy (18)

inlets places where the ocean flows through the Outer Banks toward the mainland (1)

Inner Coastal Plain that part of North Carolina that stretches from the Tidewater to the Fall Line (1)

integration the process of bringing different groups or races into society as equals (24)

internal improvements improvements in transportation, such as roads or canals (11)

interstate highways limited-access highways that extend through more than one state and are therefore part of the federal highway system (23)

ironclads armored ships used during the Civil War (15)

J

joint-stock company a company that sold shares to investors who expected to receive a share of the company's profits (5)

judicial branch the branch of government that consists of the courts; the major duty of the courts is to judge the actions of people in light of the laws of the state (26)

judiciary court system (10)

jurisdiction the area over which legal authority extends (26)

jury a group of people chosen to hear evidence on a legal case and to make a decision based on the evidence provided (26)

K

Kansas-Nebraska Act a law passed in 1854 by which Kansas and Nebraska were made territories and allowed to decide upon the slavery issue for themselves locally (14)

Kirk-Holden War the name given to Governor William W. Holden's attempts to put down the Ku Klux Klan with military forces under the command of Colonel George W. Kirk (17)

Ku Klux Klan a secret, racist organization that tried to restore political and social control to native whites through violence and intimidation (17)

L

labor union an organization of workers formed to improve their wages, benefits, and working conditions (20)

land grant a piece of land given to a settler who agreed to move onto it (5)

latitude a measure of the distance north or south of the equator (1)

legislative branch that branch of government responsible for writing laws and appropriating or setting aside the funds necessary to run the government; North Carolina's legislative branch is called the General Assembly (26)

lieutenant governor an elected official of the executive branch of government who presides over sessions of the senate and who would assume the duties of the governor if the governor were to die or leave office during his or her term (26)

livestock horses, mules, oxen, cattle, sheep, and hogs (6)

longitude a measure of the distance east or west of the prime meridian at Greenwich, England (1)

Lords Proprietor eight supporters of King Charles II of England who received from him a charter to a colony that included what later became North Carolina (5)

Loyalist a colonist who supported the crown during the American Revolution; also known as a Tory (8)

M

maize the Native American word for corn (2)

majority one more than half (12)

martial law the use of military forces to keep order in an emergency or when civilian forces cannot (17)

mass production the manufacture of great quantities of an item through the assembly of interchangeable parts (21)

mayor-council form a form of municipal government in which the people elect both the mayor and the council members for two-year terms; the council governs the city, while the mayor performs certain arranged duties (26)

Mecklenburg Resolves a document issued by North Carolina patriots in 1775 urging independence from Great Britain (8)

mediate to bring about an agreement between two sides (25)

Medicaid a federal program that provides free health care for people with very low incomes (25)

microelectronics the high-tech electronics industry, which produces silicon chips for computers (25)

middleman a trader who buys goods from producers and sells those goods to other traders or to consumers (3)

militia a citizen army (5)

minimum wage the least amount an employer can legally pay for each hour worked (22)

mint a place where coins are made (12)

misdemeanor a crime that is less serious than a felony and is usually punishable by a jail term of less than one year (26)

Missouri Compromise the 1820 agreement in Congress that allowed Missouri to enter the Union as a slave state and Maine as a free state and that prohibited slavery in any state formed north of a line even with Missouri's southern border (14)

monarch a ruler, usually a king or a queen (3)

Moral Majority a movement by evangelical religious groups in the late 1970s to elect public officials who would oppose the equal rights amendment, restore prayer to the schools, and fight abortion and homosexual rights (25)

Mountain that part of North Carolina lying between the Piedmont and the state of Tennessee (1)

mulatto a person with one white and one black parent (6)

municipality a city or town that has an organized government (18)

N

naval stores products used to preserve the wood and ropes of ships; tar, pitch, rosin, and turpentine (6)

navigable passable by boat (5)

neutral not favoring either side in a disagreement (20)

New Deal the name given to the series of laws passed during President Franklin D. Roosevelt's terms that were intended to deal with the conditions caused by the Great Depression (22)

Northwest Passage an all-water route to Asia explorers thought existed through the North American continent (3)

nullify to take away something's value or legal status; to declare that a law need not be obeyed (16)

O

Outer Banks a series of barrier islands bordering the ocean along the coast of the Tidewater (1)

overseer a person who was responsible for seeing that slaves performed the tasks assigned to them (13)

P

pacifist one who does not believe in war and will not bear arms (6)

partisan politics actions that are biased in support of or devoted to a single political party or cause (19)

partisans independent bands of military men during the Revolutionary War (9)

patent an official document giving its holder certain rights (4)

patriot a colonist who resisted the tighter controls imposed by the British; one who favored independence from Great Britain (8)

per capita income the average income earned per worker (25)

persecution being subjected to unjust or cruel treatment or constant hostility, especially because of religious or political beliefs (5)

picket to protest outside an establishment to try to convince others not to enter it (24)

Piedmont that part of North Carolina lying between the Fall Line and the Blue Ridge Mountains (1)

Piedmont Crescent the industrial, urban corridor slicing across central North Carolina (18)

plank road a road made by laying down large pine planks and covering them with sand (12)

plantation a large farm or estate (6)

planter a slaveholder who owned twenty or more slaves (13)

platform a document that outlines the principles, programs, and policies that a political party supports (14)

popular sovereignty the right of the people who live within a territory to decide upon an issue, such as whether to allow slavery (14)

Populists members of the People's party, which was formed in 1892 (19)

president of the senate the presiding officer of the senate; the lieutenant governor (26)

president pro tempore an officer of the senate who presides over the sessions when the lieutenant governor is absent (26)

price supports guaranteed prices for specified crops or other items (22)

primary an election to nominate candidates for office in which all of a party's members vote for the candidates of their choice (20)

privateer a privately owned ship that was armed during wartime and expected to capture enemy vessels (4)

progressive movement a series of political and social movements whose members believed that government was best equipped to correct the ills of society and who worked to improve society (20)

prohibition forbidding by law the making or selling of alcoholic beverages (20)

propaganda ideas, facts, or rumors spread to help a cause or to hurt an opposing cause (19)

Protestants Christian non-Catholics (3)

public works local government facilities built for public use such as roads and courthouses (13)

Q

Quakers members of a religious group who did not believe in churches or ceremonies and who were pacifists (5)

R

Radicals people, mostly small farmers and westerners, who wanted a more democratic government during the Revolutionary period (9)

ratify to approve or make valid (10)

ration to limit the use or consumption of something (22)

Reconstruction the steps taken to restore the southern states to the Union and to rebuild the South after the Civil War (16)

Reconstruction Act a law passed in 1867 by Congress that placed all southern states but Tennessee under military rule and that laid out the steps those states had to follow to be restored to the Union (16)

referendum a vote of the people on a particular law before it can be put into effect (12)

Regulators westerners who tried to regulate corrupt government officials and illegal high taxes and fees before the Revolutionary War (8)

relief money and goods given to people in special need (22)

repeal to officially withdraw or cancel a law (8)

Republican party a political party formed in 1854 mainly to oppose slavery (14)

Republicans members of Thomas Jefferson's and James Madison's political party in the late 1700s, which later became today's Democratic party (11)

revenues income from taxes and other sources (26)

right-to-work law a law that allows workers to get and keep jobs without having to join a union (25)

Rip Van Winkle state North Carolina's nickname in the early 1800s, so called because the state supposedly fell asleep and made little social and economic progress (11)

royal colony a colony governed directly by the crown (5)

rural outside the city; the countryside (1)

rural electrification the process of bringing electric power to the nation's farmers (22)

S

sabotage the deliberate damaging or destruction of machinery, materials, or property (22)

satellite a man-made object that orbits Earth (23)

scalawag a native white southerner who belonged to the Republican party during Reconstruction (16)

secede to withdraw from the Union (14)

secretary of state an elected member of the executive branch of state government who is the keeper of all official state papers and records, including the laws passed by the General Assembly (26)

sectionalism an exaggerated allegiance to local interests (1)

segregation separation of the races (19)

Senate the upper house of Congress (10); the upper house of the General Assembly

separate-but-equal concept the legal practice of allowing separate public facilities for blacks and for whites (24)

service sector that part of the economy concerned with providing services to others for a fee; services include food services, medical care, financial services, and retailing (25)

sharecroppers landless farmers who rented land and purchased goods on credit, paying the landlord or merchant back with a share of the crop (18)

shoals shallows along the continental shelf (1)

shopping center a group of retail stores in one location with abundant parking (23)

sit-in a type of demonstration where people enter a public facility and refuse to leave under their demands are heard (24)

slave a person bound to a lifetime of service to others (5)

slave code a set of laws that define the social, economic, and physical rights of slaves (13)

slave state a state that permitted slavery (14)

smuggling bringing goods into an area illegally (5)

Social Security Act federal legislation passed in 1935

to provide old-age benefits and survivors' insurance (22)

software instructions that enable a computer to perform a variety of tasks (25)

sounds shallow bodies of water between the Outer Banks and the mainland (1)

sovereignty the supreme power or source of authority; in the United States, the people are sovereign (26)

Spanish Armada the Spanish fleet that attacked England in the 1580s (4)

speaker of the house an officer of the house of representatives who presides over sessions of the house (26)

specie gold or silver (7)

squatter a person who settles on land without a clear title to it (7)

Stamp Act a law passed by Parliament in 1765 levying taxes on all kinds of documents (8)

states' rights a principle that supports the rights of the individual states over the rights of the federal government (10)

stock market a place where the stock (shares of ownership) of corporations is bought and sold (22)

strategy a detailed plan for using military forces or for achieving a goal (15)

strike workers' refusal to work, usually as a protest over some grievance (21)

suburb a residential area outside city limits (23)

suffrage the right to vote (12)

superintendent of public instruction an elected member of the executive branch of state government who oversees the state's public school system, including teacher certification and textbook adoption (26)

superior court court of original jurisdiction that hears civil cases involving property worth more than $10,000 and criminal felony cases (26)

supreme court the highest court in the state; only hears cases on appeal from lower courts and from the Utilities Commission (26)

synthetic man-made or manufactured; not made from natural products (23)

T

tariff a tax on imported goods (10)

taxes the money given by businesses and citizens to the government to pay for services the government provides (5)

technology the practical use of scientific knowledge, especially in business and industry (25)

tenancy system the rental of farmland at an agreed-upon price or a share of the crop (18)

Tennessee Valley Authority a federal agency established to control flooding and improve conditions in the seven states drained by the Tennessee River (22)

termination the federal government's policy in the 1950s of ending monetary support for Native American tribes (24)

textile industry the activities involved in producing textile products (18)

Tidewater that part of coastal North Carolina that extends 20 to 30 miles inland from the Atlantic Ocean (1)

tobacco industry the activities involved in growing and curing tobacco and in producing tobacco products (18)

tornado a severe windstorm whose winds can reach speeds of up to 500 miles an hour; characterized by a funnel-shaped cloud (1)

Tory War a civil war fought between Whigs and Tories in the Carolinas during the Revolutionary period (9)

Townshend Acts laws passed by the British Parliament in 1767 that taxed certain imports into the American colonies (8)

Trail of Tears refers to the route followed by the Cherokee when removed from their land to reservations in Oklahoma (12)

treasurer an elected member of the executive branch of state government who receives state revenues and pays the state's bills (26)

treaty a formal agreement between nations (7)

tribe a group of people who share a common ancestry, language, name, and way of living (2)

tributary a stream or river that flows into a larger river (3)

truce a suspension of fighting (15)

trust a group of firms that works together to control all or nearly all of the business in an industry so there is little, if any, competition (20)

U

underground railroad a secret way of helping slaves escape to the North and Canada in the period before the Civil War (14)

unicameral one house, as a legislature (5)

Union League an organization used by Republicans after the Civil War to bring blacks into the party (16)

universal manhood suffrage the right of all men to vote (16)

urban pertaining to a city (1)

U.S. Constitution the plan of government for the United States (10)

V

veto to refuse to approve legislation (10)

W

War Hawks members of Congress in the early 1800s who wanted the United States to declare war on Great Britain in order to capture Canada and eliminate British influence in America (11)

Whig party a political party formed in the early 1800s to oppose President Andrew Jackson; it favored internal improvements, a national bank, and a tariff on foreign goods (12)

Whigs patriots in the American Revolution (9)

Whiskey Rebellion a revolt in the 1790s by farmers protesting the federal government's excise tax on whiskey (11)

white supremacy the belief that the white race is superior to the black race, or any other race (17)

Wilmot Proviso a proposal introduced in the U.S. House of Representatives by David Wilmot of Pennsylvania that barred slavery from any territory gained from Mexico (14)

Women's Christian Temperance Union (WCTU) an organization that worked to stop the sale of alcoholic beverages (20)

worker's compensation a form of government insurance for accidental death or injuries in the workplace (21)

World War I the war fought from 1914 to 1918 between the Central Powers (led by Germany and Austria-Hungary) and the Allied Powers (led by France, Great Britain, Russia, and the United States) (20)

World War II the war fought from 1939 to 1945 between the Axis Powers (Germany, Japan, and Italy) and the Allied Powers (Great Britain, France, the United States, and others) (22)

writ of habeas corpus a court order releasing imprisoned people if the authorities cannot show why they are being held (15)

Y

yeoman a small farmer (6)

INDEX

The purpose of the index is to help you locate information quickly. The index contains references to not only text, but also photographs and maps. A page number with an **m** before it indicates a map; a page number with a **p** before it indicates a photograph or illustration.

Cumberland County, 165, 426, 495, 603
currency, 197, 202, 222
currents, 24
Currituck County, 603
Currituck Lighthouse, p8
Currituck Sound, 24, 25, 451

D

da Gama, Vasco, p73, 73
Daniels, Josephus, 422, 427, 439, p440
Dare, Virginia, 96, p97
Dare County, 603
Darwin, Charles, p423, 423, 463
Dasamunguepeuk, 94
Davidson, William Lee, 190
Davidson College, 19, 253, 399, 439, 511
Davidson County, 603
Davie, William R., 190, p197, 197, 203-204, p209, 209, 212, 215, 219, 223, 225, 608
Davie County, 603
Davis, Benjamin O., 529
Davis, Burke, 516
Davis, James, 142
Davis, Jefferson, 300, p317, 317, 328, 334, 342
Day, John, 191
Day, Thomas, 279
de Leon, Juan Ponce, 76
de Soto, Hernando, p77, 77-78
Declaration of Independence, 184, 185, 222
Declaration of Rights, 187, 216, 580
Democratic party, 248, 354, 396, 422, 426, 530
    in North Carolina, 256, 314, 403, 404, 422, 592-595
    and progressive reforms, 422-439
    return to power by, 256-257, 403-404, 411-412
    and slavery issue, 294, 298
    southern, 298, 530
    and white supremacy issue, 367, 403, 408, 409-411, 413
denominations, 570
Denson, Daisy, 469
depression, 473.
    See also Great Depression.
deserters, 324, 324
development, regional, 568-570
dialect, 50
Diaz, Bartholomew, 72
dictator, 489
Discovery Place, 514-515
discrimination, 278, 410, 523-524

disease, 82-83, 383, 507
disfranchisement, 412
Dismal Swamp, 9, 276
dissenters, 115
district courts, 590
diversified, 559
Division of Archives and History, 120, 517
Dix, Dorothea L., p254, 254
Dixon, Thomas, 465
Dobbs, Arthur, p152, 152-153, 154, 157, 607
Dockery, Alfred, 352
Dole, Elizabeth, 549
Douglas, Stephen A., p295, 295, 298
draft, 314
draft resister, 324
Dragging Canoe, 184, p186
Drake, Sir Francis, 87, 94, p96
dramas, outdoor, 515, 568
Dred Scott decision, 296
drivers, 271
drought, 24, 31
Drummond, William, 110, p111, 606
Dudley, Edward B., 248, p250, 250
Duke, Benjamin, 386, 455
Duke, James Buchanan ("Buck"), 386, p432, 432, 455
Duke, Washington, p386, 386
Duke Power, 455
Duke University, p18, 18, 511, 560
Duplin County, 603
Durant, George, 112
Durham, 16, 18, p384, 385, 390, 399, 459, 494, 503, 505, 527, 534
Durham County, 603
duties, 172. *See also* taxes.

E

Easley, Michael F., 560, p588, 610
East, John, 594
East Carolina University, 14, 511
Eastchurch, Thomas, 112, 606
Eastern Band of Cherokee, 546
economy, 39, 555, 559-561, 562-563
    in antebellum period, 258-261
    colonial, 139-140
    during Great Depression, 474, 475, 477, 478-482, 484, 486
    in postwar period, 504, 510
    regional development, 568-570
    after Revolutionary War, 202
    after War of 1812, 229
    See also industry.
Edenton, 12, 119, 151, 185, 275, 312
Edenton Tea Party, p174, 175

Edgecombe County, 188, 408, 603
education, 204, 231
    Accountability Act, 572
    Aycock's plan for, 425
    Basic Education Program, 510, 572
    for blacks, 350, 363, 533, 534
    church-sponsored schools, 363
    community colleges, 510-511
    funding for, 425, 509, 593
    higher, 203, 253, 396-397, 511-512
    and integration, 531-534
    Literary Fund, 235, 253
    Murphey's plan for, 234, 235
    and Pearsall Plan, 533
    public, 234, 252, 257, 362, 396, 508-510
    reforms, 257, 509, 510, 572, 574
    state superintendent of, 257, 574
    technical colleges, 510-511
    See also schools.
Edwards, Weldon N., p302, 302
Ehle, John, 516
Ehringhaus, J. C. Blucher, 480, 487, 610
election reform, 405-406, 411, 433
electric power, 455-456, 486,
elevation, 6, 16, 20
Elizabeth City, 12, 277, 311, 494, 496
Elizabeth City State University, 12, 397, 534
Elizabeth I, Queen, p86, 87, 88, 92, 97
Elizabeth II, pcover, p69, 517
Ellis, John W., 252, 257, 299, 300, p301, 302, 303, 314, 609
emancipate, 279
Emancipation Proclamation, 307, 308
embargo, 227
Emergency Relief Administration, 483
England,
    colonies of, 92-95, 96-97, 99, 103, 104, 105
    conflict with Spain, 87, 94, 97
    exploration by, 87-88
    trade with, 105, 111-112, 119
    See also Great Britain.
Eno River, 49
entertainment, 517-518
environment, 3, 4, 36, 574
Episcopal Church, 253, 363
Equal Suffrage League, 438
Ericsson, Leif, 73
ethnic groups, settlement by, 130-136, m131
evangelicalism, 233, 234, 571
Evans, Henry, 275, 279
evolution, 423, 463, 464

p165, 168-169, 176-177
Reid, David S., p256, 256, 609
Reidsville, 459
relief, 477, 483-484
religion, 132
    among blacks, 233-234, 360-361, 571
    in colonial North Carolina, 109-110,
        113, 115, 118, 143
    denominations, 570
    Great Revival, 233-234
    among Native Americans, 80, 82
    in North Carolina, 570-572
    and politics, 234, 249, 572
    and social issues, 287, 289
    and televangelism, 571
repeal, 172
Republican party, 298, 342, 592
    birth of, 296
    and fusion, 405, 413
    and Ku Klux Klan, 368
    in North Carolina, 296, 300, 353-354,
        362-366, 412, 413, 421, 593, 594
    and railroad bond scandal, 365-367
    and Reconstruction, 351, 352, 353,
        361, 372
    and southern strategy, 542
Republicans, Jeffersonian, 222, 225
Research Triangle Park, 560
reservation, Indian, 118, 247
resources, 36, 259-260, m617
revenues, 588
Revolutionary War, 176-179, 183
    aftermath, 196, 201
    battles in, 192, m193, 193, 194
    events leading to, 173-175
    and Loyalists, 188, 190
    and Native Americans, 184-186
    in North Carolina, 190-195
    and Tory War, 195-196
Reynolds, Richard Joshua, p385, 385
Rhett, William, 119
Ribaut, Jean, 78, p79
rice, 12, 258, 266, 271
Richland Balsam Mountain, p37
Richmond, David, p535
Richmond County, 6, 495, 605
right-to-work law, 561-562
Rip Van Winkle state, 230-233
rivers, p26, 26, p27, 35, 39, 235, m615.
    See also specific rivers.
roads, 143, p230, 235, m454, 569, m612
    building, 453, 504
    financing, 468
    plank, 257
Roanoac Indians, 49, 88, 93, 94

Roanoke colony, 92-95, 96-97, 99
Roanoke Island, p9, 92-95, 96, 311, 360,
    363
Roanoke River, 26, 99, 118, 235
Robeson County, pix, 99, 258, 599, 605
Rockingham, 331, 517, 564
Rockingham County, 605
Rockwell, Kiffin Y., 440, p444
Rocky Mount, 14, 231
Rogers, John, 154
Roosevelt, Franklin D., 439, 478, p479,
    p480, 480, 507, 529
Rough Riders, 410
Rowan County, 130, 159, 165, 187, 259,
    605
royal colony, 123
rural, 20, 260, 503
rural electrification, 487
Russell, Daniel L., p406, 406, 410, 609
Rutherford, Griffith, 185, 186
Rutherford County, 193, 259, 605

S
Sabin, Albert B., 507
sabotage, 494
Said, Omar ibn, 136, p137
Saint Mary's School, 253, 398
Salem, p126, 231, 257
Salem College, 253
Salisbury, 165, 168, 223, 261, 324, p333,
    334, 382, 427
Salk, Jonas, 507
Salmon Creek, 107
Sampson County, 605
Sandburg, Carl, home, 23
Sandhills, area, p14, 14
Sanford, p452
Sanford, Terry, 508, 509, p509, 511, 560,
    562, 593, 610
Saponi Indians, 50
satellite, 508
Sawyer, Eugene, 451
scalawags, 353
Schiele Museum of Natural History, pviii
schools, 201, 254
    for blacks, p362, 363, 423, p425, 524
    charter, 510
    church-sponsored, 363-364
    colleges and universities, 253, 363
    community colleges, 510-511
    consolidated, 508
    early, 203
    freedmen's, p362, 363
    Governor's School, 509
    high schools, 425

    integration of, 531-534, 542-543
    kindergarten, 509
    Murphey's plan for, 234, 235
    public, 253, 355, 396, 424, 425, 468
    reforms, 425,
    School of the Arts, 509
    School of Science and Mathematics, 520
    tax support for, 355, 509
    technical, 510-511
    term, 365, 396, 424, 425
Scopes, John T., p463, 463
Scotch-Irish settlers, 131-132
Scotia Seminary, 364
Scotland County, 495, 605
Scots, Highland, settlers, 132-133, 156,
    176, 178, 189
Scott, Dred, 296
Scott, Robert W., p511, 512, 521, 560, 610
Scott, W. Kerr, p592, 592, 610
Seaboard Airline Railway, 382, 430
seashores, national, 9
secession, 285-299, 299-300, 302, 303,
    344
Secotan Indians, 49
secretary of state, 588
sectionalism, 35, 149-150, 208-210, 285
Securities Exchange Act, 484
segregation, 403, 410, 412, 524, 531, 533,
    551
Seneca Falls Women's Rights Convention,
    277
Senate,
    federal, 214
    state, 187, 581, 582-583, m582
separate-but-equal concept, 410, 524, 533
service sector, 563
Settle, Thomas, p373, 373
settlement, 8, 34
    of America, 103-104, 106, 170
    of North Carolina, 106-108, 111, 113,
        118, 122-123, 129-136, m131, 143,
        152
Seven Year's War, *see* French and Indian
    War.
Sevier, John, 193, 209, p210, 210
Seymour-Johnson Air Force Base, 6, 494
sharecroppers, 393, 461
Sharp, Susie, 549
Shaw University, 363, 536
Shelby, 382, 487
Shelby, Isaac, 193
Sheridan, Louis, 279
Sherman, William T., 292, p331, 331, 335
Sherman Anti-Trust Act, 432
Shining Rock, 23

shoals, 8, 24
Shoffner, T. M., 368
Shoffner Act, 22-23, 369
shopping centers, 505
Sickles, Daniel, 353, 354
Simmons, Furnifold M., 408, p409, 412, p422, 422, 439
Sims, George, 164
Siouan tribes, 49-50
sit-ins, 525, 535-536
skills, building
    analyzing illustrations, 181
    analyzing state interests, 599
    comparing costs and benefits, 577
    conducting interviews, 377
    decision making, 521
    detecting bias, 499
    distinguishing fact from opinion, 401
    finding causes, 159
    finding information, 125
    finding main idea, 67
    generalizations and conclusions, 305
    notetaking, 447
    reaching compromises, 219
    reading news articles, 551
    recognizing propaganda, 417
    studying historical documents, 357
    traveling through time, 239
    understanding cause and effect, 339
    using graphs, 145
    using maps, 281, 471
    using mathematics, 263
    using mileage charts, 199
    using primary sources, 101
    using textbook, 39
    using timelines, 85
slave codes, 267-268, 274
slavery, 285
    and antislavery movement, 287, 288, 289
    and Civil War, 307-308
    compromises over, 214, 286-287, 293, 294
    growth of in North Carolina, 35, 136, 137, 139, 265-266, m266
    end of, 307, 308, 344
    life under, 138, 269-275
    and Native Americans, 116-117, 118
    and politics, 255, 291, 295
    resistance to, 261, 265, 276, 277
    slave code, 267-268, 274
    See also African Americans, Africans, blacks, slaves.
slaves, 106
    in antebellum period, 265-279

brought from Africa, 136
and discrimination, 359
freeing, 277, 307-308
life of, 269-275
population of, 129, 265
and religion, 136, 233-233, 275
revolts by, 178, 276
in Revolutionary War, 178, 196, 199
and slave codes, 267-268, 274
and underground railroad, 287
work done by, 271-273
See also slavery.
slave states, 286
slave trade, 266-267, p267
Smithfield, 204, 333, 413
smuggling, 119
Snow, Ernest Ansel, 390
snowfall, 30-31
social classes, 137
Social Security Act, 484
software, 554, 555
soils, 14, 33
Somerset Place, p270
Sothel, Seth, 112-113
sounds, 24-26, 118
Southern Appalachian Repertory Theater, 514
Southern Christian Leadership Conference (SCLC), 525, 538
Southern Railway Company, 382, 430
Southern Rights party, 302
Southport, 12, 311, 363
sovereignty, 578
Soviet Union, 490, 491, 492, 519
Spaight, Richard Dobbs, Sr., 205, 212, 215, 608
Spain, 76-79, 155, 157, 209, 244
Spangenberg, Bishop August, 130, 133
Spanish Armada, 97, 98
Spaulding, Asa Timothy, p527, 527
Spaulding, Charles Clinton, 527
speaker of the house, 583
specie, 148
Spencer, Samuel, 203, 216
Spencer Shops, 19
sports, 398, 407, 517
Spotswood, Alexander, p122, 122
squatters, 151
St. Augustine's College, 363, p364
Stafford, Lillian Exum Clement, p469, 469
Stamp Act, 163, 170, 171, 172, 181
Stanford, Richard, 227-228
Stanly, Edward, 248
Stanly, John Carruthers, 279
Stanly County, 605

state government, see government.
state symbols, 201, 261, 601
State Normal and Industrial School, p397, 397
states' rights, 208, 221, 225, 285
Statesville, 154, 390, 427
steam power, 388
steamships, p236, 236, 251
Stephens, John W., p368, 369
stock car racing, 517
stock market, 473, 475, 484
Stokes County, 605
Stoneman, George H., p334, 334
Storey, Ellen, p364
Strange, Robert, 261
strategy, 309
stretch-out, 459, 479
strikes, labor, 459, 562
Stuart, John, 157, 184
Student Non-Violent Coordinating Committee (SNCC), 536, 538, 541
suburbs, 504, 505-506
suffrage, 187, 249, 354, 537-538, 595
    amendment, 412, 424, 523
    and blacks, 187, 278, 354, 523, 524, 537-539
    free, 256, 257
    grandfather clause, 412
    laws affecting, 404, 523, 538, 595
    and property requirement, 187, 256, 355
    universal manhood, 355
    woman's, 434-435, 438-439
Sugar Act, 170
Sunny Point, 6
superintendent of common schools, 257
superintendent of public instruction, 364, 574, 588-589
superintendent of public works, 355
superior courts, 590
Supreme Court,
    federal, 410
    state, 590
Surry County, 365, p366, 605
Swain, David L., p231, 231, p248, 248, 608
Swain County, p378, 605
Swann v. Charlotte-Mecklenburg Board of Education, 534
Swepson, George W., 366
symbols, state, 601
synthetic fibers, 504

T
Taliaferro, H. E., 261
Tallmadge amendment, 286

ACKNOWLEDGMENTS

SURVEY PARTICIPANTS: Joyce Kilby, Northwest Ashe, Warrenville, Ashe County; Terry N. Everett, Bath Elementary School, Bath; Gwen Jones, Belhaven Junior High School, Belhaven, Beaufort County; Jacquelyn H. Breece, Tar Heel Jr. Sr. High School, Tar Heel; Betty Butler, Dublin Elementary School, Dublin; Darrel Melvin, Clarkton School of Discovery, Clarkton, Bladen County; Fay Rogers, Shallotte Middle School, Shallotte, Brunswick County; Ramona Henderson Bryson, Valley Springs Middle School, Arden, Buncombe County; Shanda McFarlin, Liberty Middle School, Burke County; Linda Deal, H. M. Arndt Middle School, Hickory, Catawba County; Thomas S. Edwards, Chatham Middle School, Silver City, Chatham County; Brenda Wright, Havelock Middle School, Havelock, Craven County; Margaret F. Harris, South Davidson High School, Denton; Christine Hunt, Ledford Middle School, Thomasville, Davidson County; J. Thomas Terry, Lowe's Grove Middle School, Durham, Durham County; B. Davis, Ashley Middle School, Winston-Salem, Darlene L. Gardner, Atkins Middle School, Winston-Salem; Ray A. Winn, Paisley Middle School, Winston-Salem, Forsyth County; Danny Amos, Northwest Middle School, Greensboro; Jean R. Botzis, Aycock Middle School, Greensboro; Andrea McGuire, Northwest Middle School, Greensboro; Gwen Willard, Northwest Middle School, Greensboro, Guilford County; DeLois H. Borders, East Hoke Middle School, Raeford, Hoke County; Patricia W. Newman, Fairview Elementary School, Sylva; Mary Goddard Slagle, Smokey Mountain Elementary School, Whittier, Jackson County; Sue G. Miller, EastLee Middle School, Sanford, Lee County; Billy M. Hamm, Jr., Woodington Middle School, Kinston, Lenoir County; Karen Wiggins, Macon Middle School, Franklin, Macon County; Pat Nelson, Robersonville Middle School, Robersonville. Martin County; Shirley Jakeman, Quail Hollow Middle School, Charlotte, Mecklenberg County; Shirley S. Evers, Westmoore Elementary School, Seagrove; Mamie Murray, Highfalls Elementary School, Highfalls; Sandy Sackmann, Aberdeen Middle School, Aberdeen, Moore County; Cynthia S. Lloyd, Conway Middle School, Conway; Alan J. Stimpson, Gaston Middle School, Gaston, Northampton County; Carol Connelly, Jacksonville Middle School, Jacksonville, Onslow County; Ann Collins, Grey Culbreth Middle School, Chapel Hill, Orange County; Linda L. Hill, Pamlico Junior High School, Bayboro, Pamlico County; Judy K. Harrelson, Ellerbe Junior High School, Ellerbe, Richmond County; Jacob Godwin, Fairmont Middle School, Fairmont, Robeson County; James C. Pope, Jr., Corriher-Lipe Middle School, Landis, Rowan County; Franklin D. Head, R. S. Middle School, Rutherfordton, Judith Helton, East Middle School, Bostic; Art Sigmon, Mt. Vernon Elementary School, Forest City, Rutherford County; Maurice M. Floyd, Henderson Middle School, Henderson; Alice Hinson, Eaton Johnson School, Henderson, Vance County; ; Faye G. Beal, West Cary Middle School, Cary; Yetive Capps, East Millbrook Middle School, Raleigh, Wake County; Susan Lawrence, Parkway School, Boone, Wautauga County; Ginger Price, Spring Creek School, Seven Springs; Dianne Thornton, Grantham Middle School, Goldsboro, Wayne County; Ken Greene, C. B. Eller Elementary School, Elkin; Lori Martin, Union Elementary/Middle School, N. Wilkesboro; Sheila Richardson, Roaring River Elementary School, Roaring River, Wilkes County; F. T. Franks, Jr., Toisnot Middle School, Wilson, Wilson County; Gary Swain, Jonesville Elementary School, Jonesville, Yadkin County

PICTURE CREDITS: The following abbreviations are used for sources from which several illustrations were obtained.

NCDAH – North Carolina Department of Archives and History
NCC – North Carolina Collection, University of North Carolina Library at Chapel Hill
NCTT – North Carolina Department of Travel and Tourism
UNCP – John White paintings reprinted, by permission of the publisher, from *The Complete Drawings of John White*, by Paul Hulton. Copyright © 1983 by The University of North Carolina Press.

FRONT MATTER: Cover Bruce Roberts. i Robin McDonald. ii-iii Bruce Roberts. iv-v Robin McDonald. vii Robin McDonald. viii (top) NCTT, (above) Bruce Roberts. ix (top) Robin McDonald, (above) Bruce Roberts. **UNIT ONE:** x-1 (both) Bruce Roberts. **CHAPTER ONE:** 2-3 Bruce Roberts. 3 Billy Barnes. 4 NCTT. 5 Bruce Roberts. 6 Robin McDonald. 7 Bruce Roberts. 8 (top) Robin McDonald, (above) Bruce Roberts. 8-9 Robin McDonald. 10-11 (all) Bruce Roberts. 12-13 Bruce Roberts. 13 (both) NCTT. 14 (both) NCTT. 15 (both) Billy Barnes. 16-17 Bruce Roberts. 17 NCTT. 18 (top) Billy Barnes, (above) NCTT. 19 Bruce Roberts. 20 NCTT. 20-21 Robin McDonald. 21 (left) Bruce Roberts, (above) NCTT. 22 (top) NCTT, (bottom) Bruce Roberts. 23 Bruce Roberts. 24 (top) Bruce Roberts, (above) Robin McDonald. 26 Robin McDonald. 27 (top and left) Robin McDonald (right), Bruce Roberts. 28 Robin McDonald. 29 Bruce Roberts. 30 Bruce Roberts. 31 UPI/Corbis-Bettmann. 32-33 Bruce Roberts. 34 NCDAH. 36 Robin McDonald. 37 (both) Robin McDonald. **CHAPTER TWO:** 40 Bruce Roberts. 42 Patrick Brady. 43 Pinson Mounds State Archeological Area, Tennessee. 44 (both) Red Mountain Museum. 45 Pinson Mounds State Archeological Area, Tennessee. 46 Robin McDonald. 46-47 Robin McDonald. 48 Robin McDonald. 50 UNCP. 51 (both) UNCP. 52 (both) UNCP. 53 (both) UNCP. 54 Smithsonian Institution. 54-55 Billy Barnes. 56 Smithsonian Institution. 57 Robin McDonald. 58 NCTT. 59 Thomas Gilcrease Museum of American Art and History. 60 Tennessee State Museum. 61 University of Alabama Special Collections. 62 NCTT. 63 Cherokee Historical Association. 64 (left) NCTT, (right) Billy Barnes. 65 Bruce Roberts. **UNIT TWO:** 68 Bruce Roberts. 68-69 Robin McDonald. **CHAPTER THREE:** 70 Corbis-Bettmann. 70-71 Architect of the Capitol. 73 (both) Corbis-Bettmann. 74 Bruce Roberts. 75 (both) Library of Congress. 76 Library of Congress. 77 (top) Library of Congress, (above) University of Alabama Special Collections. 78 Corbis-Bettmann. 79 Corbis-Bettmann. 80 Library of Congress. 81 National Museum of American Art/Art Resources. 82 Organization of American States. 83 NCC. **CHAPTER FOUR:** 86 Corbis-Bettmann. 87 Corbis-Bettmann. 89 (left) UNCP, (right) NCDAH. 90 (both) NCC. 91 NCC. 92 (top) National Portrait Gallery/Art Resources, (below) NCDAH. 93 Robin McDonald. 94 UNCP. 95 UNCP. 96. Corbis-Bettmann. 97 NCDAH. 98 Library of Congress. 99 Billy Barnes. **CHAPTER FIVE:** 102 Corbis-Bettmann. 104 (both) Corbis-Bettmann. 105 Corbis-Bettmann. 106 National Portrait Gallery/Art Resources. 107 NCDAH. 108 NCDAH. 109 NCDAH. 111 Corbis-Bettmann. 112 National Portrait Gallery/Art Resources. 113 National Portrait Gallery/Art Resources. 114 (both) Robin McDonald. 115 NCDAH. 116 NCDAH. 117 NCC. 118 NCDAH. 119 NCDAH. 120 (both) NCDAH. 121 NCDAH, photo by Diane Hardy. 122 (left) West Virginia State Archives, (right) NCDAH. 123 Robin McDonald. **UNIT THREE:** 126 Robin McDonald. 126-127 Bruce Roberts. **CHAPTER SIX:** 128-129 NCDAH. 131 NCDAH. 132 Library of Congress. 133 NCDAH. 134 (both) Bruce Roberts. 135 (left) NCTT, (below) Bruce Roberts. 136 Library of Congress. 137 NCC.